que®
CERTIFICATION

# MCSE
## Planning and Maintaining a Microsoft Windows Server 2003 Network Infrastructure

### Exam 70-293

**Will Schmied**

**Robert J. Shimonski**

**Training Guide**

# MCSE TG 70-293: PLANNING AND MAINTAINING A MICROSOFT WINDOWS SERVER 2003 NETWORK INFRASTRUCTURE

International Standard Book Number: 0-7897-3013-8

Library of Congress Catalog Card Number: 2003109280

Printed in the United States of America

First Printing: December 2003

06   05   04   03          4   3   2   1

## Trademarks

All terms mentioned in this book that are known to be trademarks or service marks have been appropriately capitalized. Que Publishing cannot attest to the accuracy of this information. Use of a term in this book should not be regarded as affecting the validity of any trademark or service mark.

## Warning and Disclaimer

Every effort has been made to make this book as complete and as accurate as possible, but no warranty or fitness is implied. The information provided is on an "as is" basis. The authors and the publisher shall have neither liability nor responsibility to any person or entity with respect to any loss or damages arising from the information contained in this book or from the use of the CD or programs accompanying it.

## Bulk Sales

Que Publishing offers excellent discounts on this book when ordered in quantity for bulk purchases or special sales. For more information, please contact

**U.S. Corporate and Government Sales**
**1-800-382-3419**
corpsales@pearsontechgroup.com

For sales outside of the U.S., please contact

**International Sales**
**1-317-428-3341**
international@pearsontechgroup.com

**PUBLISHER**
Paul Boger

**EXECUTIVE EDITOR**
Jeff Riley

**DEVELOPMENT EDITOR**
Steve Rowe

**MANAGING EDITOR**
Charlotte Clapp

**PROJECT EDITOR**
Sheila Schroeder

**COPY EDITOR**
Chuck Hutchinson

**INDEXER**
Heather McNeill

**PROOFREADER**
Juli Cook

**TECHNICAL EDITORS**
Richard Coile
Will Willis

**PUBLISHING COORDINATOR**
Pamalee Nelson

**MULTIMEDIA DEVELOPER**
Dan Scherf

**INTERIOR DESIGNER**
Louisa Adair

**COVER DESIGNER**
Charis Ann Santillie

**PAGE LAYOUT**
Michelle Mitchell

**Que**®
CERTIFICATION

Que Certification • 800 East 96th Street • Indianapolis, Indiana 46240

## A Note from Series Editor Ed Tittel

Congratulations on your purchase of MCSE Training Guide 70-293 exam, the finest exam preparation book in the marketplace!

As Series Editor of the highly regarded Training Guide series, I can assure you that you won't be disappointed. You've taken your first step toward passing the MCSE Training Guide 70-293 exam, and we value this opportunity to help you on your way!

As a "Favorite Study Guide Author" finalist in a 2002 poll of CertCities readers, I know the importance of delivering good books. You'll be impressed with Que Certification's stringent review process, which ensures the books are high-quality, relevant, and technically accurate. Rest assured that at least a dozen industry experts—including the panel of certification experts at CramSession—have reviewed this material, helping us deliver an excellent solution to your exam preparation needs.

Favorite Study Guide Author

We've also added a preview edition of PrepLogic's powerful, full-featured test engine, which is trusted by certification students throughout the world.

As a 20-year-plus veteran of the computing industry and the original creator and editor of the Exam Cram series, I've brought my IT experience to bear on these books. During my tenure at Novell from 1989 to 1994, I worked with and around its excellent education and certification department. At Novell, I witnessed the growth and development of the first really big, successful IT certification program—one that was to shape the industry forever afterward. This experience helped push my writing and teaching activities heavily in the certification direction. Since then, I've worked on more than 70 certification related books, and I write about certification topics for numerous Web sites and for *Certification* magazine.

In 1997 when Exam Cram was introduced, it quickly became the best-selling computer book series since "...*For Dummies*," and the best-selling certification book series ever. By maintaining an intense focus on the subject matter, tracking errata and updates quickly, and following the certification market closely, Exam Cram was able to establish the dominant position in cert prep books.

You will not be disappointed in your decision to purchase this book. If you are, please contact me at etittel@jump.net. All suggestions, ideas, input, or constructive criticism are welcome!

*Ed Tittel*

# Contents at a Glance

## Appendixes

# Table of Contents

# About the Authors

**Will Schmied** (BSET, MCSE, CWNA, TICSA, MCSA, Security+, Network+, A+) is the president of Area 51 Partners, Inc., a provider of wired and wireless networking implementation, security, and training services to businesses in the Hampton Roads, Virginia, area. Will holds a bachelor's degree in mechanical engineering technology from Old Dominion University, along with his various IT industry certifications. In addition to his activities with Area 51 Partners, Inc., Will operates the MCSE certification portal MCSE World located at www.mcseworld.com.

Will has previously authored and contributed to several other publications from Que Publishing, including *MCSA/MCSE Planning, Implementing, and Maintaining a Microsoft Windows Server 2003 Environment Exam Cram 2 (Exam 70-296)*; *MCSA/MCSE 70-291 Training Guide: Implementing, Managing, and Maintaining a Windows Server 2003 Network Infrastructure (2003)*; *MCSA Training Guide (70-218): Managing a Windows 2000 Network Environment (2002)*; *MCSE Windows 2000 Server Exam Cram 2 (Exam 70-215) (2003)*; *Special Edition Using Windows XP Professional, Bestseller Edition (2003)*; *and Platinum Edition Using Windows XP (2003)*. Will has also worked with Microsoft in the MCSE exam-development process.

Will currently resides in Newport News, Virginia, with his wife, Chris; their children, Christopher, Austin, Andrea, and Hannah; their dogs, Peanut and Jay; and their cat, Smokey. When he's not busy working, you can find Will enjoying time with his family or reading a Douglas Adams book. You can visit Area 51 Partners at www.area51partners.com.

**Robert J. Shimonski** (TruSecure TICSA, Cisco CCDP, CCNP, Cisco Firewall Specialist, Nortel NNCSS, Microsoft MCSE, MCP+I, Novell Master CNE, CIP, CIBS, CNS, IWA CWP, DCSE, Prosoft MCIW, SANS GSEC, GCIH, CompTIA Server+, Network+, Inet+, A+, e-Biz+, Security+, HTI+, Symantec SPS, and NAI Sniffer SCP) is a Lead Network and Security Engineer for a very large conglomerate.

Robert has planned, designed, maintained, and managed very large network infrastructures for more than 50 companies around the world. Solutions deployed include but are not limited to Cisco and Nortel routing and switching equipment, Check Point and Cisco Security solutions, Microsoft and Novell Directory deployments, and many others. Robert's specialties include network infrastructure design with the Cisco and Nortel product line; network security design and management with CiscoSecure and PIX firewalls; network management and troubleshooting with CiscoWorks, CiscoSecure, and Sniffer-based technologies.

Robert is the author of many security-related articles and more than 25 published books, including the Sniffer Network Optimization and Troubleshooting Handbook and the Security+ Study Guide and DVD Training System. You can contact Robert at www.rsnetworks.net or at rshimonski@rsnetworks.net.

# We Want to Hear from You!

As the reader of this book, *you* are our most important critic and commentator. We value your opinion and want to know what we're doing right, what we could do better, what areas you'd like to see us publish in, and any other words of wisdom you're willing to pass our way.

As an executive editor for Que Publishing, I welcome your comments. You can email or write me directly to let me know what you did or didn't like about this book—as well as what we can do to make our books better.

*Please note that I cannot help you with technical problems related to the topic of this book. We do have a User Services group, however, where I will forward specific technical questions related to the book.*

When you write, please be sure to include this book's title and author as well as your name, email address, and phone number. I will carefully review your comments and share them with the author and editors who worked on the book.

Email:     feedback@quepublishing.com

Mail:      Jeff Riley
           Executive Editor
           Que Publishing
           800 East 96th Street
           Indianapolis, IN 46240 USA

For more information about this book or another Que Publishing title, visit our Web site at www.examcram2.com. Type the ISBN (excluding hyphens) or the title of a book in the Search field to find the page you're looking for.

# Introduction

*MCSE 70-293 Training Guide: Planning and Maintaining a Windows Server 2003 Network Infrastructure* is designed for advanced end users, network engineers, and systems administrators who are seeking to pass Exam 70-293 in pursuit of a Microsoft certification. Passing the Planning and Maintaining a Microsoft Windows Server 2003 Network Infrastructure exam qualifies you as a Microsoft Certified Professional (MCP) and counts as core credit toward the Microsoft Certified Systems Engineer (MCSE) certification.

This exam measures your ability to perform more advanced planning and implementation of security solutions, TCP/IP, DNS and WINS infrastructures, routing, remote access, highly available solutions through clustering and network load balancing, secure administration methods, secure data transmission methods, and digital certificates. It is already assumed that you understand the basics of all these topics and all the supporting areas that would be required to be at this stage of your career and experience with Windows Server 2003.

## WHO SHOULD READ THIS BOOK

This book is designed to help you meet your certification goals by preparing you for the Planning and Maintaining a Microsoft Windows Server 2003 Network Infrastructure exam (70-293). In a Windows Server 2003 network, the ability to plan, install, support, and troubleshoot the various networking components and services included with Windows Server

2003 is critical to an administrator's success. Windows Server 2003 tightly integrates services such as DHCP and DNS into the core operating systems as well as the Active Directory, and requires that they be configured correctly to function. This exam touches on all the major networking components critical to a successful Windows Server 2003 implementation. Although volumes of information are available on the history, theory, and underlying applications related to the networking services provided by Windows Server 2003, this book does not cover these portions of the services in detail. The purpose of this book is to provide you with an introduction to these services in general, provide you with an in-depth look at the Windows Server 2003 implementations of these network services, and prepare you to take the exam.

One additional area that is new to the Windows exams is the emphasis on network security. Keeping in line with the Microsoft Trustworthy Computing initiatives, Microsoft is putting a much greater emphasis on the security facets of all its Windows Server 2003 exams.

Recognizing that a great deal of information exists on these topics that this book cannot cover, each chapter in this book contains a section called "Suggested Readings and Resources" that provides you with recommended sources for filling in the blanks. So, although you may not be an expert at planning and implementing complex, multiple-site DNS architectures to support Active Directory, by the time you complete this book, you will know how to start and how to avoid many common pitfalls you might otherwise fall into. Additional resources are presented so that you can further your understanding and take your skills to the next level. (Chapter 3, "Planning, Implementing, and

Maintaining a Name Resolution Infrastructure," discusses planning new DNS namespaces.)

One of the most common questions with any of the Microsoft certification tests is, "Do I need to take a class to pass this test?" Although the information you need to pass the exam is in this book, one thing that is difficult for any book to provide is hands-on experience with the product. If you can set up an environment that enables you to perform the exercises outlined in this book (hardware and software recommendations for this environment are included at the end of this introduction), you will be in good shape. You'll be in especially good shape if you have the opportunity to work with Windows Server 2003 in a production environment. To pass the exam, you do not need to take a class in addition to buying this book. However, depending on your personal study habits or learning style, you may benefit from taking a class in conjunction with studying from this book.

Microsoft specifies the following audience profile for this exam, which also summarizes the experience level that a typical MCSE candidate should possess:

▶ The MCSE on Windows Server 2003 credential is intended for IT professionals who work in the typically complex computing environment of medium to large companies.

▶ Candidates should have experience implementing and administering a network operating system in environments that have the following characteristics:

- 250 to 5,000 or more users

- Three or more physical locations

- Three or more domain controllers

- Network services and resources such as messaging, database, file and print, proxy server, firewall, Internet, intranet, remote access, and client computer management

- Connectivity requirements such as connecting branch offices and individual users in remote locations to the corporate network and connecting corporate networks to the Internet

▶ In addition, candidates should have experience in the following areas:

- Implementing and administering a desktop operating system

- Designing a network infrastructure

# HOW THIS BOOK HELPS YOU

This book takes you on a self-guided tour of all the areas covered by the Planning and Maintaining a Microsoft Windows Server 2003 Network Infrastructure exam and teaches you the specific skills you need to achieve your MCSE certification. It also provides helpful hints, tips, real-world examples, and exercises, as well as references to additional study materials. Specifically, this book is set up to help you in the following ways:

▶ **Organization**—The book is organized by individual exam objectives. Every objective you need to know for the Planning and Maintaining a Microsoft Windows Server 2003 Network Infrastructure exam is covered in this book. We have attempted to present the objectives in an order that is as close as possible to that listed by Microsoft. However, we have not hesitated to reorganize where needed to make the material as easy as possible for you to learn. We have also attempted to make the information accessible in the following ways:

- The full list of exam topics and objectives is included in this introduction.

- Each chapter begins with a list of the objectives to be covered.

- Each chapter also begins with an outline that provides you with an overview of the material and the page numbers where particular topics can be found.

- The objectives are repeated where the material most directly relevant to it is covered (unless the whole chapter addresses a single objective).

- The CD-ROM included with this book contains, in PDF format, a complete listing of the test objectives and where they are covered within the book.

▶ **Instructional Features**—This book has been designed to provide you with multiple ways to learn and reinforce the exam material. Following are some of the helpful methods:

- **Objective Explanations**—As mentioned previously, each chapter begins with a list of the objectives covered in the chapter. In addition, immediately following each objective is an explanation in a context that defines it more meaningfully.

- **Study Strategies**—The beginning of the chapter also includes strategies for approaching the study and retention of the material in the chapter, particularly as it is addressed on the exam.

- **Exam Tips**—Exam tips appear in the margin to provide specific exam-related advice. Such tips may address the material covered (or not covered) on the exam, the way it is covered, mnemonic devices, or particular quirks of that exam.

- **Summaries**—Crucial information is summarized at various points in the book in lists or tables. Each chapter ends with a summary as well.

- **Key Terms**—A list of key terms appears at the end of each chapter.

- **Notes**—These notes appear in the margin and contain various kinds of useful information, such as tips on technology or administrative practices, historical background on terms and technologies, or side commentary on industry issues.

- **Warnings**—When you're using sophisticated information technology, the potential for mistakes always exists; catastrophes can even occur because of improper application of the technology. Warnings appear in the margin to alert you to such potential problems.

- **Case Studies**—Each chapter concludes with a case study. The cases are meant to help you understand the practical applications of the information covered in the chapter.

- **Step by Steps**—These hands-on tutorial instructions walk you through a particular task or function relevant to the exam objectives.

- **Exercises**—Found at the end of each chapter in the "Apply Your Knowledge" section, exercises are performance-based opportunities for you to learn and assess your knowledge.

▶ **Extensive practice test options**—The book provides numerous opportunities for you to assess your knowledge and practice for the exam. The practice options include the following:

- **Review Questions**—These open-ended questions appear in the "Apply Your Knowledge" section at the end of each chapter. They enable you to quickly assess your comprehension of what you just read in the chapter. Answers to the questions are provided later in the section.

- **Exam Questions**—These questions also appear in the "Apply Your Knowledge" section. They reflect the kinds of multiple-choice questions that appear on the Microsoft exams. Use them to practice for the exam and to help you determine what you know and what you need to review or study further. Answers and explanations for them are provided.

- **Final Review**—This part of the book provides you with valuable tools for preparing for the exam.

- **Fast Facts**—This condensed version of the information contained in the book is extremely useful for last-minute review.

- **Study and Exam Prep Tips**—Read this section early on to help you develop study strategies. It also provides you with valuable exam-day tips and information on exam/question formats such as adaptive tests and case study–based questions.

- **Practice Exam**—A practice test is included. Questions are written in styles similar to those used on the actual exam. Use it to assess your readiness for the real thing.

The book includes several other features, such as a section titled "Suggested Readings and Resources" at the end of each chapter that directs you toward further information that could aid you in your exam preparation or your actual work. Valuable appendixes are included as well, such as a glossary (Appendix A), a description of what is on the CD-ROM (Appendix B), and an overview of the PrepLogic Practice Tests Software (Appendix C).

For more information about the exam or the certification process, contact Microsoft at

Microsoft Education: 800-636-7544

Internet: `ftp://ftp.microsoft.com/Services/MSEdCert`

World Wide Web: `http://www.microsoft.com/train_cert`

CompuServe Forum: `GO MSEDCERT`

# PLANNING AND MAINTAINING A MICROSOFT WINDOWS SERVER 2003 NETWORK INFRASTRUCTURE EXAM (70-293)

Planning and Maintaining a Microsoft Windows Server 2003 Network Infrastructure exam (70-293) covers the Windows Server 2003 networking topics represented by the conceptual groupings or units of the test objectives. The objectives reflect job skills in the following areas:

▶ Planning and Implementing Server Roles and Server Security

▶ Planning, Implementing, and Maintaining a Network Infrastructure

▶ Planning, Implementing, and Maintaining Routing and Remote Access

▶ Planning, Implementing, and Maintaining Server Availability

▶ Planning and Maintaining Network Security

▶ Planning, Implementing, and Maintaining Security Infrastructure

Before taking the exam, you should be proficient in the job skills represented by the following objectives and subobjectives.

## Planning and Implementing Server Roles and Server Security

The Planning and Implementing Server Roles and Server Security objective is designed to make sure that you understand and thus can plan and implement secure servers based on their roles in the network. You need to understand the default security configuration of new computers as well as how to incrementally tighten security to meet your needs. The objectives are as follows:

▶ Configure security for servers that are assigned specific roles.

▶ Plan a secure baseline installation.

• Plan a strategy to enforce system default security settings on new systems.

• Identify client operating system default security settings.

• Identify all server operating system default security settings.

▶ Plan security for servers that are assigned specific roles. Roles might include domain controllers, Web servers, database servers, and mail servers.

• Deploy the security configuration for servers that are assigned specific roles.

• Create custom security templates based on server roles.

▶ Evaluate and select the operating system to install on computers in an enterprise.

• Identify the minimum configuration to satisfy security requirements.

## Planning, Implementing, and Maintaining a Network Infrastructure

The Planning, Implementing, and Maintaining a Network Infrastructure objective is designed to make sure that you can adequately plan, implement, configure, and troubleshoot a complex network infrastructure consisting of multiple protocols, multiple name resolution services, and the physical and logical placement of objects and resources. The objectives are as follows:

▶ Plan a TCP/IP network infrastructure strategy.

• Analyze IP addressing requirements.

• Plan an IP routing solution.

• Create an IP subnet scheme.

▶ Plan and modify a network topology.

• Plan the physical placement of network resources.

• Identify network protocols to be used.

▸ Plan an Internet connectivity strategy.

▸ Plan network traffic monitoring. Tools might include Network Monitor and System Monitor.

▸ Troubleshoot connectivity to the Internet.

- Diagnose and resolve issues related to Network Address Translation (NAT).

- Diagnose and resolve issues related to name resolution cache information.

- Diagnose and resolve issues related to client configuration.

▸ Troubleshoot TCP/IP addressing.

- Diagnose and resolve issues related to client computer configuration.

- Diagnose and resolve issues related to DHCP server address assignment.

▸ Plan a host name resolution strategy.

- Plan a DNS namespace design.

- Plan zone replication requirements.

- Plan a forwarding configuration.

- Plan for DNS security.

- Examine the interoperability of DNS with third-party DNS solutions.

▸ Plan a NetBIOS name resolution strategy.

- Plan a WINS replication strategy.

- Plan NetBIOS name resolution by using the Lmhosts file.

▸ Troubleshoot host name resolution.

- Diagnose and resolve issues related to DNS services.

- Diagnose and resolve issues related to client computer configuration.

# Planning, Implementing, and Maintaining Routing and Remote Access

The Planning, Implementing, and Maintaining Routing and Remote Access objective is designed to make sure that you can adequately plan, implement, configure, and troubleshoot a remote access and routing solution. The objectives are as follows:

▸ Plan a routing strategy.

- Identify routing protocols to use in a specified environment.

- Plan routing for IP multicast traffic.

▸ Plan security for remote access users.

- Plan remote access policies.

- Analyze protocol security requirements.

- Plan authentication methods for remote access clients.

▸ Implement secure access between private networks.

- Create and implement an IPSec policy.

▸ Troubleshoot TCP/IP routing. Tools might include the `route`, `tracert`, `ping`, `pathping`, and `netsh` commands and Network Monitor.

# Planning, Implementing, and Maintaining Server Availability

The Planning, Implementing, and Maintaining Server Availability objective is designed to make sure that you can adequately plan, implement, configure, and troubleshoot complex highly available solutions including clustering and network load balancing. You also are expected to understand and be able to plan and manage disaster recovery operations for your network in addition to monitoring your network for signs of trouble using available monitoring and logging tools. The objectives are as follows:

▶ Plan services for high availability.

- Plan a high availability solution that uses clustering services.

- Plan a high availability solution that uses network load balancing.

▶ Identify system bottlenecks, including memory, processor, disk, and network-related bottlenecks.

- Identify system bottlenecks by using System Monitor.

▶ Implement a cluster server.

- Recover from cluster node failure.

▶ Manage network load balancing. Tools might include the Network Load Balancing Monitor Microsoft Management Console (MMC) snap-in and the WLBS cluster control utility.

▶ Plan a backup and recovery strategy.

- Identify appropriate backup types. Methods include full, incremental, and differential.

- Plan a backup strategy that uses volume shadow copy.

- Plan system recovery that uses Automated System Recovery (ASR).

## Planning and Maintaining Network Security

The Planning and Maintaining Network Security objective is designed to make sure that you can

adequately plan, implement, configure, and troubleshoot complex network data security solutions that use the IP Security (IPSec) protocol. The objectives are as follows:

▶ Configure network protocol security.

- Configure protocol security in a heterogeneous client computer environment.

- Configure protocol security by using IPSec policies.

▶ Configure security for data transmission.

- Configure IPSec policy settings.

▶ Plan for network protocol security.

- Specify the required ports and protocols for specified services.

- Plan an IPSec policy for secure network communications.

▶ Plan secure network administration methods.

- Create a plan to offer Remote Assistance to client computers.

- Plan for remote administration by using Terminal Services.

▶ Plan security for wireless networks.

▶ Plan security for data transmission.

- Secure data transmission between client computers to meet security requirements.

- Secure data transmission by using IPSec.

▶ Troubleshoot security for data transmission. Tools might include the IP Security Monitor MMC snap-in and the Resultant Set of Policy (RSoP) MMC snap-in.

## Planning, Implementing, and Maintaining Security Infrastructure

The Planning, Implementing, and Maintaining Security Infrastructure objective is designed to make sure that you can adequately plan, implement, configure, and troubleshoot a complex Certificate Services infrastructure for your network. You also are expected to understand change and configuration management basics. Lastly, you will be tested on basic security management tools such as Microsoft Baseline Security Analyzer (MBSA) and Microsoft Software Update Services (SUS). The objectives are as follows:

► Configure Active Directory directory service for certificate publication.

► Plan a public key infrastructure (PKI) that uses Certificate Services.

  • Identify the appropriate type of certificate authority to support certificate issuance requirements.

  • Plan the enrollment and distribution of certificates.

  • Plan for the use of smart cards for authentication.

► Plan a framework for planning and implementing security.

  • Plan for security monitoring.

  • Plan a change and configuration management framework for security.

► Plan a security update infrastructure. Tools might include Microsoft Baseline Security Analyzer and Microsoft Software Update Services.

# HARDWARE AND SOFTWARE YOU WILL NEED

As a self-paced study guide, *MCSE 70-293 Training Guide: Planning and Maintaining a Windows Server 2003 Network Infrastructure* is meant to help you understand concepts that must be refined through hands-on experience. To make the most of your studying, you need to have as much background on and experience with Windows Server 2003 as possible. The best way to do this is to combine studying with working on real networks, using the products on which you will be tested. This section gives you a description of the minimum computer requirements you need to enjoy a solid practice environment.

The minimum computer requirements to ensure that you can study everything on which you'll be tested are one or more workstations running Windows 2000 Professional or Windows XP Professional, and two or more servers running Windows Server 2003—all connected by a network. Many of these examples, exercises, and references refer to Internet Web sites, so an Internet-connected network would be a benefit. Because we look at some of the higher level capabilities of the Windows Server 2003 family, the minimum requirements listed are specific to Windows Server 2003 Enterprise Edition. It has all the features that are covered by this exam and the lowest minimum hardware requirements.

## Windows 2000 Professional

If you are using Windows 2000 Professional on your client workstations, they need to meet the following *minimum* requirements:

- Major hardware listed on the Hardware Compatibility List at www.microsoft.com/ whdc/hcl/search.mspx

- 133MHz or higher Pentium (or compatible) CPU

- At least 64MB of RAM required

- Hard drive of at least 2GB with 650MB free space minimum

- CD-ROM or DVD drive required

- 3.5-inch 1.44MB floppy drive recommended

- VGA or higher resolution monitor and video adapter

- Keyboard and mouse required

- Network adapter required for networking

## Windows XP Professional

If you are using Windows XP Professional on your client workstations, they need to meet the following *minimum* requirements:

- Major hardware listed in the Windows Catalog at www.microsoft.com/windows/catalog/

- 300MHz or higher Pentium (or compatible) CPU recommended, minimum of 233MHz CPU required

- 128MB of RAM recommended, minimum of 64MB of RAM required

- Hard drive with at least 1.5GB of free space minimum

- CD-ROM or DVD drive required

- 3.5-inch 1.44MB floppy drive recommended

- Super VGA or higher resolution monitor and video adapter

- Keyboard and mouse required

- Network adapter required for networking

## Windows Server 2003 Enterprise Edition

Windows Server 2003 computers need to meet the following minimum requirements. You should strive to exceed these requirements where possible to provide for enhanced performance and stability.

- Major hardware listed in the Windows Server Catalog at www.microsoft.com/windows /catalog/server/

- 733MHz or higher Pentium (or compatible) CPU recommended for Intel x86–based computers, minimum of 133MHz CPU required

- 256MB of RAM recommended, minimum of 128MB of RAM required

- Hard drive with at least 1.5GB of free space minimum for Intel x86–based computers

- CD-ROM or DVD drive required

- 3.5-inch 1.44MB floppy drive recommended

- Super VGA or higher resolution monitor and video adapter

- Keyboard and mouse required

- Network adapter required for networking

You can more easily obtain access to the necessary computer hardware and software in a corporate business environment. Allocating enough time within the busy workday to complete a self-study program, however, can be difficult. Most of your study time will occur after normal working hours, away from the everyday interruptions and pressures of your regular job.

# ADVICE ON TAKING THE EXAM

You can find more extensive tips in the section titled "Study and Exam Prep Tips," but keep this advice in mind as you study:

▶ Read all the material. Microsoft has been known to include material not expressly specified in the objectives. This book includes additional information not reflected in the objectives in an effort to give you the best possible preparation for the examination—and for the real-world network experiences to come.

▶ Do the Step by Steps and complete the exercises in each chapter. They help you gain experience using the specified methodology or approach. All Microsoft exams are task- and experienced-based and require you to have experience actually performing the tasks on which you will be tested.

▶ Use the questions to assess your knowledge. Don't just read the chapter content; use the questions to find out what you know and what you don't. If you are struggling at all, study some more, review, and then assess your knowledge again.

▶ Review the exam objectives. Develop your own questions and examples for each topic listed. If you can develop and answer several questions for each topic, you should not find it difficult to pass the exam.

▶ Find a "study-buddy." Okay, this tip sounds pretty corny, but it works: Find a coworker or friend who is also preparing for the exam and use that person to improve your knowledge. Quiz each other and assist each other with sections where you feel your knowledge is weak.

**NOTE**

**Exam Taking Advice**   Although this book is designed to prepare you to take and pass the Planning and Maintaining a Microsoft Windows Server 2003 Network Infrastructure exam (70-293), there are no guarantees. Read this book, work through the questions and exercises, and when you feel confident, take the Practice Exam and additional exams using the PrepLogic Practice Tests software. This should tell you whether you are ready for the real thing.

When taking the actual certification exam, make sure you answer all the questions before your time limit expires. Do not spend too much time on any one question. If you are unsure, answer the question the best you can; then mark it for review after you have finished the rest of the questions. However, this advice does not apply when you are taking an adaptive exam. In that case, take your time on each question. There is no opportunity to go back to a question.

Be sure to read each question carefully and read all the answers before making a selection. Questions may have an answer that is close, but one of the other answers may, in fact, be a better answer. If you select your answer before reading all the choices, you may miss the "best" answer.

Get a good night's sleep before the exam. If you don't know the information by the night before the exam, an all-night cram session will just make you tired when you are taking the exam. You need to be at your sharpest when you take this exam; don't handicap yourself with sleep deprivation.

Remember, the primary objective of this book is not the exam; it is to ensure that you understand the material. After you understand the material, passing the exam should be simple. Knowledge is a pyramid; to build upward, you need a solid foundation. This book and the Microsoft Certified Professional programs are designed to ensure that you have that solid foundation.

Good luck!

This element of the book provides you with some general guidelines for preparing for any certification exam, including Exam 70-293, "Planning and Maintaining a Microsoft Windows Server 2003 Network Infrastructure." It is organized into four sections. The first section addresses learning styles and how they affect preparation for the exam. The second section covers exam preparation activities and general study tips. This is followed by an extended look at the Microsoft certification exams, including a number of specific tips that apply to the various Microsoft exam formats and question types. Finally, changes in Microsoft's testing policies and how they might affect you are discussed.

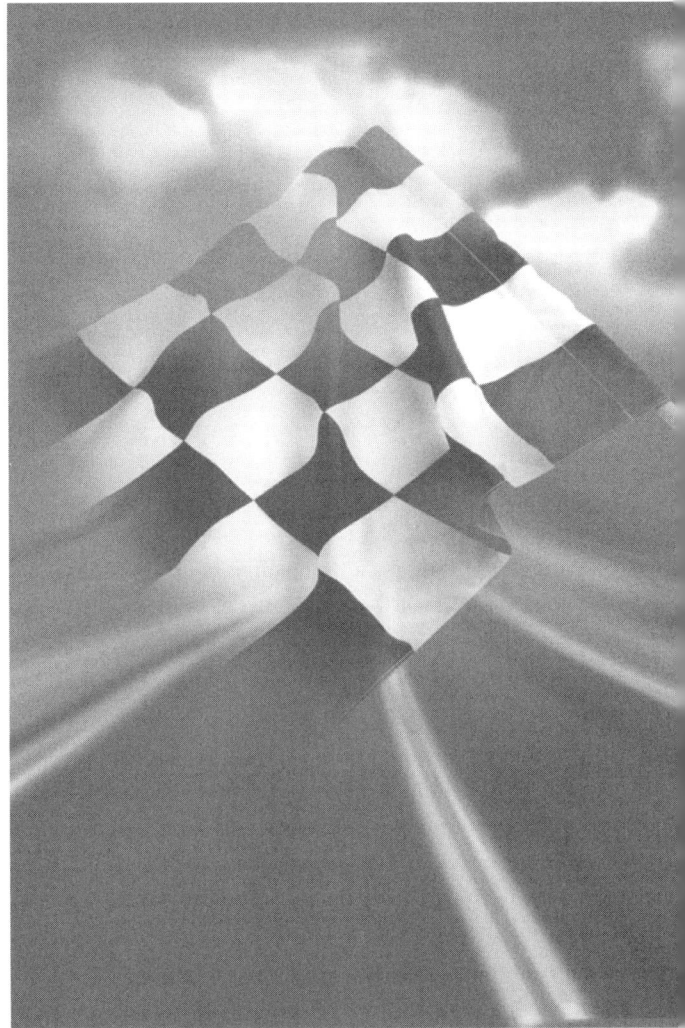

# Study and Exam Prep Tips

# LEARNING STYLES

To best understand the nature of preparation for the test, you need to understand learning as a process. You are probably aware of how you best learn new material. You might find that outlining works best for you, or, as a visual learner, you might need to see things. Or you might need models or examples, or maybe you just like noodling around. Whatever your learning style, test preparation takes place over time. Obviously, you shouldn't start studying for a certification exam the night before you take it; it is very important to understand that learning is a developmental process. Understanding learning as a process helps you focus on what you know and what you have yet to learn.

Thinking about how you learn should help you recognize that learning takes place when you are able to match new information to old. You have some previous experience with computers and networking. Now you are preparing for this certification exam. Using this book, software, and supplementary materials will not just add incrementally to what you know; as you study, the organization of your knowledge actually restructures as you integrate new information into your existing knowledge base. This leads you to a more comprehensive understanding of the tasks and concepts outlined in the objectives and of computing in general. Again, learning happens as a result of a repetitive process rather than a singular event. If you keep this model of learning in mind as you prepare for the exam, you will make better decisions concerning what to study and how much more studying you need to do.

# STUDY TIPS

There are many ways to approach studying, just as there are many different types of material to study. However, the tips that follow should work well for the type of material covered on Microsoft certification exams.

# Study Strategies

Although individuals vary in the ways they learn information, some basic principles of learning apply to everyone. You should adopt some study strategies that take advantage of these principles. One of these principles is that learning can be broken into various depths. Recognition (of terms, for example) exemplifies a rather surface level of learning in which you rely on a prompt of some sort to elicit recall. Comprehension or understanding (of the concepts behind the terms, for example) represents a deeper level of learning than recognition. The ability to analyze a concept and apply your understanding of it in a new way represents further depth of learning.

Your learning strategy should enable you to know the material at a level or two deeper than mere recognition. This will help you perform well on the exams. You will know the material so thoroughly that you can go beyond the recognition-level types of questions commonly used in fact-based multiple-choice testing. You will be able to apply your knowledge to solve new problems.

## Macro and Micro Study Strategies

One strategy that can lead to deep learning includes preparing an outline that covers all the objectives and subobjectives for the particular exam you are working on. You should delve a bit further into the material and include a level or two of detail beyond the stated objectives and subobjectives for the exam. Then you should expand the outline by coming up with a statement of definition or a summary for each point in the outline.

An outline provides two approaches to studying. First, you can study the outline by focusing on the organization of the material. You can work your way through the points and subpoints of your outline, with the goal of learning how they relate to one another. For example, you should be sure you understand how each of the main objective areas for Exam 70-293 is similar to and different from another. Then you should do the same thing with the subobjectives; you should be sure you know which subobjectives pertain to each objective area and how they relate to one another.

Next, you can work through the outline, focusing on learning the details. You should memorize and understand terms and their definitions, facts, rules and tactics, advantages and disadvantages, and so on. In this pass through the outline, you should attempt to learn detail rather than the big picture (the organizational information that you worked on in the first pass through the outline).

Research has shown that attempting to assimilate both types of information at the same time interferes with the overall learning process. If you separate your studying into these two approaches, you will perform better on the exam.

## Active Study Strategies

The process of writing down and defining objectives, subobjectives, terms, facts, and definitions promotes a more active learning strategy than merely reading the material does. In human information-processing terms, writing forces you to engage in more active encoding of the information. Simply reading over the information leads to more passive processing.

You need to determine whether you can apply the information you have learned by attempting to create examples and scenarios on your own. You should think about how or where you could apply the concepts you are learning. Again, you should write down this information to process the facts and concepts in an active fashion.

The hands-on nature of the exercises at the ends of the chapters provides further active learning opportunities that will reinforce concepts as well.

## Common-Sense Strategies

You should follow common-sense practices when studying: You should study when you are alert, reduce or eliminate distractions, and take breaks when you become fatigued.

## Pretesting Yourself

Pretesting allows you to assess how well you are learning. One of the most important aspects of learning is what has been called *meta-learning*. Meta-learning has to do with realizing when you know something well or when you need to study some more. In other words, you recognize how well or how poorly you have learned the material you are studying.

For most people, assessing this can be difficult. Review questions, practice questions, and practice tests are useful in that they reveal objectively what you have learned and what you have not learned. You should use this information to guide review and further studying. Developmental learning takes place as you cycle through studying, assessing how well you have learned, reviewing, and assessing again until you feel you are ready to take the exam.

You might have noticed the practice exam included in this book. You should use it as part of the learning process. The PrepLogic Practice Exams, Preview Edition, test simulation software included on this book's CD-ROM also provides you with an excellent opportunity to assess your knowledge.

You should set a goal for your pretesting. A reasonable goal would be to score consistently in the 90% range.

See Appendix C, "Using PrepLogic, Preview Edition Software," for further explanation of the test simulation software.

In the next section, you'll learn more about the format of Microsoft test questions and how to answer them.

# EXAM LAYOUT AND DESIGN

The format of Microsoft exams can vary. In addition to the eight exam question types we will examine next, Microsoft has publicly announced that it may include adaptive testing technology and simulation items in the certification exams. You may not know ahead of time what you are getting into, so you should prepare the same regardless.

## Active Screen Questions

The active screen question is one of several new types introduced with the Windows Server 2003 MCP exams. This question type requires you to configure a dialog box by changing one or more of its options, as shown in Figure 1.

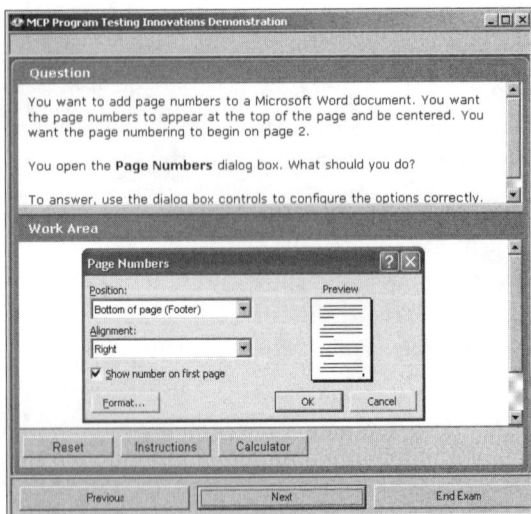

**FIGURE 1**
The active screen question type requires you to manipulate a dialog box to achieve the desired results.

To answer the active screen question, you may need to do one of several things, including selecting and unselecting options, changing values in drop-down menus, and dragging text elements into text areas within the dialog box. When you are done with your configuration actions, you simply need to click the Next button to progress to the next question. You can use the Reset button to reset the dialog box back to its original configuration.

It is important to note that not every element in the dialog box will be active; this can be helpful if you have trouble figuring out where to start with the question. You can use the scrollbars to view the entire text or dialog box area. The splitter bar can also be used to resize the panes as desired.

## Build List and Reorder Questions

The build list and reorder question type is not new to the Windows Server 2003 MCP exams, but Microsoft has redefined it since its initial introduction. In the build list and reorder question, shown in Figure 2, you are required to build a list in the correct order that represents the steps required to achieve the required result.

You can move objects to the workspace by dragging them. You can rearrange objects in the workspace by dragging them up and down within the list. Should you need to remove an object from the workspace, simply drag it out of the workspace. The Reset button can be used to reset the workspace back to its original configuration. You can use the scrollbars to view the entire text or dialog box area. The splitter bar can also be used to resize the panes as desired.

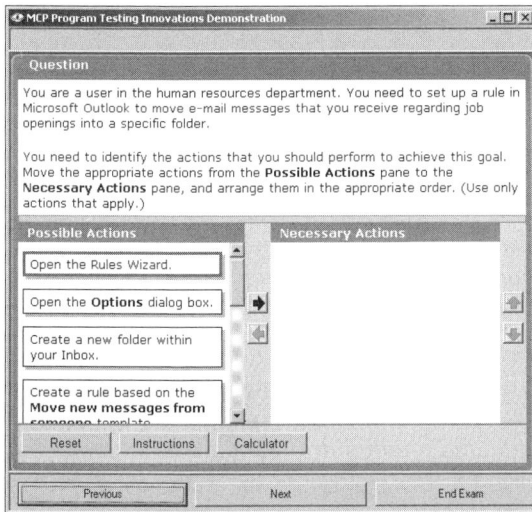

**FIGURE 2**
The build list and reorder question type requires you to indicate the correct answer by building an answer list.

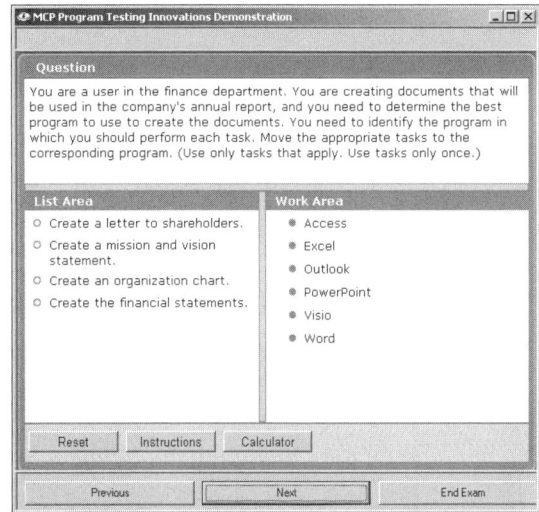

**FIGURE 3**
The create a tree question type requires you to create a tree structure to answer the question.

## Create a Tree Questions

The create a tree question type is also not new to the Windows Server 2003 MCP exams, but Microsoft has refined it since its initial introduction. In the create a tree question, shown in Figure 3, you are required to create a tree structure to achieve the required result or answer the question at hand.

You answer this type of question by dragging source nodes into the answer tree in the correct locations. Entries that are present in the answer tree cannot be moved from their initial locations. Answer trees can include five levels of nodes and thus can grow quite complex for some questions. When a source node can no longer be used, it is no longer available to select and drag. If a source node is still available to select and drag, it can be used again as required. You can remove nodes by dragging them out of the answer tree or by selecting them and pressing Delete. The Reset button can be used to reset the answer tree back to its original configuration. The + and – icons can be used to expand or hide the child nodes that are under a parent node.

## Drag-and-Drop Questions

The drag-and-drop question type requires you to drag source objects into their proper place in the work area. In the drag-and-drop question, shown in Figure 4, you are required to place the correct text labels under the items they are associated with.

You answer this type of question by dragging source objects into the work area and placing them in the correct locations. Place the source object into the correct target when the target area turns gray. You can delete source objects by dragging them back to their initial location or by clicking on them and pressing Delete. The Reset button can be used to reset the work area back to its original configuration.

## Hot Area Questions

The hot area question type asks you to select one or more areas on a graphic to indicate the correct answer to a question, as shown in Figure 5. The hot spots on the graphic are shaded when you move the mouse over them and are marked with an obvious border. To select or deselect an element, just click it.

**FIGURE 4**
The drag-and-drop question type requires you to place items in the correct location to answer the question.

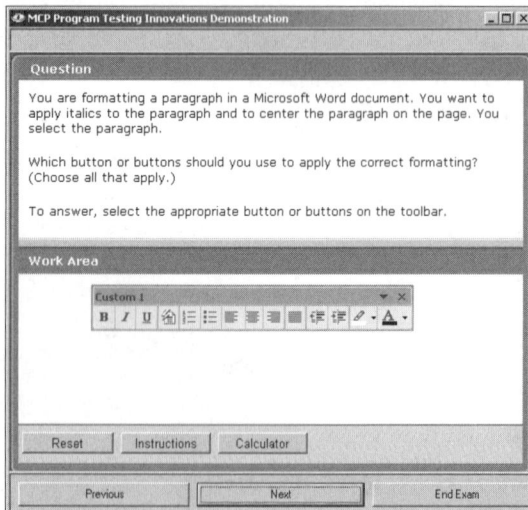

**FIGURE 5**
The hot area question type requires you to select one or more areas to answer the question.

After selecting an area, you can unselect it by clicking it again. To unselect all selected areas, click the Reset button.

# Multiple-Choice, Single-Answer, and Multiple-Choice, Multiple-Answer Questions

Some exam questions require you to select a single answer, whereas others ask you to select multiple correct answers. Both are standard question types that Microsoft and most other vendors have used for years. Single-answer questions provide radio buttons (circles) for your answer selection. Multiple-answer questions provide check boxes for your answer selections and usually are indicated by one of the following phrases:

▶ Select two correct answers.

▶ Select all correct answers.

▶ Select three correct answers; each answer represents a part of the solution.

# Testlet (Quizlet) Exam Format

The testlet is more of an exam format than a question format and is used on the design exams. The testlet format is also known as the quizlet or case study format. Testlets typically consist of 10 or more questions of varying types (from those discussed previously) as well as a significant amount of background material that must be read and understood for you to be able to successfully answer the questions. Figure 6 shows the new testlet format Microsoft is using in the Windows Server 2003 MCP exams.

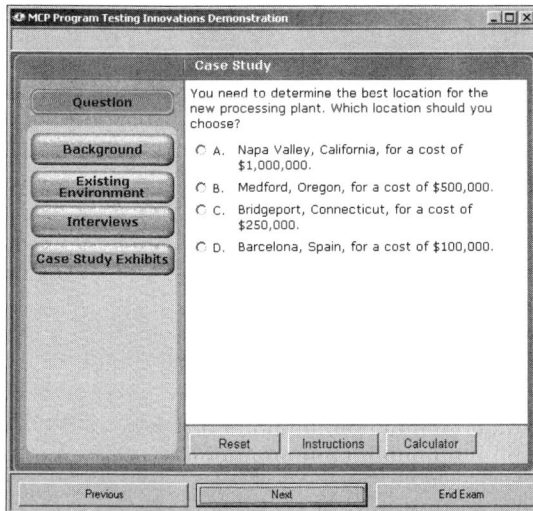

**FIGURE 6**
The testlet is composed of several questions and their related background information.

Each testlet is its own self-contained test. Although you can move back and forth between questions with the testlet, you cannot go back and rework testlet questions you have completed and moved past. Typically, you might expect to find three to five testlets on any one exam, each with around 5–20 questions and with a timer that is appropriate for the number of questions contained within that specific testlet.

The left pane of the quizlet window presents several areas that contain the required reading and necessary illustrations to answer the questions correctly. Note that each button in the left pane of the quizlet window may actually reveal multiple subselections below it.

## Putting It All Together

As you can see, Microsoft is making an effort to utilize question types that go beyond asking you to simply memorize facts. These question types force you to know how to accomplish tasks and understand concepts and relationships. You should study so that you can answer these types of questions rather than those that simply ask you to recall facts.

Given all the different pieces of information presented so far, the following sections present a set of tips that will help you successfully tackle the exam.

# QUESTION-HANDLING STRATEGIES

For those questions that have only one right answer, usually two or three of the answers are obviously incorrect, and two of the answers are plausible. Unless the answer leaps out at you (if it does, reread the question to look for a trick; sometimes those are the ones you're most likely to get wrong), begin the process of answering by eliminating those answers that are most obviously wrong.

At least one answer out of the possible choices for a question can usually be eliminated immediately because it matches one of these conditions:

▶ The answer does not apply to the situation.

▶ The answer describes a nonexistent issue, an invalid option, or an imaginary state.

After you eliminate all answers that are obviously wrong, you can apply your retained knowledge to eliminate further answers. Look for items that sound correct but refer to actions, commands, or features that are not present or not available in the situation that the question describes.

If you're still faced with a blind guess among two or more potentially correct answers, reread the question. Try to picture how each of the possible remaining answers would alter the situation. Be especially sensitive to terminology; sometimes the choice of words (*remove* instead of *disable*) can make the difference between a right answer and a wrong one.

You should guess at an answer only after you've exhausted your ability to eliminate answers and are still unclear about which of the remaining possibilities is correct. An unanswered question offers you no points, but guessing gives you at least some chance of answering a question right; just don't be too hasty when making a blind guess.

Numerous questions assume that the default behavior of a particular utility is in effect. If you know the defaults and understand what they mean, this knowledge will help you cut through many Gordian knots. Simple "final" actions may be critical as well. If a utility must be restarted before proposed changes take effect, a correct answer may require this step as well.

## MASTERING THE INNER GAME

In the final analysis, knowledge gives confidence, and confidence breeds success. If you study the materials in this book carefully and review all the practice questions at the end of each chapter, you should become aware of those areas where additional learning and study are required.

After you've worked your way through the book, take the practice exam in the back of the book. Taking this test provides a reality check and helps you identify areas to study further. Make sure you follow up and review materials related to the questions you miss on the practice exam before scheduling a real exam. Don't schedule your exam appointment until after you've thoroughly studied the material and feel comfortable with the whole scope of the practice exam. You should score 80% or better on the practice exam before proceeding to the real thing (otherwise, obtain some additional practice tests so you can keep trying until you hit this magic number).

> **EXAM TIP**
> If you take a practice exam and don't get at least 80–90% of the questions correct, keep practicing. Microsoft provides links to practice exam providers and also self-assessment exams at `http://www.microsoft.com/traincert/mcpexams/prepare/`.

Armed with the information in this book and with the determination to augment your knowledge, you should be able to pass the certification exam. However, you need to work at it, or you'll spend the exam fee more than once before you finally pass. If you prepare seriously, you should do well.

## More Exam Preparation Tips

Generic exam-preparation advice is always useful. Following are some tips:

▶ Become familiar with the product. Hands-on experience is one of the keys to success on any MCP exam. Review the exercises and the Step by Steps in the book.

▶ Review the current exam-preparation guide on the Microsoft Training & Certification Web site. The documentation Microsoft makes available on the Web identifies the skills every exam is intended to test.

▶ Memorize foundational technical detail, but remember that MCP exams are generally heavier on problem solving and application of knowledge than on questions that require only rote memorization.

▶ Take any of the available practice tests. We recommend the one included in this book and the ones you can create by using the PrepLogic software on this book's CD-ROM. As a supplement to the material bound with this book, try the free practice tests available on the Microsoft MCP Web site.

▶ Look on the Microsoft Training & Certification Web site for samples and demonstration items (as of this writing, check `www.microsoft.com/traincert/mcpexams/faq/innovations.asp`, but you might have to look around for the samples because the URL may have changed). These items tend to be particularly valuable for one significant reason: They help you become familiar with new testing technologies before you encounter them on MCP exams.

## Tips for During the Exam Session

The following generic exam-taking advice that you've heard for years applies when you're taking an MCP exam:

▶ Take a deep breath and try to relax when you first sit down for your exam session. It is very important that you control the pressure you might (naturally) feel when taking exams.

▶ You will be provided scratch paper. Take a moment to write down any factual information and technical detail that you have committed to short-term memory.

▶ Carefully read all information and instruction screens. These displays have been put together to give you information relevant to the exam you are taking.

▶ Accept the nondisclosure agreement and preliminary survey as part of the examination process. Complete them accurately and quickly move on.

▶ Read the exam questions carefully. Reread each question to identify all relevant details.

▶ In fixed-form exams, tackle the questions in the order in which they are presented. Skipping around won't build your confidence; the clock is always counting down.

▶ Don't rush, but also don't linger on difficult questions. The questions vary in degree of difficulty. Don't let yourself be flustered by a particularly difficult or wordy question.

Besides considering the basic preparation and test-taking advice presented so far, you also need to consider the challenges presented by the different exam designs, as described in the following sections.

## Tips for Fixed-Form Exams

Because a fixed-form exam is composed of a fixed, finite set of questions, you should add these tips to your strategy for taking a fixed-form exam:

▶ Note the time allotted and the number of questions on the exam you are taking. Make a rough calculation of the number of minutes you can spend on each question, and use this figure to pace yourself through the exam.

▶ Take advantage of the fact that you can return to and review skipped or previously answered questions. Record the questions you can't answer confidently on the scratch paper provided, noting the relative difficulty of each question. When you reach the end of the exam, return to the more difficult questions.

▶ If you have session time remaining after you complete all the questions (and if you aren't too fatigued!), review your answers. Pay particular attention to questions that seem to have a lot of detail or that require graphics.

▶ As for changing your answers, the general rule of thumb here is *don't!* If you read the question carefully and completely and you felt as though you knew the right answer, you probably did. Don't second-guess yourself. If, as you check your answers, one clearly stands out as incorrect, however, of course you should change it. But if you are at all unsure, go with your first impression.

## Tips for Adaptive Exams

If you are planning to take an adaptive exam, keep these additional tips in mind:

▶ Read and answer every question with great care. When you're reading a question, identify every relevant detail, requirement, or task you must perform and double-check your answer to be sure you have addressed every one of them.

▶ If you cannot answer a question, use the process of elimination to reduce the set of potential answers and then take your best guess. Stupid mistakes invariably mean that additional questions will be presented.

▶ You cannot review questions and change answers. When you leave a question, whether you've answered it or not, you cannot return to it. Do not skip any question, either; if you do, it's counted as incorrect.

## Tips for Case Study Exams

The case study exam format calls for unique study and exam-taking strategies:

▶ Remember that you have more time than in a typical exam. Take your time and read the case study thoroughly.

▶ Use the scrap paper or whatever medium is provided to you to take notes, diagram processes, and actively seek out the important information.

▶ Work through each testlet as if each were an independent exam. Remember that you cannot go back after you have left a testlet.

▶ Refer to the case study as often as you need to, but do not use that as a substitute for reading it carefully initially and for taking notes.

## FINAL CONSIDERATIONS

Finally, a number of changes in the MCP program affect how frequently you can repeat an exam and what you will see when you do:

▶ Microsoft has an exam retake policy. The rule is "two and two, then one and two." That is, you can attempt any exam twice with no restrictions on the time between attempts. But after the second attempt, you must wait two weeks before you can attempt that exam again. After that, you are required to wait two weeks between subsequent attempts. Plan to pass the exam in two attempts or plan to increase your time horizon for receiving the MCP credential.

▶ New questions are always being seeded into the MCP exams. After performance data is gathered on new questions, the examiners replace older questions on all exam forms. This means that the questions appearing on exams regularly change.

▶ Any of the current MCP exams may be republished in adaptive form. The exception to this may be the case study exams because the adaptive approach does not work with that format.

These changes mean that the brute-force strategies for passing MCP exams have lost their viability. So if you don't pass an exam on the first or second attempt, it is likely that the exam's form could change significantly by the next time you take it. It could be updated from fixed-form to adaptive, or, even more likely, it could have a different set of questions or question types.

Microsoft's intention is not to make the exams more difficult by introducing unwanted change, but to create and maintain valid measures of the technical skills and knowledge associated with the different MCP credentials. Preparing for an MCP exam has always involved not only studying the subject matter but also planning for the testing experience itself. With the continuing changes, this is now truer than ever.

Starting a text devoted to networking with a chapter on security might seem odd, but only if you are still working with the assumption that security is only for secret government research laboratories. Security is now front and center in Windows Server 2003, permeating it from front to back, top to bottom. Thus, it is only fitting that we discuss security and server roles before anything else in this training guide.

Microsoft defines the "Planning and Implementing Server Roles and Server Security" objectives as follows:

**Configure security for servers that are assigned specific roles.**

▶ The key to configuring and implementing role-based server security is to recognize the different levels at which security must be implemented. Servers should be grouped in Organizational Units (OU) by role for the purpose of applying security settings to them in an administratively efficient manner.

**Plan a secure baseline installation.**

▶ Plan a strategy to enforce system default security settings on new systems.

▶ Identify client operating system default security settings.

▶ Identify all server operating system default security settings.

• **Windows Server 2003 is the most secure network operating system, out of the box, ever produced by Microsoft. While planning and implementing your overall network security plan, you need to be able to identify and, if necessary, enforce the default security settings on servers and client computers.**

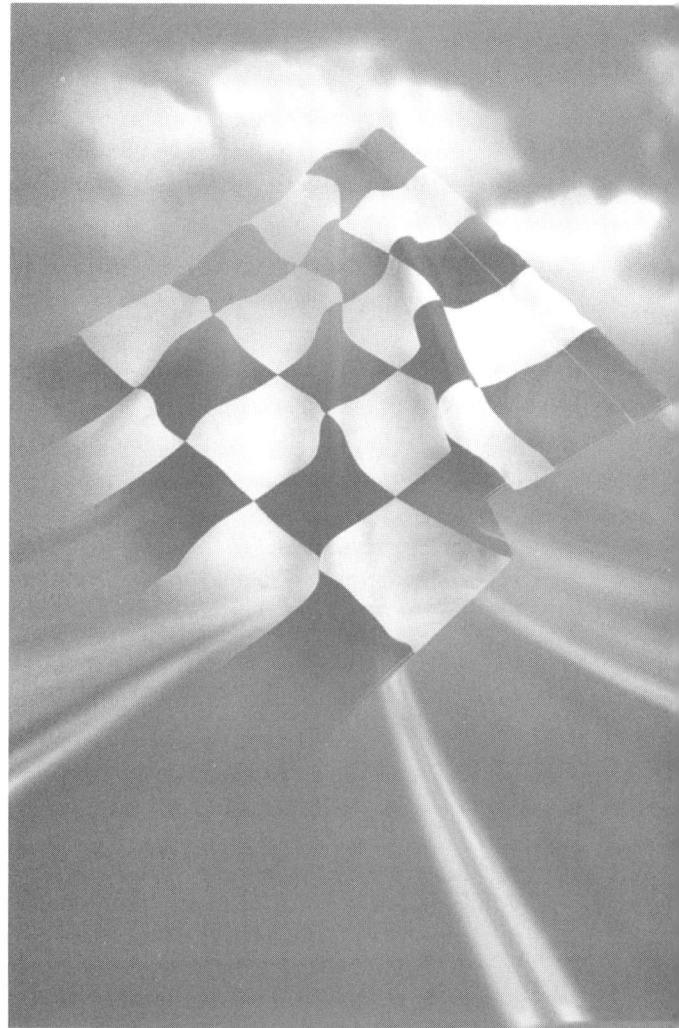

CHAPTER 1

# Planning and Implementing Server Roles and Server Security

**Plan security for servers that are assigned specific roles. Roles might include domain controllers, Web servers, database servers, and mail servers.**

▶ Deploy the security configuration for servers that are assigned specific roles.

▶ Create custom security templates based on server roles.

• **Not all servers are created alike; this simple fact has been proven time and again to administrators who got caught with their proverbial pants down. To effectively secure servers with varying roles, you need to identify the threats and vulnerabilities that each server faces.**

**Evaluate and select the operating system to install on computers in an enterprise.**

▶ Identify the minimum configuration to satisfy security requirements.

• **A default, out of the box, installation of Windows Server 2003 may not be the best choice for your particular security requirements. Being able to identify the best operating system and the optimal security configuration for that operating system is an important part of your overall network security plan.**

▶ Become familiar with the topics presented in this chapter, including security templates, Group Policy, and hierarchical organizational systems. All these topics will be important as you plan and implement a security solution for your network.

▶ Understand the strengths and weaknesses of the different security configuration tools available to you. Each has a specific purpose and can be used to secure your network.

▶ Get your hands dirty. The Step by Steps throughout this book provide plenty of directions and exercises, but you should go beyond these examples and create some of your own. If you can, experiment with each of the objectives to see how they work and why you would use each one.

# INTRODUCTION

Windows Server 2003 is inherently more secure right out of the box than any previous version of Windows to come before it. The Trustworthy Computing campaign that Microsoft is leading has shown itself directly in the intrinsic security of Windows Server 2003. Although this version is overall more secure than its predecessors, that does not relieve you of the responsibility to evaluate, plan and implement additional, custom security measures for your Windows Server 2003 network.

Whatever security plan you ultimately design and implement, you will be best served by implementing *role-based security*. Role-based security is implemented by using a layered approach to security; the most general security settings are applied at the highest level and become increasingly more restrictive as you go deeper into the organizational structure of the domain. Through the use of the preconfigured security templates included with Windows Server 2003, combined with careful planning and attentive administration of the network, you will be able to implement a role-based security solution.

Windows Server 2003 comes with a complete set of preconfigured security templates that you can use to quickly apply standardized security settings to a single computer, an Organizational Unit (OU), or a domain if desired. In addition to these preconfigured security templates, Microsoft has made available additional security templates that can be used to enforce very specific security settings on Windows Server 2003 computers, depending on their assigned role. Throughout this chapter we examine the various ways that security templates can be configured and implemented to apply both default and customized security solutions in your Windows Server 2003 network.

# IMPLEMENTING ENTERPRISE SECURITY

If any one thing could be said about Windows Server 2003, it might be that Windows Server 2003 depends on Active Directory through and through. Active Directory permeates every part of an enterprise Windows Server 2003 network and is the conduit through which the network functions efficiently and securely. Although this is not a text on Active Directory design and implementation, nor is it designed to ready you for Exam 70-294, "Planning, Implementing, and Maintaining a Microsoft Windows Server 2003 Active Directory Infrastructure," you will become acutely aware throughout this chapter how important a good Active Directory design and implementation are to your Windows Server 2003 network security plan.

Because Active Directory is so important to effectively plan and implement a solid security plan in Windows Server 2003 networks, it is critical that you understand how to effectively organize your Active Directory structure to achieve the best results, both from a security standpoint and also from an administrative one. When Windows 2000 was introduced, many network administrators mistakenly believed that the domain was a security boundary. This is simply not the case. The only absolute security boundary is that of the forest itself. In any forest environment, there exists ways for trusted administrators to acquire more privileges than they should have and abuse the power that has been granted to them.

Unfortunately, the reality is that the single forest arrangement with multiple domains is the best overall way to design, implement, and manage the vast majority of Windows Server 2003 networks—including those that you will most likely be working on. With that in mind, you must plan for security from the beginning of your design.

Organizational Units (OU), sometimes thought of as nothing more than an organizational tool to "clean" up the visual appearance of Active Directory, are actually among your most powerful tools for planning, implementing, and maintaining a secure network environment. OUs offer an easy way to segment users and other security principals, specifically computers in this instance, for the purpose of creating and enforcing administrative boundaries. Nesting OUs within each other, each with its own specific Group Policy Object (GPO), allows you to piece together the overall security solution for your network. Figure 1.1 illustrates this principle.

**FIGURE 1.1**

By nesting Organizational Units, you can create segmented and secure networks.

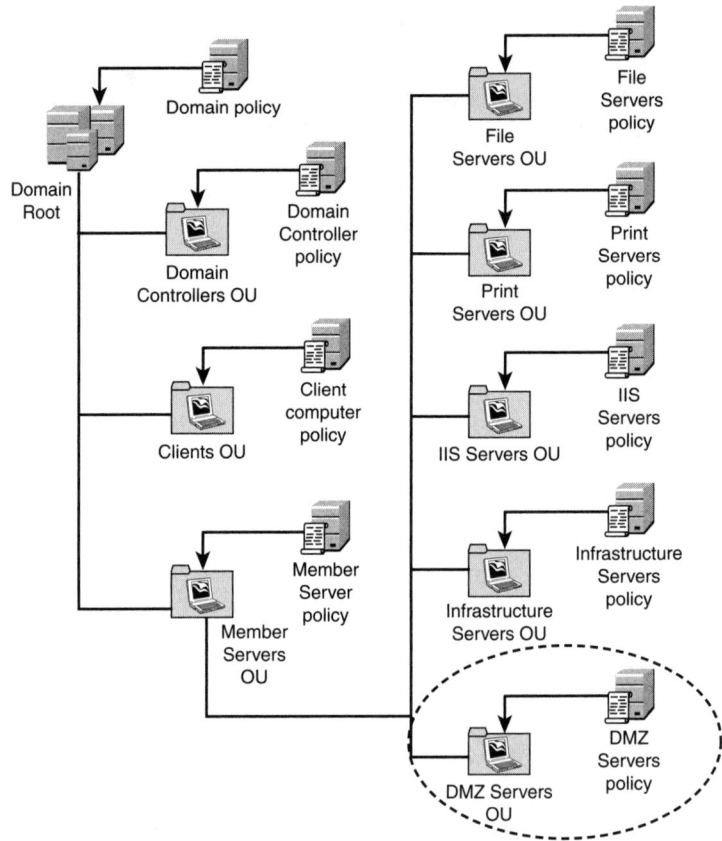

With this brief introduction to the way you might create a layered security solution, let's now move forward and start examining the tools available to you. The first step in implementing role-based security is to implement a *baseline configuration*. Before you can implement this baseline configuration, however, you must be aware of the default security settings that Windows gives you to start the process. This is the topic of the next section.

# PLANNING SECURE BASELINE INSTALLATIONS

Plan a secure baseline installation.

▶ Plan a strategy to enforce system default security settings on new systems.

Security just doesn't happen; it requires careful planning, meticulous attention to detail, and persistence. We've already talked a bit about the inherent security of Windows Server 2003 right out of the box, but what about client operating systems? Are they to be thought of as less secure? The answer: yes and no. Ultimately, the security of your servers and clients is what you make of it. To make them secure, you need a baseline—a starting point. Once you know where you are starting from, you can better see where it is that you are going to. To that end, we examine the default security settings of Windows Server 2003 after a clean installation of a member server and the default security settings of Windows XP Professional after a clean installation. By default, these security settings are applied to every clean installation that is performed. By ensuring that only authorized personnel perform operating system installations, and perform them in a prescribed and consistent manner, you can ensure that these settings are applied uniformly across all new installations.

## Identifying Windows Server 2003 Default Security Settings

Plan a secure baseline installation.

▶ Identify all server operating system default security settings.

The security you get out of Windows Server 2003 depends in part on how it is installed. Clean installations of Windows Server 2003 automatically receive the complete set of default configuration settings and thus are more secure (by default) than an upgrade installation. A computer that is upgraded to Windows Server 2003 is likely to inherit security settings that were present in the previous installation. This problem becomes even more acute when Windows NT 4.0 is upgraded to Windows Server 2003 due to the differences in the way Windows NT 4.0 handles the Registry and file system Discretionary Access Control Lists (DACLs).

You might be tempted to assume that by applying the Default security template, `Setup security.inf`, to a computer that you can easily reset it to the security settings that it would have after a clean installation. This assumption is not always correct. The default security template is automatically created during the installation of Windows Server 2003 on a computer. It represents the current security configuration at that time: either new settings for a clean installation or the resulting settings after an upgrade installation. This security template cannot accurately be used to ensure security settings are uniform unless the same type of installation is being performed on the same type of hardware. This security template, as discussed in more detail in the next section of this chapter, can however be used to reset the computer back to a known state. This capability becomes important over time as you have the need to enforce security settings on computers that may have experienced some changes.

You can identify the default security settings on a newly installed Windows Server 2003 member server through a variety of different means, such as the Local Group Policy console, the Local Security Policy console or the Resultant Set of Policy (RSoP) snap-in. Although the default security settings can be identified easily enough, they are presented in Table 1.1 for your reference.

| | |
|---|---|
| **EXAM TIP** | For a complete rundown on the security settings you can expect to find in Windows Server 2003 and Windows XP Professional in several different configurations, download "Threats and Countermeasures: Security Settings in Windows Server 2003 and Windows XP" from `http://go.microsoft.com/fwlink/?LinkId=15160`. |

**TABLE 1.1**

**WINDOWS SERVER 2003 MEMBER SERVER DEFAULT SECURITY SETTINGS**

| *Group Policy Node/Policy Item* | *Default Member Server Setting* |
|---|---|
| *Windows Settings\Security Settings\Account Policies* | |
| Enforce password history | 24 passwords remembered |
| Maximum password age | 42 days |
| Minimum password age | 1 days |
| Minimum password length | 7 characters |
| Passwords must meet complexity requirements | Enabled |
| Store password using reversible encryption for all users in the domain | Disabled |

| Group Policy Node/Policy Item | Default Member Server Setting |
|---|---|
| **Windows Settings\Security Settings\Account Lockout Policy** | |
| Account lockout duration | Not defined |
| Account lockout threshold attempts | 0 invalid login |
| Reset account lockout counter after | Not defined |
| **Windows Settings\Security Settings\Kerberos Policy** | |
| Enforce user logon restrictions | Not applicable |
| Maximum lifetime for service ticket | Not applicable |
| Maximum lifetime for user ticket | Not applicable |
| Maximum lifetime for user ticket renewal | Not applicable |
| Maximum tolerance for computer clock synchronization | Not applicable |
| **Windows Settings\Local Policies\Audit Policy** | |
| Audit account logon events | Success |
| Audit account management | No auditing |
| Audit directory service access | No auditing |
| Audit logon events | Success |
| Audit object access | No auditing |
| Audit policy change | No auditing |
| Audit privilege use | No auditing |
| Audit process tracking | No auditing |
| Audit system events | No auditing |
| **Windows Settings\Local Policies\User Rights Assignment** | |
| Access this computer from the network | Backup Operators, Power Users, Users, Administrators, Everyone |
| Act as part of the operating system | Not defined |
| Add workstations to domain | Not defined |
| Adjust memory quotas for a process | Administrators, NETWORK SERVICE, LOCAL SERVICE |
| Allow logon locally | Backup Operators, Power Users, Users, Administrators |

*continues*

**TABLE 1.1**    *continued*

**WINDOWS SERVER 2003 MEMBER SERVER DEFAULT SECURITY SETTINGS**

| Group Policy Node/Policy Item | Default Member Server Setting |
|---|---|
| *Windows Settings\Local Policies\User Rights Assignment* | |
| Allow logon through Terminal Services | Remote Desktop Users, Administrators |
| Back up files and directories | Backup Operators, Administrators |
| Bypass traverse checking | Backup Operators, Power Users, Users, Administrators, Everyone |
| Change the system time | Power Users, Administrators |
| Create a pagefile | Administrators |
| Create a token object | Not defined |
| Create global objects | SERVICE, Administrators |
| Create permanent shared objects | Not defined |
| Debug programs (SeDebugPrivilege) | Administrators |
| Deny access to this computer from the network | SUPPORT_388945a0 |
| Deny logon as a batch job | Not defined |
| Deny logon as a service | Not defined |
| Deny logon locally | SUPPORT_388945a0 |
| Deny logon through Terminal Services | Not defined |
| Enable computer and user accounts to be trusted f or delegation | Not defined |
| Force shutdown from a remote system | Administrators |
| Generate security audits | NETWORK SERVICE, LOCAL SERVICE |
| Impersonate a client after authentication | SERVICE, Administrators |
| Increase scheduling priority | Administrators |
| Load and unload device drivers | Administrators |

| Group Policy Node/Policy Item | Default Member Server Setting |
| --- | --- |
| **Windows Settings\Local Policies\User Rights Assignment** | |
| Lock pages in memory | Not defined |
| Log on as a batch job | SUPPORT_ 388945a0, LOCAL SERVICE |
| Log on as a service | NETWORK SERVICE |
| Manage auditing and security log | Administrators |
| Modify firmware environment values | Administrators |
| Perform Volume Maintenance Tasks | Administrators |
| Profile single process | Power Users, Administrators |
| Profile system performance | Administrators |
| Remove computer from docking station | Power Users, Administrators |
| Replace a process level token | NETWORK SERVICE, LOCAL SERVICE |
| Restore files and directories | Backup Operators, Administrators |
| Shut down the system | Backup Operators, Power Users, Administrators |
| Synchronize directory service data | Not defined |
| Take ownership of files or other objects | Administrators |
| **Windows Settings\Local Policies\Security Options** | |
| Accounts: Administrator account status | Enabled |
| Accounts: Guest account status | Disabled |
| Accounts: Limit local account use of blank passwords to console logon only | Enabled |
| Accounts: Rename administrator account | Administrator |
| Accounts: Rename guest account | Guest |
| Audit: Audit the access of global system objects | Disabled |
| Audit: Audit the use of Backup and Restore privilege | Disabled |

*continues*

**TABLE 1.1** *continued*

## WINDOWS SERVER 2003 MEMBER SERVER DEFAULT SECURITY SETTINGS

| *Group Policy Node/Policy Item* | *Default Member Server Setting* |
|---|---|
| *Windows Settings\Local Policies\Security Options* | |
| Audit: Shut down system immediately if unable to log security audits | Disabled |
| Devices: Allow undock without having to log on | Enabled |
| Devices: Allowed to format and eject removable media | Administrators |
| Devices: Prevent users from installing printer drivers | Enabled |
| Devices: Restrict CD-ROM access to locally logged-on user only | Disabled |
| Devices: Restrict floppy access to locally logged-on user only | Disabled |
| Devices: Unsigned driver installation behavior | Warn but allow installation |
| Domain controller: Allow server operators to schedule tasks | Not defined |
| Domain controller: LDAP server signing requirements | Not defined |
| Domain controller: Refuse machine account password changes | Not defined |
| Domain member: Digitally encrypt or sign secure channel data (always) | Enabled |
| Domain member: Digitally encrypt secure channel data (when possible) | Enabled |
| Domain member: Digitally sign secure channel data (when possible) | Enabled |
| Domain member: Disable machine account password changes | Disabled |
| Domain member: Maximum machine account password age | 30 days |
| Domain member: Require strong (Windows 2000 or later) session key | Disabled |
| Interactive logon: Do not display last user name | Disabled |
| Interactive logon: Do not require CTRL+ALT+DEL | Disabled |
| Interactive logon: Message text for users attempting to log on | Not defined |

| *Group Policy Node/Policy Item* | *Default Member Server Setting* |
|---|---|
| ***Windows Settings\Local Policies\Security Options*** | |
| Interactive logon: Message title for users attempting to log on | Not defined |
| Interactive logon: Number of previous logons to cache (in case domain controller is not available) | 10 logons |
| Interactive logon: Prompt user to change password bef ore expiration | 14 days |
| Interactive logon: Require Domain Controller authentication to unlock workstation | Disabled |
| Interactive logon: Require smart card | Disabled |
| Interactive logon: Smart card removal behavior | No Action |
| Microsoft network client: Digitally sign communications (always) | Disabled |
| Microsoft network client: Digitally sign communications (if server agrees) | Enabled |
| Microsoft network client: Send unencrypted password to third-party SMB servers | Disabled |
| Microsoft network server: Amount of idle time required before suspending session | 15 minutes |
| Microsoft network server: Digitally sign communications (always) | Disabled |
| Microsoft network server: Digitally sign communications (if client agrees) | Disabled |
| Microsoft network server: Disconnect clients when logon hours expire | Enabled |
| MSS: Number of connections to create when additional connections are necessary for Winsock applications | 0 |
| MSS: Enable dynamic backlog for Winsock applications | Disabled |
| MSS: Maximum number of 'quasifree' connections for Winsock applications | 0 |
| MSS: Minimum number of free connections for Winsock applications | 0 |
| MSS: Allow automatic detection of dead network gateways | Disabled |
| MSS: Allow automatic detection of MTU size | Enabled |
| MSS: Allow ICMP redirects to override OSPF generated routes | Enabled |

*continues*

**TABLE 1.1**   *continued*

## WINDOWS SERVER 2003 MEMBER SERVER DEFAULT SECURITY SETTINGS

| *Group Policy Node/Policy Item* | *Default Member Server Setting* |
|---|---|
| ***Windows Settings\Local Policies\Security Options*** | |
| MSS: Allow IRDP to detect and configure Default Gateway addresses | Disabled |
| MSS: Allow the computer to ignore NetBIOS name release requests except from WINS servers | Enabled |
| MSS: Disable Autorun for all drives | Disabled |
| MSS: Enable the computer to stop generating 8.3 style filenames | Disabled |
| MSS: How many dropped connect requests to initiate SYN attack protection | 5 |
| MSS: How many times unacknowledged data is retransmitted | 5 |
| MSS: How often keep-alive packets are sent in milliseconds | 7,200,000 |
| MSS: IP source routing protection level | No additional protection, source routed packets are allowed |
| MSS: Percentage threshold for the security event log at which the system will generate a warning | 0 (not configured) |
| MSS: Syn attack protection level | No additional protection, use default settings |
| MSS: SYN-ACK retransmissions when a connection request is not acknowledged | 3 and 6 seconds, half-open connections dropped after 21 seconds |
| MSS: The time in seconds before the screen saver grace period expires | 5 |
| MSS: Enable Safe DLL search mode | Disabled |
| Network access: Allow anonymous SID/Name translation | Disabled |
| Network access: Do not allow anonymous enumeration of SAM accounts | Enabled |
| Network access: Do not allow anonymous enumeration of SAM accounts and shares | Disabled |

| *Group Policy Node/Policy Item* | *Default Member Server Setting* |
| --- | --- |
| *Windows Settings\Local Policies\Security Options* | |
| Network access: Do not allow storage of credentials or .NET Passports for network authentication | Disabled |
| Network access: Let Everyone permissions apply to anonymous users | Disabled |
| Network access: Named Pipes that can be accessed anonymously | *Too numerous to list* |
| Network access: Remotely accessible registry paths | *Too numerous to list* |
| Network access: Remotely accessible registry paths and subpaths | *Too numerous to list* |
| Network access: Restrict anonymous access to Named Pipes and Shares | Enabled |
| Network access: Shares that can be accessed anonymously | COMCFG,DFS$ |
| Network access: Sharing and security model for local accounts | Classic—local users authenticate as themselves |
| Network security: Do not store LAN Manager hash value on next password change | Disabled |
| Network security: Force logoff when logon hours expire | Disabled |
| Network security: LAN Manager authentication level | Send NTLM response only |
| Network security: LDAP client signing requirements | Negotiate signing |
| Network security: Minimum session security for NTLM SSP based (including secure RPC) clients | No minimum |
| Network security: Minimum session security for NTLM SSP based (including secure RPC) servers | No minimum |
| Recovery console: Allow automatic administrative logon | Disabled |
| Recovery console: Allow floppy copy and access to all drives and all folders | Disabled |
| Shutdown: Allow system to be shut down without having to log on | Disabled |
| Shutdown: Clear virtual memory pagefile | Disabled |
| System cryptography: Force strong key protection for user keys stored on the computer | Not defined |
| System cryptography: Use FIPS compliant algorithms for encryption, hashing, and signing | Disabled |

*continues*

**TABLE 1.1**    *continued*

**WINDOWS SERVER 2003 MEMBER SERVER DEFAULT SECURITY SETTINGS**

| Group Policy Node/Policy Item | Default Member Server Setting |
| --- | --- |
| **Windows Settings\Local Policies\Security Options** | |
| System objects: Default owner for objects created by members of the Administrators group | Administrators group |
| System objects: Require case insensitivity for non-Windows subsystems | Enabled |
| System objects: Strengthen default permissions of internal system objects (e.g. Symbolic Links) | Enabled |
| System settings: Optional subsystems | Posix |
| System settings: Use Certificate Rules on Windows Executables for Software Restriction Policies | Disabled |
| **Windows Settings\Event Log\Settings for Event Logs** | |
| Maximum application log size | 16,384KB |
| Maximum security log size | 16,384KB |
| Maximum system log size | 16,384KB |
| Restrict guest access to application log | Enabled |
| Restrict guest access to security log | Enabled |
| Restrict guest access to system log | Enabled |
| Retain application log | Not defined |
| Retain security log | Not defined |
| Retain system log | Not defined |
| Retention method for application log | As needed |
| Retention method for security log | As needed |
| Retention method for system log | As needed |

> **NOTE**
>
> **File System, Registry, and Services** Information about the default settings of the file system, Registry, and services is not provided due to the large number of possible configurations of the hardware and operating system.

Of course, the defaults listed in Table 1.1 can and will change depending on the final role of the server. The Default Domain Policy will be applied to all member servers in the domain, modifying the defaults previously listed. Servers that are promoted to domain controller status will also be subjected to the additional configuration contained in the Default Domain Controller Policy. The installation and configuration of various network services and applications may also lead to additional security configuration modifications. Recall, as you saw in Figure 1.1, that the final configuration of a computer is the cumulative total of all policies applied to it at all levels, unless they have been blocked.

# Identifying Windows XP Professional Default Security Settings

Plan a secure baseline installation.

▶ Identify client operating system default security settings.

You can identify the default security settings on a newly installed Windows XP Professional workstation through a variety of different means, such as the Local Group Policy console, the Local Security Policy console, or the Resultant Set of Policy (RSoP) snap-in. Although the default security settings can be identified easily enough, they are presented in Table 1.2 for your reference.

**TABLE 1.2**

**WINDOWS XP PROFESSIONAL DEFAULT SECURITY SETTINGS**

| *Group Policy Node/Policy Item* | *Default Domain Member Client Setting* |
| --- | --- |
| *Windows Settings\Security Settings\Account Policies* | |
| Enforce password history | 0 passwords remembered |
| Maximum password age | 42 days |
| Minimum password age | 0 days |
| Minimum password length | 0 characters |
| Passwords must meet complexity requirements | Disabled |
| Store password using reversible encryption for all users in the domain | Disabled |

*continues*

**TABLE 1.2**   *continued*

## WINDOWS XP PROFESSIONAL DEFAULT SECURITY SETTINGS

| *Group Policy Node/Policy Item* | *Default Domain Member Client Setting* |
|---|---|
| ***Windows Settings\Security Settings\Account Lockout Policy*** | |
| Account lockout duration | Not applicable |
| Account lockout threshold | 0 invalid login attempts |
| Reset account lockout counter after | Not applicable |
| ***Windows Settings\Security Settings\Kerberos Policy*** | |
| Enforce user logon restrictions | Not applicable |
| Maximum lifetime for service ticket | Not applicable |
| Maximum lifetime for user ticket | Not applicable |
| Maximum lifetime for user ticket renewal | Not applicable |
| Maximum tolerance for computer clock synchronization | Not applicable |
| ***Windows Settings\Local Policies\Audit Policy*** | |
| Audit account logon events | No auditing |
| Audit account management | No auditing |
| Audit directory service access | No auditing |
| Audit logon events | No auditing |
| Audit object access | No auditing |
| Audit policy change | No auditing |
| Audit privilege use | No auditing |
| Audit process tracking | No auditing |
| Audit system events | No auditing |
| ***Windows Settings\Local Policies\User Rights Assignment*** | |
| Access this computer from the network | Everyone, Administrators, Users, Power Users, Backup Operators |
| Act as part of the operating system | Not defined |
| Add workstations to domain | Not defined |
| Adjust memory quotas for a process | LOCAL SERVICE, NETWORK SERVICE, Administrators |

| Group Policy Node/Policy Item | Default Domain Member Client Setting |
|---|---|
| ***Windows Settings\Local Policies\User Rights Assignment*** | |
| Allow logon through Terminal Services | Administrators, Remote Desktop Users |
| Back up files and directories | Administrators, Backup Operators |
| Bypass traverse checking | Everyone, Administrators, Users, Power Users, Backup Operators |
| Change the system time | Administrators, Power Users |
| Create a pagefile | Administrators |
| Create a token object | Not defined |
| Create global objects | Not applicable |
| Create permanent shared objects | Not defined |
| Debug programs | Administrators |
| Deny access to this computer from the network | Support_*xxxxxxxx*, Guest |
| Deny logon as a batch job | Not defined |
| Deny logon as a service | Not defined |
| Deny logon locally | Support_*xxxxxxxx*, Guest |
| Deny log on through Terminal Services | Not defined |
| Enable computer and user accounts to be trusted for delegation | Not defined |
| Force shutdown from a remote system | Administrators |
| Generate security audits | LOCAL SERVICE, NETWORK SERVICE |
| Increase scheduling priority | Administrators |
| Load and unload device drivers | Administrators |
| Lock pages in memory | Not defined |
| Log on as a batch job | Support_*xxxxxxxx* |
| Log on as a service | NETWORK SERVICE |

*continues*

**TABLE 1.2** *continued*

**WINDOWS XP PROFESSIONAL DEFAULT SECURITY SETTINGS**

| Group Policy Node/Policy Item | Default Domain Member Client Setting |
|---|---|
| *Windows Settings\Local Policies\User Rights Assignment* | |
| Log on locally | Administrators, Users, Power Users, Backup Operators |
| Manage auditing and security log | Administrators |
| Modify firmware environment values | Administrators |
| Perform Volume Maintenance Tasks | Administrators |
| Profile single process | Administrators, Power Users |
| Profile system performance | Administrators |
| Remove computer from docking station | Administrators, Power Users |
| Replace a process level token | LOCAL SERVICE, NETWORK SERVICE |
| Restore files and directories | Administrators, Backup Operators |
| Shut down the system | Administrators, Power Users, Backup Operators, Users |
| Synchronize directory service data | Not defined |
| Take ownership of files or other objects | Administrators |
| *Windows Settings\Local Policies\Security Options* | |
| Accounts: Administrator account status | Enabled |
| Accounts: Guest account status | Disabled |
| Accounts: Limit local account use of blank passwords to console logon only | Enabled |
| Accounts: Rename administrator account | Administrator |
| Accounts: Rename guest account | Guest |
| Audit: Audit the access of global system objects | Disabled |
| Audit: Audit the use of Backup and Restore privilege | Disabled |
| Audit: Shut down system immediately if unable to log security audits | Disabled |

| *Group Policy Node/Policy Item* | *Default Domain Member Client Setting* |
|---|---|
| ***Windows Settings\Local Policies\Security Options*** | |
| Devices: Allow undock without having to log on | Enabled |
| Devices: Allowed to format and eject removable media | Administrators |
| Devices: Prevent users from installing printer drivers | Disabled |
| Devices: Restrict CD-ROM access to locally logged-on user only | Disabled |
| Devices: Restrict floppy access to locally logged-on user only | Disabled |
| Devices: Unsigned driver installation behavior | Warn but allow installation |
| Domain controller: Allow server operators to schedule tasks | Not defined |
| Domain controller: LDAP server signing requirements | Not defined |
| Domain controller: Refuse machine account password changes | Not defined |
| Domain member: Digitally encrypt or sign secure channel data (always) | Enabled |
| Domain member: Digitally encrypt secure channel data (when possible) | Enabled |
| Domain member: Digitally sign secure channel data (when possible) | Enabled |
| Domain member: Disable machine account password changes | Disabled |
| Domain member: Maximum machine account password age | 30 days |
| Domain member: Require strong (Windows 2000 or later) session key | Disabled |
| Interactive logon: Do not display last user name | Disabled |
| Interactive logon: Do not require CTRL+ALT+DEL | Not defined |
| Interactive logon: Message text for users attempting to log on | Not defined |
| Interactive logon: Message title for users attempting to log on | Not defined |
| Interactive logon: Number of previous logons to cache (in case domain controller is not available) | 10 logons |

*continues*

**TABLE 1.2**   *continued*

**WINDOWS XP PROFESSIONAL DEFAULT SECURITY SETTINGS**

| Group Policy Node/Policy Item | Default Domain Member Client Setting |
|---|---|
| **Windows Settings\Local Policies\Security Options** | |
| Interactive logon: Prompt user to change password before expiration | 14 days |
| Interactive logon: Require Domain Controller authentication to unlock workstation | Disabled |
| Interactive logon: Smart card removal behavior | No Action |
| Microsoft network client: Digitally sign communications (always) | Disabled |
| Microsoft network client: Digitally sign communications (if server agrees) | Enabled |
| Microsoft network client: Send unencrypted password to third-party SMB servers | Disabled |
| Microsoft network server: Amount of idle time required before suspending session | 15 minutes |
| Microsoft network server: Digitally sign communications (always) | Disabled |
| Microsoft network server: Digitally sign communications (if client agrees) | Disabled |
| Microsoft network server: Disconnect clients when logon hours expire | Enabled |
| MSS: Number of connections to create when additional connections are necessary for Winsock applications | 0 |
| MSS: Enable dynamic backlog for Winsock applications | Disabled |
| MSS: Maximum number of 'quasi-free' connections for Winsock applications | 0 |
| MSS: Minimum number of free connections for Winsock applications | 0 |
| MSS: Allow automatic detection of dead network gateways | Disabled |
| MSS: Allow automatic detection of MTU size (possible DoS by an attacker using a small MTU) | Enabled |
| MSS: Allow ICMP redirects to override OSPF generated routes | Enabled |

| *Group Policy Node/Policy Item* | *Default Domain Member Client Setting* |
| --- | --- |
| ***Windows Settings\Local Policies\Security Options*** | |
| MSS: Allow IRDP to detect and configure Default Gateway addresses (could lead to DoS) | Disabled |
| MSS: Allow the computer to ignore NetBIOS name release requests except from WINS servers | Enabled |
| MSS: Disable Autorun for all drives | Disabled |
| MSS: Enable the computer to stop generating 8.3 style filenames | Disabled |
| MSS: How many dropped connect requests to initiate SYN attack protection | 5 |
| MSS: How many times unacknowledged data is retransmitted | 5 |
| MSS: How often keep-alive packets are sent in milliseconds | 7,200,000 |
| MSS: IP source routing protection level | No additional protection, source routed packets are allowed |
| MSS: Percentage threshold for the security event log at which the system will generate a warning | 0 (not configured) |
| MSS: Syn attack protection level | No additional protection, use default settings |
| MSS: SYN-ACK retransmissions when a connection request is not acknowledged | 3 and 6 seconds, half-open connections dropped after 21 seconds |
| MSS: The time in seconds before the screen saver grace period expires | 5 |
| MSS: Enable Safe DLL search mode | Disabled |
| Network access: Allow anonymous SID/Name translation | Disabled |
| Network access: Do not allow anonymous enumeration of SAM accounts | Enabled |
| Network access: Do not allow anonymous enumeration of SAM accounts and shares | Disabled |
| Network access: Do not allow storage of credentials or .NET Passports for network authentication | Disabled |
| Network access: Let Everyone permissions apply to anonymous users | Disabled |

*continues*

**TABLE 1.2** *continued*

**WINDOWS XP PROFESSIONAL DEFAULT SECURITY SETTINGS**

| *Group Policy Node/Policy Item* | *Default Domain Member Client Setting* |
| --- | --- |
| *Windows Settings\Local Policies\Security Options* | |
| Network access: Named Pipes that can be accessed anonymously | COMNAP, COMNODE, SQL\QUERY, SPOOLSS, EPMAPPER, LOCATOR, TrkWks, TrkSvr |
| Network access: Remotely accessible registry paths | *Too numerous to list* |
| Network access: Shares that can be accessed anonymously | COMCFG,DFS$ |
| Network access: Sharing and security model for local accounts | Classic—local users authenticate as themselves |
| Network security: Do not store LAN Manager hash value on next password change | Disabled |
| Network security: Force logoff when logon hours expire | Disabled |
| Network security: LAN Manager authentication level | Send LM and NTLM responses |
| Network security: LDAP client signing requirements | Negotiate signing |
| Network security: Minimum session security for NTLM SSP based (including secure RPC) clients | No minimum |
| Network security: Minimum session security for NTLM SSP based (including secure RPC) servers | No minimum |
| Recovery console: Allow automatic administrative logon | Disabled |
| Recovery console: Allow floppy copy and access to all drives and all folders | Disabled |
| Shutdown: Allow system to be shut down without having to log on | Enabled |
| Shutdown: Clear virtual memory pagefile | Disabled |
| System cryptography: Use FIPS compliant algorithms for encryption, hashing, and signing | Disabled |
| System objects: Default owner for objects created by members of the Administrators group | Object creator |

| Group Policy Node/Policy Item | Default Domain Member Client Setting |
|---|---|
| **Windows Settings\Local Policies\Security Options** | |
| System objects: Require case insensitivity for non-Windows subsystems | Enabled |
| System objects: Strengthen default permissions of internal system objects (e.g. Symbolic Links) | Enabled |
| **Windows Settings\Event Log\Settings for Event Logs** | |
| Maximum application log size | 512 KB |
| Maximum security log size | 512 KB |
| Maximum system log size | 512 KB |
| Restrict guest access to application log | Enabled |
| Restrict guest access to security log | Enabled |
| Restrict guest access to system log | Enabled |
| Retain application log | 7 days |
| Retain security log | 7 days |
| Retain system log | 7 days |
| Retention method for application log | Overwrite events older than |
| Retention method for security log | Overwrite events older than |
| Retention method for system log | Overwrite events older than |

Of course, the defaults listed in Table 1.2 can and will change depending on the final role of the workstation. The Default Domain Policy will be applied to all workstations in the domain, modifying the defaults previously listed. The installation and configuration of various network services and applications may also lead to additional security configuration modifications. Recall, as you saw in Figure 1.1, that the final configuration of a computer is the cumulative total of all policies applied to it at all levels, unless they have been blocked.

## Selecting Secure Operating Systems

Evaluate and select the operating system to install on computers in an enterprise.

▶ Identify the minimum configuration to satisfy security requirements.

The enterprise operating systems of choice these days are Windows 2000, Windows XP Professional, and Windows Server 2003. Your choice depends on several factors, including budgetary issues, licensing, and specific role requirements.

You should be aware of potential problems with legacy clients, such as Windows 95 and Windows NT 4.0, in newer Windows Active Directory domains. These legacy clients cannot participate fully in the Active Directory domain environment because they cannot utilize Group Policy Objects; you need to implement security settings on these computers through System Policies or direct editing of the Registry. Also, these legacy computers may not be able to communicate with Windows Server 2003 domain controllers due to the increased level of security of domain controller communications through server message block (SMB) signing.

If your budget allows it, you will be best served by installing all Windows Server 2003 servers and all Windows XP Professional workstations. This combination provides the greatest amount of security configuration capability, including newer items such as wireless networking security, 802.1x configuration, and Software Restriction Policies. Also, the newly improved Certificate Services in Windows Server 2003 were designed to be used with Windows XP Professional clients.

# PLANNING AND IMPLEMENTING ROLE-BASED SECURITY USING SECURITY TEMPLATES

As discussed in the beginning of this chapter, security is best achieved through careful planning and attentive administration.

Realizing that you, as a network administrator, may not have the time or detailed knowledge required to create complex security policies on your own, Microsoft has given you a leg up on the bad guys by providing several preconfigured security templates with Windows Server 2003. These preconfigured security templates can be used to implement security settings on servers and workstations quickly and easily. You can think of them in one of two ways: either as a starting point from which to make your own customized security template or as a solution in and of themselves. Neither thought is more correct than the other.

In addition to the preconfigured security templates provided within Windows Server 2003, Microsoft has also done security-minded network administrators everywhere a favor by providing additional role-based security templates in the Windows Server 2003 Security Guide, a free download that you can acquire from `http://go.microsoft.com/fwlink/?LinkId=14845`. We discuss these role-based security templates later in this chapter.

In simple terms, a security template is little more than a specially formatted flat text file that can be read by the Security Configuration Manager tools. These preconfigured templates have an `.inf` extension and can be located in the `%systemroot%\security\templates` folder on your Windows Server 2003 computer. You can use the Security Configuration and Analysis console, the `secedit.exe` tool, or the Local Security Policy console to apply these templates to a local computer. You can apply templates to an Organizational Unit or domain by importing them into the Security Settings section of the applicable Group Policy using the Group Policy Editor. You also can use these preconfigured templates as a baseline to compare an unknown system against a known set of configuration settings by using the Security Configuration and Analysis console or the `secedit.exe` tool.

We examine the security templates included with Windows Server 2003 in the next section and then move forward into how they are configured and used after that.

# Introducing the Windows Server 2003 Security Templates

Table 1.3 details the preconfigured security templates that ship with Windows Server 2003.

### TABLE 1.3

### THE PRECONFIGURED SECURITY TEMPLATES IN WINDOWS SERVER 2003

| Template (Filename) | Description |
| --- | --- |
| Default security (Setup security.inf) | This template is created during the installation of Windows Server 2003 on the computer. This template is variable between one computer to the next, depending on whether the installation was performed as a clean install or an upgrade. Setup security.inf represents the default security settings that the computer started with and thus can be used to reset portions of security as required. This template can be applied to both workstations and member servers, but not to domain controllers and should never be applied via Group Policy due to the large amount of data it contains; it can result in performance degradations. |
| Default DC security (DC security.inf) | This template is automatically created when a member server is promoted to domain controller. It represents the file, Registry, and system service default security settings for that domain controller and can be used later to reset these areas to their default configuration. |

| *Template (Filename)* | *Description* |
|---|---|
| Compatible (`compatws.inf`) | The compatible workstation/member server template provides a means to allow members of the Users group to run applications that do not conform to the Windows Logo Program. Applications that do conform to the Windows Logo Program can be, in the majority of cases, successfully run by members of the Users group without any further modifications required. For applications, that do not conform, two basic choices are available: make the users members of the Power Users group or relax the default permissions of the Users group. The compatible template solves this problem by changing the default file and Registry permissions that are granted to the Users group to allow them to run most applications that are not part of the Windows Logo Program. As a side effect of applying this template, all users are removed from the Power Users group because the basic assumption is that the template is being applied in an effort to prevent the need for Power Users. This template should not be applied to domain controllers, so be sure not to import it into the Default Domain Policy or the Default Domain Controller Policy. |
| Secure (`securews.inf`, `securedc.inf`) | The secure templates are the first ones to actually begin the process of locking down the computer to which they are applied. The two secure templates are `securews.inf`, which is for workstations and member servers, and `securedc.inf`, which is for domain controllers only. The secure templates prevent the use of the LAN Manager (LM) authentication protocol. Windows 9*x* clients need to have the Active Directory Client Extensions installed to enable NT LAN Manager (NTLM) v2 to allow them to communicate with Windows 2000 and later clients and servers using these templates. These templates also impose additional restrictions on anonymous users, such as preventing them from enumerating account and share information. The secure templates also enable server message block (SMB) signing on the server side. By default, SMB signing is enabled on client computers. When this template is applied, SMB packet signing is always negotiated between clients and servers. |

**TABLE 1.3**    *continued*

### THE PRECONFIGURED SECURITY TEMPLATES IN WINDOWS SERVER 2003

| Template (Filename) | Description |
| --- | --- |
| Highly Secure (hisecws.inf, hisecdc.inf) | The highly secure templates impose further restrictions on computers they are applied to. Whereas the secure templates require at least NTLM authentication, the highly secure templates require NTLM v2 authentication. The secure templates enable SMB packet signing; the highly secure templates require SMB packet signing. In addition to the various additional security restrictions that are imposed by the highly secure templates, these templates also make several changes to group membership and the login process. All members of the Power Users group are removed from this group. Also, only Domain Admins and the local administrative account are allowed to be members of the local Administrators group. When the highly secure templates are used, it is assumed that only Windows Logo Program–compliant applications are in use. As such, there is no provision in place for users to use noncompliant applications because the compatible template is not needed and the Power Users group has no members. Members of the Users group can use applications that are Windows Logo Program compliant. Additionally, members of the Administrators group can use any application they want. |
| System root security (Rootsec.inf) | This template defines the root permissions for the root of the system volume. Should these permissions be changed, they can be reapplied using this template. This template also can be modified to apply the same permissions to other volumes. Explicitly configured permissions are not overwritten on child objects when using this template. |
| No Terminal Server use SID (Notssid.inf) | This template is used on servers that are not running Terminal Services to remove all unnecessary Terminal Services Security Identifiers (SIDs) from the file system and Registry. This, however, does not increase the security of the server. |

**WARNING**

**Templates are incremental**   All the preconfigured security templates are incremental, meaning that they have been designed to be applied to computers that are using the default security settings. These templates do not implement the default security settings before applying their security settings.

# Using the Security Configuration Manager Tools

Plan security for servers that are assigned specific roles. Roles might include domain controllers, Web servers, database servers, and mail servers.

▶ Deploy the security configuration for servers that are assigned specific roles.

▶ Create custom security templates based on server roles.

Now that you've seen the security templates available for your use, let's take a brief look at the tools available to you for the design, testing, and implementation of these (and other) security templates. The Security Configuration Manager is not one console or tool per se, but instead is actually a collection of tools and utilities that you can use to implement security solutions across your network.

The components of the Security Configuration Manager include

▶ The Security Configuration and Analysis snap-in

▶ The Security Templates snap-in

▶ Group Policy security extensions

▶ The `secedit.exe` command

Each of these tools is examined in the following sections as they relate to implementing security solutions using the preconfigured security templates that are supplied in Windows Server 2003. At this point you need to construct a customized Microsoft Management Console (MMC) that you can use to work with these security templates, as outlined in Step by Step 1.1.

---

## STEP BY STEP

### 1.1 Creating a Customized Security Console

**1.** Open an empty MMC shell by selecting Start, Run and entering **MMC** in the Open field. Click OK. An empty MMC shell appears, as shown in Figure 1.2.

*continues*

*continued*

**FIGURE 1.2**
Starting with an empty MMC shell, you can build any number of customized configuration and management consoles.

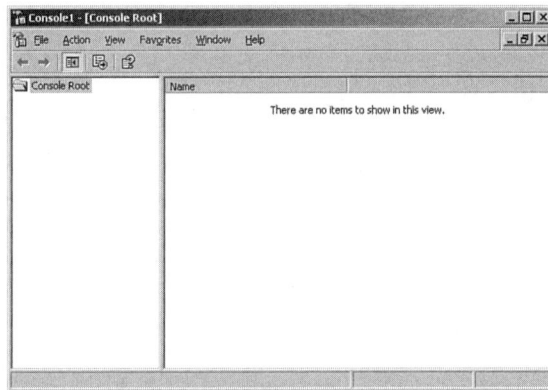

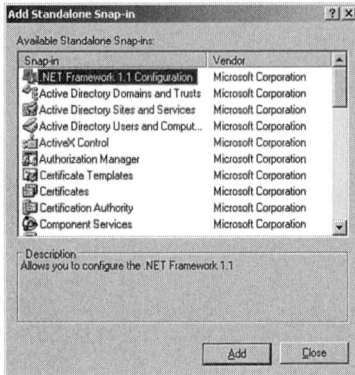

**FIGURE 1.3** ▲
You can add a number of snap-ins from here.

**FIGURE 1.4** ▶
The customized console is not as empty as it was.

2. Select File, Add/Remove Snap-in to open the Add/Remove Snap-in dialog box. Click Add to open the Add Standalone Snap-in dialog box, shown in Figure 1.3.

3. Scroll down the Snap-in list and select the Security Configuration and Analysis and Security Templates snap-ins by double-clicking each of them.

4. Click Close and then click OK to return to the MMC, shown in Figure 1.4.

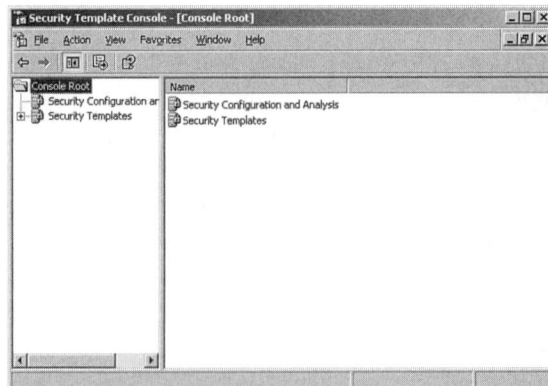

5. Save the console by selecting File, Save. A standard save dialog box appears. Specify the filename and location to save the console to. By default, the console is saved into the Administrative Tools folder of the currently logged-in user.

Armed with a custom security console, let's move forward and examine how the tools are put to work.

## The Security Configuration and Analysis Snap-in

The Security Configuration and Analysis snap-in is an important tool in any administrator's security template toolbox. By using the Security Configuration and Analysis snap-in, you can create, configure, test, and implement security template settings for a local computer. Therein lies its one real weakness: It can be used to work only with the settings of a local computer. You can, however, find ways to get around this limitation by using the other tools that are at your disposal, including `secedit.exe` and the security extensions to Group Policy, both of which are discussed later in this chapter.

The Security Configuration and Analysis snap-in can be used in two basic modes, as its name suggests—configuration and analysis—although not necessarily in that order. When you're using the Security Configuration and Analysis snap-in to analyze the current system security configuration, no changes are ever made to the computer being analyzed. The administrator simply selects a security template to compare the computer against (either a preconfigured template or a custom created template). The settings from the template are loaded into a database and then compared to the settings currently implemented on the computer. It is possible to import multiple templates into this database, thus merging their settings into one conglomerate database. In addition, you can specify that existing database settings are to be cleared before another template is imported into the database. When the desired security templates have been loaded into the database, any number of analysis actions can be performed, both by the Security Configuration and Analysis snap-in and by the `secedit.exe` command, as discussed later in this chapter.

After the database has been populated and an analysis scan has been initiated, the Security Configuration and Analysis snap-in examines each configurable Group Policy option and then reports back to you the results of the analysis scan. Each setting is marked with an icon that denotes one of several possible outcomes, such as that the settings are the same, the settings are different, or the settings do not apply. Table 1.4 outlines the possible icons that you might see and what they indicate.

### TABLE 1.4

### THE PRECONFIGURED SECURITY TEMPLATE ICONS IN WINDOWS SERVER 2003

| Icon | Description |
| --- | --- |
| Red circle with White X | The item is defined in the analysis database and on the computer but does not match the currently configured setting. |
| Green check mark | The item is defined in the analysis database and on the computer and matches the currently configured setting. |
| Question mark | The item is not defined in the analysis database and was not examined on the computer. |
| Exclamation point | The item is defined in the analysis database but not on the computer. |
| No special icon | The item is not defined in the analysis database or the computer. |

> **NOTE**
>
> **Not all computers are created equal**
> You can expect that not every computer has the same security settings initially. Your results, when performing this process, may vary depending on the initial state of the computer being used for the analysis.

The best way to begin to understand the Security Configuration and Analysis snap-in is to work with it. Step by Step 1.2 presents the process of comparing the security configuration of a Windows Server 2003 member server to that of the securews.inf template.

## STEP BY STEP

### 1.2 Using the Security Configuration and Analysis Snap-in to Analyze Settings

1. From the customized security console you created in Step by Step 1.1, select the Security Configuration and Analysis node. Notice that Security Configuration and Analysis actually provides you with some instructions as to how to proceed.

2. Right-click the Security Configuration and Analysis node and select Open Database from the context menu. The Open Database window appears, as shown in Figure 1.5.

**FIGURE 1.5**
You can either load an existing database or create a new one.

3. Because you do not have an existing database, create a new one by entering the name **security1** into the File Name field and click Open to open it.

4. On the Import Template page, shown in Figure 1.6, select the security template you are loading into the database. In this exercise, you should use the securews.inf template. If this is an existing database that you want to clear out before starting the analysis, be sure to select the Clear This Database Before Importing option. Click Open after you make your selections. The Security Configuration and Analysis snap-in appears again.

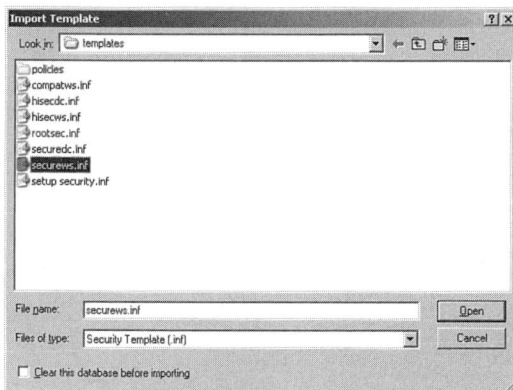

**FIGURE 1.6**
You need to select a template to load into the database.

*continues*

*continued*

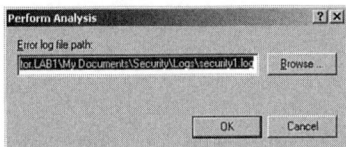

**FIGURE 1.7**
The error log keeps track of any errors encountered during the analysis process.

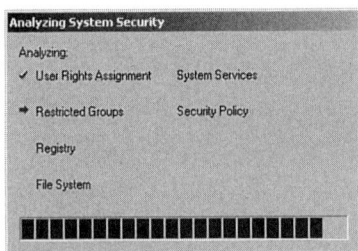

**FIGURE 1.8**
The Analyzing System Security dialog box keeps
you apprised of the computer's progress in the
analysis.

**FIGURE 1.9**
The analysis output resembles the information
shown in the Group Policy Editor.

**5.** To perform the analysis operation, right-click the Security
Configuration and Analysis node and select Analyze
Computer Now to start the analysis. The Perform Analysis
dialog box appears.

**6.** Provide a pathname and filename for an error log. In most
cases, the default pathname and filename, as shown in
Figure 1.7, are suitable, but you can change this as
required. Click OK to start the analysis process. You
briefly see the Analyzing System Security dialog box,
shown in Figure 1.8.

When the analysis is complete, you are returned to the
Security Configuration and Analysis snap-in, except that
now it has been populated and looks similar to what you
might expect to see in the Group Policy Editor, as shown
in Figure 1.9.

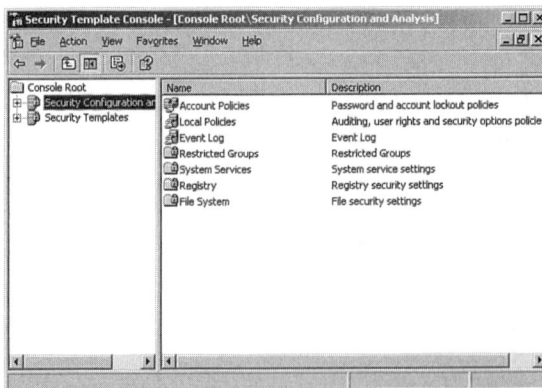

**7.** Open the Account Policies\Password Policy node, as
shown in Figure 1.10, and you can see that some items are
not in agreement between the database settings and the
computer settings.

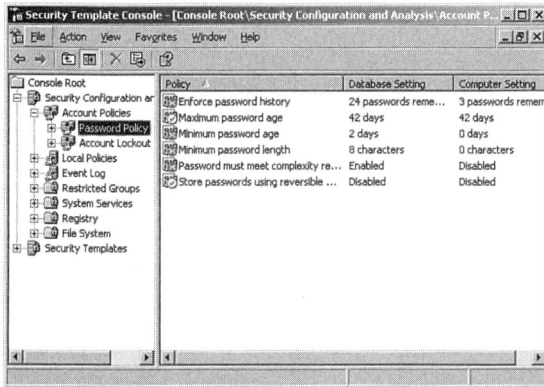

**FIGURE 1.10**
You can quickly determine the status of the computer against the settings of the security template.

As shown in Figures 1.9 and 1.10, you can analyze and configure several areas by using the Security Configuration and Analysis snap-in:

► *Account Policies*—This node contains items that control user accounts. In Windows NT 4.0, these items are managed from the User Manager for Domains. This node has two subnodes: Password Policy and Account Lockout Policy. The Password Policy node deals with account password-related items, such as minimum length and maximum age. The Account Lockout Policy node contains options for configuring account lockout durations and lockout reset options.

► *Local Policies*—This node contains policies that are applied to the local machine. This node has three subnodes: Audit Policy, User Rights Assignment, and Security Options. The Audit Policy node is relatively self-explanatory: It offers options for configuring and implementing various auditing options. The User Rights Assignment node contains miscellaneous options that deal with user rights, such as the ability to log in to a computer across the network. The Security Options node contains many other options—such as the option to set a login banner or allow the system to be shut down without being logged in first—that previously could be edited only in the Windows NT 4.0 Registry or by using System Policies.

▶ *Event Log*—This node contains options that allow you to configure the behavior and security of the event log. In this node, for example, you can include maximum log sizes and disallow guest access to the event logs.

▶ *Restricted Groups*—This node allows you to permanently configure which users are allowed to be members of specific groups. For example, company policy may provide the ability to perform server backups to a specific group of administrators. If another user who is not otherwise authorized with these privileges is added to this group and not removed after he or she has performed the intended function, you have created a security problem because the user has more rights than normally authorized. By using the Restricted Groups node, you can reset group membership to the intended membership.

▶ *System Services*—This node allows you to configure the behavior and security assignments associated with all system services running on the computer. Options include defining that a service is to start automatically or be disabled. In addition, you can configure the user accounts that are to have access to each service.

▶ *Registry*—This node allows you to configure access restrictions that specify who is allowed to configure or change individual Registry keys or entire hives. This option does not provide you with the means to create or modify Registry keys, however; that must still be done by using the Registry Editor.

▶ *File System*—This node allows you to set folder and file NTFS permissions. This is especially handy if you need to reset the permissions on a large number of folders or files.

After a security settings analysis is completed and you have examined the results, you can begin the process of determining what changes need to be made. You can configure your changes directly into the database by using the Security Configuration and Analysis snap-in, or you can create or edit a security template by using the Security Templates snap-in, as discussed in the next section. When you use the Security Configuration and Analysis snap-in to make changes, your changes reside only in the database until you do one of two things: export the database to a security template file or apply the database settings to the computer. When you work with the Security Templates snap-in, you actually make changes directly to the template and need to save it when you're finished. The result is the same no matter which way you go about it.

The second part of the Security Configuration and Analysis snap-in is configuration—the process of actually applying the settings contained in the database to the local computer. Before you apply the settings to the computer, you should have first completed the analysis as detailed in Step by Step 1.2. After you do so and are happy with the configuration (or have edited the configuration to suit your needs), you can apply the settings by right-clicking the Security Configuration and Analysis node and selecting Configure Computer Now from the context menu. You are again asked for the pathname and filename of the error log. After you provide this information, the settings in the database are applied to the computer. Running the analysis again confirms this by showing that all items are now in agreement.

As mentioned previously, if you need to get the database settings out and into the form of a security template, you need to simply right-click the Security Configuration and Analysis node and select Export Template from the context menu. The Export Template To window appears, as shown in Figure 1.11, prompting you to enter the path and filename of the security template. You should be sure to use a unique name; in other words, do not save over one of the preconfigured security templates because you might need it again in the future.

**EXAM TIP**

**For the Local Computer Only**
Remember that the Security Configuration and Analysis snap-in can be used only to apply the settings to the local computer. You need to export the database to a security template if you want to apply the settings to another computer or to a larger scope of computers, such as a domain or an OU.

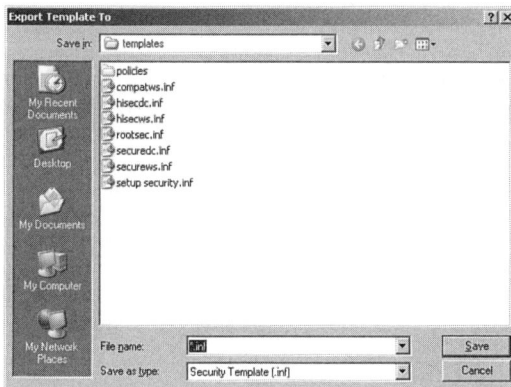

**FIGURE 1.11**
Be sure to specify a unique name for your exported template to avoid overwriting a preconfigured security template.

## The Security Templates Snap-in

The Security Templates snap-in, shown in Figure 1.12, might at first seem to have no real purpose. However, this is not the case at all. You can use this snap-in to modify existing templates or create new ones from scratch without the danger or possibility of accidentally applying the template to the computer or GPO.

**FIGURE 1.12**

The Security Templates snap-in allows you to work with existing and new templates.

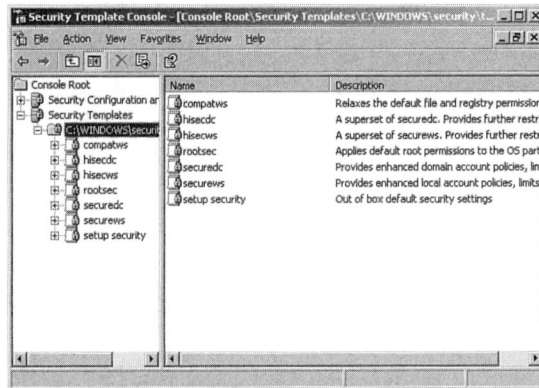

To customize an existing template, you simply begin making changes to it to suit your requirements. When you are done, you should save it with a new name by right-clicking on it and selecting Save As from the context menu. The standard save dialog box that allows you to specify the path and filename of the template appears.

To start with a completely empty template—in which no settings are preconfigured—you can right-click the template location and select New Template, as shown in Figure 1.13.

**FIGURE 1.13**

You can easily create a new (blank) template if you desire.

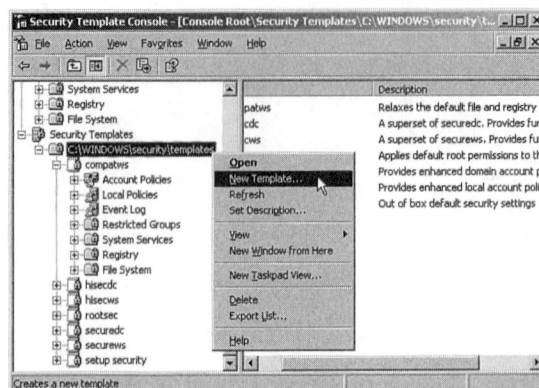

# GUIDED PRACTICE EXERCISE 1.1

In this exercise, you create your own security template to meet the following requirements:

- ▶ You want to require all users to configure passwords that are at least 10 characters long. Additionally, the users' passwords must contain characters other than letters and numbers.

- ▶ You want to prevent users from reusing the same password in the next 24 passwords they enter. You also want to force users to change their passwords after 30 days have passed.

- ▶ You want to prevent users from cycling through a list of passwords to get back to their favorite one.

- ▶ You want to lockout user accounts after five incorrect login attempts. These user accounts are to be locked out for 45 minutes, and the lockout counter also should be reset after 45 minutes.

You should try this exercise on your own first. If you get stuck, or you would like to see one possible solution, follow these steps:

1. Open or create an MMC that contains the Security Templates snap-in.

2. Right-click on the template location (that is, `C:\WINDOWS\Security\Templates`) and select New Template from the context menu.

3. Provide a descriptive name such as **Account Security Policy** and a longer description as desired; then click OK.

4. In the Security Templates snap-in, double-click the newly created security template to expand its top-level nodes.

5. Expand the Account Policies node and open the Password Policy node.

6. Double-click the Minimum Password Length item. Select the Define This Policy Setting in the Template option. Change the numerical value to **10** and click OK.

*continues*

*continued*

7. Double-click the Passwords Must Meet Complexity Requirements item. Select the Define this Policy Setting in the Template option. Select the Enabled radio button and click OK.

8. Double-click the Enforce Password History item. Select the Define This Policy Setting in the Template option. Change the numerical value to **24** and click OK.

9. Double-click the Maximum Password Age item. Select the Define This Policy Setting in the Template option. Change the numerical value to **30** and click OK.

10. When prompted to accept changes to the Minimum Password Age item, click OK.

11. Double-click the Minimum Password Age item. Ensure the Define This Policy Setting in the Template option is selected. Change the numerical value to **5** and click OK.

12. Open the Account Lockout Policy node.

13. Double-click the Account Lockout Threshold item. Ensure the Define This Policy Setting in the Template option is selected. Change the numerical value to **5** and click OK.

14. When prompted to accept changes to the Account Lockout Duration and Reset Account Lockout Counter After items, click OK.

15. Double-click the Account Lockout Duration item. Ensure the Define This Policy Setting in the Template option is selected. Change the numerical value to **45** and click OK.

16. Double-click the Reset Account Lockout Counter After item. Ensure the Define This Policy Setting in the Template option is selected. Change the numerical value to **45** and click OK.

17. Right-click on the security template name on the left side of the window and select Save from the context menu.

## Group Policy Security Extensions

Using the Security Configuration and Analysis snap-in is certainly not the only way to apply a security template to a computer. Imagine the amount of time and effort involved in applying a security template locally at each computer using the Security Configuration and Analysis snap-in. As difficult and time-consuming as that process would be, try to imagine using this approach on several different types of computers to implement a role-based security solution. In this case, you would have the added hassle of trying to remember which template goes on what computer.

Fortunately, you can easily and quickly import security templates into GPOs by using the Group Policy Editor. Step by Step 1.3 outlines this process.

---

# STEP BY STEP

### 1.3 Importing a Security Template into a GPO

1. Open the Active Directory Users and Computers console by selecting Start, Programs, Administrative Tools, Active Directory Users and Computers.

2. Locate the domain or OU to which you want to apply the security template. In this example, we apply the securews.inf template to the Sales OU.

3. Right-click the Sales OU and select Properties from the context menu. The Sales Properties dialog box appears. Switch to the Group Policy tab, as shown in Figure 1.14.

4. To create a new GPO, click the New button. Supply a name for the new GPO and press Enter.

5. Click the Edit button to open the Group Policy Editor for the selected GPO.

6. Expand the nodes as follows: Computer Configuration, Windows Settings, Security Settings. Right-click the Security Settings node and select Import Policy from the context menu, as shown in Figure 1.15.

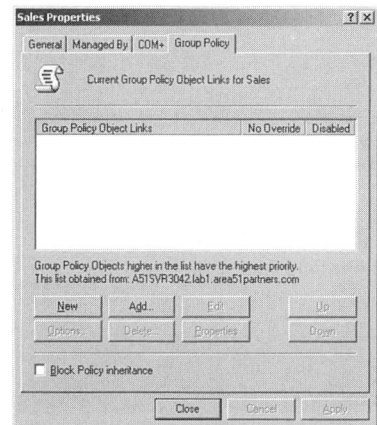

**FIGURE 1.14**
You need to create a new GPO if no GPOs exist already.

*continues*

*continued*

**FIGURE 1.15**
You can import a security template into the Group Policy Editor.

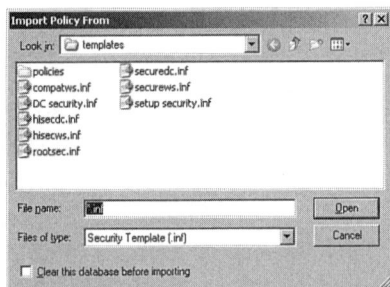

**FIGURE 1.16**
You select the security template that you want to import into the GPO.

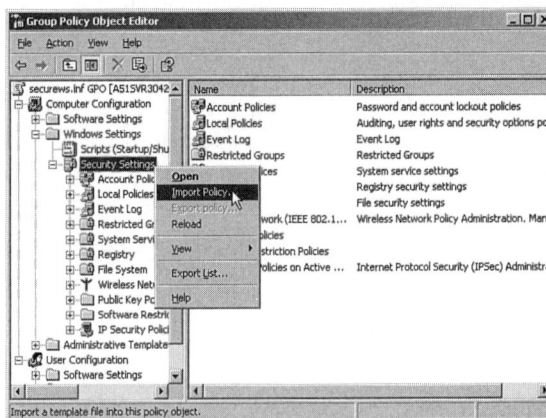

**7.** The Import Policy From dialog box, shown in Figure 1.16, appears, providing a list of the preconfigured security templates. You can navigate to another location if desired to use another security template.

The settings configured in the template are now applied to the GPO and will be applied during the next Group Policy refresh cycle.

---

Note that you can also perform this process at the domain level to apply security settings to all computers within the domain. As previously discussed, you should apply the most generic settings at the domain level and then at the OU level apply specific settings that pertain to the computers in that OU.

---

### GPO PROCESSING

Group Policy Objects (GPOs) are the basic building blocks of Group Policy. As you've seen several times in this chapter already, GPOs can be applied at several different levels within your network. Additionally, any settings that are applied to a parent object are, by default, passed along to all child objects through inheritance. Group Policy is applied and processed by Windows Server 2003 in the following order:

- **Local**—The local GPO (there can be only one) is applied first to a computer. It can be overwritten by the GPOs at the remaining processing levels.

- **Site**—GPOs linked at the site level are applied next and will, by default, be applied to objects contained within the site.

- **Domain**—GPOs linked at the domain level are applied next and will, by default, be applied to all objects contained within that domain.

- **OU**—GPOs linked at the Organizational Unit level are applied next and will, by default, be applied to all objects contained within that OU.

As mentioned, by default the GPO settings that are applied later will override the GPO settings that were applied earlier. This default behavior can be modified, however, if desired to produce different results. For a more in-depth discussion on Group Policy processing, see *MCSE 70-294 Training Guide: Planning, Implementing, and Maintaining a Microsoft Windows Server 2003 Active Directory Infrastructure* by Eric Rockenbach and Don Poulton (2003, Que Publishing; ISBN: 0789729490).

## secedit.exe

We have spent a good amount of time so far in this chapter examining the ways you can work with security templates by using the Windows GUI. But what about the command line? As you might have guessed, there is a command-line alternative to the Security Configuration and Analysis snap-in, and it comes in the form of the `secedit.exe` command.

You can use `secedit` to perform the same functions as the Security Configuration and Analysis snap-in, plus a couple of additional functions not found in the snap-in. The `secedit` command has the following top-level options available for use:

▶ `/analyze`—This option allows you to analyze the security settings of a computer by comparing them against the baseline settings in a database.

▶ `/configure`—This option allows you to configure the security settings of the local computer by applying the settings contained in a database.

**Viewing the Results of a Security Analysis**   You need to view the results of a security analysis in the Security Configuration and Analysis snap-in by opening the database created during the analysis. At first, you might feel that running the analysis from the command line and then viewing the results in the GUI is counterproductive. In reality, the opposite is the case. Say you run secedit from a script on multiple computers. You can then view the databases, one for each computer, in the GUI at your leisure to determine what changes need to be made to the security settings on the computers. You can use the %computername% variable when creating the database and log files to create one set of results for each computer being scanned.

▶ **/export**—This option allows you to export the settings configured in a database to a security template .inf file.

▶ **/import**—This option allows you to import the settings configured in a security template .inf file into a database. If you will be applying multiple security templates to a database, you should use this option before performing the analysis or configuration.

▶ **/validate**—This option validates the syntax of a security template to ensure that it is correct before you import the template into a database for analysis or configuration.

▶ **/GenerateRollback**—This option allows you to create a rollback template that can be used to reset the security configuration to the values it had before the security template was applied.

Of the available options, you will most often make use of the /analyze and /configure switches. Examples and explanations of their usage are provide here.

To analyze the current security configuration of the local computer, you issue the secedit command with the following syntax:

```
secedit /analyze /db FileName /cfg FileName /overwrite /log FileName
➥ /quiet
```

The secedit /analyze parameters are explained in detail in Table 1.5.

**TABLE 1.5**

**THE secedit /analyze PARAMETERS**

| Switch | Description |
| --- | --- |
| /db FileName | This switch specifies the pathname and filename of the database to be used to perform the analysis. |
| /cfg FileName | This switch specifies the pathname and filename of the security template that is to be imported into the database before the analysis is performed. |
| /overwrite | This switch specifies that the database is to be emptied before the security template is imported. |

| Switch | Description |
|---|---|
| /log *FileName* | This switch specifies the pathname and filename of the file that is used to log the status of the analysis process. By default, a log named `scesrv.log` is created in the `%windir%\security\logs` directory. |
| /quiet | This switch specifies that the analysis process should take place without further onscreen comments. |

For example, suppose that you want to analyze the settings on a computer compared to the settings contained in the `securews.inf` template. You could issue the following command to perform this function:

```
secedit /analyze /db c:\sectest\1.sdb
➥/cfg C:\WINDOWS\security\templates
➥\securews.inf /log c:\sectest\1.log
```

To configure the current security configuration of the local computer, you issue the `secedit` command with the following syntax:

```
secedit /configure /db FileName /cfg FileName /overwrite
➥/areas Area1 Area2 ... /log FileName /quiet
```

The `secedit /configure` parameters are explained in detail in Table 1.6.

### TABLE 1.6

### THE `secedit /configure` PARAMETERS

| Switch | Description |
|---|---|
| /db *FileName* | This switch specifies the pathname and filename of the database to be used to perform the analysis. |
| /cfg *FileName* | This switch specifies the pathname and filename of the security template that is to be imported into the database before the analysis is performed. |
| /overwrite | This switch specifies that the database is to be emptied before the security template is imported. |

*continues*

**TABLE 1.6** *continued*

**THE secedit /configure PARAMETERS**

| Switch | Description |
| --- | --- |
| /areas | This switch specifies the security areas that are to be applied to the system. By default, when this parameter is not specified, all security areas are applied to the computer. The following options are available: **GROUP_MGMT**—This area is the Restricted Group settings. **USER_RIGHTS**—This area is the User Rights Assignment settings. **REGKEYS**—This area is the Registry permissions settings. **FILESTORE**—This area is the File System permissions settings. **SERVICES**—This area is the System Service settings. |
| /log *FileName* | This switch specifies the pathname and filename of the file that is used to log the status of the analysis process. By default, a log named scesrv.log is created in the %windir%\security\logs directory. |
| /quiet | This switch specifies that the analysis process should take place without further onscreen comments. |

For example, suppose that you want to configure the settings on a computer with the settings in the securews.inf template. You could issue the following command to perform this function:

```
secedit /configure /db c:\sectest\1.sdb
➡/cfg C:\WINDOWS\security\templates\securews.inf
➡ /log c:\sectest\1.log
```

# Using Role-Based Security Templates

Configure security for servers that are assigned specific roles.

Plan security for servers that are assigned specific roles. Roles might include domain controllers, Web servers, database servers, and mail servers.

▶ Deploy the security configuration for servers that are assigned specific roles.

▶ Create custom security templates based on server roles.

Now that you have seen the preconfigured security templates provided with Windows Server 2003 and also the tools of the Security Configuration Manager, you are ready to move forward and implement role-based security solutions for your network. Looking back again at Figure 1.1, you can see how security policies are applied at several nested levels in the sample network.

Referring specifically to servers, you thus apply security policies (via security templates and GPOs) at the three following hierarchical levels:

- *Domain*—The most common security requirements, such as password and account lockout policies, are applied at the domain level. These policies are applied to all computers—servers and workstations alike—within the domain.

- *Baseline*—This policy contains security configuration items that apply to all member servers, such as auditing policies and user rights assignments. In the example shown in Figure 1.1, baseline policies are applied through the Domain Controller Policy, Client Computer Policy, and Member Server Policy.

- *Role-specific*—To address the specific security needs of each specific server role, member servers are divided into role-based groups using OUs and have specific, individual security policies applied to them. In the example shown in Figure 1.1, the role-specific policies are applied through the File Servers Policy, Print Servers Policy, and so on.

As you can see, the first step in successfully establishing role-based security is dividing computers by role. After that task has been accomplished, the Domain and Baseline Policies must be implemented by importing them into the applicable Group Policy Objects. Because these security templates are incremental in nature, you are expected to have applied these higher-level policies before attempting to subsequently apply the role-specific security policy. Also, to achieve the best results from a role-based security plan, your member servers should be performing only one specific function, such as print server, file server, IIS server, and so on. When member servers perform multiple functions, the level of complexity increases rapidly in regards to managing, maintaining, and securing them.

> **WARNING**
>
> **Test before deployment**  Although Microsoft thoroughly tested the default security templates provided with Windows Server 2003 and the additional security templates provided in the Windows Server 2003 Security Guide in a lab environment, this does not alleviate you of the same responsibility. It is nothing short of foolish to blindly apply any security template to a production environment without thorough testing and evaluation in a lab environment that closely mimics your actual production network.

As discussed earlier in this chapter, the Windows Server 2003 Security Guide (located at `http://go.microsoft.com/fwlink/?LinkId=14845`) contains several excellent security templates that can be used to quickly and uniformly create a role-based security solution for your Windows Server 2003 network. This guide actually includes the following three sets of security templates:

► *Legacy Client*—The least secure environment, these security polices are designed for networks using Windows Server 2003 or Windows 2000 Server domain controllers and member servers. Clients run Windows 98 or Windows NT 4.0, Windows 2000, or Windows XP Professional.

► *Enterprise Client*—A fairly secure environment where the network uses Windows Server 2003 domain or Windows 2000 Server controllers and member servers. Clients run Windows 2000 or Windows XP Professional.

► *High Security*—An extremely secure environment where the network uses Windows Server 2003 or Windows 2000 Server domain controllers and member servers. Clients run Windows 2000 or Windows XP Professional. Due to the extremely restrictive settings contained in these security policies, many applications may fail to function properly. Network useability will decline, and management of workstations and servers becomes very difficult.

Table 1.7 outlines the typical Windows Server 2003 server roles and the security templates supplied for each of these respective roles.

**TABLE 1.7**

**THE WINDOWS SERVER 2003 SERVER ROLES**

| Server Role | Security Template |
| --- | --- |
| Domain Controller | `Enterprise Client - Domain Controller.inf` |
| Member Servers | `Enterprise Client - Member Server Baseline.inf` (applied to all member servers) |
| Certificate Services servers | `Enterprise Client - CA Server.inf` |
| File servers | `Enterprise Client - File Server.inf` |

| Server Role | Security Template |
|---|---|
| Infrastructure servers (DHCP, WINS) | `Enterprise Client - Infrastructure Server.inf` |
| Internet Authentication Server (IAS) servers | `Enterprise Client - IAS Server.inf` |
| Internet Information Services (IIS) servers | `Enterprise Client - IIS Server.inf` |
| Print servers | `Enterprise Client - Print Server.inf` |
| Bastion Hosts (DMZ servers) | `High Security - Bastion Host.inf` |

> **NOTE**
>
> **No DNS Server Security?** Notice that DNS servers are not listed anywhere among the possible Windows Server 2003 server roles. The reason is that, in the most secure environment, all domain controllers are also DNS servers, thus providing for the best security and replication possible.

The specifics associated with the security settings applied to each server role are far too numerous to lend themselves to discussion here; however, as you might expect, they are specifically crafted for each role.

## CASE STUDY

### ESSENCE OF THE CASE

Following are the essential elements in this case:

▶ Security will be implemented in a hierarchical fashion using role-based security templates.

▶ Only one forest and only one domain will be created. Organizational Units will thus be used to segment the specific server roles.

▶ The FTP servers located in the DMZ will require extra security measures because they are susceptible to more types of attacks.

▶ A more secure initial security plan can be implemented because there are no legacy clients to be supported.

### SCENARIO

You are a network security consultant who has been hired by the ACME Rocket Company to work with its in-house network administrators to plan, develop, and implement a hierarchical role-based server security plan.

When you meet with the company president, he gives you the following information: "I want you to help our administrators get a solid security plan in place for the network. After talking with the CIO, we both agree that the best way to implement security for our network is to assign servers specific tasks and secure them appropriately."

The CIO has the following additional information for you: "We are going to use a role-based approach to secure our network's servers. Each

*continues*

## CASE STUDY

*continued*

server will be assigned one specific role that will not change. We are implementing a completely new network using all Windows Server 2003 servers and all Windows XP Professional client workstations. We will have only one forest and one domain; all segmentation will need to be accomplished within this domain."

ACME Rockets has the following types of servers planned for its new network: domain controllers, file servers, print servers, IIS intranet servers, and FTP servers that will be located in the DMZ.

### ANALYSIS

By default, all domain controllers will be automatically placed in the Domain Controllers OU.

Also, all client workstations will, by default, be placed in the Computers OU. You will want to create an OU called Member Servers and then create additional OUs inside it for the file servers, print servers, and intranet IIS servers. Lastly, you will need to create an OU in the domain root for the DMZ FTP servers.

You will next need to develop a Domain Baseline Security Policy that will be applied to the domain root itself. This security policy will be applied to all computers in the domain. Next, you will want to apply a Domain Controller Specific Security Policy that hardens your domain controllers. You should then apply a Member Server Baseline Security Policy to the Member Server OU that hardens all member servers. Lastly, you should develop and apply a High Security Policy to the DMZ server OU.

## CHAPTER SUMMARY

### KEY TERMS

Before you take the exam, make sure you are comfortable with the definitions and concepts for each of the following key terms. You can use Appendix A, "Glossary," for quick reference.

- Active Directory
- Baseline
- Compatible security template
- Default DC security template

"Quality is job one" was a common expression used by a major automotive manufacturer in years past. You can now say that, when it comes to Windows Server 2003 networks at least, security is job one. In this chapter, we only scratched the surface of the security pool. Security is a very deep and often misunderstood part of network administration—and one that you cannot afford to overlook.

Every security plan must have a starting point. By making use of the preconfigured security templates supplied with Windows Server 2003 and the additional security templates included in the Windows Server 2003 Security Guide, you can quickly and efficiently implement role-based security in your network. By configuring and testing security templates in the Security Configuration and Analysis

## CHAPTER SUMMARY

snap-in, you can avoid mistakenly applying them to a large group of computers via Group Policy until you are ready to do so. When you are happy with your security templates, you can quickly apply them to your computers by importing them into Group Policy Objects at the applicable levels within your network's organization. Because security templates are incremental, you can apply general settings at the domain root level and increase the security configuration as you navigate deeper into the network.

**KEY TERMS**

- Discretionary Access Control List
- Domain
- Forest
- Group Policy Editor
- GPO
- Highly Secure security template
- Organizational Unit
- Resultant Set of Policy
- Role-based security
- Security Configuration and Analysis snap-in
- secedit.exe
- Secure security template
- Security template
- Security Templates snap-in

## APPLY YOUR KNOWLEDGE

## Exercises

### 1.1   Analyzing a Local Computer's Security Settings

In this exercise, you use the Security Configuration and Analysis snap-in to perform an analysis of the local computer's security.

**Estimated time:** 20 minutes

1.  Open your custom security console or create one that contains the Security Configuration and Analysis snap-in.

2.  Right-click the Security Configuration and Analysis node and select Open Database from the context menu.

3.  Create a new database by entering the name **securitydb.**

4.  Select the security template you are loading into the database for this exercise.

5.  Right-click the Security Configuration and Analysis node and select Analyze Computer Now to start the analysis.

6.  Provide an error log name and pathname and click OK to start the analysis process. After the analysis is complete, you are returned to the Security Configuration and Analysis snap-in.

7.  Compare the database settings to those of the local computer. How are they different? How are they the same? What do you need to change to implement the required security?

### 1.2   Importing a Security Template into Group Policy

In this exercise, you import a security template into a Group Policy Object.

**Estimated time:** 15 minutes

1.  Open the Active Directory Users and Computers console.

2.  Locate the domain or OU to which you want to apply the security template.

3.  Right-click the appropriate OU or domain and select Properties from the context menu. The Properties dialog box appears. Select the Group Policy tab.

4.  To create a new GPO, click the New button. Supply a name for the new GPO and press Enter.

5.  Click the Edit button to open the Group Policy Editor for the selected GPO.

6.  Expand the nodes as follows: Computer Configuration, Windows Settings, Security Settings. Right-click the Security Settings node and select Import Policy from the context menu.

7.  Select the template to be imported.

## Review Questions

1.  You are trying to explain to your CIO why using security templates to configure security is a better idea than directly configuring a GPO. What are some reasons that you might present to him to support your position?

2.  You have just completed an analysis of one of your Windows Server 2003 computers using the `secedit.exe` command. How can you now most easily view the analysis output produced?

3.  Security templates in Windows Server 2003 have what file extension?

## Exam Questions

1. You are the administrator of a Windows Server 2003 Active Directory network. Your network consists of 1,500 Windows XP Professional client computers spread out over 15 OUs with approximately 100 computers each. Your network also has 300 Windows Server 2003 servers fulfilling various roles, including domain controllers, file servers, print servers, IIS servers, and Certificate Services servers. You have just finished creating a customized security template that specifies the Account Policy and auditing settings that are required by your organization's corporate policy for specific departments. What is the best way for you to apply this template to only the Sales, Marketing, Production, and Engineering OUs?

    A. Import the security template at the domain level into a GPO.

    B. Import the security template into each required OU by using a GPO.

    C. Script the `secedit.exe` command to apply the security template to the required computers.

    D. Manually apply the security template to each of the computers.

2. You are the network administrator for Just Right Tops, LLC. Your network consists of three geographically distant sites that function as three different domains. No site has a direct link to any other site. You have recently completed the creation of two custom security templates that are to be applied to all computers in all three sites of your company network. How can you most easily deploy these security templates at all three sites?

    A. Create and configure a new domain controller for each remote site. Apply the security templates to the domain controllers. Place a new domain controller in each site and allow Active Directory to replicate.

    B. Export the security templates into `.inf` files by using the Security Configuration and Analysis snap-in. Deliver the security templates to the remote location and import them into the appropriate GPOs.

    C. Establish connectivity between all sites and force the remote site domain controllers to perform replication with the local site domain controllers after implementing the new security templates.

    D. Re-create the security templates at each remote site and then import them into the appropriate GPOs.

3. You are the network administrator of the Gidget's Widgets, LLC, corporate network. You have instructed Andrea, your assistant administrator, to configure file access auditing for all files in the CorpDocs folder on your file server. In which node of the Group Policy Editor will Andrea find the auditing options?

    A. Account Policies

    B. Local Policies

    C. Restricted Groups

    D. File System

## APPLY YOUR KNOWLEDGE

4. You are the network administrator for Sunbrew Dairy Farms, Inc. You are currently interviewing a candidate for the position of assistant network administrator. You have asked Christopher, the candidate, what the `secedit.exe` command can be used for. Which of the following answers that Christopher gives you are correct? (Choose all that apply.)

   A. `secedit.exe` can be used to analyze the current security settings.

   B. `secedit.exe` can be used to apply new security settings to a computer.

   C. `secedit.exe` can be used to apply new security settings to a GPO.

   D. `secedit.exe` can be scripted, allowing it to be run on many computers across the entire network.

5. You are interviewing Austin for the position of assistant network security administrator. When you ask him what the best uses for an Organizational Unit are, what correct answers do you expect to hear from him? (Choose two correct answers.)

   A. OUs can be used to group together objects for simplified network administration.

   B. OUs can be used to create child domains within the DNS namespace.

   C. OUs can be used to create child domains with the Active Directory forest environment.

   D. OUs can be used to apply role-specific settings to groups of like objects.

6. In a Windows Server 2003 Active Directory environment, what constitutes the security boundary?

   A. The domain

   B. The Organizational Unit

   C. The forest

   D. The security principal

7. Austin is the network administrator for the Eternal Light Group, LLC. He is attempting to perform an analysis of a computer by using the Security Configuration and Analysis snap-in. What is the correct order of performance of the following steps? (Delete any steps that are not needed.)

   1. Select the security template to be used in the analysis.

   2. Right-click Security Configuration and Analysis and then select Analyze Computer Now.

   3. Select the log file to be used in the analysis.

   4. Right-click Security Configuration and Analysis and then select Open Database.

   5. Right-click Security Configuration and Analysis and then select Configure Computer Now.

   6. Select the database to be used in the analysis.

   A. 2, 1, 3, 4, 6, 5

   B. 4, 1, 6, 2, 5, 3

   C. 4, 6, 1, 2, 3

   D. 2, 6, 1, 3, 4

## APPLY YOUR KNOWLEDGE

8. You have just completed an analysis of a computer by using the Security Configuration and Analysis snap-in. When you examine the results, you notice several items that have red circle with white X icons next to them. What do they indicate?

   A. The item is not defined in the analysis database and was not examined on the computer.

   B. The item is defined in the analysis database and on the computer, and it matches the currently configured setting.

   C. The item is defined in the analysis database but not on the computer.

   D. The item is defined in the analysis database and on the computer, but it does not match the currently configured setting.

9. You are the network administrator for Gidget's Widgets, LLC. You are trying to explain to one of your assistant administrators, Hannah, how the `secedit.exe` command can be used to apply security templates to computers. Which of the following additional switches do you need to make sure she uses with the `secedit /configure` command? (Choose all that apply.)

   A. `/analyze`

   B. `/db`

   C. `/log`

   D. `/cfg`

10. Chris is creating a security plan for her network that will be using a role-based approach. If her domain has the following types of servers, how many different security policies should she plan on using?

    • Domain Controllers

    • File Servers

    • Print Servers

    • IIS Servers

    • DHCP Servers

    A. 5

    B. 6

    C. 7

    D. 8

11. Chris is creating a security plan for her network that will be using a role-based approach. What is the first step in implementing a role-based security configuration for her Active Directory network?

    A. Implementing a Domain Baseline Security Policy

    B. Implementing a Domain Controller Baseline Security Policy

    C. Implementing a Member Server Baseline Security Policy

    D. Implementing role-specific security policies for her different member servers

## APPLY YOUR KNOWLEDGE

12. Christopher is preparing to implement a role-based security solution on his Windows Server 2003 Active Directory network. He, however, does not know the starting configuration of his workstation clients. He proposes that he will just apply the `Setup Security.inf` security template located on each computer to that computer to restore the settings to a known state with all settings being the same across all client workstations. What is wrong with his proposal?

   A. The `Setup Security.inf` security template is found only on domain controllers.

   B. The `Setup Security.inf` security template is specific to the specific computer and can vary from one computer to the next.

   C. The `Setup Security.inf` security template is found only on computers that are upgraded from a previous operating system.

   D. The `Setup Security.inf` security template cannot actually be used to apply security settings to a computer; it is only a record of the initial security configuration the computer had.

13. Where can you find the preconfigured security templates that are installed with Windows Server 2003?

   A. `%systemroot%\templates`

   B. `%systemroot%\security\templates`

   C. `%systemroot%\security\`

   D. `%systemroot%\security\default\templates`

14. What limitation of the Security Configuration and Analysis snap-in can you get around by using Group Policy Objects?

   A. Security Configuration and Analysis cannot be used to implement security policies on a computer.

   B. Security Configuration and Analysis cannot be used to implement security policies at the domain level.

   C. Security Configuration and Analysis cannot be used to determine the current security configuration of a computer.

   D. Security Configuration and Analysis has no command-line equivalent.

15. Christopher is preparing to use the `secedit.exe` command to analyze the security on one of his member servers. If Christopher is using the secure workstation security template as his comparison point and needs to ensure that the analysis database is clear before importing the security template, which of the following choices represents the correct command that Christopher should enter to perform the analysis?

   A.

   ```
   secedit /analyze /overwrite /db c:\sectst\
   ➥sectst1.sdb /cfg C:\WINDOWS\security
   ➥ \templates\securedc.inf /log c:\sectst\
   ➥ sectst1.log
   ```

   B.

   ```
   secedit /configure /db c:\sectst\sectst1.sdb
   ➥/cfg C:\WINDOWS\security\templates\
   ➥securedc.inf /log c:\sectst\sectst1.log
   ```

## APPLY YOUR KNOWLEDGE

C.

```
secedit /analyze /db c:\sectst\sectst1.sdb /
➦ cfg C:\WINDOWS\security\templates
➦ \securews.inf /log c:\sectst\sectst1.log
```

D.

```
secedit /analyze /overwrite /db c:\sectst
➦ \sectst1.sdb /cfg C:\WINDOWS\security
➦ \templates\securews.inf /log c:\sectst
➦ \sectst1.log
```

# Answers to Review Questions

1. By using security templates, you can perform configuration and testing on a computer that will not result in changes being applied across the network until they are ready. In addition, by using a security template, you are in effect using a script: You can ensure that all changes will be identical to all computers they are applied to, even if they are in different OUs or domains. For more information, see the section "The Windows Server 2003 Security Templates."

2. Although secedit.exe allows you to analyze and configure computers throughout the network from the command line, you cannot easily view the analysis reports created from it except through Security Configuration and Analysis. Although you can view the log file in a text editor, such as Notepad, accurately determining the results of the analysis is not easy. For more information, see the section "The Security Configuration and Analysis Snap-in."

3. Security templates are flat text files that have the .inf file extension. For more information, see the section "The Windows Server 2003 Security Templates."

# Answers to Exam Questions

1. **B.** The best way to apply the settings to only computers that require them is to import the template into a GPO associated with each OU that requires the settings. Importing the security template into the domain-level GPO would apply the settings to all computers in the domain, most likely with unwanted side effects. For more information, see the section "Group Policy Security Extensions."

2. **B.** Because you created custom security templates using the Security Configuration and Analysis snap-in, you can simply export them into .inf files and transfer them to the remote sites via any available means. When they are at the remote sites, the security templates can be imported to the appropriate GPOs, thus placing them into effect. For more information, see the section "Group Policy Security Extensions."

3. **B.** The Local Policies node of the Group Policy Editor contains three subnodes: Audit Policy, User Rights Assignment, and Security Options. Andrea will find the auditing items she will need to configure in the Audit Policy subnode. For more information, see the section "The Security Configuration and Analysis Snap-in."

4. **A, B, D.** The secedit.exe command can be used to analyze a computer, configure a computer, export a computer's security settings to a template, import the settings from a template, validate the context of a template, and create a rollback template. Because secedit.exe is a command-line tool, you can script it and use it on many computers across an entire network. For more information, see the section "secedit.exe."

## APPLY YOUR KNOWLEDGE

5. **A, D.** Organizational Units can be used, very efficiently in fact, to group together objects that are similar in nature for easier administration. As well, you can apply security and other configuration settings to an OU to quickly have these settings applied to the objects within the OU itself. OUs should not be thought of as just containers to hold objects for the sake of better organizing Active Directory from a visual standpoint; they are actually very powerful administrative tools when properly used. Permissions to perform administrative functions can be assigned through delegation to nonadministrators at the OU level as well, further enhancing the administrative benefit of OUs. For more information, see the section "Implementing Enterprise Security."

6. **C.** Contrary to the popular belief in the past, the forest is the only absolute security boundary in a Windows Server 2003 Active Directory domain. Domains are only administrative boundaries: A user with Domain Admin credentials in one domain could possibly gain domain administrative credentials in other domains through unscrupulous actions. For more information, see the section "Implementing Enterprise Security."

7. **C.** The correct steps to be used to perform an analysis of a computer with the Security Configuration and Analysis snap-in are as follows: Select Open Database, select the database, select the security template, select Analyze Computer, and select the log file. For more information, see the section "The Security Configuration and Analysis Snap-in."

8. **D.** A red circle with white X icon next to an item in the Security Configuration and Analysis snap-in results indicates that the item is present in both the database and the computer but does not match the currently configured setting. For more information, see the section "The Security Configuration and Analysis Snap-in."

9. **B, C, D.** The /db switch specifies the pathname and filename of the database to be used, the /log switch specifies the pathname and filename of the error log to be used during the process, and the /cfg switch specifies the pathname and filename of the security template to be loaded into the database. For more information, see the section "secedit.exe."

10. **C.** Chris should be using seven (7) different security policies as follows: Domain Baseline Policy, Domain Controllers OU Policy, Member Servers OU Baseline Policy, File Servers OU Policy, Print Servers OU Policy, IIS Servers OU Policy, and DHCP Servers OU Policy. Each type of server has specific security requirements that necessitate different security policies. The domain itself needs a Baseline Security Policy that takes care of things such as password and account lockout policies. Also, the Member Servers OU needs a Baseline Security Policy to configure items that apply to all member servers such as auditing and user rights assignments. For more information, see the section "Using Role-Based Security Templates."

11. **A.** The first step to successfully implementing a role-based security solution is to create the baseline—the starting point. Thus, Chris needs to implement a Domain Baseline Security Policy before she moves on. For more information, see the section "Implementing Enterprise Security."

12. **B.** Christopher's mistake is in the fact that he proposes to use the `Setup Security.inf` security template located on each client workstation to apply the same settings across all his workstations. The `Setup Security.inf` security template is created during the installation of Windows on the computer—either clean or upgrade—and varies from one computer to the next. For more information, see the section "The Windows Server 2003 Security Templates."

13. **B.** The preconfigured security templates that install with Windows Server 2003 can be found in the `%systemroot%\security\templates` directory. Typically, this is `C:\WINDOWS\security\templates`. For more information, see the section "Planning and Implementing Role-Based Security Using Security Templates."

14. **B.** The only real failing in Security Configuration and Analysis is that it cannot be used to analyze or configure security on anything other than the local computer. It does not have the capability to be targeted at a remote computer like some of the other MMC snap-ins. For more information, see the section "The Security Configuration and Analysis Snap-in."

15. **D.** Only option D meets all the specified requirements that Christopher has for performing this analysis: He must use the secure template for a member server (`securews.inf`), and he must ensure that the database is cleared prior to importing the security template. Response C appears to meet these requirements but does not provide for clearing the database before importing the security template. For more information, see the section "`secedit.exe`."

---

### Suggested Readings and Resources

1. Windows Server 2003 Security Guide, `http://go.microsoft.com/fwlink/?LinkId=14845`.

2. Threats and Countermeasures: Security Settings in Windows Server 2003 and Window XP, `http://go.microsoft.com/fwlink/?LinkId=15159`.

3. "Security Configuration Manager Overview," `www.microsoft.com/technet/prodtechnol/windowsserver2003/proddocs/server/se_scm_overview.asp`.

4. "Security Configuration Manager," `www.microsoft.com/technet/prodtechnol/windowsserver2003/proddocs/entserver/SEconcepts_SCM.asp`.

Your network is the road by which your data travels from point to point. Quite simply, if your network is flawed or not functioning properly, your day is going to be unhappy at best. At worst, your network services will not function, and if the network is down, most applications and services you are trying to deliver will not be deliverable. Good network designs do not just happen, nor are they necessarily hard to implement. A thorough knowledge of the mechanics of Transmission Control Protocol/Internet Protocol (TCP/IP), Internet Protocol (IP) routing, IP subnetting, and Internet connectivity goes a long way toward creating and maintaining a network that not only works, but also can evolve and grow as business and user needs change and/or become more complex.

Microsoft has defined the TCP/IP connectivity portion of the "Planning, Implementing, and Maintaining a Network Infrastructure" objectives as follows:

**Plan a TCP/IP network infrastructure strategy.**

- **Analyze IP addressing requirements.**

- **Plan an IP routing solution.**

- **Create an IP subnet scheme.**

▶ Good networks begin with good planning and good designs. To plan and design a good network, you need to understand the IP addressing and routing requirements of your organization. With this knowledge in mind, you can move forward and start planning the IP subnets you require. This creates a solid backbone from which the rest of your network will be built.

**Plan and modify a network topology.**

- **Plan the physical placement of network resources.**

- **Identify network protocols to be used.**

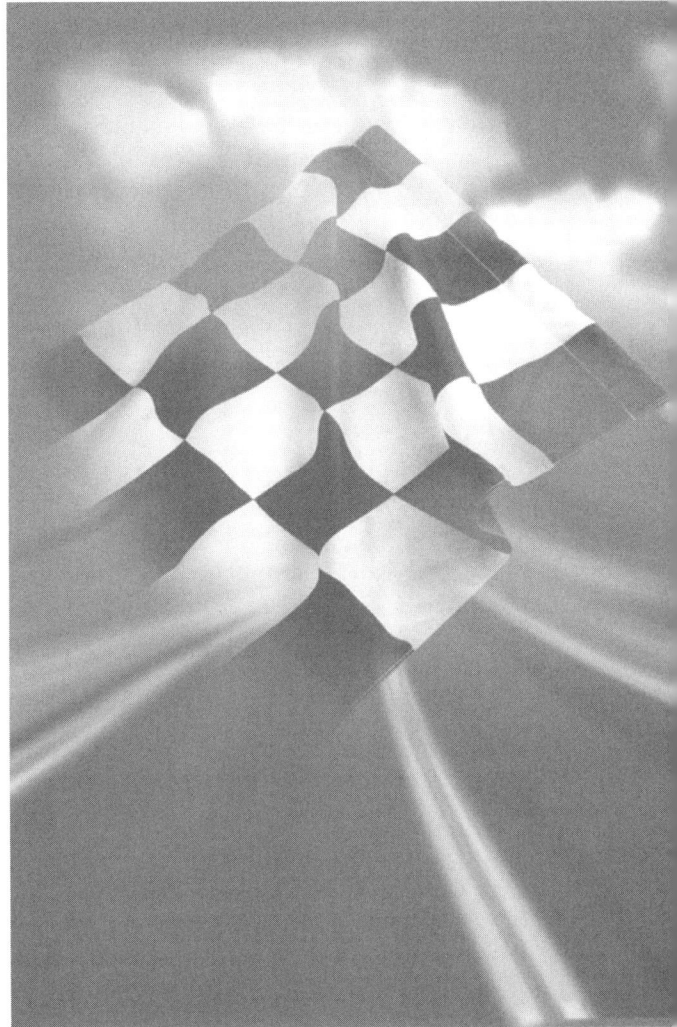

CHAPTER 2

# Planning, Implementing, and Maintaining a Network Infrastructure

▶ As mentioned before, all networks should have a design and/or plan. A large part of that plan should address where to physically and logically place network resources (file servers, print servers, Internet access, and so on) and identify protocols that will be used to connect to and access these resources.

### Plan an Internet connectivity strategy.

▶ Reliable, available Internet access has become a required commodity in the vast majority of networks today. Email, Web browsing, and a plethora of other business functions need Internet access to function. Thus, not having Internet connectivity would likely become a big problem in a short amount of time. In this chapter, we cover the importance of planning an Internet connectivity strategy.

### Plan network traffic monitoring. Tools might include Network Monitor and System Monitor.

▶ Networks have problems that at times are hard to solve or reproduce for one reason or another, but still need to be solved nonetheless. Using tools such as Network Monitor and System Monitor helps you to locate, identify, and troubleshoot issues as well as monitor traffic traversing your local area network (LAN).

### Troubleshoot connectivity to the Internet.

- **Diagnose and resolve issues related to Network Address Translation (NAT).**

- **Diagnose and resolve issues related to name resolution cache information.**

- **Diagnose and resolve issues related to client configuration.**

▶ After you are connected to the Internet, you may encounter many problems. You must address issues with Network Address Translation planning and implementation, issues with the domain name system (DNS), and, of course, issues with clients trying to connect to and use the Internet.

### Troubleshoot TCP/IP addressing.

- **Diagnose and resolve issues related to client computer configuration.**

- **Diagnose and resolve issues related to DHCP server address assignment.**

▶ All great network administrators need to know, understand, and embrace TCP/IP. This objective covers what you need to know abut TCP/IP from a client perspective. You need to know how to troubleshoot TCP/IP issues, as well as those issues resulting from problems with a Dynamic Host Configuration Protocol (DHCP) server.

# STUDY STRATEGIES

▶ Focus on the objectives. Make sure you understand what each objective is asking you to do or learn. Read over the objectives a few times and try to understand what they are asking for; then think about how to plan, design, and troubleshoot problems resulting from each one.

▶ Memorize all TCP/IP charts, numbering, and standards as they map to the objectives. For instance, if your knowledge of subnetting is weak, you will most likely want to mark this as a weak spot. Make sure you attack your weak spots and get these issues under your belt for this exam.

▶ Get your hands dirty. The Step by Steps throughout this book provide plenty of directions and exercises, but you should go beyond these examples and create some of your own. If you can, experiment with each of the objectives to see how they work and why you would use each one.

# INTRODUCTION

In this chapter, we look at how to plan, implement, and maintain a Windows Server 2003 network infrastructure. Before we delve into the specifics of "how" to do this, we first introduce the "why." Why should you worry so much about your network infrastructure? The answer is simple: If you don't have a well-developed network infrastructure, the rest of your applications, services, and systems will fail. Don't believe it? Let's look at an example from a client with a poorly designed network infrastructure.

ABC Corporation has been in business for 10 years. It is the primary producer of widgets for the world. ABC Corp. needs to merge with three new companies by the end of the year to broaden its widget inventory. The four widget companies will form one network after the merger is complete. You are the network administrator responsible for making this happen. Following are issues you will most likely see arise:

▶ Wasteful IP numbering schemes

▶ Routing loops and problems with routing tables from improperly designed networks or networks connected improperly

▶ A need to connect internal DNS namespaces, WINS servers, and Active Directory

▶ A need to have email systems work together

▶ A need to tie applications and databases together and make them accessible to all users in all plants

The whole point to this example is that without a "rock solid" network infrastructure, you are assured to see problem after problem arise from lack of planning and design. Some of the items listed here are business solutions that your users demand and expect. It's up to you to understand the infrastructure well enough so that you can implement these solutions easily enough.

The goal of this chapter is not only to present you the information you need to pass this exam, but also to introduce you to the importance of actually doing this work for real.

**Implementing Windows Server 2003 in a TCP/IP-based network**
For the 70-293 exam, you are responsible for knowing how to implement Windows Server 2003 in a TCP/IP-based network and troubleshoot any issues that arise. If you know how a TCP/IP network is designed, how TCP/IP works, and how to troubleshoot it, you will have few problems with the exam, as well as real-word scenarios in which you have to implement this technology on the job.

# PLANNING A TCP/IP NETWORK INFRASTRUCTURE STRATEGY

Planning a TCP/IP network infrastructure strategy is no simple task. Accomplishing this task can take many years of experience and good a understanding of the mechanics of TCP/IP. This makes TCP/IP one of the exam items that many candidates shy away from because this topic deals with numbers and you may have to do some basic math or understand many concepts just to complete one specific item or task. For example, let's look at a possible problem you may have to contend with.

You are the administrator of ABC Corporation and need to connect another network to your own and plan a way for the other network to communicate with you. By itself, this problem is not very difficult, but when looking at the topology map, as shown in Figure 2.1, you start to see where the complexity surfaces.

**FIGURE 2.1**
Viewing a TCP/IP infrastructure.

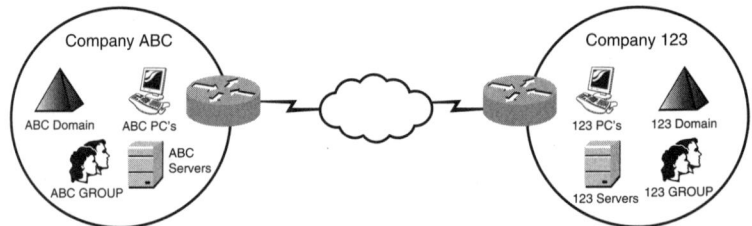

The true complexity surfaces when you start to examine the following issues:

1. How will the two domains work together?

2. Will DNS namespaces need to be connected?

3. Are any of the client computers Windows 9*x* legacy clients?

4. Will you need to implement WINS?

5. Does the company you are connecting to use DHCP, and what IP ranges does it have in its scopes?

6. Are the IP addresses and DHCP ranges duplicate to what you use in ABC Corporation?

7. How are you going to make the two routers communicate?

8. What wide area network (WAN) topology are you going to use between them?

9. What routing protocol are you going to use, or should you use static routes?

10. Are there any firewalls, Access Control Lists (ACLs), or filtering devices present that could potentially block specific transmissions?

These questions are not meant to scare you; instead, they are meant to help you start thinking about the multitude of issues that surround the design and deployment of TCP/IP networks. Before we go any further, let's spend some time reviewing the fundamentals of TCP/IP.

# TCP/IP Fundamentals

To successfully plan a TCP/IP-based network infrastructure strategy, you need to understand TCP/IP addressing and routing fundamentals. We examine these topics further in this section.

TCP/IP stands for *Transmission Control Protocol/Internet Protocol*, which is actually two separate protocols, one called TCP and the other called IP. TCP/IP is really two protocols within a "suite" of protocols that map to a model. Two models you have most likely heard of are the Open System Interface (OSI) model and the Department of Defense (DoD) model. This chapter does not contain a detailed explanation of these models because most of the information you need for the exam is not based on your memorizing the OSI model; however, you should understand it (if you don't already) before we cover the TCP/IP suite. You can find detailed information on the OSI model from the Microsoft Web site at `www.microsoft.com/technet/prodtechnol/windows2000serv/reskit/ tcpip/part4/tcpappa.asp`.

TCP/IP maps to both the OSI and DoD models but actually maps more closely with the DoD model because the Department of Defense was the original creator and user of the protocol.

The real importance of understanding the fundamentals of the OSI model becomes apparent when you try to troubleshoot TCP/IP base

**EXAM TIP**

**Understanding the OSI and DoD models**  You are not expected to know a great deal about either the OSI or DoD models for the 70-293 exam. They exist simply to break a complex topic into smaller pieces.

communications and services. Understanding what is happening at each layer makes it easier to determine where the fault may lie.

TCP/IP is the basic communication language or protocol of the Internet. There are many other protocols in use, some of which you may be familiar with, such as AppleTalk, IPX/SPX, even SNA. All these protocols have been displaced by TCP/IP, however. Because most networks today are connected to the Internet somehow, using only TCP/IP on internal networks makes more sense.

You can see a good example of a TCP/IP-based network in Figure 2.2, which displays some of the TCP/IP concepts you will be working with both on this exam and also during your day-to-day network administration.

**FIGURE 2.2**
Viewing a complex TCP/IP infrastructure.

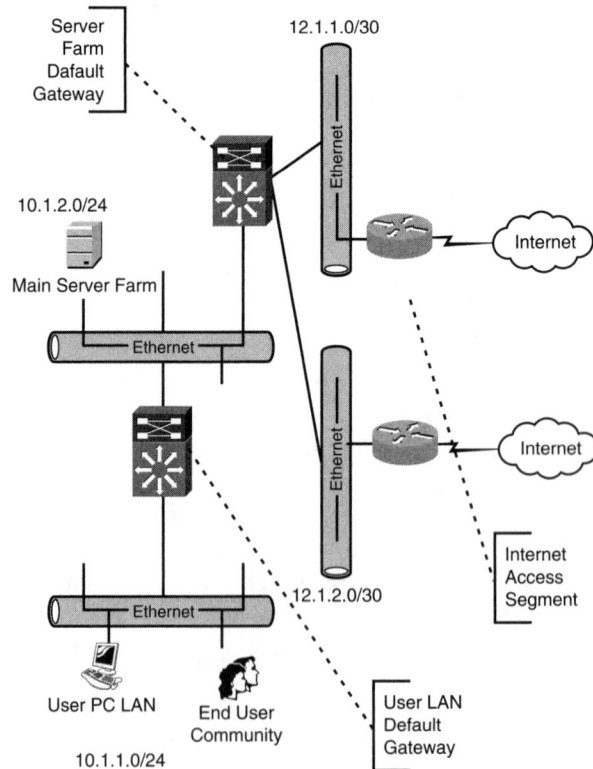

Notice that all end users on the Internet access segment in the user LAN in Figure 2.2 are on the 10.1.1.0/24 network, which is a privately addressed segment because you are using a 10.0.0.0 network address. This end-user segment accesses file, print, and application servers on the 10.1.2.0/24 segment.

A Layer 3 switch, which has a router built into the device, separates the user LAN from the server farm. The Layer 3 switch's IP address is 10.1.1.1, which makes it the default gateway for the user LAN.

Although a proxy server is not documented in the diagram, one is available in the server farm; it provides Internet access for the network users. This server has an IP address of 10.1.2.30. The proxy server points to a firewall and then out to the external routers on a publicly routable IP address segment.

To tie these two segments together, a PC on the user LAN would need to have an IP address on that segment that is in the same subnet (10.1.1.0) and a default gateway assignment of 10.1.1.1. If you need to access a server with an IP address of 10.1.2.30 (the proxy server for Internet access), the packets would be sent to the default gateway for processing.

You can run the `ipconfig /all` command to see how this configuration will look on the client end. The output is as follows:

```
C:\>ipconfig/all

Windows 2000 IP Configuration
        Host Name . . . . . . . . . . . : SHIMONSKI-LAPTOP
        Primary DNS Suffix  . . . . . . :
        Node Type . . . . . . . . . . . : Hybrid
        IP Routing Enabled. . . . . . . : No
        WINS Proxy Enabled. . . . . . . : No
        DNS Suffix Search List. . . . . : rsnetworks.net

Ethernet adapter Local Area Connection:
        Connection-specific DNS Suffix  . : rsnetworks.net
        Description . . . . . . . . . . : 3Com 3C920
        ➡ (3C905C-TX Compatible)
        Physical Address. . . . . . . . : 00-08-74-56-0A-34
        DHCP Enabled. . . . . . . . . . : Yes
        Autoconfiguration Enabled . . . . : Yes
        IP Address. . . . . . . . . . . : 10.1.1.10
        Subnet Mask . . . . . . . . . . : 255.255.255.0
        Default Gateway . . . . . . . . : 10.1.1.1
        DHCP Server . . . . . . . . . . : 10.1.1.12
        DNS Servers . . . . . . . . . . : 10.1.1.15
                                          10.1.1.16
                                          10.1.1.17
        Lease Obtained. . . . . . . . . : Sunday,
        ➡August 24, 2003 11:30:00 AM
        Lease Expires . . . . . . . . . : Monday, August 25, 2003
        ➡ 11:30:00 AM
```

So, now that you have viewed a common network setup, let's look at some relevant terminology:

▶ **IP address**—A 32-bit binary address that is used to identify a TCP/IP host's network and host ID.

▶ **Physical address (MAC address)**—A 48-bit alphanumeric number, such as 00-08-74-97-0B-26, that denotes the host's physical address. Also called a Media Access Control (MAC) address, the physical address is unique to the device to which it is assigned.

▶ **Network interface card (NIC)**—A device installed into a PC or other host device to allow it to have a MAC address and be assigned an IP address. This device connects you to the network.

▶ **Default gateway**—The configured router on a TCP/IP-enabled system that allows all packets destined for a remote network to be forwarded out of the local network.

▶ **Layer 3 switch (router)**—A Layer 3 switch is nothing more than a router and a switch integrated into the same chassis, which makes it faster, easier to manage, and more secure. In today's network infrastructures, the line between switches, routers, and firewalls is becoming blurred because most of them are being integrated into one single device (chassis) that can perform all these tasks.

▶ **Subnet mask**—In TCP/IP, a mask that is used to determine what subnet an IP address belongs to. A subnet mask enables a host or router to determine which portion of an IP address is the network ID and which is the host ID. The host can then use this information to determine whether to send a packet to a host on the local network or to a router.

▶ **Public IP address**—An IP address for use on the Internet or a private network that must be assigned via an organization or Internet service provider (ISP) so that no duplicates will exist.

▶ **Private IP address**—An IP address range reserved for private (non–Internet-connected) networks. There are private address ranges in the Class A, Class B, and Class C address blocks.

► **Network Address Translation (NAT)**—A process by which private IP addresses are mapped to public IP addresses and vice versa. The device that performs this translation keeps a table of which IP addresses given from the NAT pool map to the one that was distributed.

► **Proxy server**—A server-based application that serves as a go-between for the internal LAN clients and the public Internet. A proxy server also caches pages so that Internet response seems faster to internal clients.

► **Firewall**—A device that protects the internal network from the external Internet, WAN, business partner, or anything else you may want to protect against.

So, how exactly does IP work? In the following sections, we examine in more detail IP, IP addressing, ranges, classes, and other related terminology.

## Internet Protocol Fundamentals

By now, you should have a good idea of what an IP network might look like, and more important, you should know what to do with one come exam time. If not, fear not. As we progress through the rest of this chapter, we will continue to lay out scenarios for you to enhance your understanding. Right now, however, we need to dig a little deeper into how IP addressing works so that you fully understand it.

The vast majority of production networks currently use IPv4, which stands for Internet Protocol version 4. More often than not, you don't even notice the v4 when discussing IP—and rightfully so. With the exception of the relatively new IPv6, which some networks are beginning to adopt, there is no other IP to talk about. In reality, you will not be tested on IPv6 on the 70-293 exam, but you need to know of its existence because it is a standard part of the Windows Server 2003 networking suite.

---

**WARNING**

**Unique IP addresses**  Duplicate IP addresses do not work. All IP addressing must be unique on each segment. If you have duplicates, your systems will know and give you error messages that duplicate addressing exists somewhere on your network.

---

**EXAM TIP**

**Using RFCs**  For detailed information on any protocol standard, you should become familiar with *Requests For Comments,* which are commonly called *RFCs.* They are the documents that depict a protocol's standards and fundamentals. Although their content is highly technical, they are the definitive information source on any protocol standard you need to research. For more information, check out the following RFCs:

Transmission Control Protocol (TCP) RFC: `ftp.isi.edu/in-notes/std/std7.txt`

Internet Protocol (IP) RFC: `ftp.isi.edu/in-notes/std/std5.txt`

## IPV6...COMING SOON TO A NETWORK NEAR YOU!

It's no secret that we're running out of IP addresses under the current IPv4 addressing system. Under IPv4, IP addresses are 32-bit numbers consisting of four binary octets separated from each other by periods. For example, 11000000.10101000.00000000.10011010 is 192.168.0.154 in decimal notation. This way of providing IP addresses provides for $2^{32}$, or 4,294,967,296 possible addresses, of which a small number are reserved for private networks and cannot be routed in the Internet.

The IPv6 addressing system aims to solve this problem by making use of 128-bit numbers to represent unique IP addresses. Using 128 bits gives you $2^{128}$ or 340,282,366,920,938,463,463,374,607,431,768,211,456 ($3.4 \times 10^{38}$) possible addresses. That is enough IP addresses to provide 655,570,793,348,866,943,898,599 ($6.5 \times 10^{23}$) addresses for every square meter of the earth's surface. That *should* help solve the shortage of available public IP addresses. Of course, the true power of the IPv6 addressing system is that it allows multiple hierarchical levels of organization and flexibility in design that is currently lacking from today's IPv4 Internet.

A 128-bit IPv6 address, as you might suspect, looks different from what you are used to seeing in IPv4. An IPv6 address in binary form looks like

```
0010000111011010 0000000011010011 0000000000000000 0010111100111011
0000001010101010 0000000011111111 1111111000101000 1001110001011010
```

which translates into

```
21DA:00D3:0000:2F3B:02AA:00FF:FE28:9C5A
```

in hexadecimal.

The IPv6 protocol and addressing system should all but put an end to memorizing IP addresses! With the advent of the IPv6 protocol, IP classes and classless interdomain routing (CIDR) will be things of the past. The three commonly used private IP ranges (10.0.0.0/8, 172.16.0.0/12, and 192.168.0.0/16) will be replaced by one site-local address range (FEC0::/48). The familiar loopback address of 127.0.0.1 will be replaced by ::1.

In the interest of making things ever easier, you can use double colons (::) to represent contiguous strings of zero value. So, the loopback address 0:0:0:0:0:0:0:1 becomes simply ::1. Of course, you can use double colons only once in an IPv6 IP address—for obvious reasons.

Additionally, you can use leading zero suppression to remove the leading zeros within an individual 16-bit string. Thus, 21DA:00D3:0000:2F3B:02AA:00FF:FE28:9C5A becomes 21DA:D3:0:2F3B:2AA:FF:FE28:9C5A. Of course, the drivers within the operating system and the infrastructure hardware devices (routers, switches, and so on) handle all these conversions automatically, invisible to you.

For more information on IPv6, visit the official IPv6 site, located at `http://www.ietf.org/html.charters/ipv6-charter.html`, or visit the Microsoft Web site on IPv6, located at `http://www.microsoft.com/windowsserver2003/technologies/ipv6/default.mspx`.

With that brief detour into IPv6 out of the way, let's dig deeper into the mechanics of IP (IPv4, to be proper) and see how it all works together.

As we mentioned earlier, an IP address is a 32-bit number that denotes a node or host on a network. The number, which resembles 10.1.1.1/24, is a unique host on a single network. If you have two nodes, one numbered 10.1.1.1 and the other numbered 10.1.1.2, they can communicate if they are connected to the same network segment and no other outstanding issues stop communication.

An IP address is broken down into two specific parts: the network identifier and host identifier. Let's look at the following IP address to understand it better:

IP address: 10.1.1.1

Subnet mask: 255.255.255.0

You need to break down this number into binary bits to truly see what we mean by masking. First, consider the fact that you have a 32-bit address written in decimal format. If you want to see the subnet mask 255.255.255.0 in binary, you have to change the format from decimal to binary, or base 2, numbering, as follows:

255.255.255.0 = 11111111.11111111.11111111.00000000

Remember, binary uses only 1s and 0s, either on or off. No other numbers are used, so you can see how the network is masked. All 1s in the network portion denote the actual network you are working on. This leaves the host portion (the 0s at the end) available for assignment. This way, any device can know what network it's on, or better, what subnet. Because we've used 24 1s here, we denote the IP address as 10.1.1.0/24. Using this form of notation is an easier way to show a subnet mask assignment. If you see /30, for example, the address appears like this in binary:

11111111.11111111.11111111.11111100

This concept can be confusing because, although you now have to perform an operation called *subnetting* on the exam, you need to know what network a host is on, and being able to see it in this format can help you pass this portion of the exam.

How did we get this subnet mask? Easy. First, you must understand what makes up a single octet. An octet is 8 bits out of 32 denoted and separated by a single period. Take one single octet and break it down as shown:

| 128 | 64 | 32 | 16 | 8 | 4 | 2 | 1 |
|-----|----|----|----|---|---|---|---|

If you can duplicate this chart, then you can figure out a subnet mask. First, you have to know where this chart comes from. Remember how we described base 2 numbering as being 0s and 1s? We also use base 10 numbering, and to go from one to the other, you can use this chart. Remember, a single octet is broken down into 8 bits. Now, take this same chart and plug in the last octet that you don't know because you obviously know that the first three octets have all their bits turned on (1s) so they are all 255 in decimal.

| 128 | 64 | 32 | 16 | 8 | 4 | 2 | 1 |
|-----|----|----|----|---|---|---|---|
| 1   | 1  | 1  | 1  | 1 | 1 | 0 | 0 |

Now, all you have to do is add the table elements, but to make your task even easier, you need to know that all the bits up to the last two should equal 255 because they were all turned on. So, you can simply subtract the last two bits shown as 0s (which adds up to 3) from the number 255. This equals 252, which is a common subnet for a WAN link because you need only a network, a broadcast address, and two useable hosts on the subnet, one for each link from each router. This concept is illustrated in Figure 2.3.

**FIGURE 2.3**
*Viewing a point-to-point link.*

So what exactly did we mean by a single network, a broadcast, and two useable nodes? When you subnet, you have to remember one major point: You always need a network address and a broadcast address for each subnet you create.

If any one thing is universally true when you are dealing with TCP/IP networks, it might be that each and every one is different from the next. Each network varies in size, complexity, physical and logical layout—just to name a few key points of interest. So how will you go about planning a new TCP/IP network? What IP class will you choose to implement? How will you go about properly subnetting it? Will you use private or public IP addresses? You must consider all these questions—and more.

We start our examination of these questions by discussing public versus private IP addressing systems.

## Public Versus Private IP Addressing

Public IP addressing uses three major spaces: Classes A, B, and C. There are also two more classes: Class D, which is used for multicast-based networks, and Class E, which is still experimental. Class A is for very large networks, Class B is for medium-sized networks, and Class C is used for networks that have no more than a couple hundred nodes. Public ranges run as shown in Table 2.1.

**TABLE 2.1**

**VIEWING IP ADDRESS CLASSES**

| Class | Range |
| --- | --- |
| Class A | 1–126 |
| Class B | 128–191 |
| Class C | 192–223 |

Although the private IP address ranges shown in Table 2.2 fall within the Class A, B, and C public IP addresses, note that private IP

NOTE

**Loopback addressing** The IP address 127.0.0.0 is reserved for loopback network and testing. 127.0.0.1 is also located in your HOSTS file, which allows you to test the IP connectivity of your own machine. If you use the command **ping localhost** (which is the host-name located in the HOSTS file), you can resolve to 127.0.0.1, and you should see a reply. This way, you know that TCP/IP is configured properly—at least on your own system.

addresses are not routable on the Internet by design (and by default) and should never be seen outside an internal network.

**TABLE 2.2**

**VIEWING PRIVATE IP CLASSES**

| Class | Range |
|-------|-------|
| Class A | 10.0.0.0–10.255.255.255 |
| Class B | 172.16.0.0–172.31.255.255 |
| Class C | 192.168.0.0–192.168.255.255 |

Now you are familiar with the IP address ranges that you will see both in public and private IP networks, but one question remains: Why do we have "private IP addresses"? IP addresses are a limited commodity—as difficult a concept as that may seem. Had ISPs and private organizations been allowed to use public IP addresses within their large internal networks, the number of useable IP addresses would have quickly vanished into nothing but a memory. Of course, you might argue that this is still a problem—hence the arrival of IPv6—and it is to a certain extent. Private IP addressing has allowed us to avoid this problem until now, thus negating the need for a newer and better IP addressing system.

By assigning a single public IP address to a company, you can then use multiple private IP addresses (tens, hundreds, thousands) internally without any problem, thanks to Network Address Translation (NAT). NAT provides a translation service allowing multiple private IP addresses to access Internet resources as if they indeed had a publicly routable IP address. This also helps explain why private IP addresses are not meant to be routable because it's entirely likely that IP address 192.168.0.100 (one of my internal network servers) is used several hundred thousand times in many other private IP networks.

So how does a device know on which class another device is numbered? The device (a router, for example) examines the first octet of the incoming packet and can determine from the first few bits of the packet what class the packet came from and is using. The first few bits of each IP address indicate which of the address class formats it is using. The address structures are shown in Table 2.3.

If you have a Class A address, the first number is a 0, the network bits are at 7, and the local address makes up the corresponding 24 bits: 1 bit for the identifier, 7 for the network (8 in total) and 24 for host addressing. Table 2.3 shows all the identifiers used for classes A, B, and C.

**TABLE 2.3**

**VIEWING IDENTIFIER LIST FOR CLASS A–C IP ADDRESSING**

| Class | Identifier |
| --- | --- |
| Class A | 0 |
| Class B | 10 |
| Class C | 110 |

You should now be familiar with the basic operation of IP. We can now begin to really get exam specific. Because we have already covered several of the terms and scenarios you are likely to see on the exam, we can cover each objective without having to go into very granular detail.

# ANALYZING IP ADDRESSING REQUIREMENTS

**Plan a TCP/IP network infrastructure strategy.**

▶ **Analyze IP addressing requirements.**

In this section, we look at what you need to know to analyze IP addressing requirements and how to plan a TCP/IP-based network strategy. If you think about the exam objective, what comes to mind? This would be a scenario-based discussion, much like the ones we had earlier. For instance, if you were to analyze requirements for a network infrastructure, you would need to use every skill taught to you since starting this chapter. Let's look at a sample situation:

You are the administrator of 300 Windows XP Professional workstations and a server farm consisting of 25 Windows Server 2003 systems. You need to develop an IP addressing scheme to assign IP addresses to all 300 Windows XP workstations and all 25 servers, set up Internet Access, and set up business-to-business connections or remote sites.

Sounds like a lot of work, doesn't it? Handling this situation really isn't too bad, so let's break down what you may need to know:

1. You need to set up TCP/IP, so you start by picking an IP range that works for you. You may not have the flexibility of picking a brand new one (a network specialist within your group may assign it if you do not manage addresses), so let's say the corporate office assigns the two class C addresses 10.10.1.0/24 and 10.10.2.0/24. This assignment gives you more than 500 addresses you can use.

2. Next, you need to set up a topology map like the one shown in Figure 2.4. Such a map will most likely be provided for you in the exam, but knowing how to create one solves two problems: passing the exam and working on the job. Remember, exam questions don't come up on the job; real-world experience does, so make this topology map as if you were going to see it in the actual question.

3. After laying out a map, you can assign the IP addresses. First, you need to assign IP addresses to the user LAN. Because they are all connected to the Layer 3 switch in the middle of the network topology map, you can assign a set of Virtual LANs (VLANs). A VLAN is used to logically segment the network into different subnets for security and manageability. You can either use this approach or make a DHCP super scope of two subnets. Either way, make sure that you have enough IP addresses to provide to all your hosts. Take into account that you will most likely have closet switches, printers, or other devices that may also need to utilize an IP address.

4. Next, you should make sure you have a default gateway. Because the Layer 3 switch is also a router, you can make it the default gateway for your network.

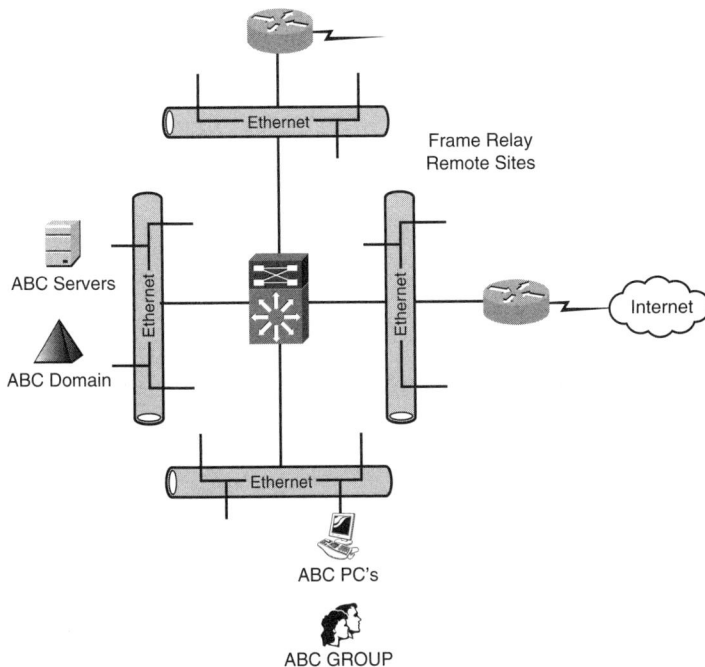

**FIGURE 2.4**

*Planning a complex IP environment.*

5. Next, you can assign IP addresses to your servers. You should assign static IP addresses to your servers, printers, and any other resource that will not change. Say you have a proxy server with an IP address of 10.10.1.40. If DHCP somehow gives it another IP address when its leases expires, you need to change all your client assignments. This is something you would never do, so make certain that you assign your resources static IPs.

6. Next, make sure that the Layer 3 switch has a route over to the Frame Relay Network, as well as the segment where your Internet access router is.

7. Finally, make sure that you have an IP helper address (better known as a DHCP relay agent) configured on your router because, by default, a router does not pass a broadcast across. Therefore, you would have to make sure that your users in the LAN can access and get DHCP addresses from the server farm where the server is located.

That's it! You have analyzed a problem and set up a basic IP addressing solution. Now you can get your network up and running.

## Planning an IP Configuration Strategy

For the final step, you need to consider how you will lay out your IP configuration strategy. Because every computer on your network needs to be able to connect via an IP address, you must know how to get each one an IP address if you do not have addresses set statically. A DHCP server dynamically assigns addresses from a manually designated range of addresses called a *scope* that you predetermine when you deploy your DNS server. Because we already discussed static assignments, let's look at one last option that you may come across and will most likely be tested on during the 70-293 exam.

*Automatic Private IP Addressing (APIPA)* allows a workstation that cannot reach a DHCP server to assign its own IP address so that it can participate on a network. APIPA uses a range from 169.254.0.1 to 169.254.255.254. This is a great strategy if you do not have any other IP addresses on the network. This is true because the workstations can configure themselves, but, most times, this strategy proves to be useless and only gives you a clue that for some reason this workstation cannot get an IP address from the DHCP server. In any case, make certain that you remember this range and what APIPA is used for.

> **EXAM TIP**
>
> **APIPA** Automatic Private IP Addressing (APIPA) is a feature that allows DHCP clients to automatically configure themselves with an IP address and subnet mask when a DHCP server isn't available. The IP address range that APIPA uses is from 169.254.0.1 to 169.254.255.254. When the DHCP server is available, the client can switch back to DHCP.

## PLANNING AN IP ROUTING SOLUTION

### Plan a TCP/IP network infrastructure strategy.

▶ **Plan an IP routing solution.**

In this section, we analyze how to plan an IP routing solution. First, let's briefly review what *IP routing* is. A *router* is a device that looks at a packet that comes in one of its interfaces, analyzes the packet against its routing table (which can be dynamically or statically configured), and decides what segment of the network the packet needs to go to based on that table. In other words, if you have a router configured on your network (as your default gateway), and packets coming from the 10.10.1.0 segment need to get to 10.10.2.0, the router makes that decision. You can set up the router with static IP routes, which means that you hand-pick specific routes and enter them into the table manually, or you can have the router set up dynamically via a routing protocol such as *Routing Information Protocol (RIP)* or *Open Shortest Path First (OSPF)*. So, before we get into specifics, let's look at what you can use as a router.

If you have a large environment or depend heavily on your routing infrastructure, you may opt to use a hardware routing device such as one from Cisco, Nortel, or 3Com. If you are interested in saving money and using a software-based router, Windows Server 2003 can provide such a tool. A software-based routing solution, such as one using the Routing and Remote Access Service (RRAS) can be ideal on a small, properly segmented network with relatively light traffic between subnets. This doesn't mean you should use one over the other; it just means you can select one based on preference or the best price solution after you have performed a cost analysis. Regardless, knowledge of general routing and routers is needed for the 70-293 exam.

RRAS can provide a software-based router on top of Windows Server 2003. We will examine using RRAS to configure routing in detail in Chapter 4, "Planning, Implementing, and Maintaining Routing and Remote Access."

# PLANNING AND MODIFYING A NETWORK TOPOLOGY

In this section, we cover ways to plan and modify a network topology. Why is this important? If you need to add on to or alter your network topology, you need to focus on the following areas before you do:

▶ You need to plan the physical placement of your network resources.

▶ You need to identify network protocols to be used.

# Planning Physical Placement of Network Resources

**Plan and modify a network topology.**

▶ **Plan the physical placement of network resources.**

Now that you are familiar with how to plan a TCP/IP network, let's look at where you may want to place devices on a network. Before we get into the exact details you need to know, let's talk about why planning the placement is so important in the first place.

First, you should know how a network is laid out before you deploy it. You should know what you want a network to look like before you even contemplate ordering gear to populate it. This step is important because you must consider many factors before implementation. These factors include the following:

▶ Do you want redundancy and high availability?

▶ Do you want security?

▶ Where will the application flows be generated from?

▶ How do you stop or contain bottlenecks from occurring?

Looking at these questions before you plan anything is critical because you may change your mind during the implementation. It is possible that before you are even done rolling it out you will find something you would have done differently or better. Long story short, you need to plan physical placement of resources before you deploy them, and the best way to do this is to use a topology map.

Now you can answer the questions that you posed to yourself. Let's look at each in detail:

▶ **Do you want redundancy and high availability?** When you design a network, you have to think about device failure. This chapter describes how to place network devices where they belong as well as how to design them properly. If you consider all the situations that can happen on a network, you surely should consider some redundancy in your network solution. You should look at all points of failure; for example, if something fails, you could be down and off the network for several hours, so you must consider if that's okay for your business. Always get managers' approvals as well because the redundant hardware may cost extra; however, the expense is worthwhile if you have to keep your network up and running all the time with minimal downtime. Examples of redundancy can be anything from redundant servers in a cluster, redundant routers for a default gateway, all the way to redundant power supplies in devices in case of failure. Today, you can order just about anything redundant for failure.

▶ **Do you want security?** You have to plan your security infrastructure well in advance. The security infrastructure includes routers and switches, firewalls, proxy servers, even the Windows Server 2003 system you will deploy. Consider their placement in the network with an eye on security because where you place them (whether on a perimeter network or a VLAN) can actually increase or decrease the security on their network.

▶ **Where will the application flows be generated from?** You have to consider where you will place your resources on your network. If you have a file server, a print server, two domain controllers, a WINS server, a DNS server, and a DHCP server to populate your network, where does it make the most sense to locate them? In other words, you would want a server farm segment with a high-speed backbone (perhaps gigabit Ethernet) with high-speed connections to the Internet or remote sites. You would want to make sure that your user LAN segment is also able to reach this backbone with little trouble. (Later in the chapter, we describe network monitoring and ways you locate problems with this type of solution.)

▶ **How do you stop or contain bottlenecks from occurring?** You can follow the existing rules, one of which is called the 80/20 rule. In this rule, you make sure that 80% of your clients are closest to your network resources (such as email, file and print, and so on) and only 20% of the other clients have to cross over a network router or other device to reach those resources. In other words, you must make sure that you design your network so that you have the fastest possible paths to all resources needed; if you do not, bottlenecks may occur. Bottlenecks also may occur if you mismatch your network speeds. For example, say you use 10BaseT rather than 100BaseTX so that you have Fast Ethernet on your user LAN but only a 10Mbps connection to the Internet; this could create a bottleneck.

## Selecting Network Protocols

**Plan and modify a network topology.**

▶ **Identify network protocols to be used.**

Now that you know how to place devices on your network, let's look at what protocols to use. Besides TCP/IP, we also mentioned other protocols earlier in this chapter. Here, we discuss routing and routed protocols and when or why to choose them. We also describe how to manage the protocols you are using, as well as why you may or may not want to use them.

When you want to plan for protocols besides TCP/IP (which we have covered throughout this chapter), you may need to consider the following protocols in your network infrastructure:

▶ IPX/SPX

▶ SNA

▶ NetBIOS/NetBEUI

We cover only these three because the point behind the whole objective is not to be an expert in any other protocol but TCP/IP, but to be able to recognize a need for other protocols in your network infrastructure, how to identify them, and how to plan for them.

## IPX/SPX

IPX/SPX, which stands for *Internetwork Packet Exchange/Sequence Packet Exchange*, is similar to TCP/IP. You can think of IP mapping to IPX and TCP mapping to SPX. These protocols perform similar operations. IPX/SPX was originally created and used extensively by Novell with its NetWare platform of network operating systems. Although IPX/SPX was a great protocol, TCP/IP became the protocol of the Internet. To avoid missing out on the Internet revolution, all NOS vendors chose to develop TCP/IP into all their solutions moving forward, leaving in other protocols such as IPX/SPX only for backward compatibility. Novell NetWare version 5.0 was the first version to be shipped with a real version of TCP/IP, whereas the older versions of NetWare (versions 4.x and earlier) used add-on packs and NetWare IP (NWIP).

Because IPX/SPX was more readily adopted into the earlier network system platforms, Novell NetWare versions 4.x and earlier and some Novell Directory Services (NDS) functions did not work without IPX/SPX installed. Wherever you work in the field, you may run into older systems on a network running NetWare 4.x and earlier; therefore, IPX/SPX will be running as well. Consequently, you, the Microsoft Certified Professional, need to know how and when to deploy IPX/SPX into or out of your network if necessary.

## SNA

Systems Network Architecture (SNA) is an old but still widely used protocol. Developed by IBM, SNA is a protocol suite that runs on most mainframes used today. Microsoft professionals who know only Microsoft may be shocked to learn that in today's networks they most likely will be confronted with some form of mainframe and may also be responsible for network connectivity to it.

SNA Server was an older Microsoft Backoffice product that helped Windows users connect to and print on an IBM mainframe via the SNA protocol. This solution has since been renamed Host Integration Server (HIS) 2000. Again, it is important that you understand that SNA may exist in your network and that you need to know how to work with it.

## NetBIOS

Another old protocol, the Network Basic Input/Output System (NetBIOS) is a session layer communications service used by client and server applications in IBM-based token-ring and PC LAN Ethernet-based networks. NetBIOS is really just a way for application programming interface–based communications to take place. This means that higher-level services can run over lower-level protocols such as IP. This process is known as *NetBIOS over TCP/IP (NBT)*. The NetBIOS service contains three main sections: the name, session, and datagram services.

Why do you need to know about such a protocol? You will be using NetBIOS names if you have older systems running WINS because they are not on DNS, which would require a Windows 2000 (or newer) network. Older systems rely on NetBIOS, so until you can upgrade all your systems, you will have to use it.

# PLANNING FOR NETWORK TRAFFIC MONITORING

**Plan network traffic monitoring. Tools might include Network Monitor and System Monitor.**

For this objective, you need to look at a network with a critical eye toward packet-level analysis. Although you do not need to know all the details about packet-level analysis, you are responsible for knowing how to troubleshoot networks and systems with the tools that Microsoft provides with the base-level operating system. Windows Server 2003 provides both System Monitor and Network Monitor. System Monitor resides in the Performance Management console, and Network Monitor must be installed separately after a default installation. You can install Network Monitor from the Windows Components Wizard under the Network Management Tools group.

System Monitor helps you to troubleshoot network issues, but few look to System Monitor for help. Why? People mainly don't look to it because they do not know that some of the network monitoring features are in it. For example, an MCP should know that System Monitor can monitor network card I/O, error packets, IP datagram error checking, and so on. You can use this tool to troubleshoot problems going in and going out of the network interface. This is a way for you to troubleshoot errors that may be coming from a bad NIC or from excessive broadcasts hitting your server. Having that many broadcasts hit your server could mean a network problem; you may need to replace a hub with a switch, for example. Either way, you can see why System Monitor is helpful.

Network Monitor, shown in Figure 2.5, captures frames, or packets, to and from the local computer and the network.

Graph pane          Total Stats pane

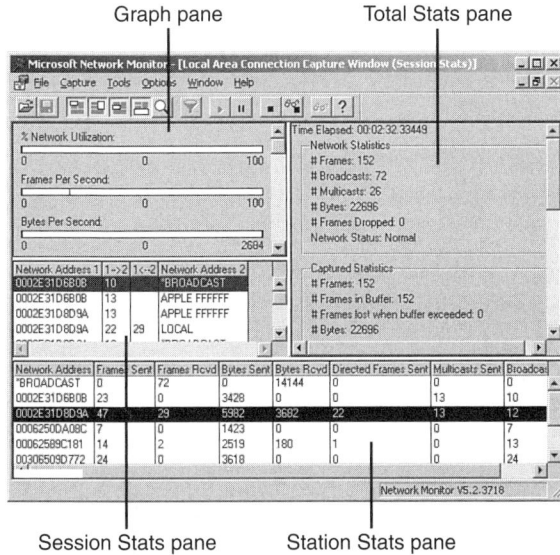

**FIGURE 2.5**
The Network Monitor's four panes display information about network traffic.

Session Stats pane          Station Stats pane

The four panes in Network Monitor report information about current network activity or a captured file:

- ▶ **Graph pane**—This pane reports percentages of activity, in bar chart format.

- ▶ **Session Stats pane**—This pane reports individual statistics of client-to-server activity during a capture or live activity.

- ▶ **Station Stats pane**—This pane reports information on each workstation's activity on a network. Keep in mind that this is actually activity between the specific workstation and the server on which Network Monitor is installed when using the Windows Server 2003 version of Network Monitor.

- ▶ **Total Stats pane**—This pane reports the totals of the stats for all the other panes.

Network Monitor, which comes with Windows Server 2003, is a protocol analyzer that allows you to "sniff" the network traffic traversing the network. This capability is important because, without a good picture of what is running through your network, you can't accurately talk about how to remove unneeded protocols, what protocols are creating problems, what protocols are incorrectly configured, or what network interface card repeatedly broadcasts packets because it has a hardware problem. All these issues, including an accurate statement of what your bandwidth utilization would be, are hidden from you without the use of Network Monitor.

One limitation of the Network Monitor is that it captures and contains only traffic sent to and from the computer in which it is installed. If you need a more robust solution, you can either use a third-party product such as Sniffer Pro or Ethereal. If you opt to move to a Microsoft solution, you must purchase Microsoft Systems Management Server (SMS), which can capture frames sent to or from any computer on which the Network Monitor driver is installed.

# TROUBLESHOOTING TCP/IP ADDRESSING

**Troubleshoot TCP/IP addressing.**

For this objective, you are responsible for knowing how to troubleshoot basic client-based TCP/IP issues. This means that you must know all the things that can go wrong on a client workstation based on IP addressing and the ways to isolate these problems as well as to resolve them. You have to know basic TCP/IP troubleshooting techniques as well as ways to figure out whether the problem is DHCP based.

## Troubleshooting Client Computers

**Troubleshoot TCP/IP addressing.**

▶ **Diagnose and resolve issues related to client computer configuration.**

When troubleshooting client-based TCP/IP problems, you really need to develop a good troubleshooting methodology; otherwise, you will just be wasting your time. You have to know what to check in what order, based on certain triggers you are looking for. For example, if a user tells you that she cannot log in to the network, that information is a trigger for a troubleshooting methodology. If the user cannot log on, you should then think about what the problem could be. Is only one user unable to log on, or are more users having the same problem? I usually ask this question first because if all the users are unable to log on, it's a big problem.

Assuming only this user is unable to log on, you may be prompted to ask whether she keyed in the proper password, whether she had Caps Locks on, or whether she entered her password wrong a few times and locked herself out. If none of these are the case, your troubleshooting usually warrants a walk down to the user's desk for some investigation. From that trigger, you find out that not everyone has this problem; it is isolated to just this user. You also figure out that this is not a problem with a server; it is a problem with the client workstation. The user checked to make sure that she had the PC powered on and that she was, in fact, at the login screen and could not log in, even after checking to see whether she had used Caps Locks. Now, you have a problem.

When you get to the user, you can try to repeat her steps first, then check her password again, and so on. After you move past these common problems, you can turn your attention to the network connection. You look at the back of the PC to check the link lights on the NIC and find that they are not on. You then check the cable plugged into the back of the PC, directly into the NIC. Lastly, you move to the wall jack where the cable plugs into the wall to find it dislodged. Somehow it became unplugged. After you plug it back in and check the link lights on the NIC, the user is able to log on to the network a few seconds later.

The whole point behind this story is that a problem triggered a chain of responses from you to solve that problem.

Let's look at an IP-based issue now. If you have a server that cannot get on the network, and you are able to isolate the problem down to the bottom two layers (Network Access or Physical and Data Link), your only other option is to start troubleshooting layer three. So, how would you troubleshoot? First, look at any client that cannot access the network and for which you have isolated a layer three problem. What would you do? You can use the ping command as follows from the workstation to see what the problem could be:

```
C:\> Ping 10.10.10.1 with 32 bytes of data:

Request timed out.
Request timed out.
Request timed out.
Request timed out.

Ping statistics for 10.10.10.1:
    Packets: Sent = 4, Received = 0, Lost = 4 <100% loss>,
Approximate round trip times in milli-seconds:
    Minimum = 0ms, Maximum = 0ms, Average= 0ms

C:\> Ping 10.10.5.1 with 32 bytes of data:

Reply from 10.10.5.1: bytes=32 time=10ms TTL=255
Reply from 10.10.5.1: bytes=32 time=10ms TTL=255
Reply from 10.10.5.1: bytes=32 time=10ms TTL=255
Reply from 10.10.5.1: bytes=32 time=10ms TTL=255

Ping statistics for 10.10.5.1:
    Packets: Sent = 4, Received = 4, Lost = 0 (0% loss),
Approximate round trip times in milli-seconds:
    Minimum = 10ms, Maximum =  10ms, Average =  10ms
```

Here, you can see the output of a simple ping command run to test the default gateway of a LAN. The ping tool is used to test IP connectivity to other hosts on the network. You use ping (which uses Internet Control Message Protocol, or ICMP, echo-based error reporting) to get an idea of what may be wrong. In this case, the ping to a default gateway timed out. You ping this device because you need to see whether the network has IP connectivity. As you can see from this output, it does not. This example also pings another host on the network, which is a mainframe in the same VLAN. As you can see, the problem doesn't have anything to do with the workstation, which you may have assumed. The problem lies with the default gateway, which is bad. This result means something may be wrong with the router.

Are you beginning to understand how troubleshooting works? Problems can go many ways, so the best way to arm yourself is to memorize not only the tool, but also the methodology behind it to isolate and resolve problems, and to identify the triggers you get from others that help you to reduce your troubleshooting time.

You can, of course, use other tools such as ipconfig. Typing this command at the command prompt provides a great deal of information, as you can see here:

```
Windows 2000 IP Configuration

Ethernet adapter Local Area Connection:
        Connection-specific DNS Suffix  . : rsnetworks.net
        IP Address. . . . . . . . . . . : 192.168.2.100
        Subnet Mask . . . . . . . . . . : 255.255.255.0
        Default Gateway . . . . . . . . : 192.168.2.1
```

The `ipconfig` command returns your IP address, DNS domain, subnet mask, and default gateway. All this information is very important to troubleshooting client computers. If you do not see the proper information (such as an IP address of 0.0.0.0), you likely have some sort of problem.

There are a host of switches that can be used with the `ipconfig` command. Here, we cover only the `/all` switch. This switch, when used in conjunction with `ipconfig`, gives you even more TCP/IP-based information. We looked briefly at the use of this switch earlier in the chapter; remember that this switch provides more detailed information, such as DHCP, DNS, and WINS servers used, as well as your physical address and DHCP lease information. Understanding this command is important not only for the exam, but also for your job because you will be using it all the time. We cover the `ipconfig` command further in the following sections, where we cover more switches as they relate to DHCP and DNS.

> **EXAM TIP**
>
> **`ipconfig` questions**  Be prepared to look for questions with an `ipconfig` output like the example shown here. You may be shown an `ipconfig` screen with an IP address of 192.168.2.100 and a topology map that shows you trying to communicate on a subnet of 192.168.1.0. It should be obvious to you now that you are not able to communicate if you are not on the same subnet.

# Troubleshooting DHCP Server Issues

### Troubleshoot TCP/IP addressing.

▶ **Diagnose and resolve issues related to DHCP server address assignment.**

Working through DHCP client-based issues is actually easy. The available scope either doles out an IP address to you, or it doesn't. It's that easy. You know if a client is configured to accept an IP address by using the `ipconfig /all` command. The results show a DHCP-enabled column with either Yes or No selected. If you see Yes, and you don't have an IP address assigned, you can try a few options. Always start with the easiest option first. You should consider `ipconfig` your tool of choice when trying to troubleshoot IP-based problems on clients and servers alike. When you want to troubleshoot a DHCP server issue, you can simply use one of the following two `ipconfig` switches:

```
ipconfig/ release
ipconfig/ renew
```

The `release` switch releases the IP address for the specified adapter, and likewise, the `renew` switch asks the DHCP server to renew the lease and to get your IP address back so you can participate on the network.

If you do not receive an answer from your DHCP server, you may have one of a few different problems. You may not have client connectivity, so you must make sure that you do. You cannot `ping` anything because you do not have an IP address, and you need that to communicate to the other host via ICMP. You can statically assign an IP to verify connectivity. You can also see whether you are on a segment with a DHCP server. If not, you may need an IP helper address assigned to the router; the helper agent is also known as a *DHCP relay agent*, which pushes the DHCP-based broadcasts over the router and points them to the DHCP server on the appropriate segment where it is located. If this relay agent is not configured, your client more than likely will not get a DHCP address. These are the most common issues you are likely to see on the 70-293 exam, and also in production environments.

# PLANNING AND TROUBLESHOOTING INTERNET CONNECTIVITY

In this section, we discuss your network infrastructure's Internet connectivity options, design issues, the reasons NAT is used, and the reasons the Internet and connectivity are so important. We also look at client-specific issues as well as issues relating to DNS. These are some of the more complicated issues to resolve, especially when you are dealing with NAT and DNS.

## Planning Internet Connectivity

### Plan an Internet connectivity strategy.

To connect your LAN to the Internet, you need to plan for the following issues:

▶ What type of connection do you want? What media, what technology?

▶ How much bandwidth do you need to provide?

▶ What hardware will you use?

▶ Will security be involved?

▶ Who provides DNS?

▶ Will you be doing Network Address Translation?

▶ Where does Windows Server 2003 fit into network connectivity?

These questions are often asked before a deployment because deploying an Internet connection strategy is easier if you plan for it. Not planning or making up the plan as you are deploying can lead to an unsecured connection with the wrong bandwidth, which causes nothing but problems. Let's look at each question in depth to plan your Internet connection strategy:

▶ **What type of connection do you want? What media, what technology?** You need to consider what type of connection to the Internet you will have installed because the type of Internet connection you select determines what the connection media will be (WISP, T1, DSL, cable, and so on) as well as what signaling method, what additional hardware (modem, router, CSU/DSU) you will need. Each connection type selected also dictates the bandwidth you will have available to you in most instances. Therefore, you need to plan your Internet connection method well.

▶ **How much bandwidth do you need to provide?** You need to consider what type of traffic and how much of it will be traversing your Internet connection. Without applications to limit what can leave or enter your network via the Internet, most of your bandwidth will likely be consumed by outbound email and Internet Web browsing.

▶ **What hardware will you use?** Will you use a Cisco router? A 3Com router? You need to know what to use for an Internet connection before you purchase the hardware because it is imperative that you plan the hardware around the connection type. You need specific interface types depending on what technology you select (T1, DSL, and so on), so you must make sure you plan your hardware accordingly.

▶ **Will security be involved?** Whether a firewall will be used dictates how you deploy your Internet connection. If you want to use a firewall, you must plan for it as well. If a firewall is used, you must plan what traffic you need to pass; otherwise, the firewall will block it out. For instance, if you were to use the Remote Desktop Protocol or Terminal Services over the Internet, you would need to configure the firewall to allow this traffic to pass.

▶ **Who provides DNS?** The domain name system is the lifeblood of the Internet. Without it, everyone would have to memorize IP addresses to get to everything they needed; instead, easy-to-remember and -use names such as Que.com are used. Your ISP normally provides DNS, or you can move the DNS into your network (preferably on your Demilitarized Zone, DMZ) and have an internal namespace forward out to the public DNS servers. Either way, you need to consider this issue when deploying your Internet solution.

▶ **Will you be doing Network Address Translation?** NAT translates one set of IP addresses to another. If NAT is to be used, you must plan for it. Because setting up NAT is somewhat complex if you have never done it before, you must make sure you properly plan what you need before you deploy it. For example, say you want to have a 10.1.1.0/24 LAN access the Internet via a translatable pool of addresses to the Internet via 12.1.1.1, 12.1.1.2, and 12.1.1.3. You must plan this configuration so you know what IP addresses you will need and how to deploy them so that they work.

▶ **Where does Windows Server 2003 fit into network connectivity?** Windows Server 2003 can be used as an Internet connection, but it is advised that for larger implementations you get dedicated devices to do specific tasks.

## Troubleshooting Client Configuration Issues

**Troubleshoot connectivity to the Internet.**

▶ **Diagnose and resolve issues related to client configuration.**

If you cannot connect to the Internet with a client PC, you have a few options to think about. First, you need to consider that the Internet may be inaccessible. Sometimes the line that supplies the traffic to and from your organization has problems with the ISP. Although such problems can be deemed inexcusable, you may see the line go down for maintenance or for an unpredicted outage.

As a client, you also may see that your IP address is not on the same subnet (if you have a static assignment on a laptop and move to another subnet) or your network connection is disconnected. Make sure that you know how to troubleshoot client issues for the 70-293 exam.

## Troubleshooting DNS Issues

**Troubleshoot connectivity to the Internet.**

▶ **Diagnose and resolve issues related to name resolution cache information.**

Here, we discuss ways to troubleshoot DNS connectivity on a client workstation that is having problems with name resolution on a Windows network. You need to know how to diagnose and resolve problems related to name resolution cache information. To do this, you need to know the `ipconfig` command, which was discussed previously. `ipconfig` has several switches associated with it, so if you are working from a Windows workstation, and you cannot get a client to resolve names properly because the client-side DNS cache is either corrupted or not updated to a change already made on the DNS server, you can easily flush out that information by using one of the following commands:

▶ `ipconfig /flushdns`—This command purges the DNS resolver cache.

▶ `ipconfig /displaydns`—This command displays the contents of the DNS resolver cache.

▶ `ipconfig /registerdns`—This command refreshes all DHCP leases and reregisters DNS names.

Everything you need to know is done at the command prompt.

## Troubleshooting Network Address Translation (NAT) Issues

### Troubleshoot connectivity to the Internet.

▶ **Diagnose and resolve issues related to Network Address Translation (NAT).**

We covered NAT in great detail throughout the chapter, so this section covers what you need to know about NAT for the exam. You need to be aware of the changes that have been made to the IPSec protocol and NAT in Windows Server 2003.

First, you need to understand why such changes were needed in the first place. Network Address Translation does not allow IPSec to work. IPSec is a security-based protocol that allows you to secure communications across your network. The problem is that the IPSec packet, by design, does not work well with NAT. Because NAT breaks down the packets to change the IP address, it also causes problems with the IPSec packet, which is essentially encrypted and cannot be changed. With Windows Server 2003, the biggest change is that IPSec and L2TP are both supported through NAT. Revised IPSec clients are available for Windows XP and 2000 Professional as well. Using Windows Server 2003 and NAT dramatically reduces problems with IPSec.

## CASE STUDY

### ESSENCE OF THE CASE

Following are the essential elements in this case:

- ▶ Timeout problems
- ▶ Times when no connectivity exists at all
- ▶ Loss of connectivity
- ▶ Use of hubs

### SCENARIO

You have been hired as a consultant to work for ABC, Inc., because the company is having specific problems with its network. The problems range from clients timing out, loss of connectivity when trying to access network resources, to no connectivity to the network during peak hours. The network consists of four core switches, eight closets to connect the user segments consisting of four 24-port hubs each, and two redundant core routers. You need to analyze the network, find the problems, and implement a solution.

### ANALYSIS

As a consultant going to ABC, Inc., you immediately start to look at the network documentation and network topology maps. You need to make sure that there aren't any obvious errors in design (such as using stacked hubs in closets) and so on. It is your responsibility to check the network layout to see if there are any bottlenecks anywhere, choke points on the network, or mismatched bandwidth speeds going into critical areas. For example, you should make sure that you have a backbone segment with your critical servers that runs on Gigabit Ethernet and then move to the desktop users, most likely coming out of switch closets located around the building you may be working in. These connections should run at a minimum of 100Mbps.

In today's networks, most businesses send around very large files, both video and voice, so you can't get away with using hubs running at 10Mbps anymore. The nature of a hub is to broadcast data out of every port, whereas a

*continues*

## CASE STUDY

*continued*

switch keeps a MAC-to-port memory map to keep the number of broadcasts down to a minimum. Not using switches is a design flaw. Using hubs can cause massive collision counts, and if the collision counts are too high, your clients may experience time outs, disconnects, or just bad performance.

In any case, by running a protocol analyzer on your network, you can find any excessive broadcasts, collisions, or extra protocols that

may be traversing the network. As a solution, you should run a protocol analyzer in the closet hubs, determine that traffic volume is way too high with collisions and broadcast traffic, and put in switches to control the traffic better. By doing so, you upgrade the network desktop users from 10Mbps to 100Mbps, a connection speed 10 times faster than they were using before. These changes solve all four network problems the company was experiencing.

## CHAPTER SUMMARY

### KEY TERMS

Before taking the exam, make sure you are comfortable with the definitions and concepts for each of the following key terms. You can use Appendix A, "Glossary," for quick reference.

- TCP/IP
- Network Address Translation (NAT)
- Physical address
- Network interface card (NIC)
- Layer 3 switch
- Router
- Default gateway
- Subnet mask

In this chapter, we described TCP/IP planning, design, and basic implementation. We also covered ways to troubleshoot TCP/IP. Now you can look at workstation problems with more confidence because you know how to ping devices on your network (and know what you are pinging). You also know how to see whether you have an IP address or find what IP address you do have. You learned ways to plan a TCP/IP network as well as the devices that populate a network.

Good networks begin with good planning and good designs. To plan and design a good network, you need to understand the IP addressing and routing requirements of your organization. With this knowledge in mind, you can move forward and start planning the IP subnets you need. This creates a solid backbone from which the rest of your network can be built. In this chapter, we looked at planning an IP-based network from many different angles. All networks should have a design and/or plan, and included in that plan should be information regarding where you would place your network resources (file, print, Internet access, and so on) as well as what protocols will be used to connect to and access such resources.

## CHAPTER SUMMARY

In all networks today, not connecting to the Internet would massively hamper a company's growth. Email, Web browsing, and a plethora of other solutions need Internet access to function, so not having Internet connectivity would be a huge problem. In this chapter, we also covered the importance of planning an Internet connectivity strategy. We looked at strategy, planning, and design. Networks have problems that at times are hard to solve or reproduce for one reason or another, but still need to be solved nonetheless. Using tools such as Network Monitor and System Monitor can help you find problems as well monitor traffic traversing your LAN. Once your network is connected to the Internet, many things can happen. You may have problems with Network Address Translation planning and implementation, with DNS, and of course, with clients trying to connect to and use the Internet.

All network administrators need to know, understand, and embrace TCP/IP. You need to know how to troubleshoot TCP/IP issues, as well as those issues resulting from problems with a DHCP server.

**KEY TERMS**

- Public address
- Private address
- Proxy server
- Firewall
- Protocol analyzer

## APPLY YOUR KNOWLEDGE

# Exercises

### 2.1 Using `ping`

In this exercise, you learn how to use the `ping` utility. Ping can be used if you have a connectivity problem. In exercise 2.2, we look at dealing with a connectivity issue and using `ping` to resolve it.

**Estimated time:** 5 minutes

1. You are the administrator for ABC, Inc. You are responsible for 30 Windows Server 2003 systems, 300 XP Professional clients, and all connecting network infrastructure. A client asks you to see why she can't connect to the network.

2. To perform this test, you can use the `ping` utility. Choose Start, Run. Type CMD in the Run dialog box and then press Enter. Type `ping` at the command prompt and enter the IP address of your default gateway.

3. You are able to successfully `ping` the router, so you are connected via IP.

### 2.2 Renew an IP Address

In this exercise, you learn how to renew an IP address from a DHCP server.

**Estimated time:** 5 minutes

1. You are the senior administrator for 123 Inc. You are responsible for 300 Windows Server 2003 systems, 2000 XP Professional clients, and all connecting network infrastructure. A client asks you why she can't access any network resources.

2. You try to `ping` the default gateway, and you receive hardware errors.

3. You use the `ipconfig` command and see that you have an IP address of 0.0.0.0.

4. You know you have a DHCP server on your network, so you should have an IP address.

5. To find the IP address, choose Start, Run. Type CMD in the Run dialog box and then press Enter. Type `ipconfig /renew` to get a new IP address from the DHCP server.

### 2.3 Using `ipconfig`

In this exercise, you learn how to view all IP-related information associated with your workstation.

**Estimated time:** 5 minutes

1. You are the administrator for ABC, Inc. You are responsible for 30 Windows Server 2003 systems, 300 XP Professional clients, and all connecting network infrastructure. A client asks you to see why he cannot connect to the network.

2. You can't `ping` anything from the workstation.

3. You need to check whether you have an IP address assigned to the workstation.

4. To check the address, choose Start, Run. Type CMD in the Run dialog box and then press Enter. Type `ipconfig /all` and see whether you have an IP address assigned.

# Review Questions

1. You have 20 network clients who cannot access any network resources. You try to `ping` the default gateway but cannot hit it; however, you are able to `ping` other devices on a different subnet. What could be the problem?

## APPLY YOUR KNOWLEDGE

2. Several of your Windows XP Professional clients are having trouble connecting to an Internet Web site. You suspect that they have local DNS cache data that is preventing them from contacting the correct IP address. What can you do to quickly resolve this problem?

3. Four Windows workstations cannot access the network. You have DHCP enabled on the segment, and everyone else is okay. If nothing is wrong with the server, what could be the problem?

4. You are the senior administrator of your company. Your CIO cannot access the network. She checks to see whether the link lights are on and the cable is attached, and they are. What would be your next step to troubleshoot this problem?

5. One workstation cannot access the network. You want to run a simple test to see whether the workstation can communicate with other devices on the network. What utility could you use?

## Exam Questions

1. As the lead administrator for the ABC LLC network, you are responsible for planning a TCP/IP network that is robust and functional. You have a total of 450 clients spread out over three locations. You have 150 clients per location, and at one central location, you have approximately 25 servers. You are asked to select an IP addressing scheme that maps to your needs. Select the best option to subnet and IP address this network.

   A. Use a Class A network of 10.1.1.0/8.

   B. Use a Class B network of 172.16.0.0/16.

   C. Use three Class C networks of 192.168.1.0/24, 192.168.2.0/24, and 192.168.3.0/24.

   D. Use a single Class A subnetted network of 10.1.1.0/16.

2. Jake is the senior network administrator for your organization. Jake is responsible for 200 Windows XP Professional clients and 15 Windows Server 2003 systems located on a network backbone running at 100Mbps. All 200 clients complain of slow response times on the network and have difficulty doing the simplest of tasks, such as browsing the Internet, especially during the mid-morning and mid-afternoon periods of the day. The clients are running at 10Mbps. What can Jake do to increase the performance of his network? (Choose two answers.)

   A. Upgrade the backbone to 1000Mbps.

   B. Install hubs in the network closets to segment the network.

   C. Upgrade the clients to 100Mbps.

   D. Install a network monitor to adjust the network for better performance.

3. You are the network administrator of the ABC Company, and you currently have a network client that cannot access the network. When you talk to the user on the phone, you find out that there is no break in the cable and the link lights on the NIC are operational. You then go down to the user's workstation to troubleshoot. Because you have determined that this is not a lower-layer problem, you are convinced it may be a IP-based problem. What two tools can you use to see whether this is a layer three problem?

## APPLY YOUR KNOWLEDGE

A. `Ping` the default gateway.

B. Use `ipconfig` to see whether you have a valid IP address.

C. Use `ipconfig /release` to get a valid IP address.

D. Use `ipconfig /flushdns` to clear your cache because it may be corrupted.

4. Marshall is the network administrator for QBC Corp. He runs a network of 20 Windows Server 2003 systems on a network backbone, as well as 200 Windows XP Professional clients. Marshall is worried about connectivity to the Internet. For some reason, none of the internal clients can resolve anything in the company's Web browsers. Marshall runs some checks on the Internet connection, and it appears to be okay. He then runs some checks and finds out that if he enters the URL `http://www.que.com` in a browser, he cannot resolve this address, but if he enters the URL `http://64.12.107.4`, he can access the site. What could be the possible problem with the network?

A. Marshall is having a problem resolving DNS. He should check the DNS settings.

B. The network core switch is down. Marshall should check the device and reboot it.

C. A bad route in the Internet router keeps Marshall from getting on the Internet. He should add the correct route.

D. WINS is misconfigured. Marshall needs to reconfigure it and try again.

5. Pete is the systems administrator for RDT, Inc. He runs a network of 25 Windows Server 2003 systems on a network backbone, as well as 300 Windows XP Professional clients. Pete cannot get a server to connect to the network. He was given an IP address of 10.1.1.12/24 for the server. He has the server plugged into the network backbone (Gigabit Ethernet), which is on the 10.0.1.0/24 subnet. This subnet does not have a DHCP server located on it. What could be the problem?

A. Pete has the correct IP address, but the subnet mask is incorrect.

B. Pete has the correct IP address, but the DHCP server from another segment is interfering with his communications.

C. Pete has the wrong IP address; he needs one for that backbone segment.

D. Pete set up the wrong server and has a duplicate address on the network.

6. Sally is the senior network administrator for Runners Corp. She runs a network of 20 Windows Server 2003 systems, as well as 250 Windows XP Professional clients. Sally is worried about a client that cannot connect to the network. She does not have an IP address assigned. Sally used `ipconfig` and found an IP address of 0.0.0.0. She knows that a DHCP server is present on the subnet in which she is located and that all lower-level troubleshooting has been performed, such as checking link lights and cable connectivity. What is the most likely solution to this problem?

## APPLY YOUR KNOWLEDGE

A. Sally can issue the `ipconfig /renew` command to get a new IP address.

B. Sally can issue the `ipconfig /flushdns` command to get a new IP address.

C. Sally can issue the `ipconfig /dsiplayip` command to get a new IP address.

D. Sally can issue the `ipconfig /release` command to get a new IP address.

7. You are the network administrator for QBC Corp. The company has a network of 25 Windows Server 2003 systems on a network backbone, as well as 150 Windows XP Professional clients. You need to design a network with a new IP range given to you by your supervisor. You are given a range of 129.0.1.0/24 to use for your clients. What is the proper class that this IP address range falls into?

A. Class A

B. Class B

C. Class C

D. Class D

8. Marshall is the network administrator for QBC Corp. He runs a network of 20 Windows Server 2003 systems on a network backbone, as well as 200 Windows XP Professional clients. Marshall is worried about a single PC that cannot connect to the network. Which would be the most logical troubleshooting step to start with?

A. Marshall can use Network Monitor to see whether the network is congested.

B. Marshall can use System Monitor to see whether the network interface card is defective.

C. Marshall can `ping` localhost.

D. Marshall can use the `ipconfig /ipinfo` command to see whether he has a valid IP address.

9. Pete is the systems administrator for RDT, Inc. He runs a network of 25 Windows Server 2003 systems on a network backbone, as well as 300 Windows XP Professional clients. Pete has been tasked with deploying an IP addressing solution to a remote network. He has to remain within the standards dictated by the networking group to use a private range within the private network. Which private range can he use within the network?

A. Class A: 12.0.0.0–12.255.255.255

B. Class B: 172.15.0.0–172.31.255.255

C. Class C: 192.169.0.0–192.169.255.255

D. Class A: 10.0.0.0–10.255.255.255

10. Sally is the Senior Network Administrator for Runners Corp. She runs a network of 20 Windows Server 2003 systems, as well as 250 Windows XP Professional clients. Sally has started to troubleshoot a workstation located on subnet 10.1.2.0/24. When Sally started to troubleshoot, she realized after running `ipconfig` that the workstation is not on the same subnet, which is what is keeping it from communicating. From running `ipconfig`, she finds an IP address of 169.254.0.1. What is the problem?

A. The NIC failed, and this is the IP address given to show a NIC failure.

B. There is nothing wrong at all; the workstation should communicate without error.

C. The APIPA range 169.254.0.1 to 169.254.255.254 is being used probably because the DHCP server failed.

D. The DHCP server is working fine but is doling out the wrong IP address scope.

11. A router on your network received packets from the LAN destined to remote networks. Your router will make a decision on what class a packet's source and destination IP addresses are from simply from viewing the first few bits of the address. What prefix accurately shows a Class C network?

A. 0

B. 10

C. 110

D. 1110

12. Marshall is the network administrator for QBC Corp. He runs a network of 20 Windows Server 2003 systems on a network backbone, as well as 200 Windows XP Professional clients. Marshall is worried about whether to use static routes or dynamic routes in his routers. He wants to keep the router overhead low, and only one route (a default route) is needed. What course of action should Marshall take?

A. Marshall can use static routes but add a routing protocol as a backup.

B. Marshall can use the dynamic routing protocol OSPF.

C. Marshall can use a single static route.

D. Marshall can use Access Control Lists for reduced routing overhead.

13. Pete is the systems administrator for RDT, Inc. He runs a network of 25 Windows Server 2003 systems on a network backbone, as well as 300 Windows XP Professional clients. Pete is worried about configuring the right range of IP addresses for his network. Basically, he is given the choice to select a single Class C range from the private range of IP addresses. What range would fit this need?

A. Pete should assign a private range of 192.165.2.0/24 to the network segment.

B. Pete should assign a private range of 192.167.3.0/24 to the network segment.

C. Pete should assign a private range of 192.169.1.0/24 to the network segment.

D. Pete should assign a private range of 192.168.5.0/24 to the network segment.

14. Sally is the senior network administrator for Runners Corp. She runs a network of 20 Windows Server 2003 systems, as well as 250 Windows XP Professional clients. Sally is asked to troubleshoot a server that cannot connect to the network. Starting from the most obvious to the most difficult, Sally begins to troubleshoot her server. Sally has isolated the issue to the NIC on the server. What troubleshooting technique makes the most sense to solve this problem?

A. The NIC has no link lights present.

B. `ipconfig` returns the `Hardware error` message.

C. `ping` returns the `Destination not found` message.

D. `ipconfig /renew` returns an `NIC failure` message.

## APPLY YOUR KNOWLEDGE

15. You are the network administrator for QBC Corp. The company has a network of 25 Windows Server 2003 systems on a network backbone, as well as 300 Windows XP Professional clients. You need to test a workstation's capability to get, maintain, and then release an IP address. What two commands would you use to get and then give up an IP address on a host? (Choose only one answer.)

   A. `ipconfig /off`, `ipconfig /on`

   B. `ipconfig /release`, `ipconfig /renew`

   C. `ipconfig /fluship`, `ipconfig /renewip`

   D. `ipconfig /release`, `ipconfig /getip`

## Answers to Review Questions

1. A switch on that segment is powered off or has failed. Because you can get to other areas of your network, there is a good chance that you have a simple hardware problem. For more information, see the section "Planning Physical Placement of Network Resources."

2. Use the `ipconfig /flusndns` command on the affected computers to purge the local DNS resolver cache and allow the computer to query a DNS server for the correct IP address. For more information, see the section "Troubleshooting DNS Issues."

3. The DHCP client leases may have expired on these four workstations, so use the `ipconfig /renew` command to get a new lease period. For more information, see the section "Troubleshooting TCP/IP Addressing."

4. Because you have link lights (layer two is good), you would want to move to layer three and see whether you have an IP address. Use the `ipconfig` command to see whether you have an IP address. For more information, see the section "Troubleshooting Client Computers."

5. You can use `ping` to test basic layer three connectivity on the network. `Ping` the default gateway, a server, or any other device you know is up and operational. For more information, see the section "Troubleshooting TCP/IP Addressing."

## Answers to Exam Questions

1. **C.** You can solve this issue by using three Class C networks of 192.168.1.0/24, 192.168.2.0/24, and 192.168.3.0/24. For more information, see the section "Troubleshooting TCP/IP Addressing."

2. **A, C.** To get this network to operate faster and more effectively, Jake should upgrade the backbone to 1000Mbps and upgrade the clients to 100Mbps on the desktop. For more information, see the section "Planning Physical Placement of Network Resources."

3. **A, B.** To solve this problem, you can use two tools: the `ping` utility and `ipconfig`. `Ping` the default gateway to test connectivity and use `ipconfig` to see whether you have a valid IP address. For more information, see the section "Troubleshooting TCP/IP Addressing."

4. **A.** In this situation, Marshall is having a problem resolving DNS. He needs to check DNS settings and resolve any issues with them. For more information, see the section "Troubleshooting DNS Issues."

## APPLY YOUR KNOWLEDGE

5. **C.** Pete has the wrong IP address; he needs one for that backbone segment. For more information, see the section "Analyzing IP Addressing Requirements."

6. **A.** Sally can issue the `ipconfig /renew` command to get a new IP address from the DHCP server. Basically, she needs to know that if she sees certain indicators that point to a lack of connectivity but can be solved by renewing an IP address, she needs to renew the lease on a system that may have been released after the time period. For more information, see the section "Troubleshooting DHCP Server Issues."

7. **B.** This IP address range falls into Class B. The Class B range is set from 128–191. For more information, see the section "Analyzing IP Addressing Requirements."

8. **C.** The IP address 127.0.0.0 is reserved for loopback networks and testing. 127.0.0.1 is also located in the HOSTS file, which allows Marshall to test the IP connectivity of his own machine. If he uses the command **ping loopback** (which is the hostname located in the HOSTS file), he can resolve to 127.0.0.1 and should see a reply. This way, Marshall knows that IP is configured properly—at least on his own system. For more information, see the section "Troubleshooting TCP/IP Addressing."

9. **D.** Class A falls between 10.0.0.0 and 10.255.255.255. Pete can use this entire Class A for internal network private IP addressing. Class B falls between 172.16.0.0 and 172.31.255.255, and Class C falls between 192.168.0.0 and 192.168.255.255. These numbering assignments are kept at www.iana.org. For more information, see the section "TCP/IP Fundamentals."

10. **C.** The APIPA range 169.254.0.1–169.254.255.254 is being used probably because the DHCP server failed. This happens when Sally has a client set to get an IP address from a DHCP server, but there is no DHCP server answering requests for service. For more information, see the section "Analyzing IP Addressing Requirements."

11. **C.** The prefix the router looks at would be the first few bits of the IP address, and this is how it knows the class. If you see a 0 as the first bit, it would be a Class A. If the first bit is a 1, it would be Class B. Class C would be two bits turned on, so the prefix would look like 110; thus, Answer C is correct. For more information, see the section "Planning an IP Routing Solution."

12. **C.** Marshall can use a single static route. The best option in this case is to use just a single route statement. Routing protocols are complex and offer significant overhead; they can also be a security risk in some instances. If Marshall needs only a single route, he should simply add that one route, not an entire protocol that would learn more routes than needed and advertise them unnecessarily. For more information, see the section "Planning an IP Routing Solution."

13. **D.** Pete should assign a private range of 192.168.1.0/24 to the network segment. The other answers are all in the public range of IP address assignments, so he should use the 192.168.01.0–192.168.255.255 range. Anything in this range is considered a private IP address. For more information, see the section "Analyzing IP Addressing Requirements."

## APPLY YOUR KNOWLEDGE

14. **A.** In this situation, the NIC card has no link lights present, which indicates that there is a break somewhere on the network. All other answers given were layer three issues dealing with IP addressing. Sally should always troubleshoot the lower layers first before moving up the model. For more information, see the section "Planning Physical Placement of Network Resources."

15. **B.** To solve this problem, you can use the `ipconfig/release` or `ipconfig/renew` command to get a new IP address for use. For more information, see the section "Troubleshooting DHCP Server Issues."

### Suggested Readings and Resources

1. Microsoft Corporation. 2003. *Microsoft Windows Server 2003 Resource Kit*. Redmond, WA: Microsoft Press. ISBN: 0735614717.

2. Microsoft Corporation. 2003. *Microsoft Windows Server 2003 Deployment Kit*. Redmond, WA: Microsoft Press. ISBN: 0735614865.

3. Davies, Joseph, and Thomas Lee. 2003. *Microsoft Windows Server 2003 TCP/IP Protocols and Services Technical Reference*. Redmond, WA: Microsoft Press. ISBN: 0735612919.

4. Windows Server 2003 RFC Checklist at `www.rfc-editor.org/rfc.html`:

   - 768 User Datagram Protocol (UDP)
   - 783 Trivial File Transfer Protocol (TFTP)
   - 791 Internet Protocol (IP)
   - 792 Internet Control Message Protocol (ICMP)
   - 793 Transmission Control Protocol (TCP)
   - 826 Address Resolution Protocol (ARP)
   - 854 Telnet Protocol (TELNET)
   - 950 Internet Standard Subnetting Procedure
   - 959 File Transfer Protocol (FTP)
   - 1001, 1002 NetBIOS Service Protocols
   - 1065, 1035, 1123, 1886 Domain Name System (DNS)
   - 1256 ICMP Router Discovery Messages
   - 1518 Architecture for IP Address Allocation with CIDR
   - 1519 Classless Inter-Domain Routing (CIDR)
   - 1812 Requirements for IP Version 4 Routers
   - 2131 Dynamic Host Configuration Protocol
   - 2136 Dynamic Updates in the Domain Name System (DNS UPDATE)
   - 2581 TCP Congestion Control

In today's well-connected network-centric world, name resolution is a critical component of any Windows Server 2003 network. The domain name system (DNS) is often considered one of the "critical" core network services—and rightfully so. The Windows Internet Naming Service (WINS) has fallen out of favor with the move away from the Network Basic Input/Output System (NetBIOS) and NetBIOS Extended User Interface (NetBEUI), but it is still lingering in the background for many administrators who are faced with maintaining a heterogeneous network environment. Despite the fact that Windows Server 2003 (and Windows 2000 Server for that matter) runs on Transmission Control Protocol/Internet Protocol (TCP/IP) through and through, many networks still must support legacy Windows 9x and NT clients; thus, WINS still has a small place in Windows Server 2003 and therefore in this MCSE exam.

Microsoft has defined the name resolution portion of the "Planning, Implementing, and Maintaining a Network Infrastructure" objectives as follows:

**Plan a host name resolution strategy.**

- **Plan a DNS namespace design.**

- **Plan zone replication requirements.**

- **Plan a forwarding configuration.**

- **Plan for DNS security.**

- **Examine the interoperability of DNS with third-party DNS solutions.**

▶ DNS is king when it comes to name resolution in Windows Server 2003 networks. Proper prior planning is essential to implementing a functional DNS environment for your network. Planning for DNS involves many different processes and steps, however, and you must be aware of them all to be able to create the correct DNS infrastructure you require.

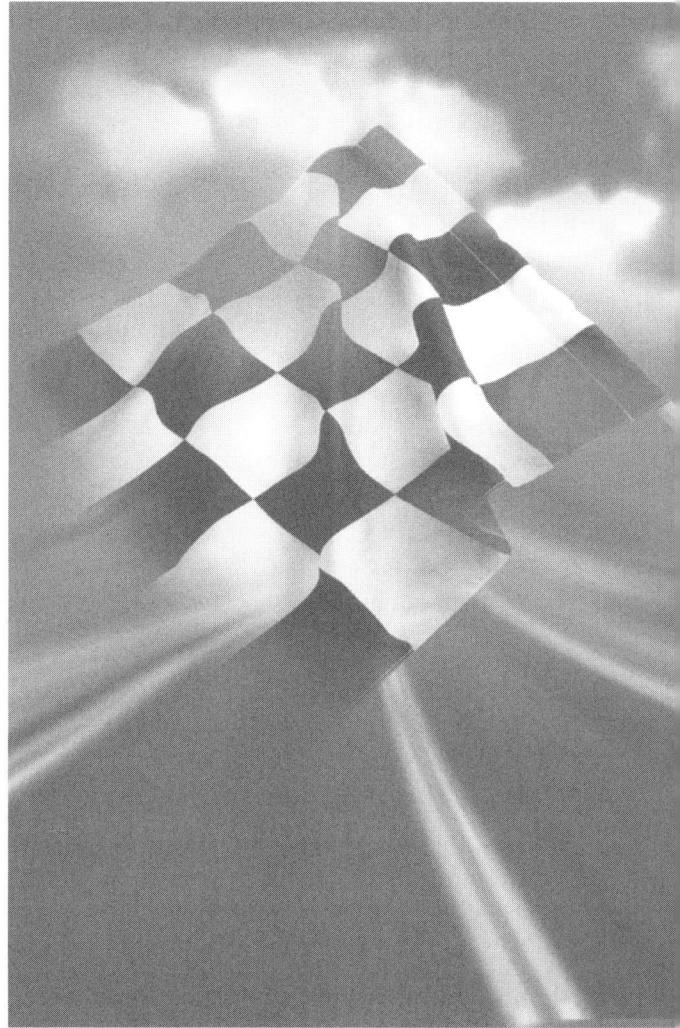

CHAPTER 3

# Planning, Implementing, and Maintaining a Name Resolution Infrastructure

**Plan a NetBIOS name resolution strategy.**

- **Plan a WINS replication strategy.**

- **Plan NetBIOS name resolution by using the** LMHOSTS **file.**

▶ Even though Microsoft has officially moved away from WINS as the primary name resolution, it still exists to provide backward compatibility with legacy clients, such as Windows 98 and Windows NT 4.0 computers. You need to have a basic understanding of how WINS is configured to provide name resolution for your legacy clients—and do well on the exam.

**Troubleshoot host name resolution.**

- **Diagnose and resolve issues related to DNS services.**

- **Diagnose and resolve issues related to client computer configuration.**

▶ DNS is one of those core network services that works right almost all the time. However, when the day comes that "DNS is broken," you will most certainly hear about it. In addition to the complaints your users will undoubtedly flood you with, your network may very well come to a screeching halt because Active Directory is extremely dependent on a functional DNS infrastructure. Being able to quickly identify and correct DNS-related problems is an essential part of your duties as the network administrator.

## STUDY STRATEGIES

▶ Be sure that you have a thorough understanding of the WINS service and NetBIOS name resolution. Although this is a legacy Microsoft protocol, it is still required in many environments, and Microsoft wants to be absolutely sure you understand how it works.

▶ Review the use of the monitoring tools and the different parameters of WINS that can be monitored. In its exams, Microsoft has focused a great deal of attention on the monitoring and troubleshooting of the different services, including the WINS service.

▶ Get your hands dirty. The Step by Steps throughout this book provide plenty of directions and exercises, but you should go beyond these examples and create some of your own. If you can, experiment with each of the objectives to see how they work and why you would use each one.

# INTRODUCTION

Just 10 years ago, TCP/IP was not the king when it came to network communications protocols. Windows NT 3.51 relied on the venerable NetBIOS Extended User Interface (NetBEUI) protocol by default, and NetWare servers could be counted on to understand only IPX/SPX. With the recent widespread adoption of the Internet by the masses, TCP/IP slowly started to creep into private networks of all sizes and purposes. Administrators and network designers began to see the power and flexibility that TCP/IP offered them, and Microsoft and Novell took note of the shift. It wasn't long before all operating systems provided support for TCP/IP, but it still was not the networking protocol of choice. With the introduction of Windows 2000, Microsoft made TCP/IP and the domain name system (DNS) integral parts of Windows Active Directory networks.

# INTRODUCTION TO DNS

You probably use DNS every day, whether or not you are familiar with the underlying mechanism. Domain names are easy to use and remember. The ease with which you can access a Web site using domain names (such as www.microsoft.com or www.quepublishing.com) is a built-in simplicity that comes with a price: The DNS namespace is complex. DNS names are created as part of a hierarchical database that functions much like the directories in a file system. Hierarchies are powerful database structures because they can store tremendous amounts of data while making it easy to search for specific bits of information. Before examining the specifics of the DNS namespace hierarchy, let's review some rules about hierarchies in general.

## Hierarchies

Before getting into the details of a hierarchy, we should review some terms:

▶ **Tree**—This is a type of data structure with each element attached to one or more elements directly beneath it. In the case of DNS, this structure is often called an inverted tree because it is generally drawn with the root at the top of the tree.

▶ **Top-level domain (TLD)**—TLD refers to the suffix attached to Internet domain names. There is a limited number of predefined suffixes, and each one represents a top-level domain. The more popular TLDs include `.COM`, `.EDU`, `.GOV`, `.MIL`, `.NET`, and `.ORG`.

▶ **Node**—A node is a point at which two or more lines in the tree intersect. In the case of DNS, a node can represent a TLD, a subdomain, or an actual network node (host).

▶ **Fully qualified domain name (FQDN)**—A domain name that includes all domains between the host and the root of DNS is an FQDN. For example, `www.microsoft.com` is an FQDN.

▶ **Leaf**—A leaf is an item at the bottom of a hierarchical tree structure, and it does not contain any other objects.

▶ **Zone**—A DNS zone is a logical grouping of hostnames within DNS. For example, `quepublishing.com` is considered the forward lookup zone for Que Publishing. It is the place where the information about the Que Publishing hosts is contained within DNS.

In DNS, containers called domains hold the information. The hierarchy starts with a root container, called the *root domain*. The root domain doesn't have a name, so it is typically represented by a single period, as shown in Figure 3.1. The root domain contains pointers to all TLDs, which are directly below the root domain. These domains are also sometimes called *first-level domains*. Lower-level domains are second-level, third-level, and so on. Every domain name has a suffix that indicates which TLD domain it belongs to. There is only a limited number of such domains as defined by Request for Comment (RFC) 1591. Following are some of the more common TLDs:

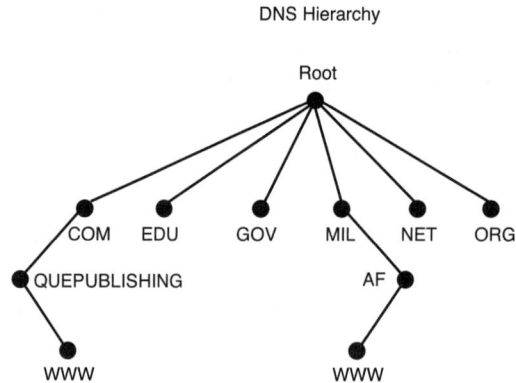

DNS Hierarchy

**DNS country codes** Two-letter country code TLDs also exist for nearly all countries on the planet. Examples include .US for the United States, .CA for Canada, .JP for Japan, and .UK for the United Kingdom. New TLDs are constantly being added to meet the requirements for new domain names on the Internet. Recent additions include .BIZ and .INFO, among others.

▶ **.COM**—Intended for commercial entities, but it has become the overwhelming favorite top-level domain (example of .COM: `area51partners.com`)

▶ **.EDU**—Intended for higher-education institutions, such as four-year colleges and universities (example of .EDU: `berkeley.edu`)

▶ **.GOV**—Intended for use by agencies of the U.S. Federal Government (example of .GOV: `whitehouse.gov`)

▶ **.MIL**—Intended for use by agencies of the U.S. military (example of .MIL: `af.mil`)

▶ **.NET**—Intended for use by network providers and organizations dedicated to the Internet, such as Internet service providers (example of .NET: `ibm.net`)

▶ **.ORG**—Intended for nonprofit or noncommercial establishments, such as professional groups, charities, and other such organizations (example of .ORG: `npr.org`)

## Fully Qualified Domain Names (FQDNs)

As we have discussed, DNS is used to translate a hostname to an IP address. The FQDN name typically looks something like the following:

`filesvr042.corporate.mcseworld.com`

This is known as the host's fully qualified domain name (FQDN) because it lists the host's precise location in the DNS hierarchy. The DNS name in the example represents the host FILESVR042 in the subdomain CORPORATE (this is frequently a department or division in a company), which is in the subdomain MCSEWORLD (this is frequently the name of the company or organization that has registered the domain), which is in the TLD .COM.

**EXAM TIP**

**Fully qualified domain names**
Make sure you have a good understanding of what an FQDN is and how it is represented.

# PLANNING A DNS NAMESPACE DESIGN

### Plan a host name resolution strategy.

> ### ▶ Plan a DNS namespace design.

Up to this point in our discussion about DNS, we have looked at only the historical and design aspects of DNS—and for good reason. Only by understanding how DNS was created and designed can you effectively plan and implement a DNS design in a Windows Server 2003 Active Directory domain. Because DNS permeates Windows Server 2003, you should deliberately and carefully plan your DNS namespace *before* you ever perform the first installation of Windows Server 2003 on a computer.

The following list represents some questions you should ask yourself when planning your namespace needs:

> ▶ **Is your DNS namespace to be used for internal purposes only?** If so, you can use characters that are not typically used in DNS names, such as those outside the RFC 1123 standards. An example might be bigcorp.local.

> ▶ **Is your DNS namespace to be used on the Internet as well?** If you are currently using a corporate DNS namespace on the Internet, or think that you might at any point in the future, you should register your own domain name and conform to Internet naming standards.

**EXAM TIP**

The following discussion about DNS assumes that you are already familiar with installing the DNS service and performing basic management and configuration tasks. If you need a review, see Chapter 2 of *MCSA/MCSE 70-291 Training Guide: Implementing, Managing, and Maintaining a Windows Server 2003 Network Infrastructure*, (2003, Que Publishing; ISBN: 0789729482) by Will Schmied and Dave Bixler.

▶ **Will you be implementing Active Directory?** The design and implementation of Active Directory on your network play a critical role in determining how domains should be created and nested within each other.

You have the following three basic options to consider when planning the DNS namespace you will be using:

▶ **Use an existing DNS namespace**—This option uses the same namespace for both the internal (corporate network) and external (Internet) portions of your network. If your domain name is bigcorp.com, you would use it for both internal and external use. Although this method is the easiest and provides simple access to both internal and external resources, it poses additional administrative requirements because an administrator must ensure that the appropriate records are being stored on the internal and external DNS servers as a security precaution.

▶ **Use a delegated DNS namespace**—This option uses a delegated domain of the public namespace. If your domain name is bigcorp.com, you might consider using corp.bigcorp.com for the internal namespace. When you use this option, the corp.bigcorp.com domain becomes the root of the Active Directory forest and domain structure. Internal clients should be allowed to resolve external namespace addresses; however, external clients should not. Using a delegated DNS namespace provides a namespace that is easy to understand and remember, and that fits in nicely with the existing registered domain name. All internal domain data is isolated in the domain or domain tree, thus requiring its own DNS server for the delegated internal domain. The downside to delegated namespaces is that this adds length to the total FQDN.

▶ **Use a unique DNS namespace**—This option uses a completely separate but related domain name for your internal namespace. As an example, if you are using bigcorp.com for your external namespace, you might use bigcorp.net for your internal namespace. This configuration provides the advantage of improving security by isolating the two namespaces from each other. Additionally, the administrative burden is relatively low because zone transfers do not need to be performed between the two namespaces, and the existing DNS namespace remains unchanged. In addition, this option prevents internal resources from being exposed directly to the Internet.

Consider the following example of a fictitious company that is in the planning stages of a major worldwide network reorganization and upgrade to Windows Server 2003 Active Directory. Gidget's Widgets, Inc., is a major manufacturer of household goods and already owns the gidgets.com domain name for its Internet Web site. Gidget's makes everything from bath towels to kitchen sinks. Gidget's corporate headquarters are located in the United States, with regional field offices in Canada, Mexico, England, Germany, India, Japan, and Australia. Gidget's corporate structure has the following major departments: Executive, Administrative, Engineering, Manufacturing, Facilities, Sales, Legal, and Information Services. Within each department are one or more individual divisions. How would you go about designing a DNS namespace for the Gidget's Widgets internal network?

You have several options; let's assume for the sake of argument that you are going to first create a delegated domain named corp to serve as the root of the internal network and also as the Active Directory root. Starting with the corp.gidgets.com domain, you could create fourth-level domains by country code. Within these domains, you could create fifth-level domains, as required, for each of the major departments. You might end up with a configuration that looks something like that shown in Figure 3.2.

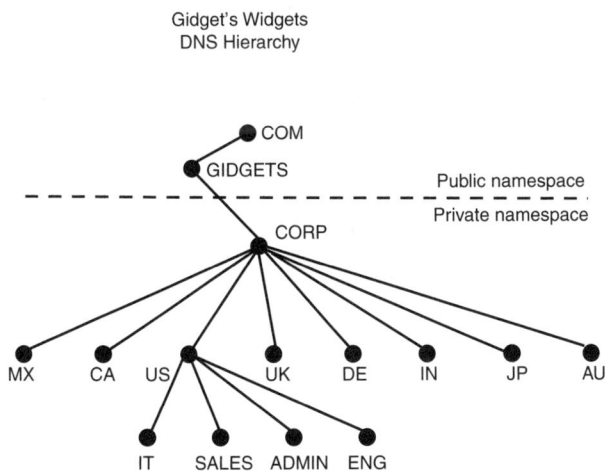

Gidget's Widgets
DNS Hierarchy

**FIGURE 3.2**
Gidget's network has been nicely organized by using countries as fourth-level domains and major departments as fifth-level domains.

**Designing the DNS hierarchy**
Several of the examples presented in this chapter do not represent "best design practices" in that they have many levels of depth. This is done for illustrative purposes to help you gain a better understanding of how DNS works. In reality, you may want to consider placing resources within Organizational Units instead of fifth-level domains and below. Having too many levels in your domain architecture can lead to slower authentication, among other issues.

If you were a network administrator in the United States working from a computer called GREENGUY42, your FQDN would be greenguy42.it.us.corp.gidgets.com. Of course, you could also design the DNS namespace using continents instead of countries, if desired. When creating DNS namespaces that are several levels deep like the example in Figure 3.2, you must keep in mind some general DNS restrictions as outlined in Table 3.1.

**TABLE 3.1**

**DNS NAME RESTRICTIONS**

| *Restriction* | *Standard DNS* | *DNS in Windows Server 2003 (and Windows 2000)* |
|---|---|---|
| Characters | Supports RFC 1123, which permits *A* to *Z*, *a* to *z*, 0 to 9, and the hyphen (-). | Supports several different con figurations: RFC 1123 standard, as well as support for RFCs 2181 and the character set specified in RFC 2044. |
| FQDN length | Permits 63 bytes per label and 255 bytes for an FQDN. | Permits 63 bytes per label and 255 bytes for an FQDN. Domain controllers are limited to 155 bytes for an FQDN. |

No matter what design you settle on, you must (in most cases) get it right the first time. Redesigning a DNS namespace is a difficult and time-consuming task after the fact, at best. In addition, failing to properly design the namespace for Active Directory compatibility can lead to functionality problems in the future.

After you've planned your namespace, you're ready to get down to business and start working out the finer points of your DNS implementation. The next thing you need to plan for is the types of zones you will be using. But what exactly is a zone?

# PLANNING DNS ZONE REQUIREMENTS

**Plan a host name resolution strategy.**

▶ **Plan zone replication requirements.**

You can easily get lost in the maze of acronyms and buzzwords surrounding DNS, especially if you are having a conversation with someone who has been working with IP networking and DNS for a while. You have a standard primary server for each zone, which might also be a domain, unless it's a reverse lookup zone; then you have zone transfers happening when you least expect it. To the uninitiated, this discussion can sound alarmingly like some arcane networking ritual, paying homage to the DNS deities.

Working with DNS is not nearly as bad as it sounds. But before we get any deeper into the Windows Server 2003 DNS infrastructure, we must discuss what exactly is meant when we refer to a *DNS zone*. First, although it is typically abbreviated in the world of DNS, a zone is actually a *zone of authority*, which means that it contains the complete information on some part of a domain namespace. In other words, it is a subset or root of that portion of namespace. The nameserver is considered to have authority for that zone, and it can respond to any requests for name resolution from that zone. So, when you look at the DNS name `www.quepublishing.com`, `quepublishing.com` is a DNS zone within the `.com` hierarchy. The `www` denotes the DNS record of a host contained within the `quepublishing.com` zone.

This conceptual representation of a zone also has a physical counterpart: All the information relating to a particular zone is stored in a physical file known as the *zone database file*, or more commonly the *zone file*, that can be found at `%systemroot%\system32\dns` for zones that are not stored in Active Directory. The following types of zones are supported by Windows Server 2003:

▶ **Standard primary**—A standard primary zone holds a master copy of a zone and can replicate it to all configured secondary zones in standard text format. Any changes that must be made to the zone are made on the copy stored on the primary.

**NOTE**

**"What's the difference between a zone and a domain?"**    Although the two terms can seem as if they are used interchangeably, there is a difference. A DNS domain is a segment of the DNS namespace. A zone, on the other hand, can contain multiple contiguous domains.

For example, `quepublishing.com` is a DNS domain. It contains all the information for that specific portion of the DNS namespace. `sales.quepublishing.com` is another example of a domain, which is contiguous with the `quepublishing.com` domain; in other words, the two domains "touch." So, if you were to create a DNS forward lookup zone on your DNS server, it could contain records for both domains. Zones allow for the logical grouping and management of domains and resource records on your DNS servers.

▶ **Standard secondary**—A standard secondary zone holds a read-only copy of the zone information in standard text format. Secondary zones are created to increase performance and resilience of the DNS configuration. Information is transferred from the primary zone to the secondary zones.

▶ **Active Directory–integrated**—Active Directory–integrated zones are available only on Windows 2000 Server and Windows Server 2003 DNS servers in an Active Directory domain. The zone information is contained within the Active Directory database and is replicated using Active Directory replication. Active Directory–integrated zones provide an increased level of replication flexibility as well as security. Active Directory–integrated zones also operate in a multimaster arrangement because they are hosted within Active Directory itself; this way, any DNS server (domain controller) hosting the Active Directory–integrated zone can update the zone data.

▶ **Stub**—Microsoft has introduced support for stub zones for the first time in Windows Server 2003. A stub zone contains only those resource records that are necessary to identify the authoritative DNS servers for that zone. Those resource records include Name Server (NS), Start of Authority (SOA), and possibly glue host (A) records. (Glue host records provide A record pointers to ensure that the master zone has the correct nameserver information for the stub zone.)

Although determining the zone type might not seem to be an important part of planning your DNS solution, nothing could be further from the truth. The type of DNS zone that you implement ultimately determines the placement of the DNS servers in your network. In addition, the type of DNS zone that you create will, in part, affect the construction of the network and the interoperability with other DNS servers, such as Unix Berkeley Internet Name Domain (BIND) servers.

When you are using a standard primary/standard secondary DNS zone implementation, the following points are of concern:

▶ A single DNS server is the master, holding the only writable copy of the DNS zone file.

▶ Zone transfers can be conducted using either incremental or full zone transfer.

▶ This implementation is fully compatible with BIND DNS servers by using the standard DNS zone transfer methods in place.

When you are using an Active Directory–integrated DNS zone implementation, the following points are of concern:

▶ A multimaster arrangement allows any DNS server to make updates to the zone file.

▶ Zone data is replicated with Active Directory data.

▶ Increased security is provided on the zone file.

▶ Redundancy is provided for DNS dynamic update.

▶ The administrator can adjust replication scope. Additionally, the zone file can be replicated to a standard secondary DNS server—a common practice for DNS servers placed on screened subnets.

▶ This implementation appears to be a standard primary zone to a BIND DNS server, thus allowing the use of BIND DNS servers as standard secondary zone servers.

Table 3.2 provides a comparison of Active Directory–integrated zones and standard DNS zones.

**TABLE 3.2**

**DNS ZONE TYPE COMPARISON**

| DNS Feature | Standard DNS Zones | Active Directory–Integrated Zones |
|---|---|---|
| Complies with Internet Engineering Task Force (IETF) specifications | Yes | Yes |
| Uses Active Directory for replication | No | Yes |
| Increases availability by providing a multimaster arrangement | No | Yes |
| Allows for zone updates after the failure of a single DNS server | No | Yes |
| Supports incremental zone transfers | Yes | Yes |

Regardless of whether you create standard or Active Directory–integrated DNS zones, you should be aware of the benefits of also using standard secondary zones. The following list presents some of the benefits you can realize by placing secondary zones on your network:

▶ The addition of standard secondary zone servers increases the redundancy of the zone by proving name resolution even if the primary zone server is unresponsive.

▶ When remote locations are connected to the core network over WAN links, secondary zone servers can greatly reduce costs and network traffic. By placing standard secondary zones in these remote locations or in locations with a high number of clients, you can improve overall network performance.

▶ Standard secondary zone servers reduce the load on the primary servers by distributing name resolution requests among more DNS servers.

At this point, you have a fair amount of information in hand to start planning your DNS zone requirements. Depending on what types of zones you implement, your zones will use either transfers or replication. Zone transfers occur in standard zones, whereas zone replication occurs in Active Directory–integrated zones.

Unlike WINS, which allows for a push/pull arrangement, zone transfers always originate with the secondary server polling the primary zone at the configured interval. It does so by checking the zone version number on the primary server to see whether it has changed in comparison to the version number on the secondary server. As changes are made to the zone file, the zone version number is incremented. When the zone version number on the primary server has been incremented, a zone transfer is required and will be performed. If the secondary zone supports incremental zone transfers (which Windows Server 2003 does), the secondary zone pulls (from the primary zone) only the changes made to resource records for each incremental zone version—meaning that a resource record could potentially be updated one or more times in a single zone transfer. When you use incremental zone transfers, network traffic is reduced and zone transfer speed is increased.

Active Directory–integrated DNS zones replicate data among all domain controllers, allowing any domain controller to modify the zone file and replicate the changes to the rest of the domain controllers that are running the DNS service. Replication occurs on a per-property basis, meaning that only the relevant changes will be replicated. Active Directory–integrated zones replicate only the final result of multiple changes to a resource record, unlike standard zones, which transfer the changes to a resource record that occurred in each zone version number.

With your namespace and zone type plans complete, you must next evaluate the need for forwarder and slave DNS servers. That is the topic of the next section.

# PLANNING DNS FORWARDING REQUIREMENTS

**Plan a host name resolution strategy.**

▶ **Plan a forwarding configuration.**

Before a discussion of forwarding and slave DNS servers can be undertaken, some general knowledge of how DNS clients query a DNS server to resolve IP addresses is of some use.

In a TCP/IP network, a *DNS resolver* is any system that has been configured with one or more DNS server IP addresses and that performs queries against these DNS servers. The DNS resolver is part of the DNS Client service, which is automatically installed when Windows is installed. The resolver can request one of two types of queries from a DNS server: recursive or iterative.

A *recursive query* is a DNS query that is sent to a DNS server from a DNS resolver asking the DNS server to provide a complete answer to the query, or an error stating that it cannot provide the information. If the DNS server is also configured as a forwarder, the query can be forwarded directly to another DNS server. If the query is for a name outside the local DNS server's zone of authority, it performs an iterative query against a root DNS server, which then responds with the IP address of the DNS server whose zone of authority includes the desired IP top-level domain. Additional iterative queries are then performed until the name is resolved into its IP address or an error is produced.

An *iterative query* is a DNS query that is sent by a DNS server to another DNS server in an effort to perform name resolution. Consider the example of a workstation (DNS resolver) in the `bigcorp.com` domain that wants to communicate with a Web server located in the `smallcorp.com domain`. Figure 3.3 illustrates the process by which the IP address for `www.smallcorp.com` will be resolved to its IP address. Recall that `www` is a typical alias for a Web server or bank of clustered Web servers.

**FIGURE 3.3**

The initial recursive query results in several iterative queries in an effort to resolve the name to an IP address.

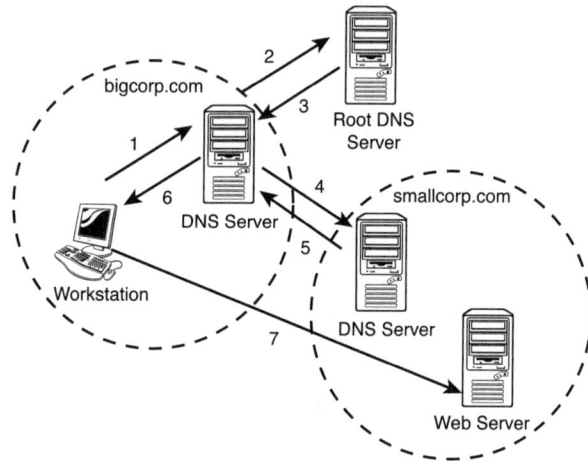

The process illustrated in Figure 3.3 follows these basic steps:

1. The DNS resolver (the local workstation) sends a recursive query to its local DNS server requesting the IP address of `www.smallcorp.com`.

2. The local DNS server, which is also configured as a forwarder, does not have information about `www.smallcorp.com` in its zone of authority and thus issues an iterative query to a root DNS server for the IP address of `www.smallcorp.com`.

3. The root DNS server does not have the requested information about the IP address of `www.smallcorp.com`, but it does know the IP address of a nameserver for the `smallcorp.com zone`. It provides this information back to the requesting DNS server.

4. The local DNS server next issues an iterative query to the DNS server for the `smallcorp.com` zone asking it for the IP address of `www.smallcorp.com`.

5. The `smallcorp.com` DNS server is authoritative for that zone, so it provides the requested IP address back to the local DNS server for `www.smallcorp.com`.

6. The local DNS server next passes the IP address of `www.smallcorp.com` back to the requesting workstation.

7. The client can now make a connection to `www.smallcorp.com`.

So, with the discussion of how DNS queries are performed and resolved under your belt, you can begin to plan for configuration and use of DNS forwarders on the network.

A *DNS forwarder* is a DNS server that accepts forwarded recursive lookups from another DNS server and then resolves the request for that DNS server. This capability can be useful if you do not have local copies of your internal DNS zone and want to have your local DNS server forward DNS queries to a central DNS server that is authoritative for your internal DNS zone. Caching-only servers make good DNS forwarders. If the DNS forwarder does not receive a valid resolution from the server that it forwards the request to, it attempts to resolve the client request itself.

A *DNS slave server* is a DNS forwarder server that does not try to resolve a resolution request if it doesn't receive a valid response to its forwarded DNS request. You typically see this type of DNS server implemented in conjunction with a secure Internet connection.

A new feature in Windows Server 2003, *conditional forwarding*, enables administrators to direct DNS requests to other DNS servers based on domain. Previous versions of Microsoft DNS supported only one forwarder, so if forwarding were enabled, all requests would be sent to a single server. This feature is used frequently when you want requests made to the internal network to be forwarded to a master DNS server that stores internal DNS zones, but have resolution requests that are made to Internet domains be sent to the Internet using the standard resolution process.

Figure 3.4 shows the Forwarders tab of the DNS server Properties dialog box.

> **EXAM TIP**
>
> **Know conditional forwarding**
> Because enabling conditional forwarding is a new capability with Windows Server 2003's DNS service, you need to be familiar with how it works and when you might need to use it.

**FIGURE 3.4**
On the Forwarders tab, you can configure where this server will send DNS requests if another DNS server will be supplying some or all of the DNS resolution for that server.

**Don't disable recursion** If you disable recursion in the DNS server properties, you cannot use a forwarder. Forwarding DNS requests requires that the DNS server be capable of making recursive queries.

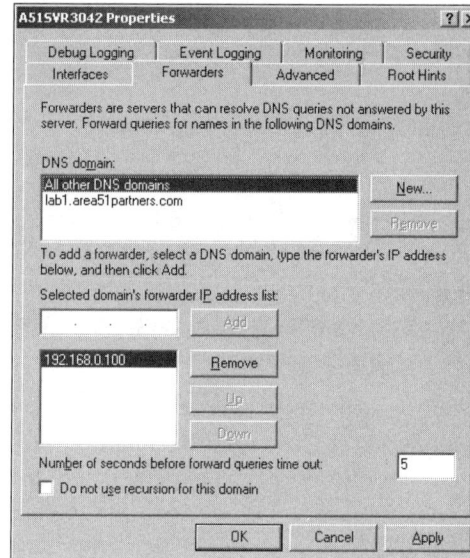

Say that you have a single internal domain called `lab1.area51partners.com`. You need to forward any queries to that domain directly to the primary DNS server for the `lab1.area51partners.com` domain. The Windows Server 2003 DNS service enables you to configure forwarding for a single domain, a group of domains, or all domains. Earlier versions of the Windows DNS service supported only forwarding of all domains; it was an all-or-nothing proposition. The functionality of being able to split forwarding among multiple servers while still resolving some domains locally is known as *conditional forwarding*. Figure 3.5 shows the different IP address that has been configured for conditional forwarding to the internal domain.

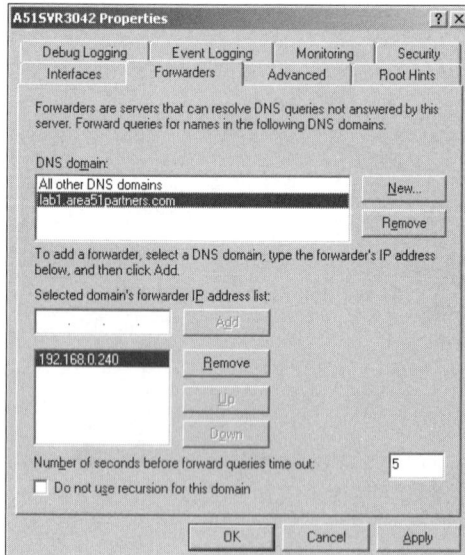

A common implementation of DNS forwarders in a Windows Server 2003 network has one specific DNS server being allowed to make queries to DNS servers outside the firewall. This implementation allows the firewall to be configured to allow DNS traffic only from this specific DNS server to leave the protected network, and allows only valid replies back to the DNS server to enter the protected network. Through this approach, all other DNS traffic—both inbound and outbound—can be dropped at the firewall, adding to the overall security of the network and the DNS service. Figure 3.6 illustrates this concept.

**FIGURE 3.5**
Conditional forwarding enables you to configure specific DNS servers by domain.

Forwarders can be used to ensure that DNS queries have the best possible chance of being answered with the requested information.

As you have seen, they also can be implemented to increase security of the DNS service on your network. With security in mind, we examine other ways you can configure additional security to your DNS servers.

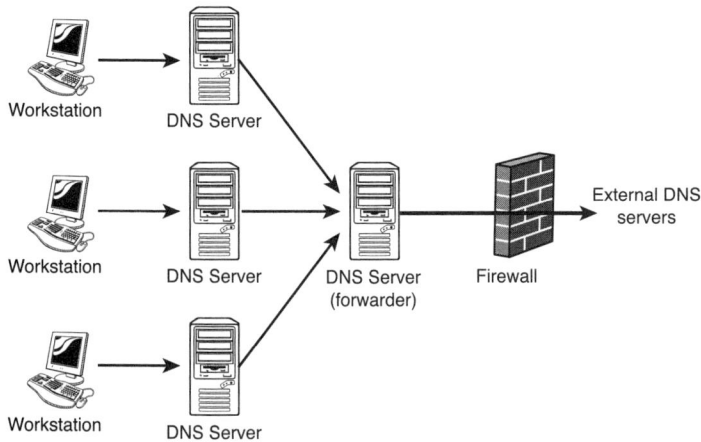

**FIGURE 3.6**
DNS forwarders can be implemented to control DNS traffic into and out of the protected network.

# GUIDED PRACTICE EXERCISE 3.1

In this exercise, you'll be planning and implementing a DNS forwarding solution.

▶ You have been hired as a network consultant for ACME Widgets, Incorporated.

▶ ACME has offices and manufacturing facilities located in the United States, Canada, Mexico, England, and France. All locations are connected via permanent VPN connections over the Internet.

▶ All resources for each country are located in a child domain under the acmewidgets.com domain. All zones are Active Directory integrated.

▶ Each child domain contains two DNS servers that are responsible for the DNS information for resources in that child domain's zone file. The DNS server IP addresses are 172.16.10.56 and 172.16.10.57 (United States), 172.16.12.56 and 172.16.12.57 (Canada), 172.16.13.56 and 172.16.13.57 (Mexico), 172.16.15.56 and 172.16.15.57 (England), and 172.17.15.56 (France).

*continues*

*continued*

▶ You have two external DNS servers at each location that are maintained by the local ISP providing the Internet connection.

▶ You need to provide a DNS forwarding solution that provides the best overall resolution speeds for all Internal and External name queries. You are configuring the DNS servers in the United States first.

You should try doing this on your own first. If you get stuck, or you would like to see one possible solution, follow these steps:

1. Open the DNS console.

2. Right-click the first DNS server in the United States (172.16.10.56) and select Properties from the context menu.

3. Select the Forwarders tab in the Server Properties dialog box.

4. Enter the DNS domain `ca.acmerockets.com` using the New button on the Forwarders tab.

5. Enter the IP addresses of the Canada DNS servers (172.16.12.56 and 172.16.12.57) to this entry using the Add button on the Forwarders tab.

6. Enter the DNS domain `mx.acmerockets.com` using the New button on the Forwarders tab.

7. Enter the IP addresses of the Mexico DNS server (172.16.13.57) to this entry using the Add button on the Forwarders tab.

8. Enter the DNS domain `uk.acmerockets.com` using the New button on the Forwarders tab.

9. Enter the IP addresses of the England DNS servers (172.16.15.56 and 172.16.15.57) to this entry using the Add button on the Forwarders tab.

10. Enter the DNS domain `fr.acmerockets.com` using the New button on the Forwarders tab.

11. Enter the IP addresses of the France DNS server (172.17.15.56) to this entry using the Add button on the Forwarders tab.

12. Select the All Other DNS Domains entry.

13. Enter the IP addresses of the United States public DNS servers for this entry. This will direct all DNS queries that do not match any of your internal domains to be forwarded to your external DNS servers.

14. Close the Server Properties dialog box.

# CONFIGURING DNS SECURITY

**Plan a host name resolution strategy.**

▶ **Plan for DNS security.**

With the majority of your planning already accomplished, you now need to plan the security of the DNS service. Providing security for DNS is not a task that you can accomplish by performing one action or by configuring one item. DNS is a dynamic service that, by its very nature, must be capable of interacting with network clients on several different levels. Not only must clients be capable of retrieving information from a DNS server through queries, but authorized clients must also be capable of having their resource records entered or updated when they acquire a Dynamic Host Configuration Protocol (DHCP) lease on the network. Thus, DNS security is a multifaceted area that takes some preplanning to implement properly.

Configuring DNS security can be broken into the following five general areas of concern:

- ▶ Dynamic updates
- ▶ Active Directory DNS permissions
- ▶ Zone transfer security
- ▶ DNS server properties
- ▶ DNS Security (DNSSEC)

Each of these concerns is addressed in the sections that follow.

**NOTE**

**Implementing secure dynamic updates**   If you are planning to use secure dynamic updates on your network and also plan to have multiple DHCP servers, you must ensure that all your DHCP servers have been placed in the DnsUpdateProxyGroup group. Adding all your DHCP servers to this group allows them to perform proxy updates for all your network's DHCP clients.

The addition of the DHCP servers to the DnsUpdateProxyGroup is required to prevent records from being inaccessible to one DHCP server because a different DHCP server previously updated it, thus taking ownership of it. This process works the same as any other shared network resource, such as documents on a network file share.

# Dynamic Updates

Dynamic updates occur when a DHCP server or a DNS client computer automatically updates the applicable DNS resource records when a DHCP lease is granted (or expires). Three types of dynamic updates exist in Windows Server 2003, each with its own security specifics.

*Secure dynamic updates* are available when Active Directory–integrated zones are in use. Using secure dynamic updates, the DNS zone information is stored in Active Directory and thus is protected using Active Directory security features. When a zone has been created as or converted to an Active Directory–integrated zone, Access Control List (ACL) entries can be used to specify which users, computers, and groups can make changes to a zone or a specific record.

*Dynamic updates from DHCP* can be configured to allow only specific DHCP servers to update DNS zone entries. The configuration takes place on the DHCP server by configuring it with the DNS zone that is responsible for automatically updating. It takes place on the DNS server by configuring it with the DHCP servers that are to be the only authorized computers to update the DNS entries. Dynamic updates from DHCP are best implemented when the DHCP client computers are not Windows 2000 or later—such as when the client computers are Windows 98 computers. You also can implement dynamic updates from DHCP if you determine that managing individual NTFS permissions for users, computers, and groups to update their respective DNS entries becomes an administrative burden. Finally, dynamic updates from DHCP can overcome the security risks that could potentially come from allowing unauthorized computers to impersonate authorized computers and populate the DNS zone file with bad information.

*DNS client dynamic updates* are performed by clients running Windows 2000 or later. When these client computers start, their DNS client service automatically connects to the DNS server and registers the DNS client with the DNS server. Allowing DNS clients to perform dynamic updates is the least preferred method of dynamic updating and is hampered by manageability issues and potential security problems. You should typically plan to have DNS clients perform dynamic updates only when the computer has a static IP address and the assignment of the required permissions is manageable.

By default, dynamic updates are not enabled for standard zones, thus providing increased security by preventing an attacker from updating DNS zone information with bad entries. This setting is the most secure, but it offers the least functionality because all dynamic updates are disabled in this configuration. Dynamic updates are required for Active Directory–integrated zones and should be configured to allow secure dynamic updates or dynamic updates from DHCP instead of DNS client dynamic updates wherever possible, to increase security of the DNS zone data.

## Active Directory DNS Permissions

If the zone is integrated with Active Directory, the Discretionary Access Control List (DACL) for the zone can be used to configure the permissions for the users and groups that may change or control the data in the DNS zone. Table 3.3 lists the default group and user permissions for Active Directory–integrated DNS zones.

**NOTE** **DHCP on domain controllers** You should not configure the DHCP service on a computer that is also a domain controller to perform dynamic DNS updates. If a DHCP server exists on a domain controller, the DHCP server has full control over all DNS objects stored in Active Directory because the account it is running under (the domain controller computer account) has this privilege. This configuration creates a security risk that you should avoid. You should not install the DHCP server service that is configured to perform dynamic DNS updates on a domain controller; instead, you should install it on a member server if you're performing dynamic DNS updates.

As an alternative, you can use a new feature in Windows Server 2003 DHCP, which allows for the creation of a dedicated domain user account that all DHCP servers will use when performing dynamic DNS updates.

### TABLE 3.3

#### DEFAULT GROUP AND USER PERMISSIONS ON ACTIVE DIRECTORY–INTEGRATED DNS ZONES

| Group or User | Permissions |
| --- | --- |
| Administrators | Allow: Read, Write, Create All Child Objects, Special Permissions |
| Authenticated Users | Allow: Create All Child Objects |
| Creator Owner | Allow: Special Permissions |
| DnsAdmins | Allow: Full Control, Read, Write, Create All Child Objects, Delete Child Objects, Special Permissions |
| Domain Admins | Allow: Full Control, Read, Write, Create All Child Objects, Delete Child Objects |
| Enterprise Admins | Allow: Full Control, Read, Write, Create All Child Objects, Delete Child Objects |
| Enterprise Domain Controllers | Allow: Full Control, Read, Write, Create All Child Objects, Delete Child Objects, Special Permissions |

*continues*

**TABLE 3.3**    *continued*

**DEFAULT GROUP AND USER PERMISSIONS ON ACTIVE DIRECTORY–INTEGRATED DNS ZONES**

| Group or User | Permissions |
|---|---|
| Everyone | Allow: Read, Special Permissions |
| Pre-Windows 2000 Compatible Access | Allow: Special Permissions |
| System | Allow: Full Control, Read, Write, Create All Child Objects, Delete Child Objects |

You can modify these default values to suit your particular needs.

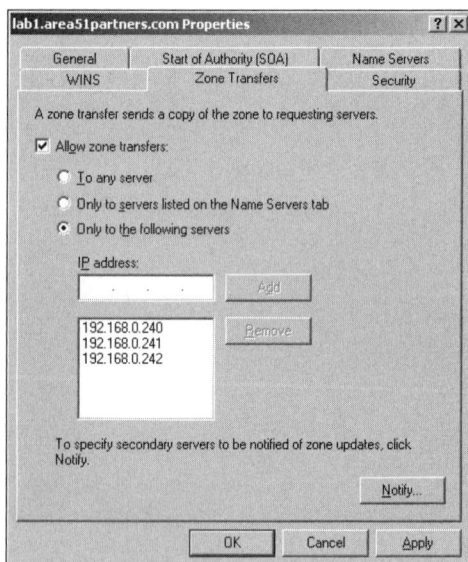

**FIGURE 3.7**
You can configure which DNS servers participate in zone transfers.

## Zone Transfer Security

You can use several methods to increase the security of zone transfers—and thus increase the security of your DNS servers overall. If attackers cannot capture your zone data from a zone transfer—once a very common method of gathering information about a domain (called *footprinting*)—they will not be able to easily determine the makeup of your network. In addition, zone transfer security prevents the injection of unauthorized data into the zone files through zone transfer from an unauthorized DNS server.

By default, Windows Server 2003 DNS performs zone transfers only with the DNS servers that are listed in a zone's Name Server (NS) resource records. Even though this configuration is fairly secure, you should consider changing this setting to allow zone transfers to be carried out only with specific IP addresses that you have explicitly configured. Figure 3.7 shows how you might make this configuration for a DNS server. Although you are still subject to IP address spoofing with this option configured, you have taken one more step toward a more secure DNS implementation. The task of identifying and defeating spoofed IP addresses lies at your perimeter security devices: firewalls, screening routers, and proxy servers.

If you must perform zone transfers across an untrusted network, you should consider implementing and using a VPN tunnel between the two DNS servers. Encrypted zone information traveling inside the tunnel is safe from prying eyes, thus providing an uncompromised zone transfer. When using a VPN tunnel for zone transfer data, you should use the strongest possible level of encryption and authentication supported by both sides of the tunnel.

Your last option to secure zone data is to use only Active Directory–integrated zones. Because the DNS zone data is stored in Active Directory, it is inherently more secure. When Active Directory–integrated zones are in use, only Active Directory–integrated DNS servers participate in zone replication. In addition, all DNS servers hosting Active Directory–integrated zones must be registered with Active Directory. All replication traffic between Active Directory–integrated DNS servers is also encrypted, further adding to the level of security provided.

## DNS Server Properties

By default, Windows Server 2003 DNS is configured to prevent unrequested resource records from being added to the DNS zone data, thus increasing zone security. From the Advanced tab of the DNS server Properties dialog box (see Figure 3.8), you can see the Secure Cache Against Pollution option, which is checked by default.

By default, Windows Server 2003 DNS servers use a secure response option that eliminates the addition of unrelated resource records that are included in a referral answer to the cache. The server typically caches any names in referral answers, thus expediting the resolution of subsequent DNS queries. However, when this feature is in use, the server can determine whether the referred name is polluting or insecure and discard it. The server thus determines whether to cache the name offered in the referral depending on whether it is part of the exact DNS domain tree for which the original name query was made. As an example, a query made for `sales.bigcorp.com` with a referral answer of `smallcorp.net` would not be cached.

## DNS Security (DNSSEC)

RFC 2535 provides for DNS Security (DNSSEC), a public key infrastructure (PKI) based system in which authentication and data integrity can be provided to DNS resolvers. Digital signatures are

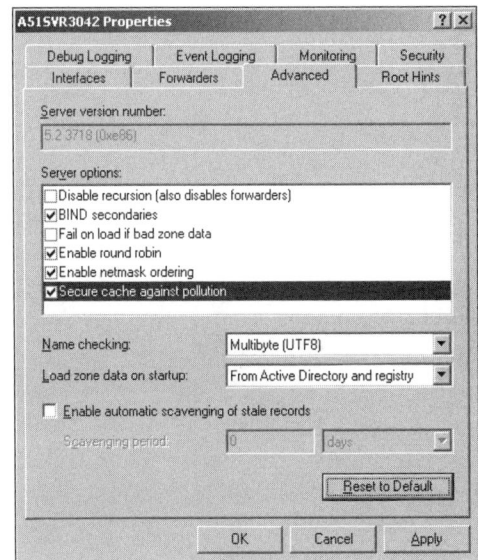

**FIGURE 3.8**
The Secure Cache Against Pollution option prevents unrequested resource records from being added to the zone data.

used and encrypted with private keys. These digital signatures can then be authenticated by DNSSEC-aware resolvers by using the corresponding public key. The required digital signature and public keys are added to the DNS zone in the form of resource records.

The public key is stored in the KEY RR (Resource Record), and the digital signature is stored in the SIG RR. The KEY RR must be supplied to the DNS resolver before it can successfully authenticate the SIG RR. DNSSEC also introduces one additional RR, the NXT RR, which is used to cryptographically assure the resolver that a particular RR does not exist in the zone.

DNSSEC is only partially supported in Windows Server 2003 DNS, providing basic support as specified in RFC 2535. A Windows Server 2003 DNS server could, therefore, operate as a secondary to a BIND server that fully supports DNSSEC. The support is partial because DNS in Windows Server 2003 does not provide any means to sign or verify the digital signatures. In addition, the Windows Server 2003 DNS resolver does not validate any of the DNSSEC data that is returned as a result of queries.

# INTEGRATING WITH THIRD-PARTY DNS SOLUTIONS

**Plan a host name resolution strategy.**

▶ **Examine the interoperability of DNS with third-party DNS solutions.**

It's a fact of life that many organizations already have existing DNS solutions in place, such as Unix BIND. In some cases, these existing BIND servers might not meet the DNS requirements of Active Directory. Table 3.4 outlines the features of some of the more common versions of BIND in use.

**TABLE 3.4**

**FEATURES OF VARIOUS BIND VERSIONS**

| BIND Version | Features |
|---|---|
| 4.9.4 | Support for fast zone transfers |
| 4.9.6 | Support for Service (SRV) resource records |
| 8.1.2 | Support for dynamic DNS (DDNS) |
| 8.2.1 | Support for incremental zone transfer (IXFR) between DNS Servers |
| 8.2.2 | Full support for all Active Directory features |

If you are faced with a situation in which you are dealing with other DNS systems, you have two basic choices of implementation:

▶ Upgrade existing DNS systems to meet the DNS requirements of Active Directory. For BIND, versions 8.1.2 and later are sufficient.

▶ Migrate existing DNS zones to Windows Server 2003 DNS.

Although it is recommended that you use only Windows Server 2003 DNS servers to ensure full support for Active Directory, you can use any DNS system that meets the following specifications:

▶ Support for SRV resource records

▶ Dynamic updates per RFC 2136

Although support for dynamic updates is highly recommended, it is not mandatory. Support for SRV resource records is mandatory, however, because they are required to provide DNS support to Active Directory.

If you have Unix BIND servers in your DNS infrastructure, you should consider placing them as secondaries instead of primaries. By default, Windows Server 2003 DNS servers use a fast zone transfer format whereby compression is used and multiple records can be sent in a single TCP message. BIND versions 4.9.4 and later support fast zone transfers. If you are using an earlier version of BIND or another third-party DNS system that does not support fast zone transfers, you must disable fast zone transfers. When you select the

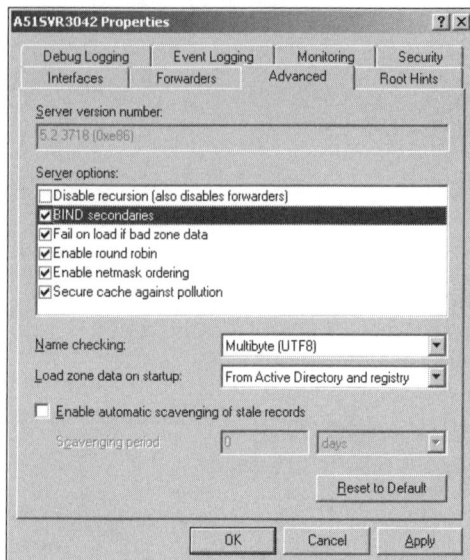

**FIGURE 3.9**
The BIND Secondaries option prevents fast zone transfers from occurring.

---

**"I don't need WINS"**   This statement is accurate only if the client computer is running DNS. Don't make the mistake of assuming that DNS is implied when you get WINS questions.

EXAM TIP

---

BIND Secondaries option (see Figure 3.9), fast zone transfers are disabled for that server.

# INTRODUCTION TO WINS

If you are at all familiar with Windows NT 4.0 networks, you are undoubtedly familiar with the intricacies of a WINS infrastructure. You may also be wondering why Microsoft didn't get rid of WINS in Windows Server 2003. Well, the good news is that with Windows Server 2003, WINS is used for backward compatibility only. Windows Server 2003 Active Directory networks do not need WINS at all.

So that means we don't need to talk about WINS, right? Sorry, but you don't get off that easily. Until your network is 100% Windows 2000 or later, you still need WINS to provide backward compatibility for legacy Windows operating systems, particularly with your NT domains. With that in mind, let's talk about what WINS is and how it works.

In the Internet-centric environment that most companies are designing and maintaining, Transmission Control Protocol/Internet Protocol (TCP/IP) has become the ubiquitous networking protocol. For old-time Unix users, using TCP/IP is a good thing. TCP/IP came out of the Unix arena and has been the native protocol for Unix systems since the late 1980s.

Microsoft, on the other hand, started with a different protocol as its LAN Manager operating system's native protocol—NetBIOS Extended User Interface (NetBEUI). NetBEUI was a pretty good protocol for small networks; it required no configuration and didn't require complex addressing like TCP/IP does. However, NetBEUI cannot handle routing and does not perform well in large environments. Microsoft needed to add TCP/IP support.

When Microsoft began to add TCP/IP support to its LAN server products, the company ran into a little problem. The naming system used on Microsoft networks at that time would not function on routed TCP/IP networks. Microsoft LAN Manager computers used the computer's NetBIOS names for identification. Although this makes maintaining the network very simple for an administrator— because servers are automatically advertised on the network by name—this naming system was a problem with TCP/IP.

NetBIOS has a design limitation that shows up in routed networks because NetBIOS relies heavily on broadcast messages to advertise servers and their shared resources. *Broadcast messages* are messages that are received by every computer on a network segment, rather than by a specific computer. This paradigm is useable on smaller networks but can add overwhelming amounts of broadcast traffic on an enterprise network. If you have ever suffered from a broadcast storm on your network, you are familiar with the issue. To confine the impact of broadcast messages on a TCP/IP network, IP routers do not forward broadcast messages. Unlike the Microsoft NWLink protocol for IPX compatibility, which was written by Microsoft to support broadcasts, TCP/IP conforms to very strict standards. To function in a TCP/IP environment, Microsoft's TCP/IP implementation had to conform to the standard. Therefore, Microsoft had to find a way to make NetBIOS naming work in a standard TCP/IP network.

Microsoft's first solution, introduced in its older LAN Manager server, was to use a LAN Manager HOSTS (LMHOSTS) file on each computer on the network. Similar to the HOSTS file used before DNS was available, LMHOSTS consists of records matching NetBIOS names to IP addresses. When a computer couldn't find a particular NetBIOS computer on the local network, it would consult its LMHOSTS file to see whether the computer could be found elsewhere.

An LMHOSTS file is a text file that must be edited manually. After creating a master LMHOSTS file, an administrator must copy the file to every computer on the network. Every time a computer was installed or removed, the master LMHOSTS file had to be updated and redistributed. The architects of TCP/IP faced a similar issue with HOSTS files before the DNS specification was written.

---

**WINS AND DNS INTEGRATION**

Although it would be nice if you no longer had to support WINS clients, this is not always the case—thus the reason that Microsoft still provides a very robust and powerful WINS server in Windows Server 2003. What's more, DNS and WINS can be integrated to provide a more complete name resolution solution for all clients on your network.

*continues*

*continued*

You can configure a DNS server to query a WINS server by configuring a DNS zone setting. This is helpful when some of the clients you support require NetBIOS name resolution, such as legacy Windows 9*x* clients, or cannot register themselves with DNS. In effect, you are providing a means for DNS clients to look up WINS client names and IP addresses without needing to contact the WINS server directly. This is accomplished by adding a WINS lookup record to the authoritative zone. After it is configured, the DNS server will query a WINS server for every request made to it for which it does not have a valid record. If the requested name is located on the WINS server, the information is returned to the requesting client via the DNS server. The process is invisible to all clients. Note that you can configure this for both forward and reverse lookup zones.

If you have a mixture of Windows and third-party DNS servers in your organization, you will run into problems if you attempt to replicate WINS lookup records to these third-party DNS servers. Only Microsoft DNS servers support WINS lookup records; thus, zone transfers to third-party DNS servers will fail. In this situation, you should use WINS referral to create and delegate a special "WINS zone" that refers queries to WINS when needed. This zone does not perform any registrations or updates. Clients need to be configured to append this additional WINS referral zone to their queries for unqualified names, thus allowing clients to query both WINS and DNS as required. You also need to ensure that this WINS referral zone is not configured to transfer to any third-party DNS servers.

---

Microsoft also needed a dynamic name service that would keep itself current on computers on the network—a name service that could work in routed TCP/IP environments. Microsoft's answer was the WINS. Four elements can be found in a WINS network:

- ▶ **WINS servers**—When WINS client computers enter the network, they contact a WINS server using a directed message. The client computer registers its name with the WINS server and uses the WINS server to resolve NetBIOS names to IP addresses.

- ▶ **WINS client computers**—WINS client computers use directed (P-node) messages to communicate with WINS servers and are typically configured to use H-node communication. Windows 2000, Windows NT, Windows 95 and 98, and

Windows for Workgroups computers can be WINS client computers.

▶ **Non-WINS client computers**—Older Microsoft network client computers that can't use P-node can still benefit from WINS. Their broadcast messages are intercepted by WINS proxy computers that act as intermediaries between the B-node client computers and WINS servers. MS-DOS and Windows 3.1 client computers function as non-WINS clients.

▶ **WINS proxies**—Windows NT, Windows 95 and 98, and Windows for Workgroups client computers can function as WINS proxies. They intercept B-node broadcasts on their local subnet and communicate with a WINS server on behalf of the B-node client computer.

As we discuss in the "Implementing WINS Replication" section of this chapter, WINS servers can replicate their databases so that each WINS server can provide name resolution for the entire network. Whenever possible, it is desirable to have at least two WINS servers. This way, name resolution can take place when one name server is down. Also, administrators can distribute WINS activity across multiple servers to balance the processing loads. WINS server addresses are one of the configuration settings that can be issued with DHCP.

# What's New in Windows Server 2003 WINS

If you're moving from a Windows NT 4.0–based WINS implementation, some great changes are in store for you in Windows Server 2003. The following improvements have been made to WINS since Windows 2000 Server:

▶ **Record filtering**—Using improved filtering and search functions, you can quickly locate records by showing only the records that fit the specified criteria. This capability can be useful when you are managing larger WINS databases. You can now specify multiple criteria to perform advanced searches. Also, you can combine filters for customized results. The available filters include record owner, record type, NetBIOS name, and IP address (with or without the subnet mask).

Lastly, because the results of the query are stored in the local NetBIOS cache on your computer, the performance of subsequent queries and name lookups is improved.

▶ **Specified replication partners**—You can define a list of WINS servers that are allowed to be the source of incoming WINS records during pull replication events. You can opt to block specific WINS servers from being able to replicate with your WINS servers. Alternatively, you can opt to allow a specific list of WINS servers to perform replication, blocking all other WINS servers from replicating with your WINS servers.

The following improvements were also made to WINS in Windows 2000 Server and are carried over into the WINS implementation in Windows Server 2003:

▶ **Command-line management**—You can use the `netsh` command with the WINS context to manage WINS servers from the command line and to use batch files.

▶ **Persistent connections**—Each WINS server can be configured to maintain a persistent connection with one or more of its replication partners. This configuration increases replication speed and eliminates network overhead associated with building and tearing down connections for replication.

▶ **Manual tombstoning**—Records can be marked for deletion (tombstoning). This tombstoned state is replicated to all WINS servers preventing an active copy of the record on a different WINS server from being propagated.

▶ **Improved management**—The WINS console is Microsoft Management Console based and can be added to customized MMCs, resulting in a user-friendly, powerful, and customized management interface.

▶ **Dynamic record deletion and multiselect**—Using the WINS console, you can you easily manage the WINS database. You can point, click, and delete one or more WINS static or dynamic entries.

▶ **Record verification**—Record verification performs a comparison of the IP address returned by a NetBIOS query of different WINS servers. This feature helps to check the consistency of names stored and replicated on your WINS servers.

- ▶ **Version number validation**—Version number validation examines the owner address–to–version number mapping tables. This feature helps to check the consistency of names stored and replicated on your WINS servers.

- ▶ **Export function**—The WINS database can be exported to a comma-delimited text file for importation into Excel or another application for offline analysis.

- ▶ **Increased fault tolerance**—Windows 98 and later clients can specify up to 12 WINS servers per interface, up from the previous limit of 2. These extra WINS servers can be queried should the primary and secondary WINS servers not respond.

- ▶ **Dynamic renewal**—WINS clients are no longer required to restart after renewing their NetBIOS name registration.

- ▶ **Nbtstat -RR option**—The Nbtstat -RR option provides the ability to release and renew the NetBIOS name registration.

- ▶ **WINS Users group**—A special local group, WINS Users, is created when WINS is installed; this group provides read-only use of the WINS console. Members of this group can view but not change information and properties of the WINS servers.

# IMPLEMENTING **WINS** REPLICATION

### Plan a NetBIOS name resolution strategy.

### ▶ Plan a WINS replication strategy.

In most environments that rely on WINS for name resolution for legacy systems, it is important to ensure that more than one WINS server exists so that you provide redundancy and availability. To ensure that each server has a current copy of the database, it is important to configure replication between your WINS servers. Let's quickly look at the different types of replication you can configure for the WINS service:

- ▶ **Pull replication**—In pull replication, your server pulls the database from the replication partner. A pull replication is time based and occurs at the time you have configured. You can decide whether to establish a persistent connection for

**EXAM TIP**

The following discussion about WINS assumes that you are already familiar with installing the service and performing basic management and configuration tasks. If you need a review, see Chapter 4 of *Deploying Network Services*, part of the Windows Server 2003 Deployment Kit at www.microsoft.com/technet/ prodtechnol/windowsserver2003/ proddocs/deployguide/dpgdns_ overview.asp.

EXAM TIP

**WINS Replication** Recall that one of the improvements in WINS since Windows NT 4.0 is the capability to maintain a persistent connection with one or more of the replication partners, enabling real-time replication. Because this is one of the new features of the WINS service, you will probably find it on the exam. Microsoft is more likely to test your familiarity with new features of the service than your understanding of the general WINS functionality because WINS has been part of the Windows server operating systems since its inception.

replication, and you can set the start time and interval for replication.

▶ **Push replication**—In push replication, your server pushes its database to the replication partner. A push replication is event driven, and the number of database updates determines when the event occurs. You can decide whether to use a persistent connection for push activities, and you can set the number of changes in version ID before replication.

▶ **Replication partner type**—The partner type can be push, pull, or push/pull, depending on your requirements. (In push/pull replication, database replication can occur using either method—push or pull.)

To configure WINS replication with another WINS server, perform the process outlined in Step by Step 3.1.

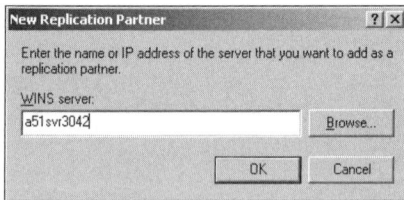

**FIGURE 3.10**
You can create a new replication partner by IP address or DNS name.

# STEP BY STEP

### 3.1 Configuring WINS Replication

1. Open the WINS console by clicking Start, Programs, Administrative Tools, WINS.

2. In the right pane, right-click Replication Partners and select New Replication Partner. The New Replication Partner dialog box opens, as shown in Figure 3.10, and asks you to enter the address of another WINS server. You can enter either the server name or IP address. If the server name cannot be resolved, you are prompted to enter the address of the server.

3. Enter the name or IP address of the server and click OK.

4. Click Replication Partners in the left pane of the WINS console. You should see your new replication partner in the right pane (see Figure 3.11).

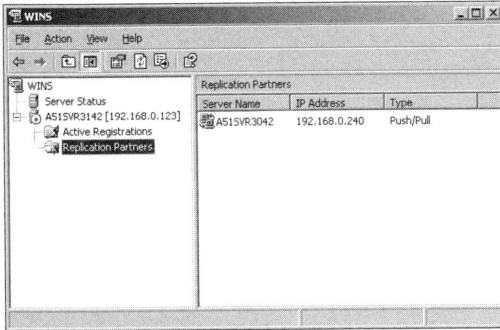

**FIGURE 3.11** ◀
All configured replication partners are listed here.

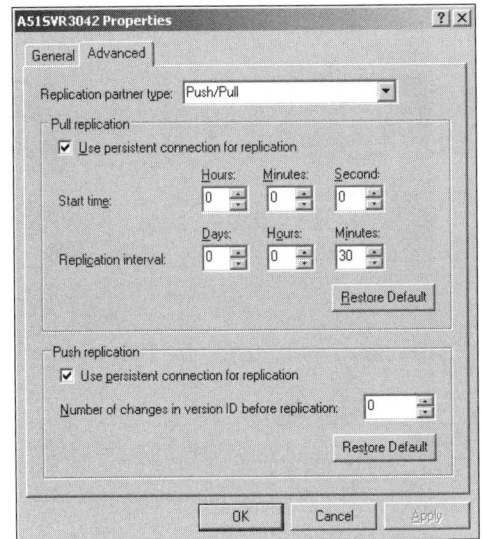

5. Right-click the newly created replication partner. Then select Properties from the context menu to open the eplication partner Properties dialog box, as shown in Figure 3.12.

6. Click the Advanced tab, shown in Figure 3.13. On this tab, you can configure the replication properties for the replication partner. You can choose from Push/Pull (the default), Push, or Pull. You can also specify the options to control how and when the replication is to occur. As discussed earlier, you should consider using a persistent connection because it will increase performance and decrease network usage.

7. Click OK when the settings meet your requirements.

**FIGURE 3.12** ▲
The General tab doesn't contain anything you can configure.

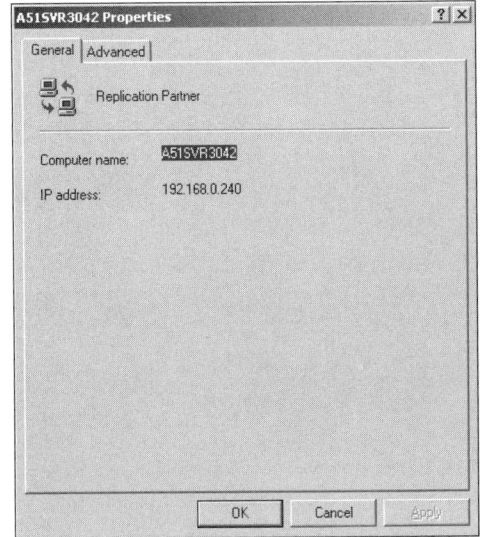

You have now configured replication with a WINS replication partner. Now let's look at the global replication properties that you can configure for replication on the WINS server. To review the global replication properties, open the WINS console application as described in Step by Step 3.1 and select the Replication Partners folder in the left pane. Right-click; then select Properties from the context menu to open the Replication Partners Properties dialog box, shown in Figure 3.14.

**FIGURE 3.13** ▲
On the Advanced tab, you can configure replication between your server and the selected partner.

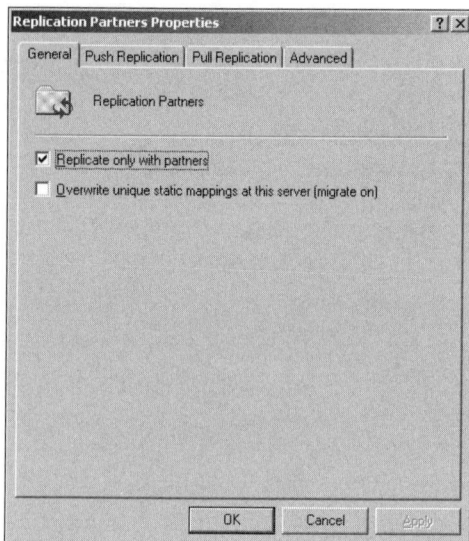

**FIGURE 3.14**
On the General tab, you can control with whom your server replicates and what to do about static entries.

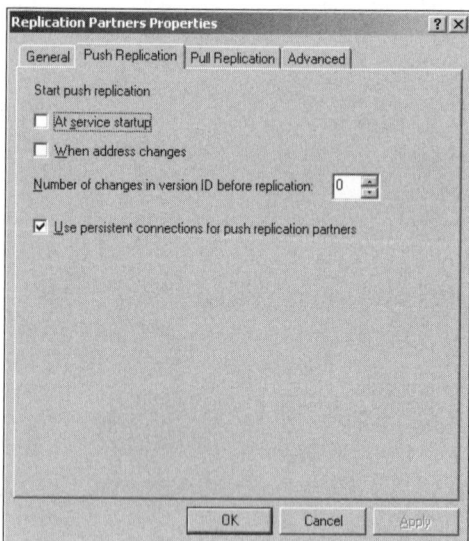

**FIGURE 3.15**
On the Push Replication tab, you can configure how the server should perform push replication.

You can configure the replication properties for the server from the following four tabs:

▶ **General**—The General tab allows you to restrict replication to configured replication partners as well as configure the server to allow the overwriting of static mappings on the server. If you have static mappings currently in use on your network, you can benefit from allowing the WINS server to overwrite these static mappings with their dynamic counterparts. This option serves to ensure that all records are up to date and computers and services are reachable.

▶ **Push Replication**—As you can see in Figure 3.15, you can use the Push Replication tab to establish whether replication will start at system startup. You also can use this tab to establish when an address changes (and you can configure the number of changes required to trigger the push replication). Lastly, you can configure the server to use persistent connections for the push replication.

▶ **Pull Replication**—As you can see in Figure 3.16, you can use the Pull Replication tab to establish whether pull replication starts at system startup, the time the replication should start, the interval between replications, and the number of times replication should be retried. Lastly, you can configure the server to use persistent connections for the pull replication.

▶ **Advanced**—The Advanced tab, shown in Figure 3.17, allows you to configure a list of WINS servers that you want to allow or block from being able to replicate to your server. You can also specify that your WINS server is to configure itself to automatically replicate with other WINS servers that it discovers on the network. Be aware, though, that this option may be a security risk if you cannot account for all the WINS servers on your network. Also, because this option relies on multicasting, you may want to consider it only for small networks. If you configure this option, you also can configure the interval at which the WINS server will multicast as well as the time to live (TTL) for the multicast messages.

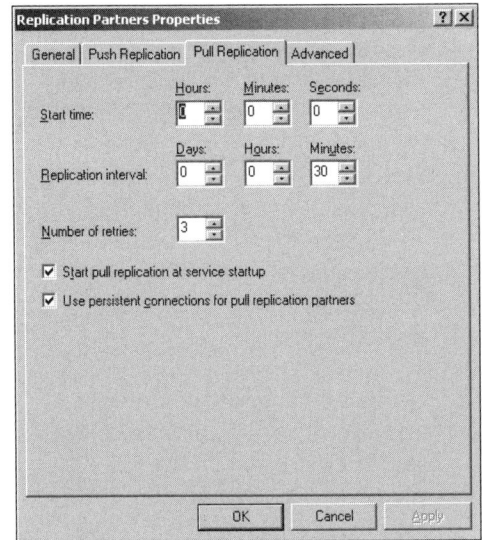

**FIGURE 3.16**
On the Pull Replication tab, you can configure how the server should perform pull replication.

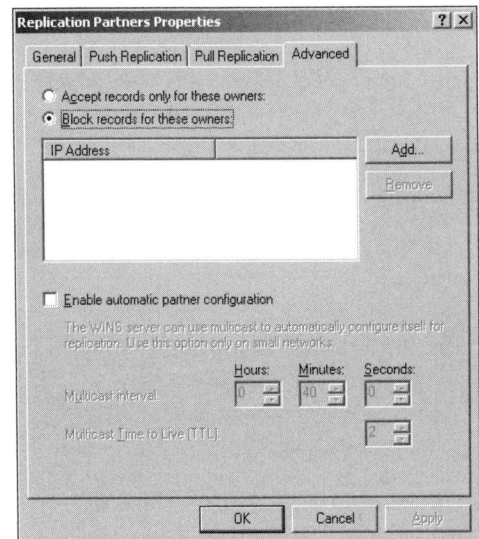

**FIGURE 3.17**
On the Advanced tab, you can specify with which WINS servers your server will or will not replicate, among other items.

N O T E

**What's multicasting?** Multicasting is the act of transmitting a message to a select group of recipients. This is in contrast to the concept of a broadcast, where traffic is sent to every host on the network, or a unicast, where the connection is a one-to-one relationship, and there is only one recipient of the data. Think about sending an email message. If you send an email message to your manager, it is an example of a unicast message. If you send an email message to every user on the system, it is a broadcast. Send an email message to a mailing list, and you have sent a multicast message, which falls between the previous two. Teleconferencing and videoconferencing use the concept of multicasting, as does broadcast audio, where the connection is one to a selected group. At this time, only a few applications take advantage of this feature, but with the growing popularity of multicast applications, you may see more multicast applications in the future. WINS is one that you can keep on the list, but only for small networks.

**EXAM TIP**

**Global replication settings** Because we just finished discussing configuring replication partners, these parameters should look familiar. However, in this section the changes apply to any replication partners created after the modifications are made. They are not applied to existing replication partners.

# IMPLEMENTING NETBIOS NAME RESOLUTION

**Plan a NetBIOS name resolution strategy.**

▶ **Plan NetBIOS name resolution by using the** LMHOSTS **file.**

Microsoft TCP/IP uses NetBIOS over TCP/IP (NetBT) as specified in RFC 1001 and 1002 to support the NetBIOS client and server programs in the local area network (LAN) and wide area network (WAN) environments. Before we look at the specifics of NetBIOS name resolution, let's briefly review how computers communicate on the network. This review should help you understand how the different NetBIOS modes work and why some are preferable to others.

Computers can use two ways to communicate on a network:

▶ Through broadcast messages, which every computer receives

▶ Through directed messages, which are sent to a specific computer

Whenever possible, communicating through directed messages is preferable. This approach cuts down on the amount of network traffic and ensures that only the affected hosts receive the message. It also ensures that the messages propagate across routers. So, Microsoft needed to make sure that WINS communicated primarily with directed messages. The company accomplished this by allowing several types of NetBIOS naming methods. These naming methods are commonly called node types. A node is simply a device on a network. Every computer on a Microsoft computer is configured as one of four node types. The node type determines whether the computer will learn names through broadcast messages, directed messages, or some combination of broadcast and directed messages. Before you can work with WINS, you need to know what the node types are and when they are used:

▶ **B-node (broadcast node)**—This node relies exclusively on broadcast messages and is the oldest NetBIOS name resolution mode. A host needing to resolve a name request sends a message to every host within earshot, requesting the address associated with a hostname. B-node has two shortcomings: Broadcast traffic is undesirable and becomes a significant user of network bandwidths, and TCP/IP routers don't forward broadcast messages, which restricts B-node operation to a single network segment.

▶ **P-node (point-to-point node)**—This node relies on WINS servers for NetBIOS name resolution. Client computers register themselves with a WINS server when they come on the network. They then contact the WINS server with NetBIOS name resolution requests. WINS servers communicate using directed messages, which can cross routers, so P-node can operate on large networks. Unfortunately, if the WINS server is unavailable, or if a node isn't configured to contact a WINS server, P-node name resolution fails.

▶ **M-node (modified node)**—This hybrid mode first attempts to resolve NetBIOS names using the B-node mechanism. If that fails, an attempt is made to use P-node name resolution. M-node was the first hybrid mode put into operation, but it has the disadvantage of favoring B-node operation, which is associated with high levels of broadcast traffic.

▶ **H-node (hybrid node)**—This hybrid mode favors the use of WINS for NetBIOS name resolution. When a computer needs to resolve a NetBIOS name, it first attempts to use P-node resolution to resolve a name via WINS. Only if WINS resolution fails does the host resort to B-node to resolve the name via broadcasts. Because it typically results in the best network utilization, H-node is the default mode of operation for Microsoft TCP/IP client computers configured to use WINS for name resolution. Microsoft recommends leaving TCP/IP client computers in the default H-node configuration.

**WARNING**

**It takes two to replicate**
Remember that you must configure both partners in a replication relationship to replicate with each other; otherwise, replication does not occur.

**EXAM TIP**

**Microsoft does test on backward compatibility** Don't be fooled. Just because WINS is a legacy technology, that doesn't mean it won't be tested on the exam. Microsoft recognizes the importance of backward compatibility, and as a result, you can expect to see questions on WINS for this exam. If you have not worked with it in a legacy environment, make sure you understand how WINS works.

**IN THE FIELD**

### THE METHOD WINS USES TO RESOLVE A NAME

The time may come when you need to understand exactly how WINS resolves a name. (Because H-node is not only the default but is also the recommended configuration, we restrict our discussion to the H-node name resolution.) When a WINS client computer configured for hybrid node needs to resolve a hostname, it goes through the following series of steps:

*continues*

*continued*

1. The WINS client computer checks its NetBIOS name cache. If the name is found, that name is returned.

2. The client queries the WINS server. If the name is found, that name is returned.

3. The client issues a broadcast to find the host on the local network. If the name is found, that name is returned.

4. The client looks for the LMHOSTS file to check for an entry. If the name is found, that name is returned.

5. The client looks for the HOST file to check for an entry. If the name is found, that name is returned.

6. The client queries the DNS server for the entry. If the name is found, that name is returned.

7. If all these methods fail, the WINS client computer issues an error message saying that it cannot communicate with the host.

---

**EXAM TIP**

**Registering with WINS** When your Windows client computer enters the network, it registers with WINS so that other Microsoft client computers can resolve its name to an address. For the exam, you should be aware that although a WINS proxy server can be used to resolve names for hosts that have registered with WINS, it cannot be used to register with WINS. You need access to the WINS server to successfully register.

Another point that many people have a misconception about is how clients actually contact the WINS server. Unlike DHCP clients, WINS clients cannot locate a WINS server through broadcasts. A WINS server IP address needs to be provided to a client ahead of time either though DHCP or by manual configuration.

Although networks can be organized using a mixture of node types, Microsoft recommends against doing so. B-node client computers ignore P-node directed messages, and P-node client computers ignore B-node broadcasts. Therefore, it is conceivable that two client computers could separately be established with the same NetBIOS name. If WINS is enabled on a Windows 2000 or XP computer, the system uses H-node by default. Without WINS, the system uses B-node by default. Non-WINS client computers can access WINS through a WINS proxy, which is a WINS-enabled computer that listens to name query broadcasts and then queries the WINS server on behalf of the requesting client computer.

The actual configuration of a computer to use LMHOSTS for NetBIOS name resolution is not done by using the WINS console or a Group Policy Object, as you might expect. You must actually configure it computer by computer by setting the options available to you on the WINS tab of the Advanced TCP/IP Settings dialog box, as shown in Figure 3.18.

You have the following options available to you to allow the use of the LMHOSTS file on the local computer:

▶ **Enable LMHOSTS lookup**—This option, which is selected by default, specifies that an LMHOSTS file is to be used to resolve NetBIOS hostnames to an IP address.

▶ **Default**—This option, which is selected by default, specifies that this network connection is to obtain the NetBIOS over TCP/IP (NetBT) setting from the Windows DHCP server that granted its lease.

▶ **Enable NetBIOS over TCP/IP**—This option specifies that this network connection is to use NetBT and WINS.

▶ **Disable NetBIOS over TCP/IP**—This option specifies that this network connection is not to use NetBT and WINS.

LMHOSTS files typically contain entries similar to the following ones, which are examples given the default LMHOSTS file located in the `%systemroot%\System32\Drivers\Etc` folder:

```
102.54.94.97    rhino
102.54.94.123   popular
102.54.94.117   localsrv
```

Each entry maps a NetBIOS name to an IP address for hosts that are not located on the local subnet, thus allowing legacy clients to locate other legacy clients on the network.

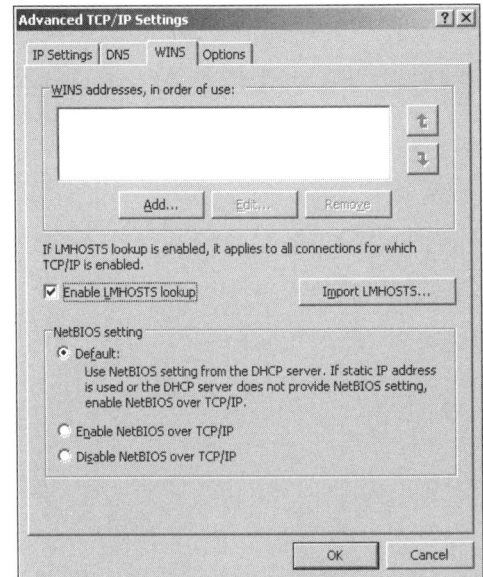

**FIGURE 3.18**
On the WINS tab of the Advanced TCP/IP Settings dialog box, you can configure the network connection to use an LMHOSTS file.

# TROUBLESHOOTING NAME RESOLUTION PROBLEMS

**Troubleshoot host name resolution.**

▶ **Diagnose and resolve issues related to DNS services.**

▶ **Diagnose and resolve issues related to client computer configuration.**

Troubleshooting name resolution is a sometimes tricky art that you may well need to master. Fortunately, Windows Server 2003 provides a wealth of tools that you can use to quickly determine and correct the cause of the problems at hand. You have five basic tools at your disposal when it comes to troubleshooting name resolution issues:

- ▶ `ipconfig`

- ▶ `ping`

- ▶ `nbtstat`

- ▶ `tracert`

- ▶ `pathping`

- ▶ `nslookup`

We will briefly examine the use of each of these tools in the following sections.

## ipconfig

The first, and easiest, step in troubleshooting any TCP/IP–related network problem is to gather information about the computer on which the problem is occurring or has been reported. The `ipconfig` command makes this process easy. To get a complete report of the computer's IP configuration properties, enter the **ipconfig/all** command at the command line. A typical output might look something like that shown here:

```
c:\>ipconfig/all

Windows IP Configuration

        Host Name . . . . . . . . . . . : a51svr3142
        Primary Dns Suffix  . . . . . . : lab1.area51partners.com
        Node Type . . . . . . . . . . . : Hybrid
        IP Routing Enabled. . . . . . . : Yes
        WINS Proxy Enabled. . . . . . . : No
        DNS Suffix Search List. . . . . : lab1.area51partners.com
                                          area51partners.com

Ethernet adapter Cluster:
        Media State . . . . . . . . . . : Media disconnected
        Description . . . . . . . . . . : Linksys LNE100TX
        Physical Address. . . . . . . . : 02-BF-0A-00-00-01

Ethernet adapter Administration:
        Connection-specific DNS Suffix  . :
        Description . . . . . . . . . . : Realtek RTL8139
        Physical Address. . . . . . . . : 00-E0-7D-C1-3E-70
```

```
DHCP Enabled. . . . . . . . . . . : No
IP Address. . . . . . . . . . . . : 192.168.0.123
Subnet Mask . . . . . . . . . . . : 255.255.255.0
Default Gateway . . . . . . . . . : 192.168.0.1
DNS Servers . . . . . . . . . . . : 192.168.0.240
                                    192.168.0.100
Primary WINS Server . . . . . . . : 192.168.0.240
Secondary WINS Server . . . . . . : 192.168.0.241
```

You can learn several key pieces of information about your computer's network connections just from examining the output of the `ipconfig/all` command. First, the top of the output tells you the hostname and domain that the computer belongs to as well as the DNS suffixes that have been configured for the computer. Note that additional connection-specific DNS suffixes are listed later in the detail. Moving down to the first network connection, `Cluster`, notice that its status is shown as `Media disconnected`, which means that either the network cable is disconnected at one or both ends or that the device the cable is attached to (a switch or hub) is not powered on. This might be your first sign of a problem.

The second network connection, `Administration`, shows the full gamut of information that can be gleaned from the `ipconfig/all` command, including whether DHCP is enabled for the adapter, the IP address assigned, the default gateway (always a prime concern when problems arise with computers on different subnets), and other critical information including the IP addresses for the DNS servers in use by the network connection. All this information can be used to identify where the problem lies by determining simply "what doesn't look right." Usually, the problem jumps right out at you after you start to look around for it.

You also can use the `ipconfig` command to display and purge the contents of the local DNS resolver cache, as shown in the following output:

```
c:\>ipconfig/displaydns

Windows IP Configuration
    1.0.0.127.in-addr.arpa
    ----------------------------------------
    Record Name . . . . . : 1.0.0.127.in-addr.arpa.
    Record Type . . . . . : 12
    Time To Live  . . . . : 276808
    Data Length . . . . . : 4
    Section . . . . . . . : Answer
    PTR Record  . . . . . : localhost
```

```
a51svr3042.lab1.area51partners.com
----------------------------------------
    Record Name . . . . . : A51SVR3042.lab1.area51partners.com
    Record Type . . . . . : 1
    Time To Live  . . . . : 2721
    Data Length . . . . . : 4
    Section . . . . . . . : Answer
    A (Host) Record . . . : 192.168.0.240

    Record Name . . . . . : A51SVR3042.lab1.area51partners.com
    Record Type . . . . . : 1
    Time To Live  . . . . : 2721
    Data Length . . . . . : 4
    Section . . . . . . . : Answer
    A (Host) Record . . . : 10.0.0.10

    Record Name . . . . . : A51SVR3042.lab1.area51partners.com
    Record Type . . . . . : 1
    Time To Live  . . . . : 2721
    Data Length . . . . . : 4
    Section . . . . . . . : Answer
    A (Host) Record . . . : 10.0.0.1

c:\>ipconfig/flushdns

Windows IP Configuration
Successfully flushed the DNS Resolver Cache.

c:\>ipconfig/displaydns

Windows IP Configuration
    1.0.0.127.in-addr.arpa
    ----------------------------------------
    Record Name . . . . . : 1.0.0.127.in-addr.arpa.
    Record Type . . . . . : 12
    Time To Live  . . . . : 276751
    Data Length . . . . . : 4
    Section . . . . . . . : Answer
    PTR Record  . . . . . : localhost

    localhost
    ----------------------------------------
    Record Name . . . . . : localhost
    Record Type . . . . . : 1
    Time To Live  . . . . : 276751
    Data Length . . . . . : 4
    Section . . . . . . . : Answer
    A (Host) Record . . . : 127.0.0.1
```

This command can be helpful in situations in which the local DNS cache is corrupt or contains invalid information. This cache will rebuild itself over time as the computer queries DNS servers.

# ping

The ping command is practically as old as TCP/IP networking itself. You can use the ping command to test basic network connectivity between two computers, over local and remote networks. The basic syntax of the ping command looks something like ping *computerIP* or ping *HostName*. This command causes Windows to send four special Internet Control Message Protocol (ICMP) packets to the remote computer that are then returned to the local computer. You can instruct Windows to send a continuous stream of ping packets by using the ping -t command. Using the ping -a command specifies that name resolution is to be performed during the ping process.

You can see the standard output of the ping command here without the use of any modifying switches:

```
C:\>ping mcseworld.com

Pinging mcseworld.com [207.44.182.13] with 32 bytes of data:

Reply from 207.44.182.13: bytes=32 time=57ms TTL=46
Reply from 207.44.182.13: bytes=32 time=53ms TTL=46
Reply from 207.44.182.13: bytes=32 time=52ms TTL=46
Reply from 207.44.182.13: bytes=32 time=51ms TTL=46

Ping statistics for 207.44.182.13:
    Packets: Sent = 4, Received = 4, Lost = 0 (0% loss),
Approximate round trip times in milli-seconds:
    Minimum = 51ms, Maximum = 57ms, Average = 53ms
```

Note, however, that some remote firewalls and routers have been configured to block ICMP packets (once commonly used to stage Denial of Service attacks), and you might see output like this:

```
C:\>ping microsoft.com

Pinging microsoft.com [207.46.245.222] with 32 bytes of data:

Request timed out.
Request timed out.
Request timed out.
Request timed out.

Ping statistics for 207.46.245.222:
    Packets: Sent = 4, Received = 0, Lost = 4 (100% loss)
```

You can also test the TCP/IP stack on the local network adapter by using the ping loopback or ping 127.0.0.1 command, as shown here:

**NOTE**

**The story of ping**  If you want to see the history of the ping command and learn some other interesting ping-related trivia, be sure to visit the page of the late Mike Muuss, creator of the ping application. You can find it located at

```
C:\>ping loopback

Pinging a51svr3142.lab1.area51partners.com [127.0.0.1] with 32
➥bytes of data:

Reply from 127.0.0.1: bytes=32 time<1ms TTL=128
Reply from 127.0.0.1: bytes=32 time<1ms TTL=128
Reply from 127.0.0.1: bytes=32 time<1ms TTL=128
Reply from 127.0.0.1: bytes=32 time<1ms TTL=128

Ping statistics for 127.0.0.1:
    Packets: Sent = 4, Received = 4, Lost = 0 (0% loss),
Approximate round trip times in milli-seconds:
    Minimum = 0ms, Maximum = 0ms, Average = 0ms
```

If pinging the loopback address works, but you cannot successfully
ping an outside address, you might try pinging the default gateway
for the specific computer. How do you know what the default gateway is? Look back at the output of the ipconfig/all command to
gather this information. Pinging the default gateway's IP address lets
you know if any problems you are having are being caused by the
default gateway itself. Of course, the ipconfig/all command shows
only the private IP address of the default gateway; you also need to
know and ping the public IP address of publicly addressable gateways, such as border routers and firewalls.

## nbtstat

If your problem seems to be WINS and NetBT specific, you might
consider using the nbtstat command to gather information and
troubleshoot the problem at hand. nbtstat can be used to display
the local NetBIOS table on the computer, display the content of the
local NetBIOS cache on the computer, or even purge the local
NetBIOS cache.

You can use several different switches with nbtstat to determine
how it returns information to you. Using the nbtstat -n command
returns the local NetBIOS name table, as shown here:

```
C:\>nbtstat -n

Cluster:
Node IpAddress: [0.0.0.0] Scope Id: []
    No names in cache

Administration:
Node IpAddress: [192.168.0.123] Scope Id: []
                NetBIOS Local Name Table
```

```
      Name              Type      Status
      ------------------------------------------------
      A51SVR3142    <00>  UNIQUE      Registered
      LAB1          <00>  GROUP       Registered
      A51SVR3142    <20>  UNIQUE      Registered
      LAB1          <1E>  GROUP       Registered
```

If you need to list the contents of the NetBIOS name cache, use the
nbtstat -c command to produce the following output:

```
C:\>nbtstat -c

Cluster:
Node IpAddress: [0.0.0.0] Scope Id: []
    No names in cache

Administration:
Node IpAddress: [192.168.0.123] Scope Id: []
                NetBIOS Remote Cache Name Table

      Name              Type      Host Address   Life [sec]
      -------------------------------------------------------
      A51SVR3042.LAB1<2E>  UNIQUE        192.168.0.240       525
      A51SVR3042    <20>  UNIQUE        192.168.0.240       97
      W2KSVR001     <00>  UNIQUE        192.168.0.101       537
```

To examine the NetBIOS name table of a remote computer, use the
nbtstat -a *RemoteComputerName* command to produce the following
output:

```
C:\>nbtstat -a a51svr3042

Cluster:
Node IpAddress: [0.0.0.0] Scope Id: []
    Host not found.

Administration:
Node IpAddress: [192.168.0.123] Scope Id: []
         NetBIOS Remote Machine Name Table

      Name              Type      Status
      ------------------------------------------------
      A51SVR3042    <00>  UNIQUE      Registered
      LAB1          <00>  GROUP       Registered
      LAB1          <1C>  GROUP       Registered
      A51SVR3042    <20>  UNIQUE      Registered
      LAB1          <1B>  UNIQUE      Registered
      LAB1          <1E>  GROUP       Registered
      LAB1          <1D>  UNIQUE      Registered
      .._MSBROWSE__.<01>  GROUP       Registered

      MAC Address = 00-E0-7D-C1-3E-0E
```

To display a listing of client and server connections, use the nbtstat
-s command to produce the following output:

```
C:\>nbtstat -s

Cluster:
Node IpAddress: [0.0.0.0] Scope Id: []

    No Connections

Administration:
Node IpAddress: [192.168.0.123] Scope Id: []

                    NetBIOS Connection Table

    Local Name        State      In/Out  Remote Host      Input   Output

    ................................................................

    A51SVR3142 <00>  Connected   Out    W2KSVR001 <20>   97MB     92MB
```

You can also clear the contents of the cache and reload it from the LMHOSTS file by using the nbtstat -R command. You must use an uppercase R in this command. To release and subsequently refresh name records on a WINS server, issue the nbtstat -RR command.

## tracert

tracert is another of the old standby tools that network administrations have grown to love over time. tracert routes tracing from the source to the destination, showing all intermediate hops (routers) that are used to forward and deliver the packets to their destination. As well, tracert calculates how long each hop takes. The basic use of tracert yields output like the following:

```
C:\>tracert mcseworld.com

Tracing route to mcseworld.com [207.44.182.13]
over a maximum of 30 hops:

  1    16 ms    13 ms    22 ms  ip68-0-16-1.hr.hr.cox.net [68.0.16.1]
  2    74 ms    47 ms    19 ms  68.10.8.41
  3    19 ms    14 ms    16 ms  nrfksysr02-atm151103.hr.hr.cox.net
     ➡ [68.10.8.53]
  4    16 ms    14 ms    35 ms  nrfkdsrc02-gew0304.rd.hr.cox.net
     ➡ [68.10.14.17]
  5    17 ms    18 ms    12 ms  nrfkbbrc02-pos0101.rd.hr.cox.net
     ➡ [68.1.0.26]
  6    18 ms    18 ms    18 ms  nrfkdsrc02-gew03010999.rd.hr.cox.net
     ➡ [68.1.0.31]
  7    27 ms    24 ms    18 ms  ashbbbpc01pos0100.r2.as.cox.net
     ➡ [68.1.1.19]
  8    23 ms    16 ms    28 ms  68.105.30.70
  9    60 ms    53 ms    61 ms  hrndva1wcx2-pos0-0.wcg.net [64.200.89.1]
```

```
10    80 ms    54 ms    61 ms   drvlga1wcx2-pos4-0.wcg.net
   ➦ [64.200.232.125]
11    60 ms    51 ms    54 ms   drvlga1wcx1-oc48.wcg.net [64.200.127.49]
12    53 ms    61 ms    56 ms   dllstx1wcx3-oc48.wcg.net [64.200.240.21]
13    62 ms    61 ms    58 ms   dllstx1wcx2-pos10-0.wcg.net
   ➦ [64.200.110.133]
14    63 ms    56 ms    58 ms   hstntx1wce2-pos4-0.wcg.net
   ➦ [64.200.240.74]
15   124 ms    67 ms    56 ms
   ➦hstntx1wce2-everyonesinternet-gige.wcg.net [65.77.93.54]
16    74 ms    55 ms    55 ms   39.ev1.net [207.218.245.39]
17    62 ms    56 ms    56 ms   www.mcseworld.com [207.44.182.13]

Trace complete.
```

# pathping

The pathping command is a new tool first introduced in Windows 2000 that combines the capabilities of ping and tracert into one tool. pathping is used to gather information about network latency and network loss at the intermediate hops between the source and destination. It accomplishes this by sending multiple ICMP messages to each router between the source and destination over a period of time and then computing results based on the packets returned from each router. pathping can thus be used to quickly determine the operational status of each router or subnet the packets must cross. A pathping output is presented here:

```
C:\>pathping mcseworld.com

Tracing route to mcseworld.com [207.44.182.13]
over a maximum of 30 hops:
  0  a51svr3142.lab1.area51partners.com [192.168.0.123]
  1  ip68-0-16-1.hr.hr.cox.net [68.0.16.1]
  2  ip68-0-16-1.hr.hr.cox.net [68.0.16.1]
  3  nrfksysr02-atm151103.hr.hr.cox.net [68.10.8.53]
  4  nrfkdsrc02-gew0304.rd.hr.cox.net [68.10.14.17]
  5  nrfkbbrc02-pos0101.rd.hr.cox.net [68.1.0.26]
  6  nrfkdsrc02-gew03010999.rd.hr.cox.net [68.1.0.31]
  7  ashbbbpc01pos0100.r2.as.cox.net [68.1.1.19]
  8  68.105.30.70
  9  hrndva1wcx2-pos0-0.wcg.net [64.200.89.1]
 10  drvlga1wcx2-pos4-0.wcg.net [64.200.232.125]
 11  drvlga1wcx1-oc48.wcg.net [64.200.127.49]
 12  dllstx1wcx3-oc48.wcg.net [64.200.240.21]
 13  dllstx1wcx2-pos10-0.wcg.net [64.200.110.133]
 14  hstntx1wce2-pos4-0.wcg.net [64.200.240.74]
 15  hstntx1wce2-everyonesinternet-gige.wcg.net [65.77.93.54]
 16  39.ev1.net [207.218.245.39]
 17  host6.wfdns.com [207.44.182.13]
```

```
                Computing statistics for 425 seconds...
                      Source to Here   This Node/Link
         Hop  RTT     Lost/Sent = Pct  Lost/Sent = Pct  Address
          0                                              a51svr3142.lab1.
        ➥area51partners.com [192.168.0.123]
                                        0/ 100 =  0%    |
          1   22ms     0/ 100 =  0%     0/ 100 =  0%    ip68-0-16-1.hr.hr.
        ➥cox.net [68.0.16.1]
                                        0/ 100 =  0%    |
          2   22ms     0/ 100 =  0%     0/ 100 =  0%    ip68-0-16-1.hr.hr.
        ➥cox.net [68.0.16.1]
                                        0/ 100 =  0%    |
          3   17ms    18/ 100 = 18%    18/ 100 = 18%    nrfksysr02-
        ➥atm151103.hr.hr.cox.net [68.10.8.53]
                                        0/ 100 =  0%    |
          4   20ms     0/ 100 =  0%     0/ 100 =  0%    nrfkdsrc02-
        ➥gew0304.rd.hr.cox.net [68.10.14.17]
                                        0/ 100 =  0%    |
          5   17ms     1/ 100 =  1%     1/ 100 =  1%    nrfkbbrc02-
        ➥pos0101.rd.hr.cox.net [68.1.0.26]
                                        0/ 100 =  0%    |
          6   23ms     2/ 100 =  2%     2/ 100 =  2%    nrfkdsrc02-
        ➥gew03010999.rd.hr.cox.net [68.1.0.31]
                                        0/ 100 =  0%    |
          7   26ms     1/ 100 =  1%     1/ 100 =  1%
        ➥ashbbbpc01pos0100.r2.as.cox.net [68.1.1.19]
                                        0/ 100 =  0%    |
          8   24ms     0/ 100 =  0%     0/ 100 =  0%    68.105.30.70
                                        0/ 100 =  0%    |
          9   23ms     0/ 100 =  0%     0/ 100 =  0%    hrndva1wcx2-pos0-0.wcg.net
        ➥[64.200.89.1]
                                        0/ 100 =  0%    |
         10   35ms     0/ 100 =  0%     0/ 100 =  0%    drvlga1wcx2-pos4-0.wcg.net
        ➥[64.200.232.125]
                                        0/ 100 =  0%    |
         11   35ms     1/ 100 =  1%     1/ 100 =  1%    drvlga1wcx1-oc48.wcg.net
        ➥[64.200.127.49]
                                        0/ 100 =  0%    |
         12   53ms     1/ 100 =  1%     1/ 100 =  1%    dllstx1wcx3-oc48.wcg.net
        ➥[64.200.240.21]
                                        0/ 100 =  0%    |
         13   52ms     2/ 100 =  2%     2/ 100 =  2%    dllstx1wcx2-pos10-0.wcg.net
        ➥[64.200.110.133]
                                        0/ 100 =  0%    |
         14   58ms     0/ 100 =  0%     0/ 100 =  0%    hstntx1wce2-pos4-0.wcg.net
        ➥[64.200.240.74]
                                        0/ 100 =  0%    |
         15   59ms     0/ 100 =  0%     0/ 100 =  0%    hstntx1wce2-
        ➥everyonesinternet-gige.wcg.net [65.77.93.54]
                                        0/ 100 =  0%    |
         16   58ms     1/ 100 =  1%     1/ 100 =  1%    39.ev1.net [207.218.245.39]
                                        0/ 100 =  0%    |
         17   59ms     0/ 100 =  0%     0/ 100 =  0%    mcseworld.com
        ➥[207.44.182.13]

        Trace complete.
```

As you can see from this `pathping` output, the network connectivity between source and destination is overall very good. The only (small) problem appears to be that the router located at 68.10.8.53 is dropping about 18% of the packets sent to it; this, however, does not appear to be adversely affecting the transmission as a whole.

## nslookup

The `nslookup` command can be used to look up and display information for troubleshooting DNS issues. `nslookup`, however, is not a simple tool that you can jump right into with a fair amount of DNS knowledge. Unlike other troubleshooting tools, `nslookup` has an interactive and noninteractive usage mode—much the same as the `netsh` command.

When looking up a single item, you would be best off using the noninteractive mode by issuing a command similar to the following:

```
nslookup mcseworld.com 192.168.0.100
```

In this example, the first parameter specifies the DNS name or IP address of the computer you want to look up, and the second parameter specifies the DNS name or IP address of the DNS server you want to use. If you do not specify a DNS server, the default DNS server for the requesting computer will be used. This sample `nslookup` query might return a result such as this:

```
U:\>nslookup mcseworld.com 192.168.0.100
Server:  w2ksvr001.dontpanic.local
Address:  192.168.0.100

Non-authoritative answer:
Name:    mcseworld.com
Address:  207.44.182.13
```

If you need to look up multiple pieces of information or more complex information, such as information about specific resource records contained in a zone, you need to use `nslookup` in interactive mode. You can see how interactive mode can be used to gain more advanced information, such as the list of all name servers (NS resource record) and mail exchangers (MX resource record) for the `microsoft.com` zone.

```
U:\>nslookup
Default Server:  w2ksvr001.dontpanic.local
Address:  192.168.0.100
```

```
> server ns2.hr.cox.net
Default Server:  ns2.hr.cox.net
Address:  68.10.16.25

> set type=ns
> microsoft.com
Server:  ns2.hr.cox.net
Address:  68.10.16.25

Non-authoritative answer:
microsoft.com    nameserver = dns1.tk.msft.net
microsoft.com    nameserver = dns3.uk.msft.net
microsoft.com    nameserver = dns1.cp.msft.net
microsoft.com    nameserver = dns1.sj.msft.net

dns1.cp.msft.net        internet address = 207.46.138.20
dns1.sj.msft.net        internet address = 65.54.248.222
dns1.tk.msft.net        internet address = 207.46.245.230
dns3.uk.msft.net        internet address = 213.199.144.151
> set type=mx
> microsoft.com
Server:  ns2.hr.cox.net
Address:  68.10.16.25

:
microsoft.com    MX preference = 10, mail exchanger = mailb.microsoft.com
microsoft.com    MX preference = 10, mail exchanger = mailc.microsoft.com
microsoft.com    MX preference = 10, mail exchanger = maila.microsoft.com

microsoft.com    nameserver = dns1.cp.msft.net
microsoft.com    nameserver = dns1.sj.msft.net
microsoft.com    nameserver = dns1.tk.msft.net
microsoft.com    nameserver = dns3.uk.msft.net
maila.microsoft.com     internet address = 131.107.3.124
maila.microsoft.com     internet address = 131.107.3.125
mailb.microsoft.com     internet address = 131.107.3.123
mailb.microsoft.com     internet address = 131.107.3.122
mailc.microsoft.com     internet address = 131.107.3.121
mailc.microsoft.com     internet address = 131.107.3.126
dns1.cp.msft.net        internet address = 207.46.138.20
dns1.sj.msft.net        internet address = 65.54.248.222
dns1.tk.msft.net        internet address = 207.46.245.230
dns3.uk.msft.net        internet address = 213.199.144.151
>
```

The Non-authoritative answer label indicates that this information
was retrieved from the selected DNS server's local cache and was not
directly queried as a result of the nslookup query.

You can exit interactive mode at any time by typing **exit**.

The nslookup command has an extremely large feature set, too large
to do justice to it here in this space. You can get more information

on the full use and functionality of `nslookup` at www.microsoft.com/
technet/prodtechnol/windowsserver2003/proddocs/standard/
nslookup.asp.

## CASE STUDY

### ESSENCE OF THE CASE

Following are the essential elements in this case:

▶ You will need to plan a new DNS name-space that meets the requirements outlined by the CEO and CIO.

▶ You will need to use a delegated name-space to provide the required results.

▶ Secure dynamic updates in an Active Directory–integrated zone will be required to provide the DNS data protection required while still allowing clients to update their IP address information in DNS.

▶ Conditional forwarding will be configured to forward all name resolution requests for the `ricksrockets.com` domain to the external DNS servers provided by the ISP.

### SCENARIO

Rick's Rockets is a leading manufacturer of toy rocket kits. Rick's currently owns the `ricksrockets.com` domain name and uses its ISP to host its Web, FTP, and email services through that domain name. Rick's current internal network is extremely decentralized and disorganized and is actually still functioning as a Windows 2000 workgroup. All workstations are Windows 2000 Professional, and all servers are Windows 2000 Advanced Server.

You have been hired by Rick, the CEO of Rick's Rockets, to plan and implement a completely new network infrastructure to include an internal DNS namespace to support the rollout of Windows Server 2003 and Active Directory. Rick's Rockets will not be purchasing any additional publicly accessible domain names. Rick's will be upgrading its Windows 2000 Advanced Server licenses to Windows Server 2003 Enterprise Edition licenses to support the new network plan.

Roger, the CIO of Rick's Rockets, has informed you that he wants the new internal DNS namespace to be easy for users to remember but to provide complete isolation from the external DNS namespace. Internal clients should be allowed to resolve IP addresses for external resources, but external clients should not be able to resolve IP addresses for internal resources. All clients should automatically update their IP addresses in DNS, and DNS should accept updates only from

*continues*

## CASE STUDY

*continued*

authorized clients to increase security of the internal DNS servers. The internal DNS servers should not be able to resolve external IP addresses directly but should provide forwarding to the external DNS servers maintained by Rick's ISP.

### ANALYSIS

You propose to create a delegated namespace, such as `corp.ricksrockets.com` for the internal network. It will provide an easy-to-remember namespace for users while still isolating the internal network from the external network.

If you create Active Directory–integrated zones using secure dynamic updates, all Windows 2000 workstation clients will be able to automatically update their DNS information after receiving a DHCP lease. Secure dynamic updates also prevent unauthorized clients from polluting the DNS data with bad information.

By configuring conditional forwarding for the `ricksrockets.com` zone, you can ensure that all name resolution requests are performed as quickly as possible for your clients without having to host the zone on your internal DNS servers.

## CHAPTER SUMMARY

### KEY TERMS

Before taking the exam, make sure you are comfortable with the definitions and concepts for each of the following key terms. You can use Appendix A, "Glossary," for quick reference.

- Active Directory
- Active Directory–integrated zone
- B-node
- Conditional forwarding

In the TCP/IP network of today's connected world, DNS is no longer a nicety; it's a requirement. Originally created to replace the antiquated and difficult-to-maintain HOSTS file, the domain name system (DNS) has quickly seen its popularity rise as TCP/IP has become the king of all networking protocols. Microsoft has lead the charge to make TCP/IP and DNS the de facto standards for all networks, small and large.

Because DNS is so critical to a Windows Server 2003 network, it is important that you prepare adequately before implementing your DNS solution. Only through proper prior planning can you be reasonably well assured of not having any problems down the road. The first decision you will need to make is what your DNS namespace will look like. You will need to choose from using an existing, delegated, or unique namespace.

# CHAPTER SUMMARY

After choosing your namespace, you can determine what types of zones you will require as well as how you will configure forwarding to occur. You will, of course, also want to look into securing your DNS infrastructure from attack and compromise. By choosing an Active Directory–integrated zone, you can ease administrative burden and increase DNS security.

If you have other DNS systems in use on your network, you will need to decide what their role is to be in your Windows Server 2003 network. Will you upgrade these servers to a newer version that is compatible with and supports the DNS requirements of Windows Server 2003? If not, you should consider migrating their DNS zones over to your Windows Server 2003 DNS servers and then retiring these legacy DNS servers or making them secondaries for improved redundancy.

Although Windows Server 2003 networks do not normally require WINS, WINS is still very much alive and available for use to ensure that legacy Windows clients can actively participate in newer networks that use the more robust DNS for name resolution. You should have a good understanding of the basics of WINS, including the LMHOSTS file, and how to maintain and monitor WINS. WINS servers do not perform zone transfers, as do standard DNS zones; they replicate—the same term used for Active Directory–integrated DNS zones. You must be able to configure and manage WINS replication if your network is distributed over more than one site or has more than one WINS server.

When something goes awry with a TCP/IP configuration, you need to be able to determine the cause and required corrective action. Windows Server 2003 (and Windows XP) provide a suite of tools that you can use to troubleshoot TCP/IP configuration. You will most commonly find yourself relying on the ipconfig, ping, nbtstat, tracert, pathping, and nslookup command-line tools.

## KEY TERMS

- Discretionary Access Control List (DACL)
- Domain name service (DNS)
- Dynamic Host Configuration Protocol (DHCP)
- DNS client dynamic update
- DNS forwarder
- DNS resolver
- DNS Security (DNSSEC)
- DNS slave server
- Dynamic updates from DHCP
- Fully qualified domain name (FQDN)
- H-node
- Internet Control Message Protocol (ICMP)
- ipconfig
- Iterative query
- LAN Manager HOSTS (LMHOSTS)
- Leaf
- M-node
- NetBIOS
- nbtstat
- pathping
- ping

## CHAPTER SUMMARY

- P-node
- Push replication
- Pull replication
- Push/pull replication
- Recursive query
- Replication partner
- Secure dynamic update
- Standard primary zone
- Standard secondary zone
- Stub zone
- Top-level domain (TLD)
- tracert
- Transmission Control Protocol/Internet Protocol (TCP/IP)
- Tree
- Windows Internet Naming Service (WINS)
- Zone
- Zone transfer

| APPLY YOUR KNOWLEDGE | |
|---|---|

## Exercises

### 3.1 Testing TCP/IP

This exercise guides you through the process of retrieving IP address information. Then you use a few command-line entries to test the configuration and connectivity of the IP address.

**Estimated time:** 10 minutes

1. Select Start, Run. Then type **CMD** and press Enter.

2. At the command prompt, type the command **ipconfig** and press Enter. What is your IP address? What is your subnet mask? Can you determine the IP address of the DNS server?

3. Enter **ipconfig/all**. What additional information can you now see?

4. Enter **ping 127.0.0.1**. This is a special loopback test that tells you whether your network interface card is dead, just playing sick, or, you hope, just fine.

5. Enter **ping XX**, where *XX* is your favorite Web site.

6. If you have another computer on this network, ping the IP address of that computer.

7. ping the name of the computer.

8. Did all your communications occur successfully? If not, you may need to perform some additional investigation and troubleshooting to determine where your problem lies. Note that more and more publicly accessible networks (such as microsoft.com) now actively drop ICMP packets, thus preventing the ping command from working properly.

### 3.2 Configuring a Replication Partner

In this exercise, you configure a replication partner.

**Estimated time:** 10 minutes

1. Open the WINS console by clicking Start, Programs, Administrative Tools, WINS.

2. In the right pane, right-click Replication Partners and select New Replication Partner. The New Replication Partner dialog box opens and asks you to enter the address of another WINS server. You can enter either the server name or IP address. If the server name cannot be resolved, you are prompted to enter the address of the server.

3. Enter the name or IP address of the server and click OK.

4. Click Replication Partners in the left pane of the WINS console. You should see your new replication partner in the right pane.

5. Right-click the newly created replication partner. Then select Properties from the context menu to open the Replication Partner Properties dialog box.

6. Click the Advanced tab. On this tab, you can configure the replication properties for the replication partner. You can choose from Push/Pull (the default), Push, or Pull. You can also specify the options to control how and when the replication is to occur.

7. Click OK when the settings meet your requirements.

## APPLY YOUR KNOWLEDGE

### 3.3   Performing a Manual Push Replication

In this exercise, you manually perform a push replication.

**Estimated time:** 10 minutes

1. Open the WINS console by clicking Start, Programs, Administrative Tools, WINS.

2. Right-click WINS Server and select Start Push Replication.

3. Enter the DNS name or IP address of the other WINS server and click OK.

4. Select Start for This Partner Only as the replication method. You can select Propagate to All Partners as the other method. Click OK. You receive a message that the replication request has been queued.

5. Check the event log for the status of the request and to see when it is completed.

### 3.4   Performing a Manual Pull Replication

In this exercise, you manually perform a pull replication.

**Estimated time:** 10 minutes

1. Open the WINS console by clicking Start, Programs, Administrative Tools, WINS.

2. Right-click the WINS Server and select Start Pull Replication.

3. Enter the DNS name or IP address of the other WINS server and click OK.

4. When asked to confirm the request, click Yes. You receive a message stating that the replication request has been queued.

5. Check the event log for the status of the request and to see when it is completed.

## Review Questions

1. You need to determine if one of the routers between your network and your partner's network is dropping packets. What command-line utility can you use to make this determination?

2. You are planning a new Windows Server 2003 Active Directory network for your organization. The organization currently uses three Unix BIND DNS servers. What minimum version of BIND do you need to have to support Active Directory?

3. You have been directed to create a new DNS namespace for your company. The namespace must be as short as possible and be easily accessible from inside and outside your organization. The namespace will be used within a screened subnet to host a publicly accessible e-commerce application. What type of namespace should you implement?

4. You are considering setting up WINS for your network. You feel you need a better understanding of how NetBIOS works and how the different node types work. What are the four NetBIOS node types, and how do they work?

5. What is the major difference between push replication and pull replication?

## Exam Questions

1. You are currently planning the DNS namespace for a new Windows Server 2003 deployment. The namespace will be used only for the internal network. There will be a separate public network located in a DMZ with a different DNS namespace. Which of the following DNS namespaces

## APPLY YOUR KNOWLEDGE

would be acceptable on the internal network but not on the public network? (Choose all that apply.)

A. `bigcorp.com`

B. `bigcorp.corp`

C. `bigcorp.local`

D. `corp.bigcorp.com`

E. `local.bigcorp.com`

2. You are the network administrator for Rick's Rockets, a leading aerospace manufacturing corporation. You have several dozen legacy clients on your network that require WINS to be available. You are configuring a new Windows Server 2003 computer to act as WINS servers for your network. You also have one existing Windows 2000 Server computer providing WINS services. You want replication to occur after a certain number of changes have occurred. What configuration do you need to make?

A. Configure a push partner on the Advanced tab of your WINS server properties page.

B. Configure a pull partner on the Advanced tab of your WINS server properties page.

C. Configure a push partner on the Settings tab of your WINS server properties page.

D. Configure a pull partner on the Settings tab of your WINS server properties page.

3. You are a network consultant who has been hired by Carmen's Clown College, Inc. You have been given the task of designing a delegated DNS namespace for Carmen's new Windows Server 2003 network. Carmen's already owns the `clowncollege.com` domain, and its ISP is hosting

its Web site. Which of the following options represents a valid delegated DNS namespace?

A. `clowncollege.net`

B. `corp.clowncollege.com`

C. `clowncollege.corp.com`

D. `clowncollege.com.corp`

4. You are the network administrator for a five-location pet food manufacturer. You have WINS servers at all five locations, and you would like them to replicate with each other automatically. What should you do?

A. Configure each WINS server as a replication partner. In Replication Partner properties, select Replicate with All Partners.

B. Configure each WINS server as a replication partner. In Replication Partner properties, select Replicate Only with Partners.

C. In Replication Partner properties, deselect Replicate Only with Partners. The server will automatically replicate with any WINS servers.

D. Install WINS. Any WINS servers on the network will automatically replicate.

5. You are interviewing Chris, a candidate for an assistant administrator position in your company. When you ask her what a standard secondary zone is, what answer should she tell you?

A. A zone that holds a writable copy of the zone data and that can transfer it to all configured servers

B. A zone that holds a read-only copy of the zone data

## APPLY YOUR KNOWLEDGE

C. A zone that has its zone data held within Active Directory

D. A zone that contains only those resource records necessary to identify the authoritative DNS servers for a zone

6. You are the network administrator for Blue Sky Air, and you are training another administrator to assist with maintaining the network. She is having a hard time understanding the different NetBIOS node types, especially what type the Windows 2000 Professional and Windows XP Professional computers use. What is the default node type for these computers?

A. H-node

B. M-node

C. P-node

D. B-node

7. You are a senior consultant for Legacy Systems, Inc., a leading consultancy that helps organizations integrate their existing networks with newer technologies, such as Windows Server 2003. You are currently trying to get the existing BIND DNS implementation working with the newer Windows Server 2003 DNS service. Eventually, you will be able to migrate the existing BIND DNS zones to Windows Server 2003, but the customer wants this to occur over a six-month period, to prepare for any troubles. There are several different BIND servers, all of different versions. You are not sure what the version is on each of them. What setting can you change in the Windows Server 2003 DNS configuration to ensure that zone transfers succeed between the Windows Server 2003 DNS servers and the BIND servers?

A. BIND Secondaries

B. Enable Round-robin

C. Enable Netmask Ordering

D. Secure Cache Against Pollution

8. You are the system administrator for Widgets and Things, Inc. You are installing a WINS server on your Windows Server 2003 server. Your end users are all using DHCP. What is the best way to configure the workstations to utilize the WINS server?

A. Make sure the WINS server is installed on a domain controller. WINS resolution will happen automatically.

B. Modify the DHCP scope options for the WINS server to include the address of the new WINS server.

C. Open the Network applet and open the TCP/IP properties. On the WINS tab, modify the TCP/IP properties to point to the WINS server. Repeat this procedure for each machine.

D. Update the LMHOSTS file to include the address of the new WINS server.

9. A client computer that makes a DNS query to a DNS server for name resolution of a remote host is referred to as what?

A. A recursive query

B. An iterative query

C. A DNS resolver

D. A DNS forwarder

## APPLY YOUR KNOWLEDGE

10. The WINS service was created to replace what?

    A. The domain name service

    B. The HOSTS file

    C. The LMHOSTS file

    D. The WINS file

11. You are a senior consultant for Legacy Systems, Inc., a leading consultancy that helps organizations integrate their existing networks with newer technologies, such as Windows Server 2003. You are currently trying to get the existing BIND DNS implementation working with the newer Windows Server 2003 DNS service. Eventually, you will be able to migrate the existing BIND DNS zones to Windows Server 2003, but the customer wants this to occur over a six-month period, to prepare for any troubles. There are several different BIND servers, all of different versions. You are not sure what the version is on each of them. What is the minimum version of BIND that you will require on these BIND servers to ensure that they meet the DNS requirements of Active Directory?

    A. 4.9.4

    B. 4.9.6

    C. 8.1.2

    D. 8.2.1

12. You are the WAN administrator for the Women's Place clothing store. You have six satellite locations all connected with low bandwidth WAN links. Each location has its own WINS server for name resolution and will need to be replicated to. What is the best configuration for the WINS replication from the corporate WINS server to those in the field?

    A. Configure a pull replication from the remote servers to the central server and schedule it to occur whenever 100 entries have been added to the table.

    B. Configure a push replication from the remote servers to the central server and schedule it to occur whenever 100 entries have been added to the table.

    C. Configure a pull replication from the central server to the remote servers and schedule it to occur whenever 100 entries have been added to the table.

    D. Configure a push replication from the central server to the remote servers and schedule it to occur whenever 100 entries have been added to the table.

13. By default, with what DNS servers will a Windows Server 2003 DNS server perform zone transfers?

    A. Only those servers listed on the Zone Transfers tab of the zone properties dialog box.

    B. Only those servers listed on the Name Servers tab of the zone properties dialog box.

    C. All servers listed on the Name Servers and Zone Transfers tabs of the zone properties dialog box.

    D. All servers not listed on the Name Servers and Zone Transfers tabs of the zone properties dialog box.

## APPLY YOUR KNOWLEDGE

14. You are troubleshooting network connectivity between two computers on a routed IP network. What command can you use to send a continuous flow of ICMP echo request packets to the destination IP address?

    A. `ping -a`

    B. `ping -t`

    C. `ping -l`

    D. `ping -f`

15. You are configuring your Windows Server 2003 DNS servers for increased security. You are concerned about the possibility of queries' responses containing resource records that are not pertinent to the original queries. What option can you select that will prevent this from occurring by allowing the DNS server to not cache a resource record if it is not part of the exact DNS domain tree for which the original query was made?

    A. BIND Secondaries

    B. Enable Round-robin

    C. Enable Netmask Ordering

    D. Secure Cache Against Pollution

# Answers to Review Questions

1. The `pathping` command combines the functionality of the `ping` and `tracert` commands and allows you to quickly determine which routers or subnets are dropping packets. For more information, see the section "`pathping`."

2. The BIND servers need to be at version 4.9.6 (support for SRV resource records). For more

   information, see the section "Integrating with Third-Party DNS Solutions."

3. You should implement a unique DNS namespace. This option uses a completely separate but related domain name for your internal namespace. As an example, if you are using `bigcorp.com` for your external namespace, you might use `bigcorp.net` for your internal namespace. This configuration provides the advantage of improving security by isolating the two namespaces from each other. For more information, see the section "Planning a DNS Namespace Design."

4. The main differentiator between the four node types is the methods they use for name resolution (broadcast versus direct connection). The four types are as follows:

   B-node (broadcast node), which relies exclusively on broadcast messages and is the oldest NetBIOS name resolution mode. A host needing to resolve a name request sends a message to every host within earshot, requesting the address associated with a hostname. B-node has two shortcomings: broadcast traffic is undesirable and becomes a significant user of network bandwidths, and TCP/IP routers don't forward broadcast messages, which restricts B-node operation to a single network segment.

   P-node (point-to-point node, which relies on WINS servers for NetBIOS name resolution). Client computers register themselves with a WINS server when they come on the network. They then contact the WINS server with NetBIOS name resolution requests. WINS servers communicate using directed messages, which can cross routers, so P-node can operate

## APPLY YOUR KNOWLEDGE

on large networks. Unfortunately, if the WINS server is unavailable or if a node isn't configured to contact a WINS server, P-node name resolution fails.

M-node (modified node) is a hybrid mode that first attempts to resolve NetBIOS names using the B-node mechanism. If that fails, an attempt is made to use P-node name resolution. M-node was the first hybrid mode put into operation, but it has the disadvantage of favoring B-node operation, which is associated with high levels of broadcast traffic.

H-node (hybrid node) is also a hybrid mode that favors the use of WINS for NetBIOS name resolution. When a computer needs to resolve a NetBIOS name, it first attempts to use P-node resolution to resolve a name via WINS. Only if WINS resolution fails does the host resort to B-node to resolve the name via broadcasts. Because it typically results in the best network utilization, H-node is the default mode of operation for Microsoft TCP/IP networks configured to use WINS for name resolution. Microsoft recommends leaving TCP/IP client computers in the default H-node configuration. For more information, see the section "Implementing NetBIOS Name Resolution."

5. The main difference between push and pull replication (besides the direction the database is replicated) is the trigger for the event. In the case of a push replication, the trigger is event based. When a specified number of changes are made to the database, the replication is triggered. A pull replication is triggered by the time configured for the replication. This is user configured. For more information, see the section "Implementing WINS Replication."

## Answers to Exam Questions

1. **B, C.** The `bigcorp.corp` and `bigcorp.local` namespaces are not allowable public DNS namespaces, per RFC 1123. However, they are perfectly acceptable for an internal namespace. Answers A, D, and E represent valid external (public) namespaces and could thus be used internally or externally. Only Answers B and C represent namespaces that are valid only on an internal network. For more information, see the section "Planning a DNS Namespace Design."

2. **A.** If you want your WINS server to send notification to replication partners that a number of changes have happened on your WINS server, you need to select the Push option for the WINS server. For more information, see the section "Implementing WINS Replication."

3. **B.** The `corp.clowncollege.com` namespace represents a delegated DNS namespace. `corp.clowncollege.com` would thus become the root of the Active Directory forest and domain structure. Internal network clients should be allowed to resolve both internal and external domain names; however, external (Internet) clients should not be allowed to resolve internal hostnames. The namespace `clowncollege.net` represents a unique namespace; thus, Answer A is incorrect. The namespaces `clowncollege.corp.com` and `clowncollege.com.corp` are not delegated namespaces of the `clowncollege.com` namespace; thus, Answers C and D are incorrect. For more information, see the section "Planning a DNS Namespace Design."

4. **B.** After the WINS servers have been configured as replication partners, they will replicate with each other based on the replication configuration. For more information, see the section "Implementing WINS Replication."

## APPLY YOUR KNOWLEDGE

5. **B.** A standard secondary zone holds a read-only copy of the zone information in standard text format. Secondary zones are created to increase performance and resilience of the DNS configuration. Information is transferred from the primary zone to the secondary zones. A master zone is one that holds the only writable copy of the zone data; thus, Answer A is incorrect. An Active Directory–integrated zone operates in a multi-master mode, whereby all name servers can make changes to the zone data; thus, Answer C is incorrect. A stub zone contains only those resource records necessary to identify the authoritative DNS servers for a zone; thus, Answer D is incorrect. For more information, see the section "Planning DNS Zone Requirements."

6. **A.** Windows 2000 Professional and Windows XP Professional computers use H-node (hybrid) for NetBIOS name resolution. This node type favors the WINS server for name resolution but attempts to resolve the name by broadcast if the WINS server is unavailable. For more information, see the section "Implementing NetBIOS Name Resolution."

7. **A.** By selecting the BIND Secondaries option, you disable fast zone transfers and ensure that zone transfers are compatible and can succeed with older DNS implementations that do not support fast zone transfers. BIND version 4.9.4 and later do support fast zone transfers. Selecting the Enable Round-robin option configures the DNS server to use a round-robin rotation to rotate and reorder resource records if multiple records exist; thus, Answer B is incorrect. The Enable Netmask Ordering option configures the DNS server to reorder its host records in the response it sends to a query based on the IP address of the DNS resolver from which the query came; thus, Answer C is incorrect. The Secure Cache Against Pollution option configures the DNS server to prevent the addition of resource records that are unrelated to the original query; thus, Answer D is incorrect. For more information, see the section "Integrating with Third-Party DNS Solutions."

8. **B.** Because this is a DHCP environment, just add/update the WINS option for the DHCP scope. Answer C might work, but it is much more labor intensive than the one-time scope update. For more information, see the section "Implementing WINS Replication."

9. **C.** A DNS resolver is any system that has been configured with the IP addresses of one or more DNS servers and that performs name resolution queries against these servers. Recursive and iterative represent the types of name resolution queries that are performed. A recursive query is a DNS query that is sent to a DNS server from a DNS resolver asking the DNS server to provide a complete answer to the query, or an error stating that it cannot provide the information; thus, Answer A is incorrect. An iterative query is a DNS query that is sent by a DNS server to another DNS server in an effort to perform name resolution; thus, Answer B is incorrect. A DNS forwarder is a DNS server that has received a forwarded name resolution request from another DNS server; thus, Answer D is incorrect. For more information, see the section "Planning DNS Forwarding Requirements."

10. **C.** WINS is a dynamic replacement for the LMHOSTS file. For more information, see the section "Introduction to WINS."

## APPLY YOUR KNOWLEDGE

11. **C.** BIND 8.1.2 meets all the DNS requirements to support Active Directory by adding support for dynamic DNS. BIND 4.9.4 introduces support for fast zone transfers and does not meet the requirements for Active Directory; thus, Answer A is incorrect. BIND 4.9.6 introduces support for SRV resource records but does not meet all the requirements for Active Directory; thus, Answer B is incorrect. BIND 8.2.1 introduces support for incremental zone transfers—although this is not a requirement for Active Directory; thus, Answer D is also incorrect. For more information, see the section "Integrating with Third-Party DNS Solutions."

12. **D.** For this question, keep two components in mind: the trigger (when a certain number of entries are added, this is the least bandwidth-intensive mechanism) and the direction the information must travel. Answer D is the only one with the right combination of these factors. For more information, see the section "Implementing WINS Replication."

13. **B.** By default, Windows Server 2003 DNS servers perform zone transfers only with the DNS servers that are listed on the Name Servers tab of the zone properties dialog box; thus, Answers A,

C, and D are incorrect. All DNS servers that are considered to be authoritative for the DNS zone are listed on the Name Servers tab. Although this configuration is fairly secure, you can make it more secure by explicitly configuring DNS servers by IP address on the Zone Transfers tab for which you want to allow zone transfers to occur. For more information, see the section "Zone Transfer Security."

14. **B.** By issuing the `ping -t` command, you can send a continuous stream of ICMP echo request packets to the destination IP address. You can stop the stream of packets by pressing the Ctrl+C key combination. For more information, see the section "`ping`."

15. **D.** DNS servers typically cache any names in referral answers, thus expediting the speed of resolving subsequent DNS queries. However, when this feature is in use, the server can determine if the referred name is polluting or insecure and discard it. The server thus determines whether to cache the name offered in the referral depending on whether it is part of the exact DNS domain tree for which the original name query was made. For more information, see the section "DNS Server Properties."

# APPLY YOUR KNOWLEDGE

## Suggested Readings and Resources

1. Microsoft Corporation. 2003. *Microsoft Windows Server 2003 Resource Kit.* Redmond, WA: Microsoft Press. ISBN: 0735614717.

2. Microsoft Corporation. 2003. *Microsoft Windows Server 2003 Deployment Kit.* Redmond, WA: Microsoft Press. ISBN: 0735614865

3. Davies, Joseph, and Thomas Lee. 2003. *Microsoft Windows Server 2003 TCP/IP Protocols and Services Technical Reference.* Redmond, WA: Microsoft Press. ISBN: 0735612919.

4. "Technical Overview of Windows Server 2003 Networking and Communications," www.microsoft.com/windowsserver2003/ techinfo/overview/netcomm.mspx.

5. "Deploying Network Services," www.microsoft.com/technet/prodtechnol/ windowsserver2003/evaluate/cpp/reskit/ netsvc/default.asp.

Microsoft has defined the Routing and Remote Access portion of the "Planning, Implementing, and Maintaining Routing and Remote Access" objectives as follows:

**Plan a routing strategy.**

- **Identify routing protocols to use in a specified environment.**

- **Plan routing for IP multicast traffic.**

▶ Routing is the process of moving packets from one network to another. To do this efficiently, you must know how to plan a strategy that works for your business needs and ensure that it is implemented properly. You need to identify which routing strategy you may need (static versus dynamic routing) and what protocols you want to use. You also need to understand what multicast traffic is and how to plan routing for it.

**Plan security for remote access users.**

- **Plan remote access policies.**

- **Analyze protocol security requirements.**

- **Plan authentication methods for remote access clients.**

▶ Remote access can be a great thing for your users— if planned and implemented properly, including security. To fully secure your remote access solution, you need to understand the authentication methods available as well as how to configure and implement remote access policies.

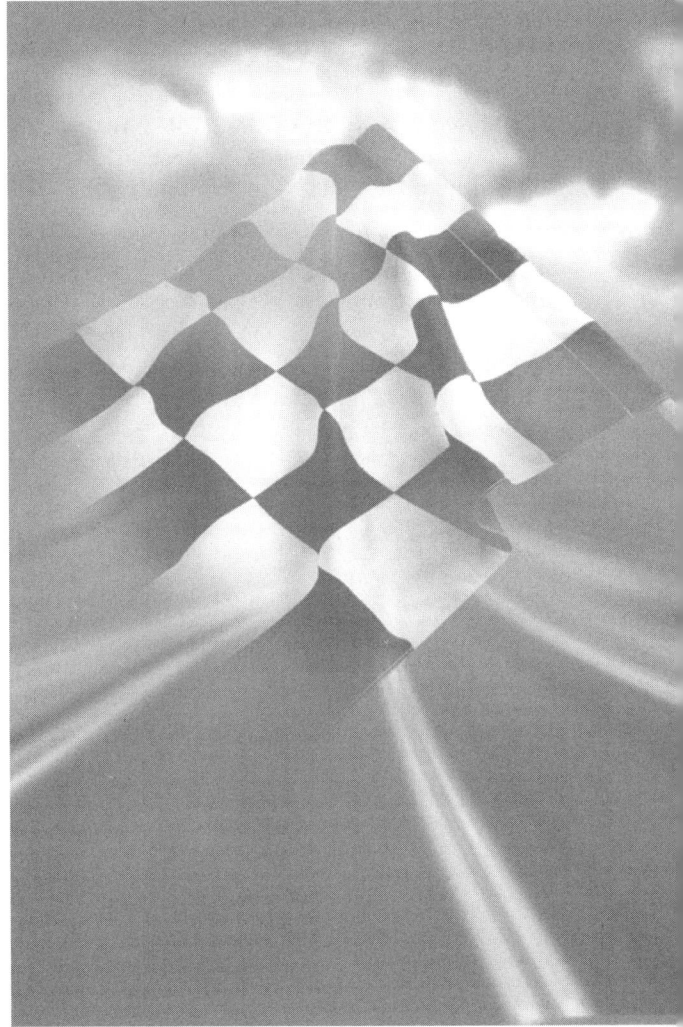

CHAPTER 4

# Planning, Implementing, and Maintaining Routing and Remote Access

**Troubleshoot TCP/IP routing. Tools might include the** route, tracert, ping, pathping, **and** netsh **commands and Network Monitor.**

▶ After your network infrastructure has been designed, planned, and implemented, you need to know how to troubleshoot it. Windows Server 2003 provides quite a few tools to help you troubleshoot, so you need to know how to use them not only to solve problems, but also to take the 70-293 exam. Here, you learn how to use route, tracert, ping, pathping, netsh, and Network Monitor.

## STUDY STRATEGIES

▶ Focus on understanding what protocols are used for what solution. In other words, if you are asked to create a hub and spoke network with static routes on the spokes and a routing protocol in the core, which would you use? What routing protocol? If you are asked to make it secure, what would you use? These are the questions you need to know how to answer from a design and planning standpoint.

▶ Take some time to review network security planning. This exam focuses on security as well, so make sure you study not only how to plan a network infrastructure, but also how to secure your network infrastructure.

▶ Get your hands dirty. The Step by Steps throughout this book provide plenty of directions and exercises, but you should go beyond these examples and create some of your own. If you can, experiment with each of the objectives to see how they work and why you would use each one.

# INTRODUCTION

In times gone by, it was considered safe practice to build a castle with a moat, drawbridge, and very high walls to keep your enemies out. If business was to be done in your land, a visitor would have to enter the castle under guard, show or claim credentials or services, and then be allowed in to do business.

Things haven't changed much. In today's corporate network, the same basic procedures are still in place as were utilized in the past. The only real change is that networks are much more complex and at risk than any castle ever was. It is for this reason that as you plan and design your network, you must know how to analyze potential holes and pitfalls for security and implement a network security strategy to stop these potential problems. One of the key goals of this chapter is to do just that: to help you learn how to secure remote access to your network.

In the interconnected business environment of today, businesses cannot survive as isolated kingdoms. The trend is for companies to integrate, merge, as well as buy and sell each other. During any one of these processes, the likelihood that you will need to implement a secure remote access solution is extremely high.

First, this chapter looks at how Microsoft provides Routing and Remote Access Service (RRAS) solutions. You also learn how to plan a routing strategy. *Routing* is the process of moving packets from one network to another. To route efficiently, you need to know how to properly configure RRAS for routing. To do this, you need to identify which routing strategy you may need (static versus dynamic routing) and what protocols you want to use. You also need to understand what multicast traffic is and how to plan routing for it.

Of course, RRAS is good for more than just simple routing; its primary function is to provide remote access connectivity for your network. Unfortunately, just providing remote access is no longer good enough; you have to take steps to secure it as well. You need to know how to plan remote access policies with Windows Server 2003, analyze protocol security requirements, plan authentication methods for your remote access clients, as well as plan and modify a network topology and integrate all these items into your overall network solution.

Of course, planning, implementing, and securing do not constitute all of your work; you will undoubtedly spend some time troubleshooting your solution both during its implementation and also after this point. Being able to identify the right troubleshooting tool for the job will make this process quicker and more efficient for you, thus bringing back critical business services to your network in a timely fashion. Some of the tools you need to become familiar with include the `route`, `tracert`, `ping`, `pathping`, and `netsh` commands and the Network Monitor.

# PLANNING A ROUTING STRATEGY

In this section, you discover how to plan a routing strategy. It is imperative that you first cover some basic material to be able to understand what you are planning and why you are planning it that way. As you are planning a routing strategy, you must also identify the routing protocols you will need to use in normal environments, as well as what protocols to implement while using multicast-based traffic.

## What Is Routing?

*Routing* is the process of taking data from one network and moving it to another network. If you recall, in Chapter 2, "Planning, Implementing, and Maintaining a Network Infrastructure," you learned the differences in subnets and how networks are identified by devices, such as by using the subnet mask. We also covered how a routing decision is made—for example, when a packet has a destination address that does not match the network it is currently on and needs to get to the network it is destined for. This is why you need a *default gateway*, which can be a router or a device acting as a router. It is at the default gateway where the routing process truly takes place.

Chapter 2 also covered the Open System Interface (OSI) and Department of Defense (DoD) models and TCP/IP. You learned how important these items are in today's network environment. You also learned about routing in general. Let's quickly review a simple network diagram showing one user accessing a single Web server. In

Figure 4.1, it is clear that a user is accessing a Web page on a remote Web server.

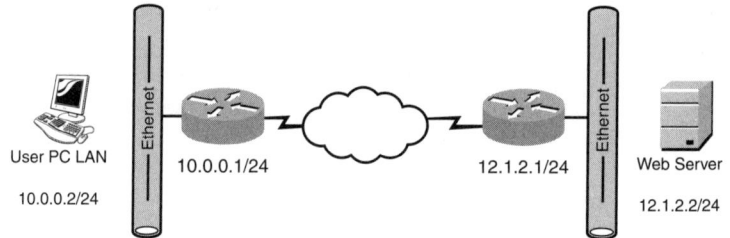

User PC LAN  Ethernet  10.0.0.1/24  12.1.2.1/24  Ethernet  Web Server

10.0.0.2/24  12.1.2.2/24

Let's look at the details of the request in Figure 4.1. From this information, you can gain a fundamental understanding of routing and how data is routed from one network to another.

▶ First, the user on the PC LAN accesses a Web page by opening his Web browser (Internet Explorer) and entering the domain name or IP address of the server on which the page resides. In this case, that would be `http://12.1.2.2/index.htm`.

▶ Next, the user's computer, which is on the 10.0.0.0/24 subnet, makes a request to a server on the 12.1.2.0/24 subnet. Because they are two different subnets, the packets need to be sent to the default gateway configured on the client LAN. The default gateway is set to 10.0.0.1, which is where routing takes place.

▶ The packets enter the router's Ethernet port, which is connected to the local area network (LAN). This interface (the one connected to the LAN) is nothing more than a network interface card (NIC) that gives access to and from the Ethernet-based network. After the packets enter the router, the router strips them down to look inside. This is done to view the destination address, which is 12.1.2.2 on the destination network of 12.1.2.0/24.

▶ Next, the router (10.0.0.1) looks in its routing table. A *routing table* is nothing more than a list of networks that the router will service. In this case, the router has been configured with a routing entry to do the following: If a packet comes from the LAN and is destined to go to the 12.1.2.0 network, it sends the traffic out interface 1. This interface is connected to the far-side router, which is labeled 12.1.2.1. As such, after the packets come in, they are forwarded to the 12.1.2.1 router, where the Web server is located.

▶ After the 12.1.2.1 router receives the packets, it also looks inside the packets to see where the packets need to go. When the router opens and reads the packets, it sees that the packets are destined to go to the 12.1.2.0 network, and it is a host with an IP address of 12.1.2.2. What makes this process even easier is that a router also holds an Address Resolution Protocol (ARP) cache; as long as that router is up and directly connected to the same subnet as the Web server, the packet will more than likely be sent directly to the Web server.

▶ Finally, the Web server receives the packets (which are a request to see a Web page named index.htm) and answers that request by producing the Web page to the remote client. The same process happens again, except in reverse order, to return the page to the requesting machine.

In Figure 4.2, the scenario has been expanded to show a routing environment over a larger network.

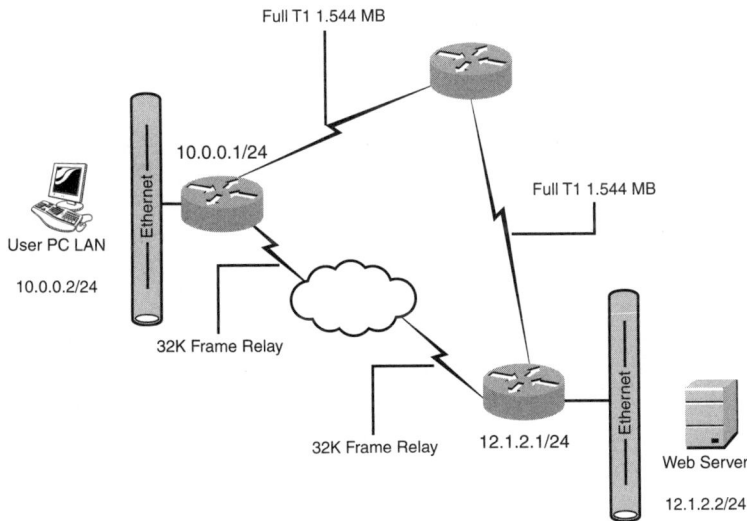

**FIGURE 4.2**
Complex routing environments offer multiple paths to the destination.

Based on the previous example, you should be somewhat familiar with the basic process of getting the packets from the source to the destination. Now, however, you have a problem because more than one router separates the two networks that need to interact. So, how are the required routing decisions made in this situation?

As you can see, there is a one-hop connection via Frame Relay to the Web server with 32KB of bandwidth. Also, you can see a two-hop connection from the client to the Web server that is separated by two T1 lines. So, in general, where would the router send the traffic? Over the one-hop connection, which is technically shorter, or over the two-hop connection, which has much more bandwidth? A router also makes decisions that are very complex, including deciding what could be faster—a slower link over fewer hops or a multihop link that utilizes high bandwidth links.

## Static Versus Dynamic Routing

Now we will look at what actually does the routing for you and what your involvement in the process is. For one, routing is not as simple as it was made to sound. This process can become very complex and, without a proper design, could actually ruin your network. We will describe the problems that can occur throughout the chapter, but you need to understand that you must plan your network for routing before you implement it. Major problems could arise if you don't plan. Following are some planning questions you should consider:

▶ Will you use a static or dynamic routing environment, and why would you use one over the other?

▶ Which routing environment is more secure?

A *static routing* environment is one in which all routing entries in the routing table are entered manually. When static routing is used, the administrator responsible for the router must manually enter information into the router to allow it to perform its function. If you want the router to route packets intended for remote destinations, you need to configure its routing table so the router will forward the packets to the next hop along the path to their destination. This may be simply something such as "all traffic that is not addressed for the local subnet is to be forwarded out of the router on Interface 1" or perhaps something more complex if the router has multiple interfaces connected to different networks.

A *dynamic routing* table is one that you create with a routing protocol such as *Routing Information Protocol (RIP)* or *Open Shortest Path First (OSPF)*, which we will explore more shortly. When dynamic routing is used, the chosen routing protocol actually builds the routing table on the fly by "learning" about the routes that are available to it and maintaining an accurate status on these routes. Should a route fail when dynamic routing is in use, all nearby routers will adjust their routing tables to prevent sending packets along the failed route. A simple example of a routing table is shown in Table 4.1.

**TABLE 4.1**

**SAMPLE ROUTING TABLE**

| *Destination Network* | *Interface to Use* | *Number of Hops* |
| --- | --- | --- |
| 172.16.0.0/16 | Via 10.0.2.1 | 1 hop |
| 10.0.0.0/8 | Via 10.0.2.1 | 1 hop |
| 12.1.2.0/24 | Via 10.0.2.1 | 1 hop |
| 0.0.0.0/0 | Via 10.0.2.1 | 1 hop |

The router keeps this table in memory so that, when a packet comes in, it can look at the prefix (the first few bits), hop count, and destination network. It's that easy. A routing table tells packets where to go, and it can be created manually or dynamically.

Routing tables compute the next hop for a packet. You must remember that a routing table needs to have two fields to function: the *IP prefix* and the *next hop address* (which must be a valid address). The router from which the packet is leaving and going to must be able to reach this valid address; you must be connected, or the route will not work. If you do not have a match (a packet comes in and does not have a routing table entry match), the packet is discarded, and you will most likely get an *Internet Control Message Protocol (ICMP)* notification that the destination host was unreachable.

Following are some key points to consider about static versus dynamic routing:

▶ Static routing is tedious. You have to know exactly what you want to do because any mistake causes the router to not work properly, resulting in routing errors that can prevent network connectivity.

▶ You may want to implement static routing if you have only a few routes to maintain. Remember, each time a packet enters the router, the router needs to process it, so tables that are very long can cause the router to take longer to make a routing decision, which in turn could slow down your network. When you use dynamic routing protocols, it is possible to have a router learn as many as hundreds of routes, depending on network size.

▶ Static routes are more secure because only a few required routes are in the table, so no one can see too much information. In this case, if the router is compromised by an attacker, he or she cannot glean too much information from your compromised router. The attacker may know only a default route back to the core network, for example; whereas if the attacker compromises a core router with 300 networks in the table, he or she can map your whole network from that one router.

▶ Dynamic routing is easy to configure and, once configured, is easy to maintain. If changes are made to the network, more than likely the routers will learn the changes, and they can quickly establish convergence on the network. *Convergence* occurs when all routers know all other routers on the network, and the topology is accurate.

▶ Dynamic routing is becoming more secure as more and more routing protocols provide ways to encrypt and authenticate updates between peers. However, configuring dynamic routes requires that the administrator have a greater level of knowledge and experience than when configuring static routes.

One of the key elements required to design and implement efficient routing solutions is to understand the differences between your available options and then to implement the correct one. You might be wondering whether static and dynamic routing protocols can be used at the same time. The answer to that question is yes.

# Distance Vector Versus Link State

Now that you understand dynamic and static routing, let's dig deeper into dynamic routing and the complexities it offers. You need to know this information for the 70-293 exam because Microsoft Windows Server 2003 allows you to configure either static or dynamic routing. If you choose dynamic, you have the option of using either a Link State dynamic routing protocol or a Distance Vector dynamic routing protocol. You need to know the specifics of each and which one to select in a production environment.

## Link State

Link State protocols are highly functional routing protocols that allow routers to pass information efficiently. A Link State routing protocol ensures that each router on the network maintains a map of the network. You should also know that any network is prone to have a problem or failure occur at any time. Frame Relay links have problems, Telcos have problems, and all of them affect your networks. For example, assume that one of your T1 lines experiences a failure that separates two routers on a subnet across the Internet. Both would be able to (through the routing protocol) adjust for this loss of the link between them because that is what they are programmed to do. When your router link fails, it is programmed to sense the loss of carrier on the line and then, through the routing protocol, send updates to the other routers adjacent to them so that they all know that the link is down and the IP subnet where they are maintained is no longer available for destination packets on the wire.

When a network link changes state (up to down, or vice versa), a notification, called a *link state advertisement (LSA)*, is flooded throughout the network. Routers all over the network address this change and make sure that their routing tables are adjusted accordingly. Another configurable option of Link State protocols is that they can use something other than hop count to determine their path through the network. Link State protocols can also determine that going over more routers may be quicker if the available bandwidth is higher instead of choosing the shortest path deemed solely on how many routers away the destination is.

So, what is so great about a Link State routing protocol? It is highly reliable and much less bandwidth intensive than a Distance Vector routing protocol. Also, it is highly configurable. Now, let's look at a Distance Vector protocol.

## Distance Vector

Distance Vector protocols are easy to configure and maintain, but not as reliable or efficient as Link State protocols. Distance Vector protocols (such as RIP) allow for simple design and simple maintenance, but your bandwidth may suffer as a result.

A Distance Vector protocol lets every router that is configured to use it inform every other adjacent router of its entire routing table. This means that each router on the network gets a full routing table from each neighboring router. These tables are used to create a metric based on hop count. Each router knows how far it is to another subnet in the network so that when incoming packets (when the router strips the header and reads the destination address) are read, the router will know the quickest way to get the packet there. This simplicity comes at the cost of more bandwidth utilized to keep the routing tables updated as compared to Link State protocols.

## Planning the Correct Routing Protocol to Use

**Plan a routing strategy.**

▶ **Identify routing protocols to use in a specified environment.**

With that lengthy but necessary routing introduction behind you, let's move forward now and examine the routing protocols available for use in Windows Server 2003. Windows Server 2003 provides three routing protocols to choose from: *RIP*, *RIPv2*, and *OSPF*. RIP and RIPv2 are Distance Vector based, and OSPF is Link State based.

## RIP

Although not commonly used as a protocol of choice for new network designs, the *Routing Information Protocol (RIP)* is still widely used throughout the world. The reason is that RIP was deployed widely in the past. RIP is not a proprietary protocol either; it is universal between just about every router (or routing device) ever made, so your knowledge and understanding of RIP are critical. RIP is also part of just about every Windows-based server ever created. Consequently, you need to know about RIP—how to design it and how to troubleshoot problems that may occur when using it.

As mentioned previously, RIP is a Distance Vector routing protocol. Remember that RIP is easy to configure and maintain, and should be used for smaller networks; it should not be used for very large enterprise deployments that span several routers. RIP is defined in Request for Comments (RFC) 1058 and updated by RFC 1388. To keep the amount of information you need down to a minimum (you will be asked about RIP on the 70-293 exam), we describe what you need to know for the exam here:

▶ RIP is limited to 15 router hops, with 16 hops being infinity. What does this mean? Picture a LAN with a PC that needs to communicate with a server on another LAN that is 15 routers away. The routers keep a list of which subnets are no more than 15 routers away, and if you try to expand the network past the $16^{th}$ router, communications do not happen. Remember, you have a 15-hop maximum between networks, and the $16^{th}$ is deemed infinity.

▶ RIP has problems with subnetted networks. In Chapter 2, we briefly covered what subnetted networks would resemble in your design. RIP was created and deployed before networks were subnetted to the degree that they are today, and because they have no direct support for RIP, your networks cannot support it. It really comes down to the information that each router sends to each other and what that packet contains. If the routing update does not contain a field in the packet to allow for subnetted networks, it does not carry over the information you may need it to. In other words, RIP is configured to look at the prefix of the IP address in the routing update and know whether it's either A, B, or C, and nothing more. If you subnet, your subnet will not be supported because RIP understands only that if a packet with an IP address of 10.0.0.1 comes in, it is automatically assigned a subnet of 255.0.0.0, even if you have it subnetted down to 255.255.255.0.

▶ RIP is bandwidth intensive, and although that isn't a problem on most networks, a smaller network with WAN links that are set small (such as Frame Relay links set with a 32KB committed information rate) could feel the effect of constant broadcasts every 30 seconds, especially if the routing table is large. If the routing table is too large, more than one update could be sent every 30 seconds, making it even more bandwidth intensive. By default, RIP broadcasts to its neighbors every 30 seconds lists of networks and subnets it can reach.

▶ RIP is not very secure. RIP contains no security features or configurable parameters to make it secure. Other protocols used today have configurable parameters to make them more secure; however, RIP does not contain any solution to make it secure by default.

In sum, RIP is a Distance Vector–based protocol that is available on Windows Server 2003 for configuration. It is easy to set up and configure for use, but is limited in what it can do for you. For larger networks, therefore, using RIP would not be wise. In real-world production environments, you most likely will not use RIP in a new deployment, but because so much of it still exists today, you would be wise to know it and understand it well, especially for the 70-293 exam.

Some of the most important features of troubleshooting RIP and the reasons it is so important to think about RIP's limitations when considering design are covered in the section "Other Problems with Routing" later in this chapter.

## RIPv2

RIP was not the greatest protocol ever designed, but due to its ease of use, it was widely deployed and used. RIPv2, or RIP version 2, was created for RIP users to overcome problems with security. This version adds an option for authentication to the RIP packet as well as support for subnetted networks. RIPv2 allows for variable-length subnetted networks to be passed through routing updates.

RIPv2 offers an opportunity for growth if a company feels that it is either underskilled to deploy a routing protocol such as OSPF or that it will never grow to a larger-sized company that could benefit more from a routing protocol like OSPF. RIPv2 is supported by Windows Server 2003 as well.

EXAM TIP

**Know the differences** For the 70-293 exam, make sure you are at least familiar with the major differences between RIP and RIP version 2.

# OSPF

Open Shortest Path First (OSPF) is a Link State–based nonproprietary routing protocol. For today's networks growing in size and
complexity, OSPF is a wise choice. It is configurable, scalable, and
easy to troubleshoot. However, it is not easy to plan, design, and
deploy. Understanding OSPF can take some time and effort because
half of what you need to know is in the underlying terminology
used to explain and use OSPF.

For the 70-293 exam, you need to know how to configure and use
OSPF on a Windows Server 2003 system; more importantly, however, you need to know how to design it, know its nomenclature, and
know when to use it. You can get a detailed explanation on OSPF
by reading RFC 1247. OSPF Version 2 is documented in RFC
1583. As mentioned previously, OSPF is a Link State routing protocol with a complex set of options and features. So, what is so great
about OSPF that makes up for its high difficulty level in planning
and design? Let's look at it further:

▶ OSPF is highly scalable. You will be hard pressed to build (or
  support) a network large enough to outdo OSPF. OSPF was
  designed to work in very large networks, and it works very
  well at that. It does not have a hop count restriction as RIP
  does. With OSPF's use of areas and a subdivided domain, the
  design possibilities are almost seemingly infinite.

▶ With RIP, you cannot use subnetted networks; with OSPF,
  you can.

▶ With OSPF, your bandwidth is spared. With RIP, an entire
  routing table is broadcast from every router on the network
  every 30 seconds. With OSPF (in stable environments that do
  not suffer from many changes), packets (called hello packets)
  are sent out intermittently to verify links between adjacent
  routers. This way, less bandwidth is used, and a major update
  check is performed only every 30 minutes.

So, now you can see where the trade-off comes in. If you want to
use a more configurable and scalable protocol, you should use OSPF,
but you need to remember that all its benefits equal added work on
your part. You have to put more effort into the design, rollout, and
maintenance of an OSPF network.

For the 70-293 exam, you should also remember the disadvantages to using OSPF. It adds complexity, and its demands on memory and computation for the routers that use it can be devastating if you do not have the proper router hardware to maintain it.

What else do you need to know about OSPF? You should know how it is laid out in a design. OSPF divides the network (what it considers a routing domain) into areas. An *area* is a subdivision of the entire network and is given a label. *Area 0* (zero) is considered the backbone of an OSPF network. If your network is small enough, you can set up the entire network to use Area 0, which is very important. For example, if the network becomes more subdivided (say you have three areas, including Area 0), you need to know that if all traffic must travel between areas, the packets are first routed to the backbone, or Area 0. When you plan a network this way, the design keeps subnets consolidated to areas, thus reducing the size of the link state database that is updated on every router in an OSPF network. This keeps your OSPF network running optimally.

With OSPF, you also need to know which class of network you are using. There are three:

- ▶ **Point-to-point**—A WAN serial link connecting two routers on a single subnet can be considered a point-to-point link.

- ▶ **Multiaccess**—An Ethernet or token-ring segment is a multiaccess link. Because the class is multiaccess (like Ethernet), you need to consider that each router on the connected network wants to know about it; it is not good for this to happen because not every router needs to form an adjacency with every other router. This would diminish the benefits of using a protocol like OSPF. To avoid this problem, OSPF assigns a Designated Router (DR) to manage all the link state advertisements (LSAs) that are sent from router to router. Also, you need to know that there is a Backup DR (called the BDR), which is also selected from the available routers on the network to take over if the DR fails.

- ▶ **Nonbroadcast multiaccess (NBMA)**—A Frame Relay or X.25 cloud is classified as NBMA. Nonbroadcast multiaccess networks use DRs just like multiaccess, but you must remember that because broadcasts lack support on a Frame Relay network, for instance, you must manually configure each router with its neighbor. If you do not manually configure the routers, you suffer from loss of connectivity between the routers running OSPF.

Why is this information so important? Again, the focus of the 70-293 exam is planning and design. You must understand how a protocol works entirely before you plan to deploy it. You have to know its nuances, what makes it tick, what makes it run under the hood. Understanding what kinds of networks can be connected to utilize OSPF is just as important as knowing how to configure and maintain it. If you do not design this protocol correctly, no matter how helpful it was programmed to be, you won't reap any benefits from it.

So, now that you understand the Link State routing protocol OSPF, what do you need to remember for the exam? For the 70-293 exam, you need to know the basic design features of OSPF. Most importantly, you need to remember the following points:

> ▶ OSPF sends out hello packets to each adjacent router connected to the network. OSPF uses hello packets to verify that the network is always ready to work as advertised. These hellos are sent out of every router interface every 10 seconds but are so small in size that they do not adversely affect your available bandwidth.

> ▶ Link state advertisements provide other functionality, such as providing a solution for a scenario in which a router does not hear from its neighboring router for more than 40 seconds. The router then sends out LSAs marking the other router as down so that all the other routers can adjust their tables with the change.

> ▶ Hellos can be adjusted. A hello has a timer value that, when configured properly throughout the OSPF network, allows proper and accurate communications to take place. It is important to know that if a hello timer is misconfigured (not all timers are identical), problems can occur. Make sure that when you plan an OSPF network, you ensure that all the hello timers match. They must all be consistent across all routers on a network segment.

> ▶ Because LSAs age, it is important to get a refreshed routing table (or database) from a neighboring router just in case

**EXAM TIP**

**Take it easy**   When designing, you can bypass the DR and NBMA network design by utilizing a series of point-to-point links. They may be more intensive to configure, but they take the intricacies of DR election out of your equation.

anything has changed. If nothing has changed on a particular router for 30 minutes, the router flushes its information and seeks an updated database from its adjacent routers. This means that the network reconverges every 30 minutes—a far cry from the forced reconvergence in a RIP network every 30 seconds!

In sum, OSPF is a Link State–based routing protocol that is difficult to plan, design, manage, and maintain, but is highly configurable and scalable, making it the best choice for large networks.

Now that you are familiar with RIP and OSPF, as well as what routing is and all the other details that surround it, let's discuss how to plan a routed environment, one of the objectives of exam 70-293.

---

### OSPF VERSUS RIP

As a Microsoft Certified Professional, you must know how to design networks. No longer can you be a simple server jockey; now you need to know the connecting highway, which is the underlying network that allows your domain controllers to communicate with each other. You can't have WINS push/pull partners if you don't have a WAN. And when you have a WAN, you have routers, and when you have routers configured to use a dynamic routing protocol, you have either RIP or OSPF. So, which do you choose? Because we discussed all the details of RIP and OSPF in the preceding sections, we provide a distilled list of OSPF versus RIP here. This information will help you to decide which protocol you should use over the other. You can consider this information a summary of what you have already read in this chapter.

RIP can no longer handle the growth of business as we know it today. No business today has boundaries. A business that currently (from a network view) has only one core network and 10 remote sites could easily be acquired by another company through a merger and become part of that company's network overnight. Because most large companies that acquire other smaller companies generally have large networks, it would be safe to say that they use advanced routing protocols on their networks to handle their current size as well as their rapid growth. Your RIP-based network would be a thorn in their side, with route redistribution having to take place to communicate, or a complete network overhaul to take place to bring you into compliance with their network. RIP simply can't keep pace with businesses today; therefore, newly designed networks should not be configured to use RIP because RIP's lack of scalability does not match the nature of business.

If you decide to use RIP, you must consider that your network could never span any size larger than 15 hop counts. Remember that 16 is infinity.

Another vital flaw of RIP is that it cannot use subnetted networks other than the default subnetted classes, which are 255.0.0.0, 255.255.0.0, and 255.255.255.0. Any other variable-length subnet will not work in a RIP environment, and in today's networks this is not something you can afford. Subnetting the private IP address ranges within your network allows a large number of hosts to be used. You should not waste a single host, and being able to efficiently subnet allows you to spare every single IP needed. RIP cannot route between links that are variably subnetted, so it is not wise to deploy RIP in any network you feel may grow to that size.

RIP is bandwidth intensive on networks that are built with very slow WAN links. This means that if you use very small circuit sizes (such as 32KB) per link, you are more than likely going to feel the effects of RIP on your wide area network. Remember that RIP tries to update its neighbors with its entire routing table every 30 seconds.

RIP is slower to converge than OSPF. This problem is felt only in very large networks due to the size it could span in router hops. If the network design is poorly laid out, you, as an end user, could experience timeouts on your PC if network convergence takes too long. Having this happen every time a Frame Relay link drops could prove annoying to everyone in your company. Very large networks using RIP and dealing with very slow convergence do not work well and may need a protocol such as OSPF to handle the distributed nature of the network it is made to manage. Remember that RIP should not be used on very large networks because everyone on the network will be affected if convergence becomes a problem.

RIP understands hop count only as a routable metric. If you want to get from one LAN to another over a few router hops, the shortest hop count from LAN 1 to LAN 2 will win. What happens if there is also another path to LAN 2? What if you have another path that consists of two router hops both separated by a T1 link? This means that you would have 1.544MB of transfer on each link. Say that nothing else is utilizing this path. Now, say the other one-hop path is an analog dial-up connection between two routers over 56Kbps. Which would be faster? Of course, the two T1 lines not being used would be the fastest option, but RIP believes the single hop path is faster because it has a shorter path via hop counts,

*continues*

*continued*

which in this situation is actually the slowest path RIP could choose. Through OSPF's configurable metrics, it would know the shortest path because it is smart enough (or configurable enough) to be able to know that the T1 link is, of course, the shortest path.

RIP also has a spin-off called RIP version 2, or RIPv2 for short. If you are thinking of using RIPv2, you might want to consider using OSPF instead if your network will likely experience future growth. RIPv2 fixes the problems that RIP had—which are subnetted networks and authentication for security—but it still has slow convergence problems and a hop count limitation.

OSPF is harder to plan, design, and implement, but once you do, you gain a world of flexibility and control not offered by protocols such as RIP. OSPF addresses all the problems that RIP experiences. OSPF can handle any kind of routed environment you can design because it was made to do so. If you are going to stay with a vendor-neutral routing protocol, all new networks designed and built today should use OSPF. It offers scalability and control over a corporation of just about any size.

OSPF provides the following great enhancements over RIP: no hop count limitations; handling of variable-length subnetted networks; and the use of multicast packets (instead of broadcast packets) to give and send updates, which means less processing power used on routers not meant for the updates to process broadcast packets, which in turn eats CPU cycles for nothing. By using multicast packets, OSPF saves router CPU time. Bandwidth is also saved because routing updates are sent only as needed, not every 30 seconds. With OSPF, the network reconverges every 30 minutes, but that's to be expected and nowhere near as bandwidth consuming as every 30 seconds with RIP.

With OSPF, you can set up areas. Area 0 is always the backbone, but as far as expansion, you can expand your network into other areas such as Area 1, Area 2, and Area 3. You could configure all four areas as separate subnets and set up a logical definition of subnetted networks to limit the number of link state updates needed per area. If you separate your network into areas, not every router needs to know what every other router does; if it did, a router 29 hops away would need to exchange a database with every other router on the network, and this would make convergence really slow. OSPF allows you to create areas so that such a problem never happens.

# Planning a Routing Environment

Now that you are familiar with what routing is, how it is performed, what a router is, and what different protocols you can choose from, you need to know how to plan a routing environment. This section briefly covers what you can do to plan for your new routing environment. For one, you can plan your network logically. This section briefly describes some of the more common routing topologies, such as *ring*, *mesh* and *star* so that you understand what they mean as they are mentioned in the book as well as on the exam.

The simplest routing topology to consider is the *ring*, which is also the least efficient and reliable of the common routing topologies. In the ring topology, shown in Figure 4.3, each site is connected to its two closest neighbors with a WAN link; thus, two WAN connections and two routers are needed at each site. The ring topology is fairly easy to install and configure, but is less efficient than the next topology we will explore, the mesh, because no one site can communicate directly with any other site except its neighbor on either side.

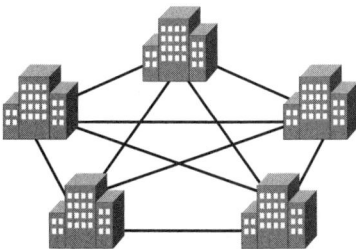

**FIGURE 4.3**
The ring topology is easy to implement and configure, but not efficient when compared to the mesh.

In a *mesh* topology, a shown in Figure 4.4, every site in the network is connected to every other site in the network by a WAN link. This arrangement is costly because it uses a high number of links and may become difficult to manage as the number of sites, and thus the number of links, grows. The benefit to this arrangement is complete redundancy against failure. If you lose a link anywhere in the network, the entire network is always up, no matter what. The drawbacks are cost and maintainability.

**FIGURE 4.4**
The mesh topology is expensive to implement and maintain, but provides complete redundancy.

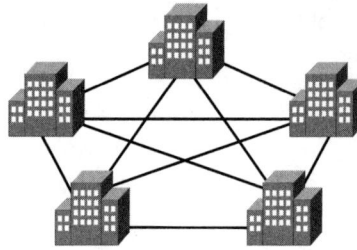

The last topology we examine here, the *star*, as shown in Figure 4.5, is essentially a core location with remote sites linked to it. Remote sites are normally other business units, smaller locations, or business partners and need to access data from the core over the WAN. All communication from one remote site to another occurs via the core location. Having all resources centralized logically in a core location (such as the headquarters) makes the design easy to maintain from a routing perspective because every site, after it is connected, is only one hop away.

**FIGURE 4.5**
The star topology is very efficient and inexpensive to implement and maintain.

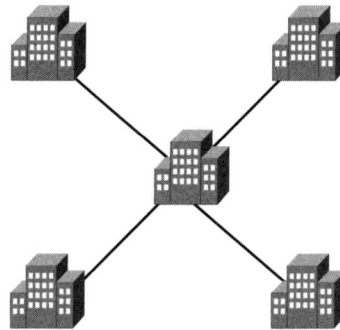

When planning a routing environment, other than planning for the topology you will use, you also have to plan your routing protocols, which we discussed previously in great detail. Remember all this information not only for the 70-293 exam, but also for all real-world production deployment scenarios.

# Windows Server 2003 Routing Solutions

As far back as Windows NT and its variations, you could always (and still can today) build a router out of a server. Remember that all routers do is connect networks together. So, if you have a switch with 10 PCs connected using the subnet 10.0.0.0/24 and another switch with another 10 PCs connected using the subnet 10.0.1.0/24, all you would need to make them communicate is a router in between the two switches. You can use either a router with two Ethernet interfaces or a Windows server with two NICs installed to connect the two subnets. You could conceivably connect the two subnets, turn on RIP, and be routing in no time.

Windows Server 2003 can act as a fully functional router using static routes or dynamic routing protocols, such as RIP (both versions) and OSPF. Would you use Windows Server 2003 for a router? Of course, you can; the only setback is that most routers today come with specialized hardware that allows them to contain telecom link–based interfaces such as ISDN, Serial, T1 lines, T3 lines, and so on. If you want to connect two or more Ethernet-based networks and route between them, you could set a Windows Server 2003 system to do that task, but can you connect to the Internet via a T1? Not so easily said and done. Remember, Windows Server 2003 is fully functional as a router, but you also need to remember its weaknesses for the exam.

Before you can configure RIP or OSPF routing to occur, you must first enable the Routing and Remote Access Service on the server, as outlined in Step by Step 4.1.

---

## STEP BY STEP

### 4.1 Enabling Routing and Remote Access Services

  **1.** Open the Routing and Remote Access console by choosing Start, Control Panel, Administrative Tools, and then Routing and Remote Access. By default, the local computer is listed as a server (see Figure 4.6). Notice the red arrow that indicates that the Routing and Remote Access Service is not presently enabled.

*continues*

*continued*

**FIGURE 4.6**
The Routing and Remote Access console is used to configure the Routing and Remote Access Service for a variety of functions, including acting as a router.

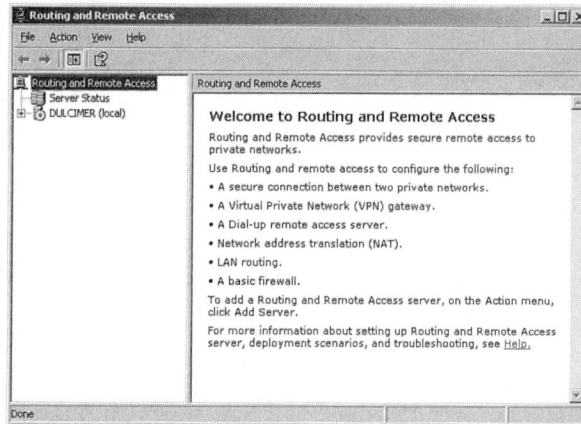

2. Right-click the server you want to configure and select Configure and Enable Routing and Remote Access. The Routing and Remote Access Server Setup Wizard starts.

3. Click Next to start configuring the Routing and Remote Access Service. The Configuration dialog box opens, as shown in Figure 4.7.

**FIGURE 4.7**
The Routing and Remote Access Server Setup Wizard includes the most common configuration options to make the configuration process as easy as possible.

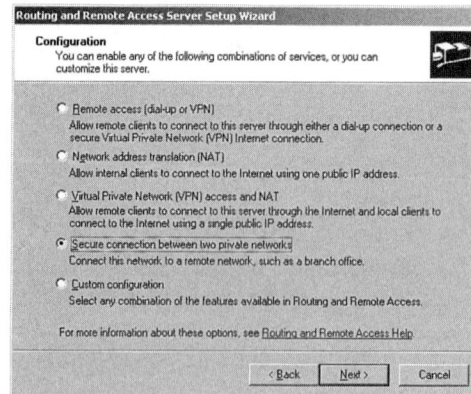

4. Select the Secure Connection Between Two Private Networks option and click Next to continue. The Demand-Dial Connections dialog box opens, as shown in Figure 4.8.

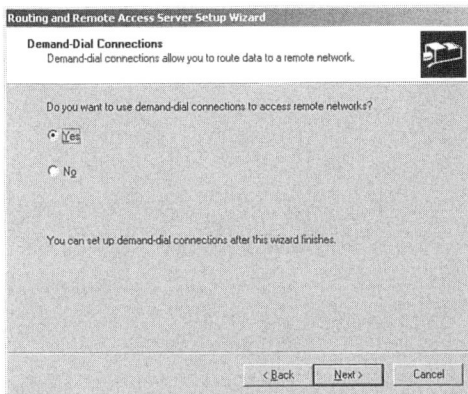

**FIGURE 4.8**
Demand-dial routing allows you to open connections between routers when traffic needs to pass through the router and disconnect connections when not needed.

**5.** On the Demand-Dial Connections dialog box, select No and click Next to continue. The Completing the Routing and Remote Access Server Setup Wizard summary dialog box opens, as shown in Figure 4.9.

**FIGURE 4.9**
The last screen of the setup wizard summarizes the changes made, lists the next steps, and allows you one final opportunity to cancel the configuration changes.

**6.** Click Finish to complete the enabling of routing services.

With your Windows Server 2003 computer now enabled to provide routing, you must decide whether you will use static routing or dynamic routing.

# Using the `route` Command to Configure Static Routes

The `route` command is primarily used to configure static routes within a network. It can also be used for troubleshooting by listing all the routes that this computer knows about.

The syntax of the `route` command is as follows:

```
route [-f] [-p] [command [destination] [mask subnetmask] [gateway]
➡ [metric costmetric]]
```

The `-f` parameter clears the routing tables of all entries. The `-p` parameter makes the route persistent. When a route is added to the router, by default the entry is not kept across reboots of the system. The `-p` parameter ensures that the entry is maintained in the routing table across reboots of the system.

The following commands are used to specify what can be done with the `route` command:

- ▶ **print**—Prints the existing entries in the routing table.

- ▶ **add**—Adds a new route to the routing table.

- ▶ **delete**—Deletes an existing route from the routing table.

- ▶ **change**—Modifies an existing route in the routing table.

The destination parameter specifies the destination that you want to reach. The destination parameter can contain the following:

- ▶ Host address

- ▶ Subnet address

- ▶ Network address

- ▶ Default gateway

The mask parameter defines what portion of the destination address must match for that route to be used. When the mask is written in binary, a 1 is significant (must match) and a 0 need not match. For example, a 255.255.255.255 mask is used for a host entry. The mask of all 255s (all 1s) means that the destination address of the packet to be routed must exactly match the network address for this route to be used. For another example, the network address 157.57.8.0 has a netmask of 255.255.248.0. This netmask means the first two octets must match exactly, the first 5 bits of the third octet must match (248=11111000), and the last octet does not matter. Thus, any address of 157.57 and the third octet of 8 through 15 (15=00001111) will use this route.

The gateway parameter specifies where the packet needs to be sent. This can be the local network card or a router on the local subnet.

The metric parameter specifies a cost that is to be associated with that route. This cost is used in the decision on how packets should be routed. Packets are routed through the route that has the lowest cost.

Step by Step 4.2 shows how to configure a static route for the network 10.100.10.0.

---

# STEP BY STEP

### 4.2 Adding a Static Route to Windows Server 2003

**1.** Open the command prompt by choosing Start, Programs, Accessories, and selecting Command Prompt. The Command Prompt window opens.

**2.** Display the system's existing routing table by typing **route print** and pressing Enter. Make note of the routes listed now to check against the routes listed after you add the static route. You should see the following information (the output will vary from computer to computer, based on your computer's interfaces, network addresses, and existing routes):

```
IPv4 Route Table
===============================================================
======
Interface List
0x1 ........................ MS TCP Loopback interface
0x10003 ...00 b0 d0 da 90 1a ...... 3Com 3C920 Integrated Fast Eth-
ernet
0x10004 ...00 20 35 e7 93 fd ...... IBM 10/100 EtherJet PCI Adapter
===============================================================
======
===============================================================
======
Active Routes:
Network Destination        Netmask         Gateway       Interface
```

*continues*

*continued*

```
Metric
        0.0.0.0          0.0.0.0     10.115.10.1      10.115.10.2
30
        0.0.0.0          0.0.0.0  10.226.136.185   10.226.136.189
20
    10.115.10.0    255.255.255.0     10.115.10.2      10.115.10.2
30
    10.115.10.2  255.255.255.255       127.0.0.1        127.0.0.1
30
 10.226.136.184  255.255.255.248  10.226.136.189   10.226.136.189
20
 10.226.136.189  255.255.255.255       127.0.0.1        127.0.0.1
20
 10.255.255.255  255.255.255.255     10.115.10.2      10.115.10.2
30
 10.255.255.255  255.255.255.255  10.226.136.189   10.226.136.189
20
       127.0.0.0        255.0.0.0       127.0.0.1        127.0.0.1
1
       224.0.0.0        240.0.0.0     10.115.10.2      10.115.10.2
30
       224.0.0.0        240.0.0.0  10.226.136.189   10.226.136.189
20
255.255.255.255  255.255.255.255     10.115.10.2      10.115.10.2
1
255.255.255.255  255.255.255.255  10.226.136.189   10.226.136.189
1
Default Gateway:    10.226.136.185
===================================================================
======
Persistent Routes:
  None
```

3. Within the Command Prompt window, type the following command and press Enter:

```
Route Add 10.100.10.0 mask 255.255.255.0 10.100.5.1 metric 2
```

A successful entry returns you to the command prompt, with no message. If the entry addition is unsuccessful, you will receive an error message.

4. To display the system's routing table with the newly added route, type **route print** and press Enter. This displays the following information (note the newly added route in boldface type):

```
IPv4 Route Table
===================================================================
======
Interface List
```

```
0x1 ......................... MS TCP Loopback interface
0x10003 ...00 b0 d0 da 90 1a ...... 3Com 3C920 Integrated Fast Eth-
ernet
0x10004 ...00 20 35 e7 93 fd ...... IBM 10/100 EtherJet PCI Adapter
=================================================================
======
=================================================================
======
Active Routes:
Network Destination        Netmask          Gateway          Interface
Metric
          0.0.0.0          0.0.0.0      10.115.10.1        10.115.10.2
30
          0.0.0.0          0.0.0.0   10.226.136.185    10.226.136.189
20
      10.100.10.0    255.255.255.0      10.115.10.2        10.115.10.2
2
      10.115.10.0    255.255.255.0      10.115.10.2        10.115.10.2
30
      10.115.10.2  255.255.255.255        127.0.0.1          127.0.0.1
30
   10.226.136.184  255.255.255.248   10.226.136.189    10.226.136.189
20
   10.226.136.189  255.255.255.255        127.0.0.1          127.0.0.1
20
   10.255.255.255  255.255.255.255      10.115.10.2        10.115.10.2
30
   10.255.255.255  255.255.255.255   10.226.136.189    10.226.136.189
20
        127.0.0.0        255.0.0.0        127.0.0.1          127.0.0.1
1
        224.0.0.0        240.0.0.0      10.115.10.2        10.115.10.2
30
        224.0.0.0        240.0.0.0   10.226.136.189    10.226.136.189
20
  255.255.255.255  255.255.255.255      10.115.10.2        10.115.10.2
1
  255.255.255.255  255.255.255.255   10.226.136.189    10.226.136.189
1
Default Gateway:     10.226.136.185
=================================================================
======
Persistent Routes:
  None
```

# Implementing RIP Routing

As discussed earlier, static routing is not necessarily a viable solution
in today's business network; thus, you should consider implementing

one of the available dynamic routing protocols that Windows Server 2003 supports. Step by Step 4.3 shows how to enable RIPv2 for routing.

---

# STEP BY STEP

### 4.3 Adding RIP to the Routing and Remote Access Service

**1.** Open the Routing and Remote Access console, as shown in Figure 4.10, by choosing Start, Control Panel, Administrative Tools, and then Routing and Remote Access.

**FIGURE 4.10**

A server with an active Routing and Remote Access Service appears in the Routing and Remote Access console with a green upward arrow.

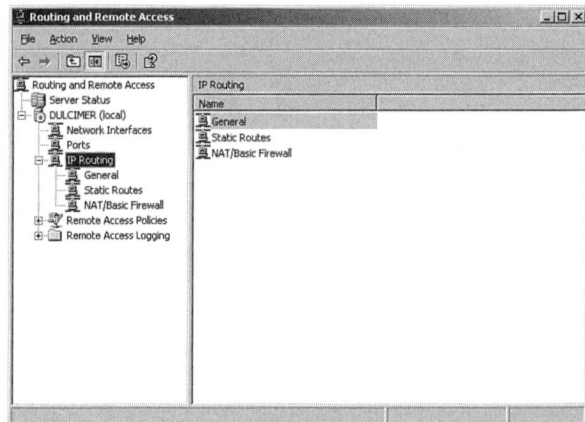

**2.** In the left pane, expand the list under IP Routing and right-click General. From the context menu, select New Routing Protocol. The New Routing Protocol dialog box opens, as shown in Figure 4.11.

**3.** Select RIP Version 2 for Internet Protocol and click OK. RIP then appears under the IP Routing entry, as shown in Figure 4.12. RIP is now installed on your Windows Server 2003 server.

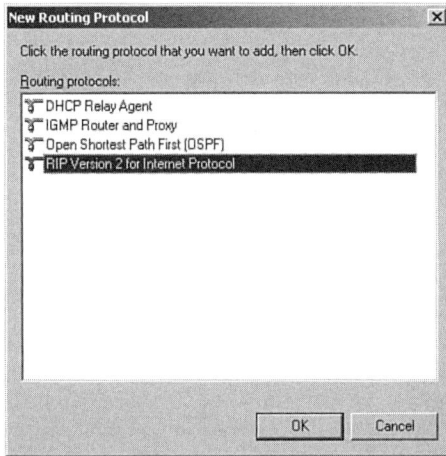

**FIGURE 4.11**
The New Routing Protocol Wizard can be used to add protocols to your Windows Server 2003 server.

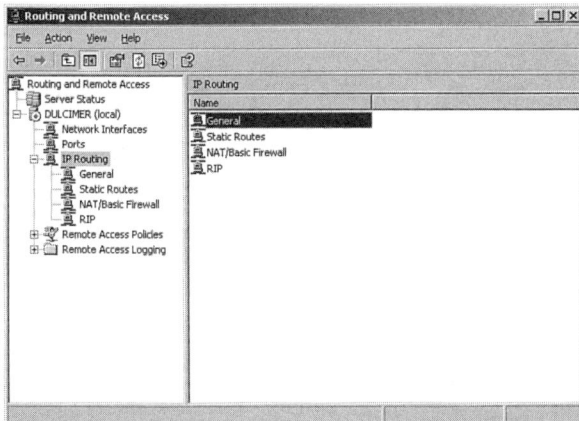

**FIGURE 4.12**
RIP appears under the IP Routing heading in the Routing and Remote Access console.

**4.** Right-click the RIP entry and select New Interface from the context menu. The New Interface for RIP Version 2 for Internet Protocol dialog box opens, as shown in Figure 4.13.

**5.** Select the appropriate Local Area Connection and click OK. The RIP Properties dialog box opens, as shown in Figure 4.14.

*continues*

*continued*

**FIGURE 4.13**
The first step in configuring RIP is to create a RIP interface.

**FIGURE 4.14**
The RIP Properties dialog box allows you to configure the RIP protocol to work in your network environment.

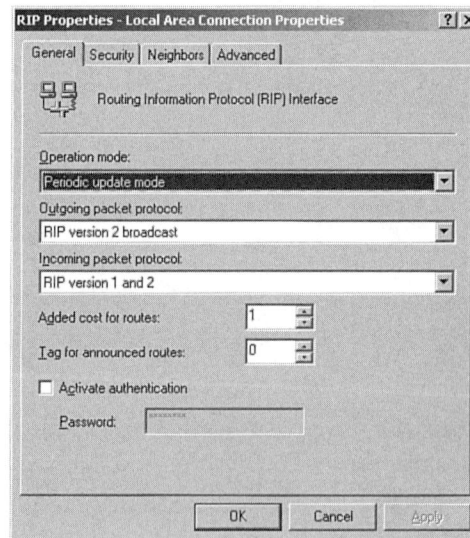

6. On the General tab, under Outgoing Packet Protocol, select RIP Version 1 Broadcast. Under Incoming Packet Protocol, select RIP Version 1 and 2. Click OK to return to the Routing and Remote Access console and activate the changes. You have just configured the server to work with any legacy RIP version 1 routers that might still be on the network.

## Implementing Silent RIP

RIP also has a feature known as *silent RIP* that allows a server running RRAS to build a routing table by listening to the RIP broadcasts on the network, but the host doesn't broadcast any updates to the network. A silent RIP router processes RIP announcements but does not announce its own routes.

To enable silent RIP on your Windows Server 2003 router, perform the steps outlined in Step by Step 4.4.

---

# STEP BY STEP

### 4.4 Enabling Silent RIP on Windows Server 2003

1. Open the Routing and Remote Access console.

2. Expand the console tree and select RIP. The list of available interfaces running RIP appears in the right pane of the console, as shown in Figure 4.15.

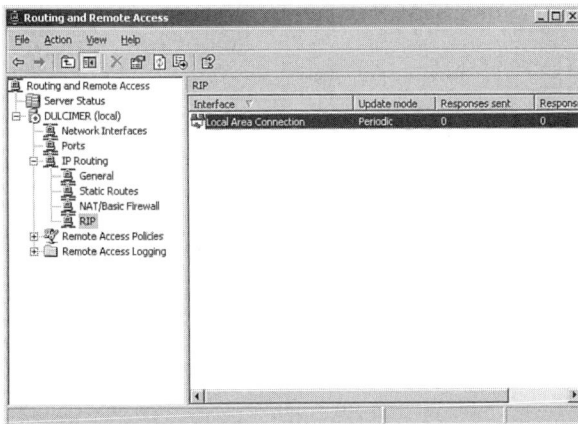

**FIGURE 4.15**
You can find the complete list of interfaces supporting a particular protocol by looking in the right pane of the console.

3. Right-click the interface that you want to configure for silent RIP mode, and from the context menu, select Properties. The Local Area Connection Properties opens, as shown in Figure 4.16.

*continues*

*continued*

**FIGURE 4.16**
The Silent RIP setting can be found in the Outgoing Packet Protocol pull-down, due to the fact that the configuration is related to which routes are broadcast, not received.

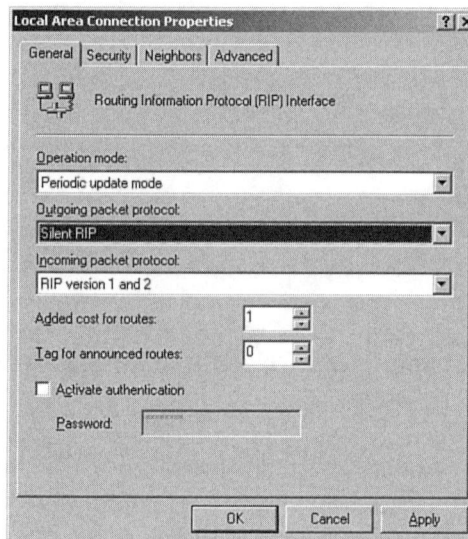

**4.** On the General tab, under Outgoing Packet Protocol, select Silent RIP from the pull-down menu. Click OK to return to the Routing and Remote Access console and apply the changes.

### Additional RIP Configuration Options

Before we move on to implementing and configuring the OSPF protocol, let's look at some of the other RIP settings you might need to set. Step by Step 4.5 shows how to set these options.

## STEP BY STEP

### 4.5 Setting Additional RIP Configuration Options with Windows Server 2003

**1.** Open the Routing and Remote Access console.

**2.** Expand the console tree and select RIP. The list of available interfaces running RIP appears in the right pane of the console.

**3.** Right-click the interface that you want to configure, and from the context menu, select Properties. The Local Area Connection Properties opens.

**4.** As you saw in Step by Step 4.4, the General tab deals with the way routes are broadcast and received. Click the Security tab, shown in Figure 4.17. Look at how the RIP updates can be managed.

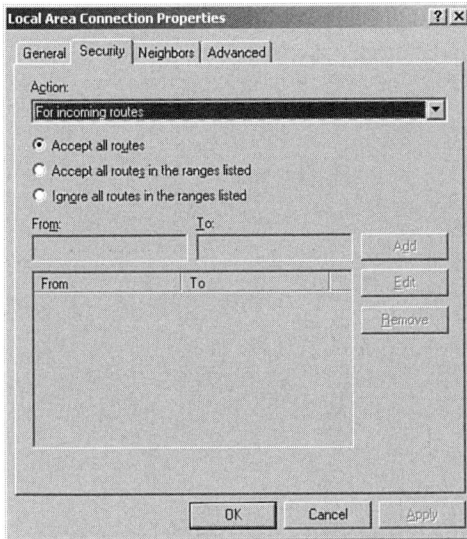

**FIGURE 4.17**
The Security tab allows you to restrict the networks that can send/receive RIP updates.

**5.** Click the Neighbors tab, shown in Figure 4.18. Review the settings that can be configured pertaining to how the router interacts with its RIP neighbors.

**6.** Click the Advanced tab, shown in Figure 4.19. The Advanced tab allows you to configure the more complex settings associated with RIP and the way Windows Server 2003 supports it. Click OK to return to the Routing and Remote Access console.

*continues*

*continued*

**FIGURE 4.18**

The Neighbors tab allows you to configure how RIP broadcasts are sent by your Windows Server 2003 router.

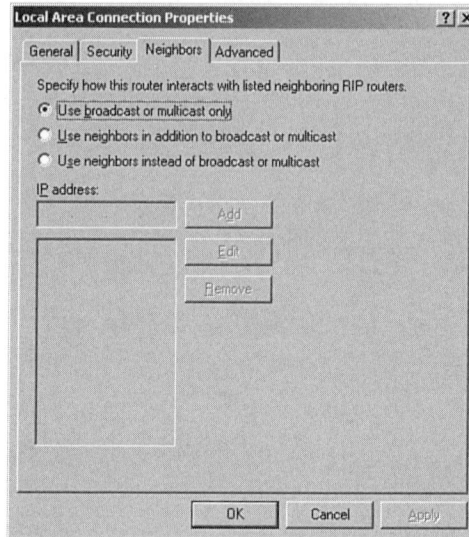

**FIGURE 4.19**

The Advanced tab allows you to configure advanced settings such as split horizon, poison reverse, and triggered updates.

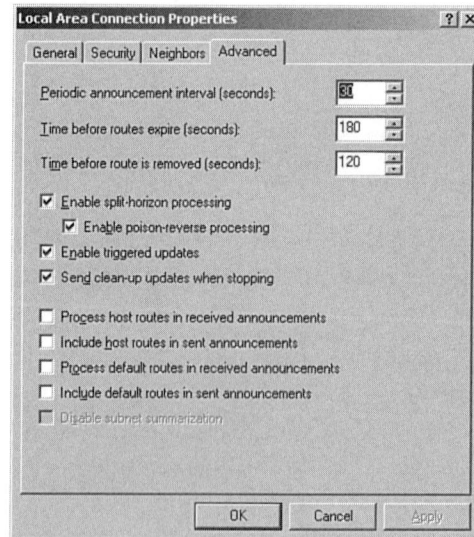

## Implementing OSPF Routing

If your network is growing or expected to grow, or you want to provide a more robust routing solution, you should consider implementing OSPF routing. Step by Step 4.6 outlines the process to configure OSPF routing on your Windows Server 2003 computer.

## STEP BY STEP

### 4.6 Installing and Configuring OSPF on Windows Server 2003

1. Open the Routing and Remote Access console.

2. Expand the console tree, and under IP Routing, right-click General. From the context menu, select New Routing Protocol. The New Routing Protocol dialog box opens.

3. Select Open Shortest Path First and click OK to install it. It now appears under IP Routing in the Routing and Remote Access console, as shown in Figure 4.20.

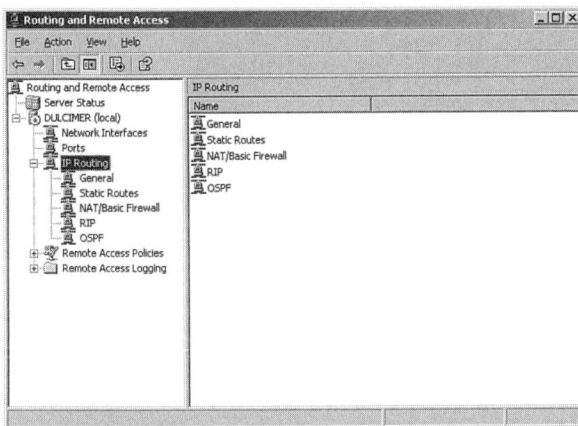

**FIGURE 4.20**
The OSPF protocol appears under the IP Routing node of the Routing and Remote Access console.

4. Select the newly installed OSPF protocol and right-click. From the context menu, select New Interface. The New Interface for Open Shortest Path First (OSPF) dialog box opens, as shown in Figure 4.21.

*continues*

*continued*

**FIGURE 4.21**
The OSPF protocol can be tied to a single interface or to multiple interfaces.

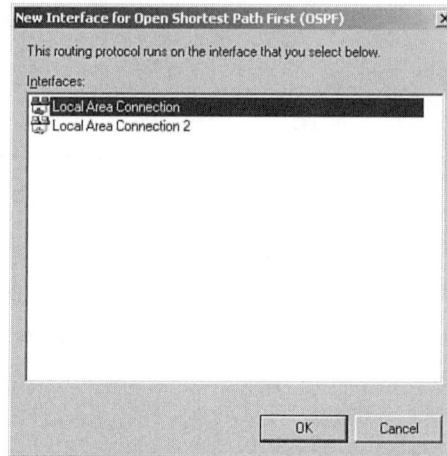

**5.** Select Local Area Connection and click OK. The OSPF Properties dialog box opens, as shown in Figure 4.22.

**FIGURE 4.22**
From the OSPF Properties dialog box, you can complete the configuration of the OSPF protocol.

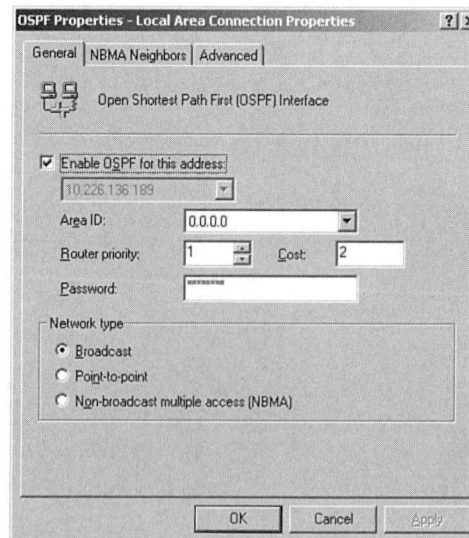

**6.** On the General tab, select the Enable OSPF for This Address option. In Area ID, click the ID of the area to which the interface belongs (for this exercise, it should be

0.0.0.0). In Router Priority, click the arrows to set the priority of the router over the interface to 1. In Cost, click the scroll arrows to set the cost of sending a packet over the interface to 2. In the Password text box, type a password. Under Network Type, set the type of OSPF interface as Broadcast. Click OK to complete the installation of the interface and return to the Routing and Remote Access console.

## Routing Hierarchies

Unlike RIP, OSPF operates within a hierarchy. The basic structure to this hierarchy includes areas, autonomous systems, and the OSPF backbone. The largest entity within the hierarchy is the autonomous system. An *autonomous system (AS)* is a collection of networks and routers under common administration, sharing a common routing protocol.

### Areas

An autonomous system can be further divided into *areas*. Each area is identified by an area ID. This identifier has no relation to an IP address or IP network ID, although it uses the same dotted decimal formula. Area IDs are not used to reflect routing data, and are actually convenient labels to simplify the management of the area. Although the area ID does not signify any IP routing information, if all the networks within an area correspond to a single subnetted network ID, the area ID can be set to the network ID. This can be convenient for administration of the areas. For example, if an area contains all the subnets of the IP network 10.1.0.0, the area ID can be set to 10.1.0.0. The reason for defining areas within an autonomous system is to reduce the size of a Link State Database.

To keep the size of LSDBs to a minimum, LSAs for an area's networks and routers are flooded within the area, but not to routers outside the area. Each area becomes its own link state domain with its own topological database.

Routers with multiple interfaces can participate in multiple areas. These routers, which are called *area border routers*, maintain separate LSDBs for each area. The routing tables within these routers are a

> **NOTE**
>
> **When do I need more than one area?** A good rule of thumb is to start creating a multiple area OSPF network when you reach 50 routers. If you have 50 routers on your network, your network is probably complex enough to warrant creating additional areas.

> **EXAM TIP**
>
> **OSPF is a complex routing protocol** If it seems as though OSPF is a really complex routing protocol, it is. Engineers who architect OSPF networks for large companies usually have extensive training and experience. For the exam, you should have a general understanding of the concepts associated with OSPF. You will not be asked to design a complex OSPF network as part of the exam.

NOTE

**The Link State Database (LSDB)**
The LSDB provides the overall picture of networks in relationship to routers within an area. The LSDB contains the collection of LSAs received from all routers in the same area. In an autonomous system with a large number of networks, each OSPF router must keep the LSA of every other router in its topological database.

combination of the routing table entries of all the SPF trees for each topological database, as well as static routes, Simple Network Management Protocol (SNMP) configured routes, and routes learned from other routing protocols. To reduce the number of entries in the routing table, the networks inside the area can be advertised outside the area using summary route advertisements. When you keep area topologies separate, OSPF passes less routing traffic than it would if the autonomous system were not partitioned.

## The Default Route

Each area within an OSPF network can be configured with a default route. A *default route* has a destination address of 0.0.0.0 with a subnet mask of 0.0.0.0. The default route is used to route any packets that are destined for an address not explicitly listed in the routing table. Default routes are typically used to reduce the size of routing tables because they can be used to summarize all routes external to the area into a single route. Default routes typically point to the OSPF backbone.

## OSPF Backbone

Every OSPF network must have at least one area. An OSPF network with more than one area must have a *backbone area* to interconnect all other areas within the network. The backbone area always has an area ID of 0.0.0.0 and acts as the hub for all the other areas on the network. All other areas must communicate their routing information to the backbone area so that it can distribute the information to all other areas. Figure 4.23 shows an example of an internetwork with several areas and a backbone.

Backbone routers not only route host traffic between areas, but can also provide summary routes within areas to other routers on the backbone. They, in turn, provide those summaries to the other routers within their areas. This configuration ensures that any host within an area can reach any host in another area. This capability ensures that no area's routing tables contain detail information about another area's topology. This minimizes the size of routing tables and ensures that the backbone handles all inter-area traffic.

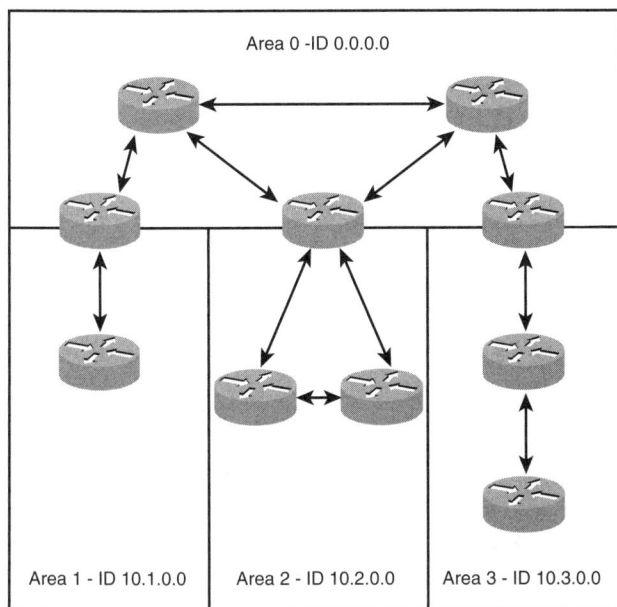

**FIGURE 4.23**
An OSPF network with multiple areas.

## Virtual Links

In rare cases an area may not have direct physical access to the backbone. In this instance, you need to configure a connection from the new area to the backbone through a connection called a virtual link. A virtual link provides the disconnected area a logical path to the backbone. The virtual link has to be established between two area border routers that have a common area, with one area border router connected to the backbone. Virtual links are configured over a non-backbone area known as a transit area.

Step by Step 4.7 shows how to configure a virtual link within RRAS. You need at least two OSPF areas to configure this interface.

## STEP BY STEP

### 4.7 Configuring a Virtual Routing Link for Windows Server 2003

1. Open the Routing and Remote Access console.

*continues*

*continued*

2. Expand the console tree and select IP Routing. Right-click OSPF and select Properties from the context menu. The OSPF Properties dialog box opens, as shown in Figure 4.24.

**FIGURE 4.24**
To setup a virtual routing link, you need to edit the OSPF properties.

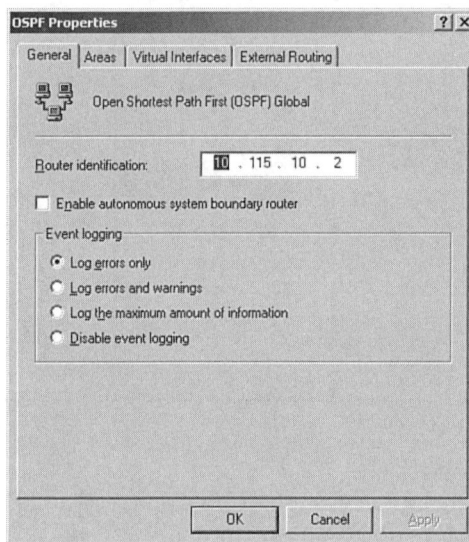

3. On the Virtual Interfaces tab, click Add. In Transit Area ID, click the transit area over which you are connecting the virtual link. The OSPF Virtual Interface Configuration dialog box opens, as shown in Figure 4.25.

4. In Virtual Neighbor Router ID, type the OSPF router ID of the router at the other endpoint of the virtual link. In Transit Delay (Seconds), click the arrows to set the transit delay in seconds. In Retransmit Interval (Seconds), click the arrows to set the retransmit interval in seconds. In Hello Interval (Seconds), click the arrows to set the hello interval in seconds. In Dead Interval (Seconds), click the arrows to set the dead interval in seconds. Click OK to add the virtual interface, and click OK again to return to the Routing and Remote Access console.

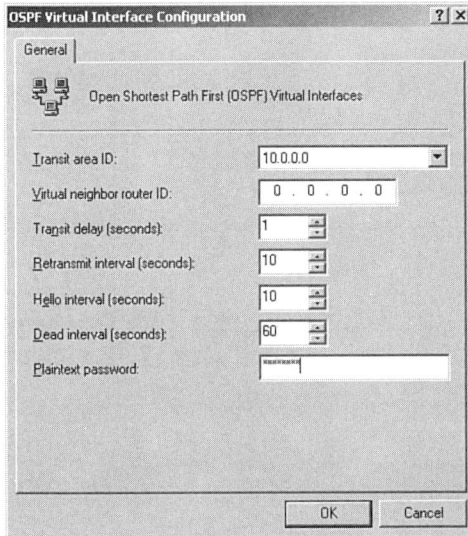

**FIGURE 4.25**
Be sure you know the network parameters and characteristics of your virtual link before configuring the virtual interface.

## Area Routing

Area partitioning creates the following two types of OSPF routing, depending on whether the source and destination are in the same area or in different areas:

▶ **Intra-area**—Intra-area routing occurs when the source and destination are in the same area. With intra-area routing, the source routes the packet to its default gateway (an internal area router). The internal area router then makes use of the explicit routes (as calculated by the SPF algorithm) maintained in the area routers and routes the packet through the appropriate interface to the destination internal area router. The destination internal area router then forwards the packet to the destination host.

▶ **Inter-area**—Inter-area routing occurs when the source and destination are in different areas. When routing between areas, the source routes the packet to its default gateway (an internal area router); the area router then forwards the packet to an area border router using the shortest path. The area border router then forwards the packets through backbone routers using the shortest path to the area border router for the destination host. The area border router for the destination host then forwards the packets through internal area routers using the shortest path, until the packets reach their destination.

Step by Step 4.8 allows you to create additional OSPF areas.

---

## STEP BY STEP

### 4.8 Creating an OSPF Area with Windows Server 2003's Routing and Remote Access Service

1. Open the Routing and Remote Access console.

2. Expand the console tree and select IP Routing. In the details pane, right-click OSPF and select Properties from the context menu. The OSPF Properties dialog box opens.

3. Select the Areas tab.

4. Click Add to open the OSPF Area Configuration dialog box, as shown in Figure 4.26.

**FIGURE 4.26**
Be sure you know the network parameters and characteristics of your area before adding it to your OSPF network.

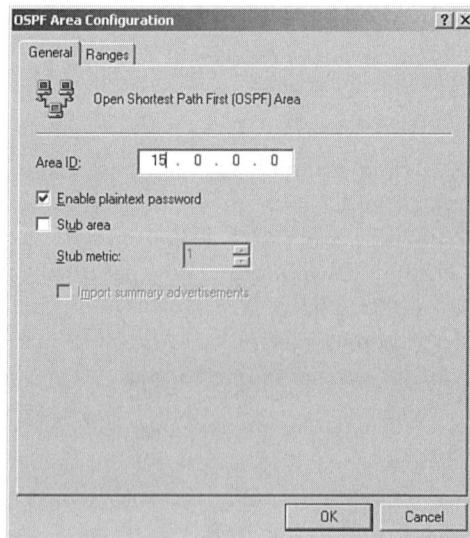

**5.** On the General tab, type a dotted decimal number that identifies the area. To use a plain-text password, verify that the Enable Plaintext Password option is selected. To mark the area as a stub, select the Stub Area option. In Stub Metric, click the arrows to set the stub metric. To import routes of other areas into the stub area, select the Import Summary Advertisements option. Click OK twice to apply the changes and return to the Routing and Remote Access console.

> **NOTE**
>
> **What is a stub area?**  A stub area is an OSPF area that doesn't advertise individual network routes from external areas. Instead, it relies on a default route (0.0.0.0 with a subnet mask of 0.0.0.0) to route all traffic out of the area. This is done to reduce the amount of memory required on the routers located in the stub area; they don't need to maintain a topology database.

## Autonomous System Routing

Routing does not occur only within areas using OSPF. When internetworks are connected to other internetworks that are under different administrative control, routing must be established. This type of routing between autonomous systems is established using external routes. Autonomous system border routers running OSPF learn about exterior routes through other routing protocols, such as Interior Gateway Routing Protocol (IGRP), RIP, or Border Gateway Protocol (BGP). Autonomous system border routers are similar to area border routers, except that they route between different autonomous systems.

> **EXAM TIP**
>
> **Supported protocols**  Some of the more common border protocols such as Interior Gateway Routing Protocol or Border Gateway Protocol are not supported by Windows Server 2003. They are important to know as general information, because they are commonly used in production networks, but will not be on the exam.

By default, autonomous system border routers advertise all external routes within their autonomous system. This allows all areas and networks within areas to reach destination networks that may lie outside the autonomous system. As a network manager, you may find it necessary to restrict the external routes that are advertised within the autonomous system. Using Windows Server 2003 Router and Remote Access Services, you can configure the autonomous system border router to accept or ignore the routes of certain external sources, such as routing protocols (RIPv2) or other sources (static routes or Simple Network Management Protocol). You can also configure the autonomous system border router to accept or discard specific routes by configuring one or multiple (Destination, Network Mask) pairs. Step by Step 4.9 shows how to enable autonomous system border routing.

## STEP BY STEP

### 4.9 Configuring Autonomous System Border Routing in Windows Server 2003's Routing and Remote Access Service

**1.** Open the Routing and Remote Access console.

**2.** Expand the console tree and select IP Routing. In the details pane, right-click OSPF and select Properties from the context menu. The OSPF Properties dialog box opens.

**3.** On the General tab, shown in Figure 4.27, click Enable Autonomous System Boundary Router.

**FIGURE 4.27**
You need to enable the Autonomous System Boundary Router parameter to accept routing information from RIP.

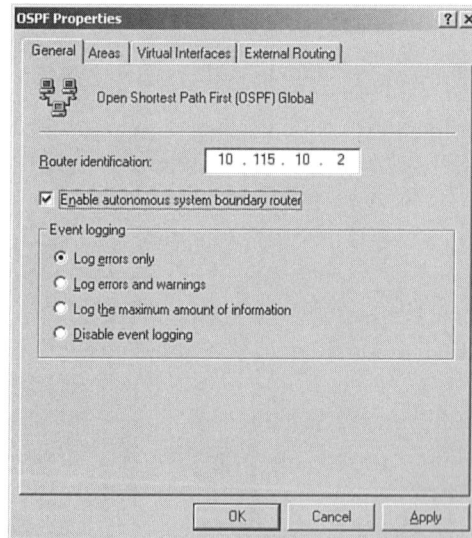

**4.** Select the External Routing tab, shown in Figure 4.28, and click Accept Routes from All Route Sources Except Those Selected. If you want to exclude a specific route source, select it in the window below. You can also select Ignore Routes from All Route Sources Except Those Selected if you want to accept routes from only one or two sources.

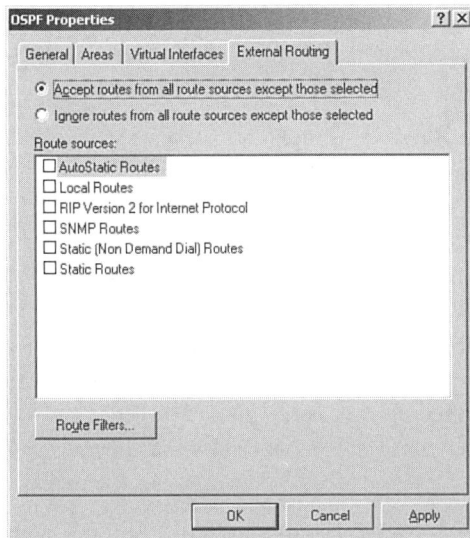

5. Click OK to return to the Routing and Remote Access console and enable the OSPF boundary routing.

# Other Problems with Routing

Our last routing topic addresses problems that may occur and what the protocols themselves can do to fix those problems after they are configured. Here, we cover hop count issues, Split Horizons and Poison Reverse, and convergence problems.

▶ **Hop count limit**—Hop count limitations restrict the network's scalability. This is a problem in design. If you have to keep building your network outward, and you suddenly can't route to a location, or the network starts experiencing major routing problems, you may have surpassed the maximum hop count limit. RIP permits a maximum hop count of 15, whereas OSPF does not have this hop count limitation. Remember that any packet traveling on a RIP network with a hop count greater than 15 hops is tagged as unreachable.

▶ **Split Horizons**—Split Horizons is a service that RIP performs to stop two node routing loops; it should prevent routing loops between adjacent routers. Split Horizons does not advertise routing information on the interface in which it was learned.

▶ **Poison Reverse**—The Poison Reverse service tries to stop routing loops in the larger internetwork, instead of just two nodes, as Split Horizons does. If a routing loop is occurring, Poison Reverse sends updates to adjacent routers to put that route (the one in question) in a hold-down state, which can be set by a timer. If these metrics are not fine-tuned, routing loops can occur. In this case, Poison Reverse is activated, and the network is put in a hold-down state. Depending on the timer, this problem could go on long enough to cause network timeouts that are experienced by the clients your network services.

▶ **Convergence issues**—If you have a problem with convergence, you need to analyze a topology map of your network as it currently operates and figure out where (and why) the network is having this problem. As stated previously, convergence occurs when all routers on the network know all other routers, and the topology is accurate. If major activity occurs in your network so that it needs to constantly reconverge (perform updates and verify routing information), you may also experience problems in which routes are unknown and data cannot be accessed. In this case, you need to adjust your network settings or redesign the network so that it converges quickly or stays in a state of convergence longer. By using OSPF instead of RIP, you are already ahead of the game because RIP reconverges the entire network every 30 seconds, by default.

# PLANNING ROUTING FOR IP MULTICAST TRAFFIC

**Plan a routing strategy.**

▶ **Plan routing for IP multicast traffic.**

This section covers IP multicast routing. We spend some time examining what multicast means and why knowing this information is important. To do that, we have to compare and contrast other forms of traffic traversing your LAN or WAN, which includes unicast, broadcast, and multicast.

▶ **Unicast**—When a single node on the network sends data to its destination node under one single packet, it knows where the destination node is and gets the data to it. Remember *uni* as being a single transmission.

▶ **Broadcast**—Broadcasting (think of the word *broad*) occurs when the destination is not known or cannot be found, and that node (which needs to find the destination node) sends out packets to all nodes on the network segment to see whether it can find its destination node. This process is conducive to increased traffic, collisions on hubbed networks, and so on. Broadcasts are at times a necessary evil, but most of the time you should prevent them from happening often or control their number. Basically, broadcast traffic adds overhead to your network (bandwidth utilization) and its devices (processing packets they don't need to look at).

▶ **Multicast**—Multicast is the happy medium but still can cause problems. A multicast transmission is based on a group. In simple terms, think of 20 nodes on a network, 5 of which need to communicate at all times and 15 of which do not need to ever know what the other 5 are doing. Say these nodes are OSPF routers. OSPF routers send out updates to each other via a multicast, so you might ask, "What about devices that do not need to know this information?" If you use a multicast address, such as 224.0.0.5 (the all-OSPF routers multicast address) for OSPF-based networks, only those devices listen for transmissions from other nodes using this service. This reduces the problems caused by broadcast traffic and enables you to cause one sender to get information to multiple (group) nodes without that message going to every node on the network. Consequently, multicasting is good, but as with any other technology, it can cause problems as well or require an advanced level of administration to make it work properly. This section focuses on these issues and how they revolve around the Windows Server 2003 platform.

**EXAM TIP**

**Get more information** For more information on this technology, you can visit the following RFCs:

- RFC 1075 defines the Distance Vector Multicast Routing Protocol (DVMRP).

- RFC 1584 defines the Multicast Open Shortest Path First (MOSPF) protocol.

Neither protocol is tested on the 70-293 exam; this information is provided just so you know how to plan for such protocols in your environment.

So now that you are familiar with the concept of multicast networks, let's consider the problems with routing such networks. Routing of multicast information is important, but first you should know why you need to route it.

Considering multicast routing is very important because your network must be able to build packet distribution trees that allow sources to send packets to all receivers. These trees ensure that each packet on the network exists one time only and is found only on a specific network. If this limitation did not exist, you would have problems with IP multicast routing. Also, multicast routing, which is the propagation of multicast listening information, is provided by multicast routing protocols such as Distance Vector Multicast Routing Protocol (DVMRP) and Multicast Open Shortest Path First (MOSPF), which is an extension to OSPF that allows it to support IP multicasting. Such protocols ease manual configuration of VPN- and OSPF-based networks and are becoming the standard for these types of networks.

As a Windows Server 2003 administrator, you need to know this information. For example, if you set up a remote access solution with Windows Server 2003 (such as a router), this router would need to know what to do with multicast traffic that approaches it. In other words, if you were to set up a Windows Server 2003 router on a multicast network, it could participate if configured properly.

The Windows Server 2003 family does not provide any multicast routing protocols like DVMRP. Other vendors, such as Cisco, are leaders in this arena. The purpose of Microsoft's product line is to conform with industry trends, vendor-neutral functionality, and so on; therefore, it is important for the server to at least be able to "participate." How can it participate then? It can use technologies to make sure that IP multicast routing does happen, even though it may not be directly responsible for routing of such information. Windows Server 2003 handles multicast traffic and its routing by forwarding this traffic. To do this, you can use the Internet Group Management Protocol (IGMP).

IGMP, which is described in RFC 2236, is an Internet protocol that allows nodes which are configured to use it to communicate as a group, instead of individually. IGMP allows a node to report its multicast group membership (the group to which it is assigned) to adjacent routers. Multicasting allows a node to send data to multiple other nodes that have also identified themselves as being part of that group. This cuts down on broadcast traffic and bandwidth consumption.

Now that you know what IGMP does, let's look at the features you must plan and design into your infrastructure to work with Windows Server 2003, especially because it can't natively route multicast traffic based on the multicast routing protocol. If you run Windows Server 2003 in your environment to help with multicast traffic, you can set it up to use the IGMP routing protocol, IGMP router mode, and IGMP proxy mode to provide multicast forwarding in a single router-based network or when connecting a single router-based LAN to the Internet. This means that you can use a Windows Server 2003 system on your network to participate in multicast routing as a forwarding service.

With a service such as multicast forwarding, a router is able to forward multicast traffic to any network where nodes also configured to use the multicast service are listening. Only multicast-capable nodes can forward multicast traffic across an internetwork. A multicast-capable node must be able to send and receive multicast network traffic as well as be able to register the multicast address that it and other routers are listening to. Again, Windows Server 2003 is capable of doing this.

**EXAM TIP**

**What are multicast packets?**
Multicast packets are IP-based packets. They must contain the right multicast address as the destination IP address. Remember the previous OSPF example in which the multicast address used to inform neighboring routers was 224.0.0.5. Only nodes listening for this destination address in the IP packet can receive multicast traffic.

# Windows Server 2003 Multicast Specifics

Windows Server 2003 enables you to use TCP/IP (refer to Chapter 2); therefore, it can work with multicast traffic. Windows Server 2003 uses a multicast forwarding table to make decisions about where to forward its incoming multicast traffic as well as to listen for IGMP report messages thus provided by the IGMP routing protocol on a single interface operating in IGMP router mode. You can plan to use the multicast routing protocol to propagate to other multicast-capable routers any information, such as multicast group listening information. Remember, though, RRAS does not provide a routing protocol for multicasting; it provides forwarding only.

**The IGMP routing protocol** Do not be confused by the IGMP routing protocol provided by Windows Server 2003. This protocol is NOT a multicast routing protocol.

---

**The MBone** The multicast-capable portion of the Internet is known as the Internet multicast backbone, or *MBone*. This is the place where all the multicast forwarding messages and reports go.

The Windows Server 2003 IGMP routing protocol is used for the maintenance of entries found in the multicast forwarding table on the router. When you add this component in RRAS, plan to configure them in one of two possible ways: IGMP router mode or IGMP proxy mode.

IGMP router mode allows you to set Windows Server 2003 to listen for IGMP Membership Report packets as well as to track group membership.

IGMP proxy mode allows you to configure your router (you must have two or more interfaces or NICs) with different settings on different interfaces—one acting as a proxy multicast host that sends IGMP membership reports on one of its interfaces.

# PLANNING AND IMPLEMENTING REMOTE ACCESS SECURITY

In this section, we examine the process of planning and implementing security for remote access solutions. In general, if you were to think about overall network security when dealing with a remote access solution, the most important consideration would be that remote access means "remote" sites, users, and so on will be entering your protected core network to access resources needed to perform business. Therefore, you need to consider how to authenticate them and make sure that you are giving access to these critical resources to the right people and that they are logged as doing such, so if a problem occurs, it can be traced back to the source.

To implement remote access security, you need to follow a general process similar to this: First, determine what risks and problems you are likely to encounter. Next, choose a solution that fits your business needs (Windows Server 2003 RRAS for this discussion), and then implement the solution. After you have implemented the solution, test it—to try to break it, in effect, looking for weaknesses in its design and implementation. This section focuses on planning and creating secure remote access solutions using remote access policies and the various user authentication methods available in Windows Server 2003.

Windows Server 2003 provides remote access for both dial-in connections and virtual private network (VPN) connections and includes a set of features that provide flexibility and security for your remote access solution. If you need to review the basics of implementing and configuring remote access, be sure to see *MCSA/MCSE 70-291 Training Guide: Implementing, Managing, and Maintaining a Windows Server 2003 Network Infrastructure* by Dave Bixler and Will Schmied (Que Publishing, 2003).

Before you go any further with your plan for secure remote access, you should ask yourself the following questions to gain an insight into what security you may need:

▶ Do all your users require remote access? In the majority of networks, only a small group of users actually needs to have remote access capabilities. Your remote access policies should take this into account and prevent unauthorized users from making remote access connections to your network.

▶ Of the users who *do* need remote access, do they need differing levels of remote access? You need to plan for this if you have users who require differing levels of remote access.

▶ Of the users who *do* need remote access, do they need to access network resources or only the resources located on the Remote Access Server? If users do not need to access any internal resources, you can contain them to the Remote Access Server for increased security and accountability.

Remote access allows users with remote computers to create a logical connection to an organization's network or the Internet. In this chapter, we do not look at the specifics of how connections are created (that is the scope of the 70-291 exam), but instead at how to authenticate and secure these connections.

# Planning Authentication Methods

**Plan security for remote access users.**

▶ **Analyze protocol security requirements.**

▶ **Plan authentication methods for remote access clients.**

To handle network traffic (and to know what to do with it via security), you need to select a protocol to use with your remote access setup in Windows Server 2003. This section highlights your options, which one seems best to utilize, what differences they have and why, as well as what you can use if you don't want a high-end security solution. Regardless, you need to know these options for the 70-293 exam.

Remote access authentication methods are configured on the Authentication Methods dialog box, as shown in Figure 4.29. In this section, we cover EAP, CHAP, MS-CHAP, MS-CHAP v2, SPAP, PAP, and nonauthorized access.

**FIGURE 4.29**
You can select any number of available remote access authentication methods.

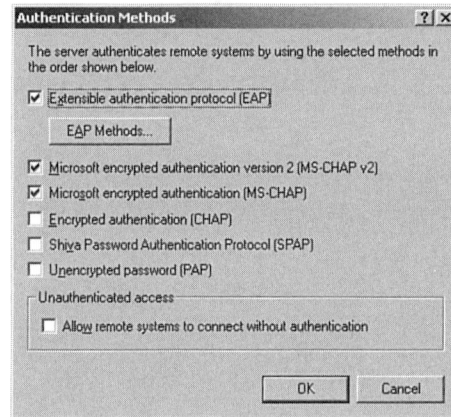

## Extensible Authentication Protocol (EAP)

Extensible Authentication Protocol (EAP) is a commonly used protocol on networks today. It is responsible for creating an authentication method in which the authentication scheme to be used is negotiated by the remote access client and the authenticator, which could be either the Remote Access Server or even a RADIUS server. Windows Server 2003 Routing and Remote Access (RRAS) includes support for EAP-TLS by default; TLS stands for *Transport Layer Security*. It could be considered an EAP type, much like the wireless access protocol called LEAP, which is provided by Cisco systems. There are many types of EAP, although they all perform similar functions, such as authentication; they just use different methods to do so. Following are some of the more common forms of EAP:

▶ **EAP-MD5 CHAP (Extensible Authentication Protocol–Message Digest 5 Challenge Handshake Authentication Protocol)**—This form of EAP uses the same type of CHAP authentication that is explained in the next authentication method, but wraps the authentication in EAP packets for increased security during transmission.

▶ **PEAP (Protected Extensible Authentication Protocol)**—This relatively new form of EAP is used in wireless networks.

▶ **EAP-TLS (Extensible Authentication Protocol–Transport Layer Security)**—This derivative of EAP uses smart cards or digital certificates to perform the authentication.

## Challenge Handshake Authentication Protocol (CHAP)

Challenge Handshake Authentication Protocol (CHAP) uses the industry standard Message Digest 5 (MD5) protocol. MD5 is a hashing scheme that encrypts your data in transit over the remote access network. CHAP is supported by virtually all remote access clients and servers. This protocol uses a user's password to perform authentication; by default, Windows Server 2003 does not allow CHAP to access a user's password. If you plan to use CHAP, you must configure the user's password for CHAP by selecting the Store Passwords Using Reversible Encryption option either on a specific user's account or in Group Policy. After this change has been made, all applicable users must then change their passwords so that they will be stored in a form that CHAP can access.

## Microsoft Challenge Handshake Authentication Protocol (MS-CHAP)

MS-CHAP provides one-way authentication of the user to the Remote Access Server and uses a single encryption key for all transmitted and received messages. Windows 95 and Windows NT 3.51 clients cannot make use of the newer, more secure, MS-CHAP version 2 (discussed next); thus, MS-CHAP is provided in Windows Server 2003 for backward compatibility with these clients.

## MS-CHAP Version 2

MS-CHAP version 2 is a stronger version of the MS-CHAP protocol that provides for mutual authentication by both the user and the server using encrypted passwords. MS-CHAP v2 is the simplest remote access authentication method to employ if all your clients are Windows 98 or newer.

## Shiva Password Authentication Protocol (SPAP)

The Shiva Password Authentication Protocol (SPAP) is an authentication protocol originally used by the Shiva LAN Rover line of products. If a Shiva client tries to connect to a Windows Server 2003 Remote Access Server, or a Windows client connects to a Shiva LAN Rover, SPAP must be used. Because Shiva was prominent in the remote access market at one time, support is still included in Windows Server 2003 even though SPAP is extremely insecure. SPAP is susceptible to replay attacks (such attacks occur when data packets are captured in transit, examined, and then replayed to the server to gain access) because the same user password is always sent over the network in the same reversibly encrypted way each time. You should use SPAP only when you absolutely have to.

## Password Authentication Protocol (PAP)

The Password Authentication Protocol (PAP) is the weakest authentication method available in Windows Server 2003. PAP sends your credentials in plain text, not encrypted or otherwise protected from compromise. Any network sniffing tool could pick up a packet with your credentials in it and, by simply looking at the packet, you could log in to a network with someone else's ID. PAP is most commonly used as a method of last resort in the event that a client and server cannot agree on any other method. Even PAP authentication is better than no authentication at all, as discussed next. You should plan to never use sensitive accounts, such as administrative accounts, when PAP is the authentication method in place.

## Using Unauthenticated Access

Windows Server 2003 supports the use of Guest access, better known as *unauthorized access,* which allows a connection attempt to be granted without need for credentials. You should avoid the use of unauthenticated access if at all possible.

# Using Dial-in Properties for Access Control

Even though Windows Server 2003 provides a full array of encrypted authentication methods, there are several basic dial-in properties that you can configure on a user-by-user basis, as shown in Figure 4.30.

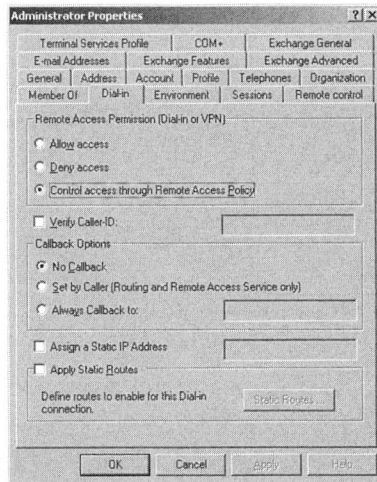

**FIGURE 4.30**
You can use these basic dial-in properties as your first line of defense.

You can use the following options on the dial-in tab to control how remote access connections are made:

▶ **Remote Access Permission**—This option enables you to allow or deny remote access to the user. Alternatively, you can leave the default selection of Control Access through Remote Access Policy. (We will discuss remote access policies shortly.)

▶ **Verify Caller ID**—If you enter a phone number in this area, the Remote Access Server will not accept any calls from any other number.

▶ **Callback Options**—This option group allows you to specify how callback should be handled for the user. This is both a cost-saving measure and a means of security.

Now that you've seen the available methods of authenticating remote access, you're ready to start creating remote access policies.

# Planning and Creating Remote Access Policies

**Plan security for remote access users.**

▶ **Plan remote access policies.**

Remote access policies are a set of conditions and connection settings that give network administrators more flexibility in authorizing connection attempts. They provide both granular and flexible configuration settings for both RAS and VPN connections. This granularity and flexibility unfortunately come at the expense of ease of use: Remote access policies can be very complex, and you need an in-depth understanding of them if you are going to successfully provide secure remote access to your users. With remote access policies, you can grant remote access by individual user account or through the configuration of specific remote access policies.

Windows Server 2003 uses three types of remote access policies to control access:

▶ **Group Policies**—Access can be controlled by group policies created on each Windows Server 2003 Routing and Remote Access Server. This is the simplest method for authenticating users as long as you are using a single server for remote access.

▶ **Local Internet Authentication Services policies**—These local policies are derived from RADIUS and can be used to define access permissions based on a number of client attributes. This mechanism requires that the Internet Authentication Service be installed on the Windows Server 2003 Remote Access Server. This is typically the best solution if you are planning on adding additional Windows Server 2003 Remote Access Servers and don't want to have to replicate the policies to each new server.

▶ **Central Internet Authentication Services policies**—A Windows Server 2003 Routing and Remote Access Service server can be configured to use a central Internet Authentication Server (IAS) RADIUS server to provide its policies. This allows multiple Routing and Remote Access dial-up servers to use the same policies without requiring the manual replication of policies and settings. This is the most practical solution for companies deploying multiple Windows Server 2003 Remote Access Servers.

Windows Server 2003 supports two methods for creating a remote access policy: utilizing a wizard to create commonly used remote access policies and using a custom method that allows you to create less common remote access policies. Step by Step 4.10 walks you through the process of creating a new remote access policy to allow VPN access to anyone in the Domain Users group using the wizard.

**NOTE** **Use Windows authentication methods** To ensure the success of Step by Step 4.10, make sure that the authentication method set on the server properties Security tab is set to Windows Authentication. Setting up a remote access policy under the Internet Authentication Service for centralized policy management works in exactly the same way as setting up the policy locally, but complicates any testing you might want to do.

## STEP BY STEP

### 4.10 Using the Remote Access Policy Wizard to Create a VPN Access Policy

1. Log on to Windows Server 2003 using the Administrator account or another account that has administrator privileges.

2. Open the Routing and Remote Access console by choosing Start, Administrative Tools, and selecting Routing and Remote Access.

3. Right-click Remote Access Policies in the left pane (see Figure 4.31) and select New Remote Access Policy from the context menu. The New Remote Access Policy Wizard opens, as shown in Figure 4.32.

4. Click Next to continue. The Policy Configuration Method dialog box opens, as shown in Figure 4.33. Select the Use the Wizard to Set Up a Typical Policy for a Common Scenario option. In the Policy Name field, type `Allow Remote Access to Remote Users`. If you are in a complex environment that uses many remote access policies, you may need a naming convention for these policies to keep them straight.

*continues*

*continued*

**FIGURE 4.31**
Remote access policies are managed locally through the Routing and Remote Access console.

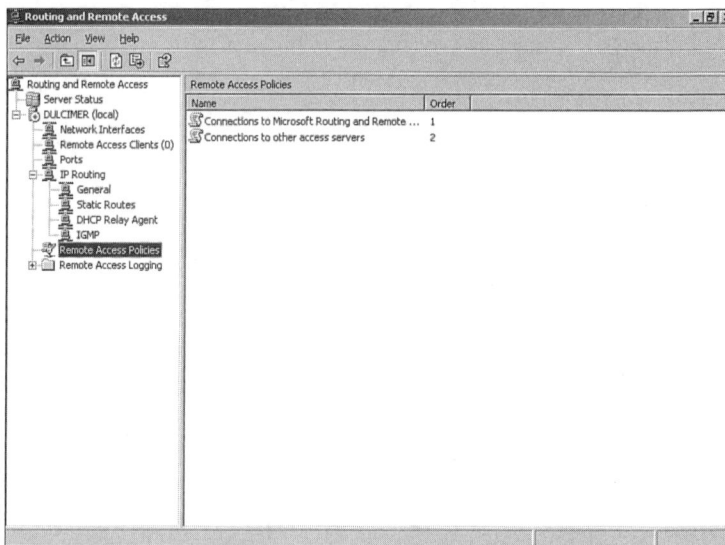

**FIGURE 4.32**
The New Remote Access Policy Wizard enables you to create new remote access policies.

**5.** Click Next to continue. The Access Method dialog box opens, as shown in Figure 4.34. For this exercise, select VPN. Be aware of the additional options for your information; it is good to know what can be done with this wizard.

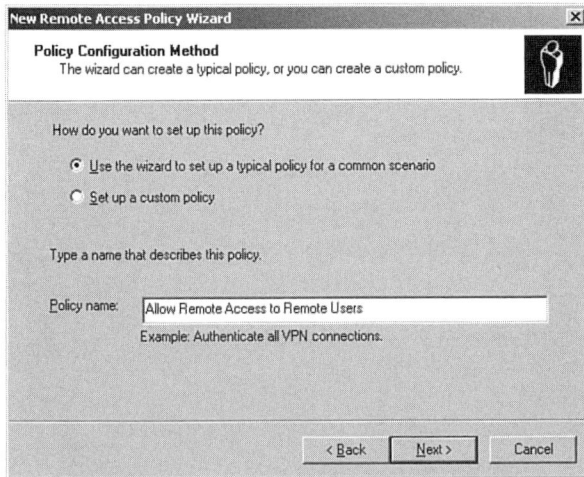

**FIGURE 4.33**
The Policy Configuration Method dialog box allows you to decide whether to use the wizard or manual configuration to create a remote access policy.

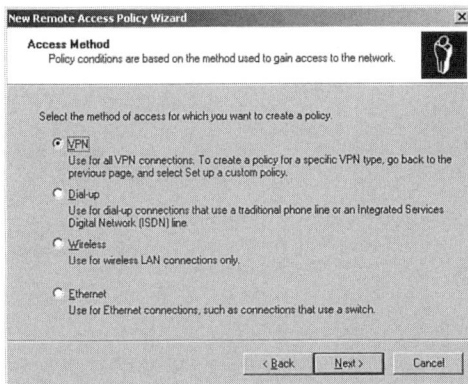

**FIGURE 4.34**
The Access Method dialog box allows you to select how users can connect to the Windows Server 2003 Remote Access Server.

6. Click Next to continue to the User or Group Access dialog box. Select the Group option and click Add to open the Select Groups dialog, as shown in Figure 4.35. Type **Domain Users** in the Enter the Objects Names to Select field. Clicking Check Names confirms that the object exists in the Active Directory.

7. Click OK to return to the User or Group Access dialog box, as shown in Figure 4.36. Notice that the group you entered in step 6 now appears in the list of groups.

*continues*

*continued*

**FIGURE 4.35**
The Select Groups dialog box allows you to populate the list of groups that will be affected by this policy.

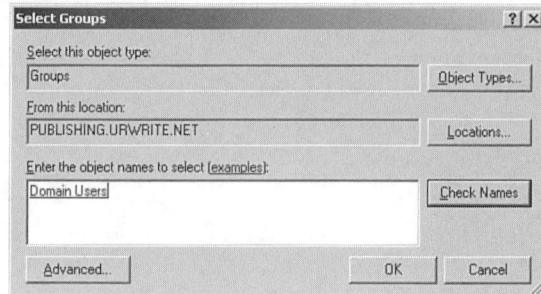

**FIGURE 4.36**
Any groups added appear in the Group Name field of the User or Group Access dialog box.

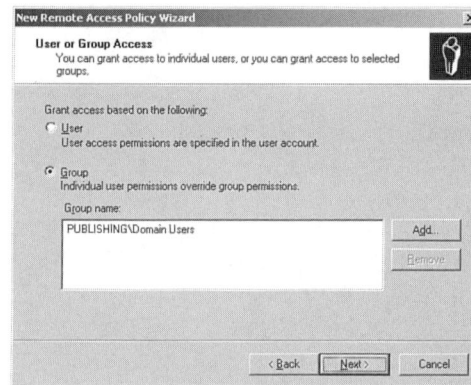

8. Click Next to continue. The Authentication Methods dialog box opens, as shown in Figure 4.37. Notice that the only authentication types allowed are EAP, MS-CHAPv2, and MS-CHAP. To use other authentication types, you need to use a custom remote access policy. Make sure that MS-CHAPv2 is selected.

9. Click OK to continue. The Policy Encryption Level dialog box opens, as shown in Figure 4.38. Because this will be a VPN connection, select Strongest Encryption. If this were a dial-up connection, you would have an additional option—No Encryption.

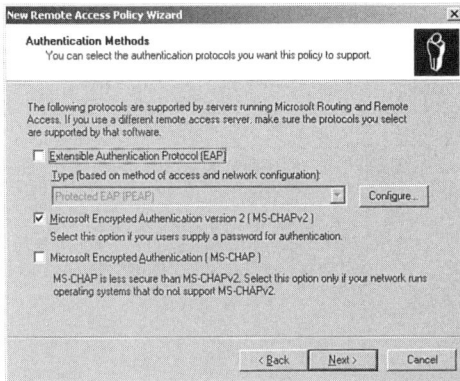

**FIGURE 4.37**
In the Authentication Methods dialog box, you can select which authentication methods will be permitted for accessing the Windows Server 2003 Routing and Remote Access Service server using this remote access policy.

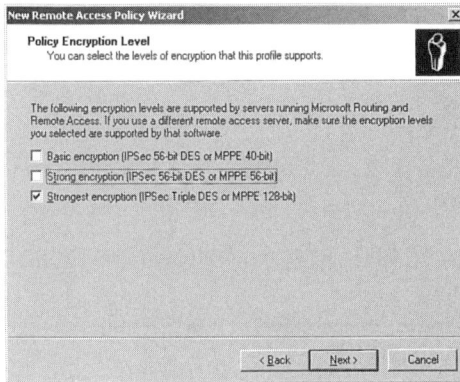

**FIGURE 4.38**
The Windows Server 2003 Routing and Remote Access Service supports three different encryption strengths.

**10.** Click Next to continue. The Completing the New Remote Access Policy Wizard dialog box opens, as shown in Figure 4.39.

**FIGURE 4.39**
The Completing the New Remote Access Policy Wizard dialog box summarizes the configuration of the policy.

*continues*

*continued*

**11.** Click Finish to complete the policy creation. Figure 4.40 shows the newly created remote access policy.

**FIGURE 4.40**
The Remote Access Policy folder shows all the policies that are in effect on the local server.

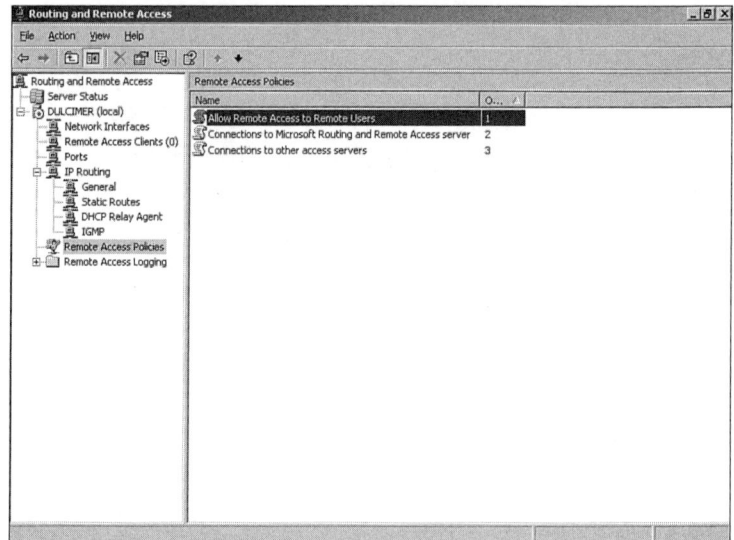

## Remote Access Profiles

In conjunction with the remote access policy, there is also a component known as the *remote access profile*. This profile contains a number of variables that allow you to further refine the parameters of the remote access policy. You can modify a remote access profile during the creation of a remote access policy, or you can review/modify a profile for an existing remote access policy by right-clicking the policy in either the Routing and Remote Access console or in the Internet Authentication Service console, selecting Properties, and then selecting the Edit Profile button. When the Settings dialog box opens, you can add additional conditions to the policy, edit the profile, or review/change the Allow/Deny Access settings on the policy. Six tabs are available in the Edit Profile dialog box; let's look at them one at a time.

## Dial-in Constraints

The parameters that you can configure on the Dial-in Constraints tab, shown in Figure 4.41, are as follows:

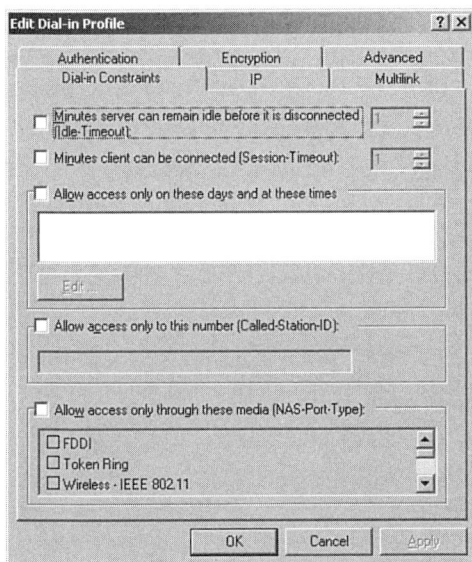

**FIGURE 4.41**
On the Dial-in Constraints tab, you can restrict how dial-in access can be used.

▶ **Minutes server can remain idle before it is disconnected (Idle Timeout)**—The Idle Timeout setting allows you to set the number of minutes of inactivity users have before the system disconnects them. This setting can be used to limit toll charges being incurred by an idle system or to protect your network from the vulnerability a connected but idle system presents. This option can also be used to maximize the availability of ports if your server has a limited number. This prevents idle users from tying up ports that might be needed by another user.

▶ **Minutes client can be connected (Session Timeout)**—The Session Timeout setting allows you to set the total number of minutes a session can last. This option can be used to limit toll charges for users who may leave themselves connected for extended periods of time.

▶ **Allow access only on these days and at these times**—This setting allows you to place day and time limits on any remote access policy, without needing to make that a condition of the policy.

▶ **Allow access only to this number (Called-Station-ID)**— This setting is typically used in conjunction with a branch office connection, to ensure that the connection is originating from the appropriate number. This field can contain a phone number or IP address, so it can be used in conjunction with a site-to-site VPN as well as a branch demand-dial connection.

▶ **Allow access only through these media types (NAS-Port-Type)**—This parameter allows you to control the types of network media that can be used to connect using this profile. You might use this setting to ensure a VPN connection can be established using only LAN media and not dial-in lines.

## IP

The parameters that can be configured on the IP tab, shown in Figure 4.42, are as follows:

**FIGURE 4.42**
On the IP tab, you can configure the characteristics of the IP protocol for a remote access policy.

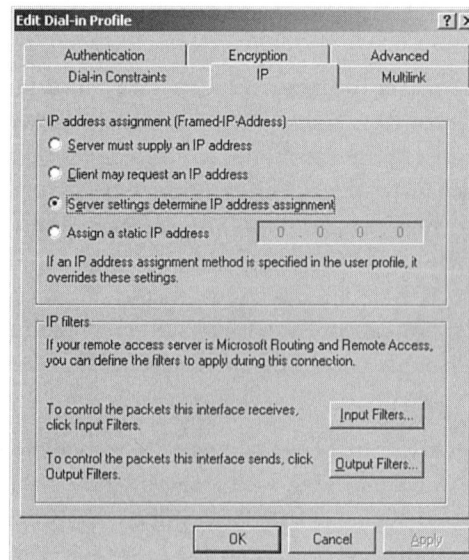

▶ **IP Address Assignment (Framed-IP-Address)**—This setting defines how users being authorized by this policy will get their IP addresses. This option is typically left at the default setting but can be used to restrict how IP addresses are assigned.

▶ **IP Filters**—This setting allows you to set IP packet filters on the connection. For example, if this connection were being used only to get Web access to your intranet server, you might set an inbound filter for port 80 (http) to access only the intranet server.

## Multilink

The parameters that you can configure on the Multilink tab, shown in Figure 4.43, are as follows:

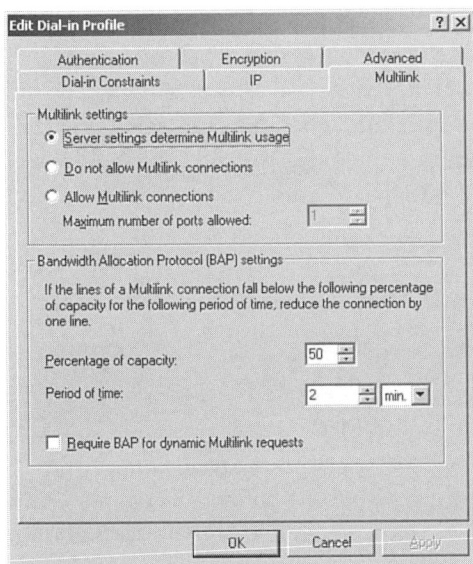

**FIGURE 4.43**
On the Multilink tab, you can configure the Multilink (aggregation of multiple physical connections into a single logical connection) capabilities of the Windows Server 2003 Routing and Remote Access Service.

▶ **Multilink Settings**—These settings control how the Multilink protocol can be used with this remote access policy:

• **Server Settings Determine Multilink Usage**—This setting enables use of the Routing and Remote Access Service server settings to determine whether Multilink is permitted.

- **Do Not Allow Multilink Connections**—This setting disables the use of Multilink.

- **Allow Multilink Connections**—This configuration allows a client computer to connect using multiple ports. Here, you can also set the maximum number of ports that can be used.

Windows 2000 and higher support the use of multiple connections to a single server, which are aggregated to provide additional bandwidth. Although multiple connections can improve performance, Multilink can be a very resource-intensive solution. Not only does it tie up multiple ports per user at the server end of the connection, but it also requires multiple modems and phone lines on the user's end.

▶ **Bandwidth Allocation Protocol (BAP) Settings**—BAP monitors the utilization on a Multilink connection and dynamically reduces the number of connected lines if the user's utilization drops below a certain amount. The utilization percentage and time before dropping one line of the Multilink connection are set here. You can (and should) require the use of BAP with any Multilink connection in this section.

## Authentication

The parameters that you can configure on the Authentication tab, shown in Figure 4.44, are as follows:

▶ **Authentication Methods**—This section allows you to select what protocols can be used to authenticate a user connecting using this remote access policy. Whenever possible, use MS-CHAP v2 or the Extensible Authentication Protocol because they provide the most secure authentication.

▶ **Unauthenticated Access**—Never enable this setting. It essentially allows clients to connect without authenticating first, and should never be used, because it bypasses all authentication security.

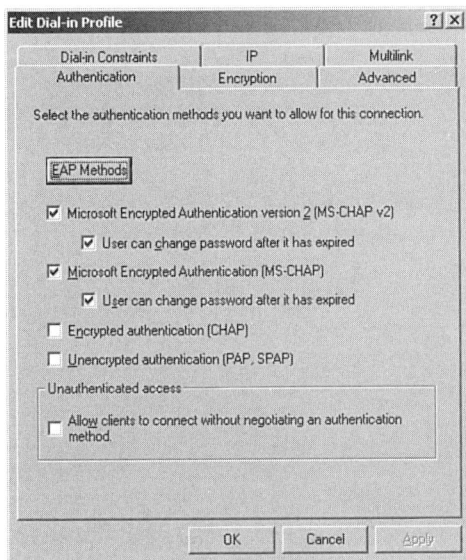

## Encryption

The purpose of the Encryption tab, shown in Figure 4.45, is to
select how strong the encryption used by this connection must be. If
you are running an entirely Windows 2000 or greater client popula-
tion, you should permit only the Strongest level of encryption. If
you have older clients, you may need to permit less strong encryption levels.

## Advanced

The Advanced tab, shown in Figure 4.46, allows you to specify additional connection attributes, typically related to RADIUS requirements for a connection. This screen is generally used only for very
complex implementations involving centralized RADIUS servers for
remote access policy storage.

**FIGURE 4.45**

On the Encryption tab, you can specify the permitted encryption strengths for a connection.

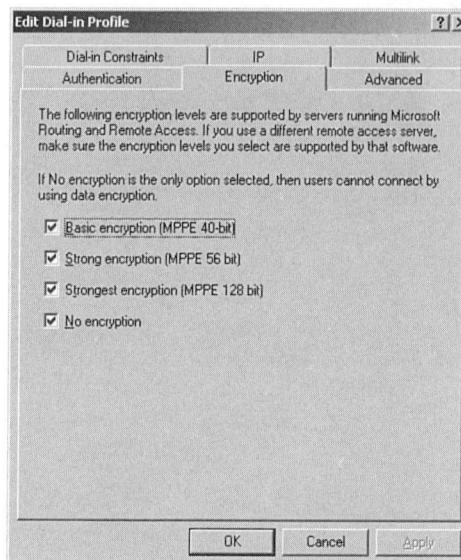

**FIGURE 4.46**

On the Advanced tab, you can specify additional connection attributes.

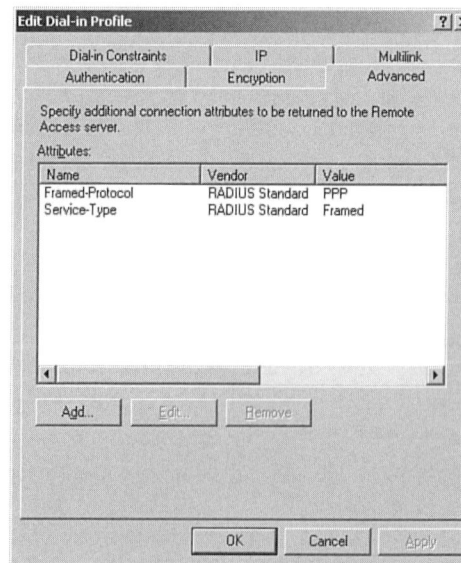

## NETWORK ACCESS QUARANTINE CONTROL

Windows Server 2003 includes a new feature called Network Access Quarantine Control. This feature allows the delay of a remote access connection attempt to the Remote Access Server until a script that verifies the configuration of the remote access computer runs. The connection attempt goes into quarantine until verified. The actual process is as follows: When a remote computer attempts to connect to the Remote Access Server, the computer is assigned an IP address to participate on the network. Then the user credentials are verified and authenticated, but the connection stays in quarantine until the remote computer is verified against the script. A script runs, and after it is completed, the server hosting quarantine releases the connection from quarantine after this information is verified. Network Access Quarantine Control is one of the newest features of Remote Access Security provided by default with Windows Server 2003.

# TROUBLESHOOTING TCP/IP ROUTING

**Troubleshoot TCP/IP routing. Tools might include the `route`, `tracert`, `ping`, `pathping`, and `netsh` commands and Network Monitor.**

To conclude this chapter, we will now spend some time examining troubleshooting of TCP/IP routing. Knowing how to skillfully troubleshoot a routing problem is key to being able to administer a WAN. You have to know how to troubleshoot problems when they occur, and Windows Server 2003 provides several tools to help you do that.

There are five commands and one utility: `route`, `tracert`, `ping`, `pathping`, `netsh`, and the Network Monitor utility. Knowing when to use which one is the key to survival in this area of the 70-293 exam. Let's start our discussion of these troubleshooting tools with the `route` command.

## The `route` Command

As mentioned earlier, routers keep routing tables. If you are using static routes, you must manually edit your routing tables; the `route` command is the means by which you do this. Although you can use the RRAS console to manipulate this data, nothing is faster or easier than using the `route` command. Within seconds, you can add a route in the routing table, adjust one, or take one out.

The `route` command is easy to manipulate. You use the `route` command, like most of the other commands we will look at, from the command line. Entering the `route` command by itself provides you with a detailed description of its use. The syntax of the `route` command is as follows and is detailed in Table 4.2:

```
ROUTE [-f] [-p] [command] [destination] [MASK netmask] [gateway]
➥[METRIC metric] [IF interface]
```

### TABLE 4.2

### route PARAMETERS

| Parameter | Description |
| --- | --- |
| -f | Instructs the `route` command to clear the routing tables of all gateway entries. |
| -p | Specifies that a route being added is to be persistent and not dumped when the computer is restarted. |
| command | Specifies the action that is to be carried out. `print` prints a route. `add` adds a route. `delete` deletes a route. `change` changes an existing route. |
| destination | Specifies the host. |
| MASK netmask | Specifies a subnet mask value for the routing entry. If a value is not specified, the default of 255.255.255.255 is used. |
| gateway | Specifies a gateway. |
| METRIC metric | Specifies the metric (route cost) of the destination. |
| IF interface | Specifies the interface number for the route. |

You can use the `route print` command to display the routing table. You need to be familiar with its output. In the following output, you can see a standard routing table that consists of `route` statements with specific details in each route:

```
C:\>route print
=========================================================================
Interface List
0x1 ........................... MS TCP Loopback interface
0x1000003 ...00 07 85 b4 0e ec ...... PCX50422 Cisco Systems352 series
```

```
0x1000004 ...00 08 74 97 0c 26 ...... EL90Xbc0 3Com EtherLink PCI
===========================================================================
===========================================================================
Active Routes:
Network Destination        Netmask          Gateway       Interface  Metric
        0.0.0.0          0.0.0.0       10.2.102.1      10.2.102.173      1
      127.0.0.0        255.0.0.0        127.0.0.1        127.0.0.1      1
     10.2.102.0    255.255.255.0    10.2.102.173      10.2.102.173      1
   10.2.102.173  255.255.255.255       127.0.0.1        127.0.0.1      1
   10.2.255.255  255.255.255.255    10.2.102.173      10.2.102.173      1
      10.2.3.31  255.255.255.255       10.2.102.3      10.2.102.173      1
 216.136.227.78  255.255.255.255       10.2.102.2      10.2.102.173      1
      224.0.0.0        224.0.0.0     10.2.102.173      10.2.102.173      1
255.255.255.255  255.255.255.255    10.2.102.173      10.2.102.173      1
Default Gateway:       134.141.102.1
===========================================================================
Persistent Routes:
  None

C:\>
```

Let's examine the first entry in the routing table to see how it is laid out:

```
  0.0.0.0          0.0.0.0       10.2.102.1    10.2.102.173        1
```

The first 0.0.0.0 is the destination, and the following 0.0.0.0 is the network subnet mask. In other words, say you need to move traffic from one network to another; to do so, you would specify the destination address with its proper subnet mask. You might want traffic from the 10.1.0.0 network to be able to get traffic across your router to the 10.2.0.0 network. This is done via a route. Here, all 0s in the destination and the netmask mean that this is a default route. A default route means that *any* destination network with *any* netmask can be sent out the other interface of your server, which should be the next hop. This is what the interface is for, as well as the gateway. The gateway IP address, 10.2.102.1, specifies the forwarding or next hop IP address over which the set of addresses defined by the network destination and subnet mask are reachable. A metric is a way to specify something specific for a route you enter. A route with the lowest metric is the one that is chosen, so if you have to weight routes with higher metrics to get them to be specified as first, or last, this is how you would do it. The interface is simply the interface index for the NIC over which the destination address can be reached.

# The tracert Command

The tracert command is one of the most important routing troubleshooting commands around. Not knowing tracert (or Traceroute for Unix and Cisco systems) is not a good thing. The tracert command helps you to find problem spots in a routed network. Consider Figure 4.47.

**FIGURE 4.47**
The tracert command will be useful in troubleshooting this complex routing environment.

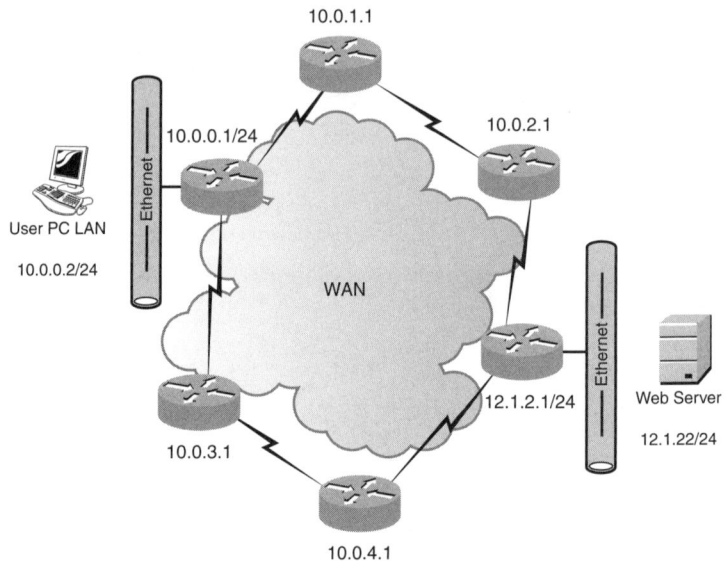

Where would you find the problem if you had one? Let's create a fictional problem that is very common on most production networks today. The clients on the 10.0.0.0 network routinely access the Web server located at 12.1.2.2 with no problems. Today, your clients suddenly can't get to this Web server at 12.1.2.2. What would you do? Well, you can do many things, but by using tracert, you can trace a route out from the 10.0.0.2 host to the 12.2.2.2 host, which is the Web server, and see where the packets drop, if they do. Here is an example:

```
C:\>tracert 12.1.2.2
Tracing route to 12.1.2.2 over a maximum of 30 hops
  1    10 ms    10 ms    10 ms  10.0.0.1
  2    10 ms    10 ms    10 ms  10.0.1.1
  3    40 ms    30 ms    40 ms  10.0.2.1
  4    40 ms    40 ms    40 ms  12.1.2.1
```

Now, you can see how useful this command is. If the 10.0.2.1 router were down (nonfunctional), you would get a request timeout or unreachable ICMP-based error message so that you would know that you have a problem there.

Another useful function of the `tracert` command is to analyze traffic routes to determine whether the most economical route is being taken. This function is especially useful for troubleshooting and tuning private networks where you can make changes (or have changes made) on the routers of concern. Recall that RIP does not differentiate between a one-hop route using a 56Kbps link or a one-hop route using a full T1 link. The `tracert` command can be used to determine exactly how traffic is moving from one point to another and correct such problems.

As with most of the other commands we will look at, you use the `tracert` command from the command line. Entering the `tracert` command by itself provides you with a detailed description of its use. The syntax of the `tracert` command is as follows and is detailed in Table 4.3:

```
tracert [-d] [-h maximum_hops] [-j host-list] [-w timeout] [-R]
➥[-S srcaddr] [-4] [-6] target_name
```

## TABLE 4.3

### tracert PARAMETERS

| Parameter | Description |
| --- | --- |
| -d | Prevents tracert from resolving IP addresses of routers to hostnames, which will increase the speed of the tracert because DNS name resolution is not required. |
| -h maximum_hops | Specifies the maximum number of router hops that will be taken to the destination host. |
| -w timeout | Specifies a timeout in milliseconds to wait for an ICMP Echo Reply or Time Exceeded message to be received. The default time is 4 seconds. If this time is exceeded, an asterisk (*) is returned instead of a time value. |
| -R | Specifies that the round-trip path is to be tested. The -R parameter is used only for IPv6. |
| -S srcaddr | Specifies the source address to start the tracert from. The -S parameter is used only for IPv6. |

*continues*

**TABLE 4.3**   *continued*

**tracert PARAMETERS**

| Parameter | Description |
| --- | --- |
| -4 | Specifies that IPv4 is to be used, which is the default. |
| -6 | Specifies that IPv6 is to be used. |
| target_name | Specifies the destination of the tracert. |

The tracert command functions by sending ICMP Echo Request packets to the specified destination, similar to the ping command (discussed next), but with a key difference. For the first group of packets sent out, the TTL (time to live) is set to 1. When the packets reach the first router, the router decrements the TTL by 1, causing the TTL to be zero. A TTL of zero results in the router discarding the packets and sending back an error message to the originating system. This error message contains the IP address of the sending router, which is then displayed as the first line of the output. The process then continues, but with the next group of three packets having a TTL of 2, thus allowing them to pass the first router, which decrements their TTL to 1, and make their way to the second router. The second router decrements the TTL to zero, and the process continues.

## The ping Command

Using ping to test connections may become something you do every day for the rest of your IT career. No other tool is used as often or as frequently as ping. PING, which stands for Packet Internet Groper, is fueled by the ICMP protocol, just as tracert is. The same ICMP Echo type messages are used as well, so learning about ping is somewhat easier if you are already familiar with the basic operation of the tracert command.

The ping command is the basic test of network connectivity. But why would you need to use ping? Let's look at an example. You are the network administrator responsible for two servers that are located on opposite sides of a WAN link (hence, two or more routers). Today you have started to get complaints that nobody at the remote site can receive email. Because the email servers are on your side of the network, you are justifiably concerned as to why nobody can get to that email. The first step in troubleshooting your problem lies with the ping command. If you can ping the email server's IP address from your location, you have confidence that the problem is no longer apparent. But what if you cannot ping the server? Your next step is to ping each hop along the route from source to destination in an attempt to determine where the problem lies. There is an inherent limitation to the ping command, though: Even though you can ping a host or router, this does not guarantee that it is performing its intended function properly. Being able to successfully ping a host indicates that basic TCP/IP connectivity exists along the route, nothing more.

To ping a host, you can simply enter the ping command followed by an IP address or DNS hostname, as shown here:

```
C:\>ping 10.0.0.1
Pinging 10.0.0.1 with 32 bytes of data:
Reply from 10.0.0.1: bytes=32 time=70ms TTL=124
Reply from 10.0.0.1: bytes=32 time=70ms TTL=124
Reply from 10.0.0.1: bytes=32 time=70ms TTL=124
Reply from 10.0.0.1: bytes=32 time=70ms TTL=124
Ping statistics for 10.0.0.1:
    Packets: Sent = 4, Received = 4, Lost = 0 (0% loss),
Approximate round trip times in milli-seconds:
    Minimum = 70ms, Maximum =  70ms, Average =  70ms
C:\>
```

The syntax of the ping command is as follows and is detailed in Table 4.4:

```
ping [-t] [-a] [-n count] [-l size] [-f] [-i TTL] [-v TOS]
➥[-r count] [-s count] [{-j HostList | -k HostList}] [-w timeout]
```

## TABLE 4.4

### ping PARAMETERS

| Parameter | Description |
| --- | --- |
| -t | Specifies that the ping command should continue sending Echo Request (ICMP) messages until manually interrupted. This is useful for establishing and monitoring a constant connection between two hosts. |
| -a | Specifies that reverse name resolution is to be performed on the destination IP address. |

*continues*

**TABLE 4.4** *continued*

**ping PARAMETERS**

| Parameter | Description |
| --- | --- |
| -n *count* | Specifies how many Echo Request messages are to be sent to the destination computer. The default is four. |
| -l *size* | Specifies the length of the data field on the Echo Request up to a maximum of 65,527 bytes. The default is 32 bytes. |
| -f | Specifies that the Echo Request messages will not be fragmented by routers along their path. This setting can be used to troubleshoot Maximum Transmission Unit (MTU) related problems. |
| -i *TTL* | Specifies the value of the TTL field in the IP header for Echo Request messages sent. The default is the default TTL value for the host. The maximum TTL is 255. |
| -v *TOS* | Specifies the value for the Type of Service (TOS) field in the Echo Request. The default value is 0, and valid values range from 0 to 255. |
| -r *count* | Specifies that the Record Route option in the IP header is used to record the path taken by the Echo Request message and corresponding Echo Reply message. The *count* must between 1 and 9. |
| -s *count* | Specifies that the Internet Timestamp option in the IP header is used to record the time of arrival for the Echo Request message and corresponding Echo Reply message for each hop. The *count* must be between 1 and 4. |
| -j *HostList* | Specifies that the Echo Request messages use the Loose Source Route option in the IP header with the set of intermediate destinations specified in *HostList*. When loose source routing is used, successive intermediate destinations can be separated by one or multiple routers. You can enter a maximum of nine addresses or hostnames in the host list. |
| -k *HostList* | Specifies that the Echo Request messages use the Strict Source Route option in the IP header with the set of intermediate destinations specified in *HostList*. When strict source routing is used, the next intermediate destination must be directly reachable. You can enter a maximum of nine addresses or hostnames in the host list. |
| -w *timeout* | Specifies the amount of time, in milliseconds, to wait for the Echo Reply message to be received. The default timeout is 4000 milliseconds (4 seconds). |

**NOTE**

**The story of ping** If you want to see the history of the ping command and learn some other interesting ping-related trivia, be sure to visit the page of the late Mike Muuss, creator of the ping application. You can find it located at http://ftp.arl.mil/~mike/ping.html.

Although the ping command has many options available, you will most often find yourself using it as demonstrated previously, perhaps appending the -t and/or -a switches to it. This command provides a constant, verifiable connection and name resolution for your troubleshooting efforts.

# The pathping Command

Testing routers by using pathping is outstanding if you want to use the best features of both ping and tracert, two tools you just learned about. Because of the similarities, you should already be familiar with what pathping can do for you. Not only does pathping use the best features of these tools, but it also has a set of excellent features of its own. First, the pathping command is a route tracing tool used to troubleshoot remote problems. The pathping command sends packets over each hop to the destination over a very specific time, and then after the time has elapsed, pathping calculates a set of results based on it. This is how pathping gets very specific results. You can test connectivity, trace a path, and more. You can now see what links as well as routers are giving you problems.

The syntax of the pathping command is as follows and is detailed in Table 4.5:

```
pathping [-n] [-h MaximumHops] [-g HostList] [-p Period] [-q NumQueries]
➥[-w Timeout] [-i IPAddress] [-4 IPv4] [-6 IPv6] [TargetName]
```

### TABLE 4.5

### pathping PARAMETERS

| Parameter | Description |
| --- | --- |
| -n | Prevents pathping from resolving the IP addresses of intermediate routers to their names. This parameter speeds up the process. |
| -h MaximumHops | Specifies the maximum number of hops in the path to search for the target. The default is 30 hops. |
| -g HostList | Specifies the that Echo Request messages are to use the Loose Source Route option in the IP header with the set of intermediate destinations specified in HostList. Successive intermediate destinations can be separated by one or multiple routers. The HostList is a series of IP addresses (in dotted-decimal notation), separated by spaces. |

*continues*

**TABLE 4.5** *continued*

**pathping PARAMETERS**

| Parameter | Description |
| --- | --- |
| -p *Period* | Specifies the number of milliseconds to wait between consecutive pings. The default is 250 milliseconds. |
| -q *NumQueries* | Specifies the number of Echo Request messages sent to each router in the path. The default is 100. |
| -w *Timeout* | Specifies the number of milliseconds to wait for each reply. The default is 3000 milliseconds. |
| -i *IPAddress* | Specifies the source address. |
| -4 *IPv4* | Specifies that pathping uses IPv4 only. |
| -6 *IPv6* | Specifies that pathping uses IPv6 only. |
| TargetName | Specifies the destination, either by IP address or hostname. |

So now that you know what pathping is, let's look at how to use it. To use pathping, you can open the command prompt and type **pathping -n 10.0.0.1**. Assuming that 10.0.0.1 is a valid host, you see the following output:

```
D:\>pathping -n 10.0.0.1
Tracing route to 10.0.0.1
over a maximum of 30 hops:
  0  172.16.2.1
  1  172.16.3,1
  2  192.168.2.1
  3  192.168.3.1

Computing statistics for 125 seconds...
              Source to Here   This Node/Link
Hop  RTT     Lost/Sent = Pct  Lost/Sent = Pct  Address
  0                                             172.16.2.1
                                0/ 100 =  0%    |
  1   41ms    0/ 100 =  0%     0/ 100 =  0%    172.16.3,1
                               13/ 100 = 13%    |
  2   22ms   16/ 100 = 16%     3/ 100 =  3%    192.168.2.1
                                0/ 100 =  0%    |
  3   24ms   13/ 100 = 13%     0/ 100 =  0%    192.168.3.1
                                0/ 100 =  0%    |
Trace complete.
```

The pathping output shows you not only what routes are experiencing packet loss, but also which routers are dropping packets. This information is valuable when you're trying to track down an Internet-related connectivity problem.

# The `netsh` Command

The `netsh` command is used on Windows 2000 and 2003 systems for troubleshooting networking-based problems. It's a very dense command that could take an entire chapter to describe, so we focus on the specifics of this command in relation to remote access and routing.

`Netsh` allows you to configure TCP/IP protocol stack options right from the command line. If you become very good at using it, you can perform just about any network-related task right from the command line. In respect to Routing and Remote Access, you simply need to navigate to those sections within the command context to adjust those settings. In other words, if you navigate to the routing context within the command, you can adjust parameters for the routing subsystem of the Windows Server 2003 system.

To use the `netsh` command, open the command prompt and type **netsh**. Doing so changes the drive letter–based prompt into the `netsh>` prompt. By typing a question mark (**?**) and pressing Enter, you can see what options you have within that context. If you see `routing`, you can change the prompt to `routing>` by typing **routing** and pressing Enter. If you type a question mark and press Enter, you see a new subset of commands you can manipulate within that prompt specific to routing functions.

The most common remote access prompt you will use within `netsh` is `ras>`. From this prompt, you can administer and work with Remote Access Servers over slow links and connections. You can use the following TechNet URL to find out all the details on the remote access `netsh` commands:

`www.microsoft.com/technet/prodtechnol/windowsserver2003/`
`proddocs/entserver/netsh_ras.asp`.

> **EXAM TIP**
>
> **Be aware of misleading results**
> Sometimes what may appear to be a router failure may not be a router failure at all, but simply a firewall that is configured to block ICMP packets. You can test by trying to ping www.microsoft.com. Microsoft has been blocking ICMP packets for years now as a means of preventing Denial of Service (DoS) attacks on its networks.

# The Network Monitor Utility

*Network traffic* is any activity to and from a host on a network. Any packet that leaves a network card, especially ones that are routed, is contributing to network traffic. The more hosts (or routers) on a network, the more services added to a network; and the more of the network that is not segmented properly, the more network traffic that network has.

Why is the issue of network traffic so important? Too much network traffic, like rush-hour traffic, clogs the speed of the network, causes the network to become a bottleneck, and can ultimately cause the network to fail. As a rule, the more network services, shares, and resources that are added to a network, the more network traffic that is generated.

You can use Network Monitor to capture packets on a network. From these packets, you can troubleshoot network problems, discern how busy a network load is, and predict how the network will grow.

Network Monitor is made up of two primary components:

▶ **Network Monitor**—Network Monitor is the tool you use to capture packets sent to and from this server. The version of Network Monitor included with Windows Server 2003 records only packets sent to and from this server and the LAN.

▶ **Network Monitor driver**—The Network Monitor driver is installed automatically when you install Network Monitor on a server. However, you might want to install just the Network Monitor driver for remote computers to be monitored through the full version of Network Monitor that is included with the Systems Management Server (SMS). If you install the Network Monitor driver on additional computers, you should make a point to install it only once per subnet.

By now you should be familiar with the basic operation of the Network Monitor. If you need a review, be sure to see *MCSA/MCSE 70-291 Training Guide: Implementing, Managing, and Maintaining a Windows Server 2003 Network Infrastructure* by Dave Bixler and Will Schmied (Que Publishing, 2003).

## Troubleshooting RIP Environments

After RIP is configured within your environment, you may be called on from time to time to troubleshoot issues that arise with routing. Although every problem is unique, Table 4.6 outlines some of the resolutions that may help when you're responding to issues within a RIP environment.

**TABLE 4.6**

## RIP PROBLEMS AND RESOLUTIONS

| Problem | Solution |
|---|---|
| Routing tables have improper routing information within a mixed RIP network. | RIP version 2 routers are configured to multicast announcements. Multicast version 1 and 2 announcements are never received by RIP version 1 routers. If you have a mixed environment of RIP version 1 and RIP version 2, ensure that the routers configured with RIP version 2 are using broadcast instead of multicast announcements. |
| Silent RIP hosts are not receiving routes. | RIP version 2 routers are configured to multicast announcements. Multicast announcements are never received by silent RIP hosts. If silent RIP hosts on a network are not receiving routes from the local RIP router, verify the version of RIP supported by the silent RIP hosts. If it is the listening service in Windows NT 4 Service Pack 4 or Windows Server 2003, you must configure the RIP routers for RIP version 1 or RIP version 2 broadcasting. |
| RIP routers are not being updated with valid routes. | You are deploying variable-length subnetting, disjointed subnets, or supernetting in a RIP version 1 or mixed RIP version 1 and RIP version 2 environment. Do not deploy variable-length subnetting, disjointed subnets, or supernetting in a RIP version 1 or mixed RIP version 1 and RIP version 2 environment because these functions are not supported. |
| RIP routers are not being updated with valid routes. | You are using autostatic RIP, and you did not properly do an initial manual update. When you use autostatic RIP on a demand-dial interface, the first time you make a connection, you must manually update routes. You must also update routes manually on the router for the corresponding interface. The routes then appear in the IP routing table. |
| Host or default routes are not being propagated. | RIP, by default, is not configured to propagate host or default routes. If they need to be propagated, change the default settings on the Advanced tab of the properties of a RIP interface. |

Table 4.6 describes only some of the problems that can arise within a RIP environment. For further troubleshooting information, refer to Microsoft Technet or the Windows Server 2003 documentation.

# TROUBLESHOOTING OSPF ENVIRONMENTS

OSPF is a more complex protocol to understand than RIP. As such, there is more risk of problems arising because of the complexity of the protocol. Because OSPF is more hierarchical than other protocols, this offers an opportunity to help troubleshoot problems that may arise; you can isolate problems with a particular area or the interconnectivity between areas more easily. Table 4.7 outlines some of the problems you may face when troubleshooting OSPF.

### TABLE 4.7

### OSPF PROBLEMS AND RESOLUTION

| *Problem* | *Solution* |
| --- | --- |
| OSPF adjacency is not forming between two neighbors. | OSPF is not enabled on the interface. Verify that OSPF is enabled on the interface on the network segment where an adjacency should form. By default, when you add an interface to the OSPF routing protocol, OSPF is disabled for the interface and must be manually enabled. |
| OSPF adjacency is not forming between two neighbors. | Ping the neighboring router to ensure basic IP and network connectivity. Use the tracert command to trace the route to the neighboring router. There should not be any routers between the neighboring routers. |
| A virtual link is not forming between two areas. | The problem is a mismatched configuration of password, hello interval, or dead interval. Verify that the virtual link neighbor routers are configured for the same password, hello interval, and dead interval. |
| A virtual link is not forming between two areas. | Virtual link neighbors are configured for the incorrect transit area ID. Verify that both virtual link neighbors are configured for the same transit area ID and that they are configured to use the correct transit area. |

| *Problem* | *Solution* |
|---|---|
| Routing tables are not being updated with OSPF routes, or improper OSPF routes are being received. | If you are not receiving summarized OSPF routes for an area, verify that the area border routers (ABRs) for the area are configured with the proper Destination, Network mask pairs summarizing that area's routes. |
| Routing tables are not being updated with OSPF routes, or improper OSPF routes are being received. | Not all ABRs are connected to the backbone. Verify that all ABRs are either physically connected to the backbone or logically connected to the backbone by using border routers, which are routers that connect two areas without going through the backbone. |

Table 4.7 lists only some of the problems that can arise within an OSPF environment. For further troubleshooting information, refer to Microsoft TechNet or the Windows Server 2003 documentation.

---

## CASE STUDY

### ESSENCE OF THE CASE

Following are the essential elements in this case:

▶ Timeouts are occurring on the LAN.

▶ Users cannot access resources.

▶ One side of the network cannot access the other side.

▶ The original side can access the other side.

### SCENARIO

You have been hired as a new network engineer to work for ABC Inc., the maker of the world's best widgets. Last week, a new segment was built on to the current LAN and connected via a Windows Server 2003 router. Now, users on the new segment are experiencing timeouts when attempting to access resources on one of the older segments. Nobody is able to get to the other side of the network. Users on the older side of the LAN report no problems at all.

### ANALYSIS

As the new network engineer, you need to analyze each problem one at a time and see whether they are all related. This step is important so that you do not waste a lot of time repeating yourself.

*continues*

## CASE STUDY

*continued*

As you look at the problems, you realize that you can solve them all within the same device because the router is causing all the problems as a result of it being misconfigured. If you notice timeouts, that means users are complaining of no connectivity, and all the applications that they are trying to open are timing out because the servers they connect to cannot be reached. Because the resources are on the other segment across the router, you know the router is at fault if no one can pass traffic over it.

Next, you see that because one side of the network can access the other side, but not the other way around, this problem may be indicative of a missing route. As a sharp network engineer, you quickly open a command prompt on the server and type `route print`. This shows you that a route is missing its routing table. You figure out that a dynamic routing protocol is not being used, only static routes, and one route is missing. After adding the missing route, you can discover that the timeout problems have disappeared, and the remote hosts can now access their resources.

## CHAPTER SUMMARY

### KEY TERMS

Before taking the exam, make sure you are comfortable with the definitions and concepts for each of the following key terms. You can use Appendix A, "Glossary," for quick reference.

- CHAP
- Distance Vector
- EAP
- IGMP
- IGMP Proxy mode
- IGMP Routing mode
- Link State
- LSA

In this chapter, you discovered the Routing and Remote Access capabilities of Windows Server 2003 and how to plan and design this feature into your network.

Understanding routing is critical because of its complexities and what Windows Server 2003 can do in the routing arena, utilizing either a static router or a dynamic routing protocol. In this chapter, you also learned how to plan either type of protocol in any environment. You learned about RIP, RIPv2, and OSPF, examining how each operates as well as looking at their strengths and weaknesses.

This chapter described both version 1 and version 2 of RIP, along with specific features such as silent RIP. Features of the RIP protocol were related to the fundamental discussion of routing covered earlier in the chapter, such as Distance Vector and Split Horizon. A discussion of how RIP functions within a network environment was provided, along with a Step by Step for implementing RIP using the RRAS features of Windows Server 2003.

The second routing protocol to be discussed was the OSPF protocol. The chapter also described the features of OSPF and how they

# CHAPTER SUMMARY

differ from RIP. The chapter then described the components and processes that make up the OSPF routing protocol. A discussion of how OSPF functions within a network environment was provided, along with a Step by Step for implementing OSPF using the RRAS features of Windows Server 2003 Advanced Server.

Later in the chapter, you learned about Routing and Remote Access, what it does with Windows Server 2003, and how to plan remote access into your network. Remember that Windows Server 2003 supports a large number of authentication protocols, such as EAP, MS-CHAPv2, and PAP. A good understanding of the basic operation and use of each will be critical to your successful remote access solution—and test day experience. Remote access is controlled through policies and profiles, and this chapter examined each.

Lastly, the chapter provided an overview of some of the tools for working with routing and diagnosing problems with routing. A discussion of the route, ping, tracert, pathping, and netsh commands and an overview of Network Monitor were provided. These are the tools that will help you to diagnose problems. In addition to an overview of the tools used, the chapter provided a brief discussion of problems that may arise with the different routing protocols and what can be done to resolve these problems. By no means was this discussion comprehensive, but it did provide insight into some of the different things to check should problems arise.

## KEY TERMS

- MPPE
- MS-CHAP version 1
- MS-CHAP version 2
- Multicast
- netsh
- OSPF
- PAP
- ping
- RIP
- RIP version 2
- route
- Routing
- RRAS
- SPAP
- TCP/IP
- tracert

## APPLY YOUR KNOWLEDGE

# Exercises

## 4.1 Enabling Routing and Remote Access

In this exercise, you enable and perform basic configuration on the Routing and Remote Access Service.

**Estimated time:** 15 minutes

1. Open the Routing and Remote Access console by choosing Start, Control Panel, Administrative Tools, and then Routing and Remote Access. By default, the local computer is listed as a server.

2. Right-click the server you want to configure and select Configure and Enable Routing and Remote Access. The Routing and Remote Access Server Setup Wizard starts.

3. Click Next to start configuring the Routing and Remote Access Service. The Configuration dialog box opens.

4. Select the Secure Connection Between Two Private Networks option and click Next to continue. The Demand-Dial Connections dialog box opens.

5. On the Demand-Dial Connections dialog box, select No and click Next to continue. The Completing the Routing and Remote Access Server Setup Wizard summary dialog box opens.

6. Click Finish to complete the enabling of routing services.

## 4.2 Adding a Static Route to the Existing Routing Table

This exercise explores using the route command to add a static route to an existing routing table. This method provides a way for you to add static routes to routing configurations.

**Estimated time:** 10 minutes

1. From the command prompt, enter route **ADD 157.0.0.0 MASK 255.0.0.0 157.55.80.1 METRIC 3 IF 2**.

2. Type **route print** to examine the new route in the routing table.

## 4.3 Adding RIP to the Routing and Remote Access Service

In this exercise, you add RIP as a dynamic routing protocol for use on your Windows Server 2003 RRAS computer.

**Estimated time:** 15 minutes

1. Open the Routing and Remote Access console.

2. In the left pane, expand the list under IP Routing and right-click General. From the context menu, select New Routing Protocol. The New Routing Protocol dialog box opens.

3. Select RIP Version 2 for Internet Protocol and click OK. RIP appears under the IP Routing entry. RIP is now installed on your Windows Server 2003 server.

4. Right-click the RIP entry and select New Interface from the context menu. The New Interface for RIP Version 2 for Internet Protocol dialog box opens.

5. Select the appropriate Local Area Connection and click OK. The RIP Properties dialog box opens.

6. On the General tab, in Outgoing Packet Protocol, select RIP Version 1 Broadcast. In Incoming Packet Protocol, select RIP Version 1 and 2. Click OK to return to the Routing and Remote Access console and activate the changes.

## APPLY YOUR KNOWLEDGE

### 4.4 Implementing Silent RIP

In this exercise, you implement silent RIP on your Windows Server 2003 RRAS computer.

**Estimated time:** 15 minutes

1. Open the Routing and Remote Access console.

2. Expand the console tree and select RIP. The list of available interfaces running RIP appears in the right pane of the console.

3. Right-click the interface that you want to configure for silent RIP mode, and from the context menu, select Properties. The Local Area Connection Properties opens.

4. On the General tab, in Outgoing Packet Protocol, select Silent RIP from the pull-down menu. Click OK to return to the Routing and Remote Access console and apply the changes.

### 4.5 Adding OSPF to the Routing and Remote Access Service

In this exercise, you add OSPF as a dynamic routing protocol for use on your Windows Server 2003 RRAS computer.

**Estimated time:** 15 minutes

1. Open the Routing and Remote Access console.

2. Expand the console tree, and under IP Routing, right-click General. From the context menu, select New Routing Protocol. The New Routing Protocol dialog box opens.

3. Select Open Shortest Path First and click OK to install it. It now appears under IP Routing in the Routing and Remote Access console.

4. Select the newly installed OSPF protocol and right-click. From the context menu, select New

Interface. The New Interface for Open Shortest Path First (OSPF) dialog box opens.

5. Select Local Area Connection and click OK. The OSPF Properties dialog box opens.

6. On the General tab, select the Enable OSPF for This Address option. In Area ID, click the ID of the area to which the interface belongs (for this exercise it should be 0.0.0.0). In Router Priority, click the arrows to set the priority of the router over the interface to 1. In Cost, click the scroll arrows to set the cost of sending a packet over the interface to 2. In Password, type a password. Under Network Type, set the type of OSPF interface as Broadcast. Click OK to complete the installation of the interface and return to the Routing and Remote Access console.

## Review Questions

1. Several of your Windows XP Professional clients are having trouble connecting to an Internet Web site labeled http://www.rsnetworks.net. You suspect that they have a connectivity issue via IP and want to perform a quick test to see why they cannot connect to the Web site. What can you do to quickly resolve this situation?

2. Several of your Windows 2000 Professional clients cannot access a server on a remote network segment that is separated by two routers. What can you do to test to see where the problem is occurring?

3. All your Windows XP Professional clients are having trouble connecting to your Windows Server 2003 Remote Access Server via VPN. The server was fine this morning, and all other clients can access the Remote Access Server. What could

## APPLY YOUR KNOWLEDGE

be the problem, and how would you try to resolve it?

4. You are running three Windows Server 2003 computers in a network that needs to participate in multicast routing. You cannot add a multicast routing protocol to your server, but you are able to add a forwarding protocol. If you needed to add a routing protocol for multicast, what protocol would you recommend to use?

5. You are a systems administrator responsible for deploying Windows Server 2003 in your network. You need a routing solution (in the form of a protocol) that will allow for massive scalability, is dynamic in nature, and will be scalable past 20 router hops. What routing protocol would you choose?

## Exam Questions

1. As the lead administrator for the ABC LLC network, you are responsible for planning a TCP/IP network that is robust and functional. You have a total of 450 clients spread out over three locations. You have 150 clients per location, and at one central location, you have approximately 25 servers. You are asked to deploy a routing solution using Windows Server 2003. Your requirements are to provide two different subnetted segments access to each other using Windows Server 2003. You would like to use a routing solution that is simple and that will forward traffic from one location to another without keeping too many unneeded routes in the table. Which of the following options represents the best choice?

A. RIP

B. OSPF

C. IGMP

D. Static Routes

2. Marshall is the network administrator for QBC Corp. He runs a network of 20 Windows Server 2003 systems on a network backbone, as well as 200 Windows XP Professional clients. Marshall is worried about connectivity to the corporate network, which extensively uses multicasting for video services. He is asked to deploy a Windows Server 2003 solution so that it can participate in the multicast routing function. Which of the following options represents the best choice?

A. IGMP Routing Mode

B. DVMRP Route Static

C. Static IP Routes

D. OSPF

3. Jake is the senior network administrator for your organization. He is responsible for 200 Windows XP Professional clients and 15 Windows Server 2003 systems located on a network backbone running at 100 Mbps. Jake needs to build a Windows Server 2003 system into a router connecting four subnets, and he needs to participate in a Cisco Router environment running the Enhanced Interior Gateway Routing Protocol (EIGRP) protocol. What can Jake configure on the Windows Server 2003 system to get it to pass routing updates from the Cisco routers to the four subnets connected?

A. RIP

B. OSPF

## APPLY YOUR KNOWLEDGE

C. EIGRP

D. Jake can't use EIGRP.

4. You are the network administrator of the ABC Company, and you currently have a network client that cannot access network resources that are on a separate subnet across the WAN. When you talk to the user on the phone, you find out that there is no break in the cable and the link lights on the NIC are operational. You then try to ping the default gateway router, and you get a response that the router is up and functional. What would be the next option you can try to find out where the breakdown in communication is coming from?

A. Ping the next hop router.

B. Run tracert to the default gateway.

C. Use netsh at the routing> prompt and type **TEST**.

D. Run pathping to the default gateway.

5. Pete is the systems administrator for RDT, Inc. He runs a network of 25 Windows Server 2003 systems on a network backbone, as well as 300 Windows XP Professional clients. Pete needs to set up a Windows Server 2003 router with multicast forwarding capabilities. He has a specific requirement to configure the router with different settings on different interfaces. To do this, Pete would have to configure the router in which mode?

A. IGMP Router mode

B. IGMP Proxy mode

C. IGMP Cancel mode

D. IGMP Split mode

6. Sally is the senior network administrator for Runners Corp. She runs a network of 20 Windows Server 2003 systems, as well as 250 Windows XP Professional clients. Sally needs to set up remote access polices so that clients with proper credentials can access the Remote Access Server and gain access to the internal network to get resources. Sally wants to ensure that all users are secure when connecting via the Internet. Which protocol can users use from a client to connect to and access a Remote Access Server securely?

A. PAP

B. SPAP

C. EAP

D. OSPF

7. Marshall is the network administrator for QBC Corp. He runs a network of 20 Windows Server 2003 systems on a network backbone, as well as 200 Windows XP Professional clients. Marshall is worried about a single PC that cannot connect to the network. He wants to ensure that all users are secure when connecting via the Internet. Which protocol can users use from a client to connect to and access a Remote Access Server securely, and is the most secure?

A. PAP

B. SPAP

C. CHAP

D. EAP

## APPLY YOUR KNOWLEDGE

8. Pete is the systems administrator for RDT, Inc. He runs a network of 25 Windows Server 2003 systems on a network backbone, as well as 300 Windows XP Professional clients. Pete needs to work on testing a router that is 16 hops away. Pete's network runs the Routing Information Protocol (RIP). Every time Pete tries to get to and connect to the router, he times out and can't connect to it. What could be the problem?

   A. The router can't be reached because it is more than 12 hops away; RIP can handle only a 12-hop count limit.

   B. The router can't be reached because it is more than 13 hops away; RIP can handle only a 13-hop count limit.

   C. The router can't be reached because it is more than 14 hops away; RIP can handle only a 14-hop count limit.

   D. The router can't be reached because it is more than 15 hops away; RIP can handle only a 15-hop count limit.

9. Sally is the senior network administrator for Runners Corp. She runs a network of 20 Windows Server 2003 systems, as well as 250 Windows XP Professional clients. Sally needs to use MS-CHAP version 1 on her Remote Access Server. She is told that this would not be wise and to use MS-CHAP version 2 instead. Why would Sally want to use version 2 over version 1?

   A. MS-CHAPv2 enables users to log in and check against a RADIUS server.

   B. MS-CHAPv2 provides for mutual authentication of both the remote access client and the remote access server for increased connection security.

   C. MS-CHAPv2 can authenticate as well as encrypt.

   D. MS-CHAPv2 allows users to send small packets across the network.

10. Jason is the network administrator for QBC Corp. He runs a network of 20 Windows Server 2003 systems on a network backbone, as well as 200 Windows XP Professional clients. Jason has a PC on a remote network segment that is separated by two routers. Users are complaining of slow connections and time-out errors when attempting to connect to this remote PC. Jason needs to see where the trouble may be occurring on the network and also needs to find out why people are complaining of timed-out sessions on their applications. There must be a bandwidth problem as well. Which tool should he use to troubleshoot and resolve this problem?

   A. tracert

   B. pathping

   C. ping

   D. route

11. Marshall is the network administrator for QBC Corp. He runs a network of 20 Windows Server 2003 systems on a network backbone, as well as 200 Windows XP Professional clients. Marshall needs to allow for the delay of a remote access connection attempt to the Remote Access Server until a script runs verifying the identity of the remote access computer. What is the new Windows Server 2003 feature called?

   A. IIS Lockdown tool

   B. Network Access Quarantine Control

## APPLY YOUR KNOWLEDGE

C. `Wscript.exe`

D. Remote Access Scripter

12. Pete is the systems administrator for RDT, Inc. He runs a network of 25 Windows Server 2003 systems on a network backbone, as well as 300 Windows XP Professional clients. Pete must use an authentication protocol on RDT's Windows Server 2003 system that will allow him to support password change during the authentication process. This way, if someone's password has expired, the person has the chance to change it if he or she wants to. Which protocol should Pete use if he wants to provide this feature?

A. SPAP

B. PAP

C. MS-CHAP

D. LDAP

13. Sally is the senior network administrator for Runners Corp. She runs a network of 20 Windows Server 2003 systems, as well as 250 Windows XP Professional clients. Sally is asked to design a network that uses RIP. She needs to span over 20 routers from one network segment to another at times. Which routing protocol should Sally recommend that the company use?

A. PAP

B. EAP

C. OSPF

D. MPPE

14. You are the network administrator for QBC Corp. The company has a network of 25 Windows Server 2003 systems on a network backbone, as well as 300 Windows XP Professional clients. You need to reset the IP address of your router quickly from the command line. Which utility should you use?

A. `ping`

B. `tracert`

C. `route`

D. `netsh`

## Answers to Review Questions

1. You can `ping` the Web site if you have DNS resolution, or `ping` it via the IP address if you know that as well. Either way, knowing how to use `ping` can quickly verify whether you have IP connectivity to a system, node, or host on the network to which you are connected. For more information, see the section "Troubleshooting TCP/IP Routing."

2. If you are not able to access a segment that is separated from you by two routers or more, you can easily see where the breakdown in communications is occurring by using `tracert`. You can also use `ping` or `pathping` for diagnostics, but `tracert` allows you to trace the route to the destination to see where the break in communication may be. For more information, see the section "Troubleshooting TCP/IP Routing."

## APPLY YOUR KNOWLEDGE

3. The default gateway (the router closest to you that you use to exit the network subnet you are on) may not be up or experiencing any problem. To resolve this issue, you should `ping` your default gateway to ensure that you have connectivity to the router closest to you, which is responsible for forwarding traffic to destinations not local to your own subnet. For more information, see the section "Troubleshooting TCP/IP Routing."

4. If you want to participate in multicast routing, you can add the IGMP routing protocol to your Windows Server 2003 system in Routing and Remote Access. For more information, see the section "Planning Routing for IP Multicast Traffic."

5. You should deploy Open Shortest Path First (OSPF), a Link State–based dynamic routing protocol that you can install and use on Windows Server 2003. You use this protocol if you want to be able to scale the network up, as well as to go beyond the 15-hop count limit that RIP imposes. For more information, see the section "OSPF."

## Answers to Exam Questions

1. **D.** RIP and OSPF are routing protocols and IGMP is a multicast protocol, so answers A, B, and C are incorrect. For more information, see the section "RIP."

2. **A.** IGMP Routing mode is not a multicast routing protocol, but a forwarding-based multicast protocol. DVMRP is a multicast routing protocol; Static IP Routes will do nothing for multicast forwarding; and OSPF is a dynamic routing protocol, not a multicast-based protocol, although it sends its updates via multicast; therefore, answers B, C, and D are incorrect. For more information, see the section "Planning Routing for IP Multicast Traffic."

3. **D.** RIP and OSPF will not work because all routing protocols must be redistributed via another routing protocol or be identical. EIGRP is not an option either because it is vendor specific and does not work with Microsoft Windows Server 2003. Therefore, answers A, B, and C are incorrect. For more information, see the section "Planning a Routing Environment."

4. **A.** Running `tracert` to the Default gateway will not give you the desired result; thus, answer B is incorrect. Using `netsh` at the `routing>` prompt and typing **TEST** will not work because it is really an invalid command; thus, answer C is incorrect. Running `pathping` to the default gateway also will not provide the desired result; thus, answer D is incorrect. For more information, see the section "The `ping` Command."

5. **B.** Although IGMP Router mode is a valid Windows Server 2003 router mode for forwarding multicast traffic, it is not the correct mode to solve the solution; thus answer A is incorrect. IGMP Cancel mode and IGMP Split mode are not valid modes; thus, answers C and D are incorrect. For more information, see the section "Planning Routing for IP Multicast Traffic."

6. **C.** PAP, SPAP, and OSPF are incorrect; thus, answers A, B, and D are incorrect. EAP is by far the most secure and up-to-date protocol Sally can use, especially because it is not vendor specific and has many extensions, such as EAP-TLS and LEAP. For more information, see the section "Extensible Authentication Protocol (EAP)."

7. **C.** PAP, SPAP, and OSPF are incorrect; thus, answers A, B, and D are incorrect. EAP is by far the most secure and up-to-date protocol Marshall can use, especially because it is not vendor specific and has many extensions, such as EAP-TLS and LEAP. For more information, see the section "Extensible Authentication Protocol (EAP)."

8. **D.** The router can't be reached because it is more than 15 hops away, and RIP can handle only a 15-hop count limit. All the other answers have the wrong hop count. For more information, see the section "RIP."

9. **B.** MS-CHAPv2 provides for mutual authentication of both the remote access client and the remote access server for increased connection security, thus making it more secure and a better choice than MS-CHAPv1. For more information, see the section "MS-CHAP."

10. **B.** The `pathping`, `tracert`, and `route` commands are all valid troubleshooting tools, but `pathping` solves the problem the best. For more information, see the section "The `pathping` Command."

11. **B.** Windows Server 2003 provides a new feature called Network Access Quarantine Control. This feature allows the delay of a remote access connection attempt to the Remote Access Server until a script runs verifying the configuration of the remote access system. The IIS Lockdown tool, `Wscript.exe`, and the Remote Access Scripter are either not valid services or are improper services for this solution; thus, answers A, C, and D are incorrect. For more information, see the section "Windows Server 2003 Routing Solutions."

12. **C.** SPAP, PAP, and LDAP are either the wrong authentication protocol or, in the case of LDAP, not even an authentication protocol to begin with; thus, answers A, B, and D are incorrect. For more information, see the section "Microsoft Challenge Handshake Authentication Protocol (MS-CHAP)."

13. **C.** OSPF is a dynamic routing protocol used to build a routing table. PAP, EAP, and MPPE are not routing protocols; therefore, answers A, B, and D are invalid. For more information, see the section "OSPF."

14. **D.** You can use `netsh` to add an IP interface and a wealth of other solutions right from the command line. This way, you can quickly change many things on your system. `ping`, `tracert`, and `route` are all incorrect tool options; thus, answers A, B, and C are incorrect. For more information, see the section "The `netsh` Command."

# APPLY YOUR KNOWLEDGE

## Suggested Readings and Resources

1. Microsoft Corporation. 2003. *Microsoft Windows Server 2003 Resource Kit.* Redmond, WA: Microsoft Press. ISBN: 0735614717.

2. Microsoft Corporation. 2003. *Microsoft Windows Server 2003 Deployment Kit.* Redmond, WA: Microsoft Press. ISBN: 0735614865.

3. Davies, Joseph, and Thomas Lee. 2003. *Microsoft Windows Server 2003 TCP/IP Protocols and Services Technical Reference.* Redmond, WA: Microsoft Press. ISBN: 0735612919.

4. Windows Server 2003 RFC Checklist at www.rfc-editor.org/rfc.html:

   - RIP RFC 1058
   - RIP (Updated) RFC 1388
   - OSPF RFC 1247
   - OSPF Version 2 RFC 1583
   - DVMRP RFC 1075
   - MOSPF RFC 1584
   - IGMP RFC 2236

High availability has become something of a buzzword in the past few years in the IT sector. People were striving for many years before that to achieve "Five Nines," or 99.999% server uptime. Microsoft makes it easier than ever before to achieve this goal with the Network Load Balancing and Clustering services provided in Windows Server 2003.

Microsoft has the following objectives for the high availability portion of the "Planning, Implementing, and Maintaining Server Availability" unit:

**Plan services for high availability.**

- **Plan a high availability solution that uses clustering services.**

- **Plan a high availability solution that uses network load balancing.**

▶ High availablity solutions are becoming more popular and more critical in today's Internet-based economy. It is important to understand and be able to work with the highly available solutions provided with Windows Server 2003.

**Implement a cluster server.**

▶ After finishing your plan for a high availability cluster solution, you need to successfully implement and manage it.

**Monitor network load balancing. Tools might include the Network Load Balancing Monitor Microsoft Management Console (MMC) snap-in and the WLBS cluster control utility.**

▶ Network load balancing (NLB) typically can be counted on to function with little to no administrative action required. You do, however, need to perform routine monitoring on your NLB clusters to ensure that they are operating properly. Windows Server 2003 contains several useful utilities that you can use to monitor NLB.

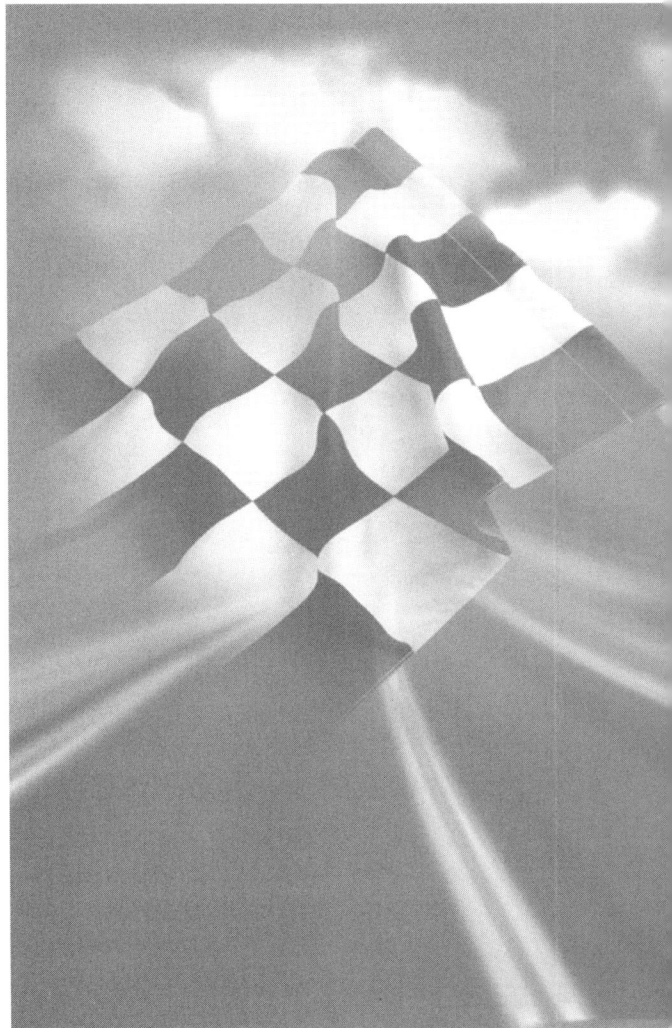

CHAPTER 5

# Planning, Implementing, and Maintaining Highly Available Servers

**Recover from cluster node failure.**

▶ Clusters are implemented to minimize the adverse effects of failure. The capability to quickly and effectively recover from the failure of one or more cluster nodes is a key part of the overall high availability solution.

## STUDY STRATEGIES

▶ For many people, the concept of high availability servers is a new one. It is important to get a good grasp of the concepts presented in this chapter, including high availability, clustering, network load balancing, failover, and failback.

▶ Ensure that you understand the specific requirements, benefits, and costs associated with high availability solutions utilizing clustering or network load balancing.

▶ Get your hands dirty. The Step by Steps throughout this book provide plenty of directions and exercises, but you should go beyond these examples and create some of your own. If you can, experiment with each of the objectives to see how they work and why you would use each one.

# INTRODUCTION

What's all the buzz about high availability? Why is everyone so intent on achieving the Utopia of high server availability: Five Nines? It really all comes down to one thing: economics. The economics of today's Internet-centric world demand that critical services and servers be available 100% of the time. In the absence of perfection, which no one has delivered yet, the bar for high availability solutions has been set at five nines: 99.999% uptime. What exactly does that equate into, though?

Five nines availability allows you to have critical services offline for 5.25 minutes per year! That's an unbelievably low number no matter how you look at it. But that's the goal of high availability solutions. As you may know, 5 minutes per year is barely enough time to apply a hot fix, much less a service pack. The answer to this problem: high availability server solutions.

When discussing high availability solutions, you can look at the problem in two distinctly different ways: hardware and software. Windows Server 2003 provides you with two types of software-based high availability: clustering and network load balancing, each of which is discussed in detail in the following sections.

# DESIGNING FOR HIGH AVAILABILITY

When it comes to creating high availability solutions, your design plans should not start at the operating system itself—in this case, Windows Server 2003. To create truly high availability server solutions, you need to start with your hardware first. An important first step in creating high availability solutions is purchasing and using high-quality hardware components from reputable first-tier vendors such as Dell, HP, or Gateway. You also need to give consideration to other issues such as power supply, power conditioning, and environmental conditioning.

## Uninterruptible Power Supplies

You might look silly if you go through all the work to create and implement a high availability solution only to have it crippled by a power failure. *Uninterruptible power supplies (UPSs)* can help prevent this problem. Not only do UPSs provide a backup source of power during power outage, but many of the better UPSs also provide *power conditioning.* Power conditioning extends the life of sensitive electronic components by removing voltage spikes, voltage dips (brownouts), and line noise.

During a power outage, UPSs automatically switch over to battery mode, providing additional time to safely—and gracefully—shut down servers and other infrastructure hardware such as switches, routers, and firewalls. It is important to closely follow the recommendations of the UPS manufacturer when connecting devices to the UPS so that it is not overloaded during a power outage condition, resulting in reduced battery operation time. Many UPS manufacturers also provide software that can be installed on critical servers to monitor the battery condition in the UPS and perform actions such as run scripts or shut down servers as the battery capacity decreases. This graceful securing of servers greatly increases your chances of recovering quickly from the casualty situation.

## Fault-Tolerant Storage Systems

Storage systems—hard drives in common vernacular—are a key part of any high availability system. Fault-tolerant disk systems can be created in one of two basic ways: either by using third-party hardware solutions or by using dynamic disks within Windows Server 2003. Either way, you should create a Redundant Array of Inexpensive Disks (RAID). There are several different variations on RAID, as discussed in the following paragraphs.

The basic premise of a RAID array is that you can use two or more relatively inexpensive hard drives to create a robust and redundant storage system that can withstand the failure of a disk and still provide disk access. Many hard drives used in RAID arrays are hotswappable, meaning they can be pulled and inserted into a server while it remains powered on. This feature, as you might expect, can greatly increase server and service uptime by allowing you to replace the failed member of an array without having to shut down the server first.

Although not all-inclusive, the following are two of the more common forms of RAID in use today:

▶ **RAID-1**—Data is written to one disk and then mirrored in its entirety to the second disk. RAID-1 mirror sets use two identical disks, called mirror volumes. The disks should be the same size. If one disk fails, the system may continue to operate using the remaining disk. Depending on which disk fails, you may experience startup problems and may need to use a boot disk containing an edited version of the boot.ini file that points toward the remaining mirror disk. No parity information is created when using a mirror set.

▶ **RAID-5**—The entire block of data is written to one data disk. The parity information for data blocks in the same rank is written to the parity disk. RAID-5 requires at least three hard drives of equal size to implement. The total capacity of a RAID-5 array is equal to $(N-1)*C$, where $N$ is the total number of disks and $C$ is the capacity of one disk.

Figure 5.1 depicts RAID-1 and RAID-5 arrays graphically.

**FIGURE 5.1**
RAID-1 and RAID-5 arrays can be used to create fault-tolerant storage systems.

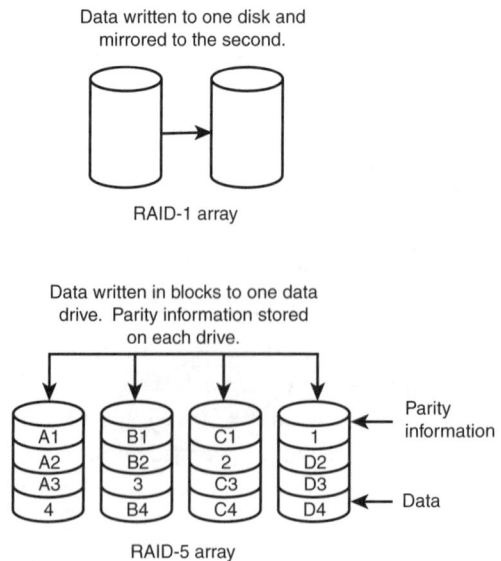

Data written to one disk and mirrored to the second.

RAID-1 array

Data written in blocks to one data drive. Parity information stored on each drive.

| A1 | B1 | C1 | 1 | Parity information |
| A2 | B2 | 2 | D2 | |
| A3 | 3 | C3 | D3 | |
| 4 | B4 | C4 | D4 | Data |

RAID-5 array

When deciding between using hardware-based RAID and software-based RAID (Windows Server 2003), you should give serious consideration to using hardware-based solutions. When you use a hardware-based RAID solution, you gain decreased headaches as well as increased performance and configurability over software-based RAID. The general problem with software-based (Windows-based) RAID solutions is that you must first reinstall and restore the operating system before you can ever get to restoring data from the RAID set—something you won't have to face if using hardware-based RAID solutions. As well, when you remove the responsibility for managing the RAID array from Windows Server 2003, the operating system will perform better overall. Also, hardware-based RAID arrays are not limited by the available options and requirements of Windows Server 2003. This allows you greater design flexibility and easier recovery should disaster strike.

# Redundant Networking Infrastructure

You should give consideration to making your network infrastructure fault-tolerant. This is usually accomplished by creating redundant routes for traffic to travel over. Also, you can utilize load-balanced or standby infrastructure hardware. Although load balancing and failover are discussed in great detail later in this chapter, a brief description is suitable here. Load-balanced devices divide the total load between two or more devices: If one fails, the remaining "living" devices pick up the load and distribute it evenly among themselves. Standby, or failover, devices kick into action after the primary device experiences a failure condition; thus, the load is transferred over to a new device entirely.

Many infrastructure devices have been designed with redundancy in mind. Vendors such as Cisco have been designing and perfecting redundancy features in their network infrastructure devices for years now. Options such as dual or even triple power supplies and the capability to configure redundancy via the Internetwork Operating System (IOS) itself ensure these devices are no longer a single point of failure (SPOF).

# PLANNING HIGH AVAILABILITY SOLUTIONS

As briefly mentioned previously, Windows Server 2003 provides support for two different types of high availability, or clustering, technologies. Of course, the ability to implement high availability solutions does not come without a price. In the case of Windows Server 2003, you must be using either the Enterprise or Datacenter Server versions to have this capability available to you. In this section we first examine the types of clustering provided in Windows Server 2003. Next, we present key terms and operational modes that will be of importance to you as you plan and implement clustering solutions. Lastly, we implement and manage clusters and network load balancing using Windows Server 2003.

## High Availability Solutions

*Clustering* is accomplished when you take a group of independent servers and assemble them together into one large collective entity that is accessed as if it were a single system. Incoming requests for service can be evenly distributed across multiple cluster members or may be handled by one specific cluster member.

The *Microsoft Cluster Service (MSCS)* in Windows Server 2003 provides high availability fault-tolerant systems through *failover*. When one of the cluster members (nodes) is unable to respond to client requests, the remaining cluster members respond by distributing the load among themselves, thus responding to all existing and new connections and requests for service. In this way, clients see little—if any—disruption in the service being provided by the cluster. Cluster nodes are kept aware of the status of other cluster nodes and their services through the use of *heartbeats*. A heartbeat is used to keep track of the status of each node and also to send updates in the configuration of the cluster. Clustering is most commonly used for database, messaging, and file/print servers. Windows Server 2003 supports up to eight nodes in a cluster.

Windows Server 2003 also provides *network load balancing (NLB)* in which all incoming connection requests are distributed using a mathematical algorithm to members of NLB cluster. NLB clustering is best used in situations in which clients can connect to any server in the cluster, such as Web sites, Terminal Services servers, and VPN servers. You can configure the way the client interacts with the NLB cluster as well, such as allowing the client to use multiple NLB cluster members during a single connection (acceptable for Web sites) or forcing the client to use the same cluster member for the entire connection period (a necessity for VPN and Terminal Services servers). Windows Server 2003 NLB clusters can contain as many as 32 nodes.

Now that we've discussed clustering technologies provided in Windows Server 2003, let's look at some of the key clustering terminology and operational modes.

> **NOTE**
>
> **Combining clustering and network load balancing** Although you can use both clustering and NLB in your final design, such as in the case of an e-commerce site that uses NLB for front-end Web servers and clustering for back-end SQL servers, you cannot use both technologies on the same server.

# High Availability Terminology

A good understanding of the following MSCS and NLB clustering terminology is key to successfully implementing and managing any clustered solution. Although the following list of terms is not all-inclusive, it represents some of the more important ones you should understand before attempting to implement any high availability solution.

- ▶ **Cluster**—A group of two or more independent servers that operate together and are viewed and accessed as a single resource.

- ▶ **Cluster resource**—A network application, service, or hardware device (such as network adapters and storage systems) that is defined and managed by the cluster service.

- ▶ **Cluster resource group**—The resources contained within a cluster. Cluster resource groups are used as failover units within a cluster; when a cluster resource group fails and cannot be automatically restarted by the cluster service, the entire cluster resource group is placed in an offline status and failed over to another node.

- ▶ **Cluster virtual server**—A cluster resource group that has a network name and IP address assigned to it. Cluster virtual servers are thus accessible by their NetBIOS name, DNS name, and IP address.

▶ **Convergence**—The process by which NLB clustering hosts determine a new, stable state among themselves and elect a new default host after the failure of one or more cluster nodes. During convergence, the total load on the NLB cluster is redistributed among all cluster nodes that share traffic handling on specific ports as determined by their port rules.

▶ **Heartbeat**—A network communication sent among individual cluster nodes at intervals of no more than 500 milliseconds that is used to determine the status of all cluster nodes.

▶ **Failback**—The process of a cluster group moving back to the preferred node after the preferred node has resumed cluster membership. For failback to occur, it must be configured for the cluster group, including the failback threshold and selection of the preferred node.

▶ **Failover**—The process of a cluster group moving from the currently active node to another still functioning node in the cluster group. Failover typically occurs when the active node becomes unresponsive for any reason and cannot be recovered within the configured failure threshold.

▶ **Node**—An individual server within a cluster.

▶ **Quorum disk**—The disk drive that contains the definitive cluster configuration data. Clustering with MSCS requires the use of a quorum disk and requires continuous access to the data contained within the quorum disk. The quorum disk contains vital data about the nodes participating in the cluster, the applications and services defined within the cluster resource group, and the status of each node and cluster resource. The quorum disk is typically located on a shared storage device.

With the discussion of key clustering terminology now behind us, we can safely move forward and begin to plan for and implement high availability solutions. Because network load balancing clusters are the simpler of the two types to understand, deploy, and support, we start our discussion with them.

**EXAM TIP**

**Clustering terminology**    Although you must understand the clustering terms presented here to be able to implement and support cluster solutions, you should not expect to be directly tested on them come exam day.

# Planning and Implementing NLB Clusters

**Plan services for high availability.**

▶ **Plan a high availability solution that uses network load balancing.**

**Implement a cluster server.**

As discussed previously, the NLB cluster is most often used to create distributed fault-tolerant solutions for applications such as Web sites, VPN servers, and Terminal Services servers. NLB clusters are composed of between 2 and 32 nodes—each of which must contain the exact same applications and content. Because NLB clusters do not replicate content among the member nodes, using applications that require users to save data locally on the node is not a good idea. In this instance, you would need to implement a clustered server environment on the back end, such as an SQL Server cluster.

The most critical part of deploying an NLB cluster is determining the operational mode that is to be used and also the port rules that will be required. To plan for these items, you must know and understand what types of applications or services will be running on the NLB cluster. Certain applications, such as an e-commerce application, make extensive use of cookies during and between client connections. Should the NLB cluster be configured to allow multiple requests during the same session to be sent to more than one server, the client may experience application failures due to the absence of the expected cookie on other NLB cluster members. We discuss port rules, filtering mode, affinity, and cluster operation modes in the following sections. When you have a good understanding of these key NLB concepts, you will be ready to start implementing an NLB clustered solution in your organization.

> **EXAM TIP**
>
> **Replicating information across NLB clusters**  Although beyond the capabilities of the normal NLB service, Application Center 2000 can be used to create NLB clusters that replicate from a master node to all other member nodes, thus ensuring that changes made to the master node are kept current on all other member nodes.

## Port Rules

When a network load balancing cluster is created, port rules are used to determine what types of traffic are to be load-balanced across the cluster nodes. Within the port rule is the additional option to configure *port rule filtering*, which determines how the traffic will be load-balanced across each of the cluster nodes.

In an NLB cluster, every cluster node can answer for the cluster's IP address; thus, every cluster node receives all inbound traffic by default. When each node receives the inbound request, it either responds to the requesting client or drops the packet if the client has an existing session in progress with another node. Should no port rule be configured to specifically define how traffic on the specific port is to be handled, the request is passed off to the cluster node having the lowest configured priority. This may result in decreased performance by the NLB cluster as a whole if the traffic is not meant to be or cannot be load-balanced.

Port rules allow you to change this behavior in a deliberate and controlled fashion. Think of port rules as the network load balancing equivalent of a firewall rule set. When you configure port rules to allow traffic on the specific ports you require to reach the NLB cluster and configure an additional rule to drop all packets not meeting any other port rules, you can greatly improve the performance of the NLB cluster by allowing it to drop all packets that are not allowed to be load-balanced. From an administrative and security standpoint, port rules allow for easier monitoring of the server due to the limited number of ports that must be monitored.

## Filtering Mode and Affinity

As mentioned briefly in the previous section, you can configure how NLB clusters load-balance traffic across cluster nodes; this action is referred to as *filtering*. By configuring filtering, you can specify whether only one node or multiple nodes within the NLB cluster are allowed to respond to multiple requests from the same client during a single session (connection).

The three filtering modes are as follows:

- ▶ **Single Host**—When this filtering mode is configured, all traffic that meets the port rule criteria is sent to a specific cluster node. The Single Host filter might be used in a Web site that has only one SSL server; thus, the port rule for TCP port 443 would specify that all traffic on this port must be directed to that one node.

▶ **Disable Port Range**—This filtering mode instructs the cluster nodes to ignore and drop all traffic on the configured ports without any further action. This type of filtering can be used to prevent ports and port ranges from being load-balanced.

▶ **Multiple Host**—The default filtering method, Multiple Host, specifies that all active nodes in the cluster are allowed to handle traffic. When Multiple Host filtering is enabled, the host affinity must be configured. *Affinity* determines how clients interact with the cluster nodes and varies depending on the requirements of the applications that the cluster is providing. Three types of affinities can be configured as follows:

   • **None**—This affinity type sends an inbound client request to all nodes within the cluster. This type of affinity results in increased speed, but is suitable only for providing static content to clients, such as static Web sites and FTP downloads. Typically, no cookies are generated by the applications running on the clusters that are configured for this type of affinity.

   • **Class C**—This affinity type causes all inbound client requests from a particular Class C address space to a specific cluster node. This type of affinity allows a user's state to be maintained but can be overloaded or fooled if all client requests are passed through a single firewall or proxy server.

   • **Single**—This affinity type maintains all client requests on the same node for the duration of the session (connection). This type of affinity provides the best support for maintaining user state data and is often used when applications are running on the cluster that generates cookies.

# NLB Cluster Operation Mode

The mathematical algorithm used by network load balancing sends inbound traffic to every host in the NLB cluster. The inbound client requests can be distributed to the NLB cluster nodes through one of two methods: *unicast* or *multicast*. Although both methods send the inbound client requests to all hosts by sending them to the media

> **EXAM TIP**
>
> **Affinity** During the exam, pay attention to questions dealing with Web applications that use cookies and other means of maintaining user session state. These are your keys to determining the required affinity type.

access control (MAC) address of the cluster, they go about it in different ways.

When you use the *unicast* method, all cluster nodes share an identical unicast MAC address. To do so, NLB overwrites the original MAC address of the cluster network adapter with the unicast MAC address that is assigned to all the cluster nodes. When you use the *multicast* method, each cluster node retains its original MAC address of the cluster network adapter. The cluster network adapter is then assigned an additional multicast MAC address, which is shared by all the nodes in the cluster. Inbound client requests can then be sent to all cluster nodes by using the multicast MAC address.

The unicast method is usually preferred for NLB clusters unless each cluster node has only one network adapter installed in it. Recall that in any clustering arrangement, all nodes must be able to communicate not only with the clients, but also among themselves. Recall that NLB modifies the MAC address of the cluster network adapter when unicast is used; thus, the cluster nodes cannot communicate among themselves. If only one network adapter is installed in each cluster node, you need to use the multicast method.

---

### SWITCH PORT FLOODING

As discussed previously, the mathematical algorithm used by network load balancing sends inbound traffic to every host in the NLB cluster. It does so by preventing the switch that the NLB cluster nodes are attached to from ever associating the NLB cluster's MAC address with a specific port on the switch. This, however, leads to the unwanted side effect of switch port flooding, where the switch floods all its ports with all packets inbound to the NLB cluster.

Switch port flooding is both a waste of valuable network resources and a nuisance to you when implementing NLB clusters. In Windows 2000, you either need to place all nodes of an NLB cluster on a dedicated switch or on a dedicated VLAN within the switch to get around the problems of switch port flooding. A new feature in Windows Server 2003, however, prevents switch port flooding from occurring. For a good introduction to Virtual LANs (VLANs), see the article at www.2000trainers.com/printarticle. aspx?articleID=65.

Internet Group Management Protocol (IGMP) support has been provided in Windows Server 2003 network load balancing to prevent flooding from occurring on those switch ports that do not have an NLB cluster node attached to them. With this feature, non-NLB cluster nodes do not ever see inbound traffic that is intended for the NLB cluster. At the same time, all NLB cluster nodes continue to receive all inbound traffic, thus meeting the requirements of the NLB algorithm. IGMP support is available only when multicast mode is configured for the NLB cluster—which presents its own set of benefits and drawbacks. As an alternative, you can utilize the dedicated switch or VLAN methods to eliminate switch port flooding with the NLB cluster in unicast mode; unicast mode does not present the same drawbacks associated with multicast mode.

---

At this point, you are ready to move forward and create an NLB cluster. After creating your NLB cluster, you can then join additional cluster nodes to it and begin managing the NLB cluster.

## Creating an NLB Cluster

By now, you've received a good introduction into network load balancing and some of its key parts. However, you still may not have a good idea in your head exactly what an NLB cluster solution might look like. Figure 5.2 shows a four-node NLB cluster arrangement.

Any good implementation needs a good plan. To successfully implement your NLB cluster, you need to identify the key parameters that require you to have information ready ahead of time. They are broken down into two major parts: *cluster parameters* and *cluster host parameters*. We examine each in turn in the following paragraphs.

The following parameters are of interest when planning for the entire cluster:

▶ **Cluster virtual IP address**—The virtual IP (VIP) address that will be assigned to represent the entire cluster must be determined. This IP address must be in the same IP subnet as the IP addresses assigned to the cluster network adapters on all cluster hosts. Also, these IP addresses should be in different IP subnets than the IP addresses chosen for the administrative IP addresses. In the example shown in Figure 5.2, the cluster VIP is 10.0.0.1/24, whereas the individual cluster network adapter IP addresses for the four nodes are 10.0.0.10/24–10.0.0.13/24.

**FIGURE 5.2**
This four-node NLB cluster provides high availability Web sites.

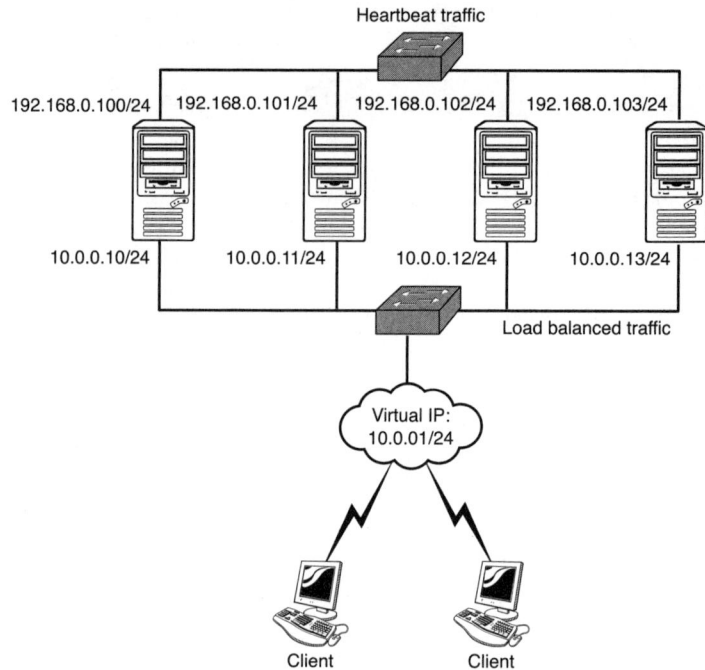

▶ **Cluster FQDN**—A fully qualified domain name (FQDN) must be assigned to the cluster, just the same as with any host on the network. This FQDN will be registered in DNS and allow clients to access the cluster as one unit. You also need to designate an FQDN for each application and service that you are running on the cluster because clients will access their FQDNs.

▶ **Cluster operation mode**—You need to choose between using unicast or multicast mode for distributing inbound client requests, as discussed previously in the "NLB Cluster Operation Mode" section.

▶ **Cluster remote control settings**—By default, remote administration of the cluster using nlb.exe is disabled. To maintain the highest level of security for your NLB cluster, you should specify that all remote administration is to be performed using the Network Load Balancing Manager. Also, you should specify that all cluster administration be done only from specified computers that are within your trusted and secured internal network to prevent compromise of cluster administrative control.

The following parameters are of interest when planning for each of the cluster nodes:

- ▶ **Cluster host priority**—Each cluster node is identified by a unique host priority number ranging from 1 to 32. During cluster convergence, the remaining cluster node with the lowest numeric host priority triggers the end of convergence and becomes the default host. No two cluster nodes can have the same host priority assignment. It's worth mentioning that you have a maximum of 32 nodes in your cluster and that the priority of each node acts as a "ranking" system, indicating the order in which you want the cluster nodes to become the default host during failure situations.

- ▶ **Administrative IP address**—These IP addresses are assigned to each non–load-balanced network adapter and should all be in the same IP subnet. These IP addresses should also be in a different IP subnet than the IP addresses chosen for the cluster IP addresses so that load-balanced and administrative traffic are completely separated, thus providing increased security for the administrative traffic.

- ▶ **Cluster IP address**—These IP addresses are assigned to each cluster network adapter and must be in the same IP subnet as the cluster VIP. These IP addresses should also be in a different IP subnet than the IP addresses chosen for the administrative IP addresses.

- ▶ **Initial Host State**—A Windows Server 2003 server configured to be an NLB cluster node starts the NLB service very early in the operating system startup process and joins the NLB cluster. If this occurs before clustered services and applications are started and available on the cluster node, clients may experience service disruptions. You need to specify whether cluster nodes will automatically start the NLB service and join the NLB cluster upon operating system load or whether the NLB service will be manually started at some later time.

With the required information in hand, you are now ready to create an NLB cluster and join additional nodes to the cluster. Step by Step 5.1 outlines the steps required to create a new NLB cluster.

**NOTE**

**Using two network adapters is best** When implementing either an NLB solution or a cluster, you should have two network adapters installed in each cluster node. All the discussion and examples that follow assume that you have two network adapters installed in your cluster nodes. As well, all network adapters that are in use should be (preferably) identical in make and model; this results in easier maintenance and upkeep in that you have only one set of drivers to keep up to date. If you cannot use identical network adapters across the cluster, you should use the same speed adapters (such as 10/100 or 100/1000) to minimize potential bottlenecks.

**FIGURE 5.3**

The Administration Properties dialog box allows you to configure network connection properties.

# STEP BY STEP

## 5.1 Creating a New NLB Cluster

1. Open the Network Connections window by selecting Start, Settings, Network Connections. The Network Connections window opens, displaying all configured connections on the computer.

2. Double-click the network adapter that you will be using as the administrative network adapter to open the network adapter Status dialog box.

3. Click the Properties button to open the Administration Properties dialog box, as shown in Figure 5.3.

4. On the General tab, select Internet Protocol (TCP/IP) and then click Properties. The Internet Protocol (TCP/IP) Properties dialog box opens, as shown in Figure 5.4.

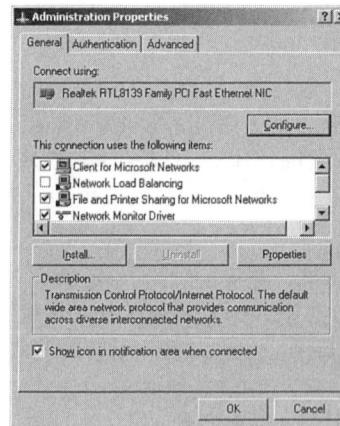

5. Enter the IP address and subnet mask to be used for the administrative interface. In most cases, these interfaces are connected only to each other, as in Figure 5.2, and thus do not require a default gateway or DNS server. You can configure this information if required, however.

6. Click Close to close the Local Area Connection Properties dialog box.

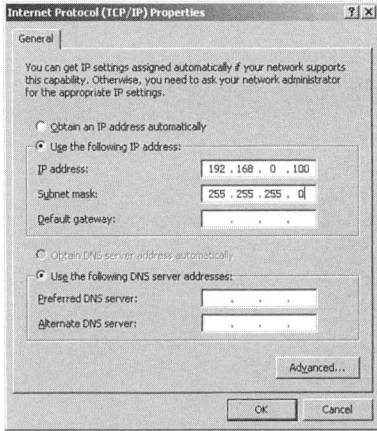

**FIGURE 5.4**
The Internet Protocol (TCP/IP) Properties dialog box allows you to configure TCP/IP settings for a network connection.

7. Configure the load balancing adapter, if not already done, by performing steps 2–6 again for the load balancing adapter.

8. Open the Network Load Balancing Manager, shown in Figure 5.5, by selecting Start, Programs, Administrative Tools, Network Load Balancing Manager.

**N O T E** **Configuring TCP/IP properties**   If you need a refresher on configuring TCP/IP properties, check out *MCSE TG 70-291: Implementing, Managing, and Maintaining a Microsoft Windows Server 2003 Network Infrastructure* (2003, Que Publishing); ISBN 0789729482.

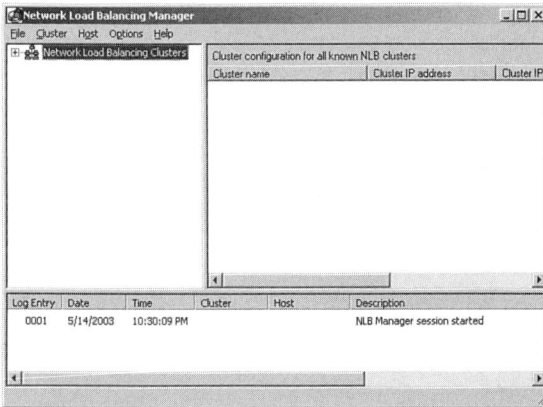

**FIGURE 5.5**
The Network Load Balancing Manager enables you to perform all administrative actions on NLB clusters.

9. Right-click on Network Load Balancing Clusters and select New Cluster from the context menu. The Cluster Parameters dialog box appears, as shown in Figure 5.6.

*continues*

*continued*

**FIGURE 5.6**
The Cluster Parameters dialog box allows you
to create a new NLB cluster.

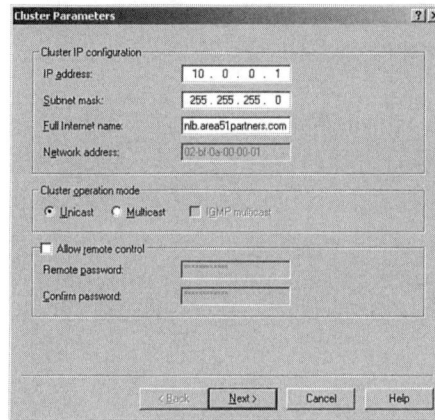

**10.** Enter the cluster's IP address, subnet mask, and cluster
domain name. The IP address configured here is the cluster's virtual IP (VIP) address. Configure the cluster for
unicast or multicast as desired. You can also configure
IGMP multicast and remote control as desired. Click
Next to continue.

**11.** On the Cluster IP Addresses dialog box, shown in Figure
5.7, enter any additional virtual IP addresses using the
Add button. Click Next when you are ready to continue.

**FIGURE 5.7**
You can enter multiple virtual IP addresses as
required by your services and applications.

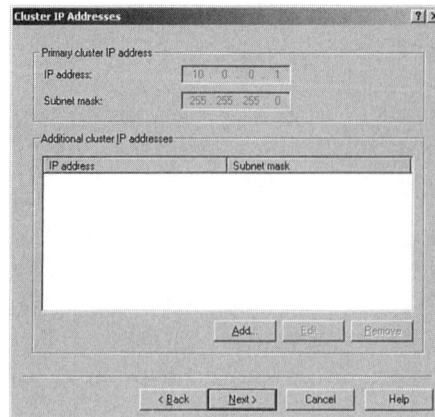

**12.** On the Port Rules dialog box, shown in Figure 5.8, configure any port rules that are appropriate for your NLB cluster installation. Clicking the Add button opens the Add/Edit Port Rule dialog box, as shown in Figure 5.9.

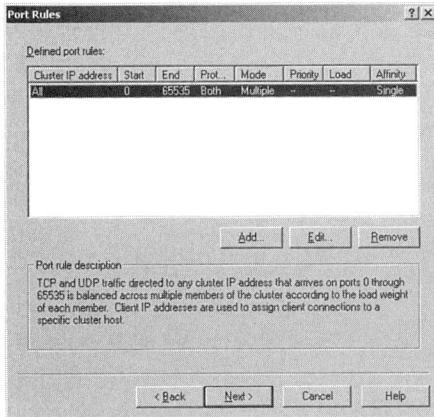

**FIGURE 5.8**
Port rules are used to quickly filter traffic from being load-balanced by the NLB cluster.

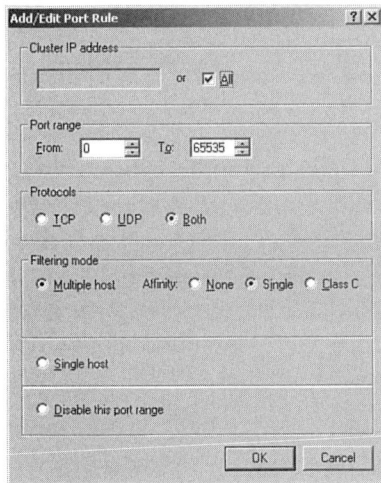

**FIGURE 5.9**
You can use port rules to allow or disallow traffic types and configure how the traffic is to be load-balanced.

**13.** Configure your port rules as discussed previously in the "Port Rules" and "NLB Cluster Operation Mode" sections of this chapter. Click OK to accept the new port rule. Click Next to continue creating the NLB cluster.

*continues*

*continued*

**14.** On the Connect dialog box, shown in Figure 5.10, type the name of the first cluster node and click the Connect button. After a brief period, all available network adapters are displayed in the bottom half of the dialog box. Select the network adapter that is to be used for load balancing and click Next to continue.

**FIGURE 5.10**
You need to select the proper network adapter to use as the load balancing adapter.

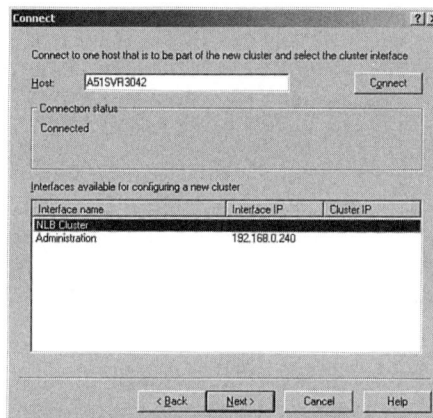

**15.** On the Host Parameters dialog box, shown in Figure 5.11, configure the host priority, cluster node dedicated IP address and subnet mask, and the initial state of the cluster node. The dedicated IP address is that of the cluster network adapter itself, and must be unique and in the same subnet as the cluster VIP. After entering all required information, click Finish to complete the NLB cluster creation process.

**16.** After a brief period of time, you can see the newly created and fully converged cluster displayed in the Network Load Balancing Manager, as shown in Figure 5.12.

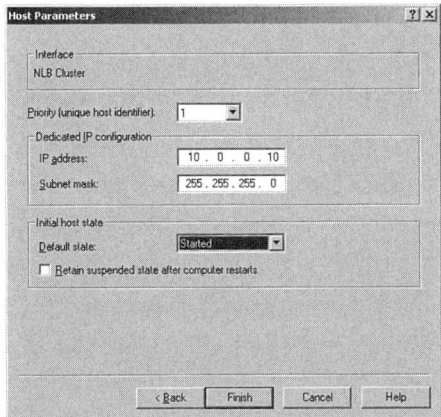

**FIGURE 5.11**
The Host Parameters dialog box contains critical configuration items that identify the specific cluster node.

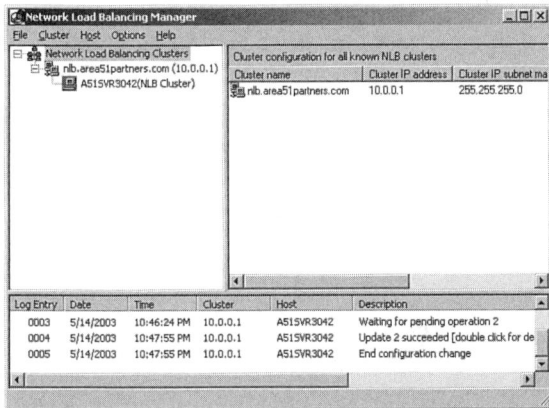

**FIGURE 5.12**
After a brief delay, the newly created NLB cluster shows up and is fully converged.

Of course, after you have created the NLB cluster, you should add at least one more cluster node to it. Step by Step 5.2 outlines the required steps to add additional nodes to the NLB cluster.

# STEP BY STEP

## 5.2 Adding Cluster Nodes to the NLB Cluster

1. On the server that is to be added to the NLB cluster, select Start, Settings, Network Connections. The Network Connections window opens, displaying all configured connections on the computer.

2. Double-click the network adapter that you want to use as the cluster network adapter to open the *network adapter* Status dialog box.

3. Click the Properties button to open the network adapter Properties dialog box.

4. On the General tab, click the Install button to open the Select Network Component Type dialog box. Double-click on Service to open the Select Network Service dialog box, as shown in Figure 5.13.

**FIGURE 5.13**
You need to ensure that Network Load Balancing is enabled for the clustering adapter.

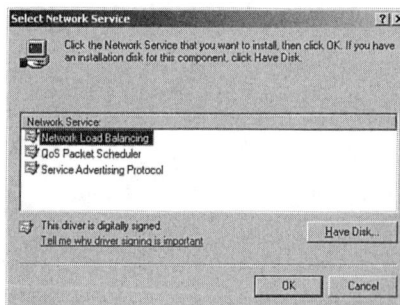

5. Select Network Load Balancing and click OK. Verify that the *network adapter* Properties now shows that Network Load Balancing is available for the clustering adapter, as shown in Figure 5.14.

6. From the cluster node where the NLB cluster was created, open the Network Load Balancing Manager.

7. If the Network Load Balancing Manager does not display the cluster, connect to it by right-clicking on Network Load Balancing Clusters and select Connect to Existing from the context menu.

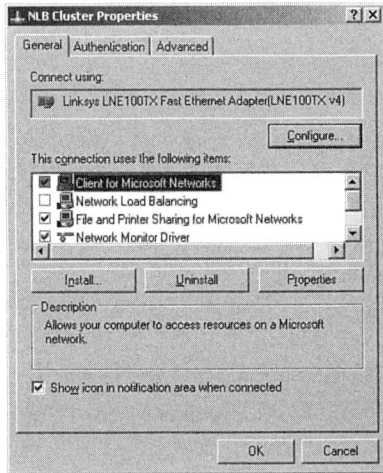

**FIGURE 5.14**
After Network Load Balancing has been made available for the clustering adapter, you can quickly add the new cluster node.

8. Right-click on the NLB cluster and select Add Host To Cluster from the context menu.

9. On the Connect dialog box, shown in Figure 5.15, type the name of the additional cluster node and click the Connect button. After a brief period, all available network adapters are displayed in the bottom half of the dialog box. Select the network adapter that is to be used for load balancing and click Next to continue.

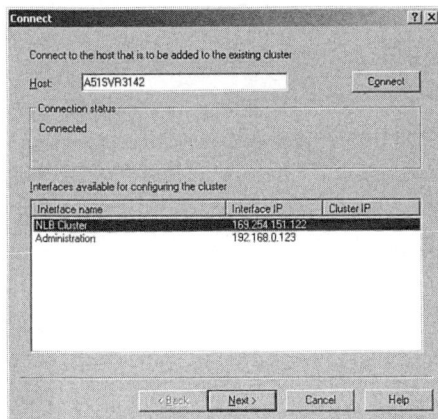

**FIGURE 5.15**
Ensure that you select the proper network adapter to use as the load balancing adapter.

*continues*

*continued*

**10.** On the Host Parameters dialog box, shown in Figure 5.16, configure the host priority, cluster node dedicated IP address and subnet mask, and the initial state of the cluster node. The dedicated IP address is that of the cluster network adapter itself, and must be unique and in the same subnet as the cluster VIP. After entering all required information, click Finish to complete the NLB cluster creation process.

**FIGURE 5.16**
The Host Parameters dialog box contains critical configuration items that identify the specific cluster node.

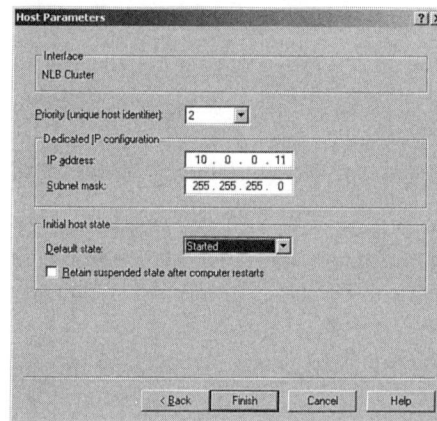

**11.** After a brief period of time, you can see the updated and fully converged cluster displayed in the Network Load Balancing Manager, as shown in Figure 5.17.

**FIGURE 5.17**
After a brief delay, the updated NLB cluster is fully converged.

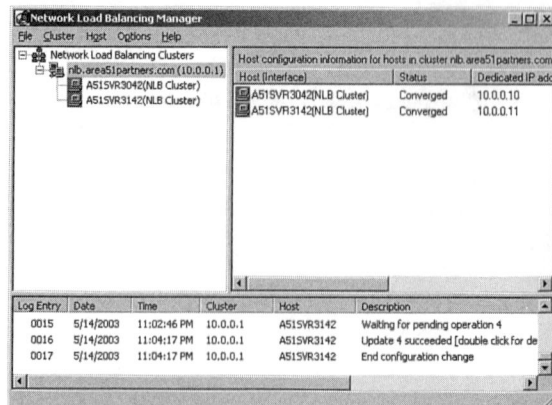

# GUIDED PRACTICE EXERCISE 5.1

In this exercise, you create a new NLB cluster. This Guided Practice helps reinforce the preceding discussion.

You should try completing this exercise on your own first. If you get stuck, or you would like to see one possible solution, follow these steps:

1. For the cluster host administrative network adapter, configure the TCP/IP properties by entering the IP address and subnet mask you have chosen. If the administrative network adapters are connected to each other only through a switch or hub, they do not need a DNS server IP address or default gateway IP address.

2. For the cluster host load balancing network adapter, configure the TCP/IP properties by entering the IP address, subnet mask, DNS server IP address, and default gateway IP address.

3. Open the Network Load Balancing Manager.

4. Right-click Network Load Balancing Clusters and select New Cluster from the context menu.

5. Enter the cluster IP address (cluster Virtual IP), subnet mask, and cluster domain name.

6. Configure the cluster for unicast or multicast as desired.

7. Configure IGMP multicast and cluster remote control as desired.

8. Add any additional cluster Virtual IP addresses as required using the Add button.

9. Configure port rules that are appropriate for your NLB cluster installation.

10. On the Connect dialog box, enter the name of the first cluster node and click the Connect button. From the displayed list, select the network adapter that is to be used for load balancing.

*continues*

**NOTE**

**Using the Network Load Balancing Manager** Although it is possible to configure NLB settings directly on a network adapter using its Properties dialog box, as shown in Figure 5.14, you should not do so. The advantages to using the NLB Manager include not having to manually duplicate settings among all hosts in the cluster. You also avoid the potential for problems and unpredictable results that often occur when attempting to manage NLB settings manually.

*continued*

11. On the Host Parameters dialog box, configure the host priority, cluster node dedicated IP address and subnet mask, and the initial state of the cluster node. The dedicated IP address is that of the cluster network adapter itself, and must be unique and in the same subnet as the cluster VIP.

12. After entering all required information, click Finish to complete the NLB cluster creation process.

---

With the discussion of creating NLB clusters behind us, we now move forward and examine MSCS clusters—commonly just referred to as *clusters*.

# PLANNING AND IMPLEMENTING MSCS CLUSTERS

**Plan services for high availability.**

▶ **Plan a high availability solution that uses clustering services.**

**Implement a cluster server.**

I made the statement earlier in this chapter that NLB clusters were the "simpler of the two types to understand, deploy, and support." This is very much a true statement. As you saw, NLB clusters require no special hardware. In fact, the only real additional requirement above meeting those to install Windows Server 2003 is that each NLB cluster should have two network adapters installed. the services and applications installed on the NLB cluster may have additional requirements, but for the most part NLB clusters are less expensive and easier to implement and maintain.

Clustering, however, has its advantages—especially in those applications where uninterrupted access to data and services is a must-have. Typical situations in which you can expect to deploy clusters are in support of Exchange Server, SQL Server, file shares, and printer shares—all services that businesses, clients, and users demand 24/7 access to.

So, what's the difference between clustering and network load balancing. As you saw previously in Figure 5.2, NLB uses a group of between 2 and 32 servers to distribute inbound requests among them in a fashion that permits the maximum amount of loading with the minimum amount of downtime. Each NLB cluster node contains an exact copy of the static and dynamic content that every other NLB cluster node has; in this way, it doesn't matter which NLB cluster node receives the inbound request, except in the case of host affinity where cookies are involved. The NLB cluster nodes use heartbeats to keep aware of the status of all nodes.

Clustering, on the other hand, uses a group of between 2 and 8 servers that all share a common storage device. Recall that a cluster resource is an application, service, or hardware device that is defined and managed by the cluster service. The cluster service (MSCS) monitors these cluster resources to ensure that they are operating properly. When a problem occurs with a cluster resource, MSCS attempts to correct the problem on the same cluster node. If the problem cannot be corrected—such as a service that cannot be successfully restarted—the cluster service fails the resource, takes the cluster group offline, moves it to another cluster node, and restarts the cluster group. MSCS clusters also use heartbeats to determine the operational status of other nodes in the cluster.

Two clustering modes exist:

▶ **Active/Passive**—One node in the cluster is online providing services. The other nodes in the cluster are online but do not provide any services or applications to clients. If the active node fails, the cluster groups that were running on that node are failed over to the passive node. The passive node then changes its state to active and begins to service client requests. The passive nodes cannot be used for any other purpose during normal operations because they must remain available for a failover situation. All nodes should be configured identically to ensure that when failover occurs no performance loss is experienced.

▶ **Active/Active**—One instance of the clustered service or application runs on each node in the cluster. If a failure of a node occurs, that instance is transferred to one of the running nodes. Although this clustering mode allows you to make use of all cluster nodes to service client requests, it can cause significant performance degradation if the cluster was already operating a very high load at the time of the failure.

You must choose from three cluster models when planning for your new cluster. They are discussed in the next section.

## Cluster Models

Three distinctly different cluster models exist for configuring your new cluster. You must choose one of the three models at the beginning of your cluster planning because the chosen model dictates the storage requirements of your new cluster. The three models are presented in the following sections in order of increasing complexity—and cost.

### Single Node Cluster

The single node cluster model, as shown in Figure 5.18, has only one cluster node. The cluster node can make use of local storage or an external cluster storage device. If local storage is used, the local disk is configured as the cluster storage device. This storage device is known as a *Local Quorum resource*. A Local Quorum resource does not make use of failover and is most commonly used as a way to organize network resources in a single network location for administrative and user convenience. This model is also useful for developing and testing cluster-aware applications.

Despite its limited capabilities, this model does offer the administrator some advantages at a relatively low entry cost:

▶ The cluster service can automatically restart services and applications that might not be able to automatically restart themselves after a failure. This capability can be used to increase the reliability of network services and applications.

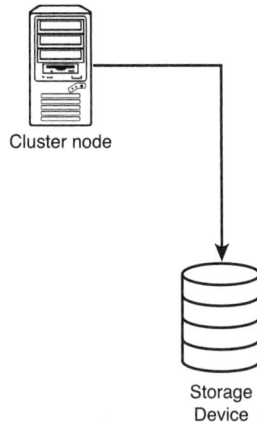

Cluster node

Storage
Device

**FIGURE 5.18**
The single node cluster can be used to increase service reliability and also to prestage cluster resource groups.

▶ The single node can be clustered with additional nodes in the future, preserving the resource groups that you have already created. You only need to join the additional nodes to the cluster and configure the failover and move policies for the resource groups to ready the newly added nodes.

> **EXAM TIP**
>
> **Creating single node clusters**   The New Server Cluster Wizard creates the single node cluster using a Local Quorum resource by default if the cluster node is not connected to a cluster storage device.

## Single Quorum Cluster

The single quorum cluster model, as shown in Figure 5.19, has two or more cluster nodes that are configured such that each node is attached to the cluster storage device. All cluster configuration data is stored on a single cluster storage device. All cluster nodes have access to the quorum data, but only one cluster node runs the quorum disk resource at any given time.

## Majority Node Set Cluster

The majority node set cluster model, as shown in Figure 5.20, has two or more cluster nodes that are configured such that the nodes may or may not be attached to one or more cluster storage devices. Cluster configuration data is stored on multiple disks across the entire cluster, and the cluster service is responsible for ensuring that this data is kept consistent across all the disks. All quorum traffic travels in an unencrypted form over the network using server message block (SMB) file shares. This model provides the advantage of being able to locate cluster nodes in two geographically different locations because they do not all need to be physically attached to the shared cluster storage device.

**FIGURE 5.19**
The single quorum cluster shares one cluster storage device among all cluster nodes.

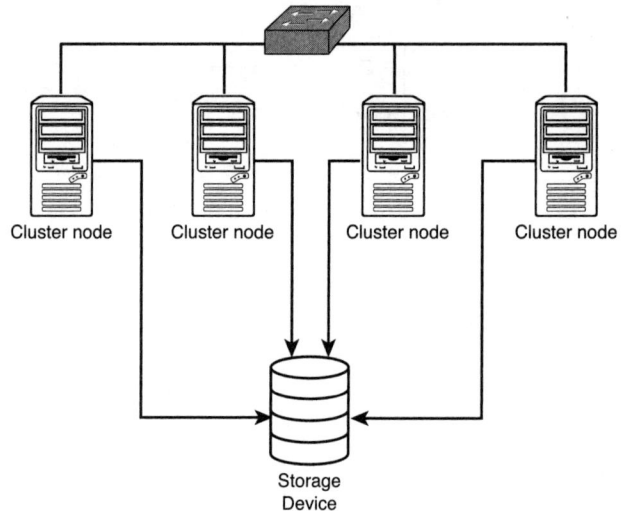

**FIGURE 5.20**
The majority node set cluster model is a high-level clustering solution that allows for geographically dispersed cluster nodes.

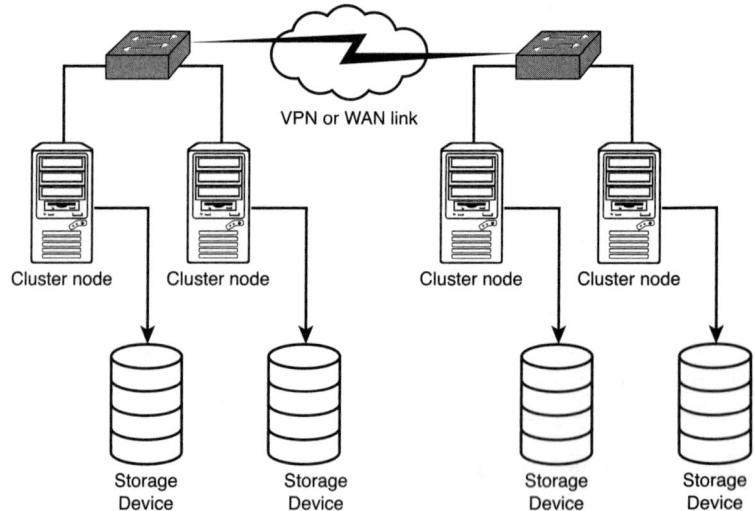

Even if all cluster nodes are not located in the same physical location, they all appear as a single entity to clients. The majority node set cluster model provides the following advantages over the other clustering models:

▶ Clusters can be created without cluster disks. This capability is useful in situations in which you need to make available applications that can failover, but you have another means to replicate data among the storage devices.

▶ Should a local quorum disk become unavailable for some reason, it can be taken offline and the rest of the cluster remains available to service client requests.

There are, however, some requirements that you must abide by when implementing majority node set clusters to ensure they are successful:

▶ A maximum of two sites can be used.

▶ The cluster nodes at either site must be able to communicate with each other with less than a 500 millisecond response time in order for the heartbeat messages to accurately indicate the correct status of the cluster nodes.

▶ A high-speed, high-quality WAN or VPN link must be established between sites so that the cluster's IP address appears the same to all clients, regardless of their location on the network.

▶ Only the cluster quorum information is replicated between the cluster storage devices. You must provide a proven effective means to replicate other data between the cluster storage devices.

The primary disadvantage to this clustering model is that if a certain number of nodes fail, the cluster loses its quorum and it then fails. Table 5.1 shows the maximum number of cluster nodes that can fail before the cluster itself fails.

> **EXAM TIP**
>
> **Don't look for Majority Node Quorums** Although this is a new technology in Windows Server 2003, you should not expect to see questions dealing with this technology on the exam. Majority Node Quorums are high-level hardware-dependent solutions that will be provided as a complete package from an OEM.

**TABLE 5.1**

**NUMBER OF FAILED NODES TO FAIL THE MAJORITY NODE SET CLUSTER**

| Number of Nodes in the Cluster | Number of Nodes to Cause the Cluster to Fail |
| --- | --- |
| 1 | 0 |
| 2 | 0 |
| 3 | 1 |
| 4 | 1 |
| 5 | 2 |
| 6 | 2 |
| 7 | 3 |
| 8 | 3 |

**Using majority node set clusters**
Majority node set clusters are most likely going to be the clustering solution of the future due to their capability to geographically separate cluster nodes, thus further increasing the reliability and redundancy of your clustering solution. Microsoft, however, at the present time recommends that you implement majority node set clustering only in very specific instances and only with close support provided by your Original Equipment Manufacturer (OEM), Independent Software Vendor (ISV), or Independent Hardware Vendor (IHV).

As shown in Table 5.1, the majority node cluster set will remain operational as long as a majority—more than half—of the initial cluster nodes remain available.

Now that you have seen the three cluster models available in Windows Server 2003, you next should give consideration to choosing the operation mode that your cluster will utilize if it is a single quorum cluster or a majority node set cluster. Cluster operation modes are discussed in the next section.

## Cluster Operation Modes

You can choose from four basic cluster operation modes when using a single quorum cluster or a majority node set cluster. These operation modes are specified by defining the cluster failover policies accordingly, as discussed in the next section. Following are the four basic cluster operation modes:

▶ **Failover Pair**—This mode of operation is configured by allowing applications to failover between only two specific cluster nodes. Only the two desired nodes should be placed in the possible owner list for the service of concern.

▶ **Hot-standby (N+I)**—This mode of operation allows you to reduce expenses and overhead associated with dedicated failover pairs by consolidating the spare node for each failover pair into a single node, thus providing a single cluster node that is capable of taking over the applications from any active node in the event of a failover. Hot-standby is often referred to as active/passive, as discussed previously in this chapter. Hot-standby is achieved through a combination of using the preferred owners list and the possible owners list. The preferred node is configured as the node that will run the application or service under normal conditions in the preferred owners list, and the spare (hot-standby) node is configured in the possible owners list.

▶ **Failover Ring**—This mode of operation has each node in the cluster running an instance of the application or service. In the event a node fails, the application or service on the failed node is moved to the next node in the sequence. The failover ring mode is achieved by using the preferred owner list to define the order of failover for a given resource group. This order should start on a different node on each node in the cluster.

▶ **Random**—This mode of operation allows the cluster to determine which node will be failed over to randomly. You define the random failover mode by configuring an empty preferred owner list for each resource group.

Now that you've been introduced to failover, let's examine cluster failover policies; this is the topic of the next section.

## Cluster Failover Polices

Although the actual configuration of failover and failback policies is discussed later in this chapter, it is important at this time to discuss them briefly so as to properly acquaint you with their use and function. Each resource group within the cluster has a prioritized listing of the nodes that are supposed to act as its host.

You can configure failover policies for each resource group to define exactly how each group will behave when a failover occurs. You must configure these three settings:

▶ **Preferred nodes**—An internal prioritized list of available nodes for resource group failovers and failbacks. Ideally, all nodes in the cluster are in this list, in the order of priority you designate.

▶ **Failover timing**—The resource can be configured for immediate failover if the resource fails, or the cluster service may be configured to try to restart the resource a specified number of times before failover actually occurs. The failover threshold value should be equal to or less than the number of nodes in the cluster.

▶ **Failback timing**—Failback can be configured to occur as soon as the preferred node is available or during a specified period of the time, such as when peak load is at its lowest so as to minimize service disruptions.

## Creating a Cluster

Now that you have a good introduction into what clustering is and how it works, you are ready to create the cluster and install the first node in the cluster. As with the NLB cluster, you should do a bit of preparation before actually starting the configuration process to ensure that your cluster is created successfully.

Any good implementation needs a good plan. To successfully implement your MSCS cluster, you need to determine and document the following pieces of information:

- All services and applications that will be deployed on the cluster.

- Failover and failback policies for each service or application that is to be deployed.

- The quorum model to be used.

- The configuration and operating procedures for the shared storage devices to be used.

- All hardware to ensure that it is listed on the Hardware Compatibility List (HCL). MSCS clusters have higher hardware requirements than NLB clusters.

- The clustering and administrative IP address and subnet information, including the cluster IP address itself.

- The cluster name, no more than 15 characters long so that it complies with NetBIOS naming requirements.

After you've configured and prepared your servers and shared storage device, you are ready to move forward with the creation of the MSCS cluster. Any installation and configuration required for the shared storage device must be completed in accordance with the manufacturers' or vendors' specifications to ensure successful deployment.

Step by Step 5.3 shows how to create a new MSCS cluster.

# STEP BY STEP

## 5.3 Creating a New MSCS Cluster

1. Open the Active Directory Users and Computers console and create a domain user account to be used by the MSCS service. Configure the password to never expire. Later during the cluster creation process, this user account will be given Local Administrator privileges on all cluster nodes and will also be delegated cluster-related user rights in the domain, including the Add Computer Accounts to the Domain user right. Figure 5.21 shows an example of what your summary page might look like after creating the domain user account.

**N O T E**

**Creating user accounts**  If you need a refresher on creating user accounts, check out *MCSE TG 70-290: Managing and Maintaining a Microsoft Windows Server 2003 Environment* (2003, Que Publishing; ISBN: 0789729350).

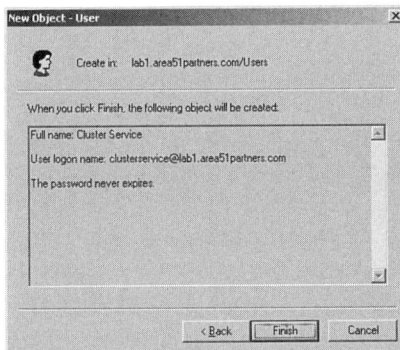

**FIGURE 5.21**
You need to ensure the cluster service domain user account's password is set to never expire.

2. Ensure that the load balancing and administrative network adapters on the first cluster node are configured correctly, as discussed previously and in Step by Step 5.1.

3. Open the Cluster Administrator by selecting Start, Programs, Administrative Tools, Cluster Administrator. You should be prompted with the Open Connection to Cluster dialog box, as shown in Figure 5.22. If not, click File, Open Connection. Select Create New Cluster and click OK to continue.

*continues*

*continued*

**FIGURE 5.22**
You need to create a new cluster because you don't already have an existing one to open.

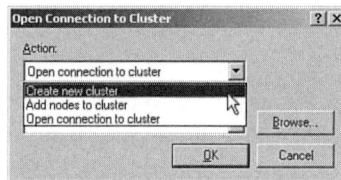

**4.** Click Next to dismiss the opening dialog box of the New Cluster Creation Wizard.

**5.** On the Cluster Name and Domain dialog box, shown in Figure 5.23, select the cluster domain from the drop-down list. Enter the cluster name in the space provided. Click Next to continue.

**FIGURE 5.23**
Only computers that are members of the selected domain can join the cluster.

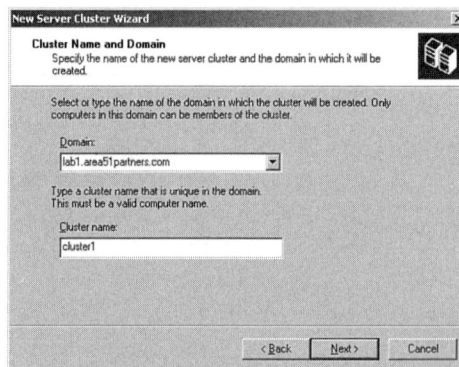

**6.** On the Select Computer dialog box, shown in Figure 5.24, select the computer that will be the first node in the new cluster. Click Next to continue.

**7.** The Analyzing Configuration dialog box, shown in Figure 5.25, appears and runs for a short period of time. You can continue with caution as long as no errors or warnings occur. You can examine the log file by clicking the View Log button. The log file is shown in Figure 5.26; notice that a local quorum is being created in this cluster. Click Next to continue after you are done viewing the output.

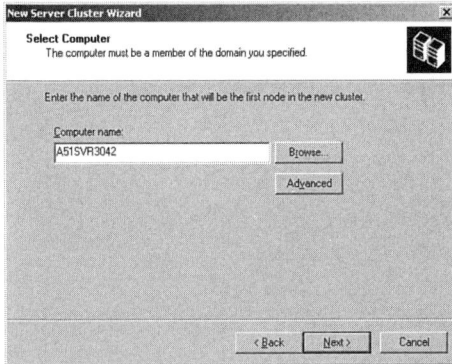

**FIGURE 5.24**
Enter or browse to the name of the first node of the cluster.

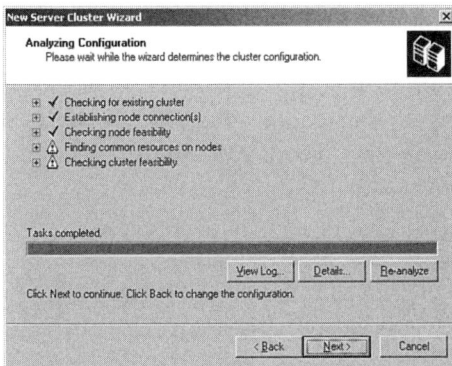

**FIGURE 5.25**
The Analyzing Cluster process alerts you to any show-stoppers encountered with your selected node.

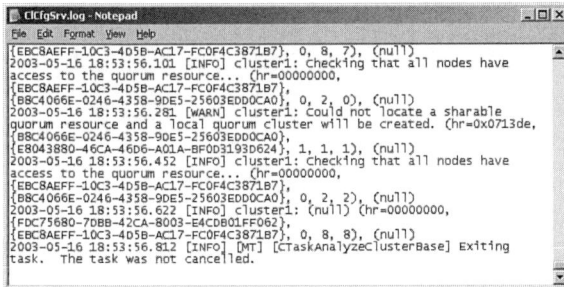

**FIGURE 5.26**
The log file, because it is very detailed, can yield some useful information.

**8.** On the IP Address dialog box, shown in Figure 5.27, enter the IP address that is being assigned to the cluster. Click Next to continue.

*continues*

*continued*

**FIGURE 5.27**
Ensure the IP address entered here is correct and in the same IP subnet as the IP addresses configured for the load balancing network adapter.

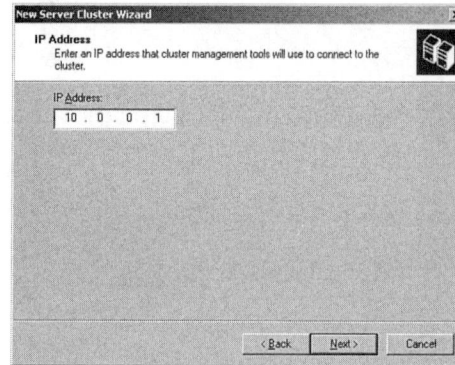

9. On the Cluster Service Account dialog box, shown in Figure 5.28, enter the proper credentials for the cluster domain user account you created previously. Click Next to continue.

**FIGURE 5.28**
You need to supply the cluster domain user account name and password to continue the cluster creation process.

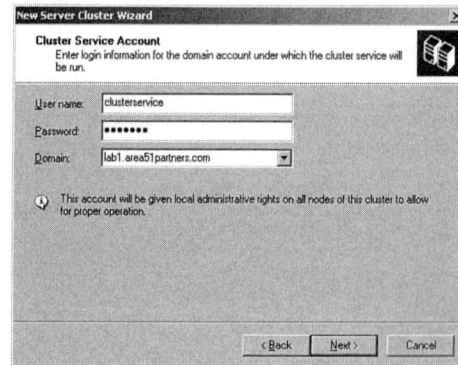

10. On the Proposed Cluster Configuration dialog box, shown in Figure 5.29, you can review the cluster configuration before continuing. Clicking the Quorum button allows you to change the type of quorum being used, as shown in Figure 5.30. When done, click Next to continue.

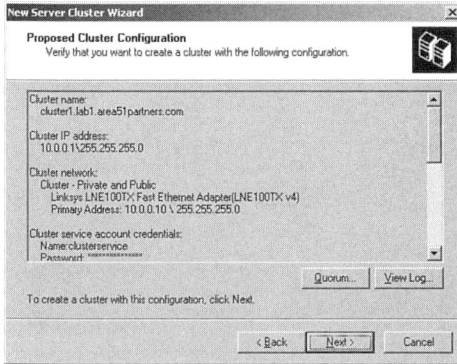

**FIGURE 5.29**
You can review the selected cluster configuration before creating it.

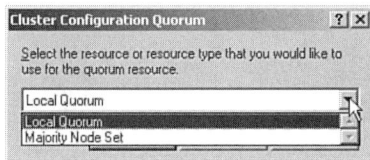

**FIGURE 5.30**
You can change the quorum type by selecting one of the available options if desired.

**11.** If all goes well—and, of course, it will—you should see results on the Creating the Cluster dialog box like those shown in Figure 5.31. Click Next to continue.

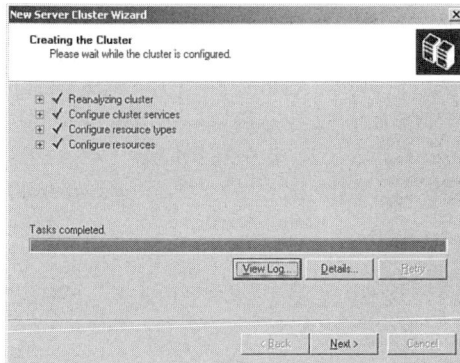

**FIGURE 5.31**
The Creating the Cluster dialog box informs you of the status of cluster creation.

**12.** Click Finish to complete the Create New Cluster Wizard.

**13.** Your new cluster appears in the Cluster Administrator, as shown in Figure 5.32.

*continues*

*continued*

**FIGURE 5.32**
The Cluster Administrator shows your new cluster now.

Congratulations, you just created your first cluster! That wasn't so difficult after you got all the preliminaries out of the way, was it? One thing you should change immediately, however, is the operational mode of the cluster node network adapters. By default, both the cluster and administrative network adapters are configured to pass both types of traffic; this is undesirable and should be corrected as soon as possible. To correct this setting, locate the Networks node of the Cluster Administrator, as shown in Figure 5.33. Right-click on each adapter to open its properties dialog box, as shown in Figure 5.34. Configure the adapter according to its role in the cluster.

**FIGURE 5.33**
You should change the network adapter operational mode as soon as possible.

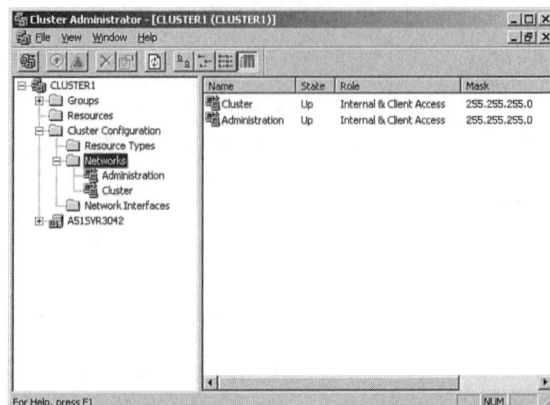

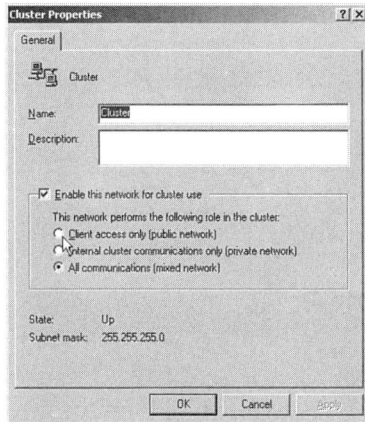

**FIGURE 5.34**
Select Client Access Only for the cluster network adapter.

You are now ready to add a second node to your new cluster. Step by Step 5.4 outlines this procedure.

## STEP BY STEP

### 5.4 Adding a Node to an MSCS Cluster

1. Ensure that the load balancing and administrative network adapters on the new cluster node are configured correctly, as discussed previously and in Step by Step 5.1.

2. Open the Cluster Administrator. If the cluster does not appear in the Cluster Administrator, click File, Open Connection and supply the required information to connect to the cluster.

3. Right-click on the cluster name in the Cluster Administrator and select New, Node from the context menu.

4. Click Next to dismiss the opening dialog box of the Add Nodes Wizard.

5. On the Select Computers dialog box, shown in Figure 5.35, enter the computer names that are to be joined to the cluster.

*continues*

*continued*

**FIGURE 5.35**
You can have up to eight nodes in a Windows
Server 2003 cluster.

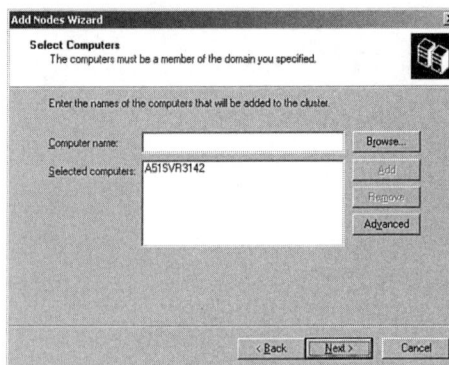

6. The Analyzing Configuration dialog box appears for the new node(s) providing information about their suitability to join the cluster. Click Next to continue.

7. On the Cluster Service Account dialog box, enter the correct password for the cluster service account. Click Next to continue.

8. On the Proposed Cluster Configuration dialog box, you can review the cluster configuration before continuing. Click Next to continue.

9. The Adding Nodes to the Cluster dialog box appears, detailing the status of the node addition. Click Next to continue.

10. Click Finish to complete the Add Nodes Wizard.

11. Your new cluster node appears in the Cluster Administrator, as shown in Figure 5.36.

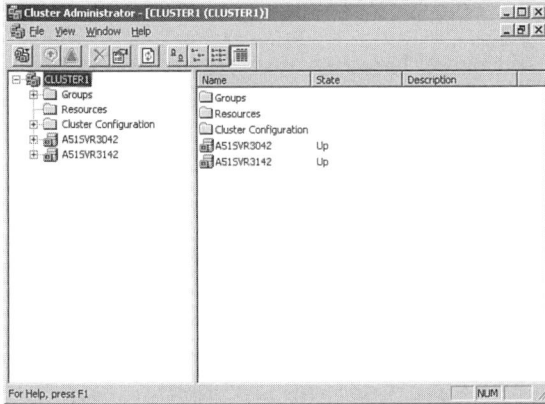

**FIGURE 5.36**
The Cluster Administrator displays the newly added cluster node.

> **EXAM TIP**
>
> **Hardcore hardware** Although this topic is way beyond the scope of this exam, you need to know how to set up and configure the storage devices required for MSCS clustering implementations. For more information, be sure to see *Server+ Certification Training Guide* (2001, Que Publishing; ISBN: 0735710872).

Now that you know how to create MSCS clusters, let's move forward and examine monitoring and managing your high availability solutions.

# GUIDED PRACTICE EXERCISE 5.2

In this exercise, you create a new MSCS cluster. This Guided Practice helps reinforce the preceding discussion.

You should try completing this exercise on your own first. If you get stuck, or you would like to see one possible solution, follow these steps:

1. From the Active Directory Users and Computers console, create a domain user account to be used by the MSCS service. Configure the password to never expire.

2. For the cluster host administrative network adapter, configure the TCP/IP properties by entering the IP address and subnet mask you have chosen. If the administrative network adapters are connected to each other only through a switch or hub, they do not need a DNS server IP address or default gateway IP address.

*continues*

*continued*

3. For the cluster host load balancing network adapter, configure the TCP/IP properties by entering the IP address, subnet mask, DNS server IP address, and default gateway IP address.

4. Open the cluster and create a new cluster.

5. On the Cluster Name and Domain dialog box, select the cluster domain from the drop-down list and enter the cluster name.

6. On the Select Computer dialog box, select the computer that will be the first node in the new cluster.

7. View the results presented in the Analyzing Configuration dialog box.

8. On the IP Address dialog box, enter the cluster Virtual IP address.

9. On the Cluster Service Account dialog box, enter the account name and password for the cluster service account you created previously.

10. On the Proposed Cluster Configuration dialog box, either accept the proposed configuration or change the quorum type being used.

---

# MONITORING AND MANAGING HIGH AVAILABILITY SOLUTIONS

After you have planned and implemented your new high availability server solution, you need to perform routine monitoring and management tasks on it to keep it operating correctly. For the most part, high availability solutions are prone to the same sorts of problems that plague regular servers: hardware failures, service stoppages, data corruption, and so on. Recall that the purpose of implementing a high availability solution is not to prevent these sorts of events from occurring (although it would be nice), but instead to minimize the impact of these occurrences on the client experience.

In this section we examine the process to recover from the failure of a cluster node as well as some of the tools that can be used to monitor network load balancing implementations.

# Recovering from Failed Cluster Nodes

**Recover from cluster node failure.**

If you've done all your planning and implementing right up to now, you are ready for the day when something—anything—happens that renders one of your cluster nodes inoperable. As mentioned previously, high availability servers are still subject to the same sorts of problems and failures that plague any server; the difference is that because you have implemented a high availability solution, your clients will continue to have access to the required applications services and should not, under most circumstances, even notice that something terrible has happened behind the scenes.

It's a nice feeling knowing that even if disaster strikes, your clients can still carry on as if nothing ever happened. However, you cannot afford to rest on your laurels when disaster does strike; you will need to get that failed cluster node back online and in the cluster in short order. How you do this will depend exactly on what the problem at hand is.

In most cases, when an MSCS cluster node has failed, you either need to rebuild it (hardware failure) or restore it (software failure or corruption) from an earlier backup set. In either case, you need to first evict the node from the cluster. To evict a node from a cluster, open the Cluster Administrator and connect to the cluster in question. Locate the node to be evicted and right-click on it. From the context menu, select Evict Node, as shown in Figure 5.37. You cannot evict a node where the Cluster Service is still running.

Evicting the last remaining node in the MSCS cluster removes the entire cluster itself, so be careful not to do so unless this is your intention. The eviction process is fairly abrupt, but it poses no problem to an already failed node because it is no longer providing service to clients.

**FIGURE 5.37**
You may need to evict a cluster node for a variety of reasons.

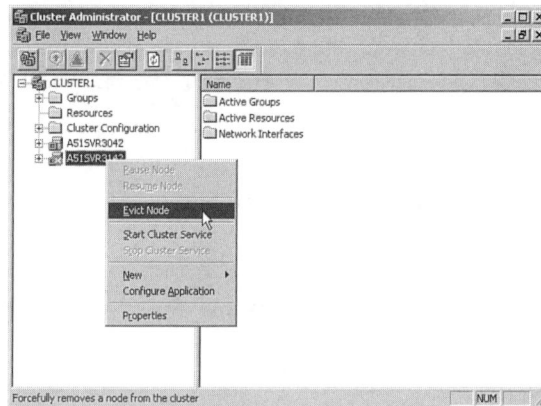

After the cluster node has been evicted, you can rebuild it or perform a restoration on it as required. Should you need to rebuild the cluster node, you need to ensure that its configuration matches exactly that of the node it is replacing. IP address, local driver letters, computer name, and domain membership are all critical to being able to successfully join the newly created node to the cluster. In the event that you need to perform a restoration from a previous backup set, you can perform this as discussed in Chapter 6, "Monitoring and Maintaining Server Availability."

In a worst-case scenario in which you cannot evict a cluster node that is still operating but is experiencing problems with the Cluster Service, you can initiate a manual removal of the Cluster Service from the node by issuing the command `cluster node` *nodename* `/ forcecleanup` from the command line, as shown in Figure 5.38.

**FIGURE 5.38**
If nothing else works to evict the cluster node, you can initiate a manual removal of the Cluster Service.

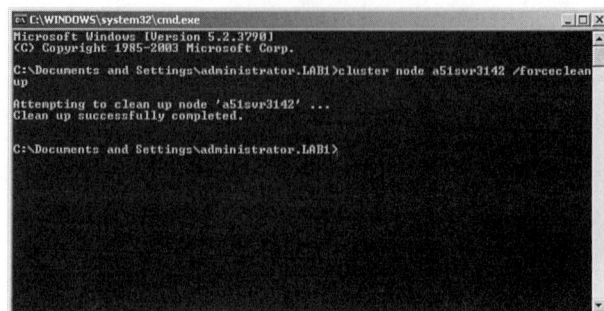

After a cluster node has failed, you should also monitor the remaining cluster nodes to ensure that they are not adversely affected or overloaded as a result. This situation can easily occur when Active/Active clustering is being used. Chapter 6 discusses monitoring server performance in Windows Server 2003. Lastly, after a cluster node has failed, you should make sure that any failovers that were configured to occur have occurred properly. If they have not already properly occurred, you need to manually move the resource group by right-clicking on it and selecting Move Group, as shown in Figure 5.39.

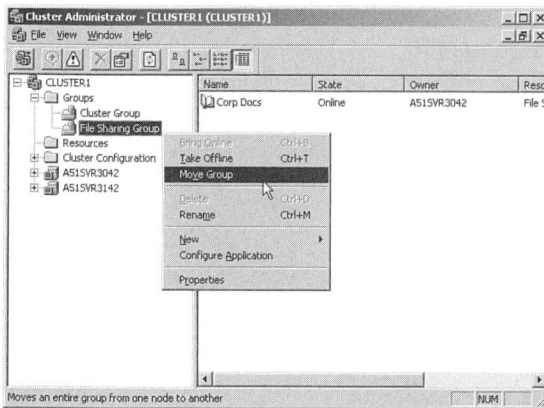

**FIGURE 5.39**
You may have to manually move a resource group if the failover has not occurred properly for some reason.

# Monitoring Network Load Balancing

**Monitor network load balancing. Tools might include the Network Load Balancing Monitor Microsoft Management Console (MMC) snap-in and the WLBS cluster control utility.**

When it comes to monitoring your NLB clusters, there is really not a whole lot to do. You should, as a standard administrative practice, perform basic performance monitoring on each of your NLB cluster nodes. You should monitor the following items:

- ▶ CPU
- ▶ Disk
- ▶ Memory
- ▶ Network
- ▶ Service or application-specific items as required

**Using `nlb.exe` remotely**   The strength of the `nlb.exe` command is that it can be used to manage NLB clusters and cluster nodes remotely across a LAN or WAN if desired. To run the `nlb.exe` command from a remote computer, you must enable remote control for the NLB cluster.

Enabling remote control presents security risks to the NLB cluster, such as data tampering, denial of service (DoS), and unintentional data disclosure to attackers. Remote control should be used only from a trusted computer inside the same firewall as the NLB cluster or over a VPN if outside the firewall.

If you choose to enable remote control despite the risks associated with it, you should take steps to protect the NLB cluster from attack as a result. The default User Datagram Protocol (UDP) control ports for the cluster, 1717 and 2504 at the cluster VIP, should be protected by a firewall. Also, you must ensure that you have configured a strong remote control password.

Using the Performance console to monitor and baseline servers is discussed at length in Chapter 6 and is not discussed here.

You can, however, also perform some monitoring of your NLB cluster and NLB cluster hosts from the command line using the `wlbs.exe` command. For those of you screaming out that the Windows Load Balancing Service was retired with Windows NT 4.0, you are very much correct; Microsoft has kept the WLBS acronym around for good measure. In reality, `wlbs.exe` and `nlb.exe` are identical in every way; therefore, we discuss `nlb.exe`.

The `nlb.exe` command has the following basic context: `nlb command [remote options]`. A complete listing of all available NLB commands can be found in the Windows Server 2003 help files or online at `www.microsoft.com/technet/prodtechnol/ windowsserver2003/proddocs/entserver/nlb_command.asp`. From a monitoring point of view, we focus only on the commands outlined in Table 5.2.

## TABLE 5.2
### THE `nlb.exe` MONITORING-SPECIFIC COMMANDS

| Command | Description |
| --- | --- |
| query | Displays the current cluster state and the list of host priorities for the current members of the cluster. This command can be targeted at a specific cluster, a specific cluster on a specific host, all clusters on the local computer, or all computers that are part of a cluster. The possible states are Unknown, Converging, Draining, and Converged. |
| queryport | Displays information about a given port rule. The command returns the following information:<br>• Whether the specified port rule was found<br>• The current state of the specified port rule<br>• The number of packets accepted and dropped on the specified port rule |
| display | Displays extensive information about the current NLB parameters, cluster state, and past cluster activity. |
| params | Displays information about the current NLB configuration. |
| ip2mac | Displays the MAC address corresponding to the specified cluster name or IP address. If multicast support is enabled, the multicast media access control address is used by network load balancing for cluster operations. Otherwise, the unicast media access control address is used. |

## CASE STUDY

### ESSENCE OF THE CASE

Following are the essential elements in this case:

- ▶ A high availability solution will be required to ensure that the Web site remains up and available to customers as much of the time as possible.

- ▶ This typical N-tier high availability solution will require a network load balancing front end and an MSCS clustering back end.

- ▶ The NLB cluster should be configured to maintain client session state when multiple client requests are sent during a single session.

### SCENARIO

You have been hired by the Think Pink Bicycle Company to implement a Windows Server 2003 powered solution for its Internet e-commerce Web site.

Think Pink has two teams of developers working to create the Active Server Pages (ASP) based application that will run the front end of the Web site and also on the SQL database that will serve as the back end of the Web site.

Customers will be able to browse the catalog and add items to their shopping carts without being signed into the Web site, but must sign in before starting the order process. Customers will have the option to sign in to their accounts at any time they like. Cookies will be used with the shopping cart and also to maintain customers' information as they move around the Web site.

The CEO of Think Pink has emphasized to you on several occasions that the overall customer experience while using the new Web site is of prime importance to him. You are to ensure that the Web site is available as much of the time as possible and also to ensure that the customer shopping experience is as smooth and flawless as possible.

### ANALYSIS

You will implement an N-tier (two-layered) solution with at least two (preferably four or more) Web servers running in an NLB cluster. The cluster should be configured for Multiple Host with the Single affinity to ensure that the client session state information in the cookies is accurately maintained over the course of the client session.

*continues*

## CASE STUDY

*continued*

The back end should use at least two (preferably four or more) SQL servers in an MSCS cluster. The cluster should be configured using a single quorum or majority node set cluster (if supported by the vendor).

Each server being used in this solution should have two network adapters installed. The load balancing network adapters in the NLB cluster should be configured in unicast mode for best results. The network adapters in the MSCS cluster should be configured appropriately so that only clustering traffic crosses the clustering adapter and administrative traffic crosses the administration adapter.

## CHAPTER SUMMARY

### KEY TERMS

Before you take the exam, make sure you are comfortable with the definitions and concepts for each of the following key terms. You can use Appendix A, "Glossary," for quick reference.

- Affinity
- Cluster
- Clustering
- Cluster resource
- Cluster resource group
- Cluster virtual server
- Convergence
- Heartbeat
- Failback
- Failover

Server reliability is a very important item in today's computer-driven world. It seems that everything from the large plasma displays in Times Square to many automatic teller machines are driven by Windows-powered servers. Being able to keep your Windows Server 2003 solution up and running as much of the time as possible is not only expected, but demanded.

It's a fact of life, however, that nothing is ever perfect. Hardware fails, software stops functioning properly, systems become unavailable. In this chapter we examined an area of server reliability that most administrators have only heard about in passing: high availability solutions.

Businesses want high availability servers to be up and operating 99.999% of the time; that's just more than 5 minutes a year of allowable downtime. For an ordinary server solution, having so little downtime would be impossible; just applying regular hot fixes and service packs takes longer than this. However, by using network load balancing and MSCS clustering, you can create high availability server solutions from multiple servers.

In the end, server reliability begins with you and your good planning.

## CHAPTER SUMMARY

**KEY TERMS**
- Network load balancing
- Node
- Port rules
- Quorum disk

## APPLY YOUR KNOWLEDGE

# Exercises

### 5.1 Creating a New NLB Cluster

In this exercise, you create a new network load balancing cluster. You will need a Windows Server 2003 Enterprise computer to complete this exercise.

**Estimated time:** 20 minutes

1. Open the Network Connections window.

2. Configure the IP address and subnet mask for the load balancing and administrative network adapters on the first NLB cluster node.

3. Open the Network Load Balancing Manager.

4. Right-click on Network Load Balancing Clusters and select New Cluster from the context menu.

5. Enter the cluster's IP address, subnet mask, and cluster domain name. Configure the cluster for unicast or multicast as desired. You can also configure IGMP multicast and remote control as desired. Click Next to continue.

6. On the Cluster IP Addresses dialog box, enter any additional virtual IP addresses using the Add button.

7. On the Port Rules dialog box, configure any port rules that are appropriate for your NLB cluster installation.

8. Configure your port rules as required.

9. On the Connect dialog box, type the name of the first cluster node and click the Connect button. Select the network adapter that is to be used for load balancing.

10. On the Host Parameters dialog box, configure the host priority, cluster node dedicated IP

address and subnet mask, and the initial state of the cluster node.

### 5.2 Adding Nodes to an Existing NLB Cluster

In this exercise, you add an additional node to an existing NLB cluster. You need to complete Exercise 5.1 before attempting this one.

**Estimated time:** 15 minutes

1. On the server that is to be added to the NLB cluster, open the Network Connections.

2. Open the network adapter Status dialog box for the network adapter that will be used for load balancing.

3. Click the Properties button to open the network adapter Properties dialog box.

4. Install the Network Load Balancing service.

5. From the cluster node where the NLB cluster was created, open the Network Load Balancing Manager.

6. If the Network Load Balancing Manager does not display the cluster, connect to it.

7. Right-click on the NLB cluster and select Add Host To Cluster from the context menu.

8. On the Connect dialog box, type the name of the additional cluster node and click the Connect button. Select the network adapter that is to be used for load balancing.

9. On the Host Parameters dialog box, configure the host priority, cluster node dedicated IP address and subnet mask, and the initial state of the cluster node.

## APPLY YOUR KNOWLEDGE

### 5.3 Creating an MSCS Cluster

In this exercise, you create a new MSCS cluster. You need a Windows Server 2003 Enterprise computer that is part of an Active Directory domain to accomplish this exercise.

**Estimated time:** 20 minutes

1. Create a domain user account to be used by the MSCS service. Configure the password to never expire.

2. Ensure that the load balancing and administrative network adapters on the first cluster node are configured correctly.

3. Open the Cluster Administrator. You should be prompted with the Open Connection to Cluster dialog box. If not, click File, Open Connection. Select Create New Cluster and click OK.

4. Click Next to dismiss the opening dialog box of the New Cluster Creation Wizard.

5. On the Cluster Name and Domain dialog box, select the cluster domain from the drop-down list. Enter the cluster name in the space provided.

6. On the Select Computer dialog box, select the computer that will be the first node in the new cluster.

7. The Analyzing Configuration dialog box appears and runs for a short period of time.

8. On the IP Address dialog box, enter the IP address that is being assigned to the cluster.

9. On the Cluster Service Account dialog box, enter the proper credentials for the cluster domain user account you created previously.

10. On the Proposed Cluster Configuration dialog box, review the cluster configuration before continuing. Change the quorum type if desired.

### 5.4 Adding a Node to an Existing MSCS Cluster

In this exercise, you add an additional node to an existing MSCS cluster. Before starting this exercise, you need to complete Exercise 5.3 and have a second computer that is part of the same domain as in Exercise 5.3.

**Estimated time:** 15 minutes

1. Ensure that the load balancing and administrative network adapters on the new cluster node are configured correctly.

2. Open the Cluster Administrator. If the cluster does not appear in the Cluster Administrator, click File, Open Connection and supply the required information to connect to the cluster.

3. Right-click on the cluster name in the Cluster Administrator and select New, Node from the context menu.

4. Click Next to dismiss the opening dialog box of the Add Nodes Wizard.

5. On the Select Computers dialog box, enter the computer names that are to be joined to the cluster.

6. The Analyzing Configuration dialog box appears for the new node(s) providing information about their suitability to join the cluster.

7. On the Cluster Service Account dialog box, enter the correct password for the cluster service account.

8. On the Proposed Cluster Configuration dialog box, you can review the cluster configuration before continuing.

## APPLY YOUR KNOWLEDGE

9. The Adding Nodes to the Cluster dialog box appears, detailing the status of the node addition.

10. Click Finish to complete the Add Nodes Wizard.

## Review Questions

1. What is network load balancing?

2. What does convergence mean?

3. What desirable function do port rules provide?

4. What ports must be made available for NLB remote control to work?

5. What is the difference between load balancing and clustering?

## Exam Questions

1. Andrea is your newly hired assistant network administrator. She has been asking you recently about high availability solutions using Windows Server 2003. She tells you that she has heard of the phrase "five nines" before but doesn't understand what it means. What is the correct answer that you should tell her in regards to the meaning of the phrase "five nines"?

   A. Five nines means that servers must be up for at least 99,999 minutes per year.

   B. Five nines means that servers cannot ever have 99.999% CPU utilization.

   C. Five nines means that servers must be up for at least 99.999% of the time per year.

   D. Five nines means that all servers must have a minimum of five 90GB hard drives.

2. Austin is interviewing for the position of assistant server reliability administrator in your organization. You are asking Austin questions during the technical proficiency portion of his interview. You have asked Austin what types of high availability solutions Windows Server 2003 provides. What two correct answers should Austin provide you?

   A. Network load balancing

   B. Windows File Protection

   C. Clustering

   D. Redundant power supplies

3. When discussing the process of convergence, what are you referring to?

   A. A network communication sent among individual cluster nodes at intervals of no more than 500 milliseconds that is used to determine the status of all cluster nodes.

   B. The process of a cluster group moving back to the preferred node after the preferred node has resumed cluster membership.

   C. The process by which NLB clustering hosts determine a new, stable state among themselves and elect a new default host after the failure of one or more cluster nodes.

   D. The process of a cluster group moving from the currently active node to another still functioning node in the cluster group.

4. You are preparing to implement a network load balancing solution for your organization's e-commerce Web site. You will be load balancing six Windows Server 2003 computers running IIS on the front end with four Windows Server 2003 computers in a cluster on the back end providing access to an SQL Server 2000 database. You are

## APPLY YOUR KNOWLEDGE

using the unicast cluster operation mode. In what two ways can you prevent switch port flooding from occurring on the NLB cluster?

A. Configure IGMP multicast support for the NLB cluster.

B. Place the NLB cluster nodes on a dedicated switch.

C. Place the NLB cluster nodes on a dedicate VLAN.

D. Configure single affinity for the NLB cluster.

5. You are preparing to implement a network load balancing solution for your organization's e-commerce Web site. You will be load balancing six Windows Server 2003 computers running IIS on the front end with four Windows Server 2003 computers in a cluster on the back end providing access to an SQL Server 2000 database. You are trying to decide which clustering mode to use for your back-end servers. What two clustering modes exist?

A. Active/Passive

B. Passive/Active

C. Passive/Passive

D. Active/Active

6. You are preparing to implement a network load balancing solution for your organization's e-commerce Web site. You will be load balancing six Windows Server 2003 computers running IIS on the front end with four Windows Server 2003 computers in a cluster on the back end providing access to an SQL Server 2000 database. Which of the following cluster models is not available in Windows Server 2003?

A. Single node cluster

B. Multiple quorum cluster

C. Single quorum cluster

D. Majority node set cluster

7. You are preparing to implement a network load balancing solution for your organization's e-commerce Web site. You will be load balancing six Windows Server 2003 computers running IIS on the front end with four Windows Server 2003 computers in a cluster on the back end providing access to an SQL Server 2000 database. Your e-commerce application makes heavy use of cookies to maintain user session state information during the active connection. Which type of filtering mode should you configure to ensure that clients receive the best possible overall service during their connection period?

A. Single Host

B. Disable Port Range

C. Multiple Host

D. Allow Port Range

8. You are preparing to implement a network load balancing solution for your organization's e-commerce Web site. You will be load balancing six Windows Server 2003 computers running IIS on the front end with four Windows Server 2003 computers in a cluster on the back end providing access to an SQL Server 2000 database. Your e-commerce application makes heavy use of cookies to maintain user session state information during the active connection. Which type of affinity should you configure to ensure that clients receive the best possible overall service during their connection period?

A. None

B. Class C

C. Multiple

D. Single

9. You are preparing to implement a network load balancing solution for your organization's e-commerce Web site. You will be load balancing six Windows Server 2003 computers running IIS on the front end with four Windows Server 2003 computers in a cluster on the back end providing access to an SQL Server 2000 database. You are using the unicast cluster operation mode. Which of the following statements are true about the load balancing adapters installed in your network load balancing servers? (Choose two correct answers.)

   A. All cluster nodes share an identical unicast MAC address.

   B. All cluster nodes retain their original MAC address. In addition, the load balancing adapters are also assigned an additional multicast MAC address.

   C. If a network load balancing server is using the unicast operational mode and has only one network adapter installed, it will be unable to communicate with the other nodes in the network load balancing cluster.

   D. Inbound client requests are sent to all cluster nodes using the multicast MAC address.

10. You are preparing to implement a network load balancing solution for your organization's e-commerce Web site. You will be load balancing six Windows Server 2003 computers running IIS on the front end with four Windows Server 2003 computers in a cluster on the back end providing access to an SQL Server 2000 database. You are using the unicast cluster operation mode. How many total IP addresses will you need to assign for the network load balancing portion of the solution?

   A. 1

   B. 6

   C. 7

   D. 12

11. Chris is creating a new cluster. She has all the required information written down so that she can enter it during the creation process except for the user account that is to be used. What user account should Chris use during the cluster creation process as the cluster service account?

   A. The built-in local Administrator account

   B. An account that is a member of the Domain Admins group

   C. An account that is a member of the Enterprise Admins group

   D. A user account that is configured for the password to never expire

12. Jeff wants to use the nlb.exe command to manage his NLB cluster from his desktop computer. What must Jeff do before he will able to manage the NLB cluster from his desktop computer?

   A. Ensure that he is a member of the Enterprise Admins group.

   B. Enable remote control on the NLB cluster.

## APPLY YOUR KNOWLEDGE

C. Disable remote control on the NLB cluster.

D. Configure the required port rules on the NLB cluster.

13. Dave is a network administrator in a large Windows Server 2003 Active Directory network. He is responsible for managing and maintaining his company's server clusters. On Monday morning during his normal monitoring cycle, he notices that one of the cluster nodes in his Exchange Server cluster has stopped responding to client requests due to the Cluster Service not running. What is the first step that Dave should perform to begin the recovery process on this failed node?

A. Initiate an ASR restoration.

B. Evict the node from the cluster.

C. Initiate a Windows Backup restoration.

D. Add a new node to the cluster.

14. Rick has just completed the planning and configuration of a new NLB cluster that is to be used as the front end of an Internet Web site. All the cluster nodes are connected to the same switch on the core network. After several days Rick has noticed an exceptionally high amount of traffic on the switch that he cannot explain. What might be the cause of this excessive traffic?

A. The switch is unmanaged and therefore cannot map the MAC address to IP address correctly for the servers attached to it.

B. The switch is experiencing port flooding.

C. The switch has an incorrectly configured VLAN on it.

D. The cluster node network adapters are configured for half-duplex operation.

15. Rick has just completed the planning and configuration of a new NLB cluster that is to be used as the front end of an Internet Web site. All the cluster nodes are connected to the same switch on the core network. After several days Rick has received several complaints from users stating that their shopping carts sometimes lose the contents as they move around the Web site. What is the most likely reason for this problem?

A. The client affinity is misconfigured.

B. The port rules are misconfigured.

C. The operational mode is misconfigured.

D. The host priorities are misconfigured.

## Answers to Review Questions

1. Network load balancing distributes all incoming connection requests using a mathematical algorithm to members of the NLB cluster. For more information, see the section "High Availability Solutions."

2. Convergence is the process by which NLB clustering hosts determine a new, stable state among themselves and elect a new default host after the failure of one or more cluster nodes. For more information, see the section "High Availability Terminology."

3. Port rules can be used to allow traffic only on specific ports to be load-balanced. If you configure explicit allow rules for specific ports and an explicit deny rule dropping all other traffic, only the desired traffic will be load-balanced. For more information, see the section "Port Rules."

## APPLY YOUR KNOWLEDGE

4. The default UDP control ports are 1717 and 2504 at the cluster VIP. For more information, see the section "Monitoring Network Load Balancing."

5. Network load balancing distributes all incoming connection requests using a mathematical algorithm to members of the NLB cluster. Clustering allows several independent servers to act and appear as a single entity to clients. For more information, see the section "High Availability Solutions."

## Answers to Exam Questions

1. **C.** The phrase "five nines" refers to server (or service/application) availability and means that the server must be available for client requests at least 99.999% of the time; this equates to only 5.25 minutes of downtime per year. For more information, see the section "Introduction."

2. **A, C.** Windows Server 2003 provides Network Load Balancing and MSCS clustering services to create high availability server solutions. For more information, see the section "High Availability Solutions."

3. **C.** Convergence is the process by which NLB clustering hosts determine a new, stable state among themselves and elect a new default host after the failure of one or more cluster nodes. For more information, see the section "High Availability Terminology."

4. **B, C.** If the multicast operation mode is configured, you can use the new IGMP multicast support function. Because unicast is being used in this case, you have the option of placing the NLB

cluster nodes on a dedicated switch or VLAN to eliminate switch port flooding. For more information, see the section "NLB Cluster Operation Mode."

5. **A, D.** You can select from either Active/Passive or Active/Active clustering mode. Active/Passive has one node in the cluster online and providing services. All other nodes are online and in a standby state, ready to assume the services if the active node fails. Active/Active has an instance of the clustered service running on all nodes in the cluster. If a node fails, the service instance is transferred to one of the remaining operational nodes. For more information, see the section "Planning and Implementing MSCS Clusters."

6. **B.** The single mode cluster, single quorum cluster, and majority node set cluster models are supported in Windows Server 2003. There is no multiple quorum cluster model. For more information, see the section "Cluster Models."

7. **C.** By using the multiple host filtering mode, you will allow all cluster nodes to handle client traffic. When the multiple host filtering mode is configured, you can also configure a client affinity setting. Client affinity determines how cluster nodes will handle repeated client requests during the same session. For more information, see the section "Filtering Mode and Affinity."

8. **D.** By configuring the single affinity setting, you will maintain all client requests on the same node for the duration of the session. Single affinity provides the best support for the maintenance of user state data and is often used when applications that are running on the cluster generate cookies. For more information, see the section "Filtering Mode and Affinity."

## APPLY YOUR KNOWLEDGE

9. **A, C.** Unicast mode should be used only when the network load balancing servers have two network adapters installed. If only one network adapter is installed, the cluster nodes will not be able to communicate with each other. When the unicast mode is used, all cluster nodes are assigned an identical unicast MAC address that overwrites the MAC address of the load balancing adapter. For more information, see the section "NLB Cluster Operation Mode."

10. **C.** You will need to assign a total of seven IP addresses for the network load balancing portion of this solution. Each load balancing network adapter in the front-end IIS servers requires a dedicated IP address, such as 10.0.25.11–10.0.25.16. Also, the entire network load balancing cluster is assigned a virtual IP (VIP) address, such as 10.0.25.10. For more information, see the section "Creating an NLB Cluster."

11. **D.** Chris should use an ordinary domain user account that has been configured to never have its password expire. During the cluster creation process, this user account will be given Local Administrator privileges on all cluster nodes and will also be delegated cluster-related user rights in the domain, including the Add Computer Accounts to the Domain user right. For more information, see the section "Creating a Cluster."

12. **B.** Before the `nlb.exe` command can be used to remotely manage an NLB cluster over a LAN or WAN, remote control must be enabled on the NLB cluster. For more information, see the section "Monitoring Network Load Balancing."

13. **B.** Dave will need to first evict the failed node from the cluster before he can begin any recovery operation on the node. For more information, see the section "Recovering from Failed Cluster Nodes."

14. **B.** The most likely reason for the excessive amount of traffic on the switch is due to switch port flooding. The mathematical algorithm used by network load balancing sends inbound traffic to every host in the NLB cluster. It does so by preventing the switch that the NLB cluster nodes are attached to from ever associating the NLB cluster's MAC address with a specific port on the switch. This, however, leads to the unwanted side effect of switch port flooding where the switch floods all its ports with all packets inbound to the NLB cluster. For more information, see the section "NLB Cluster Operation Mode."

15. **A.** Rick's problem is most likely that the client affinity is misconfigured. The affinity should be configured for single. This affinity type maintains all client requests on the same node for the duration of the session (connection). This type of affinity provides the best support for the maintaining of user state data and is often used when applications are running on the cluster that generates cookies. For more information, see the section "Filtering Mode and Affinity."

## APPLY YOUR KNOWLEDGE

### Suggested Readings and Resources

1. Windows Server 2003 Deployment Kit: Planning Server Deployments, `http://go.microsoft.com/fwlink/?LinkId=15309`.

2. Clustering Services Technology Center, `http://www.microsoft.com/windowsserver2003/technologies/clustering/default.mspx`.

This chapter helps you to learn and master some of the more common concepts associated with implementing and maintaining availability of servers through such administrative tasks as performance monitoring, log monitoring, and backups. Highly available server solutions, such as clustering and network load balancing, were discussed in Chapter 5, "Planning, Implementing, and Maintaining Highly Available Servers." Microsoft has the following objectives for the routine administrative portion of the "Planning, Implementing, and Maintaining Server Availability" unit:

**Identify system bottlenecks, including memory, processor, disk, and network-related bottlenecks.**

- **Identify system bottlenecks by using System Monitor.**

▶ Examining the inner workings of the operating system can provide an administrator with some valuable insight as to how and when future problems might occur. The System Monitor can provide information that, if used properly, can help avoid costly downtime or performance degradation on servers and client machines.

**Plan a backup and recovery strategy.**

- **Identify appropriate backup types. Methods can include the backup types full, incremental, and differential.**

- **Plan a backup strategy that uses volume shadow copy.**

- **Plan system recovery that uses Automated System Recovery (ASR).**

▶ Regardless of how much planning and effort you put into keeping your servers running smoothly, disaster may still strike. Being familiar with the use and options of the Windows Backup Utility is a critical part of a disaster recovery plan in Windows Server 2003.

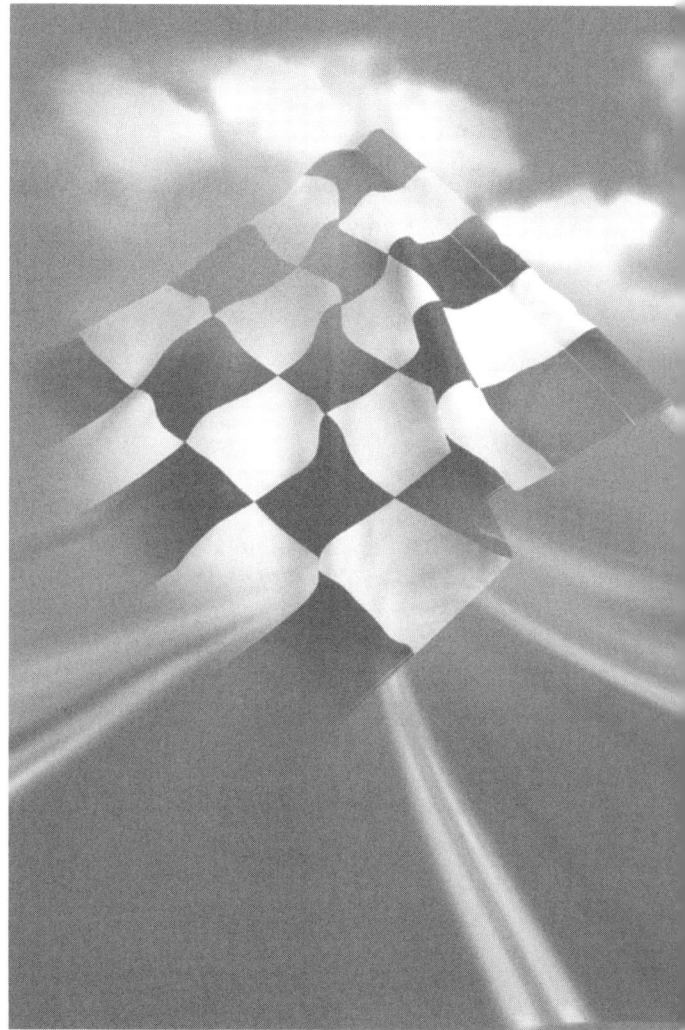

CHAPTER 6

# Monitoring and Maintaining Server Availability

▶ The key points to understand in this chapter revolve around the various means of disaster prevention and recovery available to you as an administrator. It is important to have a good grasp on ways you can identify and troubleshoot performance issues that affect your computers.

▶ It is important to understand how the Performance console is set up and what its component parts are. Know how to create a system monitor, create counter and trace logs, and configure alerts. Know specifically the main counters associated with the processor, memory, network, and disk objects as outlined in this chapter. You won't likely be tested specifically on counters, but you should be aware of them anyway.

▶ As they pertain to data backup and recovery, know how Windows Backup and Restore work, how to invoke them, and how the scheduler works. You also need to have a thorough understanding of Automated System Recovery (ASR) and volume shadow copy.

▶ Get your hands dirty. The Step by Steps throughout this book provide plenty of directions and exercises, but you should go beyond these examples and create some of your own. If you can, experiment with each of the objectives to see how they work and why you would use each one.

# INTRODUCTION

Troubleshooting is something we all wish we'd never have to do, but more often than not, we find ourselves doing it. Knowing how to properly troubleshoot and perform repairs on servers and client computers is critical for an administrator and is a task that should not be taken lightly. Knowing how to look ahead to identify problems before they occur is even more important. Unfortunately, identifying impending problems is a fine art learned over time with practice and patience.

During the course of this chapter, we look at methods to recover servers should disaster strike (despite your best efforts) and at means for identifying and correcting problems before they occur. A good understanding of these two areas will go a long way toward making your life as an administrator a happier one.

# MONITORING SYSTEM PERFORMANCE FOR BOTTLENECKS

**Identify system bottlenecks, including memory, processor, disk, and network-related bottlenecks.**

▶ **Identify system bottlenecks by using System Monitor.**

Administering a Windows Server 2003 network is not simply about making sure that people have access to resources and that information is secure. The question administrators ask themselves is not just, "Is it running?" but also, "Is it running well?" Of course, "well" is relative and can't really be quantified outside your individual context.

This section examines the assessment of server performance using the System Monitor, a tool located within the Performance console. In addition, it discusses some tips on how to tune your server before problems occur and which devices should be monitored when they do.

Periodic monitoring of your Windows Server 2003 network is important to the process of optimization. Monitoring helps to overcome the feeling-based assessment of your users. For example, by comparing current network performance against a previously established baseline, you have more information than the anecdotal "The network is slow today!" on which to base your actions. By gathering current information and comparing it against established norms for your systems (a *baseline*), you can detect bottlenecks, identify those system components that are slowing down server performance, and fix them before they become a problem to your users.

Although the actual procedure for creating a baseline is outlined later in this section, it is important to discuss the concept of a baseline here because it is the first thing you will do in practice—even if it is not the first concept that is presented here. A *baseline* is an established norm for the operation of your server as determined by normal load. This baseline can then be used as a basis of comparison for future performance to see whether repairable problems exist. As the configuration of your server changes (when, for example, a processor is added or RAM is added), new baselines are established to reflect the new expected performance.

The importance of establishing a baseline before beginning to monitor performance can't be overstated. Although there are some guidelines as to what absolute performance numbers indicate, it is as you compare current performance against past performance (the baseline) that you will really be able to evaluate how well current demand is being met and whether you require more resources on your server. In addition, it is imperative that a baseline be established before problems begin to occur. If users are already beginning to complain, "The network is slow," it is too late to establish a baseline because the statistics gathered will include whatever performance factors are contributing to the dissatisfaction.

At a minimum, you must perform periodic monitoring on the following areas of your Windows Server 2003 computers: the hard disk(s), processor(s), memory, and network adapter(s). Regardless of which type of services the server is providing, these four areas interact to make your server efficient (thereby appearing fast) or inefficient. The actual speed or efficiency of each of the components varies in importance depending on the application. In some applications, memory is more important than processor speed or availability; in other applications, disk speed and availability are more important than fast network access.

## The Performance Console

Recognizing the need to be able to monitor the performance (and thus the health) of servers and client computers, Microsoft built the Performance console into Windows Server 2003. Whether you are looking for real-time graphical views or a log you can peruse at your convenience, the Performance console can provide the type of data you need to evaluate performance and recommend system modification if necessary.

Monitoring performance begins with the collection of data. The Performance console, shown in Figure 6.1, allows you various methods of working with data, although all methods use the same means of collecting data. Data collected by the Performance console is broken down into objects, counters, and instances. An *object* is the software or device being monitored, such as the memory or a processor. A *counter* is a specific statistic for an object. Memory has a counter called Available Bytes, and a processor has a counter called % Processor Time. An *instance* is the specific occurrence of an object you are watching; in a multiprocessor server with two processors, you have three instances: 0, 1, and _Total.

**FIGURE 6.1**
The Performance console consists of four different tools.

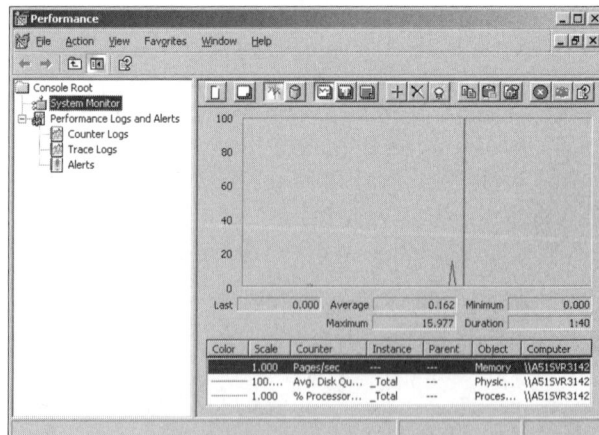

The primary difference between using the System Monitor and Counter Logs or Trace Logs is that you typically watch performance real-time in System Monitor (or playback saved logs), whereas you use Counter Logs and Trace Logs to record data for later analysis. Alerts function in real-time by providing you with alerts when a user-defined threshold is exceeded. Counter Logs, Trace Logs, and Alerts are beyond the scope of the 70-293 exam; if you want to learn more about them, however, be sure to see `www.microsoft.com/ technet/prodtechnol/windowsserver2003/proddocs/entserver/ sag_MPtopnode.asp`.

# Introduction to System Monitor

You can access the System Monitor from the Administrative Tools folder by selecting Start, Programs, Administrative Tools, Performance. When you initially open the Performance console, it looks like the console shown previously in Figure 6.1. The System Monitor enables you to view statistical data either live or from a saved log. You can view the data in three formats: graph, histogram, or report. Graph data is displayed as a line graph, histograms are displayed as bar graphs, and text-based reports show the current numerical information available from the statistics.

The basic use of the System Monitor is straightforward. You decide which object/instance/counter combinations you want to display and then configure the monitor accordingly. At that point, information begins to appear. You can also change the properties of the monitor to display information in different ways.

The best way to become familiar with the System Monitor is to start using it. Step by Step 6.1 lets you do just that by configuring monitoring for some network counters.

---

# STEP BY STEP

### 6.1 Using the System Monitor

1. Select Start, Programs, Administrative Tools, Performance to open the Performance console.

2. Click the System Monitor node.

3. To add counter items to the System Monitor, click the + icon on the toolbar, as shown in Figure 6.2.

*continues*

*continued*

**FIGURE 6.2**
To start adding counter items, you need to click the + icon on the toolbar.

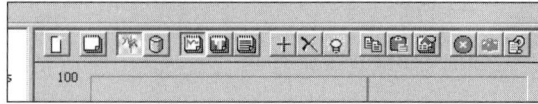

4. The Add Counters dialog box, shown in Figure 6.3, opens, allowing you to begin adding counters.

**FIGURE 6.3**
You can add counters to begin monitoring the Processor statistics.

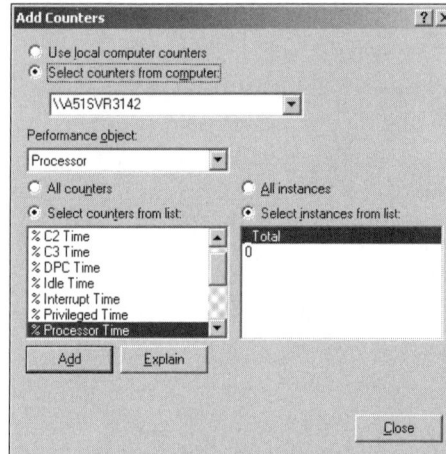

5. Select Network Interface from the Performance Object drop-down list box. The list of counters that relate to network interfaces and are available for selection appears. If you need to know what a counter means, select the counter and click the Explain button.

6. Be sure that you are adding counters for the correct network interface in your server and not for the loopback interface by selecting the Select Instances from This List option and then selecting the correct network interface, as shown in Figure 6.4.

7. After you have decided what counter you want to monitor, click Add. You can add multiple counters either by selecting each counter and clicking Add or by holding down the Ctrl key while you select all the counters you want to monitor and then clicking Add.

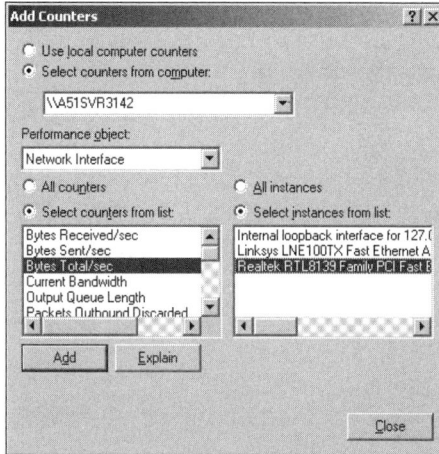

**FIGURE 6.4**
Make sure you are adding the counters for the correct instance when multiple instances exist.

8. Click Close when you are finished. Your counters are now actively graphed, like those shown in Figure 6.5.

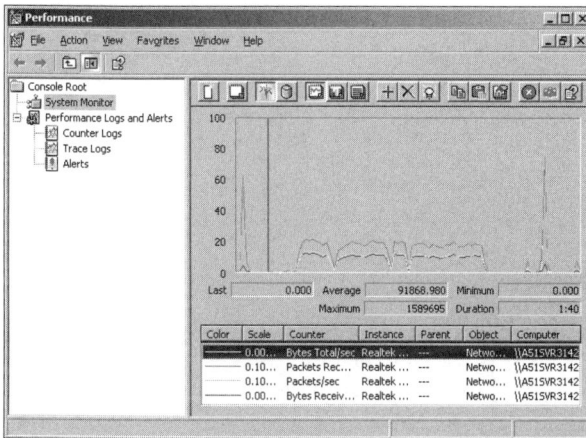

**FIGURE 6.5**
You can monitor the selected network interface statistics in real-time.

# Working with Counters

Now that you've seen how the System Monitor works from a high-level, let's dig in a little and examine the basic building block of performance monitoring: *counters*. Figure 6.6 shows a typical Add

Counters dialog box. At the top of the dialog box is a set of radio buttons with which you can obtain statistics from the local machine or a remote machine. This feature is useful when you want to monitor a computer in a location that is not within reasonable physical distance from you. Under the radio buttons is a pull-down list naming the performance objects that can be monitored. Which performance objects are available depend on the features (and applications) you have installed on your server. Also, some counters come with specific applications. These performance counters enable you to monitor statistics relating to that application from the Performance console.

**FIGURE 6.6**
The Add Counters dialog box contains many options you need to understand.

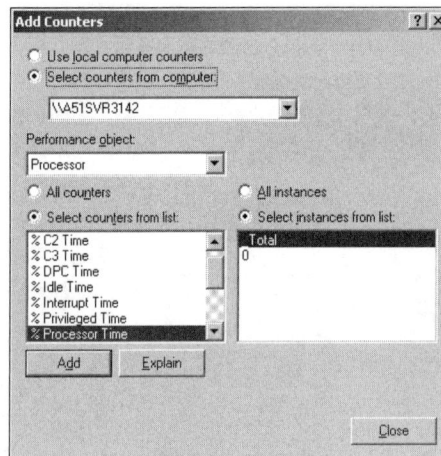

Under the performance object is a list of counters. When applied to a specific instance of an object, counters are what you are really after, and the object just narrows down your search. The counters are the actual statistical information you want to monitor. Each object has its own set of counters from which you can choose. Counters enable you to move from the abstract concept of an object to the concrete events that reflect that object's activity. For example, if you choose to monitor the processor, you can watch for the average processor time and how much time the processor spent doing non-idle activity. In addition, you could watch for %user time (time spent executing user application processes) versus %privileged time (time spent executing system processes).

To the right of the counter list is the instances list. If applicable, instances enumerate the physical objects that fall under the specific object class you have chosen. In some cases, the instances list is not applicable. For example, no instances list is available with memory. In cases in which the instances list is applicable, you see multiple instance variables (refer to Figure 6.4). One variable represents the average of all the instances, and the rest of the variables represent the values for the first physical object (number 0, 1, and so on). For example, if you have two processors in your server, you see (and can choose from) three instance variables: _Total, 0, and 1. This way, you can watch each processor individually and watch them as a collective unit.

## Using System Monitor to Discover Bottlenecks

Every chain, regardless of its strength, has its weakest link. When pulled hard enough, some point gives before all the others. Your server is similar to a chain. When it's under stress, some component cannot keep up with the others. This results in a degradation of overall performance. The weak link in the server is referred to as a *bottleneck* because it's the component that slows down everything else. As an administrator responsible for ensuring efficient operation of a Windows Server 2003 computer, you need to determine the following two things:

▶ Which component is causing the bottleneck?

▶ Is the stress on the server typical enough that action is warranted either now or in the future?

As was mentioned previously, under normal operation, only four system components typically affect system performance: memory, processors, disks, and network adapters. Therefore, you should monitor the counters that tell you the most about how those four components affect system performance. The information from these counters is critical because you can determine the answer to the two diagnostic questions listed here.

The biggest monitoring problem is not collecting the data, but interpreting it. Not only is it difficult to determine what a specific value for a particular counter means, it is also difficult to determine what that value means in the context of other counters. The biggest difficulty is that no subsystem (disk, network, processor, or memory) exists in isolation. As a result, weaknesses in one might show up as weaknesses in another. Unless you take them all into consideration, you might end up adding another processor when all you need is more RAM.

Understanding how the subsystems interact is important to understanding the significance of the counter values that are recorded. For example, if you detect that your processor is constantly running at 90%, you might be tempted to purchase a faster processor (or another processor if you have a system board that can accommodate more than one). However, it is important to look at memory utilization and disk utilization as well because the problem could be originating there instead. If you do not have enough memory, the processor must swap pages to the disk frequently. This page swapping results in high memory utilization, high disk utilization, and higher processor utilization. By purchasing more RAM, you could alleviate all these problems.

This one example illustrates how no one piece of information is enough to analyze your performance problems or your solution. You must monitor the server as a whole unit by putting together the counters from a variety of objects. Only then can you see the big picture and solve problems that might arise.

The recommended method of monitoring is to use a counter log, which captures data over a period of time. This type of monitoring helps you eliminate questions of whether the current stress on the server is typical. If you log over a period of a week or a month and consistently see a certain component under excessive load, you can be sure the stress is typical.

## Baselining Servers

As we've already discussed, monitoring the present operation of your servers and network presents you with only half of the picture. You need to create a baseline of the server performance that you can use to compare against future performance statistics to locate problematic areas. If you create baselines on servers, you can compare the present-day performance to a known value. This comparison can be very useful when you're troubleshooting, and it also aids during periods when you are modifying configurations.

A baseline is a set of typical readings that define "normal" for your servers, client computers, or network under various operating conditions, such as no load, moderate load, and heavy load. Of course, what is normal is obviously open to interpretation, but you could say that normal is a server providing users with what they want in a time frame that they think is reasonable. By creating baselines early on, you have something that you can later look back at and compare current server operating conditions to. If your system is already to the point where you are seeing system degradation, it is really too late to establish a baseline.

To establish a baseline, you pick a time (or duration of time) that represents typical user interaction with the server. Then you create a log of important counters for the duration you have determined. Some of the more commonly used (and recommended) counters are summarized in Table 6.1. For a complete reference to these counters, be sure to see www.microsoft.com/technet/prodtechnol/ windowsserver2003/proddocs/deployguide/counters1_lkxw.asp.

**EXAM TIP**

**Creating a monitoring station** Most administrators recommend that you do not perform performance monitoring locally from the server on which you are attempting to monitor and collect data. When you run the System Monitor directly on a server, you can skew the results because, of course, the actual act of monitoring consumes system resources. It's generally better to run System Monitor on a workstation pointed at the server you want to monitor (in addition to being able to monitor multiple servers from a single console).

**TABLE 6.1**

**COUNTERS TO MONITOR FOR BASELINING AND BOTTLENECK TROUBLESHOOTING**

| *Server Component* | *Recommended Counters* |
| --- | --- |
| Memory | Memory\Page Faults/sec |
| | Memory\Page Reads/sec |
| | Memory\Page Writes/sec |
| | Memory\Pages Input/sec |
| | Memory\Pages Output/sec |
| | Memory\Available Bytes |
| | Memory\Pool Nonpaged Bytes |
| | Process\Page Faults/sec |
| | Process\Working Set |
| | Process\Private Bytes |
| | Process\Page File Bytes |

*continues*

**TABLE 6.1** *continued*

**COUNTERS TO MONITOR FOR BASELINING AND
BOTTLENECK TROUBLESHOOTING**

| *Server Component* | *Recommended Counters* |
| --- | --- |
| Processor | Processor\% Processor Time |
| | System\Processor Queue Length |
| | Process\% Privileged Time |
| | Process\% Processor Time |
| | Process\% User Time |
| | Process\Priority Base |
| | Thread\% Privileged Time |
| | Thread\% Processor Time |
| | Thread\% User Time |
| | Thread\Context Switches/sec |
| | Thread\Priority Base |
| | Thread\Priority Current |
| | Thread\Thread State |
| Disk | PhysicalDisk\% Disk Time |
| | PhysicalDisk\Avg. Disk Queue Length |
| | PhysicalDisk\Current Disk Queue Length |
| | PhysicalDisk\Avg. Disk Sec/Read |
| | PhysicalDisk\Avg. Disk Sec/Write |
| | PhysicalDisk\Disk Read Bytes/sec |
| | PhysicalDisk\Disk Write Bytes/sec |
| | PhysicalDisk\Avg. Disk Bytes/Write |
| | PhysicalDisk\Disk Reads/sec |
| | PhysicalDisk\Disk Writes/sec |
| | LogicalDisk\% Disk Time |
| | LogicalDisk\Avg. Disk Queue Length |
| | LogicalDisk\Current Disk Queue Length |
| | LogicalDisk\Avg. Disk Sec/Read |
| | LogicalDisk\Avg. Disk Sec/Write |
| | LogicalDisk\Disk Read Bytes/sec |
| | LogicalDisk\Disk Write Bytes/sec |
| | LogicalDisk\Avg. Disk Bytes/Write |
| | LogicalDisk\Disk Reads/sec |
| | LogicalDisk\Disk Writes/sec |

| Server Component | Recommended Counters |
|---|---|
| Network | Network Interface\Bytes Total/sec |
| | Network Interface\Bytes Sent/sec |
| | Network Interface\Bytes Received/sec |
| | TCPv4\Segments Received/sec |
| | TCPv4\Segments Sent/sec |
| | TCPv4\Frames Sent/sec |
| | TCPv4\Frames Received/sec |
| | Server\Bytes Total/sec |
| | Server\Bytes Received/sec |
| | Server\Bytes Transmitted/sec |

The log you create should be stored in a safe place to ensure that you can refer to it in the future. Every time you perform a major hardware upgrade (such as increasing RAM or adding a processor), you should create a new set of baselines and consider deleting the old ones.

Which actual counters you want to monitor are based on the particular applications running on your server and the requirements you have for the server. Although some recommendations are given in Table 6.1, you might want to watch other objects as well if you have specific applications installed.

## Creating Baseline Counter Logs

To create a baseline, you create a counter log from the Counter Logs option of the Performance Logs and Alerts node of the Performance console. The creation of a counter log is outlined in Step by Step 6.2.

## STEP BY STEP

### 6.2 Creating and Using a Baseline Counter Log

**1.** Select Start, Programs, Administrative Tools, Performance to open the Performance console.

**2.** Expand the Performance Logs and Alerts node and click the Counter Logs entry, as shown in Figure 6.7.

*continues*

**EXAM TIP**

**Performance counters** Don't worry too much about memorizing all the different counters and their uses. The 70-293 exam is looking more for your ability to use the tools available to identify, troubleshoot, and correct problem situations.

**Don't be tricked!** When taking the 70-293 exam, carefully read each question—especially those that deal with performance monitoring—to ensure that you select the correct answer. You might find several very similar answers presented, but only one of them is correct.

*continued*

**FIGURE 6.7**
A counter log is created to keep baseline (historical) statistics about performance.

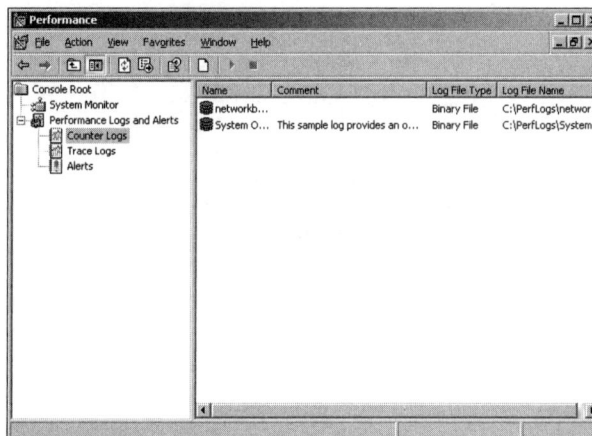

**3.** To add a new counter log, right-click the Counter Logs entry and select New Log Settings from the context menu.

**4.** Enter the name of the new counter log, as shown in Figure 6.8, and click OK. The Properties dialog box for this log appears (see Figure 6.9).

**FIGURE 6.8**
You should enter a descriptive name for the new counter log.

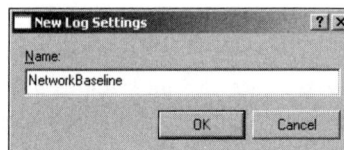

**5.** Configure new entire objects to be monitored by clicking the Add Objects button to open the Add Objects dialog box (see Figure 6.10). Alternatively, add individual counters by clicking the Add Counters button to open the Add Counters dialog box (see Figure 6.11). Add the objects or counters you want to the counter log.

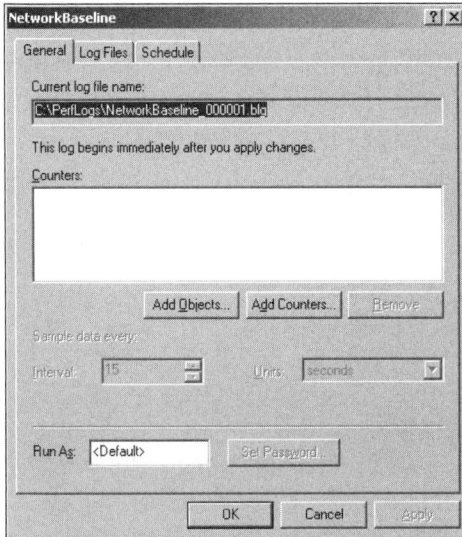

**FIGURE 6.9**
You must configure objects or counters on the new counter log before proceeding.

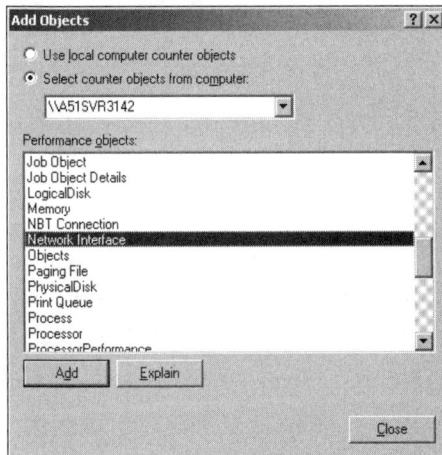

**FIGURE 6.10**
You can add entire objects to the counter log if you want.

**6.** After you have added some objects or counters, you can configure the options for sampling interval. The default is every 15 seconds—meaning that while the counter log is running, data will be collected every 15 seconds from the computers being monitored. The sampling interval has a trade-off associated with it: Smaller intervals mean larger, more accurate log files; larger intervals result in smaller, less accurate log files. In addition, the smaller the

*continues*

*continued*

sampling interval, the more resources Performance consoleing consumes. You can also configure the account to be used to run the counter log.

**FIGURE 6.11**
You can add specific individual counters to the counter log if you want.

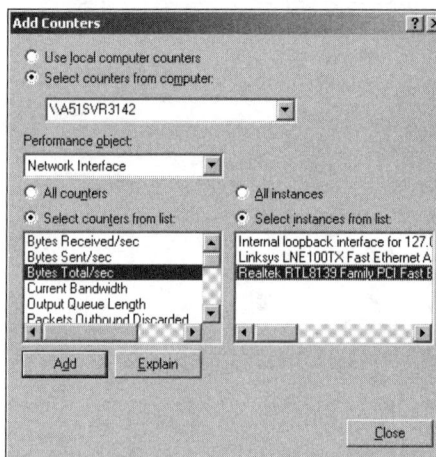

7. On the Log Files tab of the Properties dialog box, shown in Figure 6.12, select the type of log file to be created as well as the numbering system to be used. The default settings are Binary File and nnnnn. The available options are explained after this Step by Step in Tables 6.2 and 6.3. In addition, you can enter a comment that will help identify the counter log.

8. Click the Configure button to open the Configure Log Files dialog box, shown in Figure 6.13. From here, you can change the path of the log file and its maximum allowed size. Click OK after you make your changes.

9. On the Schedule tab of the Properties dialog box, shown in Figure 6.14, you can configure how and when the counter log is to run. Typically, you will run it manually, although you might opt to have it run automatically at a configured time.

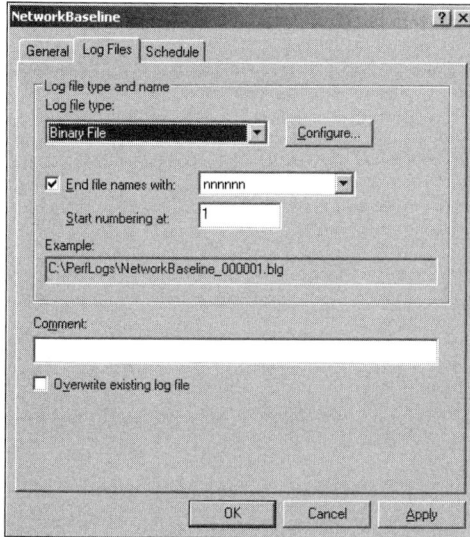

**FIGURE 6.12**
You can use the Log Files tab to configure how the log is to be saved.

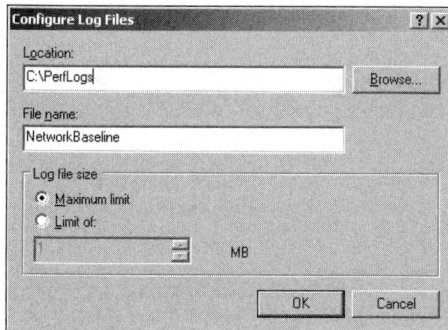

**FIGURE 6.13**
You can use the Configure Log Files dialog box to configure the maximum log file size as well as its path.

10. After you make all your configurations, click OK to save the counter log settings. After a moment, the counter log starts running if you have not configured it for manual starting.

11. After the counter log has run for a period of time adequate to capture your baseline data, click the square stop icon from the Counter Logs node to stop it.

12. Click the System Monitor node to switch back to the System Monitor. Click the database icon to open a log file, as shown in Figure 6.15.

*continues*

*continued*

**FIGURE 6.14**
You can configure the counter log to start and stop automatically if you want.

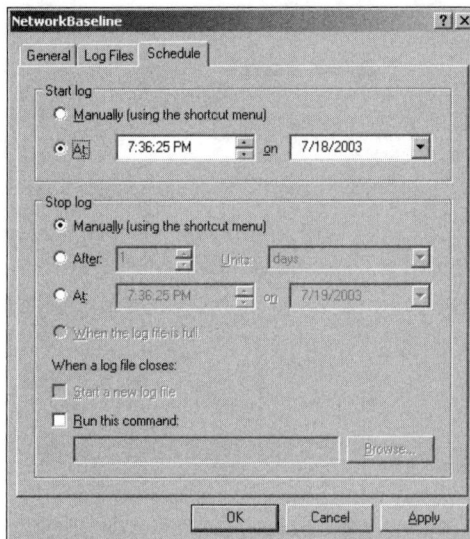

**FIGURE 6.15**
You need to load the counter log file into the System Monitor to be able to examine it.

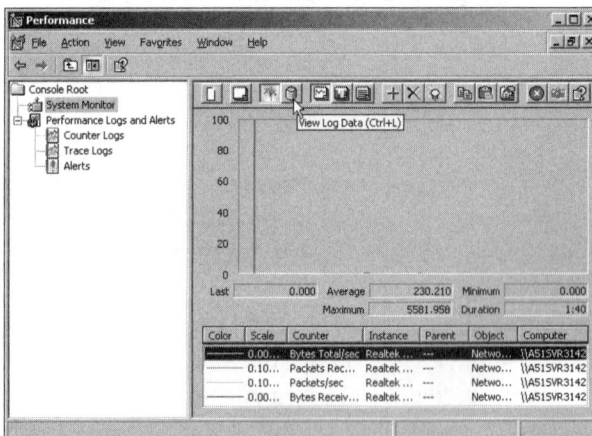

**13.** The System Monitor Properties dialog box opens, showing the Source tab, as shown in Figure 6.16. Click the Add button to locate and add the counter log file.

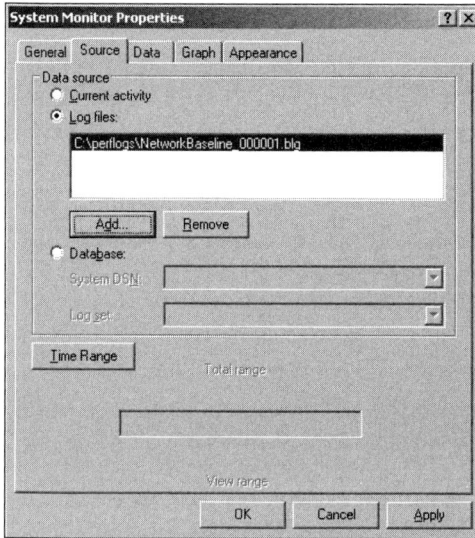

**FIGURE 6.16**
You can add one or more counter logs to the System Monitor.

**14.** Switch to the Data tab, shown in Figure 6.17, and ensure that all counters for which you are interested in seeing data are added. You will see data displayed only for counters that are selected here. Click OK when you are done.

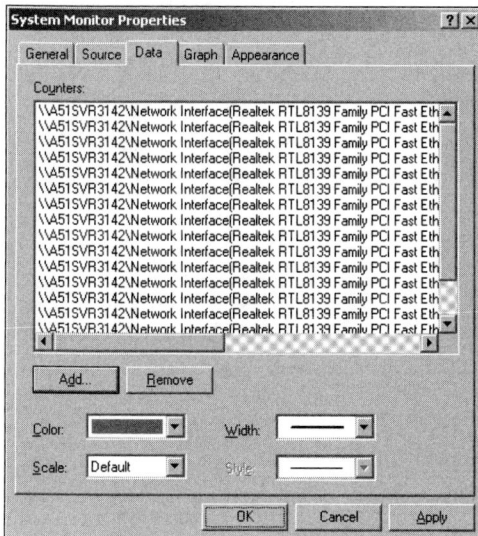

**FIGURE 6.17**
You need to ensure that all counters have been added for viewing.

*continues*

*continued*

**15.** The counter log data is now displayed in the System Monitor. If you need to display only a certain portion of the data, you can do so by configuring the Time Range option on the Source tab of the System Monitor Properties dialog box (refer to Figure 6.16).

When creating log files, you have several different file formats available to you. Table 6.2 outlines the available file formats.

**TABLE 6.2**

**COUNTER LOG FILE FORMAT OPTIONS**

| *Option* | *Description* |
| --- | --- |
| Text File (Comma Delimited) | This option defines a comma-delimited log file (with a `.csv` extension). |
| Text File (Tab Delimited) | This option defines a tab-delimited log file (with a `.tsv` extension). |
| Binary File | This option defines a sequential, binary-format log file (with a `.blg` extension). You should use this file format if you want to be able to record data instances that are intermittent—that is, stopping and resuming after the log has begun running. Only binary file formats can accommodate instances that are not persistent throughout the duration of the log. |
| Binary Circular File | This option defines a circular, binary-format log file (with a `.blg` extension). You should use this file format to continuously record data to the same log file, overwriting previous records with new data when the file reaches its maximum size. |
| SQL Database | This option allows you to save logs to an SQL database. |

When creating log files, you have several different numbering formats available to you. Table 6.3 outlines the available numbering formats.

**TABLE 6.3**

**COUNTER LOG NUMBERING SYSTEMS**

| System | Example |
| --- | --- |
| *nnnnnn* | `Network Adapter Performance_000007.blg` |
| *mmddhh* | `Network Adapter Performance_042011.blg` |
| *mmddhhmm* | `Network Adapter Performance_04201126.blg` |
| *yyyyddd* | `Network Adapter Performance_2003111.blg` |
| *yyyymm* | `Network Adapter Performance_200304.blg` |
| *yyyymmdd* | `Network Adapter Performance_20030420.blg` |
| *yyyymmddhh* | `Network Adapter Performance_2003042011.blg` |

# Daily Monitoring for Usage

On a daily basis, you may not want to monitor the full group of counters that were listed previously in Table 6.1. The counters in Table 6.4 present a smaller, and thus easier-to-manage, group of counters that you might consider monitoring on a daily basis to get a quick snapshot of your system and network performance.

**TABLE 6.4**

**COUNTERS TO MONITOR ON A DAILY BASIS**

| Server Component | Recommended Counters |
| --- | --- |
| Memory | Memory\ Available Bytes |
| | Memory\ Cache Bytes |
| | Memory\ Pages/sec |
| | Memory\ Page reads/sec |
| | Memory\ Pool Paged Bytes |
| | Memory\ Pool Nonpaged Bytes |
| Processor | Processor\ % Processor Time (all instances) |
| | System\ Processor Queue Length (all instances) |
| | Processor\ Interrupts/sec |
| Disk | Physical Disk\ Disk Reads/sec |
| | Physical Disk\ Disk Writes/sec |
| | Logical Disk\% Free Space |
| | Logical Disk\% Disk Time |
| | Physical Disk\ Current Disk Queue Length (all instances) |
| | Physical Disk\ Split IO/sec |
| Network | Network Interface\ Bytes total/sec |

As they pertain to Table 6.4, the following are descriptions of the counters:

▶ **Physical Disk\ Disk Reads/sec**—The number of disk reads that occur per second. This value is a measure of the read activity on the disk. The transfer rate of the hard drive being used determines what values you should be looking for here, so check the vendor's supplied documentation. In general, Ultra Wide SCSI disks can handle about 50–70 I/O operations per second.

▶ **Physical Disk\ Disk Writes/sec**—The number of disk writes that occur per second. This value is a measure of the write activity on the disk. The same guidelines apply for this counter as do for the Physical Disk\ Disk Reads/sec counter.

▶ **Logical Disk\ % Free Space**—The ratio of free space to total disk space on a logical drive. This value is a measurement of remaining capacity on your logical drives. You generally should track this value for each logical drive. To prevent excessive fragmentation, you should not allow the value here to drop below 15%.

▶ **Logical Disk\ % Disk Time**—The ratio of busy time to the total elapsed time. This value represents the percentage the disk is servicing read or write requests. You generally should track this value for each physical drive. If one drive is being used a lot more than another, it might be time to balance the content between the drives. The lower this number, the greater the capacity a disk has to do additional work. This value should typically not exceed 90%.

▶ **Physical Disk\ Current Disk Queue Length**—The average number of read and write requests that are waiting in queue. Optimally, this number should be no more than 2 because a larger number means the disk is a bottleneck; it is incapable of servicing the requests placed on it.

▶ **Physical Disk\ Split IO/sec**—The rate at which the operating system divides I/O requests to the disk into multiple requests. A split I/O request might occur if the program requests data in a size that is too large to fit into a single request or if the disk is fragmented. Factors that influence the size of an I/O request can include application design, the file system, or drivers. A high rate of split I/O might not, in itself, represent a problem. However, on single-disk systems, a high rate for this counter tends to indicate disk fragmentation.

▶ **Memory\ Available Bytes**—The total amount of physical memory available to processes running on the computer. This number's significance varies as the amount of memory in the computer varies, but if this number is less than 4MB, you generally have a memory deficiency.

▶ **Memory\ Cache Bytes**—The amount of cache memory available to processes running on the computer. This counter indicates growth or shrinking of the cache. The value includes not only the size of the cache but also the size of the paged pool and the amount of pageable driver and kernel code. Lower values indicate a problem, although there is no agreed-upon standard value.

▶ **Memory\ Pages/sec**—The number of hard page faults occurring per second. A hard page fault occurs when data or code is not in memory and must be retrieved from the hard drive. Each time this happens, disk activity is required, and the process is temporarily halted (because disk access is momentarily slower than RAM access). A bottleneck in memory is likely when this number is 20 or greater.

▶ **Memory\ Page reads/sec**—The number of times the disk needed to be read to resolve a hard page fault. Unlike Memory\ Pages/sec, this counter is not an indicator of the quantity of data being retrieved but rather the number of times the disk had to be consulted. This counter can give a general feeling of a memory bottleneck, whereas Memory\ Pages/sec gives a more quantifiable value to the bottleneck.

▶ **Memory\ Pool Paged Bytes**—The number of bytes of memory taken up by system tasks that can be swapped out to disk if needed. Although this counter is not a direct indicator of a memory bottleneck, if the number of Pool Paged Bytes is large, it can indicate a lot of system processes. If this number is a significant percentage of total memory, you might need to increase RAM to allow for these tasks to remain in RAM instead of being swapped out.

▶ **Memory\ Pool Nonpaged Bytes**—The number of bytes of memory taken up by system tasks that can't be swapped out to disk. This figure can indicate a bottleneck in memory, especially if the figure is a significant percentage of the total amount of RAM. Because these processes can't be swapped out, they continue to take up RAM for as long as they are running.

▶ **Network Interface\ Bytes Total/sec**—An indication of the total throughput of the network interface. This figure can be used for general capacity planning and does not necessarily indicate a network bottleneck.

▶ **Processor\ % Processor Time**—The amount of time the processor spends executing non-idle threads. This figure is an indication of how busy the processor is. The processor for a single-processor system should not exceed 75% capacity for a significant period of time. The processors in a multiple-processor system should not exceed 50% for a significant period of time. High processor utilization can be an indication of processor bottlenecks, but it could also indicate lack of memory.

▶ **System\ Processor Queue Length**—The number of processes that are ready but waiting to be serviced by the processor(s). There is a single queue for all processors, even in a multi-processor environment. A sustained queue of more than 2 generally indicates processor congestion.

▶ **Processor\ Interrupts/sec**—The number of hardware requests the processor is servicing per second. This is not necessarily an indicator of system health but, when compared against the baseline, it can help to determine hardware problems. Hardware problems are sometimes indicated by a device dramatically increasing the number of interrupts it sends.

## System Monitor Tips and Tricks

Microsoft provides some helpful tips and tricks that you should keep in mind when working with the Performance console to solve performance-related problems. Through careful analysis of data, you might be able to determine problems with the network that are not otherwise seen, such as excessive demands on resources that result in bottlenecks—and therefore slow network performance to the degree that users begin to notice that something is wrong.

The following are some of the most common causes of bottlenecks that you might encounter while troubleshooting your network:

▶ The current level of provided resources is inadequate, thus requiring additional or upgraded resources to be added to the network.

▶ The available resources are not utilized evenly, thus requiring some form of load balancing to be implemented.

▶ An available resource is malfunctioning or stopped and needs to be repaired or restarted.

▶ An available resource is incorrectly configured, thus requiring a configuration correction.

After you have identified a problem, you should take care to avoid creating new problems while correcting the old one. You should make one change at a time to avoid masking the impact of changes. After each change, you should perform additional monitoring to determine the result and the effect of the change and reevaluate the status and condition of the previously identified problem(s). In addition, you can compare the performance of applications that are run over the network to their performance when run locally to determine how the network is affecting performance.

With our discussion of performance monitoring and baselining out of the way, let's move forward and examine the second topic of this chapter: disaster recovery operations.

# PLANNING BACKUP AND RECOVERY OPERATIONS

Disasters happen. They are an administrator's worst nightmare, but they don't have to be. Even if you have the best hardware and most fault-tolerant design, nothing can replace a solid backup and restoration plan. The Backup Utility provided in Windows Server 2003, `ntbackup.exe`, is actually a "lite" version of the commercially available third-party product from Veritas Software. Although its

---

**EXAM TIP**

**Saving time by saving your configuration** No one wants to reinvent the wheel over and over. This holds true when you are configuring System Monitor with a set of counters. You can save a good amount of time and effort by setting up the System Monitor with the counters and options you want on one server and then saving the configuration file and distributing that file to each of your other servers instead of re-creating the configuration each time.

**Don't forget about the Task Manager** Even though the Task Manager is a very simple tool, don't underestimate its usefulness. You can quickly launch the Task Manager to get a real-time look at network utilization (and process performance) without having to open the System Monitor and configure counters.

capability is limited, the included Backup Utility, when used properly, can provide you with all the functionality you should need for small networks or workgroups. If you have a larger network, you may want to place some serious thought into acquiring an enterprise backup solution, such as Backup Exec.

You should keep in mind the following general points when working with Windows Backup:

- ► You can back up to either a file or tape drive.

- ► You can back up files from either the local machine or remote computers, provided that you have access to the files you want to back up on the remote computer. The limitation of backing up a computer remotely is that System State information cannot be saved.

- ► To perform a backup, you must have Read access to the files or the user right of Backup and Restore Files, which is granted by default to Administrators and Backup Operators.

- ► Special permissions are granted the Administrators and Backup Operators groups to access all files for the purposes of doing backups. Even if members of these groups cannot access the data as users, they can back it up.

The Backup Utility in Windows Server 2003 has undergone some changes from its predecessor in Windows 2000 Server. No longer will you be creating an Emergency Repair Disk (ERD); it has been replaced by the new and improved Automated System Recovery (ASR) function. Windows Server 2003 also introduces volume shadow copy in the Backup Utility. Each of these new functions is explained in more detail in the following section.

## New Windows Server 2003 Backup Features

When you use the volume shadow copy, a copy of the original volume is created instantly at the time you initiate the backup. Data is then subsequently backed up to the backup media from this shadow copy instead of the original files. This new technology provides a means to back up open files that were in use at the time of the backup being initiated. When you use volume shadow copy, files that would normally be skipped during the backup are instead backed up in their current state (at the time of the shadow copy creation) and thus appear closed on the backup media. Any applications that are running during the backup process can continue to run during the backup process. After the backup has been completed, the shadow copy is deleted. The volume shadow copy feature requires the NTFS file system to be in use and can be disabled if you want.

Another new use of the volume shadow copy feature is to create "snapshots" of shared network folders that can be used to roll back to a previous version of a file; this topic is discussed later in the "Using Volume Shadow Copy" section of this chapter.

Automated System Recovery (ASR) is an advanced restoration option of the Backup Utility that can be used to restore your system if other disaster recovery methods fail or are not available for use. Using ASR, you can restore the operating system back to a previous state, which allows you to start Window Server 2003 in the event that other methods do not work. You should always consider ASR your last resort for recovery, after Safe Mode, the Recovery Console, and Last Known Good Configuration (LKGC). You should make a point to keep your ASR media up to date as you make configuration changes to your computer. This is recommended to minimize the amount of recovery required should you ever need to use ASR. To use the ASR Wizard to create a set of ASR media, you only need to click on the Automated System Recovery Wizard button on the main page of the Backup tool, which we examine later in this section.

> **NOTE**
>
> **Limitations on disabling volume shadow copy** You cannot disable the volume shadow copy option when performing a backup of the System State data.

# Backup Methods and Media Rotation

**Plan a backup and recovery strategy.**

▶ **Identify appropriate backup types. Methods include full, incremental, and differential.**

Windows Server 2003 supports the following five backup methods:

▶ **Normal (full) backup**—Copies all selected files and marks each file as having been backed up (the archive attribute is cleared). Only the most recent copy of the backup file is required to perform restoration.

▶ **Incremental backup**—Copies only those files created or changed since the last normal or incremental backup; the archive attribute is then cleared. Using normal and incremental backups, you require the last normal backup and all incremental backups to be able to perform restoration.

▶ **Differential backup**—Copies files created or changed since the last normal (full) or incremental backup; the archive attribute is not cleared in this case. Using normal and differential backups, you need the last normal backup and the last differential backup to be able to perform restoration.

▶ **Copy backup**—Copies all selected files but does not mark each file as having been backed up (the archive attribute is not cleared). Copy backups have no effect on any other type of backup operation.

▶ **Daily backup**—Copies all selected files that have been modified the day the daily backup is performed; the archive attribute is not cleared in this case. Using normal and daily backups, you require the last normal backup and all daily backups to be able to perform restoration.

As you might guess, the true secret to effectively planning and implementing a viable backup plan is *media rotation*. When thinking about media rotation, you must consider two basic requirements:

▶ **Media lifetime**—Most backup systems use some sort of magnetic tape media. Although these tapes are very durable in most cases, they do not last forever. A good backup plan must take into account media lifetime and seek to spread wear and tear evenly over multiple tapes to both increase the lifetime of the tapes and also to increase the reliability of the tapes should they be needed to perform a restoration. A media rotation system makes this happen by preventing overly high use of one tape over another.

▶ **Data availability**—If time were not a concern, you could just perform a full backup each night, but in large networks with large amounts of critical data, performing such backups could likely take many, many hours and reduce network performance during working hours. To this end, a good backup plan includes some combination of full, incremental, daily, and differential backups. For a restoration to be successful, you must have all the correct tapes available and restore the data from them in the correct order. Using a well-documented media rotation system helps you to ensure this happens.

So, with these points in mind, let's examine three of the more common media rotation systems in use today.

## Five-Tape Rotation

As the name implies, the five-tape media rotation method uses five different tapes—one for each day of the normal workweek. Typically, these tapes would be labeled as follows: Monday, Tuesday, Wednesday, Thursday, Friday. To start this rotation, you need to perform a full backup of all data. After you complete this backup, you can perform a daily, differential, or incremental backup on the first four days of the week. On Friday of every week, you perform a full backup again. Table 6.5 outlines how the five-tape rotation method could be used.

**TABLE 6.5**

**THE SIMPLE FIVE-TAPE ROTATION METHOD**

| Sunday | Monday | Tuesday | Wednesday | Thursday | Friday | Saturday |
|---|---|---|---|---|---|---|
|  | 1<br>Monday | 2<br>Tuesday | 3<br>Wednesday | 4<br>Thursday | 5<br>Friday<br>Full | 6 |
| 7 | 8<br>Monday | 9<br>Tuesday | 10<br>Wednesday | 11<br>Thursday | 12<br>Friday<br>Full | 13 |
| 14 | 15<br>Monday | 16<br>Tuesday | 17<br>Wednesday | 18<br>Thursday | 19<br>Friday<br>Full | 20 |
| 21 | 22<br>Monday | 23<br>Tuesday | 24<br>Wednesday | 25<br>Thursday | 26<br>Friday<br>Full | 27 |
| 28 | 29<br>Monday | 30<br>Tuesday | 31<br>Wednesday |  |  |  |

As you can see, the five-tape rotation system could easily be expanded to six or seven tapes if your business needs require backups to be performed on the weekend days as well. However many tapes you use, you should always have the last one of the week set as the full backup, with each day before it being either a daily, differential, or incremental backup.

The major advantage to the five-tape rotation system is that it requires only five backup tapes. This advantage, however, comes at the cost of providing the backup history for only the past week.

## Grandfather, Father, Son (GFS)

The Grandfather, Father, Son (GFS) media rotation method is perhaps the most popular one in use today, and it provides a fairly easy method to make backup histories available for an entire year at a time. This availability does come at a cost, however: The GFS system requires 20 backup tapes to be available. As with the five-tape rotation method, to start a new GFS rotation, you should create a full backup of the data. As this method's name implies, three different generations of tapes are made using the GFS system:

▶ **Son**—These tapes are used Monday, Tuesday, Wednesday, and Thursday to perform daily, differential, or incremental backups. The son tapes require four backup tapes to be available.

▶ **Father**—These tapes are used on the last Friday of each week of the month—except for the last Friday of the month—to perform full backups. The father tapes require four backup tapes to be available for months that have five Fridays.

▶ **Grandfather**—These tapes are used on the last Friday of every month to perform a full backup. The grandfather tapes require 12 backup tapes to be available.

Table 6.6 outlines how the GFS rotation method could be used.

**TABLE 6.6**

**THE GFS ROTATION METHOD**

| Sunday | Monday | Tuesday | Wednesday | Thursday | Friday | Saturday |
|--------|--------|---------|-----------|----------|--------|----------|
|        |        |         | 1<br>Son #3 | 2<br>Son #4 | 3<br>Father #1 | 4 |
| 5 | 6<br>Son #1 | 7<br>Son #2 | 8<br>Son #3 | 9<br>Son #4 | 10<br>Father #2 | 11 |
| 12 | 13<br>Son #1 | 14<br>Son #2 | 15<br>Son #3 | 16<br>Son #4 | 17<br>Father #3 | 18 |
| 19 | 20<br>Son #1 | 21<br>Son #2 | 22<br>Son #3 | 23<br>Son #4 | 24<br>Father #4 | 25 |
| 26 | 27<br>Son #1 | 28<br>Son #2 | 29<br>Son #3 | 30<br>Son #4 | 31<br>Grandfather | |

The GFS rotation method is a middle-of-the-road solution that provides both good recoverability and also minimizes wear and tear on backup tapes. At the cost of 20 tapes per year, it is an obvious choice for most organizations.

## Tower of Hanoi

The last media rotation method—Tower of Hanoi—is based on a mathematical disk and post game of the same name. The Tower of Hanoi method is less expensive to implement in that it can be completed with a minimum of five backup tapes, but it is also very complex to implement. Tower of Hanoi also offers good data history, providing the ability to recover data as far back as 16 days—assuming that only five tapes are used.

In the five-tape Tower of Hanoi method, the tapes are used as follows:

▶ **Tape #1**—Used every other day for a full backup

▶ **Tape #2**—Used every fourth day for a full backup

▶ **Tape #3**—Used every eighth day for a full backup

▶ **Tape #4**—Used every sixteenth day for a full backup; alternates with Tape #5

▶ **Tape #5**—Used every sixteenth day for a full backup; alternates with Tape #4

As you can see, another disadvantage to this implementation is that a full backup must be performed each day. You can instead use daily, differential, or incremental backups, but you need to carefully document what type of backup is to be performed each day to make the system work correctly when it comes time for data recovery.

Table 6.7 outlines how the Tower of Hanoi rotation method could be used.

**TABLE 6.7**

**THE COMPLEX TOWER OF HANOI ROTATION METHOD**

| Sunday | Monday | Tuesday | Wednesday | Thursday | Friday | Saturday |
|---|---|---|---|---|---|---|
| | | | 1<br>Tape #1 | 2<br>Tape #2 | 3<br>Tape #1 | 4 |
| 5 | 6<br>Tape #3 | 7<br>Tape #1 | 8<br>Tape #2 | 9<br>Tape #1 | 10<br>Tape #4 | 11 |
| 12 | 13<br>Tape #1 | 14<br>Tape #2 | 15<br>Tape #1 | 16<br>Tape #5 | 17<br>Tape #1 | 18 |
| 19 | 20<br>Tape #2 | 21<br>Tape #1 | 22<br>Tape #4 | 23<br>Tape #1 | 24<br>Tape #2 | 25 |
| 26 | 27<br>Tape #1 | 28<br>Tape #3 | 29<br>Tape #1 | 30<br>Tape #2 | 31<br>Tape #1 | |

As you can see, you can easily make a mistake in the rotation when using the Tower of Hanoi method. If you implement this solution, you should create a schedule for at least three months at a time to ensure that one is always available to aid personnel in using the correct tape each day. You can also add additional tapes to this method to increase the long-term recovery capability past 16 days. Consider the effects of adding additional tapes as detailed in this list:

▶ **Six tapes**—32 days

▶ **Seven tapes**—64 days

▶ **Eight tapes**—128 days

▶ **Nine tapes**—256 days

▶ **Ten tapes**—512 days

The other major disadvantage to the Tower of Hanoi rotation method is the extreme amount of wear and tear placed on the lower-numbered tapes, such as Tape #1 and Tape #2. By replacing these tapes quarterly, for example, you can inexpensively and easily increase the reliability of the Tower of Hanoi solution.

# Using Windows Backup

**Plan a backup and recovery strategy.**

Using the Backup Utility consists of three distinct processes: creating one or more backup configurations, scheduling backups to occur automatically, and performing restorations. Each of these processes is examined in the following sections.

## Creating Backup Job Configurations

The Windows Backup Utility enables you to easily create a backup configuration. The basic steps to create the configuration are outlined in Step by Step 6.3, although your options and decisions will vary depending on how your system and backup media devices are configured.

## STEP BY STEP

### 6.3 Creating a New Backup Configuration

1. Open the Backup or Restore Wizard, shown in Figure 6.18, by selecting Start, Programs, Accessories, System Tools, Backup.

2. Click the Advanced Mode link to switch to Advanced mode of the Backup Utility, as shown in Figure 6.19.

3. Start the Backup Wizard by clicking the Backup Wizard (Advanced) button from the main page of the Backup Utility.

4. Click Next to dismiss the opening page of the wizard.

*continues*

---

**NOTE**

**System State data**  The System State data contains information that is critical to the proper startup and operation of your Windows Server 2003 computer. The following items are included in the System State data:

- Registry

- COM+ class registration database

- Critical boot and system files

- System files that are protected by Windows File Protection

- Certificate Services database if the server is a Certificate Authority

- Active Directory directory service if the server is a domain controller

- SYSVOL directory if the server is a domain controller

- Cluster service information if the server is a member of a cluster

- IIS metadirectory if IIS is installed on the server

*continued*

**FIGURE 6.18**
The Backup or Restore Wizard can be used in place of the Advanced Mode.

**FIGURE 6.19**
The Backup Utility Advanced Mode provides you with all the tools you need to create and schedule backups.

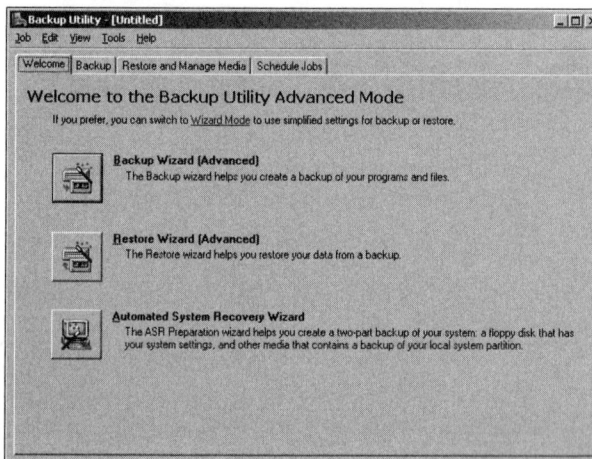

5. On the What to Back Up dialog box, shown in Figure 6.20, select the scope of the backup. Click Next to continue. If you choose to back up selected files and folders, proceed to step 6; otherwise, skip to step 7.

6. On the Items to Back Up dialog box, shown in Figure 6.21, select the files and folders to back up. Click Next to continue.

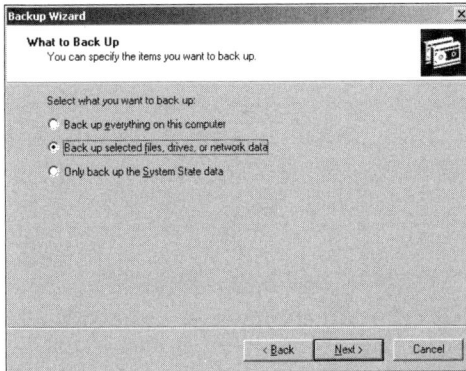

**FIGURE 6.20**
You need to select the scope of the backup that is to be performed.

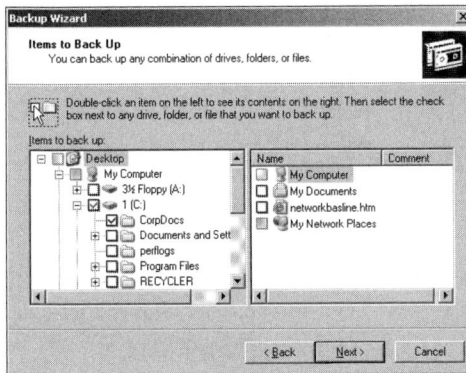

**FIGURE 6.21**
You can select entire volumes, folders, or specific files to be backed up.

**7.** On the Backup Type, Destination, and Name dialog box, shown in Figure 6.22, choose the location to save the backup file, using the Browse button if necessary, and enter the filename for the backup file. Click Next to continue.

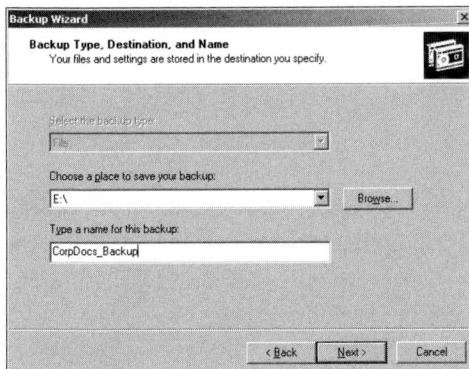

**FIGURE 6.22**
You should provide a filename for the backup file that is descriptive of its purpose or contents.

*continues*

*continued*

8. The Completing the Backup Wizard dialog box appears, as shown in Figure 6.23. To configure advanced options, including scheduling and disabling volume shadow copy, click Advanced and proceed to step 9. If you want to perform this backup immediately, click Finish.

**FIGURE 6.23**
You need to configure the Advanced options to schedule the backup to occur at a later time.

9. On the Type of Backup dialog box, shown in Figure 6.24, select the type of backup you want. The default selection is Normal. Click Next to continue.

**FIGURE 6.24**
By default, all backups are configured as Normal; you can choose from any of the five types previously discussed.

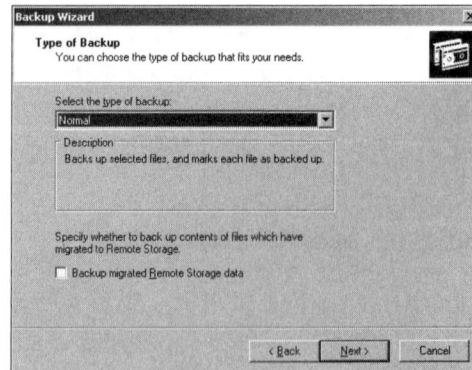

10. On the How to Back Up dialog box, shown in Figure 6.25, you can select options to verify data, enable hardware compression (if supported by your backup device), and disable volume shadow copy. Data verification and

hardware compression are usually desirable options. You should not disable the volume shadow copy unless you have a specific reason to do so. After making your selections, click Next to continue.

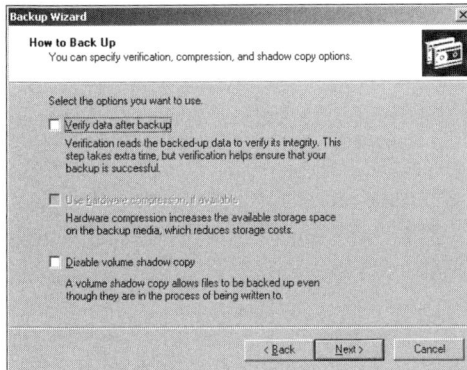

**FIGURE 6.25**
You should not disable the volume shadow copy without a valid reason to do so.

**11.** On the Backup Options dialog box, shown in Figure 6.26, you need to select whether to append existing backup data on your media or to replace it. In most cases, you simply overwrite the old data each night—especially if you are using one of the media rotation methods discussed previously in this section. After making your selections, click Next to continue.

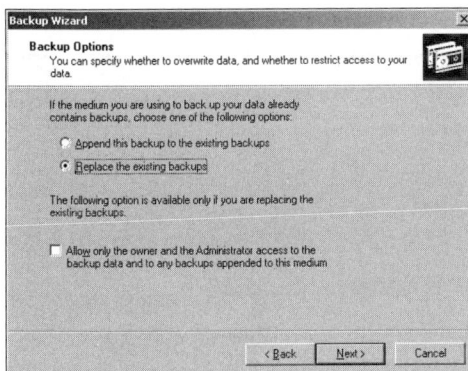

**FIGURE 6.26**
You should, in most cases, overwrite any existing data on the backup media.

**12.** On the When to Back Up dialog box, shown in Figure 6.27, you need to configure the data and time that you

*continues*

*continued*

want to perform this backup job. Using the Set Schedule button allows you to configure the scheduling options for the backup; alternatively, you can run the backup immediately by leaving the Now radio button selected. After making your selections, click Next to continue.

**FIGURE 6.27**
You can schedule backups to occur when your network will not be adversely affected.

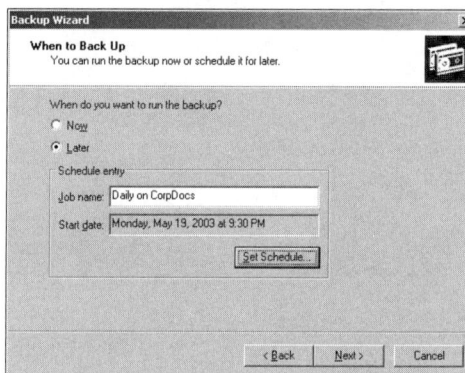

**13.** If you selected Now, click Finish to complete the Backup Wizard and start the backup. If you selected Later, you are prompted for the username and password of a domain user account authorized to perform backups. Click Finish to complete the Backup Wizard; the backup will run at the date and time you selected.

Additionally, you can choose to create a backup configuration manually; however, you still make all the same decisions as when using the Backup Wizard.

## Scheduling Backup Jobs

Managing a backup schedule is easy in Windows Server 2003. In the Backup Utility, simply switch to the Schedule Jobs tab, as shown in Figure 6.28. Each day on the calendar shows what type of backup is scheduled for that day. Holding the cursor over a backup displays the backup name. You can edit the backup properties, including rescheduling the backup by clicking it. You can also create new backup configurations by clicking the Add Job button.

**EXAM TIP**

**Scheduling backup jobs** Many administrators disable the Windows Task Scheduler because it is commonly seen as an unneeded service, and thus a security risk. If you want to schedule backup jobs using the Windows Backup Utility, you must not disable the Windows Task Scheduler.

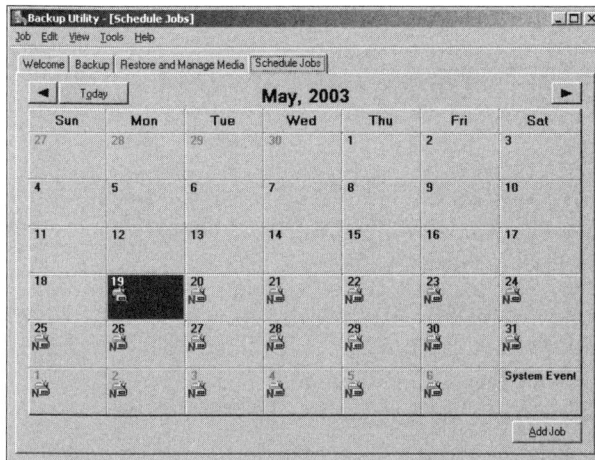

**FIGURE 6.28**
Using the Schedule Jobs tab, you can quickly determine what backup jobs are scheduled.

# GUIDED PRACTICE
# EXERCISE 6.1

In this exercise, you configure a custom backup solution for a corporate file server. This Guided Practice helps reinforce the preceding discussion.

You need to create and implement a backup plan using the Windows Backup Utility that meets the following requirements:

▶ Backup jobs should run as quickly as possible, but this requirement is not to override any other requirement.

▶ All data on the file server must be backed up completely at least once per week.

▶ Restorations should take the minimum amount of time possible and use the minimum number of backup tapes possible.

▶ You must maintain at least nine month's worth of backup archives.

▶ Backups may not be performed during business hours and cannot be running from the previous night when work starts the next morning.

The company operates Monday through Friday and has two shifts: 8:00 a.m. to 4:00 p.m. and 4:00 p.m. to 12:00 a.m.

*continues*

*continued*

You should try completing this exercise on your own first. If you get stuck, or you would like to see one possible solution, follow these steps:

1. You would be best served by creating a backup plan using the Grandfather, Father, Son tape rotation method, which requires 20 backup tapes.

2. Each night, Monday through Thursday, you should configure a differential backup to run. This backup will back up all selected data that has been modified since the last normal backup was performed.

3. Each Friday night, you should configure a normal backup to run. This will back up all selected data that has been modified since the last normal backup was performed.

4. On the last Friday of each month, you will use a different backup tape that will be rotated to offsite storage after the next Friday night normal backup has been performed.

The backup solution will provide relatively quick backups Monday through Thursday, although the backup times will increase through the week as the amount of modified data likely increases. As well, only two backup tapes, the last normal and the last differential, are required to perform the restoration, which minimizes both time and number of tapes required. By using a different backup tape (and subsequently rotating it to an offsite storage location), you can provide the required backup archival. Using the standard Grandfather, Father, Son rotation requires 20 backup tapes and provides a full year of backup history with a media rotation system.

## Performing Restorations Using Windows Backup

Should the day actually come that you need to put your backup system to the test, the actual process of performing the restoration is relatively easy in Windows Server 2003—as long as you are ready for the task. The basic steps to perform a restoration are outlined in

Step by Step 6.4, although your options and decisions will vary depending on how your system and backup media devices are configured.

---

# STEP BY STEP

### 6.4 Performing Data Restoration

1. Open the Backup or Restore Wizard by selecting Start, Programs, Accessories, System Tools, Backup.

2. Click the Advanced Mode link to switch to Advanced mode of the Backup Utility, as shown in Figure 6.19.

3. Start the Restore Wizard by clicking the Restore Wizard (Advanced) button from the main page of the Backup Utility.

4. Click Next to dismiss the opening page of the wizard.

5. On the What to Restore dialog box, shown in Figure 6.29, select the media and files that are to be restored. If your choice of media is not listed, click the Browse button to locate it. After making your selections, click Next to continue.

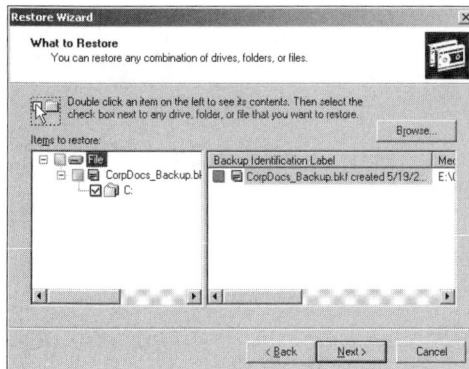

**FIGURE 6.29**
You can select to restore only certain parts of the backup file if you want.

6. The Completing the Restore Wizard dialog box appears, as shown in Figure 6.30. To configure advanced options, including where to restore the files to and what to do with existing files found in the restoration location, click Advanced and proceed to step 7. If you want to perform this restoration immediately, click Finish.

*continues*

*continued*

**FIGURE 6.30**
You need to configure the Advanced options to be able to restore the files to a different location than where they were originally located.

**7.** On the Where to Restore dialog box, shown in Figure 6.31, select the restoration location for the folders and files from the drop-down. Click Next to continue.

**FIGURE 6.31**
You can restore the files to the same or a different location if you want.

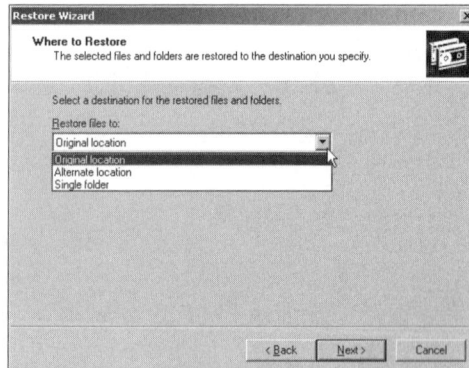

**8.** On the How to Restore dialog box, shown in Figure 6.32, decide what is to occur if existing files are found in the restoration location. Click Next to continue.

**9.** On the Advanced Restore Options dialog box, shown in Figure 6.33, you can select from several advanced restoration options, as explained in the list following this procedure. The available options are determined by the data that has been backed up, the type of hardware installed in your server, as well as the role of the server. After making your selections, click Next to continue.

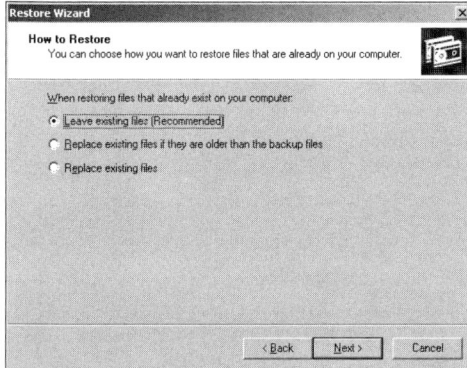

**FIGURE 6.32**
In most cases, you should leave existing files or replace older files during the restoration process.

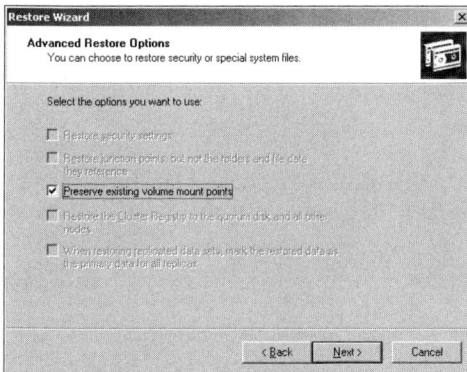

**FIGURE 6.33**
The Advanced Restore Options dialog box features several high-level configuration options.

**10.** Click Finish to start the restoration.

**11.** The Restore Progress dialog box appears, informing you of the restoration's status. When the restoration is complete, you see results similar to those shown in Figure 6.34.

**FIGURE 6.34**
In the Restore Progress dialog box, you can determine the status of your restoration process.

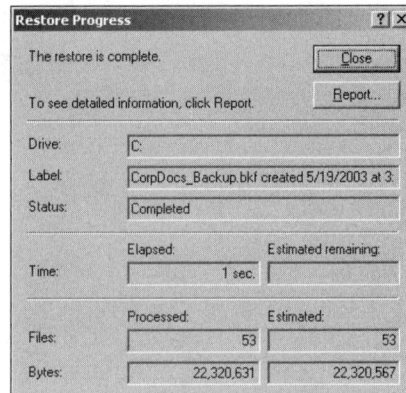

The Advanced Restore Options are as follows:

▶ **Restore security settings**—This option restores security settings for each file and folder; these settings include permissions, auditing entries, and ownership information. This option is available only for data that was backed up from an NTFS-formatted volume.

▶ **Restore junction points, and restore file and folder data under junction points to the original location**—This option restores all junction points to your hard disks as well as the data that the junction points point to. If you are restoring a mounted drive, and you want to restore the data that is on the mounted drive, you must select this check box. If you do not select this check box, you restore only the folder containing the mounted drive.

▶ **Restore junction points, but not the folders and file data they reference**—This option restores junction points only to your hard drive. This option does not restore any folders or file data that reference the junction points.

▶ **When restoring replicated data sets, mark the restored data as the primary data for all replicas**—This option performs a restoration and ensures that the restored File Replication Service (FRS) data is replicated to other configured servers.

▸ **Restore the Cluster Registry to the quorum disk and all other nodes**—This option ensures that the cluster quorum database is restored and is also replicated on all nodes in the cluster.

▸ **Preserve existing volume mount points**—This option prevents the restore operation from writing over any volume mount points you have created on the partition or volume you are restoring data to.

▸ **Restore Removable Storage database**—This option restores the Removable Storage database and deletes the existing Removable Storage database. If you are not using Removable Storage to manage storage media, you do not need to select this option.

With the discussion of the Windows Backup Utility behind us, we now move forward and examine a new feature in Windows Server 2003: Automated System Recovery.

> **NOTE**
>
> **Form of a junction point!**   A *junction point* is a physical location on a hard disk that points to data located at another location on your hard disk or another storage device. Junction points are created when you create a mounted drive.

## Using Automated System Recovery

**Plan a backup and recovery strategy.**

▸ **Plan system recovery that uses Automated System Recovery (ASR).**

Although making regular backups is an important task to accomplish, they are of no use to you should a server suffer a critical failure that prevents it from starting normally. Although you can use the `ntbackup.exe` command to create backups from the command line, you cannot perform restorations from the command line—a serious limitation should you be unable to start a Windows Server 2003 computer normally.

As discussed previously, you can use Automated System Recovery to restore the operating system back to a previous state, which allows you to start Window Server 2003 in the event that other methods do not work. You should always consider ASR your last resort for recovery, after Safe Mode, the Recovery Console, and Last Known Good Configuration (LKGC).

**WARNING**

**Keeping ASR up to date** For an ASR recovery to be effective, you must keep it up to date. You should create a new ASR set after any configuration change to the server. You should also create a new ASR set on a regular schedule—just the same as you would with a normal backup set.

**Floppy drive required** Although you can create an ASR set without having a floppy drive installed in the server, you cannot perform the ASR restoration process without one.

ASR is a two-part process that uses a startup floppy disk to boot the Windows Server 2003 computer and a backup file (that must be accessible during ASR restoration) containing the System State, system services, and all disks associated with the operating system components. The startup disk contains information about the backup, the disk configurations, and the way the restoration is to be accomplished.

To create a new ASR set, perform the steps outlined in Step by Step 6.5.

## STEP BY STEP

### 6.5 Creating an Automated System Recovery Set

**1.** Place a blank, formatted 1.44MB 3.5-inch floppy disk in your server's floppy drive.

**2.** Open the Backup or Restore Wizard by selecting Start, Programs, Accessories, System Tools, Backup.

**3.** Click the Advanced Mode link to switch to Advanced mode of the Backup Utility.

**4.** Start the Automated System Recovery Preparation Wizard by clicking the Automated System Recovery Wizard button on the main page of the Backup Utility.

**5.** Click Next to dismiss the opening page of the wizard.

**6.** On the Backup Destination dialog box, shown in Figure 6.35, provide the path and filename of the backup file to be created. Click Next to continue.

**FIGURE 6.35**
ASR creates a backup file and startup floppy disk.

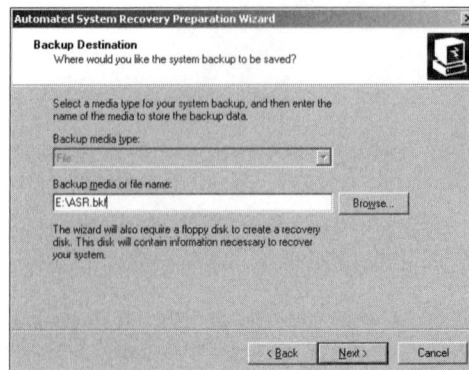

**7.** Click Finish to close the wizard and start the ASR set creation process.

**8.** Ensure that the blank, formatted floppy disk is inserted in your server's floppy drive when prompted, as shown in Figure 6.36. Click OK to create the startup floppy disk.

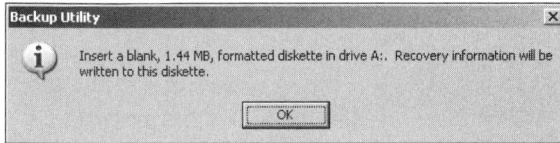

```
Backup Utility                                            [x]

   (i)   Insert a blank, 1.44 MB, formatted diskette in drive A:. Recovery information will be
         written to this diskette.

                         [      OK      ]
```

**FIGURE 6.36**
The startup floppy disk is the second part of the ASR process.

To perform an ASR recovery—after all other available methods to start the server normally have failed—you need to perform the steps listed in Step by Step 6.6. However, before starting the procedure, you need to locate the following items and have them readily available to you:

▶ The correct (up-to-date) ASR startup floppy disk.

▶ The correct (up-to-date) ASR backup media.

▶ The original Windows Server 2003 installation CD-ROM.

▶ Special drivers required for any mass storage controllers located in your server that are not available on the Windows Server 2003 CD-ROM; they also need to be available on floppy disk.

## STEP BY STEP

### 6.6 Performing Automated System Recovery

**1.** Power on the server to be recovered using ASR.

**2.** Insert your original Windows Server 2003 CD into the CD-ROM drive.

**3.** When prompted to start from the CD-ROM, press the appropriate key.

*continues*

*continued*

**4.** If you need a special mass storage driver, press F6 when prompted to install it.

**5.** Press F2 when prompted to initiate an ASR recovery.

**6.** Insert the ASR startup floppy disk.

**7.** Follow the directions that are displayed.

**8.** If you need a special mass storage driver, press F6 when prompted to install it after the server restarts.

**9.** Follow the directions that are displayed.

---

That's all there is to using Automated System Recovery. Remember, however, that ASR is your last option and should not be used without attempting all other available methods to start the server.

## Using Volume Shadow Copy

**Plan a backup and recovery strategy.**

▶ **Plan a backup strategy that uses volume shadow copy.**

As you've already seen, the volume shadow copy is another new backup feature available in Windows Server 2003. The usefulness of volume shadow copies, however, extends beyond your ability to use Windows Backup to create backups of open files; this feature also provides you with a way to archive copies of data over time, allowing users to locate and restore a specific file if they want. After the necessary configuration has been completed and the required software installed, users can view the volume shadow copies of shared network folders, including any previous versions in existence. Users can then copy any or all of the older files, allowing them to effectively restore a backup copy of the files from an earlier time.

As you might imagine, volume shadow copies can provide a number of benefits to your network users—the least of which is the ability to restore an older version should the current version of a file become corrupt or be deleted beyond recovery. You also can compare different versions of files to see what changes have occurred over time.

Files contained in a volume shadow copy are read-only while
archived, preventing them from being modified and thus nullifying
the benefits of the volume shadow copy. After a file has been extracted from a volume shadow copy archive, it can be modified or moved
to any location desired for editing.

Shadow copies are disabled by default but can be enabled and configured from the Shared Folders node of the Computer Management
console, as shown in Figure 6.37.

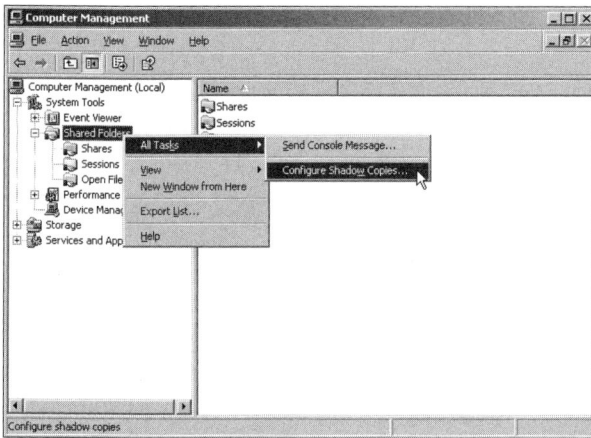

**FIGURE 6.37**
Volume shadow copies are managed from the
Computer Management console.

Windows Server 2003 allows for only 64 volume shadow copies of a
specific shared folder. When this limit is reached, the oldest copy is
deleted to make room for a newer copy. Before your network clients
can take advantage of this technology, they must have the Volume
Shadow Client software installed. The client software is available on
your Windows Server 2003 computer in the `%systemroot%\`
`system32\clients\twclient\` folder.

Step by Step 6.7 outlines the basic process to enable and configure
volume shadow copies for a volume on your Windows Server 2003
computer.

# STEP BY STEP

## 6.7 Enabling and Configuring Volume Shadow Copies

1. Open the Computer Management console by selecting Start, Programs, Administrative Tools, Computer Management.

2. Expand the System Tools node and locate the Shared Folders node.

3. Right-click the Shared Folders node and select All Tasks, Configure Shadow Copies, as shown previously in Figure 6.37.

4. The Shadow Copies dialog box opens, as shown in Figure 6.38. This dialog box displays a listing of all available volumes for which you can enable shadow copies.

**FIGURE 6.38**
Shadow copies are disabled by default for all volumes.

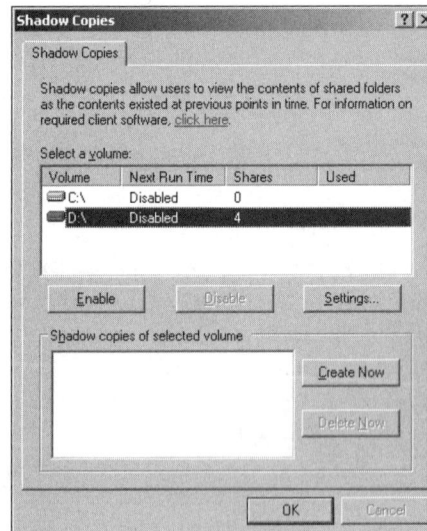

5. Select the volume for which you want to enable shadow copies and click the Enable button.

6. You are prompted with a dialog box asking for confirmation that you actually want to enable shadow copies for this volume. Click Yes to continue.

**7.** After some time, the shadow copy is completed and appears in the lower half of the Shadow Copies dialog box, as shown in Figure 6.39.

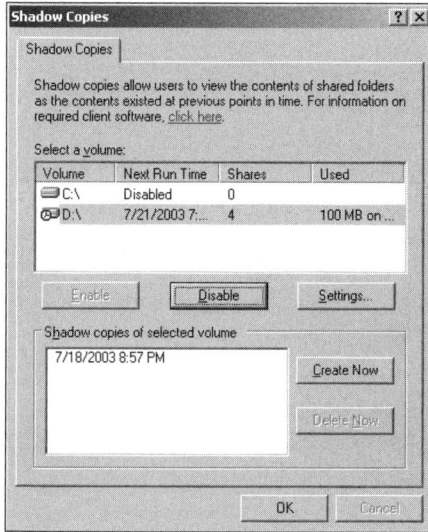

**FIGURE 6.39**
You can quickly view recent shadow copies that have been created.

**8.** If you want to change the default configuration settings, click the Settings button on the Shadow Copies dialog box. The Settings dialog box opens, as shown in Figure 6.40.

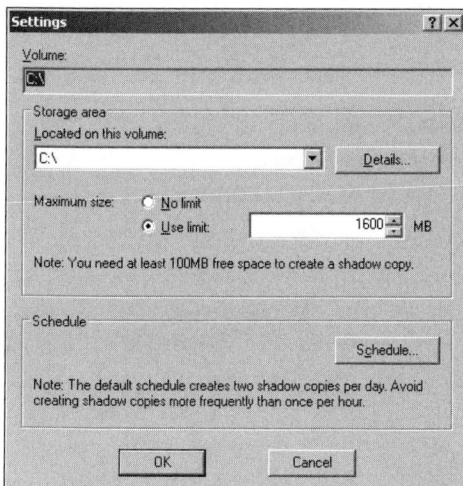

**FIGURE 6.40**
You need to configure at least 100MB of space for volume shadow copies.

*continues*

*continued*

9. On the Settings dialog box, you can change the location where the shadow copies are to be stored as well as the amount of space you want to allot to them. To configure the schedule for volume shadow copies, click the Schedule button. The schedule dialog box opens, as shown in Figure 6.41.

**FIGURE 6.41**
You can create a custom shadow copy schedule to fit your needs.

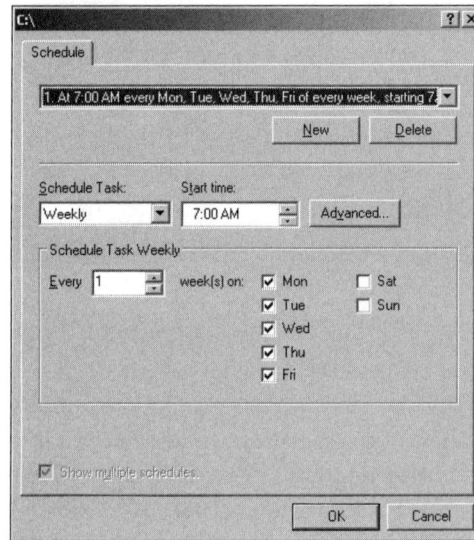

10. The default schedule creates volume shadow copies twice daily at 7 a.m. and 12 p.m. You can modify the existing schedules or delete them and create new ones as you like.

11. Click OK three times to close all the shadow copies configuration dialog boxes.

After you've configured volume shadow copies, Windows Server 2003 computers and client computers with the Volume Shadow Client software installed can view the shadow copies available for a shared network folder. You first need to locate the shared network folder, as shown in Figure 6.42, using My Network Places.

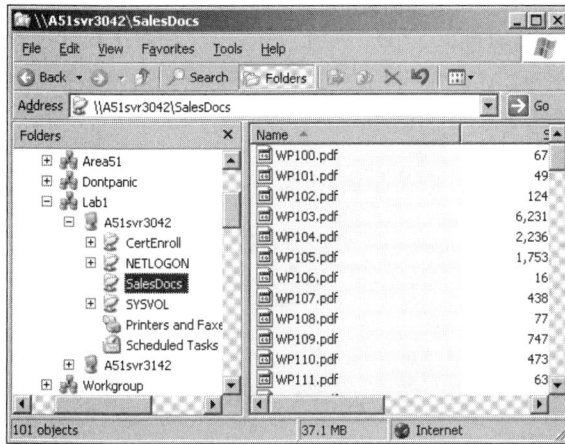

**FIGURE 6.42**
You can take advantage of the shadow copies only over the network.

Right-clicking the shared folder and selecting Properties from the context menu displays a new tab on the Properties dialog box—the Previous Versions tab, as shown in Figure 6.43.

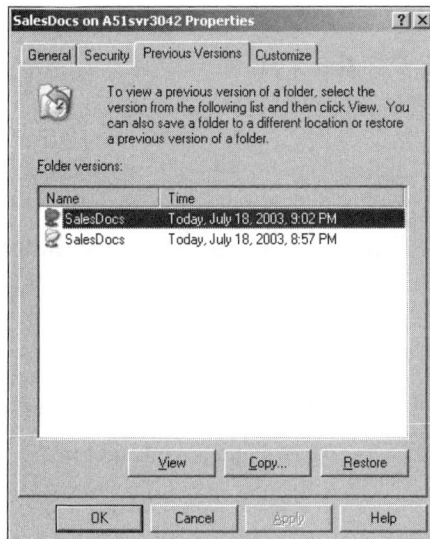

**FIGURE 6.43**
The Previous Versions tab displays all previous versions of the folder.

By selecting a previous version and clicking the View button, you can open a new Windows Explorer window displaying the previous version's contents, as shown in Figure 6.44. If you want to restore a single file or multiple files, you can simply drag them out of this location. You can also restore the entire folder by selecting it and clicking the Restore button on the Previous Versions tab. To restore the previous version of the entire folder to a different location, select the previous version and click the Copy button on the Previous Versions tab.

**FIGURE 6.44**
The Previous Versions tab displays all previous versions of the folder.

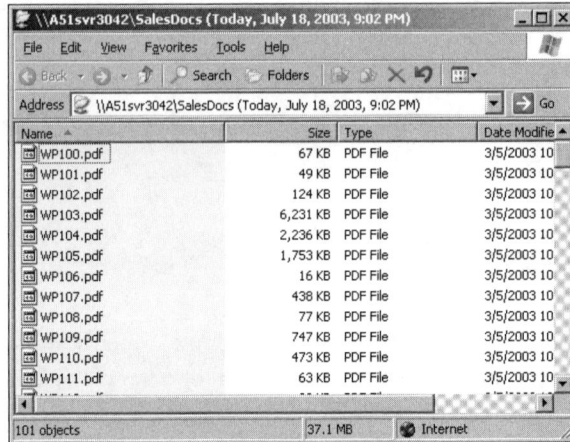

## GUIDED PRACTICE EXERCISE 6.2

In this exercise, you configure volume shadow copies for a file server. This Guided Practice helps reinforce the preceding discussion.

You should try completing this exercise on your own first. If you get stuck, or you would like to see one possible solution, follow these steps:

1. Open the Computer Management console on the file server where you are enabling shadow copies.

2. Right-click the Shared Folders node and select All Tasks, Configure Shadow Copies from the context menu.

3. On the Shadow Copies dialog box, select the volume for which you want to enable shadow copies and click the Enable button.

4. Click the Settings button to modify the default configuration of the shadow copies.

5. On the Settings dialog box, you can change the location where the shadow copies are to be stored as well as the amount of space you want to allot to the them.

6. To configure the schedule for volume shadow copies, click the Schedule button to open the Schedule dialog box.

7. Close all shadow copy dialog boxes.

## CASE STUDY: PERFORMANCE PROBLEMS WITH A NEW PROCESS

### ESSENCE OF THE CASE

The following points summarize the essence of the case study:

▶ The system has just had a new application installed.

▶ The application runs continuously as a service to local and remote users.

▶ After several days of continuous running, the system performance degrades.

▶ Rebooting the system temporarily solves the problem. However, it eventually returns.

▶ Available memory is consumed, and paging activity increases.

### SCENARIO

You have installed a new custom-developed program that runs continuously in the background as a Windows service. You and a number of remote users who are accessing data on your system use this program. When you first install it, you run the Performance console on your system to establish a baseline of performance during normal working conditions. A few days later, your system becomes sluggish and noticeably slower in all functions. You reboot your system, and it appears to be working normally again. A few days later, the same performance problems occur again. You run the Performance console and discover that the amount of available memory has dropped to almost 0 and the paging file is very active.

### ANALYSIS

When dealing with performance problems, you must remember that almost everything is inter-related with everything else. Memory problems can cause disk activity, which can manifest itself as a processor bottleneck. In this case, because the problem was apparently solved when the

*continues*

## CASE STUDY: PERFORMANCE PROBLEMS WITH A NEW PROCESS

*continued*

system was restarted, the problem is likely related to consumption of a resource rather than an elevated rate of activity. When the problem occurred again days later, the Performance console showed a higher than expected paging activity and almost no available memory. That combination would normally indicate a system that is underconfigured in memory for the process running. Because this situation did not exist when the new applica-

tion was brought online, the conclusion is that the new background service leaks memory. In this situation, memory acquired by the service during normal processing is not returned to the system. Over time, the amount of working memory assigned to the service would exceed the amount available, and Windows would begin to page to meet the needs of its normal workload. The recommendation would be to send the new service back to the developers for analysis.

## CHAPTER SUMMARY

### KEY TERMS

Before taking the exam, make sure you are comfortable with the definitions and concepts for each of the following key terms. You can use Appendix A, "Glossary," for quick reference.

- Automated System Restore
- Backup
- Baseline
- Bottleneck
- Copy backup
- Counter
- Counter log
- Daily backup
- Differential backup

This chapter covered perhaps two of the most important day-to-day activities you will be faced with as an administrator: ensuring server performance and providing disaster recovery.

Ensuring performance (and health) of servers and client computers involves using the Performance console (System Monitor, Counter Logs, Trace Logs, and Alerts), the Event Viewer, and also the Task Manager. Data gathered from these sources can be used to identify, troubleshoot, and correct problem areas.

Even with the best laid highly available server plans, disaster can and will strike when you can least afford it. Only by having a well-designed and adequate backup and restoration plan will your network live again without days of downtime. Several widely accepted backup methods and media rotation systems are available; you can, however, opt to create a customized solution that fits the unique needs of your organization. Whatever solution you end up with, you must ensure that all responsible persons are aware of its requirements and that it is tested routinely to validate its process and check for required updates and corrections.

Remember, server reliability begins with you and your good planning.

## CHAPTER SUMMARY

**KEY TERMS**

- Incremental backup
- Normal backup
- ntbackup.exe
- Performance console
- Restoration
- Volume shadow copy

## APPLY YOUR KNOWLEDGE

# Exercises

## 6.1   Creating a Baseline Counter Log

In this exercise, you use the Performance console to create a baseline counter log. You then can use the baseline as a comparison point for future performance monitoring.

**Estimated time:** 30 minutes

1. Open the Performance console.

2. Expand the Performance Logs and Alerts node and click the Counter Logs entry.

3. Create a new counter log and name it **BASLINELOG1**.

4. Add entire objects or specific counters as you like. For this example, add the Packets Sent/sec, Packets Received/sec, and Packets Received Errors counters.

5. Leave the default data collection rate and account settings as is.

6. Configure the type of log file to be used as binary. Choose the numbering system of your choice.

7. Leave the default schedule of manual activation as is.

8. Click OK to save the counter log settings.

9. Allow the counter log to run for approximately 20 minutes and then stop it.

10. Switch to the System Monitor node and click the database icon to open the counter log for viewing.

11. Click the Add button to locate and add the counter log file.

12. On the Data tab, ensure that you have configured all the same counters to be displayed as you used in the counter log itself. Click OK. The counter log data is displayed in the System Monitor.

## 6.2   Monitoring Performance

In this exercise, you monitor the current performance characteristics of a computer's network adapter.

**Estimated time:** 15 minutes

1. Open the Performance console.

2. Click System Monitor.

3. Click the + icon to open the Add Counters dialog box. Add the counters you want to monitor on your computer, such as Packets Sent/sec, Packets Received/sec, and Packets Received Errors.

4. Click Close when you are finished. Watch the configured counters for 10 minutes while performing various activities that require network transfer to and from your computer.

## 6.3   Configuring a New Backup Job

In this exercise, you configure a new backup job to be run on your Windows Server 2003 computer.

**Estimated time:** 20 minutes

1. Open the Backup or Restore Wizard.

2. Click the Advanced Mode link to switch to Advanced mode of the Backup Utility.

3. Start the Backup Wizard.

4. Click Next to dismiss the opening page of the wizard.

5. On the What to Back Up dialog box, select the scope of the backup. If you choose to back up

## APPLY YOUR KNOWLEDGE

selected files and folders, proceed to step 6; otherwise, skip to step 7.

6. On the Items to Back Up dialog box, select the files and folders to back up.

7. On the Backup Type, Destination, and Name dialog box, choose the location to save the backup file, using the Browse button if necessary, and enter the filename for the backup file.

8. To configure advanced options, including scheduling and disabling volume shadow copy, click Advanced and proceed to step 9. If you want to perform this backup immediately, click Finish.

9. On the Type of Backup dialog box, select the type of backup you want.

10. On the How to Back Up dialog box, select to verify data, enable hardware compression (if supported by your backup device), or disable volume shadow copy.

11. On the Backup Options dialog box, select whether to overwrite existing backup data on your media or overwrite it.

12. On the When to Back Up dialog box, configure the data and time that you want to perform this backup job.

13. If you selected Now, click Finish to complete the Backup Wizard and start the backup. If you selected Later, you are prompted for the username and password of a domain user account authorized to perform backups.

### 6.4   Enabling and Configuring Volume Shadow Copy

In this exercise, you enable and configure the volume shadow copy feature on your Windows Server 2003 computer.

**Estimated time:** 15 minutes

1. Open the Computer Management console.

2. Expand the System Tools node and locate the Shared Folders node.

3. Right-click the Shared Folders node and select All Tasks, Configure Shadow Copies.

4. Select the volume for which you want to enable shadow copies and click the Enable button.

5. Click the Settings button on the Shadow Copies dialog box.

6. Change the location where the shadow copies are to be stored as well as the amount of space you want to allot to them.

7. Click the Schedule button.

8. Configure the volume shadow copy schedule as required.

## Review Questions

1. What is a baseline, and why is it important to create one?

2. You have enabled the volume shadow copies on your file server using the default settings. When you try to locate a version of a file that is 42 days old, you cannot. Why is this so?

3. You create backups on Monday, Tuesday, Wednesday, and Thursday nights using differential backup. On Friday night, you perform a full backup. If you need to perform a restoration on Thursday morning, which tapes do you need?

4. Besides allowing you to create previous versions of files and folders, what other feature does the

## APPLY YOUR KNOWLEDGE

volume shadow copy provide in Windows Server 2003?

5. In general, when should you create baselines for your servers?

# Exam Questions

1. Christopher needs to back up the contents of a data folder on his server, but he does not have a tape drive. What other media can he use with Windows Backup?

   A. CD-ROM

   B. Floppy disk

   C. Text dump

   D. No other media can be used

2. You are the third-shift network administrator for Bob's Bull Riding College. You have just completed the installation and configuration of a new Windows Server 2003 file server. What should you do on this new computer over the next day or so to provide troubleshooting guidance in the future should network traffic problems occur?

   A. Remove all unnecessary protocols from the server's network adapters.

   B. Create a baseline counter log that documents what the server's performance was like at the time it was placed on the network.

   C. Check the event logs to ensure that no abnormal events occurred when the computer was joined to the network.

D. Configure and implement IPSec to secure network traffic to and from the file server.

3. You are creating a disaster recovery plan for your organization. You have decided to implement the Grandfather, Father, Son media rotation method to provide a good mix of backup history and backup media wear. Your plan has been approved by management and implemented for use on the network. After three months, you perform a comprehensive review of the disaster recovery plan and determine that it does not provide an adequate solution to protect critical operating system files. What additional information should you ensure is backed up when your backup files are created?

   A. SYSVOL directory

   B. C:\

   C. System State

   D. All files and folders on all volumes on all servers

4. You are trying to monitor the performance statistics of your Windows Server 2003 computer's network interface. You have only one network interface installed in the computer. After you have selected the desired counters from the Network Interface object and returned to the System Monitor, you see no performance statistics displayed for the selected counters, even though you have been accessing Internet Web sites and transferring files across the network. What is the most likely cause of this problem?

   A. The network interface is disabled.

   B. The network interface does not support the System Monitor.

   C. You have selected the internal loopback network interface.

D. You did not click Add to add the counters to be monitored.

5. You have enabled and configured volume shadow copies on one of your Windows Server 2003 file servers. The file server has a shared folder named `Financial` that is located at `C:\FinanceDocs`. You have deployed the Previous Versions Client to all your Windows XP Professional workstations. When you attempt to confirm that your configuration is functioning correctly by viewing the properties of the `Financial` share in Windows Explorer on your server, there is no Previous Versions tab. What is the most likely problem?

A. You forgot to install the client software on the server.

B. The client software was installed prior to enabling the shadow copies.

C. The Previous Versions tab is available only when viewing the folder over the network using My Network Places.

D. The shared folder is empty.

6. You have recently completed the configuration of a baseline counter log that you will use to collect data about the performance of a new server you have just placed on the network. You configured a maximum log file size of 1MB. You let the counter log run for approximately six hours before stopping it. When you look at the data you have collected, you see only a fraction of this total time displayed—the last 45 minutes or so that you had the counter log catching data. What is the most likely reason for this problem?

A. There has not been enough activity to generate more data than this.

B. You configured the file type as binary.

C. You configured the file type as binary circular.

D. The computer was experiencing operating system instability problems that prevented the collection of more data.

7. Deanna needs to back up critical data on her server. However, she does not have enough DAT tapes to back up everything on her server. She wants to make sure that, in addition to the user data she is backing up, she backs up the Registry on her server. What should Deanna select in addition to those data files she wants to back up?

A. C:

B. System State

C. My Documents

D. My Computer

8. You are configuring a counter log that is to run automatically each day and collect information about the performance of the network interface installed in your file server. Which of the following log numbering systems would most likely make the resulting counter logs easy to track back to the date and time they were created?

A. *nnnnnn*

B. *yyyymm*

C. *mmddhhmm*

D. *yyyymmddhh*

9. You are preparing to enable and configure volume shadow copies on one of your Windows Server 2003 file servers. All shared folders are located on Volume C of the file server. Volume C on the server has 85MB of free space available.

## APPLY YOUR KNOWLEDGE

How much space will be used by volume shadow copies?

A. 850KB

B. 8.5MB

C. 42.5MB

D. 0MB

10. Christopher wants to determine whether his server is short of memory. Under light load, users get good response. However, as load increases, so does the lack of responsiveness. Which of the following counters will aid him in determining whether memory is the bottleneck in his system?

    A. Memory\ Pages/sec

    B. Paging File\ % Usage

    C. Processor\ Interrupts/sec

    D. Network Segment\ % Net Utilization

11. Andrea is preparing a disaster recovery plan for her company. She asks you which backup option backs up only the files that have not been marked as archived and then sets the archive bit for all files that are backed up. What should you tell her?

    A. Daily backups act this way.

    B. Normal backups act this way.

    C. Copy backups act this way.

    D. Differential backups act this way.

    E. Incremental backups act this way.

12. Christopher is assisting Andrea with preparations for disaster recovery. He asks you which backup option requires only one media device for the entire backup and sets the archive bit to indicate

the data has been backed up. What should you tell him?

A. Daily backups act this way.

B. Normal backups act this way.

C. Copy backups act this way.

D. Differential backups act this way.

E. Incremental backups act this way.

13. Austin wants to monitor how much of the paging file is being used. He opens the System Monitor and starts to add the counter for this, but he is unsure which one to add. Which counter should you tell him to add to monitor the paging file usage?

    A. Paging File\ Pages/sec

    B. Memory\ Pages/sec

    C. Paging File\ % Usage

    D. Memory\ % Paging File

14. Hannah is trying to determine what could be causing her disk access to slow down over time. She opens the System Monitor and starts to add counters to help her diagnose this situation, but she is unsure what to add. Which counter should you tell her to add to help her diagnose problems with her hard drive access speed? (Select all that apply.)

    A. Physical Disk\ Disk Reads/sec

    B. Logical Disk\ % Free Space

    C. Physical Disk\ Split IO/sec

    D. Network Interface\ Bytes Total/sec

15. You are creating a disaster recovery plan for your organization. You have decided to implement the

## APPLY YOUR KNOWLEDGE

Grandfather, Father, Son media rotation method to provide a good mix of backup history and backup media wear. Your plan has been approved by management and implemented for use on the network. After three months, you perform a comprehensive review of the disaster recovery plan and determine that it does not provide an adequate solution in the event that the server cannot be started normally. What feature of Windows Server 2003 can you take advantage of to close this gap in your disaster recovery plan?

A. Volume shadow copy

B. Automated System Recovery

C. Automatic Updates

D. Safe Mode

# Answers to Review Questions

1. A baseline is a set of performance readings taken at a specific time and used to reference future readings to identify changes in performance. For more information, see the section "Baselining Servers."

2. By default, volume shadow copies create a shadow copy twice daily. Volume shadow copies can maintain only 64 previous versions, for a total of 32 days in the default configuration. For more information, see the section, "Using Volume Shadow Copy."

3. You need the full backup tape from the previous Friday night and the differential backup tape from Wednesday night. For more information,

see the section, "Backup Methods and Media Rotation."

4. Volume shadow copies also allow you to backup files that are open at the time of the backup. This way, file servers can be backed up without forcing users to close all open files. Open files are backed up in a closed state as they are at that point in time. For more information, see the section, "New Windows Server 2003 Backup Features."

5. You should create a baseline when a new server is placed in operation, after each hardware change and after each software or application modification. For more information, see the section "Baselining Servers."

# Answers to Exam Questions

1. **B.** In addition to tape drives, Windows Backup can also store to any local or network drive. Of the given choices, only the floppy disk is a valid choice. For more information, see the section "Planning Backup and Recovery Operations."

2. **B.** The best thing for you to do at this time would be to configure a counter log that collects information about the performance of the server over the next day or so to use as a baseline for future troubleshooting efforts. This baseline log should contain counters for any pertinent objects that you will likely want to monitor and troubleshoot later, including network, memory, and other objects. You also should consider creating a document that lists all applications and services that are running on the server. This document can be helpful later when you are trying to determine what might be causing changes in perfor-

mance over time. For more information, see the section "Baselining Servers."

3. **C.** You can select to have the System State information backed up to provide recovery protection for all critical operating system files, including those that are required to properly start and operate the operating system. The System State consists of the following items:

- Registry
- COM+ class registration database
- Critical boot and system files
- System files that are protected by Windows File Protection
- Certificate Services database if the server is a Certificate Authority
- Active Directory directory service if the server is a domain controller
- SYSVOL directory if the server is a domain controller
- Cluster service information if the server is a member of a cluster
- IIS metadirectory if IIS is installed on the server

For more information, see the section, "Creating Backup Job Configurations."

4. **C.** The most likely reason for this problem is that you have mistakenly selected the internal loopback interface instead of the actual network interface that the computer is using. By default, the loopback interface is selected if the name of the network interface starts with a letter after *I*. For

more information, see the section, "Introduction to System Monitor."

5. **C.** The Previous Versions tab is available in the Properties dialog box only when the share is accessed over the network or locally using the My Network Places folder. For more information, see the section, "Using Volume Shadow Copy."

6. **C.** Configuring the counter log file format as binary circular causes the log file to overwrite older information when it has reached its maximum allowed size. For more information, see the section "Baselining Servers."

7. **B.** To back up (and hence recover) the Registry, you must back up the System State information for a local server. For more information, see the section, "Creating Backup Job Configurations."

8. **D.** The *yyyymmddhh* log numbering format would provide the easiest method of determining the data and time each counter log was created. For more information, see the section "Baselining Servers."

9. **D.** Volume shadow copies requires at least 100MB of free space on the volume; therefore, you cannot enable volume shadow copies on this file server. For more information, see the section, "Using Volume Shadow Copy."

10. **A, B.** Pages/sec shows how many times per second the server has to go to the hard drive to recover information it thought ought to be in memory but has been swapped out because of a shortage of memory. % Usage of the paging file can be an indicator of low memory because, if it constantly decreases as applications run, the amount of RAM is not sufficient to fill the demand on the server, which causes the paging

file to be increased in size. For more information, see the section "Daily Monitoring for Usage."

11. **E.** Incremental backups look to see the current status of the archive bit before backing up data. If the archive bit is False, an incremental backup skips the file because it has been backed up. If the archive bit is True, an incremental backup saves the file and sets its archive bit to False. If Andrea changes a file and then runs two incremental backups in a row, only the first backs up the file. The second encounters the False archive bit set by the first incremental backup and skips the file. For more information, see the section "Backup Methods and Media Rotation."

12. **B.** Normal backups (sometimes called full backups) save all files regardless of the state of the archive bit. While saving the files, normal backups set the archive bit to False to indicate that the files have been backed up. This means that if Christopher were to do two normal backups in a row, both would save all the data, and both would set the archive bits to False. For more information, see the section "Daily Monitoring for Usage."

13. **C.** Paging File\ % Usage is the ratio of the amount of paging file being used to the total size of the paging file. A high number is desired here because it indicates that the paging file is sized correctly for the system. If this number is low, either the paging file has been set too large (and is, therefore, consuming more disk space than is necessary) or the paging file has been recently resized. For more information, see the section "Daily Monitoring for Usage."

14. **B, C.** In this case, given the counter options list-

ed, these two choices are the best options. With these two counters, Hannah can troubleshoot low disk space and fragmentation issues. Logical Disk\ % Free Space is the ratio of free space total disk space on a logical drive, which is a measurement of remaining capacity on your logical drives. Hannah usually should track this for each logical drive. To prevent excessive fragmentation, the value here should not be allowed to drop below 10%. Physical Disk\Split IO/sec reports the rate at which the operating system divides I/O requests to the disk into multiple requests. A split I/O request might occur if the program requests data in a size that is too large to fit into a single request or if the disk is fragmented. Factors that influence the size of an I/O request can include application design, the file system, and drivers. A high rate of split I/O might not, in itself, represent a problem. However, on single-disk systems, a high rate for this counter tends to indicate disk fragmentation. For more information, see the section "Daily Monitoring for Usage."

15. **B.** The Automated System Restore (ASR) feature is new in Windows Server 2003 and provides a means to restore a server in the event that all other methods fail or are not available for use. You should consider ASR as a last option and use it only after Safe Mode, Recovery Console, and the Last Known Good Configuration (LKGC) have failed. The ASR set consists of a startup floppy disk and a standard Windows Backup file. In addition to these two items, you also need your original Windows Server 2003 installation CD-ROM and any mass storage device drivers (on floppy disk) to perform an ASR recovery action. For more information, see the section

## APPLY YOUR KNOWLEDGE

### Suggested Readings and Resources

"Using Automated System Recovery."

1. Storage Services Technology Center,
   `http://www.microsoft.com/`
   `windowsserver2003/technologies/storage/`
   `default.mspx.`

2. Microsoft Corporation. 2003. *Microsoft Windows Server 2003 Deployment Kit.*

   Redmond, WA: Microsoft Press. ISBN: 0735614865.

3. Stanek, William R. 2003. *Windows Server 2003 Administrator's Pocket Consultant.* Redmond, WA: Microsoft Press. ISBN: 0735613540.

Planning and implementing network security methods do not end after you've implemented the security solutions discussed previously in Chapter 1, "Planning and Implementing Server Roles and Server Security." You still must ensure a handful of other issues are taken care of before your network is to be considered secure. Secure, however, is a relative term and one that is defined by the business and organizational requirements in place in your organization.

Microsoft defines the network security portion of the "Planning, Implementing, and Maintaining Routing and Remote Access" objective and the "Planning and Maintaining Network Security" objective as follows:

**Plan secure network administration methods.**

- **Create a plan to offer Remote Assistance to client computers.**

- **Plan for remote administration by using Terminal Services.**

▶ In today's distributed computing world, no longer can administrators easily or efficiently travel to all locations within an organization. The ability to remotely assist users and administer computers in real time gives administrators much more flexibility and offers them a means to better care for their network.

**Plan security for wireless networks.**

▶ The rapid and widespread introduction of IEEE 802.11–based wireless networks has caused serious problems for those networks without a solid wireless network security plan. The power and utility of the wireless network also account for its threat and danger. Windows Server 2003 provides new Group Policy–based features that provide a good first step toward mitigating the threats posed by wireless networks.

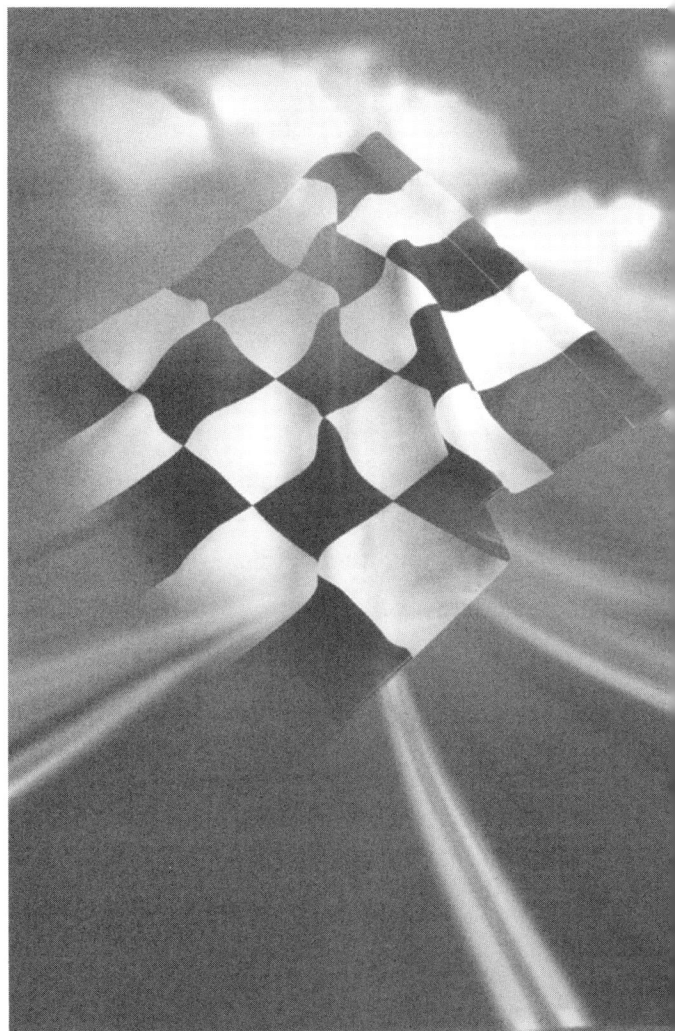

CHAPTER 7

# Planning and Maintaining Network Security

**Configure network protocol security.**

- **Configure protocol security in a heterogeneous client computer environment.**

- **Configure protocol security by using IPSec policies.**

**Configure security for data transmission.**

- **Configure IPSec policy settings.**

**Plan security for data transmission.**

- **Secure data transmission between client computers to meet security requirements.**

- **Secure data transmission by using IPSec.**

**Plan for network protocol security.**

- **Specify the required ports and protocols for specified services.**

- **Plan an IPSec policy for secure network communications.**

▶ IP Security (IPSec) is the de facto standard for security network transmissions in both heterogeneous and homogenous network environments. IPSec can be used to provide secure network connections, both internal to your network and external to your network. IPSec operates in two modes, transport and tunnel, depending on where the endpoints in a communication lie in relation to each other. IPSec is fully supported in Windows Server 2003, and three preconfigured IPSec policies are supplied to get you going quickly. It is important for you to understand not only how to implement and configure IPSec for this exam, but also for you to secure your network as well.

**Troubleshoot security for data transmission. Tools might include the IP Security Monitor MMC snap-in and the Resultant Set of Policy (RSoP) MMC snap-in.**

▶ Unfortunately, nothing works right all the time; IPSec is no exception. Using improperly configured IPSec policies is a quick way to bring all normal network traffic to a screeching halt. Windows Server 2003 provides the IP Security Monitor and the Resultant Set of Policy snap-in to monitor and troubleshoot IPSec-related traffic issues.

▶ Become familiar with the concepts of Remote Assistance and Remote Desktop for Administration. Not only will these two new technologies save you time and trouble in your daily job, but they also are very important on this exam.

▶ Set up two computers—preferably both Windows Server 2003, but one can be a Windows XP Professional computer—to practice sending and accepting Remote Assistance requests.

▶ Set up two computers—preferably both Windows Server 2003, but one can be a Windows XP Professional computer—to practice using Remote Desktop for Administration.

▶ If you have a wireless LAN at your disposal, be sure to create and implement a WLAN security policy.

▶ Carefully work your way through the material discussing the component parts of an IPSec policy. Practice creating and implementing an IPSec policy between two computers on your network.

▶ Get your hands dirty. The Step by Steps throughout this book provide plenty of directions and exercises, but go beyond these examples and create some of your own. If you can, experiment with each of the objectives to see how they work and why you would use each one.

# INTRODUCTION

Although we examined the basics of network security in Chapter 1, we have much more to talk about in regards to securing your network; that is the topic of this chapter. This chapter, however, is not the end-all when it comes to security or securing your Windows Server 2003 network. Many volumes have been written on this topic, but we seek to examine only a small sampling of the overall subject area in this chapter that is directly related to the objectives for this exam.

# PLANNING SECURE REMOTE ADMINISTRATION METHODS

One of the features that Microsoft has been slowly developing since Windows 2000 first appeared is that of built-in remote administrative capabilities. No longer do you have to purchase and install a costly third-party application to provide remote administrative access to your servers and workstations; Windows XP and Windows Server 2003 support it natively, as does the Windows 2000 Server line after you install Terminal Services in Remote Administration mode. Better yet, Windows XP and Windows Server 2003 also include Remote Desktop, which further takes advantage of the *Remote Desktop Protocol (RDP)*, allowing users to connect to a computer remotely as if they were actually using it locally.

In this section, we examine two key parts of the Terminal Services/Remote Desktop Protocol combination: *Remote Assistance* and *Remote Desktop for Administration*. Both are installed by default with an installation of Windows Server 2003; however, both must be manually enabled and configured prior to use.

## Remote Assistance

**Plan secure network administration methods.**

▶ **Create a plan to offer Remote Assistance to client computers.**

Remote Assistance, first introduced in Windows XP, provides a built-in mechanism allowing an "Expert" to lend assistance to a "Novice" whether by request or not. The Expert can be located on the same internal network or even somewhere else on the Internet. Remote Assistance allows the Expert to create a connection to the Novice's computer, view the desktop, communicate with the Novice, and even take remote control of the Novice's computer if the Novice allows. Remote Assistance can be performed only on computers running Windows XP or Windows Server 2003—a good reason to consider that desktop upgrade to Windows XP. Before a computer is eligible to receive Remote Assistance, however, it must be enabled either locally or by Group Policy.

Assuming that Group Policy has not been configured from its default setting for Remote Assistance, you can enable it on the local computer by selecting the Allow Remote Assistance Invitations to Be Sent from This Computer option on the Remote tab of the System Properties applet (located in the Control Panel), as shown in Figure 7.1.

**FIGURE 7.1**
Remote Assistance must be enabled and configured before it can be used.

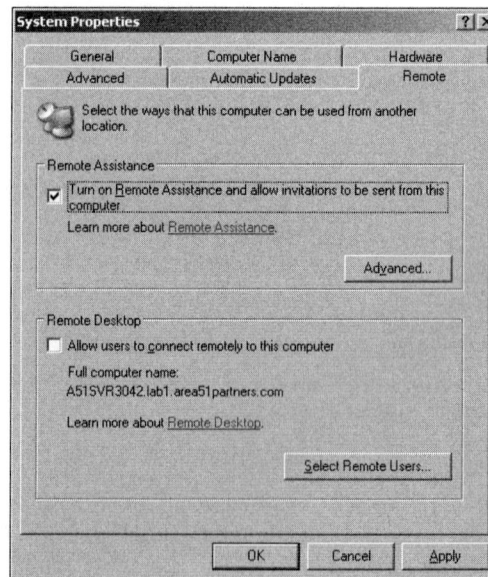

Clicking the Advanced button opens the Remote Assistance Settings dialog box, which allows you to further configure Remote Assistance settings. From this dialog box, you have the option to allow the computer to be remotely controlled during the Remote Assistance session; to do so, select the Allow This Computer to Be Controlled Remotely option. You can also configure the length of time that the Remote Assistance requests are valid.

Alternatively, you can configure Group Policy to control the Remote Assistance settings for your entire domain or by specific domains. The settings you need to configure are located in the Computer Configuration, Administrative Templates, System, Remote Assistance node, as shown in Figure 7.2. If settings are configured via Group Policy, the option to configure them locally using the System Properties applet is not available. Recall that Group Policy is applied in the following order: local, site, domain, Organizational Unit.

> **EXAM TIP**
>
> **Enabling Remote Assistance** Be sure that you know and understand the two different ways that Remote Assistance can be enabled and configured.

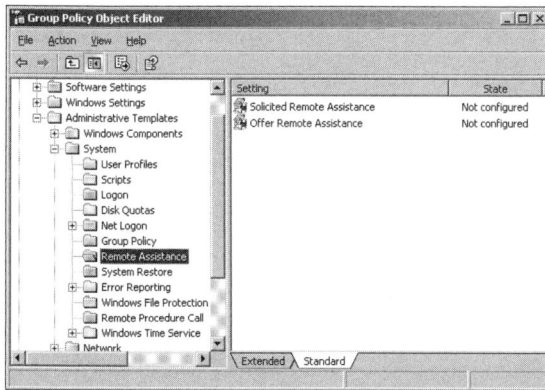

**FIGURE 7.2**
Remote Assistance can be configured using Group Policy.

The Solicited Remote Assistance setting shown in Figure 7.2 allows Remote Assistance requests to be sent from the computers that the Group Policy Object (GPO) is applied to. The Offer Remote Assistance setting shown in Figure 7.2 allows Remote Assistance to be offered without a prior request to computers that the GPO is applied to. The user (Novice) still has the option to allow or disallow the Remote Assistance offer.

## Configuring Remote Assistance Policies

To configure Remote Assistance policies using Group Policy—always the preferred method—perform the steps outlined in Step by Step 7.1.

# STEP BY STEP

## 7.1 Configuring Remote Assistance via Group Policy

1. Locate the Group Policy Object for which you want to configure the Remote Assistance settings.

2. Expand the following nodes: Computer Configuration, Administrative Templates, System, Remote Assistance.

3. Double-click the Solicited Remote Assistance setting to open its Properties dialog box, as shown in Figure 7.3.

**FIGURE 7.3**
The Solicited Remote Assistance setting allows the computer's users to request Remote Assistance.

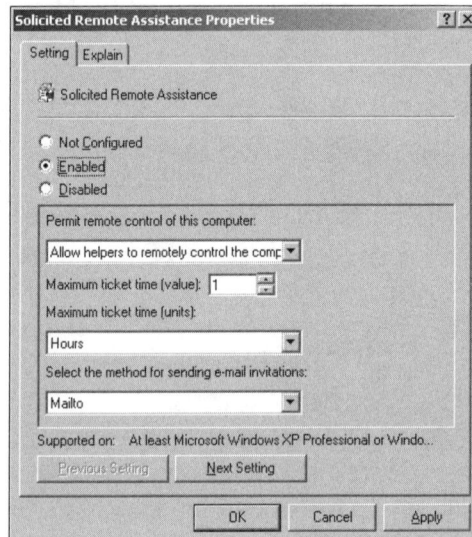

4. Select the Enabled radio button.

5. For the Permit Remote Control of This Computer option, select Allow Helpers to Remotely Control the Computer to ensure that your Experts can fully offer Remote Assistance as needed. The Expert can take control only if the Novice allows it.

6. For the Maximum Ticket Time option, configure a reasonable lifetime for the Remote Assistance request, such as one hour. This setting allows the Expert a window in which to respond to the request without creating an overly large security risk.

**7.** For the Select the Method for Sending E-mail Invitations option, your selection depends on the messaging client in use on your network. The Mailto option configures the Remote Assistance request to be sent as an Internet link and works in virtually all situations. The SMAPI (Simple MAPI) option configures the request to be attached to the message.

**8.** Click OK to close the Solicited Remote Assistance Properties dialog box.

**9.** Double-click the Offer Remote Assistance setting to open its Properties dialog box, as shown in Figure 7.4.

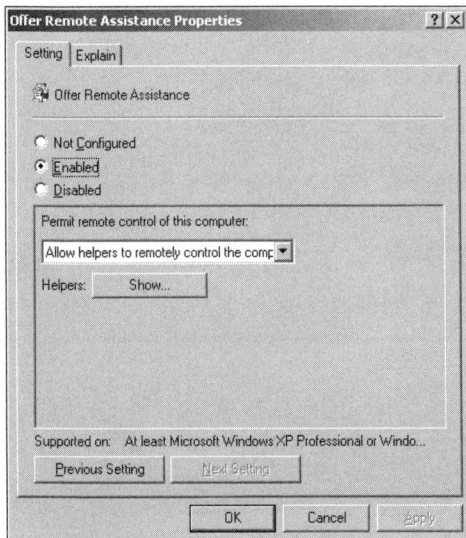

**FIGURE 7.4**
The Offer Remote Assistance setting allows Experts to offer unsolicited Remote Assistance to users.

**10.** To allow Experts to offer unsolicited Remote Assistance to users, select the Enabled radio button.

**11.** For the Permit Remote Control of This Computer option, select Allow Helpers to Remotely Control the Computer to ensure that your Experts can fully offer Remote Assistance as needed. The Expert can take control only if the Novice allows it.

**12.** Click the Show button to open the Show Contents dialog box, as shown in Figure 7.5.

*continues*

*continued*

**FIGURE 7.5**
You can allow users and groups to offer unsolicited Remote Assistance.

13. To add users and/or groups, click the Add button. You can add only one object at a time, and you must use the following format:

    *<Domain Name>\<User Name>* or

    *<Domain Name>\<Group Name>*

14. After you are done adding users and/or groups, click OK to close the Show Contents dialog box.

15. Click OK to close the Offer Remote Assistance Properties dialog box.

## Sending and Managing Remote Assistance Requests

Users can request Remote Assistance in three basic ways: Windows Messenger, email (sends a URL), or file (creates a Remote Assistance request file). Note that Windows Messenger is not the same as Microsoft Messenger, although both use similar technologies. You can most easily send Remote Assistance requests by using the Help and Support Center, which you can access by clicking Start, Help and Support. On the main page, click the Remote Assistance link under the Support Tasks column. The Remote Assistance window is shown in Figure 7.6.

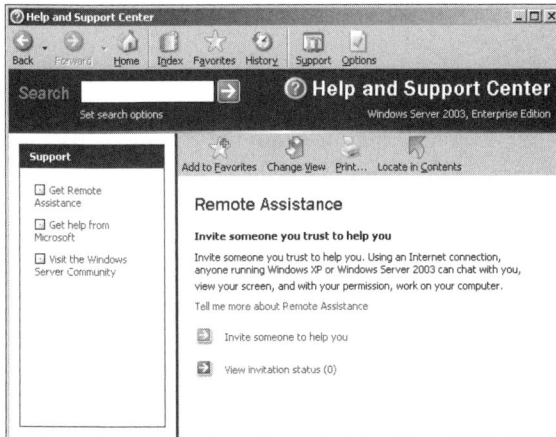

**FIGURE 7.6**
Remote Assistance requests can be easily sent and managed from within the Help and Support Center.

To send a Remote Assistance request, perform the steps outlined in Step by Step 7.2.

---

# STEP BY STEP

### 7.2 Sending a Remote Assistance Request

1. Open the Help and Support Center by clicking Start, Help and Support.

2. Click the Remote Assistance link under the Support Tasks column.

3. On the Remote Assistance window, shown in Figure 7.6, click the Invite Someone to Help You link.

4. The most common way to ask for Remote Assistance is to use Windows Messenger because you can easily see who might be available to help you. Note that Windows Messenger is not installed in Windows Server 2003, and no Windows Server 2003 version exists at the time of this writing. You can download the Windows XP version (which works perfectly in Windows Server 2003) from `microsoft.com/windows/messenger/download.asp`.

5. The Remote Assistance window changes, allowing you to pick how to contact the assistant (the Expert). As you can see, Windows Messenger, email, and file methods are available.

*continues*

*continued*

**6.** Selecting a Windows Messenger user and clicking Invite This Person opens the Windows Messenger window on the Expert's computer with the Remote Assistance request, as shown in Figure 7.7. The Expert can then accept or decline the invitation, thus beginning the Remote Assistance session.

**FIGURE 7.7**
The Expert receives the Remote Assistance request in his or her Windows Messenger window.

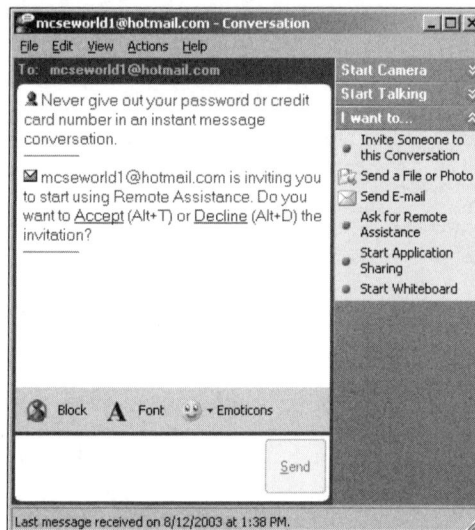

**7.** Alternatively, you can opt to send an email request using a MAPI-compliant messaging application, such as Outlook or Outlook Express, by entering the Expert's first name and clicking Continue.

**8.** On the next window, you can enter a password and duration for the request to remain valid. Click the Create E-mail Invitation button to proceed.

**9.** A new email message opens. You need to enter the correct email address and add any other notes you want before sending the message. The Expert can initiate the Remote Assistance request by clicking the URL in the message and is then required to download and install an ActiveX applet from the Microsoft Web site as part of the process.

**10.** Your last option is to create a Remote Assistance file and either give the file to the Expert or place it in a location where the Expert can access it, such as on a file share. You can create the Remote Assistance file by clicking Send Invitation as a File (Advanced). You can configure the name of the Expert, the duration the request should remain valid, and a password as well when creating the saved file. Remote Assistance request saved files have the `*.msrcincident` file extension.

---

You can view and manage Remote Assistance requests by clicking the View Invitation Status Link (*x*) shown previously in Figure 7.6. The *x* represents the number of Remote Assistance requests you have to manage. Clicking this link changes the window to the one shown in Figure 7.8.

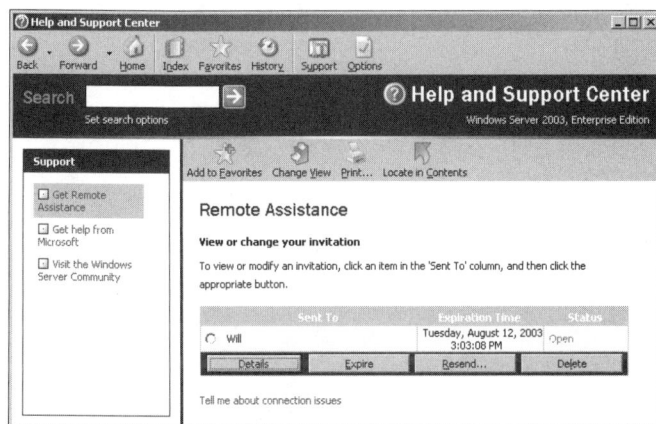

**FIGURE 7.8**
You can quickly and easily manage all your Remote Assistance requests.

For each Remote Assistance request, the following options are available:

▶ **Details**—Allows you to view details about the request, including to whom it was sent, when it was sent, when it will expire, what its current status is, and whether it is password protected.

▶ **Expire**—Allows you to force an open request to expire immediately, regardless of its configured duration.

▶ **Resend**—Allows you to resend an expired request. Resending expired requests allows you to easily send the same request again without needing to re-enter all the required details.

▶ **Delete**—Allows you to permanently delete the request.

## Using Remote Assistance

Regardless of how the Remote Assistance request is sent, the results are all the same. After the Expert accepts the request, a direct connection is made between the Expert's computer and the Novice's computer. This allows the Expert to communicate directly with the Novice and to see the Novice's desktop in view-only mode, as shown in Figure 7.9.

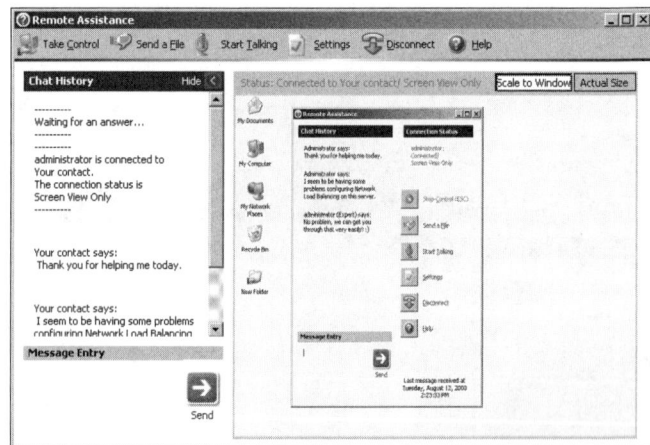

The following control buttons are available to the Expert:

▶ **Take Control**—Sends a request to the Novice to allow the Expert to take control of the Novice's computer.

▶ **Send a File**—Allows the Expert to transmit a file from the Expert's computer to the Novice's computer. This capability is useful for sending updates and such.

▶ **Start Talking**—Establishes an audio connection between the Expert and Novice similar to that offered in Windows Messenger or Net Meeting.

▶ **Settings**—Allows the Expert to configure the Remote Assistance settings for his or her computer.

▶ **Disconnect**—Terminates the Remote Assistance session and closes the direct connection between the two computers.

▶ **Help**—Displays Remote Assistance help.

The following control buttons are available to the Novice:

▶ **Stop Control**—Terminates the Expert's ability to remotely control the computer.

▶ **Send a File**—Allows the Novice to transmit a file from the Novice's computer to the Expert's computer.

▶ **Start Talking**—Establishes an audio connection between the Expert and Novice similar to that offered in Windows Messenger or Net Meeting.

▶ **Settings**—Allows the Novice to configure the Remote Assistance settings for his or her computer.

▶ **Disconnect**—Terminates the Remote Assistance session and closes the direct connection between the two computers.

▶ **Help**—Displays Remote Assistance help.

## Remote Assistance Security Concerns

Remote Assistance, like all the Terminal Services and Remote Desktop Protocol–based applications, requires that TCP port 3389 be available to make a connection. This raises the question of whether you want to leave this port open on your external firewalls. Logic says no. By closing this port on your external firewalls, you can instantly prevent the largest security risk associated with Remote Assistance: compromise by unauthorized external entities. In most cases, there is no reason why any person physically located outside your protected, private internal network should be tasked with providing Remote Assistance. Should this situation arise, consider implementing leased WAN links directly between sites or using permanent VPN connections to give some extra measure of security.

| EXAM TIP | **Remote Desktop Protocol** Don't forget that all RDP-based applications, including Remote Assistance and Remote Desktop, use TCP port 3389. This may be an important fact on your exam. |

But what do you do about the Remote Assistance request itself? The email is sent by default as a standard email message and thus is subject to capture. The Remote Assistance files are simply XML files that are easily taken apart once captured. Email messages can be, and should be, digitally signed and encrypted. If you are using Exchange 2000 or later with Outlook 2000 or later on your network, the fix is easy. If you are not, consider acquiring a personal email certificate or using Pretty Good Privacy (PGP) or some other message encryption and signing utility. The Remote Assistance files should be protected by whatever means are available, including NTFS permissions, EFS encryption, or other third-party methods. Recall that Windows XP and Windows Server 2003 allow for multiple EFS users to have access to the same file.

# GUIDED PRACTICE
# EXERCISE 7.1

In this exercise, you configure the Group Policy options for Remote Assistance. This Guided Practice helps reinforce the preceding discussion. You want to allow your users to solicit Remote Assistance. You also want to allow the Expert user to take control of the Novice's computer. However, you do not want to allow for unsolicited Remote Assistance. You want all settings to be applied to your entire domain.

You should try completing this exercise on your own first. If you get stuck, or you would like to see one possible solution, follow these steps:

1. Open the Active Directory Users and Computers console.

2. Right-click the domain node and select Properties. Create a new Group Policy Object from the Group Policy tab.

3. Expand the GPO to locate the Remote Assistance node by expanding these nodes: Computer Configuration, Administrative Templates, System.

4. Open the Solicited Remote Assistance Properties dialog box and enable solicited Remote Assistance.

5. Select the Allow Helpers to Remotely Control the Computer option to ensure that your Experts can fully offer Remote Assistance as needed. (The Expert can take control only if the Novice allows it.)

6. Configure the Maximum Ticket Time option with a reasonable lifetime, such as one hour.

7. In the Select the Method for Sending E-mail Invitations area, select the method that best suits the messaging client on your network. The Mailto option configures the Remote Assistance request to be sent as an Internet link and works in virtually all situations. The SMAPI (Simple MAPI) option configures the request to be attached to the message.

8. Close the Solicited Remote Assistance Properties dialog box.

9. Open the Offer Remote Assistance Properties dialog box and disable the ability to offer unsolicited Remote Assistance.

10. Close the Offer Remote Assistance Properties dialog box.

# Remote Desktop for Administration (RDA)

**Plan secure network administration methods.**

▶ **Plan for remote administration by using Terminal Services.**

Remote Desktop for Administration, previously referred to as Remote Administration mode in Windows 2000, provides a built-in method to remotely administer and control servers. Provided you have the correct credentials, you can even remotely restart or shut down a server. Of course, you probably ought to warn any users who might be connected to it before doing such!

You can use Remote Desktop for Administration in one of two ways. The first and simplest (although less feature-rich) method is to use the Remote Desktop Connection utility, which you can find by clicking Start, Programs, Accessories, Communications, Remote Desktop Connection. After you click the Options button, the Remote Desktop Connection dialog box opens, as shown in Figure 7.10.

**FIGURE 7.10**

The Remote Desktop Connection utility allows you to quickly and easily create a connection to a remote computer.

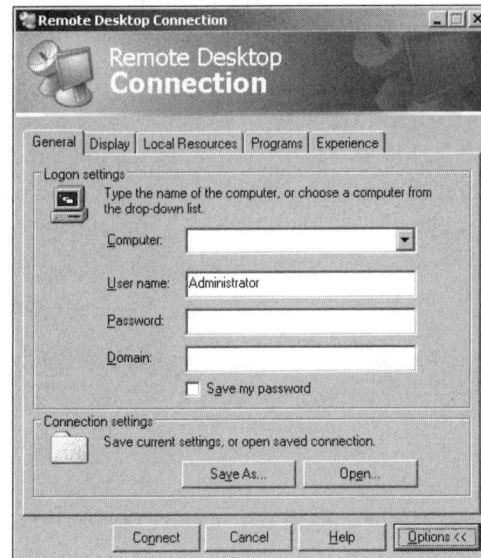

By entering the computer's name or IP address and clicking Connect, you can make a Remote Desktop for Administration connection. You may be required to supply your network credentials to complete the connection and logon process. Figure 7.11 shows what the Remote Desktop connection looks like when not in full-screen mode.

The second method for creating Remote Desktop for Administration connections is to use the new Remote Desktops console. This method offers two features that Windows administrators have been clamoring for since the introduction of Terminal Services:

▶ **Multiple connection profiles can be created.** You can configure multiple connections in the Remote Desktops console and then switch through them quickly and easily, all within the confines of a single window. The multiple windows required when using the Remote Desktop Connection utility or the Terminal Services client are not required.

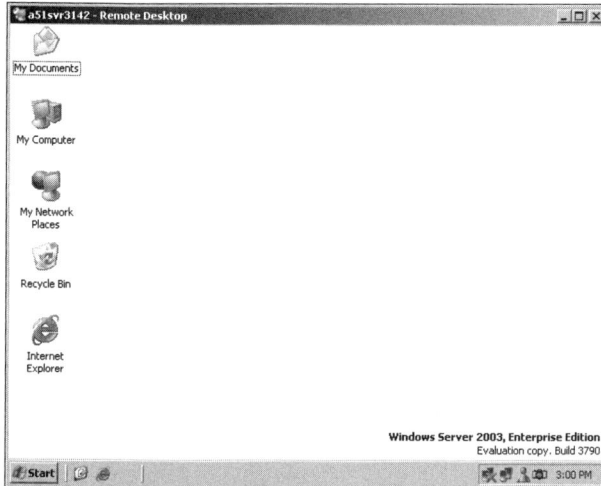

**FIGURE 7.11**
The Remote Desktop for Administration window can be full screen or smaller if you like.

▶ **Connections are made directly to the console session.** In the past, Terminal Services connections could not be made to the console session, preventing many administrators from using Terminal Services for remote administration or prompting the use of third-party applications such as PC Anywhere or VNC. Windows Server 2003, using the Remote Desktops console, now creates connections to the console session, allowing administrators to view messages and pop-ups that are not redirected to any other session. You can also use the /console switch on the Remote Desktop Client to create a console connection.

The Remote Desktops console is shown in Figure 7.12, with a connection in progress.

## RDA Security and Management Issues

Remote Desktop for Administration, like Terminal Services Administration mode before it, is fairly restrictive in who can use it and how it can be used:

▶ Only administrators can create Remote Desktop for Administration connections by default; this is a good thing. You want the number of users with this power to be as small as possible to minimize the risk of an attacker gaining complete control over your network. Access control is handled

**EXAM TIP**

**Connecting to the console** The ability to connect to the console session using the Remote Desktop Client or the Remote Desktops console is an important new feature to remember. You should keep in mind what the console session allows you that other remote connections do not—namely the ability to receive messages and pop-ups that are displayed only on the console session.

**Remote Desktop Web Connection utility** It's important to note that the Windows 2000 Terminal Services Web Client is still around in Windows Server 2003—although with a new name and many improvements. It is now known as Remote Desktop Web Connection utility.

through membership in the Remote and *both* Desktop Users group.

▶ Only two Remote Desktop sessions can exist on a computer, and both active and disconnected (but still running) sessions count toward this number. This restriction exists so that the number of concurrent changes being made to a computer is minimized to prevent configuration errors and conflicts. However, this does present a potential for a Denial of Service (DoS) attack against a computer—or at least the Remote Desktop portion. In addition to these two connections, one additional connection can exist to the server's console session.

**FIGURE 7.12**
The Remote Desktops console is the best way to manage multiple servers remotely.

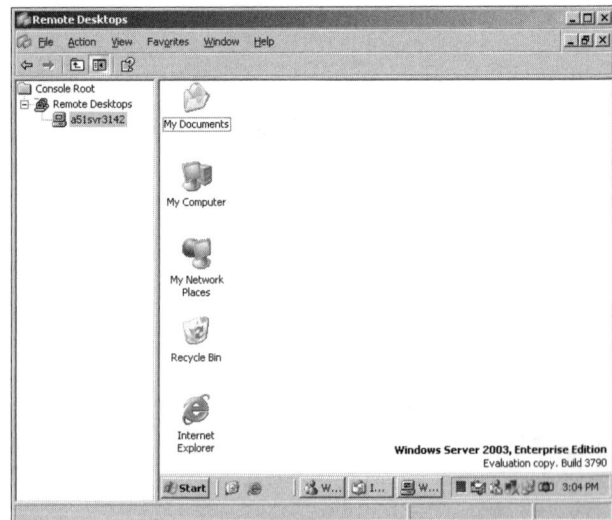

Because administrators have the ability to create Remote Desktop connections by default, the use of these accounts should be minimized. Administrators should use their administrative accounts only when absolutely required and, even then, should make judicious use of the Run As command. This just makes for good network security sense and is part of the *principle of least privilege*. Using the principle of least privilege, a compromised user account has a smaller impact on the overall security of the network than if you were to blanket-assign to users permissions that they did not need. Ideally, all normal user operations should be carried out in the context of a User account. If additional privileges are required for a specific reason, the administrator can either log in to the network with a special account

**EXAM TIP**

**Limited connections** Remember that you can establish only two regular Remote Desktop connections to a server. You can establish one additional session to a console. Additional sessions cannot be created as long as these limits have been met; this can lead to problems if administrators do not properly end their Remote Assistance sessions.

for the purpose of performing those actions or use the Run As command to perform those actions within the context of the account that has the additional privileges. You also should enforce strong security precautions and account lockout policies on all accounts that have the ability to connect using Remote Desktop; Chapter 8, "Planning, Implementing, and Maintaining Security Infrastructure," discusses this topic in more detail.

Although the Remote Desktop Connection utility offers the ability to create and save connection configurations on a local computer, this practice should be avoided if at all possible. Connection configurations are saved to a computer that contain all the Remote Desktop Connection settings in a plain-text file with the file extension of *.RDP. Although the password, if entered, is encoded, it is only a matter of time before an application is written that can quickly decode this information. Even if an attacker does not decode the password, all required information is available to establish the Remote Desktop connection and begin wreaking havoc on your network.

Questions that often arise with Remote Desktop are "What do we do about disconnected sessions?" and "How long should the timeout value be for these disconnected sessions?" There are no hard and fast answers for these questions. Consider the situation in which an administrator has made a Remote Desktop connection to a server and begun the process of applying a service pack. After starting the installation, the administrator disconnects from the server and begins working on another server. Would you really want to impose a timeout limit on this session or manually terminate the session? You must spend some time considering the requirements of your network and the ways you will meet them to avoid problems down the road.

Specific users can configure session timeout values as granular, so this is an option that you may want to configure. A special shared administrative account that has no timeout values configured on it can be used; when this account is used to create a Remote Desktop connection, all operations can proceed without danger of automatically timing out. This also allows individual administrators to make connections to the server as required to perform other tasks, provided that they log off the server when they are finished. Remember that shutting down or restarting a server from a Remote Desktop session results in that action occurring on the server if the user has the required permissions, so be careful when using the Shut Down Windows dialog box.

NOTE

**Where do Windows Server 2003 WLAN Policies fit in?** Although the Wireless LAN (WLAN) security functionality provided in Windows Server 2003 is in no way intended to replace a dedicated solution available from a company that specializes in WLAN technologies, it is a good start for smaller organizations and a nice addition to existing security measures in larger organizations.

# PLANNING WIRELESS LAN (WLAN) SECURITY

### Plan security for wireless networks.

It's an inescapable fact of today's computing environment that users want to be connected while on the move. For users, this means the power to move freely about an office or even an entire building without being wired to the wall anymore. For administrators this usually means headaches, heartaches, and visions of hackers silently sifting through the network. Fortunately, the latter doesn't have to be the case.

In Windows Server 2003, administrators can now use Group Policy to design and implement security policies to secure 802.11 Wireless LANs. The use of both Wired Equivalent Privacy (WEP) and 802.1x authentication is supported. The Group Policy options that are configured in a GPO and applied to a computer then take precedence over any user-configured settings, thus ensuring that your configuration is applied. You can create policies for three types of Wireless LANs:

▶ **Access Point (infrastructure)**—The most common type of Wireless LAN, the infrastructure mode WLAN, consists of wireless clients communicating directly with wireless Access Points (APs). No direct client-to-client communications exist. This is considered to be the most secure type of WLAN.

▶ **Computer-to-computer (ad hoc)**—Ad hoc WLANs consist of wireless clients communicating directly with each other without the use of an AP in the middle. This type of communication does not provide a direct path to the wired network.

▶ **Any available network Access Point preferred**—This option configures the policy to attempt a connection to an Access Point first if one is available. If an AP is not available, the client attempts to create an ad hoc connection if possible. This method is least preferred and usually most problematic over time.

You can locate the Wireless LAN Group Policy options, shown in Figure 7.13, in the Computer Configuration, Windows Settings, Security Settings node. By default, no policies are defined, meaning that you must create and configure them as your network requires. We examine this process later in this section.

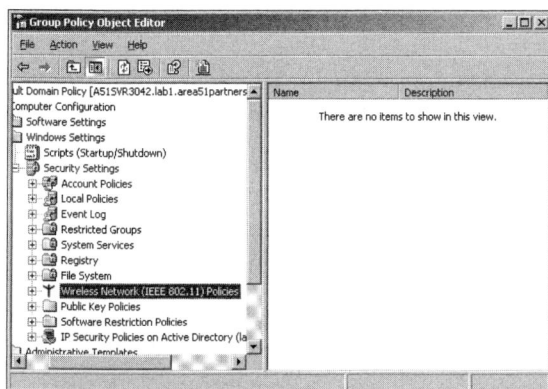

**FIGURE 7.13**
You can now configure Wireless LAN policies for your Windows Server 2003 and Windows XP Professional computers.

Before creating a policy, you should spend some time planning for it first. Wireless LANs are great when implemented and secured properly. Fail to plan properly for the security of your WLAN, and you should just as well plan to fail. When you are preparing to implement WLAN security policies, consider the following key points in regards to authentication issues:

▶ Your Access Points must support the authentication method that you intend to use, such as 802.1x.

▶ Your clients and RADIUS servers must all support the same authentication method, such as EAP-TLS or PEAP over 802.1x.

▶ Computers should always be authenticated. This setting, by default, is enabled.

▶ If using EAP-TLS (recommended), you should consider allowing the autoenrollment of certificates for users and computers. Autoenrollment makes the process much simpler.

**Authentication methods**   You should be aware of the various authentication methods afforded you in Windows Server 2003, both for wireless and wired networks. This topic was discussed in more detail in Chapter 4, "Planning, Implementing, and Maintaining Routing and Remote Access."

When configuring and implementing WLAN security policies via Group Policy, you need to keep the following points in mind about how they behave:

▶ Configurations made in Group Policy Objects take precedence over user-configured settings, with the exception of the preferred networks list. The preferred networks lists are merged together from the GPO settings and the user-configured settings to form a composite list. When the network list is merged, infrastructure networks always have higher precedence than ad hoc networks. Also, the user can change the configured Wired Equivalent Privacy (WEP) key that is assigned per Group Policy.

▶ As with all GPOs, non-administrators cannot remove or disable the policy so that it does not apply to them. This also holds true for administrators.

▶ When GPO-configured WLAN settings are changed, the client connection is momentarily broken (the client is disassociated) if the new policy takes precedence over the old policy.

▶ When GPO-configured WLAN settings are removed (when the GPO is deleted or the link is removed), the client is disassociated while the Wireless Configuration service performs a soft reset and clears its cache. When the service restarts, the client reverts to any existing client-configured settings in place.

▶ When a client is subject to multiple GPOs at various levels that assign WLAN settings, the normal Group Policy processing order applies. The GPO that is closest to the computer object takes precedence and overrides the settings that are assigned to a higher-level Active Directory container.

With your initial planning out of the way, you can begin the process of creating WLAN security policies using Group Policy as outlined in Step by Step 7.3.

## STEP BY STEP

### 7.3 Configuring a Wireless Network Policy

**1.** Using either the Group Policy Management Console (GPMC) or Group Policy Editor (GPE), locate the GPO in which you want to create the WLAN security policy.

**2.** Expand the Computer Configuration, Windows Settings, Security Settings nodes in the GPO to locate the Wireless Network (IEEE 802.11) Policies node. Right-click it and select Create Wireless Network Policy from the context menu to start the Wireless Network Policy Wizard.

**3.** Click Next to dismiss the opening page of the wizard.

**4.** Enter a name and description for the new policy on the Wireless Network Policy Name dialog box. Click Next to continue.

**5.** The Completing the Wireless Network Policy Wizard dialog box appears. Ensure that the Edit Properties option is selected and click Finish to exit the wizard and start configuring the policy's properties.

**6.** The policy Properties dialog box opens with the options available as discussed in Table 7.1. Configure your selections as you like per the information in Table 7.1 and switch to the Preferred Networks tab.

**7.** Click the Add button to open the New Preferred Setting Properties dialog box.

**8.** On the Network Properties tab, shown in Figure 7.14, configure the selections as necessary per the information in Table 7.2. When you are done, switch to the IEEE 802.1x tab.

**9.** On the IEEE 802.1x tab, shown in Figure 7.15, configure the selections as necessary per the information in Table 7.3. When you are done, click OK to commit the preferred network to the policy.

*continues*

*continued*

**FIGURE 7.14**
Creating a new preferred network starts with entering basic configuration items.

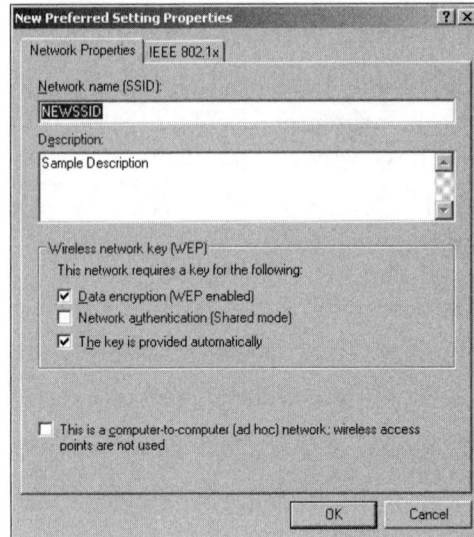

**FIGURE 7.15**
When using 802.1x authentication, you have several configuration options available to you.

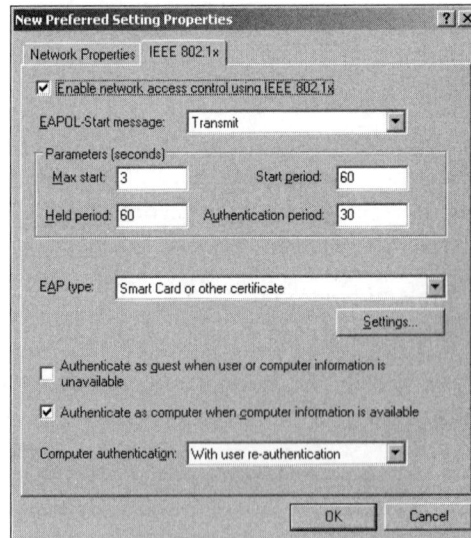

**10.** Back at the Preferred Networks tab of the policy Properties dialog box, you can add another preferred network if you want. You can also remove or edit existing preferred network entries as well as change their relative order by using the Move Up and Move Down buttons.

**11.** Click OK to close the WLAN policy Properties dialog box.

**12.** If you want to force Active Directory replication to occur, thus implementing your new WLAN policies, enter the `gpupdate /target:computer` command.

Table 7.1 outlines the configuration options that are available on the General tab of the Wireless LAN Properties dialog box, as discussed in step 6 of the Wireless Network Policy creation process.

### TABLE 7.1

### OPTIONS AVAILABLE ON THE GENERAL TAB OF THE WLAN PROPERTIES DIALOG BOX

| *Option* | *Description* |
| --- | --- |
| Name | Allows you to specify a descriptive name for the policy. |
| Description | Allows you to enter a longer description of the policy. |
| Check for policy changes every | Configures how often Active Directory should be polled to check for changes to this security policy. The default value is 180 minutes and is acceptable in most instances. |
| Network to access | Specifies the types of Wireless LANs that you want to allow clients to make connections to. You have the following available options:<br>• Any available network (access point preferred)<br>• Access point (infrastructure) networks only<br>• Computer-to-computer (ad hoc) networks only |
| Use Windows to configure wireless network settings for clients | Configures whether client settings are automatically configured for a client's 802.11 WLAN connections by the Wireless Configuration service. |
| Automatically connect to non-preferred networks | Configures whether clients can connect to other 802.11 WLANs for which they are in range. |

Table 7.2 outlines the configuration options that are available on the Network Properties tab of the New Preferred Setting Properties dialog box, as discussed in step 8 of the Wireless Network Policy creation process.

**TABLE 7.2**

**OPTIONS AVAILABLE ON THE NETWORK PROPERTIES TAB OF THE NEW PREFERRED SETTING PROPERTIES DIALOG BOX**

| Option | Description |
| --- | --- |
| Network name (SSID) | Specifies the Service Set Identifier (SSID) of the Wireless LAN. This value must exactly match the SSID value being used by your Access Points and wireless clients. |
| Description | Allows you to enter a longer description of the WLAN. |
| Wireless network key (WEP) | Specifies that a WEP key is required for the available options:<br>• **Data Encryption (WEP enabled)**—This option specifies that a WEP key is used to encrypt data sent over the WLAN.<br>• **Network authentication (Shared mode)**—This option specifies that a WEP key is used to perform authentication to the WLAN.<br>• **The key is provided automatically**—This option specifies that the WEP key is provided automatically to wireless clients by a key server of some sort, typically a RADIUS server. |
| This is a computer-to-computer (ad hoc) network; wireless access points are not used. | When selected, configures this network as an ad hoc network. If not selected, configures this network as an infrastructure network. |

Table 7.3 outlines the configuration options that are available on the IEEE 802.1x tab of the New Preferred Setting Properties dialog box, as discussed in step 9 of the Wireless Network Policy creation process.

**TABLE 7.3**

OPTIONS AVAILABLE ON THE IEEE 802.1x TAB OF
THE NEW PREFERRED SETTING PROPERTIES DIALOG
BOX

| *Option* | *Description* |
| --- | --- |
| Enable network access control using IEEE 802.1X | Specifies that 802.1x authentication is to be used when connecting to the WLAN. |
| EAPOL-Start message | Specifies how Extensible Authentication Protocol over LAN (EAPOL) start messages are to be transmitted. Options include<br>• Do not transmit<br>• Transmit (default)<br>• Transmit per IEEE 802.1X |
| Max start | Default Max start value is 3 seconds. |
| Held period | Default Held period is 60 seconds. |
| Start period | Default Start period is 60 seconds. |
| Authentication period | Default Authentication period is 30 seconds. |
| EAP type | Specifies what EAP type is to be used from the following options: Smart card or other certificate and Protected Extensible Authentication Protocol (PEAP).<br>Clicking the Settings button allows you to configure additional options, including the following:<br>• Using a smart card or certificate on the computer<br>• Validating server certificates<br>• Specifying which servers to connect to<br>• Specifying Trusted Root Certification Authorities<br>• Viewing certificates<br>• Selecting and configuring an authentication method |
| Authenticate as guest when user or computer information is unavailable | Specifies that wireless clients are to attempt to authenticate to the WLAN as a guest when user or computer information is not available. |
| Authenticate as computer when computer information is available | Specifies that wireless clients must attempt to authenticate to the WLAN even if a user is not logged on. |

*continues*

**TABLE 7.3**    *continued*

**OPTIONS AVAILABLE ON THE IEEE 802.1X TAB OF THE NEW PREFERRED SETTING PROPERTIES DIALOG BOX**

| *Option* | *Description* |
| --- | --- |
| Computer authentication | Specifies how the computer is to authenticate to the WLAN. The following options are available:<br>• With user authentication<br>• With user re-authentication (default)<br>• Computer only<br>The recommend setting is With User Re-authentication. This setting forces the computer to authenticate before a user is logged on and then performs authentication using the user's credentials when the user logs on. When the user logs off, authentication is performed again using the computer's credentials. |

# PLANNING SECURITY FOR DATA TRANSMISSION

**Plan security for data transmission.**

▶ **Secure data transmission between client computers to meet security requirements.**

▶ **Secure data transmission by using IPSec.**

IP Security (IPSec) is a framework of open standards for ensuring private, secure communications over IP networks. This protocol is rapidly becoming the underlying framework for secure communications using VPNs and will likely replace Point-to-Point Tunneling Protocol (PPTP) as Microsoft's VPN protocol of choice. IPSec takes advantage of many of the most popular encryption protocols in use today. For more information on encryption protocols, see Chapter 4. IPSec is based on an end-to-end security model, which means that the only computers that must know about IPSec are the sending and receiving computers. The packets travel the network without being affected by any of the intervening network devices. Each IPSec device handles its own security and functions with the assumption that the transport medium is not secure. The Internet is an excellent example of a transport medium that is not secure.

The Microsoft Windows Server 2003 implementation of IPSec is based on standards developed by the Internet Engineering Task Force (IETF) IPSec working group. However, it is important to note that Microsoft uses two implementations of IPSec: the IETF version, also known as Pure IPSec Tunnel mode, or just tunnel mode; and the Microsoft variant on IPSec, which Microsoft calls L2TP/IPSec mode, or transport mode. An IPSec VPN configured to use transport mode secures an existing IP packet from source to destination, using the encryption and authentication methods discussed later in this section. Tunnel mode puts an existing IP packet inside a new IP packet that is sent to a tunnel endpoint in the IPSec format. Both transport and tunnel mode can be encapsulated in Encapsulating Security Protocol (ESP) or Authentication Header (AH) headers. The original IETF Request for Comments (RFC 2401, `http://www.ietf.org/rfc/rfc2401.txt`) IPSec tunnel protocol specifications did not include mechanisms suitable for remote access VPN clients, instead focusing on site-to-site VPN implementations. For that reason, Microsoft's implementation of tunnel mode relies on the use of the L2TP protocol developed jointly with Cisco to provide this additional packet format. (An introduction to the components of IPSec comes later in this chapter.) It is worth noting that a new RFC (RFC 3193, `http://www.ietf.org/rfc/rfc3193.txt`) introduced in late 2001 discusses using L2TP with IPSec.

The following new features are supported in the Windows Server 2003 IPSec implementation:

▶ IPSec in Windows Server 2003 now supports User Datagram Protocol (UDP) encapsulation of IPSec packets to allow Internet Key Exchange (IKE) and Encapsulating Security Protocol (ESP) traffic to pass through a Network Address Translation (NAT) device—something not previously possible in Windows 2000. It is now possible for Windows 2000 and Windows XP clients to establish IPSec connections with a Windows Server 2003 server that is located behind one or more NAT devices.

▶ The IP Security Monitor is now implemented as an MMC snap-in instead of a standalone executable as in Windows 2000. Also, you can now monitor information about local and remote computers as well as several other enhancements.

**EXAM TIP**

**Protecting VPN connections** By default, client remote access VPN connections are protected using an automatically generated IPSec policy that uses IPSec transport mode (not tunnel mode) when the L2TP tunnel type is selected. You will probably see this configuration in almost every production implementation of a Windows Server 2003 IPSec implementation. To enable this configuration, configure the Routing and Remote Access Service for L2TP VPN connectivity, as described in Chapter 4.

**Understand IPSec** The exam includes questions and scenarios on IPSec. Although you don't need to memorize the minutiae surrounding the encryption protocols used by IPSec, you should be familiar with what the components of IPSec are, how to implement an IPSec tunnel, and especially how to work with IPSec policies.

▶ IPSec now supports the use of a 2048-bit Diffie-Hellman key exchange. As a result, the secret key resulting from the Diffie-Hellman exchange has greater strength. This results in a longer key length, which increases the difficulty an attacker faces when trying to determine a secret key.

▶ You can administer and control IPSec from the command line with new extensions to the `netsh` command. Using the `netsh ipsec` context, you can configure static or dynamic IPSec main mode settings, quick mode settings, rules, and configuration parameters. The `netsh ipsec` context replaces the `Ipsecpol.exe` tool that was provided with the Windows 2000 Server Resource Kit.

▶ IPSec now provides stateful filtering of network traffic during computer startup. Any outbound traffic initiated by the computer upon startup is permitted, as is any inbound reply traffic. Dynamic Host Configuration Protocol (DHCP) is exempt from this new protection provided by IPSec and is thus allowed during startup. You can also specify other types of traffic you want to exempt. Computer startup security can be configured only by using the `netsh` command with the `ipsec` context.

▶ Windows Server 2003 Enterprise Edition and Windows Server 2003 Datacenter Server Edition provide improved support for integration of IPSec with network load balancing. This allows a group of NLB servers to better provide highly available IPSec-based VPN services to clients. NLB can now accurately track IPSec-secured sessions, and the IPSec Internet Key Exchange (IKE) protocol can now detect when an IPSec-secured session is being established with a cluster server and quickly recover from a failover.

▶ IPSec provides an extension to the Resultant Set of Policy (RSoP) snap-in (another new addition to Windows Server 2003) that can be used to view IPSec policy assignments of computers or other Active Directory objects.

The following are the standard features of the Windows Server 2003 IPSec implementation:

▶ IPSec in Windows Server 2003 is policy based. It cannot be configured without an IPSec policy being in place, allowing an administrator to more easily apply settings to groups of objects such as computers or users.

▶ IPSec on Windows Server 2003 can use Kerberos v5, a digital certificate, or a shared secret (string) for user authentication.

▶ IPSec mutually authenticates computers prior to any data being exchanged.

▶ IPSec establishes a security association (SA) between the two host computers involved in the data transfer. An SA is the collection of a policy and keys, which define the rules for security settings.

▶ IPSec encrypts data using Data Encryption Standard (DES) or Triple DES (3DES).

▶ IPSec uses the MD5 or SHA1 algorithm for data hashing.

▶ IPSec is invisible to users. IPSec operates at the network level of the Open System Interface (OSI) model; therefore, users and applications do not directly interact with the protocol. After an IPSec tunnel has been created, users can connect to applications and services as if they were on the local network and not on the other side of a public network.

IPSec operates at the network layer; therefore, it is invisible to applications and computers. An understanding of the following features, however, will help you troubleshoot problems that may arise in connectivity:

▶ IPSec policies are part of Group Policy, both locally and within Active Directory. This built-in feature allows changes and management to be centralized. Settings for IPSec are enforced on the computer as the policy is enforced.

▶ The Internet Security Key Association Key Management Protocol (ISAKMP) monitors the negotiations between the hosts and provides the keys to use with security algorithms.

▶ The installed IPSec driver secures traffic between the two hosts.

# Understanding the Architecture and Components of IPSec

**Plan for network protocol security.**

▶ **Specify the required ports and protocols for specified services.**

Let's look at the underlying architecture and components of the IPSec protocol. IPSec provides data and identity protection services for each IP packet by adding a security protocol header to each IP packet. This header is made up of several components, each with its own function.

## Authentication Header (AH)

The IPSec Authentication Header (AH) provides three services as part of the IPSec protocol. First (as its name might suggest), AH authenticates the entire packet. Second, it ensures data integrity. Third, it prevents any replaying of the packet by a third party who might be trying to penetrate the IPSec tunnel. One service AH doesn't provide is payload encryption. AH protects your data from modification, but an attacker who is snooping the network would still be able to read the data. To prevent the modification of the data, AH uses two hashing algorithms to "sign" the packet for integrity:

▶ The Message Digest 5 (MD5) algorithm applies the hashing function to the data in four passes.

▶ The Secure Hash Algorithm (SHA1) is closely modeled after MD5. SHA uses 79 32-bit constants during the computation of the hash value, which results in a 160-bit key. Because SHA has a longer key length, it is considered more secure than MD5.

AH uses an IP protocol decimal ID of 51 to identify itself in the IP header. The AH header contains the following fields:

▶ **Next Header**—This field identifies the next header that uses the IP protocol ID.

▶ **Length**—This field indicates the length of the AH header.

▶ **Security Parameters Index (SPI)**—Used in combination with the destination address and the security protocol (AH or ESP), the SPI is used by the receiver to identify the cryptographic keys and procedures to be used to decode the packet.

▶ **Sequence Number**—This field provides the anti-replay functionality of AH. The sequence number is an incrementally increasing number (starting from 0) that is never allowed to cycle and that indicates the packet number. The machine receiving the packet checks this field to verify that the packet has not been received already. If a packet with this number has already been received, the packet is rejected.

▶ **Authentication Data**—This field contains the Integrity Check Value (ICV) used to verify the integrity of the message. (This is the hash value mentioned previously.) The receiver calculates the hash value and checks it against the ICV to verify packet integrity.

An IP Packet that has AH applied in transfer mode is modified with the AH header between the IP header and the TCP header, as shown in Figure 7.16.

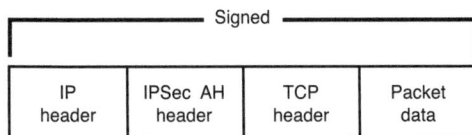

| Signed | | | |
|---|---|---|---|
| IP header | IPSec AH header | TCP header | Packet data |

**FIGURE 7.16**
An IP packet with the AH header inserted in transfer mode.

AH can be used alone or in combination with the ESP protocol, which is discussed next.

## Encapsulating Security Protocol (ESP)

Encapsulating Security Protocol (ESP) provides confidentiality in addition to authentication, integrity, and anti-replay. This portion of the IPSec protocol encrypts the data contents of the packet. The format of the ESP varies, depending on the type and mode of encryption being utilized. ESP can be used alone, in combination with AH, or using Microsoft's implementation, nested within the L2TP.

ESP appears in the IP header with an IP protocol decimal ID of 50. The ESP header contains the following fields:

**Replaying: Why Is It Bad?** You may have noticed that replaying has been included several times as part of the discussion of IPSec. Replaying is a somewhat obscure method for obtaining access to a system. A replay attack occurs when packets are intercepted by an unauthorized party, stored, and later retransmitted in an effort to trick one or both sides of the transmission into thinking that it is a valid communication. A replay attack becomes an issue because TCP/IP protocols such as Network File System (NFS) have no mechanisms to determine whether a packet is being replayed—even after several hours. Fortunately, the anti-replay mechanisms in IPSec make a replay attack a virtual impossibility.

▶ **SPI**—The receiver uses the SPI, in combination with the destination address and the security protocol (AH or ESP), to identify the cryptographic keys and procedures to be used to decode the packet.

▶ **Sequence Number**—This field provides the anti-replay functionality of ESP. The sequence number is an incrementally increasing number (starting from 0) that is never allowed to cycle and indicates the packet number. The machine receiving the packet checks this field to verify that the packet has not been received already. If a packet with this number has already been received, the packet is rejected.

The ESP trailer contains the following fields:

▶ **Padding**—Specifies 0 to 255 bytes used for 32-bit alignment and with the block size of the block cipher.

▶ **Padding Length**—Indicates the length of the Padding field in bytes.

▶ **Next Header**—Identifies the makeup of the payload, such as TCP or UDP.

The ESP Authentication Trailer contains one field: Authentication Data. This field contains the Integrity Check Value (ICV) and a media access control (MAC) used to verify the sender's identity and ensure message integrity.

ESP is inserted after the IP header and before an upper layer protocol, such as TCP, UDP, or ICMP, or before any other IPSec headers (such as AH) that have already been inserted. Everything following ESP (the upper layer protocol, the data, and the ESP trailer) is encrypted, as shown in Figure 7.17. The IP header is not signed and, therefore, not necessarily protected from modification unless tunneling mode is active, as shown in Figure 7.18.

**FIGURE 7.17**
An IP packet with the ESP header inserted in transfer mode.

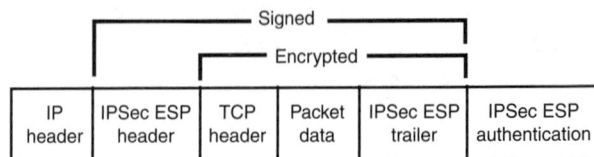

| IP header | IPSec ESP header | TCP header | Packet data | IPSec ESP trailer | IPSec ESP authentication |
|-----------|------------------|------------|-------------|-------------------|--------------------------|

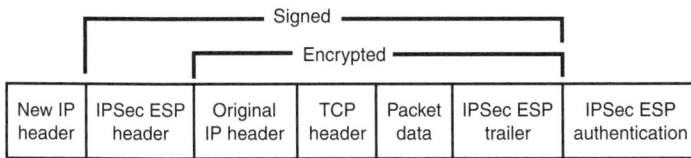

| New IP header | IPSec ESP header | Original IP header | TCP header | Packet data | IPSec ESP trailer | IPSec ESP authentication |
|---|---|---|---|---|---|---|

Signed — spans from IPSec ESP header through IPSec ESP trailer
Encrypted — spans from Original IP header through IPSec ESP trailer

**FIGURE 7.18**
An IP packet with the ESP header inserted in tunnel mode; the original IP header is now encrypted.

The final piece of the IPSec protocol is the authentication and key exchange mechanism. Authentication and key exchange are accomplished using a pair of protocols.

## Internet Security Key Association Key Management Protocol (ISAKMP/Oakley)

ISAKMP/Oakley (also known as ISAKMP/IKE, for Internet Key Exchange) provides the mechanism that allows disparate VPN servers to share encryption key information and make the IPSec protocol practical in today's environment. Before secured data can be exchanged between VPN servers, a contract between the two computers must be established. In this contract, called SA, both computers agree on how to exchange and protect information. In other words, the two servers (or the server and client computer) need to agree on how to encrypt and decrypt the data to be sent.

To enable this process, the IPSec protocol uses a standard process to build this contract between the two computers. This process combines the ISAKMP and Oakley key generation protocols. ISAKMP provides the centralized security association management, whereas Oakley actually generates and manages the encryption keys used to secure the information.

IKE actually performs a two-phase operation to establish the secure communication channel. In each phase, confidentiality and authentication are ensured by the use of encryption and authentication algorithms that are agreed upon by the computers negotiating. In the first phase (also known as main mode), the two computers establish a secure, authenticated channel called the Phase I (Main Mode) SA. The IKE provides identity protection during this phase. In the first phase (also known as quick mode), the two computers establish the rules for communication called the Phase II (Quick Mode) SA. During the second phase, a new shared key is created for use. After the Phase II SA is in place, IPSec secured communications can occur.

The final piece of this puzzle that needs to be covered is Microsoft's IPSec/L2TP implementation, which adds an additional tunneling protocol to the IPSec implementation.

## L2TP and IPSec

The major difference between the ESP tunnel and L2TP is that the L2TP tunnel performs at Layer 2 of the OSI Model, the data link layer. This way, L2TP can tunnel additional protocols, such as IPX or NetBEUI. IPSec's ESP tunneling protocol tunnels only the TCP/IP protocol, based on the standard. When L2TP and IPSec are used in combination to provide a secured tunnel, the original packet header is used to carry the packet's source and final destination, whereas the tunnel packet's IP header might contain the address of an IPSec gateway. The L2TP header carries the information needed to route the packet over the network. The Point-to-Point Protocol (PPP) header within the encapsulated packet identifies the protocol of the original packet. In other words, when using L2TP to transfer data, IPSec is used to secure the tunnel. L2TP encapsulates the packet in a PPP frame. The PPP frame is then added to a UDP-type frame assigned to port 1701. UDP, which is part of the TCP/IP suite, qualifies for IPSec to secure the contents; thus, the contents of L2TP are secure, regardless of the originating protocol and/or data type.

One additional benefit of the L2TP method is that you have a choice of additional encryption algorithms for securing the data.

Now that you have a basic introduction to the benefits and background of the IPSec protocol, you are ready to look at working with IPSec.

# Configuring and Implementing IPSec

**Configure network protocol security.**

▶ **Configure protocol security in a heterogeneous client computer environment.**

▶ **Configure protocol security by using IPSec policies.**

Before enabling IPSec on your local computer or domain, you should configure IPSec through policies. An IPSec policy is a set of rules that define how and when communication is secured between two endpoints. This is done through the configuration of various rules. Each rule contains a collection of actions and filters that begin when they encounter endpoints that match.

Policies allow you to quickly and easily configure IPSec based on the settings required within your organization. Windows Server 2003 comes with the following three preconfigured IPSec policies that may or may not meet your needs:

▶ **Client (Respond Only)**—This policy requires IPSec-provided security only when another computer requests it. This policy allows the computer to attempt unsecured communications first and switch to IPSec-secured communications if requested. This policy contains the default response rule, which creates dynamic IPSec filters for inbound and outbound traffic based on the requested protocol and port traffic for the communication that is being secured. This policy, which can be used on workstations and servers alike, provides the minimum amount of IPSec security.

▶ **Server (Request Security)**—This policy requests security from the other computer and allows unsecured communication with non IPSec-aware computers. The computer accepts inbound unsecured traffic but always attempts to secure further communications by requesting IPSec security from the sending computer. If the other computer is not IPSec-enabled, the entire communication is allowed to be unsecured. This policy, which can be used on workstations and servers alike, provides a medium level of IPSec security.

▶ **Secure Server (Require Security)**—This policy is implemented on computers that require highly secure communications, such as servers transmitting sensitive data. The filters in this policy require all outbound communication to be secured, allowing only the initial inbound communication request to be unsecured. This policy has a rule to require security for all IP traffic, a rule to permit ICMP traffic, and the default response rule to respond to requests for security from other computers. This policy, typically used only on servers, provides the highest level of IPSec security on a network. This policy can also be used on workstation computers if you want.

Non IPSec-enabled computers cannot establish any communications with computers using this policy.

You can opt to either use one of the preconfigured policies that comes with Windows Server 2003 or create your own policy. You can also modify the preconfigured policies to suit your needs if you want. Before we can go any further into our discussion about IPSec, we first need to create the tools that allow us to manage IPSec on a local computer. Step by Step 7.4 helps you to create your own IPSec management console.

## STEP BY STEP

### 7.4 Creating the IPSec Management Console

1. Open a blank MMC by clicking Start, Run. Then type **MMC** to open a blank MMC, as shown in Figure 7.19.

**FIGURE 7.19**
The MMC provides a powerful, flexible framework from which to manage Windows Server 2003.

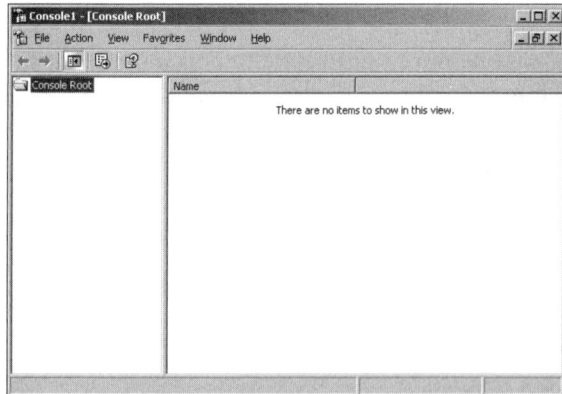

2. In your new console, click the File menu and select Add/Remove Snap-in. The Add/Remove Snap-in dialog box opens, as shown in Figure 7.20.

3. Click the Add button to open the Add Standalone Snap-in dialog box, as shown in Figure 7.21.

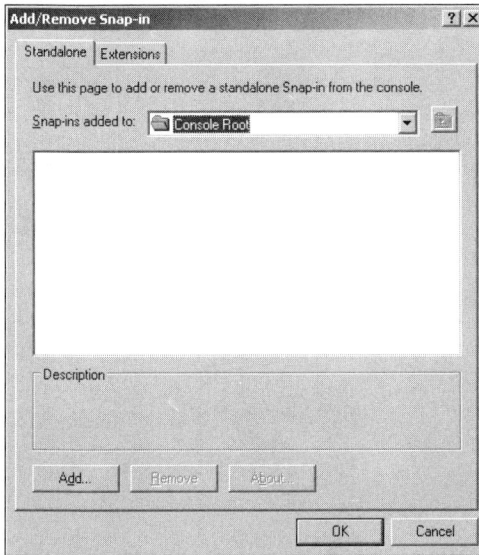

**FIGURE 7.20**
You can add snap-ins to your console to customize its management features.

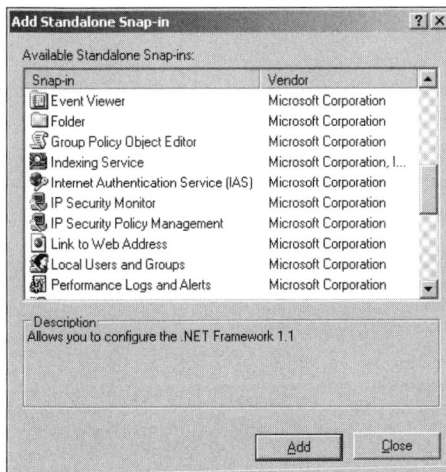

**FIGURE 7.21**
Windows Server 2003 comes with several dozen snap-ins you can choose from.

**4.** Scroll down the list, select IP Security Monitor, and click the Add button.

**5.** Select IP Security Policy Management and click the Add button. You are prompted to choose the scope that the snap-in will manage, as shown in Figure 7.22.

*continues*

*continued*

**FIGURE 7.22**
Many MMC snap-ins can be targeted at several different levels of management.

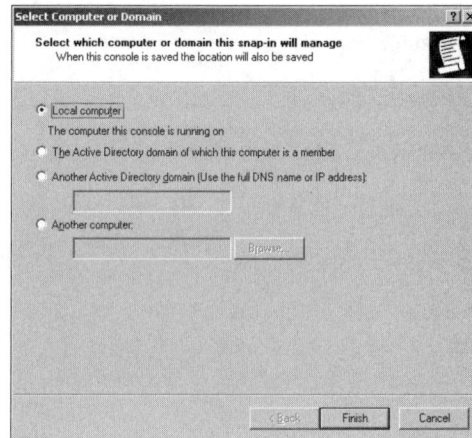

6. For this example, choose Local Computer from the Select Computer or Domain page. Notice that you have the option to select the Active Directory domain that this computer is part of, another Active Directory domain, or another computer. Click Finish to complete the addition of the IP Security Policy Management snap-in to your console.

7. Click Close on the Add Standalone Snap-in dialog box.

8. Click OK on the Add/Remove Snap-in dialog box. Your completed IPSec management console is shown in Figure 7.23.

**FIGURE 7.23**
Your completed IPSec management console contains the tools you need to manage and monitor IP Security.

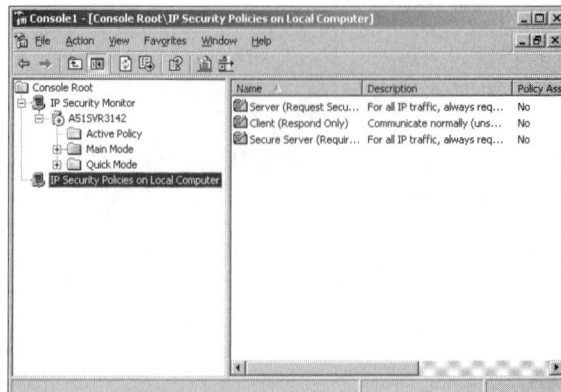

**9.** Save your newly created console by clicking File, Save. Enter a suitable name, such as `Local IPSec Management Console`, and click Save. By default, the console is saved in the Administrative Tools folder of the currently logged-in user.

Armed with your newly created IPSec management console, you can now get down to work configuring and managing IPSec. At this point, you may want to do one of two things: implement a preconfigured IPSec policy or create one of your own. We explore the latter in the next Step by Step. You can accomplish the former by right-clicking the desired policy in the right pane of the console window and selecting Assign from the context menu, as shown in Figure 7.24. Note that you can have only one IPSec policy assigned at a time.

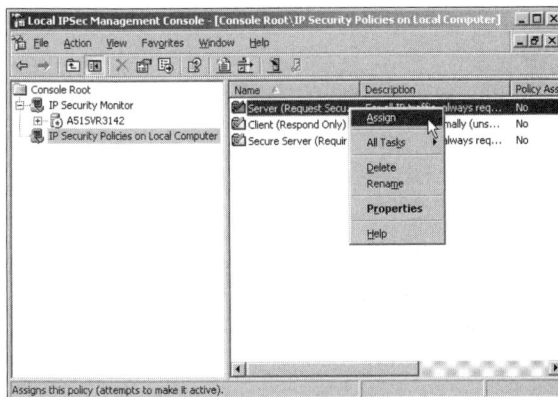

**FIGURE 7.24**
Assigning an IPSec policy to the local computer is a quick task.

You can verify that the policy is now assigned to the computer by examining the Active Policy node of the IP Security Monitor, as shown in Figure 7.25.

We examine the use of the IP Security Monitor console later in this chapter. For now, we need to look at the process to create a custom IPSec policy.

**FIGURE 7.25**
The IP Security Monitor can be used to display many bits of useful information about IPSec.

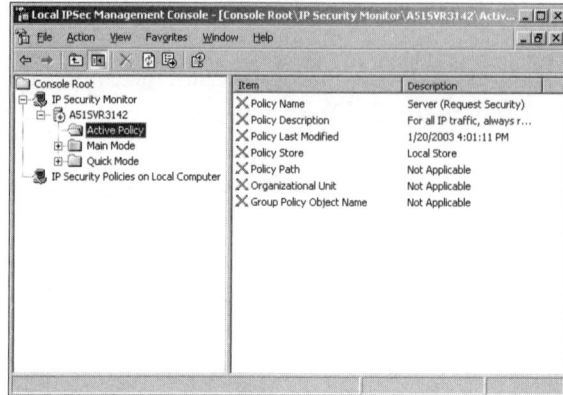

# Creating Customized IPSec Policies

**Plan for network protocol security.**

▶ **Plan an IPSec policy for secure network communications.**

**Configure security for data transmission.**

▶ **Configure IPSec policy settings.**

After you've decided to use IPSec on your network, you may realize that the preconfigured IPSec policies do not provide exactly the solution you are looking for. You can opt to either customize an existing policy or create a new one from scratch. I prefer to create policies from scratch to ensure that I have complete control over every piece of the puzzle, and that's exactly what IPSec can turn out to be if not treated with caution and respect—one large puzzle that you are left to piece together.

Before we start to actually create our own IPSec policy, let's take a few moments to examine the parts that make up an IPSec policy by dissecting the Secure Server (Require Security) policy. From within your IPSec management console, double-click this policy to open its Properties dialog box, as shown in Figure 7.26. It has two tabs: Rules and General.

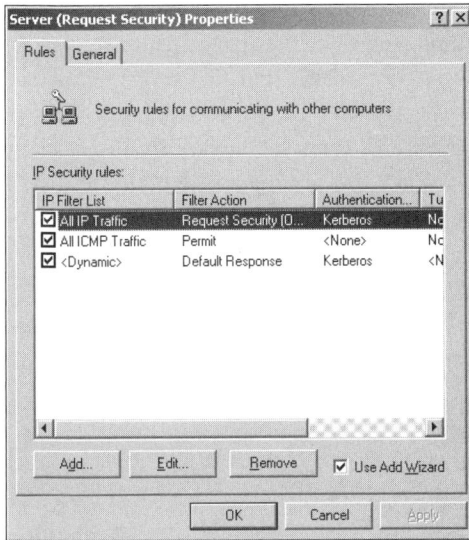

**FIGURE 7.26**
Examining the properties of a preconfigured
IPSec policy can help us to learn what makes
up such a policy.

Let's look at the Rules tab first. The IP Security Rules window lists
all the IP Security Rules that are active for that policy. Selecting a
rule and clicking the Edit button opens the Edit Rule Properties dialog box, as shown in Figure 7.27. Its five tabs contain the configuration settings for this particular rule.

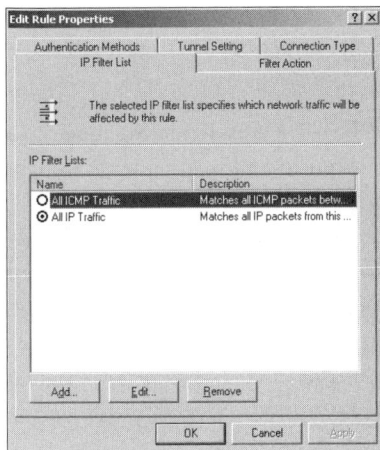

**FIGURE 7.27**
The IP Filter List tab of the Edit Rule Properties
dialog box.

The IP Filter List tab shows all IP filters configured for the selected
rule. An IP filter contains source and destination IP addresses that
apply to this rule. These IP addresses can be those of an individual

computer or that of a network subnet. If this tab identifies a network communication that has a participant listed in an IP filter, a particular filter action that is specific for that connection is applied. Selecting the All IP Traffic filter for editing opens the dialog box shown in Figure 7.28. From here, you can specify many items, including the source and destination IP addresses that this filter applies to.

**FIGURE 7.28**
You can edit the filter properties to specify the source and destination computers that they apply to.

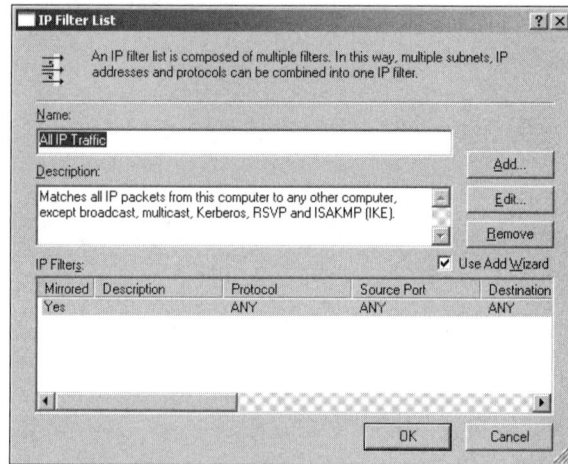

The Filter Actions tab of the Edit Rule Properties dialog box, shown in Figure 7.29, contains actions that specify the type of security and methods by which security is established.

Filter actions (see Figure 7.30) define the type of security and methods by which security is established. The default methods are Permit, Block, and Negotiate Security. The Permit option passes the traffic without the requirement for security. This action is appropriate if you never want to secure traffic to which a rule applies. The Block action silently blocks all traffic from computers specified in the IP filter list. The Negotiate Security action specifies that the computer is to use a list of security methods to negotiate the appropriate security for the communication.

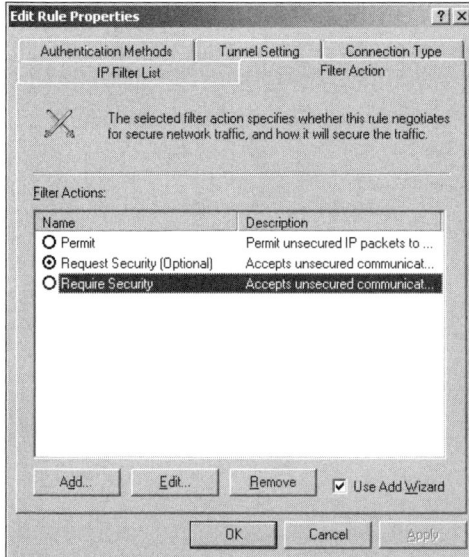

**FIGURE 7.29**
The Filter Actions tab defines the types of security and methods by which security is established.

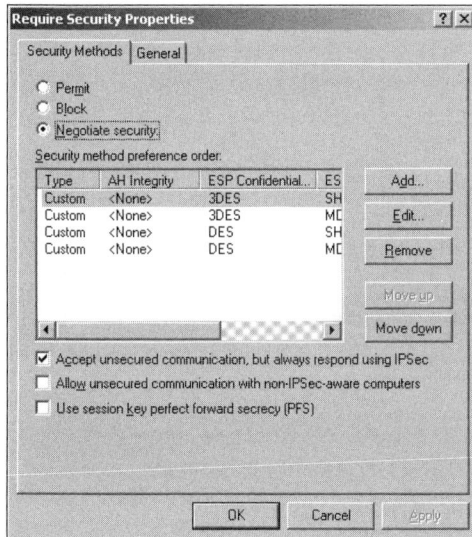

**FIGURE 7.30**
You can specify exactly what the computer will do when a filter action is processed.

If the Negotiate Security action is selected, both computers must make an agreement on the security parameters to be used, meaning that they both must support at least one common set of security parameters from those in the list. The list entries are processed in order of preference from top to bottom. The first security method shared by both computers is used.

From the Authentication Methods tab, shown in Figure 7.31, you can configure what method will be used to authenticate both sides of the communication. You can choose from Kerberos (the default setting), a digital certificate, or a shared secret (string) that will be used to protect the key exchange process. You can configure more than one method and also choose the order of precedence for your configured methods. Using the shared secret is not recommended because this static entry can be compromised.

**FIGURE 7.31**
You can specify Kerberos, digital certificate, or shared secret as the authentication methods.

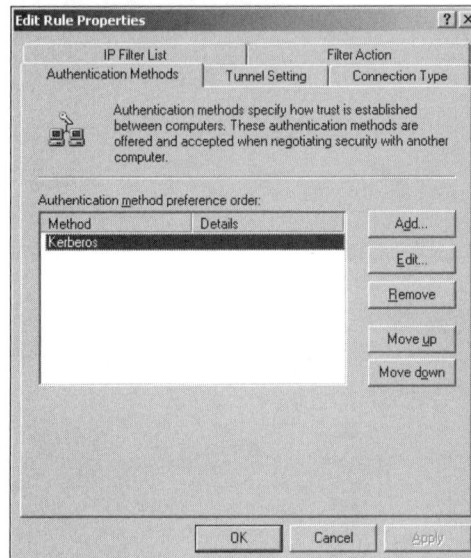

From the Tunnel Setting tab, shown in Figure 7.32, you can either have the rule apply to a tunnel by specifying an endpoint or not have it apply to a tunnel (transport mode).

The Connection Type tab, shown in Figure 7.33, determines for which types of connections the rule will be applied: LAN, Remote Access, or All Network Connections.

You can create two basic types of IPSec policies: those that specify a tunnel and those that do not specify a tunnel. Tunneling is commonly used in the creation of a VPN and is called tunnel mode. Not using a tunnel, called transport mode, is commonly used between subnets or computers on an intranet. Step by Step 7.5 shows how to create a new IPSec policy that operates in transport mode between two subnets (192.160.11.0 and 192.168.12.0) in the same intranet of the company Area 51 Partners. These two subnets represent the Accounting and Payroll departments, respectively, and they need to pass only secured traffic between their subnets.

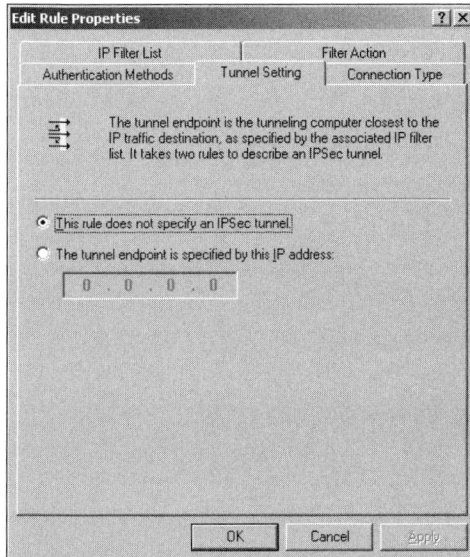

**FIGURE 7.32**
The Tunnel Setting tab allows you to configure a tunnel endpoint if required.

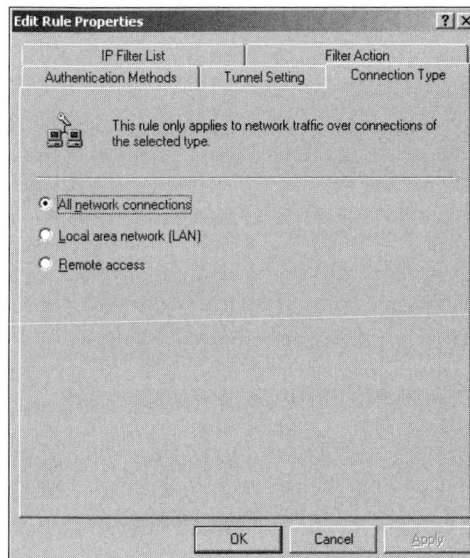

**FIGURE 7.33**
The Connection Type tab allows you to specify which connections are affected by the policy.

# STEP BY STEP

### 7.5 Creating a Custom Transfer Mode IPSec Policy

**1.** Open the IPSec management console that you created in Step by Step 7.4.

**2.** Right-click IP Security Policies and select Create IP Security Policy from the context menu.

**3.** Dismiss the opening page of the IP Security Policy Wizard by clicking Next.

**4.** On the IP Security Policy Name dialog box, enter a descriptive name for the new policy. For this example, use `Accounting to Payroll Security Policy`, as shown in Figure 7.34. Click Next after entering the required information.

**FIGURE 7.34**
You should enter a policy name and description that will make sense later.

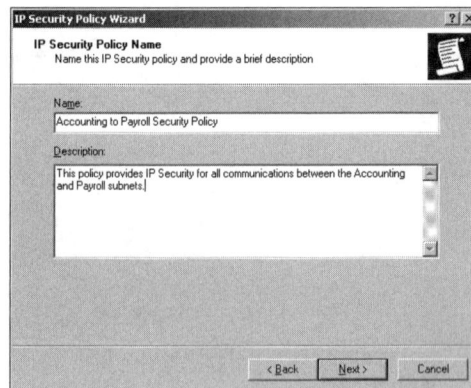

**5.** On the Requests for Secure Communication dialog box, shown in Figure 7.35, deselect Activate the Default Response Rule option. You will configure this policy entirely by yourself. Click Next to continue.

**6.** You are now at the end of the wizard portion of the creation process. Ensure that the Edit Properties option is selected, as shown in Figure 7.36, and click Finish to begin editing the policy's properties.

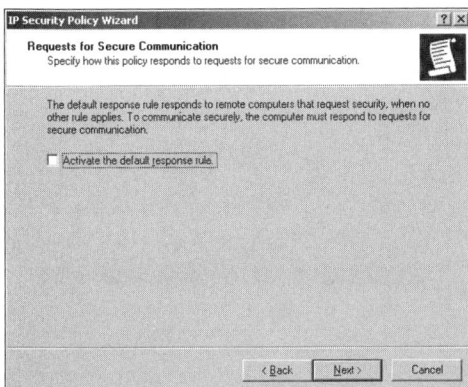

**FIGURE 7.35**
Removing the opportunity for unsecured communications to occur with the new rule.

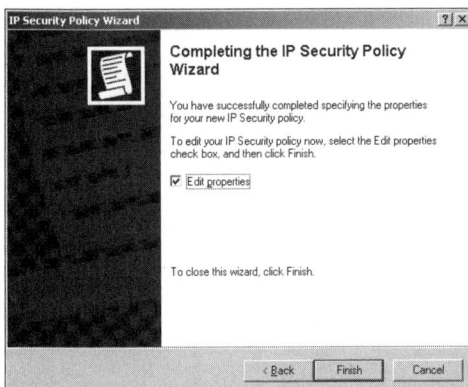

**FIGURE 7.36**
The completion of the wizard is not the completion of the policy creation process.

**7.** The Accounting to Payroll Security Policy Properties dialog box opens, as shown in Figure 7.37.

**8.** On the Rules tab, ensure that the Use Add Wizard option is selected; then click the Add button to start the Security Rule Wizard to create a new filter list and action.

**9.** Click Next to dismiss the opening page of the Security Rule Wizard.

**10.** On the Tunnel Endpoint dialog box, shown in Figure 7.38, select This Rule Does Not Specify a Tunnel (recall that this IPSec policy is being created to secure communications between two subnets on the same intranet). Click Next to continue.

*continues*

*continued*

**FIGURE 7.37**
Your new IPSec policy requires some configuration to complete.

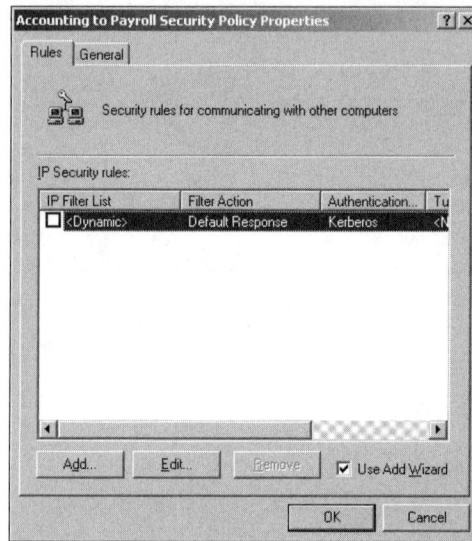

**FIGURE 7.38**
You can create a rule for either transport mode or tunnel mode.

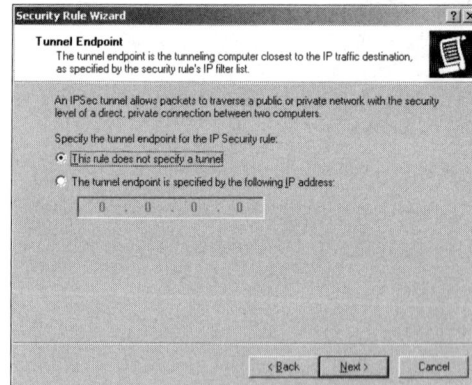

**11.** On the Network Type dialog box, shown in Figure 7.39, select the network connections to which this rule applies. For this example, select All Network Connections and click Next to continue.

**12.** The IP Filter List dialog box, shown in Figure 7.40, shows that no IP filters are configured for this rule. Click the Add button to create a filter that meets your requirements.

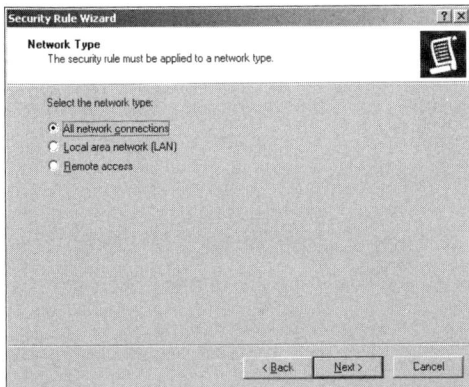

**FIGURE 7.39**
Selecting All Network Connections ensures that all communications by the server are secured using the new policy.

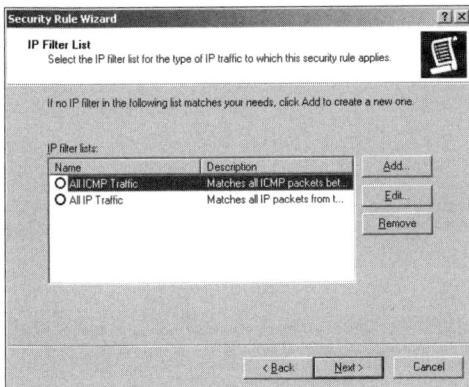

**FIGURE 7.40**
You must configure an IP filter for this rule to work properly.

**13.** From the IP Filter List dialog box, shown in Figure 7.41, you need to configure the IP filter properties for this rule. Enter a descriptive name such as **Accounting to Payroll security** in the name box and a description if you like. Ensure that the Use Add Wizard option is selected and click the Add button.

**14.** The IP Filter Wizard opens to start the process of configuring the IP filter. Click Next to dismiss the opening page of the wizard.

**15.** On the IP Filter Description and Mirrored Property dialog box, shown in Figure 7.42, enter a description of the filter. Ensure that the Mirrored option is selected. This option allows the rule to automatically match packets

*continues*

*continued*

with the exact opposite source and destination addresses to ensure that machines from the destination subnet are also included in the incoming filter. Click Next to continue.

**FIGURE 7.41**

The process to configure an IP filter begins with the IP Filter List dialog box.

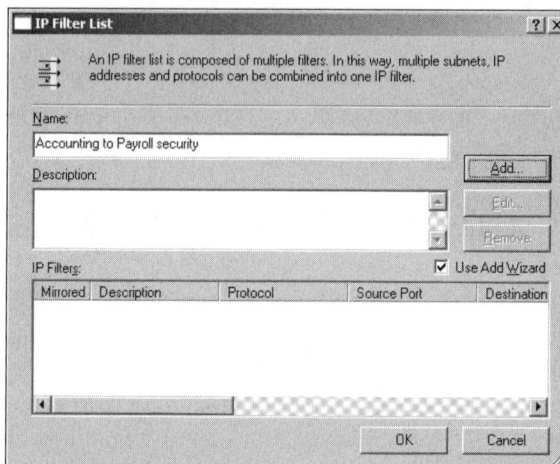

**FIGURE 7.42**

Allowing the IP filter to be mirrored saves you work.

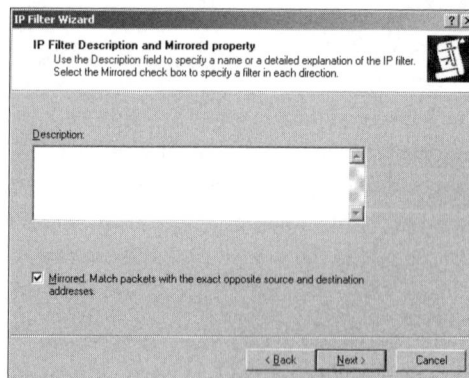

16. On the IP Traffic Source dialog box, select the A Specific IP Subnet option and configure the IP Address and Subnet mask as required. Recall that we are creating a policy between the 192.168.11.0 and 192.168.12.0 subnets. Enter **192.168.11.0** and the subnet mask of **255.255.255.0**, as shown in Figure 7.43, and click Next to continue.

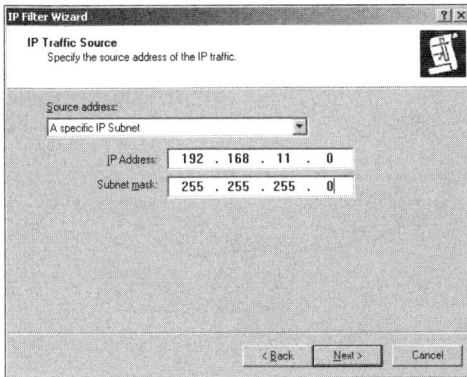

**FIGURE 7.43**
Be sure to specify the correct source address and subnet mask.

17. On the IP Traffic Destination dialog box, select the A Specific IP Subnet option and configure the IP Address and Subnet mask as required. Enter **192.168.12.0** and the subnet mask of **255.255.255.0**, as shown in Figure 7.44, and click Next to continue.

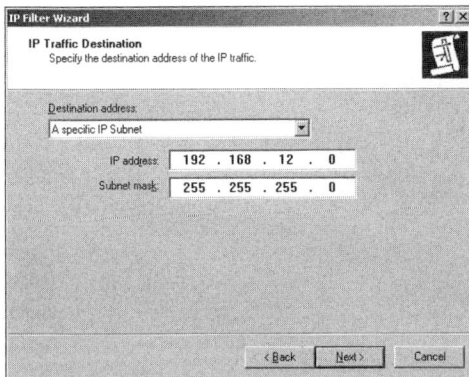

**FIGURE 7.44**
Be sure to specify the correct destination address and subnet mask also.

18. On the IP Protocol Type dialog box, shown in Figure 7.45, you can configure which IP protocol types you want to be included in the filter. We want the filter to apply to all types, so leave the default selection of Any and click Next to continue.

19. The Completing the IP Filter Wizard dialog box opens, as shown in Figure 7.46. Deselect the Edit Properties option and click Finish.

*continues*

*continued*

**FIGURE 7.45**
You can configure the filter to be very specific about what types of protocols it applies to.

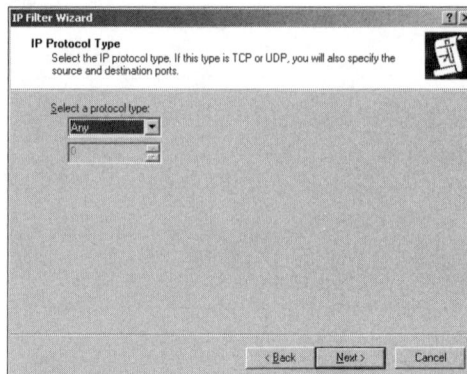

**FIGURE 7.46**
The IP filter has been created, but much work still remains.

**20.** Back at the IP Filter List dialog box, you can see your newly created IP filter. Click OK to close the filter and complete the creation process. If you click Cancel, your newly created filter will be lost, so be careful.

**21.** Select the Accounting to Payroll Security filter from the list on the IP Filter List dialog box, as shown in Figure 7.47, and click Next to continue with the Security Rule Wizard.

**22.** On the Filter Action dialog box, shown in Figure 7.48, select a filter action. Ensure that the Use Add Wizard option is selected and click Add to start the Filter Action Wizard.

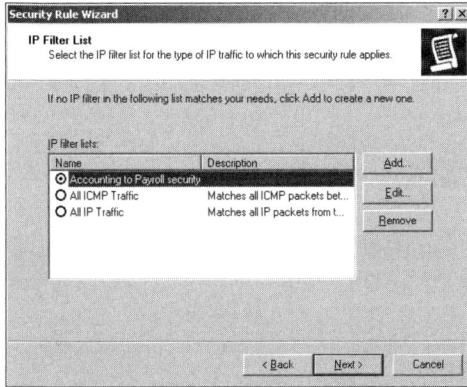

**FIGURE 7.47**
You need to select the filter for use after creating it.

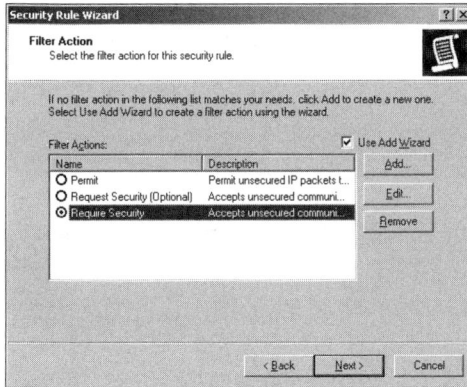

**FIGURE 7.48**
You now need to configure the action that the filter will take.

**23.** The Filter Action Wizard starts. Dismiss its opening dialog box by clicking Next.

**24.** On the Filter Action Name dialog box, enter a descriptive name and description for the filter. Click Next to continue.

**25.** On the Filter Action General Options dialog box, shown in Figure 7.49, select Negotiate Security and click Next to continue.

**26.** On the Communicating with Computers That Do Not Support IPSec dialog box, shown in Figure 7.50, you are asked whether you want to allow unsecured communications. In this case, such communications are not allowed

*continues*

*continued*

because all communications must be secured. Ensure that the Do Not Communicate with Computers That Do Not Support IPSec option is selected and click Next to continue.

**FIGURE 7.49**
Instructing the filter action to negotiate security between communication computers.

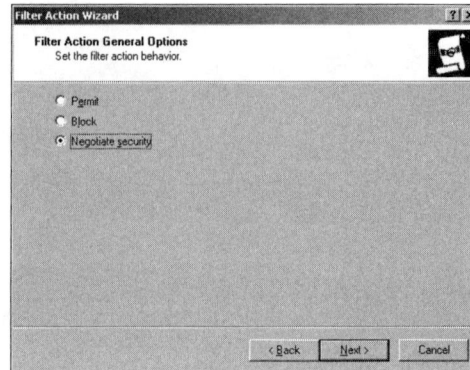

**FIGURE 7.50**
Ensure that you do not allow unsecured communications to occur.

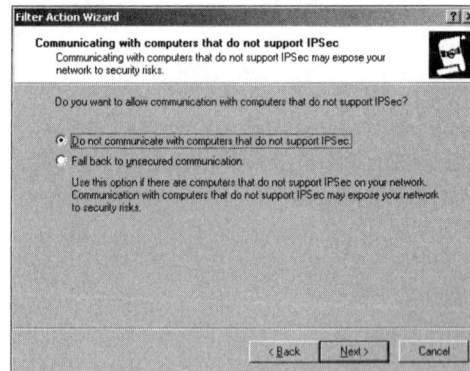

**27.** On the IP Traffic Security dialog box, shown in Figure 7.51, select Custom to specify what security methods are to be used. Click Settings to edit the security settings.

**28.** The Custom Security Method Settings dialog box, shown in Figure 7.52, opens. From here, you can specify the settings you want. Ensure that both the AH and ESP check boxes are selected. Configure the desired integrity and encryption algorithms. Do not configure settings for the session key at this time. Click OK to accept your settings.

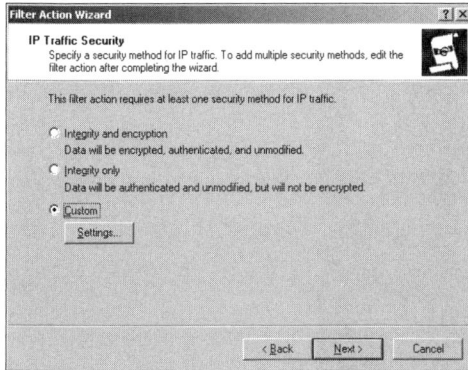

**FIGURE 7.51**
You can specify custom settings or use the standard settings provided.

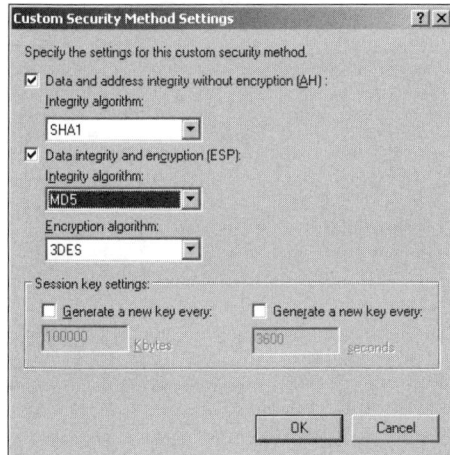

**FIGURE 7.52**
You can specify the encryption and integrity algorithms to be used in your filter action.

**29.** Back at the IP Traffic Security dialog box, click Next to continue.

**30.** On the Completing the IP Security Filter Action Wizard dialog box, shown in Figure 7.53, ensure the Edit Properties option is selected and click Finish.

**31.** Back at the filter action Properties dialog box, shown in Figure 7.54, ensure the Use Session Key Perfect Forward Secrecy (PFS) option is selected and click OK. Selecting session key PFS ensures that the master key keying material cannot be used to generate more than one session key, which adds both security and overhead to the connection. Do not click Cancel unless you want to scrap your newly configured filter action. Click OK.

*continues*

*continued*

**FIGURE 7.53**
The Filter Addition Wizard is completed, but the filter still requires a bit more configuration.

**FIGURE 7.54**
Selecting to use perfect forward secrecy to increase the security of the session key.

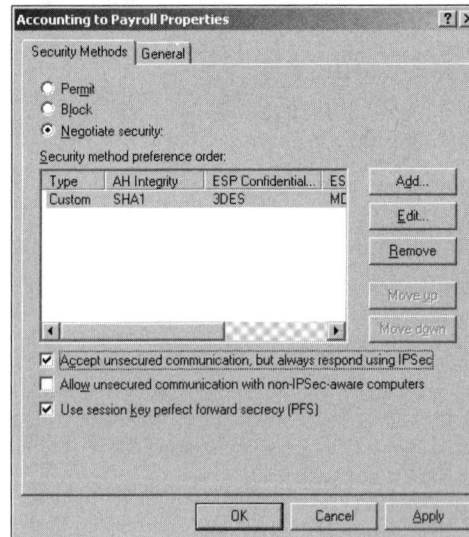

**32.** Back at the Filter Action dialog box, shown in Figure 7.55, select the newly created filter and click Next to continue.

**33.** On the Authentication Method dialog box, shown in Figure 7.56, select the primary authentication method this rule will use. The default selection of Kerberos v5 should be used in most cases. You can add additional authentication methods after the rule has been configured. Click Next to continue.

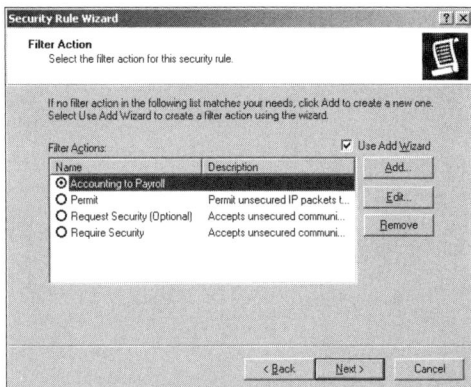

**FIGURE 7.55**
The filter action is configured, so it's time to move on.

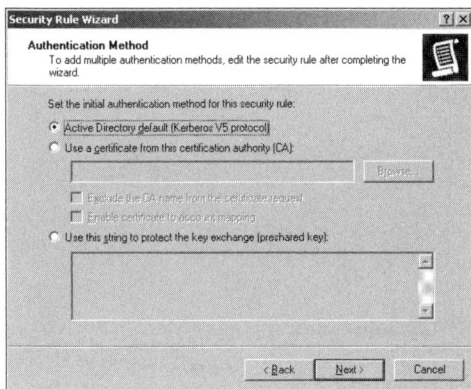

**FIGURE 7.56**
Specify the preferred authentication method; Kerberos v5 is preferred.

**34.** From the Completing the Security Rule Wizard dialog box, ensure that the Edit Properties option is deselected and click Finish to complete the rule creation process.

**35.** Finally, you are back to the policy Properties dialog box, as shown in Figure 7.57. You still have some additional configuration that you can complete, however.

**36.** On the General tab, you can configure the interval at which the computer will check for updates and changes to the security policy, as shown in Figure 7.58. The default setting of 180 minutes is usually acceptable.

*continues*

*continued*

**FIGURE 7.57**
The new security rule is displayed in the policy's properties.

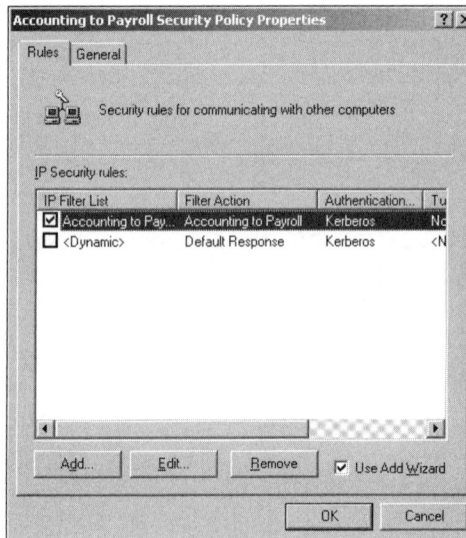

**FIGURE 7.58**
Configuring the policy update interval.

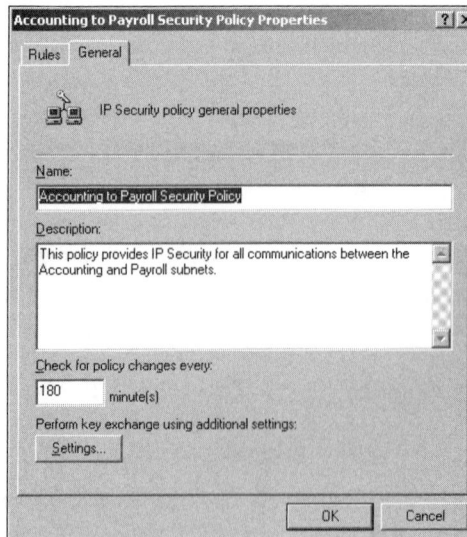

**37.** You can modify the settings used for the IKE process by clicking the Settings button at the bottom of the General tab.

**38.** On the Key Exchange Settings dialog box, shown in
Figure 7.59, you can configure for Master key perfect forward secrecy, which improves security of the keying
process. Additionally, you can change the defaults provided for key generation.

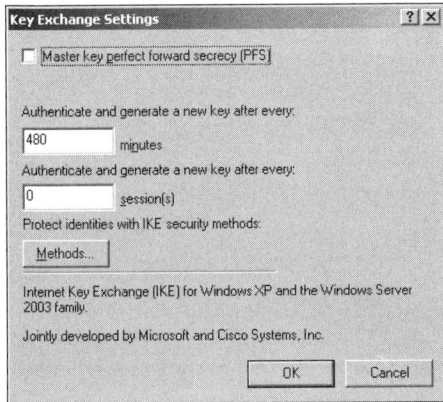

**FIGURE 7.59**
You can configure advanced IKE properties
from the Key Exchange Settings dialog box.

**39.** If you want to configure the methods used to protect the
identities, click the Methods button. The Key Exchange
Security Methods dialog box opens, as shown in Figure
7.60. Note that by default the new 2048-bit Diffie-
Hellman key exchange method is not used. You can select
it by adding or editing a security method, as shown in
Figure 7.61.

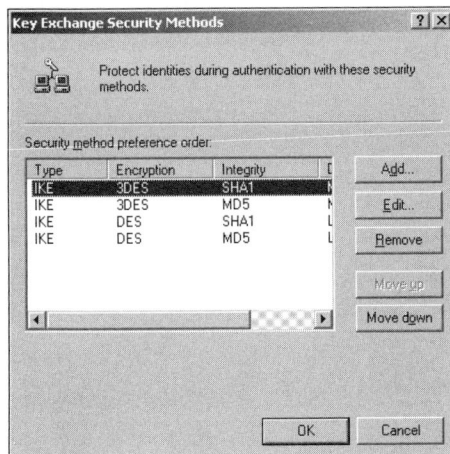

**FIGURE 7.60**
Customizing the key exchange security methods
can increase security.

*continues*

*continued*

**FIGURE 7.61**
Using the new 2048-bit Diffie-Hellman key
exchange method.

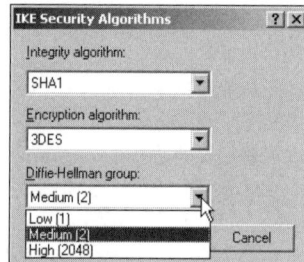

**40.** Click OK as required to return to the policy Properties
dialog box. Your new IPSec policy is now configured and
ready to use. Assign it as previously discussed at the end of
the "Configuring and Implementing IPSec" section of this
chapter.

IPSec can be deployed at any level within your organization. Thus
far, we have examined it only from the point of view of a local computer. You can just as easily apply it via Group Policy using the
Active Directory Users and Computers console, as shown in
Figure 7.62.

**FIGURE 7.62**
You can easily apply IPSec at the domain or OU
level using Group Policy.

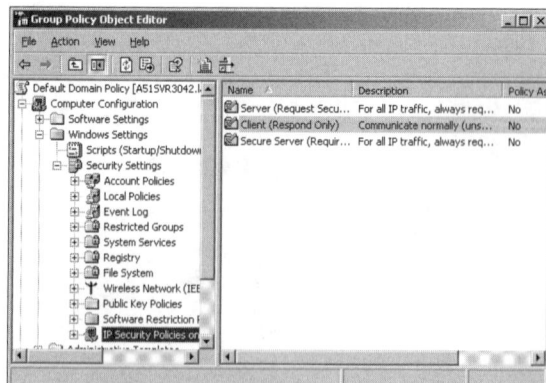

With the task of implementing IPSec out of the way, you are now
left to monitor and troubleshoot it, as we examine in the next section.

# Monitoring and Troubleshooting IPSec

**Troubleshoot security for data transmission. Tools might include the IP Security Monitor MMC snap-in and the Resultant Set of Policy (RSoP) MMC snap-in.**

With all the work behind you in configuring and deploying IPSec, you now must manage and monitor its use on your network. Fortunately, we have already seen a small bit of the monitoring tool of choice: the IP Security Monitor snap-in. Recall in Step by Step 7.4 that we constructed an IPSec management console, which contained the IP Security Monitor snap-in.

# The IP Security Monitor MMC Snap-in

The IP Security Monitor snap-in is divided into three major areas: the Active Policy node, Main Mode node, and Quick Mode node. We saw the Active Policy node previously in Figure 7.25. Table 7.4 explains each of the items in the Active Policy node of the IP Security Monitor.

**TABLE 7.4**

**ACTIVE POLICY NODE ITEMS**

| Item | Description |
| --- | --- |
| Policy Name | Provides the name of the active IPSec policy. |
| Description | Provides the description of the active IPSec policy. |
| Policy Last Modified | Provides the date and the time that the active IPSec policy was modified. |
| Policy Store | Provides the storage location for the active IPSec policy. For a local policy, it reads `Local Store`, and for a domain policy, it reads `Domain Store`. |
| Policy Path | Applies only to domain policies and provides the LDAP path to the active IPSec policy. |
| Organizational Unit | Applies only to domain policies and lists the organizational unit to which the Group Policy object is applied. |
| Group Policy Object Name | Applies only to domain policies and lists the Group Policy object to which the active IPSec policy is applied. |

The Main Mode node, shown in Figure 7.63, provides information about the Phase I security associations (SAs) as detailed in Table 7.5.

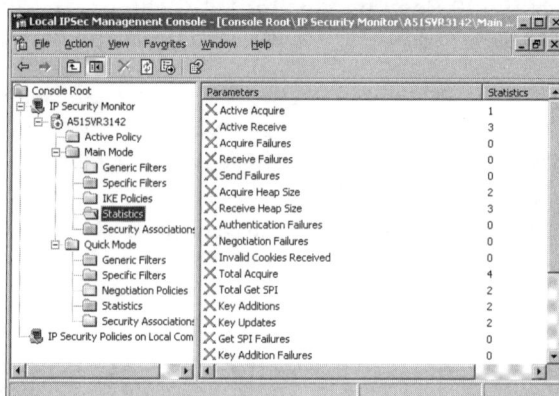

**TABLE 7.5**

## MAIN MODE (IKE) STATISTICS

| Main Mode Statistic | Description |
| --- | --- |
| Active Acquire | Displays a request by the IPSec to have IKE perform a task. This number includes all outstanding and queued requests and is typically a value of 1. Under heavy loading, this number increases. |
| Active Receive | Displays the number of IKE messages that have been received and are queued for processing. |
| Acquire Failures | Displays the number of times that an acquire has failed. |
| Receive Failures | Displays the number of times that errors have occurred in receiving IKE messages. |
| Send Failures | Displays the number of times that errors have occurred in sending IKE messages. |
| Acquire Heap Size | Displays the number of entries in the acquire heap, which stores active acquires. This number increases with heavy loading and should decrease as the heap is cleared. |
| Receive Heap Size | Displays the number of entries in the IKE receive buffers for incoming IKE messages. |
| Authentication Failures | Displays the total number of identity authentication failures that have occurred during Main Mode negotiation. This is a useful indicator to determine whether the authentication methods do not match between two computers attempting communications. |

| *Main Mode Statistic* | *Description* |
| --- | --- |
| Negotiation Failures | Displays the total number of negotiation failures that occurred during Main Mode or Quick Mode negotiation. This is a useful statistic to determine whether security and/or authentication methods do not match between two computers attempting communications. |
| Invalid Cookies Received | A value contained in a received IKE message that IKE uses to find the state of an active Main Mode. If a cookie in a received IKE message cannot be matched with an active Main Mode, it is invalid. |
| Total Acquire | Displays the total number of requests submitted by IKE to the IPSec driver to establish an SA for securing traffic. |
| Total Get SPI | Displays the total number of requests submitted by IKE to the IPSec driver to obtain a unique Security Parameters Index. |
| Key Additions | Displays the number of outbound Quick Mode SAs that IKE adds to the IPSec driver. |
| Key Updates | Displays the number of inbound Quick Mode SAs that IKE adds to the IPSec driver. |
| Get SPI Failures | Displays the number of requests submitted by IKE to the IPSec driver to obtain a unique SPI that have failed. |
| Key Addition Failures | Displays the number of outbound Quick Mode SA addition requests submitted by IKE to the IPSec driver that have failed. |
| Key Update Failures | Displays the number of inbound Quick Mode SA addition requests submitted by IKE to the IPSec driver that have failed. |
| ISADB List Size | Displays the number of Main Mode state entries, including negotiated Main Modes, Main Modes in progress, and Main Modes that have failed and have not yet been deleted. |
| Connection List Size | Displays the number of Quick Mode state entries. This number indicates the load placed on the computer. |
| IKE Main Mode | Displays the total number of successful SAs created during Main Mode negotiations. |
| IKE Quick Mode | Displays the total number of successful SAs created during Quick Mode negotiations. Typically, multiple Quick Mode SAs are created for each Main Mode SA; thus, this value may not necessarily match that of the Main Mode. |

*continues*

**TABLE 7.5** *continued*

## MAIN MODE (IKE) STATISTICS

| Main Mode Statistic | Description |
| --- | --- |
| Soft Associations | Displays the total number of negotiations that resulted in the use of unsecured traffic (also known as soft SAs). Typically, this is an indication of SAs formed with computers that do not support IPSec or were not able to negotiate a successful IPSec connection. This can be an indication of mismatched security and authentication settings. |
| Invalid Packets Received | Displays the number of received IKE messages that were invalid. Most commonly, invalid IKE messages are a result of retransmitted IKE messages or an unmatched shared key between the communicating computers. |

The Quick Mode node, shown in Figure 7.64, provides information about the Phase II SAs as detailed in Table 7.6.

**FIGURE 7.64**
The Quick Mode node displays information about the Phase II SAs.

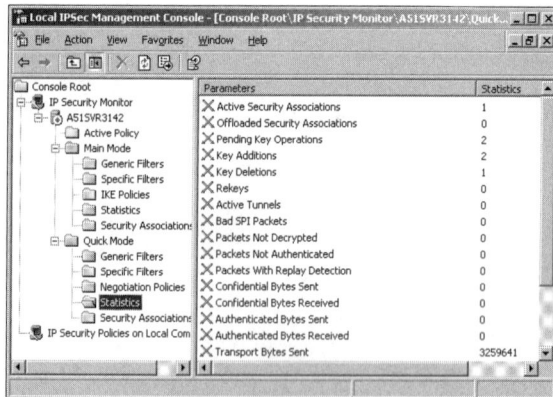

**TABLE 7.6**

## QUICK MODE (IPSEC) STATISTICS

| Quick Mode Statistic | Description |
| --- | --- |
| Active Security Associations | Displays the number of active IPSec SAs. |
| Offloaded Security Associations | Displays the number of active IPSec SAs that have been offloaded to hardware. |
| Pending Key Operations | Displays the number of IPSec key operations that are in progress. |
| Key Additions | Displays the total number of successful IPSec SA negotiations. |

| Quick Mode Statistic | Description |
| --- | --- |
| Key Deletions | Displays the number of key deletions for IPSec SAs. |
| Re-Keys | Displays the number of rekey operations for IPSec SAs. |
| Active Tunnels | Displays the number of active IPSec tunnels. |
| Bad SPI Packets | Displays the total number of packets for which the Security Parameters Index was incorrect. SPIs are used to match inbound packets with an SA. If the SPI is incorrect, the inbound SA may have expired. If rekeying intervals are set very short, this number is likely to increase very rapidly. Under normal conditions, a bad SPI packet does not mean that IP Security is failing because SAs expire normally. |
| Packets Not Decrypted | Displays the total number of packets that were not decrypted successfully. This may indicate that a packet has arrived for which the SA has previously expired. When the SA expires, the session key used to decrypt packets is removed. By itself, this does not indicate that IP Security is failing. |
| Packets Not Authenticated | Displays the total number of packets for which data could not be verified, meaning that the integrity hash verification failed. Most commonly, this is the result of an expired SA. |
| Packets With Replay Detection | Displays the total number of packets that contained a valid Sequence Number field. |
| Confidential Bytes Sent | Displays the total number of bytes sent using the ESP protocol. |
| Confidential Bytes Received | Displays the total number of bytes received using the ESP protocol. |
| Authenticated Bytes Sent | Displays the total number of bytes sent using the AH protocol. |
| Authenticated Bytes Received | Displays the total number of bytes received using the AH protocol. |
| Transport Bytes Sent | Displays the total number of bytes sent using IPSec transport mode. |
| Transport Bytes Received | Displays the total number of bytes received using IPSec transport mode. |
| Bytes Sent in Tunnels | Displays the total number of bytes sent using IPSec tunnel mode. |

*continues*

**TABLE 7.6** *continued*

## QUICK MODE (IPSEC) STATISTICS

| Quick Mode Statistic | Description |
| --- | --- |
| Bytes Received in Tunnels | Displays the total number of bytes received using IPSec tunnel mode. |
| Offloaded Bytes Sent | Displays the total number of bytes sent using hardware offload. |
| Offloaded Bytes Received | Displays the total number of bytes received using hardware offload. |

As far as configuring the IP Security Monitor, it hasn't changed much since Windows 2000. You can open the IP Security Monitor properties for any server listed in the IP Security Monitor node by right-clicking it and selecting Properties. The server Properties dialog box opens, as shown in Figure 7.65. You have the option to change the refresh interval for the IP Security Monitor statistics that are displayed and also whether you want to enable DNS name resolution; this comes into play when you are examining the SAs that are formed.

**FIGURE 7.65**
You don't have to configure very much for the IP Security Monitor's properties.

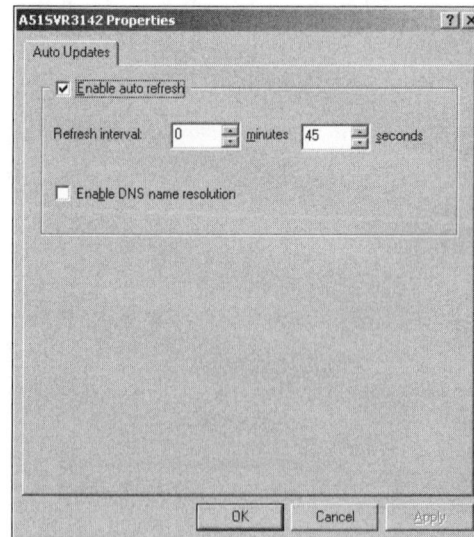

# The Resultant Set of Policy (RSoP) MMC Snap-in

The Resultant Set of Policy (RSoP) snap-in can be added to a blank or custom MMC to provide a means for you to create queries that poll Group Policy at all levels and then report the results of the query. RSoP gathers this information from the Common Information Management Object Model (CIMOM) database (otherwise known as CIM-compliant object repository) through Windows Management Instrumentation (WMI).

Often when policies are applied on multiple levels, results can conflict. Using the RSoP snap-in can easily help you to determine where the problem lies and the precedence (processing order) of the policies involved. RSoP can be used in one of two modes:

▶ **Planning Mode**—Allows you to simulate the effect of policy settings that you want to apply to a computer and user

▶ **Logging Mode**—Allows you to determine the existing policy settings for a computer and user who is currently logged on

RSoP can be added to an MMC using the same basic process as discussed in Step by Step 7.4. After you have created the custom MMC, right-click the Resultant Set of Policy object and select Generate RSoP Data to start the Resultant Set of Policy Wizard. Run the query in logging mode by following the wizard through the required steps. When you are done running the query, you can examine the results, specifically for the IPSec policies, as shown in Figure 7.66.

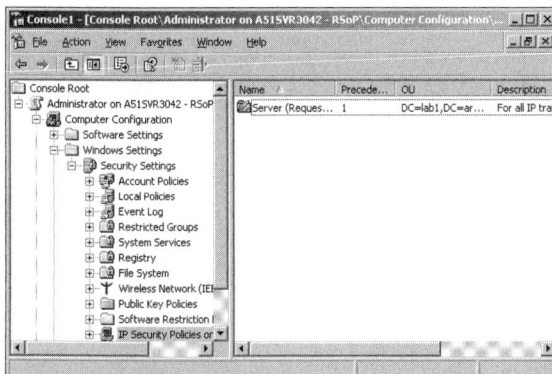

**FIGURE 7.66**
You can use RSoP to determine what policies are applied to users and computers.

# General IPSec Troubleshooting

If you have problems with IPSec, you should first verify that any routers or firewalls you may be passing through are configured to support IPSec traffic. You need to allow the following traffic:

▶ Protocol ID 50 and 51 or ESP and AH traffic

▶ UDP port 500 for IPSec negotiation traffic

Following are some other basic troubleshooting tips:

▶ **You are not able to establish any communications with a computer.** In this case, you should first verify that basic network connectivity exists between the computers in question. Ensure also that all required network services, such as DHCP and DNS, are operating properly for both computers.

▶ **You are not able to establish any communications with a computer.** This may also be the result of a computer that has been removed from the domain, which causes IPSec communications to fail.

▶ **Communications are occurring, but not as expected.** Ensure that you have the correct (and compatible) IPSec policies assigned on both computers.

▶ **No hard associations are being formed.** If soft associations are currently in place, a hard association is not formed. You need to completely stop all communications between the computers for about 5–10 minutes to allow the soft associations to time out. The easiest way to do this is to disable the network connection. After you have allowed the soft association to time out, you can check to see that a hard association has been formed. If a hard association still has not been formed, you need to examine your IPSec policy to verify that unsecured communications are not allowed.

▶ **IPSec communications are failing after configuring a digital certificate for authentication.** You must make sure that the required digital certificate is installed on the computers attempting to communicate using that IPSec policy. This can also be the result of specifying an incorrect Certificate Authority (CA).

▶ **Some computers can create IPSec connections and some cannot.** This situation is most likely caused by not having the same IPSec policy applied to all your computers. If you are intentionally using different policies, ensure that they share at least one common authentication and security method.

## CASE STUDY

### ESSENCE OF THE CASE

Following are the essential elements in this case:

▶ The current environment does not provide efficient management or operation.

▶ The workstation computers will be replaced to allow an installation of Windows XP Professional.

▶ Remote Assistance can be used to remotely assist users as long as the computers on both ends of the connection are Windows XP or Windows Server 2003.

### SCENARIO

Jeff's Jeep Tours is an Australian tour company that provides unique tours of the Australian continent. Jeff's has a central office that is located in Sydney with 20 other smaller remote offices located all over the country. Some of the remote offices have only three or four employees and no IT staff. The IT management responsibility for these offices is shared among all the IT staff in other locations. Jeff's network currently consists of a mixture of Windows 98, Windows NT 4.0 Workstation, and Windows 2000 Professional client computers with Windows 2000 Server and Windows Server 2003 domain controllers and member servers.

The CEO of Jeff's Jeep Tours, Jeff Johnson, has hired you as an outside consultant to plan and implement a solution for a new network that will allow for increased performance, security, and manageability. All workstations will be replaced with new Pentium 4 computers. No new servers will be purchased. The Sydney office uses an Active Directory domain with Windows 2000 Server domain controllers. You will be allowed to upgrade all domain controllers as required.

You propose a plan that upgrades all servers to Windows Server 2003 and installs Windows XP Professional on all client workstations. You further propose to raise the domain functional level to Windows Server 2003 and create Group Policies that provide Remote Assistance support for all remote offices that have no onsite IT personnel. You will create a top-level OU named

*continues*

## CASE STUDY

*continued*

Locations with individual OUs created inside the Locations OU for each remote site. Each client computer will be a member of its respective OU. All user accounts will also be placed in their respective OUs.

**ANALYSIS**

By installing Windows XP Professional on all client computers and placing all computer and user accounts in OUs for their location, you can easily create, configure, and implement Remote Assistance policies that will allow your IT staff to respond to user requests for assistance from any location.

## CHAPTER SUMMARY

### KEY TERMS

Before taking the exam, make sure you are comfortable with the definitions and concepts for each of the following key terms. You can use Appendix A, "Glossary," for quick reference.

- 802.1x
- Extensible Authentication Protocol (EAP)
- IPSec
- Internet Key Exchange (IKE)
- Microsoft Management Console (MMC)
- RADIUS
- Remote Assistance
- Remote Desktop for Administration

In this chapter, we examined some of the many options that are available to create and maintain more secure Windows Server 2003 networks.

Remote Assistance and Remote Desktop for Administration are both Remote Desktop Protocol–based services and can be used to remotely manage a computer. Remote Assistance is typically initiated by a user (the Novice) asking an administrator (the Expert) for help by using Windows Messenger or an email request. A file request can also be used if required. After the Expert has accepted the invitation, he or she can view and even take control of the remote computer if the Novice allows. This provides a means to help the remote user with problems on his or her computer. Remote Desktop for Administration is the replacement for Terminal Services Administration mode in Windows 2000 and does not require an invitation request to be sent. An administrator can initiate a connection to a server and remotely administer the server—even shutting it down or restarting it. Only two concurrent Remote Desktop for Administration connections can be created to any one server.

With the recent rise in popularity and availability of wireless LANs, security issues have begun to occur within organizations using WLANs. Although several vendors create full-featured security solutions for 802.11 wireless networks, Microsoft has also provided a

## CHAPTER SUMMARY

basic security implementation within Windows Server 2003. Using Group Policy, you can configure wireless network policies that can be used to determine what wireless networks your clients can connect to and how the connection must be made with respect to authentication and encryption.

IPSec can be used to secure communications both on your intranet and between endpoints over the Internet. VPNs can be created using IPSec and L2TP to ensure authenticity, integrity, and confidentiality of data in transit. The IPSec implementation in Windows Server 2003 has received several improvements since Windows 2000, most notably the capability to pass through NAT devices. Also, the Diffie-Hellman key exchange has been increased to a maximum of 2,048 bits to further increase the security of the secret key.

### KEY TERMS

- Remote Desktop Protocol (RDP)
- Terminal Services
- Transport Mode
- Tunnel Mode
- Wireless LAN (WLAN)

## APPLY YOUR KNOWLEDGE

# Exercises

### 7.1 Sending a Remote Assistance Request

In this exercise, you create and send a Remote Assistance request. You need two Windows XP Professional or Windows Server 2003 computers (or one of each) to complete this procedure.

**Estimated time:** 15 minutes

1. Open the Help and Support Center by clicking Start, Help and Support.

2. Click the Remote Assistance link under the Support Tasks column.

3. On the Remote Assistance window, click the Invite Someone to Help You link.

4. Select a Windows Messenger user and click Invite This Person.

5. To send an email request using your MAPI-compliant messaging application, enter the Expert's first name and click Continue.

6. Supply the password and duration for the Remote Assistance request.

7. Enter the correct email address and add any other notes you want before sending the message.

8. To send the Remote Assistance request using a saved file, click Send Invitation as a File (Advanced).

### 7.2 Configuring Remote Assistance Group Policy Options

In this exercise, you configure the Group Policy options for Remote Assistance. You should have at least one Windows Server 2003 computer for this procedure.

**Estimated time:** 20 minutes

1. Locate the Group Policy Object for which you want to configure the Remote Assistance settings.

2. Locate the Remote Assistance node.

3. Double-click the Solicited Remote Assistance setting to open its Properties dialog box.

4. Select the Enabled radio button.

5. For the Permit Remote Control of This Computer option, select Allow Helpers to Remotely Control the Computer to ensure that you can fully offer Remote Assistance as needed. You can take control only if the user allows it.

6. For the Maximum Ticket Time option, configure a reasonable lifetime for the Remote Assistance request, such as 1 hour. This allows you a window in which to respond to the request without creating an overly large security risk.

7. For the Select the Method for Sending E-mail Invitations option, your selection depends on the messaging client in use on your network. The Mailto option configures the Remote Assistance request to be sent as an Internet link and works in virtually all situations. The SMAPI (Simple MAPI) option configures the request to be attached to the message.

8. Click OK to close the Solicited Remote Assistance Properties dialog box.

9. Double-click the Offer Remote Assistance setting to open its Properties dialog box.

10. To allow you to offer unsolicited Remote Assistance to users, select the Enabled radio button.

## APPLY YOUR KNOWLEDGE

11. For the Permit Remote Control of This Computer option, select Allow Helpers to Remotely Control the Computer to ensure that you can fully offer Remote Assistance as needed. You can take control only if the user allows it.

12. Click the Show button to open the Show Contents dialog box.

13. To add users and/or groups, click the Add button. You can add only one object at a time, and you must use the following format:

    **<Domain Name>\<User Name>** or

    **<Domain Name>\<Group Name>**

14. Click OK to close the Offer Remote Assistance Properties dialog box.

---

### 7.3   Creating a Wireless Network Security Policy

In this exercise, you create a new Wireless network security policy. You need at least one Windows Server 2003 computer to complete this process.

**Estimated time:** 20 minutes

1. Using either the Group Policy Management Console (GPMC) or Group Policy Editor (GPE), locate the GPO in which you want to create the WLAN security policy.

2. Locate the Wireless Network (IEEE 802.11) Policies node. Right-click it; then select Create Wireless Network Policy from the context menu to start the Wireless Network Policy Wizard.

3. Click Next to dismiss the opening page of the wizard.

4. Enter a name and description for the new policy on the Wireless Network Policy Name dialog box. Click Next.

5. The Completing the Wireless Network Policy Wizard dialog box appears. Ensure that the Edit Properties option is selected; then click Finish to exit the wizard and start configuring the policy's properties.

6. The policy Properties dialog box opens. Configure your selections as you like and switch to the Preferred Networks tab.

7. Click the Add button to open the New Preferred Setting Properties dialog box.

8. On the Network Properties tab, configure the selections as necessary. When you are done, switch to the IEEE 802.1x tab.

9. On the IEEE 802.1x tab, configure the selections as necessary. When you are done, click OK to commit the preferred network to the policy.

10. Back at the Preferred Networks tab of the policy Properties dialog box, you can add another preferred network if you want. You can also remove or edit existing preferred network entries as well as change their relative order by using the Move Up and Move Down buttons.

11. Click OK to close the WLAN policy Properties dialog box.

12. If you want to force Active Directory replication to occur, thus implementing your new WLAN policies, enter the **gpupdate** **/target:computer** command.

## Review Questions

1. You need to create and implement a plan for your network that will allow you to ensure that users can always receive real-time support for their problems. What new feature of Windows Server 2003 provides this solution for you?

## APPLY YOUR KNOWLEDGE

2. You are attempting to connect to one of your Windows Server 2003 computers using the Remote Desktop Connection utility but cannot. What is the most likely reason for this trouble?

3. You are creating a new Wireless Network Security Policy. You need to ensure that your wireless clients can connect only to your Access Points and not directly to each other. What mode should you select?

4. You are planning a new IPSec policy for use on your internal network between your Financial subnet and your Accounting subnet. What authentication methods will you have to select from when creating this new policy?

5. What functions does AH provide in IPSec?

## Exam Questions

1. You are the network administrator for Joe's Crab Shack, a regional restaurant chain. You have recently begun to implement IPSec to secure communications on the internal network segments. You have just completed the configuration and implementation of the Richmond office network segment. Users in Richmond are now complaining to you that they can connect to their network resources from some computers but not from others. What do you suspect is the most likely cause of this problem?

   A. The computers do not have basic network connectivity.

   B. More than one IPSec policy is in place.

   C. The domain controller is not responding.

   D. The Kerberos key distribution center is not responding.

2. You are the network administrator for Jeff's Jeep Tours, an Australian tour company. You have a central office located in Sydney with 20 other smaller remote offices located all over the country. You have recently completed your rollout of Windows Server 2003 for all servers and Windows XP Professional for all clients in the corporate network. Some of the remote offices have only three or four employees and no IT staff. The IT management responsibility for these offices is shared among all the IT staff in other locations. When users in remote locations with no IT staff have problems with their Windows XP Professional computers, what feature should they use to get help for their problem?

   A. Terminal Services

   B. Remote Desktop for Administration

   C. Remote Desktop Protocol

   D. Remote Assistance

3. You are the network administrator for Jeff's Jeep Tours, an Australian tour company. You have a central office located in Sydney with 20 other smaller remote offices located all over the country. You have recently completed your rollout of Windows Server 2003 for all servers and Windows XP Professional for all clients in the corporate network. Some of the remote offices have only three or four employees and no IT staff. The IT management responsibility for these offices is shared among all the IT staff in other locations. You need to install a service pack on one of the Windows XP computers located in an office with no IT staff. What feature of Windows Server 2003 will you use?

## APPLY YOUR KNOWLEDGE

A. Terminal Services

B. Remote Desktop for Administration

C. Remote Desktop Protocol

D. Remote Assistance

4. You are the network administrator for Widgets and Hammerstein, LLC. Andrea, one of your users, has called you and says that she cannot connect to one of the network servers that requires secured communication. What can you do to quickly verify the IPSec policy in use on that computer?

A. Use the IP Security Monitor snap-in to see what IPSec policy is in use on the computer.

B. Use the Network Monitor to see what IPSec policy is in use on the computer.

C. Use the IP Security Policies snap-in to see what IPSec policy is in use on the computer.

D. Use the `ipconfig/all` command to see what IPSec policy is in use on the computer.

5. You are the network administrator for Joe's Crab Shack, a regional restaurant chain. While at a standards setting meeting in Redmond, Washington, you are informed that one of your newly installed Windows Server 2003 DHCP servers has stopped leasing addresses. Rick, the president of the company, has asked you to make a Remote Desktop for Administration connection to the server via your VPN connection. After you have connected to your internal network via VPN, you attempt to create a Remote Desktop for Administration connection to the affected DHCP server and cannot. The DHCP server is located on the same IP subnet as the VPN server. You can create Remote Desktop for

Administration connections to other Windows Server 2003 computers, however. What is the most likely reason for this problem?

A. Remote Desktop is not enabled on the server.

B. Your VPN server is not functioning correctly.

C. TCP port 3389 is being blocked at your firewall.

D. Remote Desktop is not enabled on your portable computer.

6. You are the network administrator for Roger's Rockets, a manufacturer of toy rocket kits. You are preparing to configure a new Wireless LAN policy for your network. You want your wireless clients to connect only to Access Points and create no other connections. Which type of network will you configure in the new WLAN security policy?

A. Ad hoc

B. Infrastructure

C. Central

D. Core

7. You are the network administrator for Sunny Day, Inc. You are creating a new IPSec policy for your internal network's financial subnet. When creating your new policy, which items can you specify as part of the IP filter? (Choose all that apply.)

A. Source IP address

B. Destination IP address

C. Network protocol

D. Operating system

## APPLY YOUR KNOWLEDGE

8. You are the network administrator for Roger's Rockets, a manufacturer of toy rocket kits. You have configured four different WLAN security policies for your network: one at the domain level, one on the Graphics OU, one on the Engineering OU, and one on the Manufacturing OU, which is a child object inside the Engineering OU. All users and computers in each department are located in the corresponding OU. For a computer located in the Manufacturing OU, which security policy will be implemented?

A. The domain WLAN security policy

B. The Engineering OU WLAN security policy

C. The Graphics OU WLAN security policy

D. The Manufacturing OU WLAN security policy

9. You are the network administrator for Roger's Rockets, a manufacturer of toy rocket kits. You have one WLAN security policy in place for your network that is configured in the Default Domain GPO. When you make a change to this WLAN security policy that changes the list of preferred networks, what will any currently connected wireless clients do?

A. The client connection will be momentarily broken if the new policy takes precedence over the old policy.

B. The client connection will be momentarily broken. When the Wireless Configuration service restarts, the client will revert to any existing client-configured settings in place.

C. The client connection will be momentarily broken. When the Wireless Configuration service restarts, the client will revert to the client settings that are configured in the next higher level WLAN security policy.

D. The client connection will broken until the radio on the wireless client has been restarted.

10. You are the network administrator for Herb's Happenings, a public relations firm. You want to create a new IPSec policy for traffic on your private network that provides the strongest secret key possible. In Windows Server 2003, what is the maximum Diffie-Hellman value that can be used?

A. 512 bit

B. 768 bit

C. 1,024 bit

D. 2,048 bit

11. You are the network administrator for Joe's Crab Shack, a regional restaurant chain. While at a standards setting meeting in Redmond, Washington, you are informed that one of your newly installed Windows Server 2003 DHCP servers has stopped leasing addresses. Your assistant administrator has verified that there are plenty of unused leases in the current DHCP scope, but is unable to determine the cause of the problem. Company policy prohibits the use of any Instant Messaging clients within your internal network. How can your assistant get Remote Assistance from you to help troubleshoot the DHCP server?

## APPLY YOUR KNOWLEDGE

A. Use Emergency Management Services to make the request.

B. Use the Recovery Console to make the request.

C. Use an email-based request.

D. Use MSN Messenger to make the request.

12. You are the network administrator for Roger's Rockets, a manufacturer of toy rocket kits. You have just completed changing the WLAN security policy that is applied to your Engineering OU. You want this policy to be enforced immediately on all clients. What command can you issue to cause Group Policy to replicate immediately?

   A. `gpupdate /target:user`

   B. `secedit /configure`

   C. `gpupdate /target:computer`

   D. `secedit /analyze`

13. You are the network administrator for Joe's Crab Shack, a regional restaurant chain. While at a standards setting meeting in Redmond, Washington, you are unsuccessfully attempting to initiate a Remote Desktop for Administration session with one of your Windows Server 2003 servers over the Internet. The server has a publicly accessible IP address, but it is located behind your network's external firewall. You can `ping` the server from your location and have verified via telephone conversation with onsite IT staff that Remote Desktop is enabled for this server. Your account is a member of the Domain Admins, Enterprise Admins, and Administrators groups for your Active Directory network. What is the most likely reason for the inability to make the Remote Desktop for Administration connection?

A. IIS 6.0 is not installed on the server in question.

B. TCP port 3389 is being blocked at the external firewall.

C. TCP port 8088 is being blocked at the external firewall.

D. Your user account does not have the required permissions to use Remote Desktop for Administration.

14. You are the network administrator for Roger's Rockets, a manufacturer of toy rocket kits. You are creating a new WLAN security policy for the wireless clients located in the Engineering OU. You have one approved 802.11b WLAN in your organization with an SSID of rogrcktint1. From time to time the Engineering department needs to use a special testing WLAN. The SSID of this testing WLAN changes each time it is implemented. What setting can you configure for the Engineering OU WLAN security policy that will allow these wireless clients to connect to the special testing WLAN when it is available?

A. You will need to update the WLAN security policy every time the special testing WLAN is available.

B. You will need to create a new WLAN security policy in the Engineering OU every time the special testing WLAN is available.

C. You will need to select the Automatically Connect to Non-preferred Networks option.

D. You will need to select the Wireless Network Key (WEP) option.

## APPLY YOUR KNOWLEDGE

15. You are the network administrator for Jeff's Jeep Tours, an Australian tour company. You are configuring one of your Windows Server 2003 computers so that it will support Remote Desktop for Administration connections. You want two additional non-administrative personnel to be able to create Remote Desktop connections to the server. To what local group do you need to add their user accounts to allow these users to create Remote Desktop for Administration connections?

    A. HelpServicesGroup

    B. Remote Desktop Users

    C. Network Configuration Operators

    D. Administrators

## Answers to Review Questions

1. Users can use Remote Assistance to request help from an Expert with their problems, provided that the computers on both ends of the connection are Windows XP or Windows Server 2003. For more information, see the section "Remote Assistance."

2. The most likely reason you cannot create the connection is that this server already has two existing Remote Desktop connections. For more information, see the section "Remote Desktop for Administration (RDA)."

3. To ensure that wireless clients create connections only to Access Points, select the Access Point (Infrastructure) Networks Only option. For more information, see the section "Planning Wireless LAN (WLAN) Security."

4. IPSec on Windows Server 2003 can use Kerberos v5, a digital certificate, or a shared secret (string) for user authentication. For more information, see the section "Planning Security for Data Transmission."

5. The IPSec AH provides three services as part of the IPSec protocol. First (as its name might suggest), AH authenticates the entire packet. Second, it ensures data integrity. Third, it prevents any replaying of the packet by a third party who might be trying to penetrate the IPSec tunnel. One service AH doesn't provide is payload encryption. AH protects your data from modification, but an attacker who is snooping the network would still be able to read the data. For more information, see the section "Authentication Header (AH)."

## Answers to Exam Questions

1. **B.** More often than not when you have some computers able to create IPSec connections and others that cannot, you have more than one IPSec policy in place. If you are intentionally using multiple policies, you need to ensure that you have at least one common authentication and security method between them; otherwise, communications will fail. Basic network connectivity, while always a potential problem, does not appear to be the problem here; thus, answer A is incorrect. The status of the domain controller is not an issue here; thus, answer C is incorrect. The status of the KDC is also not an issue here; thus, answer D is incorrect. For more information, see the section "General IPSec Troubleshooting."

## APPLY YOUR KNOWLEDGE

2. **D.** If configured to allow it, Windows XP and Windows Server 2003 computers can send Remote Assistance requests to an Expert asking for help with problems. The Novice requesting the Remote Assistance can choose from Windows Messenger, email, or a file to ask for Remote Assistance and can control the level of interaction and control the Expert has on the Novice's computer after the Remote Assistance connection has been made. Terminal Services is used in Windows Server 2003 to provide the Terminal Server role, allowing users to make connections to a Terminal Server to execute applications that are not available on their local computer, and does not provide a means for users to get help with problems on their computers; thus, answer A is incorrect. Remote Desktop for Administration is used to create administrative connections to computers and does not require a request to be sent; thus, answer B is incorrect. The Remote Desktop Protocol is used to power Remote Assistance and Remote Desktop for Administration but does not directly provide the solution required; thus, answer C is incorrect. For more information, see the section "Remote Assistance."

3. **B.** The Remote Desktop for Administration feature replaces what was previously known as Remote Administration mode of Terminal Services in Windows 2000 Server. RDA allows for a maximum of two concurrent connections to a server for the purposes of managing and maintaining it. Unlike Remote Assistance, RDA sessions do not start with a user request; an administrator can initiate an RDA connection whenever desired. Terminal Services is used in Windows Server 2003 to provide the Terminal Server role, allowing users to make connections

to a Terminal Server to execute applications that are not available on their local computer, and does not provide a means for users to get help with problems on their computers; thus, answer A is incorrect. Remote Desktop for Administration is used to create administrative connections to computers and does not require a request to be sent; thus, answer C is incorrect. Remote Assistance allows a Novice to request help from an Expert if the Novice's computer is configured to allow Remote Assistance; thus, answer D is incorrect. For more information, see the section "Remote Desktop for Administration (RDA)."

4. **A.** You need to use the IP Security Monitor snap-in to examine what IPSec policy, if any, is currently assigned to the computer. Network Monitor and the IP Security Policies snap-in will not show you what IPSec policy is assigned, and neither will the `ipconfig/all` command; thus, answers B, C, and D are incorrect. For more information, see the section "The IP Security Monitor MMC Snap-in."

5. **A.** Because you can create a connection to your network via the VPN server, the most likely problem is that Remote Desktop is not enabled on this server. The VPN server is obviously functioning correctly because you are able to connect to the network via VPN; thus, answer B is incorrect. Because you are connecting directly to your internal network via a VPN tunnel, the status of the firewall configuration is not an issue; thus, answer C is incorrect. Remote Desktop does not need to be enabled on your portable computer; thus, answer D is incorrect. For more information, see the section "Remote Desktop for Administration (RDA)."

## APPLY YOUR KNOWLEDGE

6. **B.** Infrastructure networks are those in which wireless clients create connections only to Access Points. Ad hoc networks are those in which wireless clients can create connections directly to each other without the need for an Access Point; thus, answer A is incorrect. Central and Core are not network types; thus, answers C and D are incorrect. For more information, see the section "Planning Wireless LAN (WLAN) Security."

7. **A, B, and C.** You can specify the source IP address, destination IP address, source port, destination port, and network protocol in your IP filters. The operating system is not part of the filters; thus, answer D is incorrect. For more information, see the section "Configuring and Implementing IPSec."

8. **D.** WLAN security policies are applied using the normal Group Policy processing order; thus, the security policy that is closest to the computer object takes precedence. Consequently, answers A, B, and C are incorrect. For more information, see the section "Planning Wireless LAN (WLAN) Security."

9. **A.** When a WLAN security policy is changed, the client connection will be momentarily broken if the new policy takes precedence over the old policy—that is, if the new policy changes something such as the authentication method; thus, answers B, C, and D are incorrect. For more information, see the section "Planning Wireless LAN (WLAN) Security."

10. **D.** Windows Server 2003 provides the increased Diffie-Hellman option of 2,048 bits; thus, answers A, B, and C are incorrect. The Diffie-Hellman group is used to determine the length of the base material that is actually used to generate the IPSec secret key. This increased length

increases the secret key strength and thus makes it more difficult for an attacker to break. For more information, see the section "Planning Security for Data Transmission."

11. **C.** Of the available options, the only valid one is to create and send an email request for Remote Assistance. The email request will contain a special URL that the Expert can use to initiate the Remote Assistance connection via the Microsoft Web site. The Expert will need to download and install an ActiveX applet as part of the connection process. Emergency Management Services and the Recovery Console cannot be used to send Remote Assistance requests; thus, answers A and B are incorrect. MSN Messenger is similar to Windows Messenger but cannot be used to send Remote Assistance requests; thus, answer D is incorrect. For more information, see the section "Remote Assistance."

12. **C.** You will need to use the `gpupdate /target:computer` command to immediately cause the computer configuration portion of Group Policy to refresh and update your changes. Wireless LAN security policies are not kept in the user configuration portion of Group Policy; thus, answer A is incorrect. The `secedit` command is no longer used to refresh Group Policy in Windows Server 2003; thus, answers B and D are incorrect. For more information, see the section "Planning Wireless LAN (WLAN) Security."

13. **B.** The most likely problem is that your external firewall has been configured to block traffic on TCP port 3389 and is thus preventing Remote Desktop Protocol traffic from crossing the firewall. IIS does not need to be installed to use Remote Desktop for Administration; thus, answer A is incorrect. TCP ports 8088 and 8080

## APPLY YOUR KNOWLEDGE

are used by the Web Interface for Remote Administration and are not related to Remote Desktop for Administration; thus, answer C is incorrect. Your account does in fact have the required permissions because it is a member of the Enterprise Admins, Domain Admins, and Administrators group in your domain; thus, answer D is incorrect. For more information, see the section "Remote Desktop for Administration (RDA)."

14. **C.** By creating the WLAN security policy and selecting the Automatically Connect to Non-preferred Networks option, you can enforce the settings you want (such as those for authentication and so forth) on preferred networks but still allow wireless clients to connect to non-preferred networks if required. Under normal circumstances, you might likely not configure this option because it removes some administrative control you would otherwise exercise over what networks wireless clients can connect to. You don't need to modify the existing WLAN security

policy when the special testing WLAN is available; thus, answer A is incorrect. Likewise, you don't need to create a new WLAN security policy; thus, answer B is incorrect. The Wireless Network Key (WEP) option is not related to this issue; thus, answer D is incorrect. For more information, see the section "Planning Wireless LAN (WLAN) Security."

15. **B.** You must add the user accounts for these two users to the local Remote Desktop Users group on the computer. The HelpServicesGroup is used by Remote Assistance connections; thus, answer A is incorrect. The Network Configuration Operators group is allowed to manage the networking properties of a server; thus, answer C is incorrect. You don't need to add these user accounts to the Administrators group to allow them to create Remote Desktop connections to this server; thus, answer D is incorrect. For more information, see the section "Remote Desktop for Administration (RDA)."

### Suggested Readings and Resources

1. Davies, Joseph, and Thomas Lee. 2003. *Microsoft Windows Server 2003 TCP/IP Protocols and Services Technical Reference.* Redmond, WA: Microsoft Press. ISBN: 0735612919.

2. Microsoft Corporation. 2003. *Microsoft Windows Server 2003 Resource Kit.* Redmond, WA: Microsoft Press. ISBN: 0735614717.

3. Microsoft Corporation. 2003. *Microsoft Windows Server 2003 Deployment Kit.* Redmond, WA: Microsoft Press. ISBN: 0735614865.

4. "Technical Overview of Windows Server 2003 Security Services," www.microsoft.com/windowsserver2003/techinfo/overview/security.mspx.

5. "Internet Protocol Security Overview," www.microsoft.com/technet/prodtechnol/windowsserver2003/proddocs/standard/sag_IPSECintroduct.asp.

Security is all the rage right now—and rightly so. For many years, security was thought of as something that only certain networks needed. When security was planned for a network, more often than not it included only a weak solution that the company hoped would keep external intruders out of the network. No longer can networks be exposed to the Internet without a well-thought-out and layered defense plan. In this chapter, we examine a few of the tasks that you may address in your security plan: using digital certificates, using smart cards, auditing, monitoring event logs, and keeping your Windows computers up to date with the latest security updates.

Microsoft defines the "Planning, Implementing, and Maintaining Security Infrastructure" objectives as follows:

**Configure Active Directory directory service for certificate publication.**

▶ Although you do not have to perform any direct configuration of Active Directory to make Certificate Services function, you can configure some advanced tasks, such as certificate autoenrollment for your network's users and computers.

**Plan a public key infrastructure (PKI) that uses Certificate Services.**

- **Identify the appropriate type of certificate authority to support certificate issuance requirements.**

- **Plan the enrollment and distribution of certificates.**

- **Plan for the use of smart cards for authentication.**

▶ At the heart of the Windows security solution lies Certificate Services. You use digital certificates every day in Windows Server 2003 without even realizing it. (Have you ever encrypted a file using

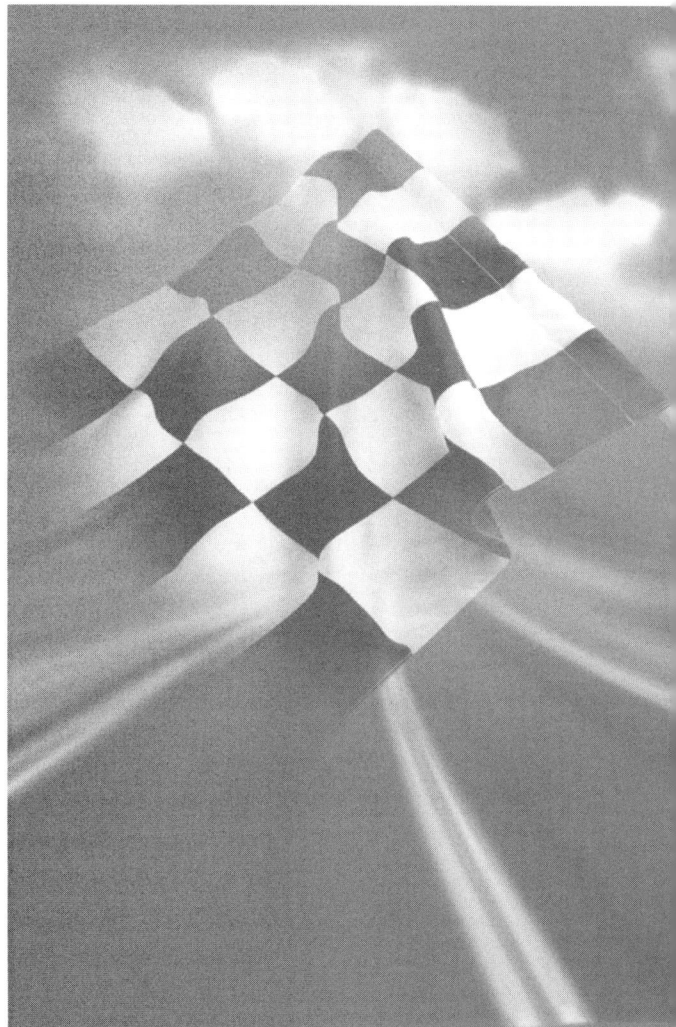

CHAPTER **8**

# Planning, Implementing, and Maintaining Security Infrastructure

EFS?) Certificate Services allows you to implement and configure one or more CAs to issue and revoke digital certificates for your network. You may also want to take your security a level further and implement a smart card authentication solution.

**Plan a framework for planning and implementing security.**

- **Plan for security monitoring.**

- **Plan a change and configuration management framework for security.**

▶ Being able to just sit back and watch the network run after implementing your security solution would be nice; however, this is not the case. You must maintain a constant watch over your network, examining many different aspects of it to determine what is occurring that should not be. By auditing and examining the event logs, you can quickly get a good idea of what is going on in your network—free, without the purchase of any advanced network monitoring tools. Also, without a change and configuration management document in place for your organization, you will likely find yourself in trouble should an ill-planned configuration change go awry.

**Plan a security update infrastructure. Tools might include Microsoft Baseline Security Analyzer and Microsoft Software Update Services.**

▶ In a perfect world, you would be able to install your server or client operating system and have it be perfect and perfectly secure right out of the box. Although Microsoft has made great progress toward meeting that ideal in Windows Server 2003, it's not quite a reality yet. Part of keeping an operating system secure involves identifying and applying updates as required. The combination of the Microsoft Baseline Security Analyzer (MBSA) and Software Update Services (SUS) makes this task easier for the Windows Server 2003 network administrator.

## STUDY STRATEGIES

▶ Become familiar with the topics presented in this chapter, including Certificate Services, auditing, event logs, SUS, and MBSA. All these topics will be important as you plan and implement a security solution for your network.

▶ Get your hands dirty. The Step by Steps throughout this book provide plenty of directions and exercises, but you should go beyond these examples and create some of your own. If you can, experiment with each of the objectives to see how they work and why you would use each one.

# INTRODUCTION

As you may realize, networks today keep growing and intermingling with other networks. This growth presents a challenge for Microsoft Certified Systems Engineers in that it increases network exposure to users and other individuals who seek to penetrate its defenses and gain entry. What makes it possible for all these networks to be vulnerable to attack? They share a common protocol.

The common protocol used in the exchange of data is Transmission Control Protocol/Internet Protocol (TCP/IP), as discussed in previous chapters of this book. Data sent via TCP/IP is broken up and sent over various routes to the final destination. Because of the design of TCP/IP, data can be intercepted easily without the sender or the receiver knowing that the data may have been intercepted. Certainly, as data passes through networks around the globe, it is susceptible to interception or forgery, and users are often the recipients of data whose content may jeopardize their own data.

We need a way to protect our outgoing data and ensure that our incoming data has not been compromised. We also need a way to verify that people and machines we may communicate with are who they say they are. Enter the *digital certificate*. This chapter introduces the fundamentals of certificates and then discusses installing and configuring CA Services.

Maintaining a secure network is not a one-step or one-day event; it is a daily, ongoing event that requires you to not only implement an initial solution but also to monitor it and massage it over time to ensure that new threats and required changes are being taken into account. Too many times in the past, administrators have tried to treat server and network security as a "set it and forget it" type of thing, but that's just not possible today. To help Windows Server 2003 administrators keep their computers and networks secure, Microsoft has provided a relatively pain-free method of identifying and installing required updates and security fixes through use of the *Microsoft Baseline Security Analyzer (MBSA)* and *Software Update Services (SUS)*.

Of course, as you might have guessed, at the heart of all your security plans must lie a solid plan to not only implement and control security, but also to monitor and manage it. Planning is key in network administration, and Windows Server 2003 networks are no different.

# WHAT'S NEW IN WINDOWS SERVER 2003 CERTIFICATE SERVICES?

Windows Server 2003, when combined with a Windows XP Professional client computer in a Windows Server 2003 Active Directory–based network, features several enhancements and improvements to Certificate Services. These features will make more sense to you as you work your way through this chapter's discussion of PKI and Certificate Services. Some of the features you will discover are listed next:

- ▶ **Version 2 certificate templates**—Version 2 templates extend the range of properties that you can configure from those provided in Version 1 templates. You now can create new certificate templates (an option sorely lacking from Windows 2000), copy existing certificate templates, and supercede certificate templates that are already in use. You need a Window Advanced Server 2003 functioning as the Enterprise Root CA.

- ▶ **Integrated and enhanced key recovery**—Windows 2000 Server relied on a Data Recovery Agent (DRA) to decrypt files following the loss or damage of an encryption key. Additionally, the Exchange 2000 Server Key Management Service (KMS) ran on top of Windows 2000 Certificate Services and did not fully integrate. Windows Server 2003 allows the archival and recovery of private keys and allows the administrator to access data encrypted with a lost or damaged private key. Now Key Recovery Agents (KRAs) are used to recover lost or damaged private keys across Windows Server 2003 and Exchange Server 2003.

- ▶ **Delta Certificate Revocation Lists**—Windows Server 2003 supports RFC 2459–compliant delta Certificate Revocation Lists (CRLs) that contain only the certificates whose status has changed since the last full (base) CRL was compiled. This results in a much smaller CRL, which can be more frequently published with no adverse effects on the network or client computers. Additionally, this provides more accurate CRLs due to reduced latency periods. In Windows 2000, CRLs were typically published once per week (the default setting). Delta CRLs allow you to publish one or more times daily as required.

**EXAM TIP**

**Delta CRLs** The Delta CRL feature of Windows Server 2003 is an important one that you should be aware of.

▶ **CA qualified subordination**—Another part of RFC 2459, qualified subordination allows a parent CA to granularly configure what a Subordinate CA is allowed to. Examples include preventing the Subordinate CA from signing a certificate for another Subordinate CA.

▶ **Common Criteria role separation**—By separating common CA-related tasks between several different levels of administration, you can meet Common Criteria requirements and enhance task delegation. Because roles are separated, no one individual should possess the ability to compromise the services or operation of the CA.

▶ **Enhanced auditing**—Windows Server 2003 provides for more detailed auditing of Certificate Services by adding two new types of events: access check and system events. System events come from seven critical areas: CA service, backup and restoration, certificate requests, certificate revocations, CA security, key archival and key recovery, and CA configuration.

After your introduction to public key infrastructure (PKI) and the enhancements found in Windows Server 2003 Certificate Services, you are ready to take the first step in implementing a PKI: planning. Remember that if you fail to plan, then you must plan to fail—especially when dealing with the sometimes confusing and complex world of PKI.

# PLANNING A WINDOWS SERVER 2003 PUBLIC KEY INFRASTRUCTURE (PKI)

So you want to install a Windows Server PKI on your network to issue and validate digital certificates? Great idea! But what exactly is a PKI, and what is it made up of? Before getting around to the planning and implementing of the often-misunderstood PKI, you should first have a good idea of what it is and how it works. After you've perused through an introduction to PKI, you then can more efficiently plan for, and subsequently implement, your PKI solution.

# Introduction to the Public Key Infrastructure (PKI)

To combat the openness of TCP/IP without losing the functionality of the protocol, PKI has been developed in tandem with TCP/IP as a means of offering security for data sent between hosts—on an intranet or on the Internet.

Using encryption, network administrators and security experts can ensure that the data is read only by the intended recipient and that data received has not been tampered with. The analogy of a physical signature and envelopes sealed with wax is an excellent parallel to how PKI is used today. In lieu of your "John Hancock" and sealing wax, you use a digital signature.

A digital signature ensures that the message is from the source it says it's from and that the message hasn't been digitally "steamed open." In addition to digital signatures, you can implement digital identifications–thus, the digital certificate.

## Certificates

What exactly is a *digital certificate*? Essentially, it's the electronic version of your passport or employee identification card. It proves that you are who you say you are. This certificate is what ultimately allows you to access resources and data.

Certificates are issued not only to individuals, but also to organizations, businesses, routers, and other entities as a way of controlling and securing data. A digital certificate contains the following information:

- ▶ The user's name
- ▶ The user's public key
- ▶ Serial number
- ▶ Expiration date
- ▶ Information on the certificate itself
- ▶ Information on the entity (called a certificate authority) that issued the certificate

When secure data is transferred, an electronic seal is inserted into the data through cryptography. When the recipient opens the data, a key verifies that the electronic seal exists and that it has not been tampered with. In addition, the recipient can be assured that the sender of the data is who he says he is.

Traditionally, when you want to send encrypted data to other users, you use your key to encrypt and secure the data. When the recipients want to open the encrypted data, they use their copy of the key to unlock the data. Should others without the key intercept the packets, they cannot decrypt the information. This method of security is not really very secure. The problem is that when unauthorized users gain access to the key, they gain access to the data—not unlike discovering your house keys in the outside lock of your door.

Digital certificates, however, use a slightly different method of locking and unlocking the data. With digital certificates, you no longer have to make copies of keys for others to unlock your data. Digital certificates use a private key to lock the data and then a different key, the public key, to unlock the data. No longer is the same key used to lock and unlock data.

With this two-key technology, your private key remains private. No one but the rightful owner should ever have access to it. However, by means of the digital certificate, you can disperse the public key to whoever may need it.

When Dick wants to send a private message to Jane, for example, Dick uses Jane's public key to encrypt the message. No one other than Jane can decrypt the message, but now the private key, Jane's key, is required to unlock the contents. When Jane responds to Dick, she can use Dick's public key to encrypt the response. Dick then uses his own private key to unlock the message.

## Certificate Authorities (CAs)

All certificates are issued by a CA, such as VeriSign or one internal to your own network. The CA verifies that the owner of the certificate is who he says he is. A CA is a trusted third party that is responsible for physically verifying the legitimacy of the identity of an individual or organization before issuing a digital certificate. A CA is also responsible for issuing certificates, revoking certificates, and publishing a list of revoked certificates.

With Windows Server 2003, you can use a third-party CA, or you can create your own CA through Microsoft's Windows Server 2003 Certificate Services, which offers four distinct types of CAs: Enterprise Root CA, Enterprise Subordinate CA, Standalone Root CA, and Standalone Subordinate CA. We take a closer look at these types of CAs throughout the chapter.

If you elect to create an internal CA for your organization, you need to establish some rules and guidelines to verify that users are employees. You can use Social Security numbers, employee badges, or an even more secure method—smart cards, which allow users to log in and access and send data, such as email and data on a network.

## The Enterprise CA

A Windows Server 2003 *Enterprise CA* provides certificates for the internal security of an entire organization, whereas an external CA (such as VeriSign) provides security for external security needs. Microsoft provides support for both, and you can mix and match to fit your business needs.

If users request a certificate in a Windows Server 2003 environment, their user accounts can act as the credentials for the user because they are logged on and recognized in the Active Directory.

A Windows Server 2003 Enterprise CA has five key characteristics:

▶ The CA server may run on any Windows Server 2003 server in the domain. You should plan for activity, network load, and physical placement of the server for best implementation. Note that you cannot use a Windows Server 2003 Web Edition server as a Certificate Authority.

▶ Because the CA name is integrated into the certificates it assigns, the name of the server should be determined before implementing CA services.

▶ The Enterprise CA Authority is integrated into the Active Directory.

▶ When you've installed an Enterprise CA, a policy module is created. An administrator can edit the policy.

▶ Because the CA is crucial for the successful implementation of the PKI, it must have a fault-tolerance scheme and a schedule of regular secure backups.

### The Standalone CA

Another type of CA that Windows Server 2003 allows you to install is a *Standalone CA*. The Standalone CA doesn't require the interaction of Active Directory, but it can use Active Directory if it's available.

A Standalone CA is useful in issuing certificates and digital signatures, and it supports secure email (S/MIME) and Secure Sockets Layer (SSL) or Transport Layer Security (TLS).

A typical Standalone CA has these key characteristics:

- It doesn't require Active Directory interaction.

- It can be used with extranets.

- It doesn't verify the requests for certificates. (All requests are pending until an administrator approves them.)

- Users requesting a certificate from a Standalone CA must supply all user account information. This information is not required within an Enterprise CA because the user is recognized by the logon account in the Active Directory.

- No certificate templates are used.

- Windows Sever 2003 logon credential certificates are not stored on smart cards. Other certificates can be, however.

- An administrator must distribute the Standalone CA certificate to the Trusted Root Certificate Store.

If Active Directory exists on the network and a Standalone CA can access it, additional options are available:

- If a domain administrator with write access to Active Directory installs the Standalone CA, the standalone is added to the Trusted Root Certification Authorities Certificate Store. In this situation, you must make certain that the default action of pending requests isn't changed to allow the Standalone CA to automatically approve all requests for certificates. Do not change the default action of pending certificate requests on a Standalone CA.

- If a domain administrator group member of the parent domain (or an administrator with write access to Active Directory) installs the Standalone CA, the Standalone CA will publish the certificate and the Certificate Revocation list to Active Directory.

With this brief PKI introduction out of the way, we can now move forward into the planning stages for your Windows Server 2003 PKI implementation.

**EXAM TIP**

**CA types**   Ensure that you have a good understanding of the characteristics, abilities, and uses of the four different CA types.

## Initial Planning for the PKI

When you are preparing to install a CA, you should start by planning how to configure your PKI. Windows Server 2003 Group Policy can allow you to publish and revoke certificates directly to user accounts. This feature can allow you to change a user's digital information and enforce it for accessing and retrieving data. Finally, your PKI scheme should include measures for your enterprise to secure email using S/MIME and SSL and/or TLS.

Before you can install the PKI and your first CA, you need to have a plan that addresses these additional questions:

▶ What type of CA or CAs do you require?

▶ How many CAs total will you require?

▶ How long will certificates be valid for?

▶ Who will manage the security?

▶ Will administrative duties be delegated?

▶ How will the CA be monitored? Who will monitor it?

▶ What kind of auditing should be in place for the CA?

▶ Where will the CA be located?

▶ Will you be using smart cards?

After you've answered these questions and have documented your answers to formulate a plan, you're ready to move into the next stages of planning.

## Planning the CA Hierarchies

Windows Server 2003 PKI allows for and encourages a dispersed hierarchy of CAs. Building a tree of CAs allows for scalability with other organizations, internal and external resources, and compatibility with third-party CA implementations.

It might seem to be the ideal solution to have only one CA—at least in terms of ease of administration. This, however, is not a realistic solution for many reasons, including size and number of domains and physical locations, along with the number of users who must be serviced by the PKI infrastructure. Each CA hierarchy begins with the *Root CA*, and multiple CAs branch from this Root CA in a parent-child relationship. The child CAs are certified by the parent CA all the way back to the Root CA. The parent CAs bind a CA public key to the child CA's identity.

In this parent-child relationship, child CAs are trusted by the parent. That parent is, in turn, trusted by its parent CA, all the way back to the originating Root CA. Also in this model, when an organization trusts a CA by adding its certificate in the Trusted Root Certification Authorities Certificate Store, the organization therefore trusts every Subordinate CA in the hierarchy. Should a Subordinate CA have its certificate revoked by the issuing CA, the revoked CA is no longer trustworthy.

Hierarchies serve many purposes. Some of the reasons for creating a CA hierarchy include

- ▶ **Varying usages**—Certificates can be issued for a number of purposes, such as secure email, SSL, and TSL. Different CAs can be responsible for different areas of security.

- ▶ **Politics**—A hierarchy allows for various departments within an enterprise to use unique policies.

- ▶ **Geography**—In a wide area network (WAN) environment, a different CA may be needed in each physical location to save network resources.

- ▶ **Security**—The Root CA requires a very secure environment with fault-tolerant devices. Subordinate CAs do not require the same amount and type of security as the root.

- ▶ **Revocation**—Most organizations need to have the capability to revoke individual CAs rather than be forced to revoke an entire enterprise.

As you're planning your hierarchy, remember that a Root CA is a CA from which all Subordinate CAs branch. This CA should be the most secure and should probably be taken offline (in the case of a Standalone CA) after the installation to ensure the security of the originating certificate and keys. Figure 8.1 illustrates how you might have multiple branching CAs in your organization.

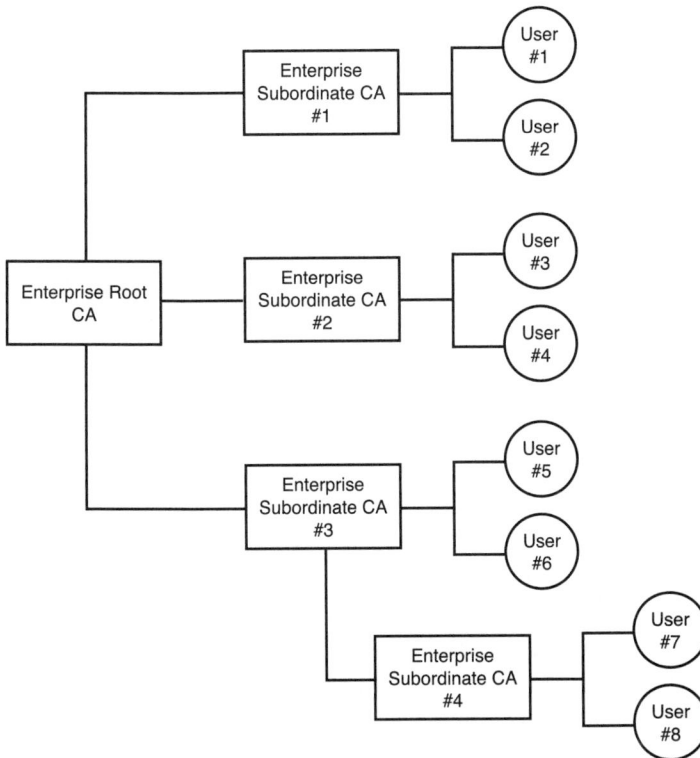

**FIGURE 8.1**
You can have certificate authorities arranged in any hierarchical order you require.

## Planning Certificate Revocation and Renewal

CAs are not only responsible for issuing and signing digital certificates, but they are also responsible for maintaining an accurate and up-to-date listing of those certificates that are no longer valid and thus should not be trusted. This listing of invalid certificates is known as a Certificate Revocation List (CRL) and is itself digitally signed by the issuing CA to verify its authenticity.

When a certificate is issued, it has a set validity period attached to it, typically five years by default. Under normal circumstances the certificate can be used for this period of time and will cease to be valid automatically should it not be renewed before the expiration date has been reached. Thus, it is only necessary to place certificates that have been revoked early for some reason on the CRL; certificates that have expired (that is, have passed their expiration date) are automatically considered invalid and do not need to be placed on a CRL.

The real decisions that you must make in relation to certificate revocation are, in most cases, limited to determining what circumstances require a certificate revocation and how to publish the CRL. Some organizations might require a certificate to be revoked only when an employee leaves the company, whereas other organizations might require a certificate to be revoked for Acceptable Use Policy (AUP) violations and the like. Also, you may need to change the interval and location to which CRLs are published. You can publish the CRL as often as once per day to any combination of the following locations: Active Directory (the default), a URL for access via a Web browser, or a CRL file that can be transported to a different location.

In direct contrast to certificate revocation, certificate renewal is just as important to your PKI implementation. Will you allow certificates to be renewed after their initial validity period has passed? When will you allow certificates to be renewed? How much of their lifetime must have passed before they can be renewed? Will you be using the same key pair for the renewed certificate—allowing users to extend the useable life of their keys—or will you require a new key pair to be created for the renewal—making any previously encrypted information unreadable?

## Renewing CAs

In a parent-child relationship between CAs, the parent CA issues a certificate as part of the relationship to designate the child CA. Just like the certificate to a client, the certificate to a Subordinate CA includes a validity period.

When the validity period expires for a CA, its own certificate must be renewed before it can grant any certification requests from client computers. When organizing your PKI, take into account the time a certification in a parent-child relationship should last.

As a safety and security measure, Windows Server 2003 PKI is set up so that a CA cannot issue certificates to requestors that will last beyond its own certificate's expiration date. This measure is handy because it ensures, for example, that a CA scheduled to expire this October cannot issue a certificate that may expire later than October.

Even the Root CA's own certificate will eventually expire. Therefore, certificates that it issues to subordinates will be staggered from its own expiration date. In other words, when the Root CA expires, all Subordinate CAs will have expired as well. No Subordinate CAs are valid beyond the date of the originating CA.

## Planning Certificate Template Usage

Windows Server 2003 comes with a wide range of preconfigured certificate templates that can be used to issue a variety of digital certificates. Although you do not need to decide which certificate templates to use before beginning your PKI implementation, you need to be aware of the certificate templates that are available and what purpose they serve. Certain applications—Exchange Server, for example—cannot be installed with full functionality unless certain optional certificate templates are made available first. Table 8.1 outlines the certificate templates that are available for use in Windows Server 2003.

**TABLE 8.1**

**THE WINDOWS SERVER 2003 CERTIFICATE TEMPLATES**

| Template | Purpose | Issued To | Published to AD? |
|---|---|---|---|
| Administrator | Provides for trust list signing and user authentication | User | Yes |
| Authenticated Session | Allows the user to authenticate to a Web server | User | No |
| Basic EFS | Allows the user to encrypt data using the Encrypting File System (EFS) | User | Yes |
| CA Exchange | Provides for key storage areas that are configured for private key archival | Computer | No |
| CEP Encryption | Allows the computer to act as a registration authority (RA) for Simple Certificate Enrollment Protocol (SCEP) requests | Computer | No |
| Code Signing | Provides a means to digitally sign software | User | No |

*continues*

**TABLE 8.1** *continued*

## THE WINDOWS SERVER 2003 CERTIFICATE TEMPLATES

| *Template* | *Purpose* | *Issued To* | *Published to AD?* |
|---|---|---|---|
| Computer | Provides a means for a computer to authenticate itself on the network | Computer | No |
| Cross-Certification Authority | Used for cross-certification and qualified subordination of CAs | CrossCA | Yes |
| Directory E-mail Replication | Provides a means to replicate email within Active Directory | DirEmailRep | Yes |
| Domain Controller | Acts as a general purpose certificate used by domain controllers | DirEmailRep | Yes |
| Domain Controller Authentication | Allows computers and users to authenticate to Active Directory | Computer | No |
| EFS Recovery Agent | Allows the user to decrypt files that have been encrypted with EFS | User | No |
| Enrollment Agent | Allows a user to request certificates on behalf of another subject | User | No |
| Enrollment Agent (Computer) | Allows a computer to request certificates on behalf of another computer subject | Computer | No |
| Exchange Enrollment Agent (Offline request) | Allows Exchange Server to request certificates on behalf of another subject and supply the subject name in the request | User | No |
| Exchange Signature Only | Allows the Microsoft Exchange Key Management Service (KMS) to issue certificates to Exchange users for digitally signing email | User | No |
| Exchange User | Allows the KMS to issue certificates to Exchange users for encrypting email | User | Yes |
| IPSEC | Provides a means for a computer to use IP Security (IPSec) to digitally sign, encrypt, and decrypt network communication | Computer | No |
| IPSEC (Offline request) | Allows IPSec to digitally sign, encrypt, and decrypt network communication when the subject name is supplied in the request | Computer | No |
| Key Recovery Agent | Provides a means to recover private keys that are archived on the certifice authority | KRA | No |
| RAS and IAS Server | Provides a means for RAS and IAS servers to authenticate their identity to other computers | Computer | No |
| Root Certification Authority | Allows the Root CA to prove its identity | CA | No |
| Router (Offline request) | Allows a router to request a certificate when requested through Simple Certificate Enrollment Protocol (SCEP) from a certificate authority that holds a CEP Encryption certificate | Computer | No |
| Smartcard Logon | Allows a user to authenticate to the domain using a smart card | User | No |
| Smartcard User | Provides a means for a user to authenticate and protect email using a smart card | User | Yes |
| Subordinate Certification Authority | Provides a means to prove the identity of the root certificate authority | CA | No |
| Trust List Signing | Allows the user to digitally sign a trust list | User | No |

| *Template* | *Purpose* | *Issued To* | *Published to AD?* |
|---|---|---|---|
| User | Provides for users for email, EFS, and client authentication to Active Directory | User | Yes |
| User Signature Only | Provides a means for users to digitally sign data | User | No |
| Web Server | Allows a Web server to prove its identity | Computer | No |
| Workstation Authentication | Allows client computers to authenticate their identity to servers | Computer | No |

With your basic PKI planning out of the way, you are now ready to move forward into more specific planning and implementation of your PKI solution.

# Planning Appropriate Certificate Authority Types

**Plan a public key infrastructure (PKI) that uses Certificate Services.**

▶ **Identify the appropriate type of certificate authority to support certificate issuance requirements.**

What exactly are the certificate requirements for your network? Will you be issuing certificates solely for use on your internal private network, or will you need to issue code signing certificates used to digitally sign applications that can be downloaded or otherwise distributed? The uses for digital certificates that you have ultimately determine the type of certificate authorities that you need to implement. Just as a note, CA types and certificate uses are directly related: The type of CA you install determines what your users and computers can do.

As a general review, let's examine each of the four basic CA types again briefly as you plan the needs for your network.

## Enterprise Root CA

Recall that the Root CA is at the top of the CA chain, as shown previously in Figure 8.1; this holds true both for Enterprise and Standalone hierarchies. The Enterprise Root CA, then, is at the top of an Enterprise—Active Directory—certificate chain and is at the top of the hierarchy. In short, all other CAs trust this Root CA.

> **EXAM TIP**
>
> **Certificate Templates** Don't worry too much about being tested on all the certificate templates Windows Server 2003 provides. This listing is provided primarily for completeness and as a reference for you to use when configuring a CA solution on your network.

The Enterprise Root CA can issue any type of certificate desired, including those for Subordinate CAs, users, and computers. However, it is usually best (and most commonly implemented) to have the Root CA issuing certificates only to its Subordinate CAs; this preserves the hierarchical nature of the certificate chain and specifies a single point that is "all knowing," so to say.

The Subordinate CAs are then charged with the responsibility of issuing certificates directly to users and computers within the organization. By implementing this parent-child relationship, you can segregate different levels of authority, providing for an overall more robust and secure CA infrastructure.

Because the Enterprise Root CA sits at the top of the certificate chain, it must therefore sign its own certificate, asserting that it is the root of the certificate chain and that all other CAs are to trust it as such.

## Enterprise Subordinate CA

The Enterprise Subordinate CA is the child in the parent-child relationship of CAs, as discussed previously. The Enterprise Subordinate CA does require Active Directory to function and can issue certificates to other (lower level) Subordinate CAs, users, and computers, as shown previously in Figure 8.1.

Enterprise Subordinate CAs can be implemented in various locations through the network to provide for increased performance and better load balancing among CAs. You can theoretically have as many Enterprise Subordinate CAs as you want, although practicality dictates that you should have only enough to ensure that all users can connect to a CA that is relatively nearby. Having unnecessary CAs on the network causes a security weakness in that a compromised CA may lead to further network compromises.

## Standalone Root CA

Just as the Enterprise Root CA is at the top of the certificate chain in an Active Directory network, the Standalone Root CA is at the top of the chain in a network that might not be using Active Directory. If Active Directory is available, the Standalone Root CA can make use of it, however. Being independent from Active Directory provides the Standalone Root CA the advantage of being able to be removed physically from the network, thus greatly increasing its security.

You can actually use a Standalone Root CA effectively to increase the security of your network by issuing from it those certificates that are very important, such as those for Subordinate CAs and those used by developers for digitally signing applications for distribution.

## Standalone Subordinate CA

The Standalone Subordinate CA behaves similarly to the Enterprise Subordinate CA—with one major difference. The Standalone Subordinate CA does not require the presence of Active Directory. Standalone Subordinate CAs are used to issue certificates directly to users; without Active Directory, you have no reason to issue certificates to computers.

---

### IT MATTERS NOT WHAT TYPE OF CA YOU IMPLEMENT...

...because you must still take the required precautions to ensure that it is as secure as can be. You must ensure first, and foremost, that all your CAs are secure from physical access by unauthorized personnel. A commonly held belief among security administrators is that physical access is the most dangerous threat to any critical server in the network. You therefore should place your CAs in a locked and access-controlled server room. Additionally, you should place them inside locked server cabinets as an added layer of protection.

Of course, physically securing your CAs is of little use should they experience a disaster situation. As with any critical business data, you must ensure that CAs are being backed up regularly using an approved and effective backup plan. The most important part of any CA is the CA's private key. Without this key, the entire CA is useless, and every certificate it has issued will have to be reissued.

Lastly, you should ensure that your network provides adequate protection for the CAs against threats both internal and external. Viruses and other malicious code run rampant today on the Internet, so you must ensure that your network is protected against these threats. You must also implement access controls to prevent unauthorized access to a CA.

---

**Internet Information Services (IIS) 6.0 in Windows Server 2003**

Unlike IIS 5.0 in Windows 2000 Server, IIS 6.0 is not installed by default in Windows Server 2003, with the exception of Windows Server 2003 Web Edition. If you have not previously manually installed IIS, you need to install it from the Windows Component Wizard under the Application Server option group before you install the Enterprise Root CA.

For best results, you should install IIS before starting the installation of Certificate Services.

At this time, we need to go above and beyond the objectives for this exam so that you gain the required knowledge. Although you won't explicitly see installing and configuring a CA listed in the objectives, understanding all the points made in the following sections is going to be very difficult without your having seen a CA installed and configured first. To that end, we will examine the installation and initial configuration of an Enterprise Root CA in the next section.

# Installing and Configuring an Enterprise Root CA

Now that you've reached this point in the chapter, you are really ready to install and perform the basic configuration of your first CA. After you've done this, you can more easily move through the remaining sections of this chapter that relate to PKI. Step by Step 8.1 outlines the process to install an Enterprise Root CA.

You should be aware of the fact that you must provide the following information during the installation of your first CA:

▶ **CA type**—You need to indicate the type of CA you will be using.

- **Enterprise Root CA**—The Enterprise Root CA is the root of all CAs in your hierarchy. Typically, an enterprise has only one. It requires Active Directory. Intermediate Subordinate CAs branch off this server. The Enterprise Root CA can only be a parent.

- **Enterprise Subordinate CA**—A Subordinate CA must obtain its certificate from a CA higher in the hierarchy. It requires Active Directory. This is the child of another CA. This CA could also be a parent to another CA.

- **Standalone Root CA**—A Standalone Root CA is like an Enterprise Root CA, except that it does not require Active Directory but can use it if it exists. Often this CA is offline to protect the validity of the originating certificates and keys.

- **Standalone Subordinate CA**—This CA does not require Active Directory but may use it if Active Directory is available. The Subordinate CA must obtain its certificate from another CA. This is the child in the relationship but may become a parent if it supplies a certificate to another CA.

▶ **Advanced options**—If you enable advanced options during the CA installation, you must provide the following:

- **The Cryptographic Service Provider (CSP)**—The CSP enables you to generate the public and private keys.

- **Key length**—The longer the key, the more secure the key.

- **Hash algorithm**—This computation produces a hash value of some piece of data. The default is Secure Hash Algorithm (SHA)-1, which is a 160-bit hash value.

▶ **CA name**—You can use just about any character you want. The name you assign the CA will also be the common name (CN) of the CA's distinguished name in Active Directory. Special characters (non–ASCII and ASCII punctuation) are stripped out in a sanitized name. Also, remember Active Directory is limited to 64 characters before it truncates names.

▶ **Organization**—You must provide the name of your organization as it is known throughout its community.

▶ **Organizational Unit**—You must indicate the division this CA manages.

▶ **City and State or Province**—You must indicate the city and state or province where the CA is located.

▶ **Country**—You need to indicate the X.500 two-character code for your country.

▶ **Location of the database**—By default, the database is stored in `\%systemroot%\system32\certlog`.

▶ **Shared folder**—You can create a shared folder for CA information if the CA is not participating in an Active Directory (such as a standalone server).

> **WARNING**
>
> **Changing the CA name**  After you install Certificate Services on the server, you cannot change its name or domain membership without first removing Certificate Services. This is, of course, for a very good reason: Changing either of these items would destroy the CA hierarchy.

# STEP BY STEP

### 8.1 Installing an Enterprise Root CA

**1.** Log in to a Windows Server 2003 that is a member of the Active Directory domain with administrative permissions.

*continues*

*continued*

2. From the Control Panel, double-click the Add or Remove Programs applet to open the Add or Remove Programs dialog box.

3. Click the Add/Remove Windows Components button located on the left side of the Add or Remove Programs dialog box to open the Windows Components Wizard.

4. Select the Certificate Services option, as shown in Figure 8.2.

**FIGURE 8.2**
You need to select the Certificate Services option to install your CA.

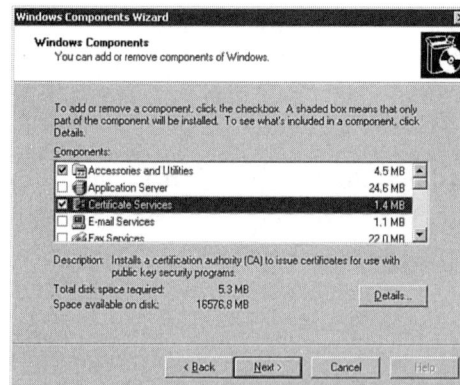

5. A warning dialog, as shown in Figure 8.3, informs you that you cannot rename the server after installing Certificate Services on it. Click Yes to continue.

**FIGURE 8.3**
You cannot rename this server after installing Certificate Services on it.

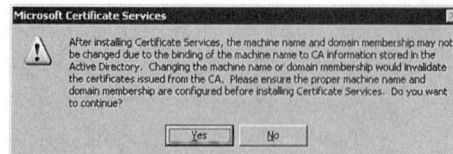

6. Click Next on the Windows Components Wizard dialog box to commence the installation process.

7. On the CA Type dialog box, shown in Figure 8.4, select the type of CA you are installing. For this example, select Enterprise Root CA and click Next to continue. If you want to customize the key pair settings, you can do so by selecting the Use Custom Settings to Generate the Key Pair and CA Certificate option.

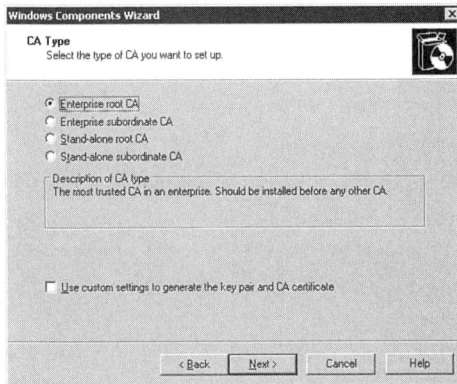

**FIGURE 8.4**
You must select one of the four available types of CAs.

8. If you selected to customize your key settings, the Public and Private Key Pair dialog box appears next, as shown in Figure 8.5. You have the opportunity to customize the installation by selecting the CSP and the Key Length. You can also use and import an existing certificate and key. Selecting the Allow This CSP to Interact with the Desktop option allows system services to interact with the desktop of the user who is currently logged on. Click Next to continue.

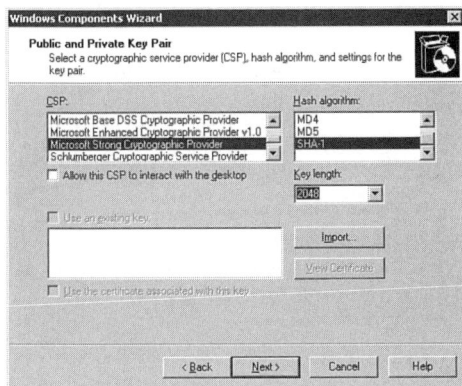

**FIGURE 8.5**
You can specify custom public and private key pair settings during the installation of the CA.

9. On the CA Identifying Information dialog box, shown in Figure 8.6, enter the common name of the CA. This name should be descriptive but should not contain any special characters. You also need to configure the Validity period; the default value is five years. After entering your selections, click Next to continue.

*continues*

*continued*

**FIGURE 8.6**
Your common name should be short and
descriptive to provide for easy identification of
the CA.

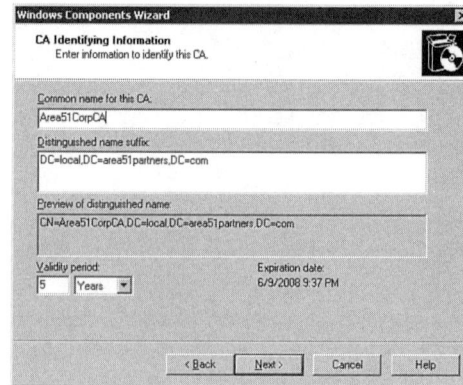

**10.** On the Certificate Database Settings dialog box, shown in
Figure 8.7, enter the database and log locations or simply
use the default selections—usually the best option in most
cases. If you have clients that are not using Active
Directory, you may want to specify that the CA maintains
a shared folder in which newly created certificates are
placed; you can do so by selecting the Store Configuration
Information in a Shared Folder option and entering the
path of the shared folder. (If you are reinstalling
Certificate Services onto a server that has already been a
CA, the Preserve Existing Certificate Database option
becomes available.) Click Next to continue.

**FIGURE 8.7**
You can specify the location of the database
and log files if desired.

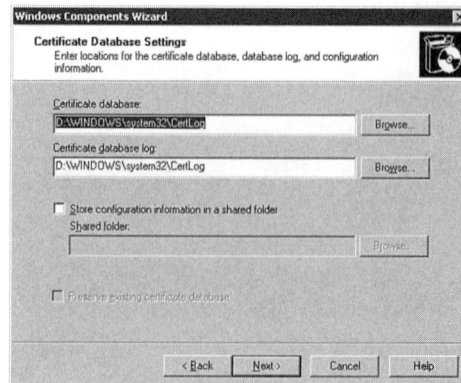

**11.** If IIS is running on the server, you are prompted to acknowledge that it will be stopped to perform the configuration of the CA. If IIS is not installed, you are prompted to install it before Web Enrollment can be used. Click Yes to acknowledge the warning.

**12.** Click Finish to close the Windows Component Wizard. The CA is now ready and available for immediate use.

---

With the knowledge of how to install the first CA in hand, you can now move forward into configuring Active Directory for certificate publication.

# Configuring Active Directory for Certificate Publication

**Configure Active Directory directory service for certificate publication.**

By default, the Enterprise CA automatically publishes all certificates directly into Active Directory. As such, there really is no need for any additional configuration in that regard. You can, however, configure two other parts of Certificate Services that deal with the publication of Certificate Revocation Lists (CRLs) and which certificates a user is allowed to submit a new certificate request for.

Recall that a CRL is used to identify all certificates that have been revoked (canceled) before their normal end of validity period. The default behavior of an Enterprise Root CA is to publish the CRL to Active Directory—as you might well expect. You can, however, perform some modification of the CRL publishing configuration to suit the needs of your network, as outlined in Step by Step 8.2.

> **NOTE**
>
> **The Key to Security**  When creating the Root CA, you also need to ensure a long validity period for the public and private key of this CA by using a long key length as a deterrent to hackers who make brute-force attacks. The longer the key, the longer you can use the private and public keys with confidence that the keys have not been compromised.
>
> Microsoft recommends using a key length of at least 2048 bits. There is, however, a trade-off between key length and CA server performance because longer key lengths require more system resources.

---

# STEP BY STEP

## 8.2 Configuring CRL Publication Properties

**1.** Select Start, Programs, Administrative Tools, Certification Authority to open your Certification Authority management console.

*continues*

*continued*

2. Locate the CA of concern in the CA management console and expand its nodes.

3. Right-click the Revoked Certificates node and select Properties from the context menu.

4. The Revoked Certificates Properties dialog box opens, as shown in Figure 8.8. You can configure the CRL publication interval as well as the Delta CRL publication interval—or disable the use of Delta CRLs completely. Click Apply to set your changes.

**FIGURE 8.8**
You can change the default values for CRL publication if you like.

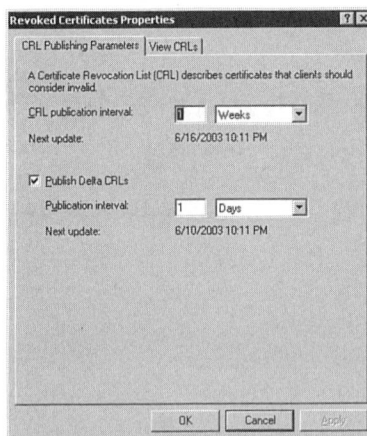

5. You can view CRLs that have been published by switching to the View CRLs tab, shown in Figure 8.9. You can examine the contents of a specific CRL by selecting it and clicking the View CRL or View Delta CRL button as applicable. After you have finished, click OK to close the Revoked Certificates Properties dialog box.

6. To change the CRL publication location, right-click the CA name and select Properties from the context menu.

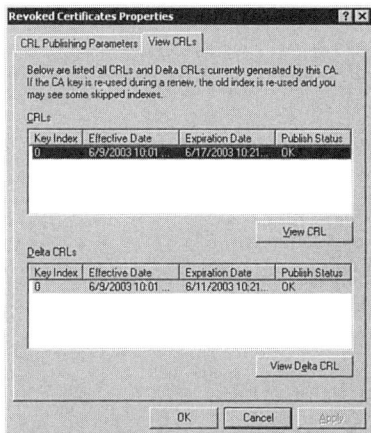

**FIGURE 8.9**
The Certification Authority management console provides a way to view CRLs.

7. After the CA Properties dialog box opens, switch to the Extensions tab, as shown in Figure 8.10. You can publish to Active Directory, a file system location, and an FTP or HTTP location. Note that not all options are available for each location. After making your configuration change, click OK. You are prompted to stop and restart Certificate Services to make the changes take effect.

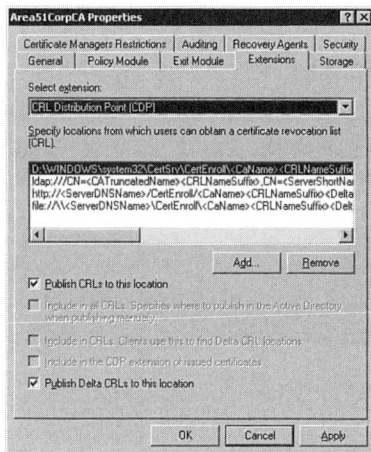

**FIGURE 8.10**
You can modify the locations to which the CRL is published from the Extensions tab of the CA Properties dialog box.

8. After you've configured the CRL publication schedule and location to your liking, you may want to immediately publish the CRL manually to all CRL Distribution Points (CDPs). To manually publish the CRL, right-click again

*continues*

*continued*

on the Revoked Certificates folder and select All Tasks, Publish. You are asked what type of CRL you want to publish, as shown in Figure 8.11. Select either a New CRL or a Delta CRL and click OK to publish it as you've previously configured.

**FIGURE 8.11**
You can select from either a New CRL or a Delta CRL.

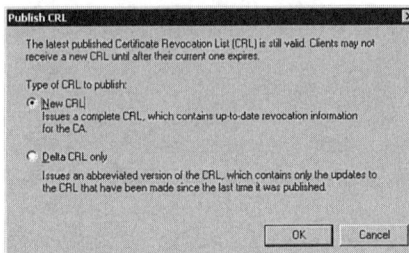

---

The only other configuration you may want to undertake in regards to certificate publication involves modifying the default configuration of the allowed certificate templates. You may want to perform the following additional actions from within the Certification Authority management console:

▶ Specify the types of certificates that each of your CAs can issue. You do so by deleting or adding (as required) certificate templates in the Certificate Templates node of the CA.

▶ Configure the Access Control List (ACL) for each template to limit its use to those users you specifically allow. To request a new certificate using a specific template, the user must have the Enroll permission enabled on the certificate template ACL.

Step by Step 8.3 outlines the process by which you can manage the certificate templates your CA is allowed to issue to your users.

# STEP BY STEP

### 8.3 Managing Certificate Templates Available for Use

1. Open the Certification Authority management console and expand the nodes under your CA.

2. Click the Certificate Templates node, which allows you to examine the certificate templates that are currently available for your CA.

3. To remove a certificate template—and thus prevent that CA from using it to issue new certificates—right-click the certificate template and select Delete from the context menu. Click Yes when prompted to confirm that you really want to remove the certificate template from the CA. Note that the certificate template is not deleted, just removed from use at that time.

4. To add a new certificate template that is not currently listed, right-click the Certificate Templates node and select New, Certificate Template to Issue from the context menu.

5. The Enable Certificate Templates dialog box, shown in Figure 8.12, opens allowing you to select the certificate template you want to make available for use. Select the certificate template and click OK. The selected certificate template now shows up in your Certificate Templates node.

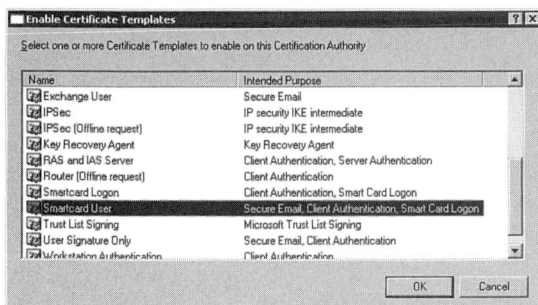

**FIGURE 8.12**
You can add additional certificate templates as you require.

*continues*

*continued*

6. If you want to configure the ACL for a certificate template, you need to first open the Certificate Templates console by right-clicking on the Certificate Templates node and selecting Manage.

7. The Certificate Templates console, new to Windows Server 2003 and shown in Figure 8.13, opens allowing you to configure the properties of all certificate templates installed on your CA.

**FIGURE 8.13**
The Certificate Templates console allows you to manage the properties of your certificate templates from a centralized location.

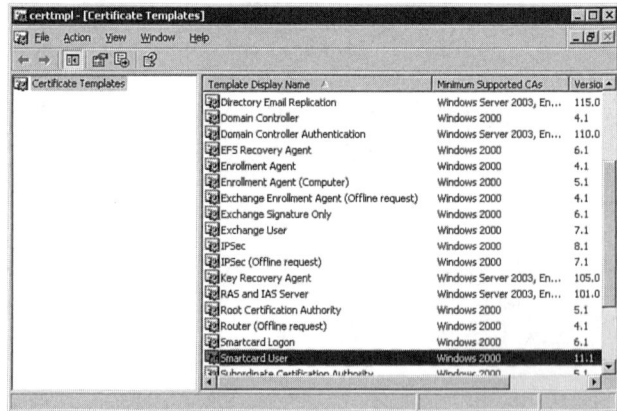

8. To modify the ACL of a certificate template, right-click it from within the Certificate Templates console and select Properties from the context menu.

9. The certificate template Properties dialog box opens. Switch to the Security tab, shown in Figure 8.14, and select the Allow box for the Enroll permission for your users and groups as required. Click OK to close the Properties dialog box when you are done.

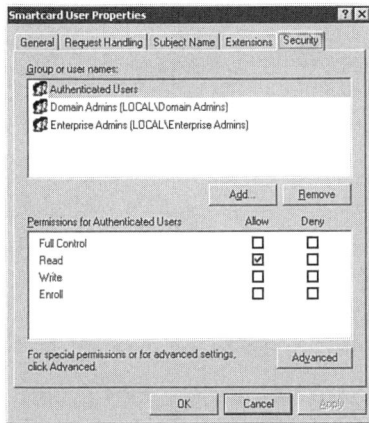

**FIGURE 8.14**
You can control who can request a certificate using a specific template by configuring the ACL.

With the discussion of CRL publication and certificate template configuration behind us, we now move on to certificate enrollment and distribution planning.

# Planning Certificate Enrollment and Distribution

**Plan a public key infrastructure (PKI) that uses Certificate Services.**

▶ **Plan the enrollment and distribution of certificates.**

With your CA installed and configured, now comes the question of how you will enroll and distribute (install) the newly requested certificates. Depending on the configuration of your network, you can choose from four different certificate enrollment options:

▶ **Certificate autoenrollment and renewal**—I mentioned at the beginning of this chapter that a Windows Server 2003 Active Directory domain with Windows XP Professional clients provides the most robust Certificate Services model. This is certainly the case when discussing certificate autoenrollment and renewal. Using these features, you can automatically issue certificates that enable PKI-based applications, such as smart card logon, EFS, SSL, and S/MIME to users and computers within your Active Directory environment. Through a combination of certificate template properties and Group Policy settings, you can opt to enroll computers when they start up and users when they log in to their domain on the network.

▶ **Certificate Request Wizard/Certificate Renewal Wizard**— Users of Windows 2000, Windows XP, and Windows Server 2003 computers can manually request certificates through the Certificates MMC snap-in. This snap-in can be added to any custom MMC. Alternatively, you can launch the Certificates console by entering `certmgr.msc` at the command prompt.

▶ **Web Enrollment Web pages**—You can connect to a CA by entering `http://CAname/certsrv` in your browser. By default, the Web Enrollment pages, which consist of ASP and ActiveX controls and thus could be considered dangerous, are installed on a CA. You can, however, install these pages on any other Windows Server 2003 computer running IIS that you want. If you're up to it, you can also customize these Web Enrollment pages to suit your specific needs. The Web Enrollment pages provide an easy way to connect clients to your CA without using the Certificates management console. Although Standalone CAs also use the Web Enrollment pages, they cannot provide certificates for smart card logon and for autoenrollment—only Enterprise CAs. Also, when Standalone CAs are used with Web Enrollment pages, the requester must specifically specify all required information because Active Directory is not available to provide the information for the certificate template. Windows 2000, Windows XP, and Windows Server 2003 computers support the use of Web Enrollment pages.

▶ **Smart Card enrollment station**—This is an advanced form of the Web Enrollment pages that allows trusted administrators to request and enroll smart card logon certificates for smart card users on the network. Only Windows XP and Windows Server 2003 computers support this form of enrollment.

Now that you've had a brief introduction into the various means available for your users to request and enroll new certificates, let's examine how the first three are used. Smart cards are discussed in the next section.

# Configuring Certificate Autoenrollment and Renewal

As already mentioned, one of the new features of Windows Server 2003 Certificate Services is the concept of autoenrollment for new certificates and automatic renewal for those approved certificates. Through the combination of Version 2 certificate templates and Group Policy settings, Windows XP and Windows Server 2003 computers and their users may automatically request and enroll new and newly renewed certificates at every Group Policy refresh. Group Policy is refreshed during computer startup, user login, and on a configured refresh interval for the network.

If you've ever been responsible for managing a PKI infrastructure, you can quickly appreciate the value in users and computers being allowed to automatically enroll and renew the most commonly used certificate types, such as those for EFS, SSL, smart cards, and S/MIME. Although users must still request the certificates manually, the task of distributing (also referred to as enrolling or installing) an approved certificate occurs automatically, thus saving the PKI administrator time and effort as well as cutting down on the number of mistakes and errors made.

Step by Step 8.4 outlines the process to configure Group Policy for autoenrollment.

---

## STEP BY STEP

### 8.4 Configuring Certificate Autoenrollment

1. On a domain controller or domain workstation running the Administration Tools, select Start, Programs, Administrative Tools, Active Directory Users and Computers to open the Active Directory Users and Computers console.

2. Expand the nodes of your Active Directory forest until you locate the specific site, domain, or Organizational Unit (OU) for which you want to configure certificate autoenrollment.

3. Right-click the desired location and select Properties from the context menu.

*continues*

*continued*

**4.** Switch to the Group Policy tab of the Properties dialog box, as shown in Figure 8.15.

**FIGURE 8.15**
You need to select the GPO to be edited or create a new one.

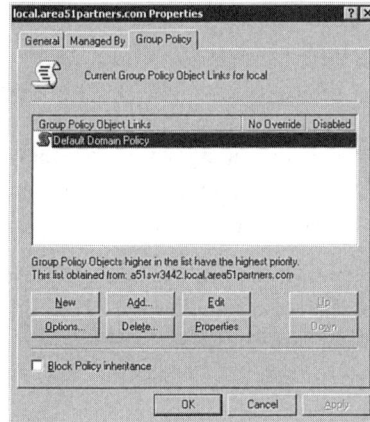

**5.** Either select an existing GPO to be edited for certificate autoenrollment options or create a new one as desired.

**6.** Within the Group Policy Editor, expand the nodes as follows to configure certificate autoenrollment for computers: Computer Configuration, Windows Settings, Security Settings, Public Key Policies (see Figure 8.16).

**FIGURE 8.16**
Certificate autoenrollment settings are located in the Public Key Policies node.

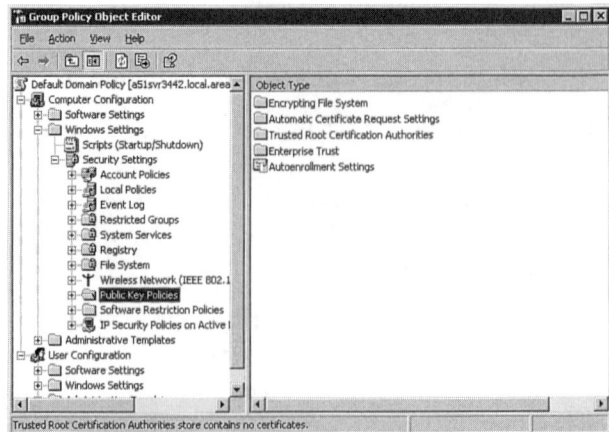

**7.** Double-click the Autoenrollment Settings option and configure computers for autoenrollment as desired, as shown in Figure 8.17.

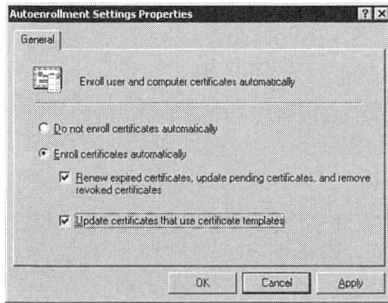

**FIGURE 8.17**
You need to select the Enroll Certificates Automatically option to enable autoenrollment.

**8.** Click OK to close the Autoenrollment Settings Properties dialog box.

**9.** If you want to configure certificate autoenrollment settings for users, do so from the User Configuration\Windows Settings\Security Settings\Public Key Policies node of the Group Policy Editor.

**10.** To refresh Group Policy immediately, run the `gpupdate` command from the command prompt. Figure 8.18 shows the update in action as the domain controller has received an autoenrollment certificate, as evidenced by Event ID 19 in the Application log of Event Viewer.

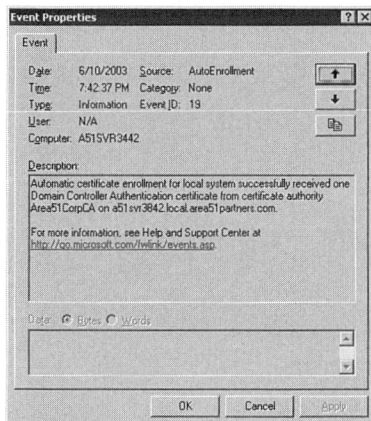

**FIGURE 8.18**
Computers will begin using certificate autoenrollment immediately after the next Group Policy refresh.

## Using the Certificate Request Wizard and Certificate Renewal Wizard

Although not as new and fancy as certificate autoenrollment, the Certificate Request Wizard and Certificate Renewal Wizard are effective ways for Windows 2000 computers (as well as Windows XP and Windows Server 2003 computers) to quickly request and renew certificates. Step by Step 8.5 outlines the use of the Certificate Request Wizard to request a new certificate from the CA.

---

## STEP BY STEP

### 8.5 Requesting a New Certificate with the Certificate Request Wizard

1. Open the Certificates console by adding it as a snap-in to a custom MMC or by entering `certmgr.msc` at the command prompt.

2. Right-click the Personal node and select All Tasks, Request New Certificate, as shown in Figure 8.19, to start the Certificate Request Wizard.

**FIGURE 8.19**
The Certificate Request Wizard allows you to quickly request a new certificate.

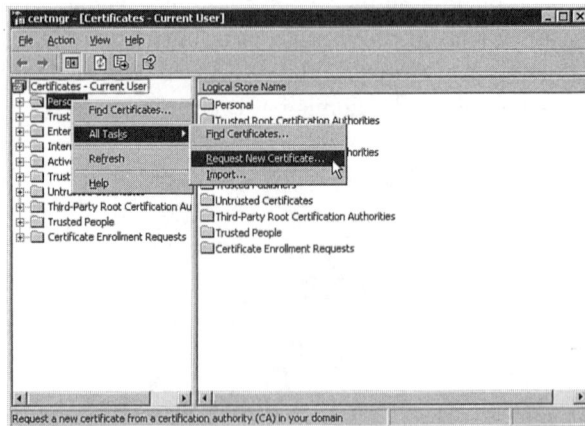

3. Click Next to dismiss the opening page of the Certificate Request Wizard.

4. On the Certificate Types dialog box, shown in Figure 8.20, select the type of certificate being requested. You can also configure advanced options, including the CSP to be used, by selecting the Advanced check box. Click Next to continue.

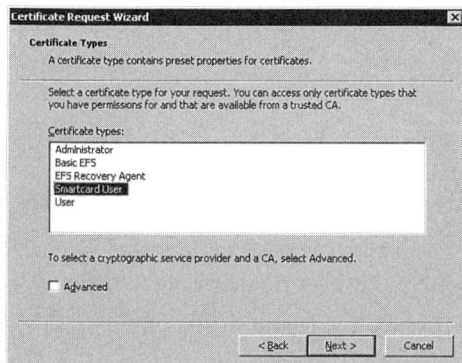

**FIGURE 8.20**
You are limited in your request by what certificate templates are available.

5. On the Certificate Friendly Name and Description dialog box, shown in Figure 8.21, enter a friendly name and description for your certificate to identify it more easily in the future. Click Next to continue.

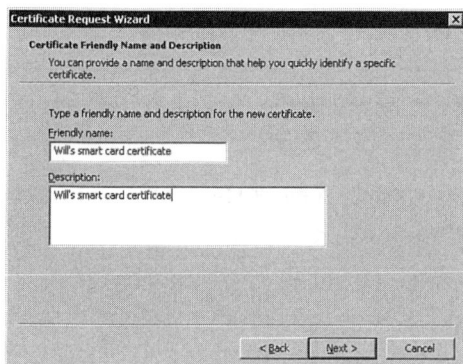

**FIGURE 8.21**
You should enter a description to help you determine what the certificate is used for.

6. Click Finish on the Completing the Certificate Request Wizard dialog box to complete the process. If your request was approved, you see the dialog box in Figure 8.22. Click OK.

*continues*

*continued*

continued

**FIGURE 8.22**
The process to request a certificate is a very easy one to complete.

## Using the Web Enrollment Web Pages

As an alternative, and sometimes more useful, means to request certificates, you can easily allow your clients to use the Certificate Services Web Enrollment pages. Assuming that you have IIS installed on the CA—which you should do before installing the CA itself—you can use Web Enrollment by connecting to the CA using the local Internet Web address `http://CAname/certsrv` in your Web browser. It is recommended that you use a current version of Internet Explorer because other browsers or older versions do not always work properly.

Step by Step 8.6 outlines the use of the Web Enrollment pages to request a new certificate from the CA.

## STEP BY STEP

### 8.6 Requesting a New Certificate via Web Enrollment

1. Open a new Internet Explorer window and enter `http://CAname/certsrv` in the address bar, where *CAname* represents the name or IP address of your CA, as shown in Figure 8.23. You may be asked to add this IP address to IE's trusted locations. Additionally, you may also be prompted to supply your network credentials for authentication.

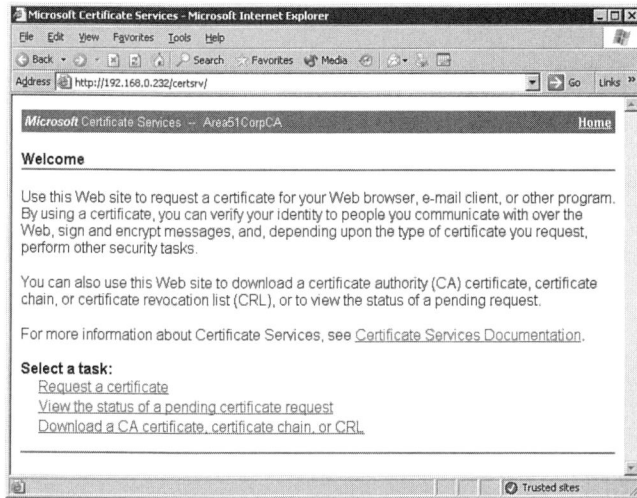

**FIGURE 8.23**
You can request new certificates, check the status of requests, and download the CRL from the Web Enrollment pages.

2. Click the Request a Certificate Link to request a new certificate. You can, if desired, also check the status of a previous certificate request or download the current CRL from this CA.

3. To request a basic user certificate, click the User Certificate link, as shown in Figure 8.24. If you want to request any other type of certificate, click the Advanced Certificate Request link. For this example, we want to request a smart card certificate, so click Advanced Certificate Request.

4. On the Advanced Certificate Request page, shown in Figure 8.25, click the Create and Submit a Request to This CA link to continue.

5. On the Advanced Certificate Request page, shown in Figure 8.26, select the type of certificate being requested and configure its properties as you require. After you have configured your certificate request as desired, click the Submit button located at the bottom of the page.

*continues*

*continued*

**FIGURE 8.24**
You need to click the Advanced Certificate Request link to request any certificate type other than a user certificate.

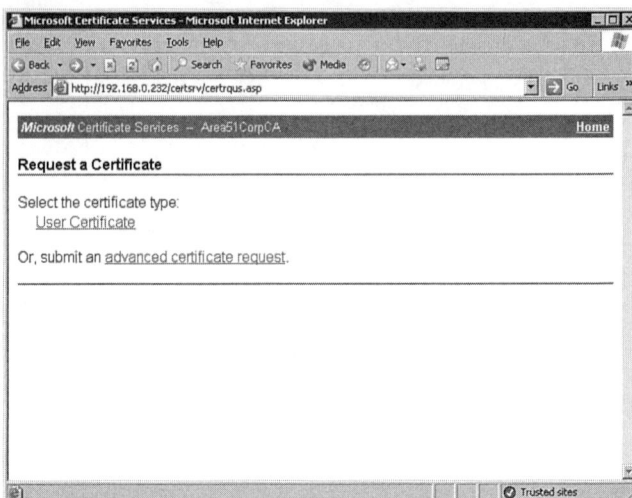

**FIGURE 8.25**
You have several request options available for your selection.

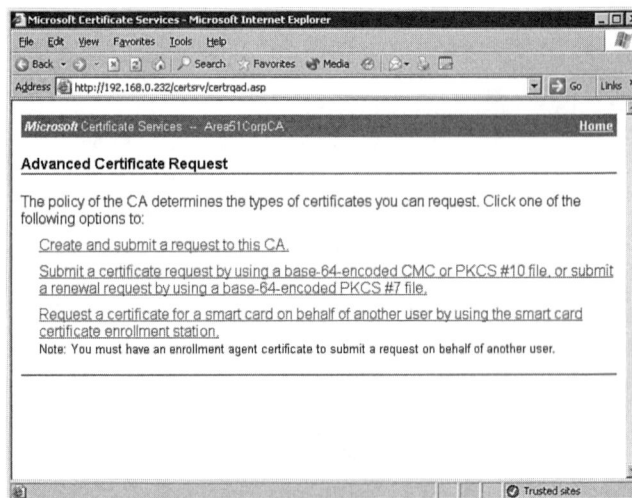

6. As part of the enhanced security of Windows Server 2003 (and Windows XP), a warning dialog indicates that a Web page is requesting a certificate on your behalf, as shown in Figure 8.27. This is not a problem unless you see this warning while surfing the Internet! Click Yes to allow this certificate to be requested.

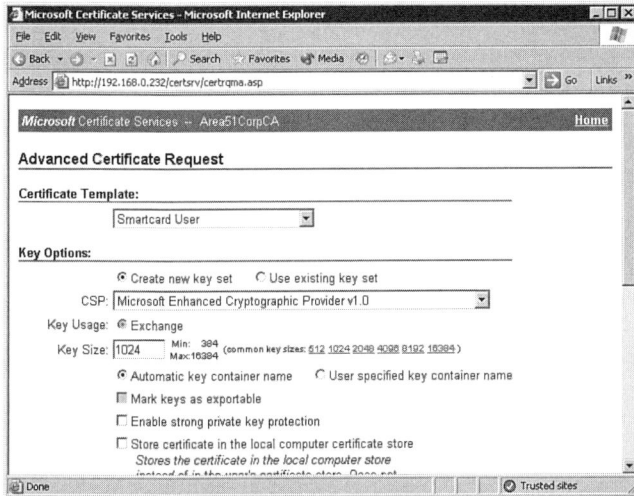

**FIGURE 8.26**
You can change the key length and several other options using an advanced certificate request.

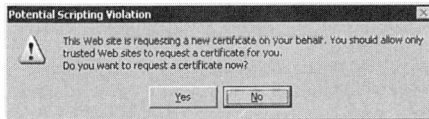

**FIGURE 8.27**
Windows warns you of the fact that a Web page is requesting a certificate for you.

**7.** If the request was successfully approved, you are next presented with the Certificate Issued page, as shown in Figure 8.28. Click Install This Certificate to install your new certificate.

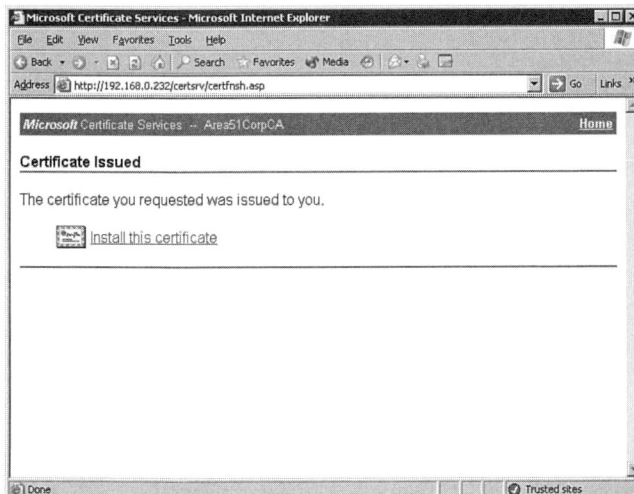

**FIGURE 8.28**
You are informed immediately as to the status of your certificate request.

*continues*

*continued*

**8.** Again, Windows alerts you to the fact that the Web page is attempting to perform some action related to a digital certificate, as shown in Figure 8.29. In this case, the Web page is attempting to install the certificate for you. Click Yes to allow the certificate to be installed.

**FIGURE 8.29**
You are warned again about the Web page's interaction with a certificate.

**9.** Your certificate is now installed, and the Web Enrollment pages will reflect this fact.

# GUIDED PRACTICE EXERCISE 8.1

In this exercise, you install and configure your first Enterprise CA with a validity period of three years. Your users need to be able to request certificates from their Web browsers. This Guided Practice helps reinforce the preceding discussion.

You should try completing this exercise on your own first. If you get stuck, or you would like to see one possible solution, follow these steps:

1. Log in to a Windows Server 2003 computer that is a member of an Active Directory domain using an account that has administrative credentials.

2. Using the Windows Components Wizard, install IIS 6.0 on a Windows Server 2003 computer that is a member of your Active Directory domain.

3. Using the Windows Components Wizard, start the installation of Certificate Services on the server.

4. Acknowledge the warning you are presented with about not being able to remain on the server after installing Certificate Services.

5. Select to install an Enterprise Root CA.

6. Supply the required identifying information about your CA. Change the validity period to three years.

7. Provide the locations to store the database and log files.

8. Acknowledge the warning that IIS will be stopped to complete the installation of the CA.

9. Finish the Windows Component Wizard.

# Planning a Smart Card Solution

**Plan a public key infrastructure (PKI) that uses Certificate Services.**

▶ **Plan for the use of smart cards for authentication.**

Introduced for the first time in Windows 2000, smart cards provided an alternative—and secure—means for user authentication. Smart cards are tamper-resistant hardware tokens that can be used to add an additional layer of security to the network. Although smart cards might at first be confused with standard credit cards, they have metallic contacts on them instead of the magnetic stripe found on a credit card. Smart cards also require specially designed readers that are attached to the computer being used for login.

Table 8.2 provides a full listing of the smart card readers that are supported in Windows Server 2003 by default.

**EXAM TIP**

**Smart Card hardware**  You should not worry about being tested on the information presented in Tables 8.2 and 8.3. It is presented here for completeness and as a reference should you later decide to implement a Smart Card solution.

**TABLE 8.2**

**WINDOWS SERVER 2003–SUPPORTED SMART CARD READERS**

| Smart Card Reader Brand | Smart Card Reader Model | Attachment Interface | Driver |
|---|---|---|---|
| American Express | GCR435 | USB | Grclass.sys |
| Bull | SmarTLP3 | Serial | Bulltlp3.sys |
| Compaq | Serial reader | Serial | grserial.sys |
| Gemplus | GCR410P | Serial | Grserial.sys |
| Gemplus | GPR400 | PCMCIA | Gpr400.sys |
| Gemplus | GemPC430 | USB | Grclass.sys |
| HP | ProtectTools | Serial | Scr111.sys |
| Litronic | 220P | Serial | Lit220p.sys |
| Omnikey AG | 2010 | Serial | Sccmn50m.sys |
| Omnikey AG | 2020 | USB | Sccmusbm.sys |
| Omnikey AG | 4000 | PCMCIA | Cmbp0wdm.sys |
| Schlumberger | Reflex 20 | PCMCIA | Pscr.sys |
| Schlumberger | Reflex 72 | Serial | Scmstcs.sys |
| Schlumberger | Reflex Lite | Serial | Scr111.sys |
| SCM Microsystems | SCR111 | Serial | Scr111.sys |
| SCM Microsystems | SCR200 | Serial | Scmstcs.sys |
| SCM Microsystems | SCR120 | PCMCIA | Pscr.sys |
| SCM Microsystems | SCR300 | USB | Stcusb.sys |
| Systemneeds | External | Serial | Scr111.sys |

Table 8.3 lists the smart cards that are supported by default in Windows Server 2003.

**TABLE 8.3**

**WINDOWS SERVER 2003–SUPPORTED SMART CARDS**

| Manufacturer | Model |
| --- | --- |
| Gemplus | GemSAFE 4k |
| Gemplus | GemSAFE 8k |
| Infineon | SICRYPT v2 |
| Schlumberger | Cryptoflex 4k |
| Schlumberger | Cryptoflex 8k |
| Schlumberger | Cyberflex Access 16k |

Smart cards are used to provide the highest level of user authentication available in Windows Server 2003 networks. For maximum security, a user can use a password or PIN to access the digital certificate on the smart card, thus further protecting the user's identity from rogue applications and attackers. Through the use of on-card digital signatures, smart cards can ensure that a user's private key is never exposed. Perhaps the single best feature of smart cards is that they—unlike software-based private keys—can be moved at will from one computer to another with ease. An administrator can prevent smart cards from being used to access the network after a preconfigured number of incorrect login attempts, protecting them further from dictionary attacks—a type of password-guessing attack in which a password is guessed from a list, or dictionary, of common words and phrases.

When implementing a smart card system, you should consider making the following certificate templates available for use. Bear in mind that none of these certificate templates are made available for use by default; you must manually add them to the Certificate Templates node of the certificate authority, as discussed earlier in this chapter in the "Configuring Active Directory for Certificate Publication" section.

▶ **Enrollment Agent**—Allows authorized users to request smart card certificates on behalf of other users

▶ **Smartcard User**—Allows a smart card user to log on to the network and digitally sign email

▶ **Smartcard Logon**—Allows a smart card user the ability to log on to the network

Smart cards can provide you with a great benefit—if they are implemented properly in your network. As you might have guessed, that means more planning for you! You should consider the following items during your smart card planning:

▶ Smart card distribution requirements

▶ Smart card enrollment options

▶ Smart card user education

▶ Smart card Group Policy options

## Smart Card Distribution Requirements

The most difficult aspect of implementing a new smart card system is determining how smart cards will be distributed. What happens if a user has a lost, damaged, or stolen smart card? What about when commonplace occurrences such as name changes, job changes, or department changes occur? All these issues need to be addressed in your smart card issuance and distribution plan. How do you handle these situations for your Windows user accounts? Perhaps you can model your smart card solution in part after your network password solution.

Another critical question that must be answered for smart cards to be a valid solution is how you will ensure that you are giving the correct credentials to the correct person. Will you require users to present validated photo identification such as corporate employee badges or driver's licenses to ensure users really are who they claim to be? What will you do if you have users who are geographically distant from your location? An ideal solution may be to issue blank smart cards to authorized users and then let them autoenroll (and thus install) the certificate to their smart card. In this way, only the authorized user has access to the smart card and the PIN required to access it. Your smart card distribution solution will be unique to the needs and organization of your company but in any case must ensure that the security of the smart card program is maintained at all times.

Although these things may not seem as though they should be part of the distribution planning, you must also ensure that you have adequately planned for public key length values, certificate validity periods, and certificate renewal policies. Be aware, however, that the memory capacity of the smart card you use can dictate the length of the public key; larger, more secure public keys require larger amounts of storage space, as you might imagine.

> **EXAM TIP**
>
> **Smart Card enrollment** Make sure you understand the basic options available to you related to Smart Card distribution and user enrollment.

## Smart Card Enrollment Options

As briefly mentioned previously, you need to ensure you have a method in place to actually enroll the smart card certificates that will be required. You can choose from two basic options when you want to enroll smart card certificates:

> ▶ **Use an enrollment agent.** The use of an enrollment agent allows a trusted administrator to process all smart card certificate requests and ensures that smart cards and their certificates are created and installed properly. Although this can be a good thing from a user's point of view, it can quickly become an overwhelming task if too few enrollment agents are designated.

> ▶ **Allow self-enrollment by smart card users.** Although using enrollment agents is usually the best (and by far the most secure) method to enroll smart cards, in some cases you may need or want to have users perform this task themselves. In cases in which you cannot physically (and safely) distribute fully ready smart cards, you may want to consider issuing blank smart cards and allowing the users to self-enroll. Should you think that self-enrollment is completely insecure, recall that you can configure your CA to hold all new requests pending a manual administrative approval, thus allowing you a chance to examine and validate the request before allowing the smart card to be enrolled with its certificate.

## Smart Card User Education

What would any security plan be without a good dose of user education? Smart cards are still a rather esoteric feature in the majority of networks today; therefore, you should take steps to ensure that your users thoroughly understand what a smart card is, how it

**Form of a Smart Card**  Without really thinking about it, you have most likely already been using a Smart Card in one way or another. ATM cards, building and parking garage access cards, and other cards with magnetic stripes are all just different forms of a Smart Card.

works, and what it provides for the network. Although not an all-inclusive listing, the following points should definitely be in your user education plan for a new smart card implementation.

▶ Ensure that users understand what special hardware and/or software they need to use their smart cards properly.

▶ Ensure that users know where to get this hardware and/or software. Additionally, ensure users know who to contact when they run into problems with their smart cards.

▶ Ensure that users understand that smart cards need to be protected from scratching, chipping, denting, and other forms of damage on the external chip area. These sorts of damages can prevent the card from being read properly, rendering it unuseable.

▶ Ensure that users understand that the card should not be exposed to temperature extremes, direct sunlight, or magnetic sources—as with any form of magnetic media.

▶ Ensure that users are instructed not to fold, spindle, or mutilate (yes, I had to say this!) their smart cards. Smart cards are fairly rugged, but they contain several internal components that can be broken by slipping the smart card into a back pocket, using the smart card to open a locked door (yes this happens), or performing other abusive actions.

## Smart Card Group Policy Options

When you are using smart cards for increased security of your network, you can configure several Group Policy options to further enhance the security of your smart card implementation:

▶ **Interactive logon: Require smart card**—This option, located in the Computer Configuration\Windows Settings\Security Settings\Local Policies\Security Options node of the Group Policy Editor can be used to prevent users from logging in to the domain by using a standard Windows username and password. Although this setting provides enhanced security, it can leave users without network access if their smart cards become unavailable for any reason. You should apply this policy at the OU level, making each smart card user a member of a domain local group and placing that group within the OU. Mistakenly applying this setting to non-smart card users will have disastrous effects.

▶ **Interactive logon: Smart card removal behavior**—This option, also located in the Security Option node, can be used to define what Windows should do when a smart card is removed from its reader with the user logged in. Possible options include No Action, Lock Workstation, and Force Logoff. This option again presents both benefits and dangers. A user who mistakenly removes her smart card with open documents may well lose any changes made since the document was last saved. On the other hand, for computers located in kiosks or other insecure areas, this setting can greatly increase the security of the computer and your network. This Group Policy setting requires training on your part to ensure that your smart card users understand the consequences of their actions. Again, this setting should be configured on an OU containing only those users who have been issued smart cards.

▶ **Do not allow smart card device redirection**—This option, located in the Computer Configuration\Administrative Templates\Windows Components\Terminal Services\Client/Server data redirection node of the Group Policy Editor, can be used to prevent users from logging in to a Terminal Server with a smart card. This can increase security and decrease loading on your Terminal Servers.

▶ **Account Lockout Policy**—The Account Lockout Policy node, located at Computer Configuration\Windows Settings\Security Settings\Account Policies\Account Lockout Policy in the Group Policy Editor, contains three useful Group Policy settings that you can use to enhance both smart card and standard Windows logins. The Account Lockout Threshold setting can be configured to specify how many failed logon attempts should be allowed before that user account is locked out. The Account Lockout Duration setting specifies how long the account is to be locked out (barring an administrator's unlocking the account early). The Reset Account Lockout Counter After option specifies how much time must pass before failed logon attempts are no longer counted against the Account Lockout Threshold setting. These policies are typically applied at a high level in your organization, such as the root of a domain to cause them to apply to all users within the domain.

# PLANNING AND IMPLEMENTING A SECURITY UPDATE INFRASTRUCTURE

**Plan a security update infrastructure. Tools might include Microsoft Baseline Security Analyzer and Microsoft Software Update Services.**

As administrators, we constantly strive to maintain a secure and functional computing environment for our users. In the perfect world, administrators would never have to update an installation of Windows; unfortunately, this is just not the case. Between weaknesses that are inherent to Windows (through coding mistakes or other issues) and the insatiable desire of Black Hats (bad hackers, as opposed to White Hats, which are good hackers) to find new and more devious ways to open up your network like a can sardines, you will soon have your hands full trying to keep your network's security stance up to date with the latest patches and hot fixes.

Realizing that it needed to become more proactive in helping Windows network administrators understand and correct the issues associated with the various security flaws that occur in the Windows operating systems, Microsoft has provided you with several tools that you can use to identify, categorize, and correct security-related issues on your network. The choice of what tool you use really depends on how you want to go about keeping your network updated. The following options are available for you to use in identifying and installing required security updates on your network's computers:

▶ **Microsoft Baseline Security Analyzer (MBSA)**—MBSA is an enhanced GUI version of the popular command-line HFNetChk application that can be used on Windows 2000, Windows XP, and Window Server 2003 computers to look for missing security updates, missing service packs, and weak security configurations in the supported Windows operating systems, Office, IIS, Structured Query Language (SQL) Server, and several other popular Microsoft applications. Even though MBSA cannot be run on a Windows NT 4.0 computer, it can be used remotely to scan a Windows NT 4.0 computer. MBSA does a good job of identifying and categorizing missing updates and security problems that it finds, but it does not provide any direct means to update required patches. The real strength of MBSA is that it can be used to scan many computers, even remote ones, at a time, providing a quick and easy-to-interpret graphical output.

▶ **Windows Update**—Windows Update, which has been around since Windows 98 arrived, provides an easy-to-use (although not always accurate) Web-based tool for determining the need to install newly available updates on a local computer. Automatic Update works in conjunction with Windows Update in instances where SUS has not been installed; it provides automatic downloading and installation of required updates.

▶ **Software Update Services (SUS)**—Introduced for Windows 2000 and improved for Windows Server 2003, SUS allows you to provide one or more Windows Update servers that run inside your protected internal network. SUS allows the administrator to exercise granular control over which updates are installed and which aren't. Only those updates specifically approved will be installed on network computers configured to use an SUS server for updating. After installing SUS, you perform all its management and configuration from within your Web browser for ease of administration.

▶ **Automatic Updates**—Automatic Updates is a new component of Windows XP SP1 and Windows 2000 SP3 that can download and install required updates from either the Windows Update Web servers or your internal SUS servers, depending on how it has been configured; the default configuration is to use the Windows Update Web servers. Automatic Updates is included in the default installation of Windows Server 2003. To configure Automatic Updates to use an internal SUS server, you must first install and configure at least one SUS server and then configure the appropriate Group Policy settings to require clients to use the designated SUS servers.

▶ **Systems Management Server**—SMS 2.0 was in use by a large number of organizations well before the release of Windows

2000 and its IntelliMirror and Active Directory technologies—the heart of software installation via Active Directory. SMS has been updated recently with the SMS 2.0 Software Update Services Feature Pack, which allows it to integrate into a SUS implementation without changing the configuration of the network clients. For many years, administrators have used SMS to manually push updates to clients; the feature pack allows this function to become more automatic. The new version of SMS is Active Directory integrated and promises many new features for software management and maintenance.

# Planning for Software Update Services

Although Windows Server 2003 provides native support for Software Update Services, it does not by default include SUS. You can easily enough acquire the SUS installation package, however, and begin work configuring and implementing SUS on a network. But what, really, is SUS? It is nothing more than a locally controlled and managed Windows Update server. Instead of configuring the Automatic Updates client on your client workstations to download updates directly from the Microsoft Windows Update servers, you can install and configure one or more SUS servers on your internal network and point your client workstations toward those servers.

As you might imagine, the ability to have your client workstations use an internal server for Windows Update can be a tremendous benefit to you because it means decreased bandwidth usage. As important as bandwidth savings might be, there is actually a larger benefit to be realized by implementing a SUS solution on your internal network: the ability to approve specific updates that are to be installed on your clients. When you use Windows Update, your client computers install any available update that matches their needs, but with SUS you can specify which of the available updates are authorized to be pushed to the clients after you are satisfied that the update will pose no problems for the systems. This is a tremendous benefit that often goes unrealized.

As previously implied, SUS is actually one part of a two-part system. The other part, the Automatic Updates client, runs on the servers and client workstations that you want to download updates. Although the Automatic Updates client was included in Windows

XP (pre–Service Pack 1), it was not the correct version to participate in SUS. You need to install Windows 2000 Service Pack 3 (or higher) or Windows XP Service Pack 1 (or higher) on client workstations to get the updated version that can interact with SUS. Alternatively, you can install the updated version of the Automatic Updates client, which you can download from `www.microsoft.com/windows2000/windowsupdate/sus/default.asp`.

You can also download the SUS installation package from this location. Unlike the previously released version of SUS, this one can be installed on a domain controller, which provides a great benefit to small organizations in which only one server is in use at some locations. The requirements to install SUS on a Windows Server 2003 computer are as follows:

▶ Pentium III 700MHz or higher CPU

▶ 512MB RAM

▶ 6GB free disk space on an NTFS partition (and the system partition on the SUS server must also be formatted with NTFS)

SUS provides the following client-side features:

▶ **Requires local administrative privileges**—Only those users who have local administrative privileges can change the settings of Automatic Updates. This prevents all other users from changing the configuration and possibly preventing required updates from being installed.

▶ **Requires digital signatures**—Only those updates that have a valid Microsoft digital signature can be downloaded and installed.

▶ **Uses just-in-time validation**—Automatic Updates can determine which of the available updates are required for the computer.

▶ **Uses minimized bandwidth**—Through the use of the Background Intelligent Transfer Service (BITS), Automatic Updates uses only idle (unused) bandwidth to download available updates, thus preventing the downloading of updates from slowing down other network activities.

▶ **Safely installs multiple updates simultaneously**—Using the same Windows Update technologies that allow for multiple updates to be installed with only a single restart, Automatic Updates can install multiple updates and request only one restart, thus improving computer availability. This feature works similarly to the way the QChain utility was used previously from the command line.

SUS provides the following server-side features:

▶ **Requires local administrative privileges**—Only those users who have local administrative privileges can change the settings of SUS. This prevents all other users from changing the configuration and possibly preventing required updates from being installed.

▶ **Requires digital signatures**—Only those updates that have a valid Microsoft digital signature can be downloaded and installed.

▶ **Update approval**—Only those updates that you have manually approved are made available to your Automatic Updates clients for download and installation. This provides for increased reliability of your network by allowing you to thoroughly test each update in a nonproduction environment before releasing it onto your live network.

▶ **Update availability**—Because the SUS server synchronizes with the Windows Update Web servers, you always have the most current list of updates available.

▶ **Remote administration**—SUS is administered from IE 5.5 or higher using either HTTP or HTTPS, allowing for an easy-to-administer interface. You need to install and configure an SSL certificate on the SUS Web site before using HTTPS connections.

▶ **Logging**—A Web server running IIS on your network can be specified as the log server and will receive statistics about updates that have been downloaded and whether the updates were installed. These statistics are placed in the log file of the configured Web server and can be used to monitor and troubleshoot the performance of SUS and Automatic Updates.

▶ **Server synchronization**—You may need to install and configure multiple SUS servers to meet the needs of your network.
SUS allows you to configure SUS servers to receive its update
packages from another SUS server if you choose.

▶ **Multiple language support**—SUS can be configured to make
available different language versions of updates. To do so, you
configure it to download specific language versions.

▶ **Diversified update hosting**—Depending on the specific
needs of your network, you can configure your SUS servers to
download the actual update packages or to have SUS servers
pointing to the Windows Update Web servers for the downloading of approved updates as required.

The actual process to install and configure SUS and Automatic
Updates is covered in Exam 70-291, "Implementing, Managing, and
Maintaining a Microsoft Windows Server 2003 Network
Infrastructure." Refer to the *MCSA/MCSE 70-291 Training Guide:
Implementing, Managing, and Maintaining a Windows Server 2003
Network Infrastructure* (2003, Que Publishing; ISBN: 0789729482)
by Dave Bixler and Will Schmied for more information on installing
and configuring your SUS solution.

---

| EXAM TIP |
|---|
| **Know SUS**  SUS is a key part of Microsoft's security update infrastructure. You need to have a very good understanding of what it does, how it works, and how you can configure it to meets your needs and requirements. |

---

# Using the Microsoft Baseline Security Analyzer

You can quickly learn to use the Microsoft Baseline Security
Analyzer. After downloading the most current version from
`www.microsoft.com/technet/security/tools/tools/mbsahome.asp`
and installing it, you are just a few mouse clicks away from performing security analysis of your network's computers.

When you launch the MBSA utility, you are presented with the
option to scan one computer, scan multiple computers, or review
previous scan reports, as shown in Figure 8.30.

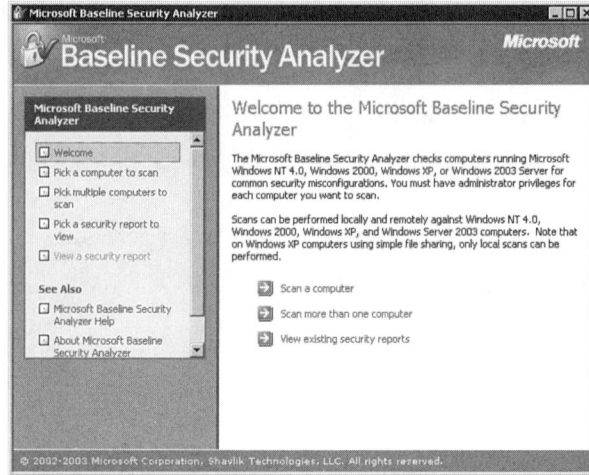

By clicking the Scan More Than One Computer link, you can enter the NetBIOS domain name or IP address range that you want scanned, as shown in Figure 8.31.

**FIGURE 8.31**
You can enter an entire domain to scan or scan a specific portion of the network.

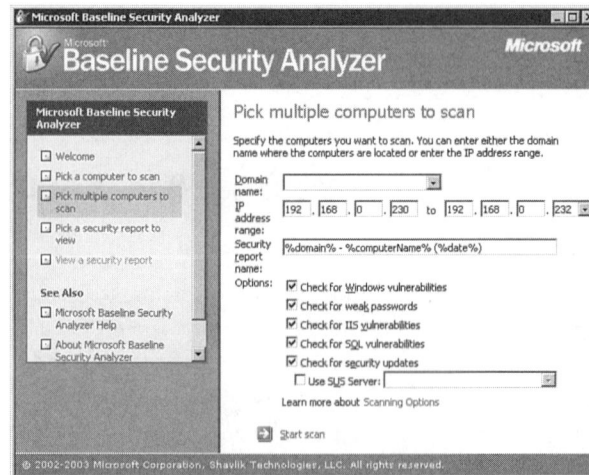

After the scan has been completed, you can see the results of each computer's scan, as shown in Figure 8.32. As you can see, this computer is missing a critical security update that creates a severe risk situation on the computer.

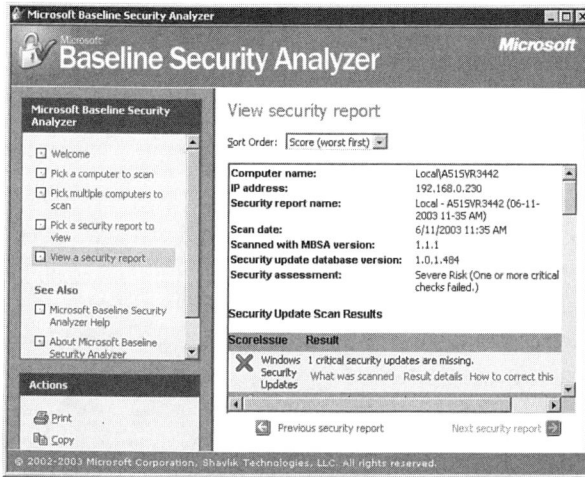

**FIGURE 8.32**
This computer is at severe risk due to a missing security update.

As mentioned previously, MBSA scans your computers not only for Windows security updates, but also for updates associated with other Microsoft products. MBSA 1.1.1 (the current version as of this writing) scans for security updates in the following products:

▶ Windows NT 4.0

▶ Windows 2000

▶ Windows XP

▶ Windows Server 2003

▶ Internet Explorer 5.01 and higher

▶ Windows Media Player 6.4 and higher

▶ IIS 4.0 and higher

▶ SQL Server 7.0 and 2000 (including Microsoft Data Engine)

▶ Exchange 5.5 and 2000 (including Exchange Admin Tools

# Maintaining a Security Update Infrastructure

In newly implemented Windows Server 2003 Active Directory networks, implementing a SUS solution to download and install approved security updates is most likely going to be your best bet. If you have an existing security update architecture in place, such as SMS or some other third-party solution, you may need to evaluate the benefits and costs of changing over to SUS. If you are relying only on Windows Update or Automatic Updates (without SUS) to keep your systems up to date, you need to seriously look into rolling out SUS.

One possible scenario for using SUS and MBSA on your network to monitor and maintain security goes like this: You install and configure one or more SUS servers on your network, as determined by the number of clients that will be accessing them (each server can handle approximately 15,000 clients) and the geographical dispersion of your network. You configure SUS to automatically synchronize content nightly when network traffic is at its lowest. You also configure Automatic Updates via a GPO to download, install, and restart computers as required nightly, thus installing any newly approved updates. You also make it a habit to review, test, and approve new security updates one or more times a week to keep your systems up to date. Lastly, you could run MBSA against your network computers twice monthly to spot-check the effectiveness of SUS in keeping your computers updated with the patches you have approved.

# PLANNING A SECURITY FRAMEWORK

As the adage goes, "fail to plan, plan to fail." Nowhere does this expression ring more true than when you are dealing with network security and change and configuration management. By now, you've undoubtedly performed quite a bit of work on your network in an attempt to increase its security. But you need to ask two questions at this point:

1. How will you verify that your security implementation is or is not functioning as desired?

2. How will you ensure that the security of your network is not reduced or compromised through changes made to the network?

Although the topics of monitoring and change and configuration management are extensive, we briefly examine both of them here.

# Planning for Security Monitoring

**Plan a framework for planning and implementing security.**

▶ **Plan for security monitoring.**

Your network is now complete. You've rolled out all your servers and clients, network links are 100% available, and all Group Policy Objects are working properly. Your network is in a Utopian state— or is it? How would you know if things weren't really as good deep down as they appear to be on the surface? If you can't see any problems, does that mean that they do not exist? Unfortunately, no.

You need to include in your administrative plan for the network a strategy to perform routine regular security monitoring of all parts of the network—from the most high profile server to the seemingly least important client workstation sitting in the lobby kiosk. But how will you go about monitoring security? It can be a big job that only increases exponentially as the number of computers on the network increases. Although you can use (and may want to at a later time) many good third-party products to centrally monitor security for your network, you can do a fair bit of monitoring yourself using only the tools provided within Windows or made available as an add-on download by Microsoft.

First and foremost, before you even start to monitor security, you should strive to always enforce the principle of least privilege for your users. This principle dictates that users are given only the minimum privileges required to perform the specific set of tasks that they have been assigned.

If you use the principle of least privilege, a compromised user account has a smaller impact on the overall security of the network than if you were to blanket-assign to users permissions that they did not need. Ideally, all normal user operations should be carried out in the context of a User account. If additional privileges are required for a specific reason, the administrator can either log in to the network with a special account for the purpose of performing those actions or use the Run As command to perform those actions within the context of the account that has the additional privileges.

After you have completely implemented the principle of least privilege, the task of monitoring network security will be greatly simplified because you can more easily determine what types of events are normal and what types of events are abnormal—indicating a possible security flaw or breach in your network.

The first part of your security monitoring plan should be to implement a well-thought-out and carefully configured auditing program. Windows Server 2003 allows you to perform auditing of the following areas:

▶ **Audit Account Logon Events**—This option configures auditing to occur for user logons and logoffs. A successful audit generates an audit entry when a user successfully logs in, and a failed audit generates an entry when a user unsuccessfully attempts to log in.

▶ **Audit Account Management**—This option configures auditing to occur for each event of account management on a computer. Typical account management events include creating a user, creating a group, renaming a user, disabling a user account, and setting or changing a password. A success audit generates an audit entry when any account management event is successful, and a failure audit generates an entry when any account management event fails.

▶ **Audit Directory Service Access**—This option configures auditing to occur when a user accesses an Active Directory object that has its own system access control list (SACL). This setting is only for Active Directory objects, such as GPOs, not for file system and Registry objects. A success audit generates an audit entry when a user successfully accesses an Active Directory object that has an SACL specified, and a failure audit generates an entry when an unsuccessful access attempt occurs.

▶ **Audit Logon Events**—This option configures auditing to occur upon each instance of a user logging on to or off a computer. The audit events are generated on domain controllers for domain account activity and on local computers for local account activity. When both the Audit Logon Events and the Audit Account Logon Events options are configured, logons and logoffs that use a domain account generate logon or logoff audit events on the local computer as well as the domain controller. A success audit generates an audit entry when a logon attempt succeeds, and a failure audit generates an audit entry when a logon attempt fails.

▶ **Audit Object Access**—This option configures auditing to occur upon each user access of an object, such as a file, folder, printer, or Registry key that has its own SACL configured. To configure auditing for object access, you also need to configure auditing specifically on each object for which you want to perform auditing. A success audit generates an audit entry when a user successfully accesses an object, and a failure audit generates an audit entry when a user unsuccessfully attempts to access an object.

▶ **Audit Policy Change**—This option configures auditing to occur upon every occurrence of changing user rights assignment policies, audit policies, or trust policies. A success audit generates an audit entry when a change to one of these policies is successful, and a failure audit generates an audit entry when a change to one of these policies fails.

▶ **Audit Privilege Use**—This option configures auditing to occur upon every occurrence of a user exercising a user right. A success audit generates an audit entry when the exercise of a user right succeeds, and a failure audit generates an audit entry when the exercise of a user right fails.

▶ **Audit Process Tracking**—This option configures auditing to occur for events such as program activation, process exit, handle duplication, and indirect object access. A success audit generates an audit entry when the process being tracked succeeds, and a failure audit generates an audit entry when the process being tracked fails.

▶ **Audit System Events**—This option configures auditing to occur when certain system events occur such as computer restarts and shutdowns. A success audit generates an audit entry when a system event is executed successfully, and a failure audit generates an audit entry when a system event is attempted unsuccessfully.

> **EXAM TIP**
>
> **Auditing options**   You must have a good understanding of these auditing options and the ways they can be used to accomplish the auditing goals set forth.

Auditing is configured through Group Policy and is discussed in more detail in *MCSA/MCSE 70-291 Training Guide: Implementing, Managing, and Maintaining a Windows Server 2003 Network Infrastructure* (2003, Que Publishing; ISBN: 0789729482) by Dave Bixler and Will Schmied because Exam 70-291 covers auditing in detail.

The second part of your security monitoring plan should be to collect, filter, and examine the event logs for all network computers in a centralized location. Several third-party applications provide this type of utility, often with many other nice features as well, but you can get good results by using the EventCombMT or DumpEL utilities. You can download EventCombMT from www.microsoft.com/technet/security/prodtech/windows/secwin2k/. Although these two tools are part of the Securing Windows 2000 Server Guide, they are still valid tools that you should have in your toolbox. Figure 8.33 shows the EventCombMT utility after the completion of a log gathering session. Note that text files are created with the output results in tab-delimited format.

**FIGURE 8.33**

The EventCombMT utility provides a quick, easy, and free method to gather event logs from the network.

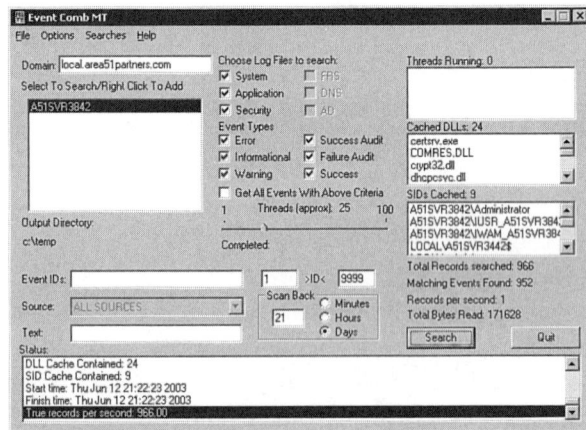

You also may want to use the DumpEL (Dump Event Log) utility which is run from the command line and be can be scripted for greater power. DumpEL provides the same basic functionality as EventCombMT, but from the command line. The best way to find DumpEL is to search for it at the Microsoft Downloads Center, located at www.microsoft.com/downloads/. If you want to enter the URL, it is www.microsoft.com/downloads/details.aspx?FamilyID=c9c31b3d-c3a9-4a73-86a3-630a3c475c1a&DisplayLang=en.

# Planning for Change and Configuration Management

**Plan a framework for planning and implementing security.**

▶ **Plan a change and configuration management framework for security.**

In today's networking environment, it's fair to say that you can no longer just go off and make changes to the configuration of the network or its computers without having documentation in hand. This documentation, more often than not, is two-fold: One set of documents details exactly what you are going to be doing and how you will back out of it should problems arise. You will create the second set of documentation as you work, documenting the new configuration that you have set in place.

The first document—the one outlining exactly what will be done, how it will be done, and what will happen should things not work out correctly—is in itself derived using yet another document: the change and configuration management policy for your network. You use the change and configuration management policy document to create all future plans for making security and configuration changes on your network. The key point that you must realize—and make all members of your organization realize—is that even the smallest change to the network can turn out to be the largest security problem you've ever seen. A good example would be a (routine) routing table change that causes PPTP traffic to take the tunnel in one direction and the regular IP subnet on the return path so that only one half of the conversation is encrypted.

As you can see from this simple example, even the smallest, most routine administrative tasks can have a large impact on the security and functionality of your network. Thus, you must implement a change and control policy that will be used when making any change to the network—whether or not the change appears to be security-related! Such a policy should require, at a minimum, the following steps:

1. As the need for change is discovered or recognized, a pending change request is filed. Such requests are reviewed and evaluated at regular intervals.

EXAM TIP

**Take control** For more information about security monitoring and change and control policies, be sure to see *TICSA Training Guide* by Mike Chapple, Debra Littlejohn Shinder, and Shawn Porter (2002, Que Publishing; ISBN: 0789727838).

2. If the change request is approved during the review process, a change order is created. In addition to describing the change and its desired results, the change order may also specify staffing, budget, and schedule requirements.

3. When the change order schedule indicates that work to incorporate the requested change is to begin, a change job or work order is enacted. Normally, such changes apply to a copy of the system being changed and do not affect changes to production environments until later in this process. The implementation group must also document its changes and file proposed changes to security policy documents at this time.

4. During the implementation process, module and unit tests make sure the change as implemented meets the requirements of the change as specified. After the implementation team decides the change is complete, it is turned over to a test group for change testing as an external check.

5. If the external testing group agrees that the change meets the specifications, that the change has no adverse effects on overall system behavior or capability, and that the documentation changes properly reflect resulting security policy, change enactment is authorized. Only at this point are changes introduced into a production environment, so only at this point do real, visible changes occur.

As you can see, this process can become lengthy and time-consuming, but no amount of planning is ever wasted. Fortunately, you do not have to reinvent the wheel to implement a good change and configuration control plan; you can find many high-quality resources both in print and on the Internet. Some of the more useful ones on the Internet include

▶ Change Management Learning Center, www.change-management.com

▶ Change Management Resource Library, www.change-management.org

▶ Kentucky Governor's Office for Technology, http://gotcm.ky.gov

## CASE STUDY

### ESSENCE OF THE CASE

Following are the essential elements in this case:

- ▶ Upload sensitive data over the Internet.

- ▶ Allow clients to securely access their own data over the Web.

- ▶ Secure data from start to finish.

### SCENARIO

Rockwell Financial Services is a company that deals in all aspects of financial management and investments. It has agents throughout North America that represent various firms for insurance and investments.

These agents use Windows XP Professional on their laptops. From the client's site, agents use the laptop to enter the investment information, and then they commute back to the their respective networks and transfer the data to their local SQL Server, which is then transferred to a centralized SQL Server in Chicago.

The company realizes the need for the security of this data, and this is why the agents currently must return to the office to transfer their information. However, the agents are complaining that they are losing valuable time that could be used to visit other clients, and in some cases, sales are lost because the market may fluctuate and opportunities are missed.

Rockwell Financial Services would like to implement a plan that would allow its agents to use the Internet to connect to the central SQL Server and upload the data through a Web interface—while securing data. In addition, the company would like to offer services to its clients that would allow the clients to access their account information online.

### ANALYSIS

Rockwell Financial Services should install Certificate Services. A hierarchy of CA could start in the central office in Chicago and then be

*continues*

## CASE STUDY

*continued*

dispersed to a child CA in each geographical location.

Sales reps would be issued a certificate from the local CA. A Web presence with a sales front and a SQL interface would be created to support secure uploads of clients' data over the Internet. In addition, a plan could be

developed to secure any data the sales reps saved on their laptops through smart cards or through EFS implementation.

A Web presence would be created for clients accessing their personal data. A certificate would be issued by a CA that would verify that the clients have access to only their data.

## CHAPTER SUMMARY

### KEY TERMS

Before taking the exam, make sure you are comfortable with the definitions and concepts for each of the following key terms. You can use Appendix A, "Glossary," for quick reference.

- Auditing
- Automatic Updates
- Certificate
- Certificate Authority
- Certificate Revocation List (CRL)
- Enterprise CA
- EventCombMT
- Group Policy Editor
- GPO
- Microsoft Baseline Security Analyzer (MBSA)

As you have seen, proper prior planning is the single most important key to success when implementing a network security plan. No effective security plan consists of only one security solution; the concept of defense in depth states that multiple, layered security solutions should be implemented to increase network security as much as possible. An example of the defense-in-depth principle would be a network that requires a username and password to gain access to the network. To further protect sensitive information, data on file servers is encrypted using EFS. Lastly, IPSec is implemented to secure network communications as they cross the network cabling itself.

Digital certificates come into play with many of these security solutions. Digital certificates can be used for smart cards to authenticate and verify the identity of the user, digital certificates are required for the use of EFS, and digital certificates can be used to provide security and authentication for IPSec communications on your network. The scope and type of PKI infrastructure you implement will be specified, in large part, by the requirements of your network's users.

## CHAPTER SUMMARY

Two basic types of CAs are available for use in Windows Server 2003. Enterprise CAs are completely integrated with Active Directory and provide some features not otherwise available in Standalone CAs. Standalone CAs do not require the presence of Active Directory, but if AD is in use, they can make use of it. Standalone CAs can be used to issue certificates and then can be removed from the network to increase their physical security. Each type of CA has two child types: Root and Subordinate. There is only one Root CA within a PKI implementation; all other CAs are Subordinate (or child) CAs. The Root CA signs its own CA certificate, as well as the CA certificate of all Subordinate CAs directly below it. Subordinate CAs issue and sign certificates for network users, computers, and other Subordinate CAs.

Microsoft introduced Software Update Services in Windows 2000 to provide an easy-to-administer way for network administrators to keep their networks up to date with required security updates. SUS has been integrated into Windows Server 2003. Using SUS and Automatic Updates, you can have approved updates automatically installed on client computers on the schedule you have configured. By allowing only administratively approved updates to be installed on client computes, SUS and Automatic Updates help you protect your network from problems that may be caused by required updates that are not compatible with your network or network applications.

After you've planned and implemented a security solution for your network, you need to ensure that your network stays secure. Microsoft has a two-step network security plan: Get Secure, Stay Secure. The Stay Secure portion requires you to maintain security after you have it in place. To maintain security, you need to monitor it. Security monitoring can be accomplished in many ways, but the most common include auditing and event logs. Also, you need to have a functional and well-thought-out change and configuration plan in place to prevent mistakes from being made that can compromise the security of your network.

---

**KEY TERMS**

- Principle of least privilege
- Revoked certificate
- Root CA
- Software Update Services (SUS)
- Standalone CA
- Subordinate CA
- Validity period

## APPLY YOUR KNOWLEDGE

# Exercises

## 8.1 Creating an Enterprise Root CA

In this exercise, you create an Enterprise Root CA for your network. You need to have a Windows Server 2003 computer that is part of an Active Directory network. If you want to use the Web Enrollment pages, you need to install IIS before installing this CA.

**Estimated time:** 20 minutes

1. Log in to a Windows Server 2003 that is a member of the Active Directory domain with administrative permissions.

2. Select Start, Settings, Control Panel, Add or Remove Programs to open the Add or Remove Programs dialog box.

3. Click the Add/Remove Windows Components button located on the left side of the Add or Remove Programs dialog box to open the Windows Components Wizard.

4. Select the Certificate Services option.

5. A warning dialog informs you that you cannot rename the server after installing Certificate Services on it.

6. Click Next on the Windows Components Wizard dialog box to commence the installation process.

7. On the CA Type dialog box, select the type of CA you are installing. For this example, select Enterprise root CA. If you want to customize the key pair settings, you can do so by selecting the Use Custom Settings to Generate the Key Pair and CA certificate option.

8. If you selected to customize your key settings, the Public and Private Key Pair dialog box appears

next. You have the opportunity to customize the installation by selecting the CSP and the Key Length. You also can use and import an existing certificate and key.

9. On the CA Identifying Information dialog box, enter the common name of the CA. This name should be descriptive but should not contain any special characters. You also need to configure the Validity period; the default value is five years.

10. On the Certificate Database Settings dialog box, enter the database and log locations or simply use the default selections—usually the best option in most cases.

11. If IIS is running on the server, you are prompted to acknowledge that it will be stopped to perform the configuration of the CA. If IIS is not installed, you are prompted to install it before Web Enrollment can be used.

12. Click Finish to close the Windows Component Wizard. The CA is now ready and available for immediate use.

## 8.2 Configuring CRL Publication Properties

In this exercise, you configure the CRL publication properties of your CA. To complete this exercise, you should first complete Exercise 8.1.

**Estimated time:** 15 minutes

1. Select Start, Programs, Administrative Tools, Certification Authority to open your Certification Authority management console.

2. Locate the CA of concern in the CA management console and expand its nodes.

3. Right-click the Revoked Certificates node and select Properties from the context menu.

## APPLY YOUR KNOWLEDGE

4. The Revoked Certificates Properties dialog box opens. Configure the CRL publication interval as well as the Delta CRL publication interval, or disable the use of Delta CRLs completely.

5. View those CRLs that have been published by switching to the View CRLs tab.

6. To change the CRL publication location, right-click the CA name and select Properties from the context menu.

7. When the CA Properties dialog box opens, switch to the Extensions tab. You can publish to Active Directory, a file system location, and an FTP or HTTP location.

8. To manually publish the CRL, right-click again on the Revoked Certificates folder and select All Tasks, Publish. You are asked what type of CRL you want to publish.

### 8.3 Requesting a Certificate with the Certificate Request Wizard

In this exercise, you request a new digital certificate from your CA using the Certificate Request Wizard. You need to complete Exercise 8.1 before attempting this exercise.

**Estimated time:** 10 minutes

1. Open the Certificates console by adding it as a snap-in to a custom MMC console or by entering `certmgr.msc` at the command prompt.

2. Right-click the Personal node and select All Tasks, Request New Certificate to start the Certificate Request Wizard.

3. Click Next to dismiss the opening page of the Certificate Request Wizard.

4. On the Certificate Types dialog box, select the type of certificate being requested. You also can

configure advanced options, including the CSP to be used, by selecting the Advanced check box.

5. On the Certificate Friendly Name and Description dialog box, enter a friendly name and description for your certificate to identify more easily in the future.

6. Click Finish on the Completing the Certificate Request Wizard dialog box to complete the process.

### 8.4 Requesting a Certificate via the Web Enrollment Pages

In this exercise, you request a new digital certificate using the Web Enrollment pages. To complete this exercise, you must first complete Exercise 8.1 and install IIS on your CA.

**Estimated time:** 10 minutes

1. Open a new Internet Explorer window and enter `http://CAname/certsrv` in the address bar, where *CAname* represents the name or IP address of your CA.

2. Click the Request a Certificate link to request a new certificate.

3. To request a basic user certificate, click the User Certificate link. If you want to request any other type of certificate, click the Advanced Certificate Request link.

4. On the Advanced Certificate Request page, click the Create and Submit a Request to This CA link to continue.

5. On the Advanced Certificate Request page, select the type of certificate being requested as well as configure its properties as you require. After you have configured your certificate request as desired, click the Submit button located at the bottom of the page.

## APPLY YOUR KNOWLEDGE

6. As part of the enhanced security of Windows Server 2003 (and Windows XP), a warning dialog indicates that a Web page is requesting a certificate on your behalf.

7. If the request was successfully approved, you are presented with the Certificate Issued page. Click Install This Certificate to install your new certificate.

8. Again, Windows alerts you to the fact that the Web page is attempting to perform some action related to a digital certificate.

## Review Questions

1. What is a certificate?

2. Why would an organization have a Standalone CA?

3. Why would a CA need to renew its certificate?

4. You are the network administrator of a large campuswide community college network. Your network is composed of computers running every version of Windows from Windows 95 to Windows Server 2003. Is SUS a good solution for your network, to ensure that all computers are up to date with the latest security patches?

5. You have configured SUS for your network, but now several client computers are not getting updates. You determine that these computers are running a Japanese localized version of Windows XP Professional. What should you do to allow the client computers to get updates from your SUS server?

6. Your CIO has instructed you to implement an SUS solution for your corporate network. He is concerned, however, about making unsecured connections to the SUS server. What can be done to provide connection security?

## Exam Questions

1. Christopher is the network administrator for the Heron Woods Resort Cottages company. Heron Woods rents vacation cottages at several locations along the Eastern Shore of Virginia and Maryland. Christopher needs to implement a solution that will keep the Windows Server 2003 and Windows XP Professional computers at all his locations up to date with the latest security updates, while at the same time installing only those updates that he has specifically approved. Heron Woods has a main office in Chincoteague, Virginia, connected to the Internet by a fractional T-1 line. All other locations are considered remote locations and have a dedicated ISDN link connecting them to the main office. What solution can Christopher implement that will allow him to meet his goals of providing available updates and allowing only approved updates to be installed? Christopher has received authorization from the CEO of Heron Woods to add only the absolute minimum number of additional servers as required to provide the best solution for meeting the requirements.

   A. Christopher should configure all servers and client workstations to connect directly to the Microsoft Windows Update Web servers weekly to download and install any new security updates that are required.

B. Christopher should install an SUS server at each of his locations, including the remote offices, that is configured to automatically synchronize each night with the Windows Update Web servers. Additionally, he should configure Automatic Updates to download and install any new security updates that are required on a nightly basis from the local SUS server.

C. Christopher should install an SUS server at each of his locations, including the remote offices. The SUS server at the main office should be configured to automatically synchronize each night with the Windows Update Web servers. The SUS servers at each of the remote offices should be configured to synchronize each night using the SUS server at the main office as its source. Additionally, he should configure Automatic Updates to download and install any new security updates that are required on a nightly basis from the local SUS server.

D. Christopher should install an SUS server at his main office that synchronizes nightly with the Windows Update Web servers. Automatic Updates for all clients, local and remote, should be configured to download and install all approved updates from the main office SUS server on a nightly basis.

2. Andrea is the network administrator for Purple Pony Wear, Inc., a leading supplier of novelty clothing items. The Purple Pony network consists of 2 Windows Server 2003 computers and 34 Windows XP Professional client computers, 30 of which are laptops in use in various remote locations by sales personnel. Andrea wants to create and implement a PKI solution so that her users can use smart cards to log on to their laptop computers, thus increasing the security of the laptops and the Purple Pony network. Priscilla, the President of Purple Pony, is concerned about users removing their smart cards from their laptop computers during their sessions and leaving their laptops logged in without being in front of them. Priscilla would like all laptops to be configured to lock the workstation when the smart card is removed so open documents will not be lost. What option does Andrea need to configure to ensure the desired result is achieved?

A. Do not allow smart card device redirection

B. Interactive logon: Require smart card

C. Account Lockout Policy

D. Interactive logon: Smart card removal behavior

3. You are the network administrator of a Windows Server 2003 Active Directory network. Your company policy states that the network access attempts of all temporary employees are to be tracked, regardless of what workstation they log on to. What auditing options do you need to configure to ensure that you can track the access of all temporary employees? (Choose two correct options.)

A. Audit Account Management

B. Audit Directory Service Access

C. Audit Logon Events

D. Audit Privilege Use

E. Audit System Events

F. Audit Account Logon Events

## APPLY YOUR KNOWLEDGE

4. You are the administrator of a large Windows Server 2003 network. Your company is a leading provider of state of the art satellite communications services for customers all over the world. The CIO of your company is very concerned about user account properties being modified by users who should not have administrative permissions. As part of your efforts to determine who might be modifying user account properties, you have decided to implement auditing. What auditing option should you configure to help you determine who is changing the user account properties on your network?

   A. Audit Account Management

   B. Audit Object Access

   C. Audit Logon Events

   D. Audit Privilege Use

   E. Audit System Events

   F. Audit Account Logon Events

5. You are the administrator of a large Windows Server 2003 network. Your company is a leading provider of state of the art satellite communications services for customers all over the world. The CIO of your company is very concerned about who is able to access files and folders located in a sensitive folder named Contacts. What auditing option should you configure to help you determine what users on your network are accessing the files and folders located within the Contacts folder?

   A. Audit Account Management

   B. Audit Object Access

   C. Audit Logon Events

   D. Audit Privilege Use

   E. Audit System Events

   F. Audit Account Logon Events

6. You are the network administrator for Nebuchadnezzar Furnaces. The company's Windows Server 2003 domain consists of domain controllers, 2 member servers, and 765 Windows XP Professional workstations. Every summer you hire 30 to 40 temporary employees to assist with additional production and sales needs for the upcoming winter season. Each employee is issued a digital certificate for smart card usage to allow him or her to securely access the network. The digital certificates have a validity period of two years by default due to the configuration of the CA that has issued them. Allison, your CIO, has told you on more than one occasion that she does not like the idea of having unused digital certificates still active. What should you do to increase your network's level of security?

   A. Change the CSP key length.

   B. Revoke the unused digital certificates.

   C. Lock the user's accounts.

   D. Disable the unused digital certificates.

7. You have just composed and sent an email message to a colleague who is located within a different Windows Server 2003 network than your own. Your email message has been digitally signed using your email certificate. Your Root CA uses a third-party certificate from a trusted third-party organization. What will your colleague need to have available to him to be able to read your email and verify it originated from you?

## APPLY YOUR KNOWLEDGE

A. Your private key

B. Your public key

C. The third-party CA's private key

D. The third-party CA's public key

8. You have just received an email message from a colleague who is located within a different Windows Server 2003 network than your own. The email message has been digitally signed by the public key for your email certificate. Her Root CA uses a third-party certificate from a trusted third-party organization. What will you need to have available to you to be able to read her email and verify it originated from her?

A. Your public key

B. Your colleague's public key

C. The third-party CA's private key

D. The third-party CA's public key

9. Rick is the network administrator for Mr. Whippy's Ice Cream. Rick has recently installed and configured an Enterprise Root CA for his Windows Server 2003 network on a server named CHOCOLATE. He performed no configuration for this new CA other than what was required during the installation process. When he tries to access the Web Enrollment Web pages at `http://CHOCOLATE/certsrv`, he receives a 404 error from Internet Explorer. What is the most likely cause of this problem?

A. Rick forgot to start the Certificate Services service following the completion of the installation process.

B. Rick has not installed Terminal Services on his CA.

C. Rick has not installed IIS on his CA.

D. Rick did not create a new CNAME record for the CA.

10. Hannah is the network administrator for the Wallops Island Rocket Company, Incorporated. Her network is required to maintain the highest level of security possible without adversely affecting the required operations of its users. For the past 10 weeks, six visiting rocket scientists have been working at her facility on a joint project with another company. Hannah issued each of these users a secure laptop including a smart card—allowing them to securely access and update the rocket systems data stored in the SQL databases. These six visiting users have completed their work and have now left the facility, leaving behind their laptop computers and smart cards as required. Hannah has just completed sanitizing their laptop computers; what should she do next?

A. Delete the data created by the scientists during their stay.

B. Degauss the hard drives installed in the laptop computers the scientists were using.

C. Perform a background check with the FBI, NSA, and NCIS on the scientists.

D. Revoke the smart card certificates the scientists were issued and immediately publish the CRL to all configured CDPs.

11. Chris is the network administrator for Island Dreams Tour and Rentals, Inc. She is preparing to implement a smart card solution for her Windows Server 2003 network. All her client computers are Windows XP Professional desktops and laptops. Some users have both a desktop computer and a laptop computer. Chris wants

## APPLY YOUR KNOWLEDGE

users to be able to use a single smart card at all times, regardless of what computer they are logging in to the network from. Chris does not want any user to be able to log on to the network without using their assigned smart cards. What can she configure to enforce this requirement on her users?

A. Do not allow smart card device redirection

B. Interactive logon: Require smart card

C. Account Lockout Policy

D. Interactive logon: Smart card removal behavior

12. Jim has recently completed a configuration change to one of his network's firewalls. Now multiple users have called the help desk complaining that they can no longer access external resources. What document did Jim most likely not have in hand which could well have prevented this problem?

A. A Security Monitoring policy

B. A Firewall Configuration policy

C. A Change and Configuration Control policy

D. A User Naming Convention policy

13. Kim has requested a new smart card certificate from one of her organization's CAs. Her request was not automatically approved and thus has been placed in a queue for administrative approval. You are the network administrator for the organization where Kim is employed. What must you do to approve her smart card certificate request?

A. You need to log in using Kim's user account and supply the approval key for her certificate request.

B. You need to use the Active Directory Users and Computers console to locate the Pending Requests folder.

C. You need to use the Certificates console to locate the Pending Requests folder.

D. You need to use the Certification Authorities console to locate the Pending Requests folder.

14. Kim has requested a new smart card certificate from one of her organization's CAs using the Web Enrollment pages. Her request was not automatically approved and thus has been placed in a queue for administrative approval. Kim wants to check on the status of her certificate request to see whether the certificate has been approved for issuance. Where can Kim most easily find this information and install the certificate if her request has been approved?

A. Active Directory Users and Computers console

B. Certificates console, Personal Store node

C. Log on to the CA Web Enrollment pages again

D. The Certificate Request Wizard

15. Chris is the network administrator for Seashell Cruises, LTD. The Seashell network has recently been upgraded from a mixed environment consisting of Windows 98 clients with Windows NT 4.0 Server and Windows 2000 Server servers. All clients now run Windows XP Professional, and all servers now run Windows Server 2003. Some

computers were upgraded in place, whereas others were clean installations. Chris has recently been hired by Seashell Cruises and wants to establish the security level of her network using the least administrative effort. She has approximately 200 client workstations and 30 servers spread over two different locations in the same geographic area all on the same IP subnet. What method can Chris use to most easily analyze all her computers and find security problems with them?

A. Use Windows Update locally on each computer to download and install required security updates.

B. Use Automatic Updates on each computer to download and install required security updates.

C. Install and configure SUS on one of her servers and configure Automatic Updates on the clients to download and install approved, required security updates.

D. Use the MBSA utility to scan her entire subnet to quickly identify security problems and missing security updates on all computers.

## Answers to Review Questions

1. A certificate is a component that allows you to send and receive secure data over a network. It assures the recipient that you are whom you claim to be, and it assures the sender that the data will reach the recipient without being jeopardized. For more information, see the section "Certificates."

2. A Standalone CA is an excellent choice when Active Directory is not present or when you want to manually approve certificate requests. For more information, see the section "The Standalone CA."

3. When a CA is created, it is assigned a certificate. This certificate, like all certificates, is set to expire. When a certificate has or is about to expire, an administrator can choose to renew the certificate. For more information, see the section "Renewing CAs."

4. If you have large numbers of pre-Windows 2000 computers (that is, legacy clients), SUS is probably not the best solution for your updating needs. In this situation, you would most likely want to examine a solution such as SMS or a third-party solution that provides the same type of functionality. For more information, see the section "Planning for Software Update Services."

5. This problem is relatively easy to solve: You simply enable support for the languages that you will be supporting from the SUS Server Options page. In this case, you should select the Japanese language option. For more information, see the section "Planning for Software Update Services."

6. You can enable SSL support on the SUS Web site and thus require that all connections be SSL secured. For more information, see the section "Planning for Software Update Services."

## Answers to Exam Questions

1. **D.** Because WAN link usage is not an issue in this scenario, and Christopher has received authorization to add only those new servers that

## APPLY YOUR KNOWLEDGE

are absolutely required, Christopher's best option is to install and configure one SUS server at the main office that synchronizes nightly with the Windows Update Web serves. All Automatic Updates clients will then be configured to receive their updates from the home office SUS server. For more information, see the section "Planning for Software Update Services."

2. **D.** By configuring the Smart card removal behavior option, located in the Computer Configuration\Windows Settings\Security Settings\Local Policies\Security Options node of the Group Policy Editor, for Lock Workstation, Andrea can achieve the desired results. For more information, see the section "Smart Card Group Policy Options."

3. **C, F.** When both the Audit Logon Events and the Audit Account Logon Events options are configured, logons and logoffs that use a domain account generate logon or logoff audit events on the local computer as well as the domain controller. A success audit generates an audit entry when a logon attempt succeeds, and a failure audit generates an audit entry when a logon attempt fails. For more information, see the section "Planning for Security Monitoring."

4. **A.** The Audit Account Management option configures auditing to occur for each event of account management on a computer. Typical account management events include creating a user, creating a group, renaming a user, disabling a user account, and setting or changing a password. A success audit generates an audit entry when any account management event is successful, and a failure audit generates an entry when any account management event fails. For more information, see the section "Planning for Security Monitoring."

5. **B.** The Audit Object Access option configures auditing to occur upon each user access of an object, such as a file, folder, printer, or Registry key that has its own SACL configured. To configure auditing for object access, you also need to configure auditing specifically on each object for which you want to perform auditing. A success audit generates an audit entry when a user successfully accesses an object, and a failure audit generates an audit entry when a user unsuccessfully attempts to access an object. For more information, see the section "Planning for Security Monitoring."

6. **B.** In this scenario, the best option for increasing security is to revoke any unused certificates and immediately publish the CRL to all CDPs. For more information, see the section "Configuring Active Directory for Certificate Publication."

7. **B.** All that is necessary to read the email and verify it came from you is your public key, which can be safely transferred to anyone you want. Your private key should never be given out. If your colleague were to install the third-party CA's root certificate, he would thus be able to verify the entire certificate chain for your digital certificate. For more information, see the section "Certificates."

8. **A.** In this scenario, because the email has been signed with your public key, you need to have access to your private key, which should not be any problem. Your private key can be used to verify messages signed with your public key and can be used to verify messages that can be decrypted with your public key. For more information, see the section "Certificates."

## APPLY YOUR KNOWLEDGE

9. **C.** To use the Certificate Services Web Enrollment pages, Rick must ensure that IIS is installed and configured properly to allow ASP pages to function properly. For best results, Rick should have installed IIS before installing the CA. For more information, see the section "Installing and Configuring an Enterprise Root CA."

10. **D.** Hannah should revoke the smart card certificates and immediately publish the CRL next. After doing so, she should also delete any unused user accounts that may have been created for the scientists' use during their visit to Hannah's facility. For more information, see the section "Configuring Active Directory for Certificate Publication."

11. **B.** By configuring the Interactive Logon: Require smart card Group Policy setting, Chris can ensure that all her users are required to log on to the network using their smart cards. Smart cards are used to provide the highest level of user authentication available in Windows Server 2003 networks. A user uses a password or PIN to access the digital certificate on the smart card, thus protecting the user's identity from rogue applications and attackers. Through the use of on-card digital signatures, smart cards can ensure that a user's private key is never exposed. Perhaps the single best feature of smart cards is that they—unlike software-based private keys—can be moved at will from one computer to another with ease. You can prevent smart cards from being used to access the network after a preconfigured number of incorrect login attempts, protecting them further from dictionary attacks—a type of password guessing attack where a password is guessed from

a list, or dictionary, of common words and phrases. For more information, see the section "Smart Card Group Policy Options."

12. **C.** Had Jim used a Change and Configuration Control policy, along with an approved change request, he most likely would not have created the problem he did as a result of his configuration change on the firewall. For more information, see the section "Planning for Change and Configuration Management."

13. **D.** Queued certificates are located in the Pending Requests folder of the Certification Authorities console. You can find and issue this certificate for Kim from this location. For more information, see the section "Installing and Configuring an Enterprise Root CA."

14. **C.** The easiest way for Kim to check on the status of her requested certificate is to go back to the CA from which she requested it via its Web Enrollment pages. If the certificate request has been approved, she also can install the certificate from that location. For more information, see the section "Using the Web Enrollment Web Pages."

15. **D.** Chris only wants to determine the security status of her network at this time, not install any updates. Using the MBSA utility is the best option because she can configure a single scan of all computers located on her subnet. After MBSA has completed the scan, she can examine each computer's results separately from the others, quickly determining what areas of their security configuration are weak in addition to determining what security updates are missing on each computer. For more information, see the section "Planning for Software Update Services."

## APPLY YOUR KNOWLEDGE

### Suggested Readings and Resources

1. SUS home page, `www.microsoft.com/windows2000/windowsupdate/sus`.

2. Windows Server 2003 online help, "Auditing Security Events," `www.microsoft.com/technet/prodtechnol/windowsserver2003/proddocs/entserver/AuditTN.asp`.

3. Windows Server 2003 online help, "Security Configuration Manager," `www.microsoft.com/technet/prodtechnol/windowsserver2003/proddocs/entserver/SEconcepts_SCM.asp`.

4. *Microsoft Windows Server 2003 Administrator's Companion* (2003, Microsoft Press; ISBN: 0735613672)

5. Microsoft Windows Server 2003 Deployment Kit, "Designing a Managed Environment," `www.microsoft.com/windowsserver2003/techinfo/reskit/deploykit.mspx`.

6. Microsoft Windows Server 2003 Deployment Kit, "Designing and Deploying Directory and Security Services," `www.microsoft.com/windowsserver2003/techinfo/reskit/deploykit.mspx`.

Now that you've finished reading this book and working through the exercises, you're ready for the exam. This section of the book is intended to be used as you're sitting in the testing center parking lot doing your "final cram" before you head in the door.

Organized by chapter, this section of the book is not only a summary, but it is also a concentrated review of the most important points. If you know and are comfortable with the content and concepts presented here, the odds are good that you are truly prepared for Exam 70-293, "Planning and Maintaining a Microsoft Windows Server 2003 Network Infrastructure."

# PLANNING AND IMPLEMENTING SERVER ROLES AND SERVER SECURITY

Role-based security is implemented by using a layered approach to security; the most general security settings are applied at the highest level and grow increasingly more restrictive as you go deeper into the organizational structure of the domain. Through the use of the pre-configured security templates included with Windows Server 2003, combined with careful planning and attentive administration of the network, you will be able to implement a role-based security solution.

Windows Server 2003 comes with a complete set of preconfigured security templates that you can use to quickly apply standardized security settings to a single computer, an Organizational Unit (OU), or a domain if desired. In addition to these preconfigured security templates, Microsoft has made available additional security templates that you can use to enforce specific security settings on Windows Server 2003 computers, depending on their assigned roles.

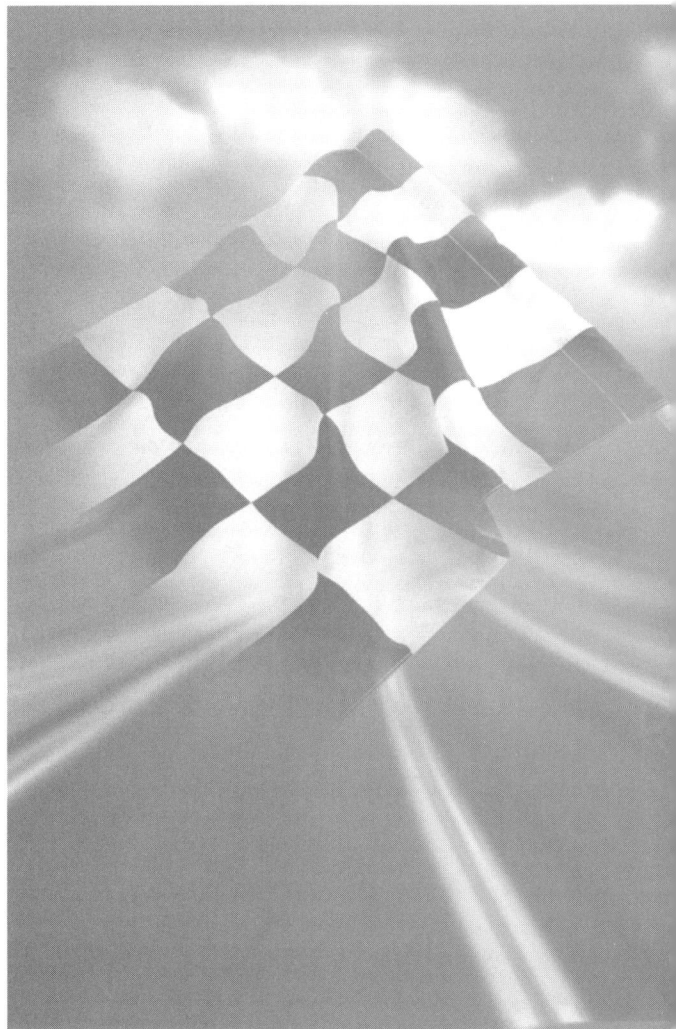

# Fast Facts

# 70-293

Organizational Units (OU), sometimes thought of as nothing more than an organizational tool to "clean" up the visual appearance of Active Directory, are actually among the most powerful tools for planning, implementing, and maintaining a secure network environment. OUs offer an easy way to segment users and other security principals, specifically computers in this instance, for the purpose of creating and enforcing administrative boundaries. By nesting OUs within each other, each with its own specific Group Policy Object (GPO), you can quickly piece together the overall security solution for your network.

You can identify the default security settings on a newly installed Windows Server 2003 member server through a variety of different means, such as the Local Group Policy console, the Local Security Policy console, or the Resultant Set of Policy (RSoP) snap-in.

A security template is little more than a specially formatted flat text file that can be read by the Security Configuration Manager tools. These preconfigured templates have the extension `.inf` and can be located in the `%systemroot%\security\templates` folder on your Windows Server 2003 computer. You can use the Security Configuration and Analysis console, the `secedit.exe` tool, or the Local Security Policy console to apply these templates to a local computer. You can apply templates to an Organizational Unit or domain by importing them into the Security Settings section of the applicable Group Policy using the Group Policy Editor. You also can use these preconfigured templates to baseline an unknown system against a known set of configuration settings by using the Security Configuration and Analysis console or the `secedit.exe` tool.

Table 1 details the preconfigured security templates that ship with Windows Server 2003.

All the preconfigured security templates are incremental, meaning that they have been designed to be applied to computers that use the default security settings.

These templates do not implement the default security settings before applying their security settings.

The Security Configuration Manager tools are to be used to design, test, and implement these (and other) security templates. The components of the Security Configuration Manager include

- ▶ The Security Configuration and Analysis snap-in
- ▶ The Security Templates snap-in
- ▶ Group Policy security extensions
- ▶ The `secedit.exe` command

The Security Configuration and Analysis snap-in is an important tool in any administrator's security template toolbox. By using the Security Configuration and Analysis snap-in, you can create, configure, test, and implement security template settings for a local computer. Therein lies its one real weakness: You can use it to work only with the settings of a local computer. You can, however, find ways to work around this limitation by using the other tools that are at your disposal, including `secedit.exe` and the security extensions to Group Policy.

The Security Configuration and Analysis snap-in can be used in two basic modes, as its name suggests—configuration and analysis—although not necessarily in that order. When you're using the Security Configuration and Analysis snap-in to analyze the current system security configuration, no changes are ever made to the computer being analyzed. The administrator simply selects a security template to compare the computer against (either a preconfigured template or a custom created template). The settings from the template are loaded into a database and then compared to the settings currently implemented on the computer. It is possible to import multiple templates into this database, thus merging their settings into one conglomerate database. In addition, you can specify that existing database settings are to be cleared before another template is imported into the database. When the desired security templates have been loaded into the database, any number of analysis actions can be performed, both by the Security Configuration and Analysis snap-in and by the `secedit.exe` command.

## TABLE 1

### THE PRECONFIGURED SECURITY TEMPLATES IN WINDOWS SERVER 2003

| Template (Filename) | Description |
| --- | --- |
| Default security (`Setup security.inf`) | This template is created during the installation of Windows Server 2003 on the computer. This template is variable between one computer to the next, depending on whether the installation was performed as a clean install or an upgrade. `Setup security.inf` represents the default security settings that the computer started with and thus can be used to reset portions of security as required. This template can be applied to both workstations and member servers, but not to domain controllers and should never be applied via Group Policy due to the large amount of data it contains; it can result in performance degradations. |
| Default DC security (`DC security.inf`) | This template is automatically created when a member server is promoted to domain controller. It represents the file, Registry, and system service default security settings for that domain controller and can be used later to reset these areas to their default configuration. |
| Compatible (`compatws.inf`) | The compatible workstation/member server template provides a means to allow members of the Users group to run applications that do not conform to the Windows Logo Program. Applications that do conform to the Windows Logo Program can be, in most cases, successfully run by members of the Users group without any further modifications required. For applications that do not conform, two basic choices are available: make the users members of the Power Users group or relax the default permissions of the Users group. The compatible template solves this problem by changing the default file and Registry permissions that are granted to the Users group to allow them to run most applications that are not part of the Windows Logo Program. As a side effect of applying this template, all users are removed from the Power Users group because the basic assumption is that the template is being applied in an effort to prevent the need for Power Users. This template should not be applied to domain controllers, so be sure not to import it into the Default Domain Policy or the Default Domain Controller Policy. |
| Secure (`securews.inf, securedc.inf`) | The secure templates are the first ones to actually begin the process of locking down the computer to which they are applied. The two different secure templates are `securews.inf`, which is for workstations and member servers, and `securedc.inf`, which is for domain controllers only. The secure templates prevent the use of the LAN Manager (LM) authentication protocol. Windows $9x$ clients need to have the Active Directory Client Extensions installed to enable NTLM v2 to allow them to communicate with Windows 2000 and later clients and servers using these templates. These templates also impose additional restrictions on anonymous users, such as preventing them from enumerating account and share information. The secure templates also enable Server Message Block (SMB) signing on the server side. By default, SMB signing is enabled on client computers. When this template is applied, SMB packet signing is always negotiated between clients and servers. |

*continues*

**TABLE 1**    *continued*

### The Preconfigured Security Templates in Windows Server 2003

| Template (Filename) | Description |
| --- | --- |
| Highly Secure (`hisecws.inf, hisecdc.inf`) | The highly secure templates impose further restrictions on computers they are applied to. Whereas the secure templates require at least NTLM authentication, the highly secure templates require NTLM v2 authentication. The secure templates enable SMB packet signing; the highly secure templates require SMB packet signing. In addition to the various additional security restrictions that are imposed by the highly secure templates, these templates also make several changes to group membership and the login process. All members of the Power Users group are removed from this group. Also, only Domain Admins and the local administrative account are allowed to be members of the local Administrators group. When the highly secure templates are used, it is assumed that only Windows Logo Program–compliant applications are in use. As such, there is no provision in place for users to use noncompliant applications because the compatible template is not needed and the Power Users group has no members. Members of the Users group can use applications that are Windows Logo Program compliant. Additionally, members of the Administrators group can use any application they want. |
| System root security (`Rootsec.inf`) | This template defines the root permissions for the root of the system volume. Should these permissions be changed, they can be reapplied using this template. This template can also be modified to apply the same permissions to other volumes. Explicitly configured permissions are not overwritten on child objects when using this template. |
| No Terminal Server use SID (`Notssid.inf`) | This template is used on servers that are not running Terminal Services to remove all unnecessary Terminal Services SIDs from the file system and Registry. This, however, does not increase the security of the server. |

After the database has been populated and an analysis scan has been initiated, the Security Configuration and Analysis snap-in examines every configurable Group Policy option and then reports back to you the results of the analysis scan. Each setting is marked with an icon that denotes one of several possible outcomes, such as that the settings are the same, the settings are different, or the settings do not apply. Table 2 outlines the possible icons that you might see and what they indicate.

**TABLE 2**

### The Preconfigured Security Template Icons in Windows Server 2003

| Icon | Description |
| --- | --- |
| Red circle with white X | The item is defined in the analysis database and on the computer but does not match the currently configured setting. |
| Green check mark | The item is defined in the analysis database and on the computer and matches the currently configured setting. |
| Question mark | The item is not defined in the analysis database and was not examined on the computer. |
| Exclamation point | The item is defined in the analysis database but not on the computer. |
| No special icon | The item is not defined in the analysis database or the computer. |

You can analyze and configure several areas by using the Security Configuration and Analysis snap-in:

▶ *Account Policies*—This node contains items that control user accounts. In Windows NT 4.0, these items are managed from the User Manager for Domains. This node has two subnodes: Password Policy and Account Lockout Policy. The Password Policy node deals with account password-related items, such as minimum length and maximum age. The Account Lockout Policy node contains options for configuring account lockout durations and lockout reset options.

▶ *Local Policies*—This node contains policies that are applied to the local machine. It has three subnodes: Audit Policy, User Rights Assignment, and Security Options. The Audit Policy node is relatively self-explanatory: It offers options for configuring and implementing various auditing options. The User Rights Assignment node contains miscellaneous options that deal with user rights, such as the ability to log in to a computer across the network. The Security Options node contains many other options—such as the option to set a login banner or allow the system to be shut down without being logged in first—that previously could be edited only in the Windows NT 4.0 Registry or by using System Policies.

▶ *Event Log*—This node contains options that allow you to configure the behavior and security of the event log. In this node, for example, you can include maximum log sizes and disallow guest access to the event logs.

▶ *Restricted Groups*—This node allows you to permanently configure which users are allowed to be members of specific groups. For example, company policy may provide the ability to perform server backups to a specific group of administrators. If another user who is not otherwise authorized with these privileges is added to this group and not removed after he or she has performed the intended function, you have created a security problem because the user has more rights than normally authorized. By using the Restricted Groups node, you can reset group membership to the intended membership.

▶ *System Services*—This node allows you to configure the behavior and security assignments associated with all system services running on the computer. Options include defining that a service is to start automatically or be disabled. In addition, you can configure the user accounts that are to have access to each service.

▶ *Registry*—This node allows you to configure access restrictions that specify who is allowed to configure or change individual Registry keys or entire hives. This option does not provide you with the means to create or modify Registry keys, however; that must still be done by using the Registry Editor.

▶ *File System*—This node allows you to set folder and file NTFS permissions. This capability is especially handy if you need to reset the permissions on a large number of folders or files.

The Security Templates snap-in might at first seem to have no real purpose. However, this is not the case at all. You can use this snap-in to modify existing templates or create new ones from scratch without the danger or possibility of accidentally applying the template to the computer or GPO.

You can easily and quickly import security templates into GPOs by using the Group Policy Editor to allow you to configure large portions of your network with the settings contained in the security template. You should apply the most generic settings at the domain level and then at the OU level apply specific settings that pertain to the computers in that OU; this is the cornerstone of role-based network security.

You can use `secedit` to perform the same functions as the Security Configuration and Analysis snap-in, plus a couple of additional functions not found in the snap-in. The `secedit` command has the following top-level switches available for use:

- **/analyze**—This option allows you to analyze the security settings of a computer by comparing them against the baseline settings in a database.

- **/configure**—This option allows you to configure the security settings of the local computer by applying the settings contained in a database.

- **/export**—This option allows you to export the settings configured in a database to a security template `.inf` file.

- **/import**—This option allows you to import the settings configured in a security template `.inf` file into a database. If you will be applying multiple security templates to a database, you should use this option before performing the analysis or configuration.

- **/validate**—This option validates the syntax of a security template to ensure that it is correct before you import the template into a database for analysis or configuration.

- **/GenerateRollback**—This option allows you to create a rollback template that can be used to reset the security configuration to the values it had before the security template was applied.

Of the available options, you will most often use the `/analyze` and `/configure` switches.

Security policies (via security templates and GPOs) are typically applied at the three following hierarchical levels to create role-based security:

- *Domain*—The most common security requirements, such as password and account lockout policies are applied at the domain level. These policies are applied to all computers—servers and workstations alike—within the domain.

- *Baseline*—This policy contains security configuration items that apply to all member servers, such as auditing policies and user rights assignments.

- *Role-specific*—To address the specific security needs of each specific server role, member servers are divided into role-based groups using OUs and have specific, individual security policies applied to them.

# Planning, Implementing, and Maintaining a Network Infrastructure

The Transmission Control Protocol/Internet Protocol (TCP/IP) maps to both the Open System Interface (OSI) and DoD (Department of Defense) models but maps more closely with the DoD model because the Department of Defense was the original creator and user of this protocol. In Table 3 you can see where TCP and IP map to the DoD model as well as some other common protocols in use on typical local area networks.

## TABLE 3

### Viewing the DoD Model with TCP/IP Mapped to It

| Process and Application Layer | SMTP (Email-based Protocol) |
|---|---|
| Host to Host Layer | TCP |
| Internet Layer | IP |
| Network Access Layer | Ethernet |

TCP/IP is the basic communication language or protocol of the Internet. Many other protocols are available out there, some of which you may be familiar with, such as AppleTalk, IPX/SPX, even SNA. All these protocols have been displaced by TCP/IP, however. Because most networks today are connected to the Internet somehow, using only TCP/IP makes more sense.

TCP/IP is responsible for creating and keeping communications between all network-connected devices that need to communicate with each other. Without the need for communication, TCP/IP would serve no true purpose, but because the whole purpose of a network is to share resources, TCP/IP is the medium that provides such communication. Couple this need for communication with some form of physical topology (cabling or wireless), and you have a network.

An IP address is a 32-bit number that denotes a node or host on a network. The number, which resembles 10.1.1.1/24, is a unique host on a single network. If you have two nodes, one numbered 10.1.1.1 and 10.1.1.2, they are able to communicate if they are connected to the same network segment and no other outstanding issues stop communication.

An IP address is broken down into two specific parts: the network identifier and host identifier. Let's look at the following IP address to understand it better:

IP address: 10.1.1.1

Subnet mask: 255.255.255.0

You need to break down this number into binary bits to truly see what we mean by masking. First, consider the fact that you have a 32-bit address written in decimal format. If you want to see the subnet mask 255.255.255.0 in binary, you have to change the format from decimal to binary, or base 2 numbering, as follows:

255.255.255.0 =
11111111.11111111.11111111.00000000

Remember, binary uses only 1s and 0s, either on or off. No other numbers are used, so you can see how the network is masked. All 1s in the network portion denote the actual network you are working on. This leaves the host portion (the 0s at the end) available for assignment. This way, any device can know what network it's on, or better, what subnet. Because we've used 24 1s here, we denote the IP address as 10.1.1.0/24. Using this form of notation is an easier way to show a subnet mask assignment. If you see /30, for example, the address appears like this in binary:

11111111.11111111.11111111.11111100

Public IP addressing uses three major spaces: Classes A, B, and C. There are also two more classes: Class D, which is used for multicast-based networks, and Class E, which is still experimental. Class A is for very large networks, Class B is for medium-sized networks, and Class C is used for networks that have no more than a couple hundred nodes. Public ranges are shown in Table 4.

## TABLE 4

### VIEWING IP ADDRESS CLASSES

| Class | Range |
| --- | --- |
| Class A | 1–126 |
| Class B | 128–191 |
| Class C | 192–223 |

Notice that 127 is not listed in the address range. The IP address 127.0.0.0 is reserved for loopback networks and testing. 127.0.0.1 is also located in the HOSTS file, which allows you to test the IP connectivity of your own machine. If you use the command `ping loopback` (which is the hostname located in the HOSTS file), you can resolve to 127.0.0.1, and you should see a reply. This way, you know that TCP/IP is configured properly—at least on your own system.

Although the private IP address ranges shown in Table 5 fall within Class A, B, and C public IP addresses, note that private IP addresses are not routable on the Internet by design (and by default) and should never be seen outside an internal network.

**TABLE 5**

**VIEWING PRIVATE IP CLASSES**

| Class | Range |
| --- | --- |
| Class A | 10.0.0.0–10.255.255.255 |
| Class B | 172.16.0.0–172.31.255.255 |
| Class C | 192.168.0.0–192.168.255.255 |

When implementing a new network, you should know what you want the network to look like before you even contemplate ordering gear to populate it. This step is important because you must consider many factors before implementation. These factors include the following:

▶ Do you want redundancy and high availability?

▶ Do you want security?

▶ Where will the application flows be generated from?

▶ How do you stop or contain bottlenecks from occurring?

IPX/SPX, which stands for Internetwork Packet Exchange/Sequence Packet Exchange, is similar to TCP/IP. You can think of IP mapping to IPX and TCP mapping to SPX. These protocols perform similar operations. IPX/SPX was originally created and used extensively by Novell with its NetWare platform of network operating systems. Although IPX/SPX was a great protocol, TCP/IP became the protocol of the Internet. To avoid missing out on the Internet revolution, all NOS vendors chose to develop TCP/IP into all their

solutions moving forward, leaving in other protocols such as IPX/SPX only for backward compatibility. Novell NetWare version 5.0 was the first version to be shipped with a real version of TCP/IP, whereas the older versions of NetWare (versions 4.x and before) used add-on packs.

Systems Network Architecture (SNA) is an old but still widely used protocol. Developed by IBM, SNA is a protocol suite that runs on most mainframes used today. Microsoft professionals who know only Microsoft may be shocked to learn that in today's networks they most likely will be confronted with some form of mainframe and may also be responsible for network connectivity to it.

Another old protocol, the Network Basic Input/Output System (NetBIOS) is a session layer communications service used by client and server applications in IBM-based token-ring and PC LAN Ethernet-based networks. NetBIOS is really just a way for application programming interface–based communications to take place. This means that higher-level services can run over lower-level protocols such as IP. This process is known as NetBIOS over TCP/IP (NBT). The NetBIOS service contains three main sections: the name, session, and datagram services.

To connect your LAN to the Internet, you need to plan for the following:

▶ What type of connection do you want? What media, what technology?

▶ How much bandwidth do you need to provide?

▶ What hardware will you use?

▶ Will security be involved?

▶ Who provides DNS?

▶ Will you be doing Network Address Translation?

▶ Where does Windows Server 2003 fit into network connectivity?

When troubleshooting client-based TCP/IP problems, you must develop a good troubleshooting methodology; otherwise, you will be wasting your time.

If you cannot make a client resolve names properly because its client-side DNS cache is either corrupted or not updated to a change already made on the DNS server, you can easily flush out that information by using one of the following commands:

- **ipconfig/flushdns**—This command purges the DNS Resolver cache.

- **ipconfig/displaydns**—This command displays the contents of the DNS Resolver cache.

- **ipconfig/registerdns**—This command refreshes all DHCP leases and reregisters DNS names.

# PLANNING, IMPLEMENTING, AND MAINTAINING A NAME RESOLUTION INFRASTRUCTURE

In the domain name system (DNS), containers called domains hold the information. The hierarchy starts with a root container, called the root domain. The root domain doesn't have a name, so it is typically represented by a single period. The root domain contains pointers to all top-level domains (TLDs), which are directly below the root domain. They are also sometimes called first-level domains. Lower-level domains are second-level, third-level, and so on. Every domain name has a suffix that indicates which TLD domain it belongs to. There are only a limited number of such domains as defined by Request for Comments (RFC) 1591. Following are some of the more common TLDs:

- **.COM**—Intended for commercial entities, but it has become the overwhelming favorite top-level domain (example of .COM: area51partners.com)

- **.EDU**—Intended for higher-education institutions, such as four-year colleges and universities (example of .EDU: berkeley.edu)

- **.GOV**—Intended for use by agencies of the U.S. Federal Government (example of .GOV: whitehouse.gov)

- **.MIL**—Intended for use by agencies of the U.S. military (example of .MIL: af.mil)

- **.NET**—Intended for use by network providers and organizations dedicated to the Internet, such as Internet service providers (example of .NET: ibm.net)

- **.ORG**—Intended for nonprofit or noncommercial establishments, such as professional groups, charities, and other such organizations (example of .ORG: npr.org)

DNS is used to translate a hostname to an IP address. The fully qualified domain name (FQDN) typically looks something like the following:

filesvr042.corporate.mcseworld.com

This is known as the host's FQDN because it lists the host's precise location in the DNS hierarchy. The DNS name in the example represents the host FILESVR042 in the subdomain CORPORATE (this is frequently a department or division in a company), which is in the subdomain MCSEWORLD (this is frequently the name of the company or organization that has registered the domain), which is in the TLD .COM.

Following are some questions you should ask yourself when planning your namespace needs:

- *Is your DNS namespace to be used for internal purposes only?* If so, you can use characters that are not typically used in DNS names, such as those outside the RFC 1123 standards. An example might be bigcorp.local.

▶ *Is your DNS namespace to be used on the Internet as well?* If you are currently using a corporate DNS namespace on the Internet, or think that you might at any point in the future, you should register your own domain name and conform to Internet naming standards.

▶ *Will you be implementing Active Directory?* The design and implementation of Active Directory on your network plays a critical role in determining how domains should be created and nested within each other.

You need to consider the following three basic options when planning the DNS namespace you will be using:

▶ *Use an existing DNS namespace*—This option uses the same namespace for both the internal (corporate network) and external (Internet) portions of your network. If your domain name is bigcorp.com, you would use this for both internal and external use. Although this method is the easiest and provides simple access to both internal and external resources, it poses additional administrative requirements because an administrator must ensure that the appropriate records are being stored on the internal and external DNS servers as a security precaution.

▶ *Use a delegated DNS namespace*—This option uses a delegated domain of the public namespace. If your domain name is bigcorp.com, you might consider using corp.bigcorp.com for the internal namespace. When you use this option, the corp.bigcorp.com domain becomes the root of the Active Directory forest and domain structure. Internal clients should be allowed to resolve external namespace addresses; however, external clients should not. Using a delegated DNS namespace provides a namespace that is easy to understand and remember and that fits in nicely with the existing registered domain name. All internal domain data is isolated in the domain or domain tree, thus requiring its own DNS server for the delegated internal domain. The downside to delegated namespaces is that this adds length to the total FQDN.

▶ *Use a unique DNS namespace*—This option uses a completely separate but related domain name for your internal namespace. As an example, if you are using bigcorp.com for your external namespace, you might use bigcorp.net for your internal namespace. This configuration provides the advantage of improving security by isolating the two namespaces from each other. Additionally, the administrative burden is relatively low because zone transfers do not need to be performed between the two namespaces, and the existing DNS namespace remains unchanged. In addition, this configuration prevents internal resources from being exposed directly to the Internet.

When creating DNS namespaces that are several levels deep, you must keep in mind some general DNS restrictions, as outlined in Table 6.

## TABLE 6

### DNS NAME RESTRICTIONS

| Restriction | Standard DNS | DNS in Windows Server 2003 (and Windows 2000) |
|---|---|---|
| Characters | Supports RFC 1123, which permits *A* to *Z*, *a* to *z*, 0 to 9, and the hyphen (-). | Supports several different configurations: RFC 1123 standard, as well as support for RFCs 2181 and the character set specified in RFC 2044. |
| FQDN length | Permits 63 bytes per label and 255 bytes for an FQDN. | Permits 63 bytes per label and 255 bytes for an FQDN. Domain controllers are limited to 155 bytes for an FQDN. |

Although it is typically abbreviated in the world of DNS, a zone is actually a *zone of authority*, which means that it contains the complete information on some part of a domain namespace. In other words, it is a subset or root of that portion of namespace. The nameserver is considered to have authority for that zone, and it can respond to any requests for name resolution from that zone. So, when you look at the DNS name www.quepublishing.com, quepublishing.com is a DNS zone within the .com hierarchy. The www denotes the DNS record of a host contained within the quepublishing.com zone.

This conceptual representation of a zone also has a physical counterpart: All the information relating to a particular zone is stored in a physical file known as the *zone database file*, or more commonly the *zone file*, that can be found at %systemroot%\system32\dns for zones that are not stored in Active Directory. The following types of zones are supported by Windows Server 2003:

▶ *Standard primary*—A standard primary zone holds a master copy of a zone and can replicate it to all configured secondary zones in standard text format. Any changes that must be made to the zone are made on the copy stored on the primary.

▶ *Standard secondary*—A standard secondary zone holds a read-only copy of the zone information in standard text format. Secondary zones are created to increase performance and resilience of the DNS configuration. Information is transferred from the primary zone to the secondary zones.

▶ *Active Directory–integrated*—Active Directory–integrated zones are available only on Windows 2000 Server and Windows Server 2003 DNS servers in an Active Directory domain. The zone information is contained within the Active Directory database and is replicated using Active Directory replication. Active Directory–integrated zones provide an increased level of replication flexibility as well as security. Active

Directory–integrated zones also operate in a multimaster arrangement because they are hosted within Active Directory itself; this way, any DNS server (domain controller) hosting the Active Directory–integrated zone can update the zone data.

▶ *Stub*—Microsoft has introduced support for stub zones for the first time in Windows Server 2003. A stub zone contains only those resource records that are necessary to identify the authoritative DNS servers for that zone. Those resource records include Name Server (NS), Start of Authority (SOA), and possibly glue host (A) records. (Glue host records provide A record pointers to ensure that the master zone has the correct nameserver information for the stub zone.)

When you are using a standard primary/standard secondary DNS zone implementation, the following points are of concern:

▶ A single DNS server is the master, holding the only writable copy of the DNS zone file.

▶ Zone transfers can be conducted using either incremental or full zone transfer.

▶ This implementation is made fully compatible with BIND DNS servers by using the standard DNS zone transfer methods in place.

When you are using an Active Directory–integrated DNS zone implementation, the following points are of concern:

▶ A multimaster arrangement allows any DNS server to make updates to the zone file.

▶ Zone data is replicated with Active Directory data.

▶ Increased security is provided on the zone file.

▶ Redundancy is provided for DNS dynamic update.

▶ The administrator can adjust replication scope. Additionally, the zone file can be replicated to a standard secondary DNS server—a common practice for DNS servers placed on screened subnets.

▶ This implementation appears to be a standard primary zone to a BIND DNS server, thus allowing the use of BIND DNS servers as standard secondary zone servers.

Table 7 provides a comparison of Active Directory–integrated zones and standard DNS zones.

## TABLE 7

### DNS ZONE TYPE COMPARISON

| DNS Feature | Standard DNS Zones | Active Directory–Integrated Zones |
|---|---|---|
| Complies with IETF specifications | Yes | Yes |
| Uses Active Directory for replication | No | Yes |
| Increases availability by providing a multi-master arrangement | No | Yes |
| Allows for zone updates after the failure of a single DNS server | No | Yes |
| Supports incremental zone transfers | Yes | Yes |

Regardless of whether you create standard or Active Directory–integrated DNS zones, you should be aware of the benefits of also using standard secondary zones. Following are some of the benefits you can realize by placing secondary zones on your network:

▶ The addition of standard secondary zone servers increases the redundancy of the zone by providing name resolution even if the primary zone server is unresponsive.

▶ When remote locations are connected to the core network over WAN links, secondary zone servers can greatly reduce costs and network traffic. By placing standard secondary zones in these remote locations or in locations with a high number of clients, you can improve overall network performance.

▶ Standard secondary zone servers reduce the load on the primary servers by distributing name resolution requests among more DNS servers.

Unlike WINS, which allows for a push/pull arrangement, zone transfers always originate with the secondary server polling the primary zone at the configured interval. It does so by checking the zone version number on the primary server to see whether it has changed in comparison to the version number on the secondary server. If the zone version number on the primary server has been incremented, a zone transfer is required and will be performed. If the secondary zone supports incremental zone transfers (which Windows Server 2003 does), the secondary zone pulls (from the primary zone) only the changes made to resource records for each incremental zone version—meaning that a resource record could potentially be updated one or more times in a single zone transfer. When you use incremental zone transfers, network traffic is reduced and zone transfer speed is increased.

Windows Server 2003 supports two zone transfer types for standard zones: full zone transfers and incremental zone transfers. You might also see them abbreviated as AXFR and IXFR, respectively. A full zone transfer causes the entire zone data file to be transferred, which is a large user of both bandwidth and time.

Active Directory–integrated DNS zones replicate data among all domain controllers, allowing any domain controller to modify the zone file and replicate the changes to the rest of the domain controllers. This form of replication is known as multimaster replication because multiple DNS servers are allowed to update the zone data—domain controllers that are running the DNS service in this case. Replication occurs on a per-property basis, meaning that only the relevant changes are replicated. Active Directory–integrated zones replicate only the final result of multiple changes to a resource record, unlike standard zones, which transfer the changes to a resource record that occurred in each zone version number.

In a TCP/IP network, a DNS resolver is any system that has been configured with one or more DNS server IP addresses and that performs queries against these DNS servers. The DNS resolver is part of the DNS Client service, which is automatically installed when Windows is installed. The resolver can request one of two types of queries from a DNS server: recursive or iterative.

A *recursive query* is a DNS query that is sent to a DNS server from a DNS resolver asking the DNS server to provide a complete answer to the query, or an error stating that it cannot provide the information. If the DNS server is also configured as a forwarder, the query can be forwarded directly to another DNS server. If the query is for a name outside the local DNS server's zone of authority, it performs an iterative query against a root DNS server, which then responds with the IP address of the DNS server whose zone of authority includes the desired IP top-level domain. Additional iterative queries are then performed until the name is resolved into its IP address or an error is produced.

An *iterative query* is a DNS query that is sent by a DNS server to another DNS server in an effort to perform name resolution. Consider the example of a workstation (DNS resolver) in the `bigcorp.com` domain that

wants to communicate with a Web server located in the `smallcorp.com domain`.

A *DNS forwarder* is a DNS server that accepts forwarded recursive lookups from another DNS server and then resolves the request for that DNS server. This capability can be useful if you do not have local copies of your internal DNS zone and want to have your local DNS server forward DNS queries to a central DNS server that is authoritative for your internal DNS zone. Caching-only servers make good DNS forwarders. If the DNS forwarder does not receive a valid resolution from the server that it forwards the request to, it attempts to resolve the client request itself.

A *DNS slave server* is a DNS forwarder server that does not try to resolve a resolution request if it doesn't receive a valid response to its forwarded DNS request. You typically see this type of DNS server implemented in conjunction with a secure Internet connection.

A new feature in Windows Server 2003, *conditional forwarding*, enables administrators to direct DNS requests to other DNS servers based on domain. Previous versions of Microsoft DNS supported only one forwarder, so if forwarding were enabled, all requests would be sent to a single server. This feature is used frequently when you want requests made to the internal network to be forwarded to a master DNS server that stores internal DNS zones, but have resolution requests that are made to Internet domains be sent to the Internet using the standard resolution process.

A common implementation of DNS forwarders in a Windows Server 2003 network has one specific DNS server being allowed to make queries to DNS servers outside the firewall. This implementation allows the firewall to be configured to allow DNS traffic only from this specific DNS server to leave the protected network, and allows only valid replies back to the DNS server to enter the protected network. Through this approach, all other DNS traffic—both inbound and outbound—can be dropped at the firewall, adding to the overall security of the network and the DNS service.

Configuring DNS security can be broken into the following five general areas of concern:

▶ Dynamic updates

▶ Active Directory DNS permissions

▶ Zone transfer security

▶ DNS server properties

▶ DNS Security (DNSSEC)

Dynamic updates occur when a DHCP server or a DNS client computer automatically updates the applicable DNS resource records when a DHCP lease is granted (or expires). Three types of dynamic updates exist in Windows Server 2003, each with its own security specifics.

*Secure dynamic updates* are available when Active Directory–integrated zones are in use. Using secure dynamic update, the DNS zone information is stored in Active Directory and thus is protected using Active Directory security features. When a zone has been created as or converted to an Active Directory–integrated zone, Access Control List (ACL) entries can be used to specify which users, computers, and groups can make changes to a zone or a specific record.

If the zone is integrated with Active Directory, the Discretionary Access Control List (DACL) for the zone can be used to configure the permissions for the users and groups that may change or control the data in the DNS zone. Table 8 lists the default group and user permissions for Active Directory–integrated DNS zones. These default values can be modified to suit your particular needs.

**TABLE 8**

**DEFAULT GROUP AND USER PERMISSIONS ON ACTIVE DIRECTORY–INTEGRATED DNS ZONES**

| Group or User | Permissions |
| --- | --- |
| Administrators | Allow: Read, Write, Create All Child Objects, Special Permissions |
| Authenticated Users | Allow: Create All Child Objects |
| Creator Owner | Allow: Special Permissions |
| DnsAdmins | Allow: Full Control, Read, Write, Create All Child Objects, Delete Child Objects, Special Permissions |
| Domain Admins | Allow: Full Control, Read, Write, Create All Child Objects, Delete Child Objects |
| Enterprise Admins | Allow: Full Control, Read, Write, Create All Child Objects, Delete Child Objects |
| Enterprise Domain Controllers | Allow: Full Control, Read, Write, Create All Child Objects, Delete Child Objects, Special Permissions |
| Everyone | Allow: Read, Special Permissions |
| Pre-Windows 2000 Compatible Access | Allow: Special Permissions |
| System | Allow: Full Control, Read, Write, Create All Child Objects, Delete Child Objects |

By default, Windows Server 2003 DNS performs zone transfers only with the DNS servers that are listed in a zone's Name Server (NS) resource records. Even though this configuration is fairly secure, you should consider changing this setting to allow zone transfers to be carried out only with specific IP addresses that you have explicitly configured.

If you must perform zone transfers across an untrusted network, you should consider implementing and using a virtual private network (VPN) tunnel between the two DNS servers. Encrypted zone information traveling inside the tunnel is safe from prying eyes, thus providing an uncompromised zone transfer. When using a VPN tunnel for zone transfer data, you should use the strongest possible level of encryption and authentication supported by both sides of the tunnel.

By default, Windows Server 2003 DNS servers use a secure response option that eliminates the addition of unrelated resource records that are included in a referral answer to the cache. The server typically caches any names in referral answers, thus expediting the resolution of subsequent DNS queries. However, when this feature is in use, the server can determine whether the referred name is polluting or insecure and discard it. The server thus determines whether to cache the name offered in the referral depending on whether it is part of the exact DNS domain tree for which the original name query was made. As an example, a query made for `sales.bigcorp.com` with a referral answer of `smallcorp.net` would not get cached.

It's a fact of life that many organizations already have existing DNS solutions in place, such as Unix BIND. In some cases, these existing BIND servers might not meet the DNS requirements of Active Directory. Table 9 outlines the features of some of the more common versions of BIND in use.

## TABLE 9

### FEATURES OF VARIOUS BIND VERSIONS

| BIND Version | Features |
| --- | --- |
| 4.9.4 | Support for fast zone transfers |
| 4.9.6 | Support for SRV resource records |
| 8.1.2 | Support for dynamic DNS (DDNS) |
| 8.2.1 | Support for incremental zone transfer (IXFR) between DNS servers |
| 8.2.2 | Full support for all Active Directory features |

If you are dealing with other DNS systems, you have two basic choices of implementation:

▶ Upgrade existing DNS systems to meet the DNS requirements of Active Directory. For BIND, versions 8.1.2 and later are sufficient.

▶ Migrate existing DNS zones to Windows Server 2003 DNS.

Although it is recommended that you use only Windows Server 2003 DNS servers to ensure full support for Active Directory, you can use any DNS system that meets the following specifications:

▶ Support for SRV (Service) resource records

▶ Dynamic updates per RFC 2136

If you have Unix BIND servers in your DNS infrastructure, you should consider placing them as secondaries instead of primaries. By default, Windows Server 2003 DNS servers use a fast zone transfer format whereby compression is used and multiple records can be sent in a single TCP message. BIND versions 4.9.4 and later support fast zone transfers. If you are using an earlier version of BIND or another third-party DNS system that does not support fast zone transfers, you must disable fast zone transfers. When you select the BIND Secondaries option, fast zone transfers are disabled for that server. You also should configure your zones to not transfer WINS-related information during zone transfers to these secondary servers.

In most environments that rely on WINS for name resolution for legacy systems, it is important to ensure that more than one WINS server exists so that you provide redundancy and availability. To ensure that each server has a current copy of the database, you need to configure replication between your WINS servers. You can configure the following types of replication for the WINS service:

► *Pull replication*—In pull replication, your server pulls the database from the replication partner. A pull replication is time based and occurs at the time you have configured. You can decide whether to establish a persistent connection for replication, and you can set the start time and interval for replication.

► *Push replication*—In push replication, your server pushes its database to the replication partner. A push replication is event driven, and the number of database updates determines when the event occurs. You can decide whether to use a persistent connection for push activities, and you can set the number of changes in version ID before replication.

► *Replication partner type*—The partner type can be push, pull, or push/pull, depending on your requirements. (In push/pull replication, database replication can occur using either method—push or pull.)

Microsoft TCP/IP uses NetBIOS over TCP/IP (NetBT) as specified in RFC 1001 and 1002 to support the NetBIOS client and server programs in the local area network (LAN) and wide area network (WAN) environments. Before we look at the specifics of NetBIOS name resolution, let's briefly review how computers communicate on the network. This review should help you understand how the different NetBIOS modes work and why some are preferable to others.

Computers can use two ways to communicate on a network:

► Through broadcast messages, which every computer receives

► Through directed messages, which are sent to a specific computer

Although networks can be organized using a mixture of node types, Microsoft recommends against doing so. B-node client computers ignore P-node directed messages, and P-node client computers ignore B-node broadcasts. Therefore, it is conceivable that two client computers could separately be established with the same NetBIOS name. If WINS is enabled on a Windows 2000 or XP computer, the system uses H-node by default. Without WINS, the system uses B-node by default. Non-WINS client computers can access WINS through a WINS proxy, which is a WINS-enabled computer that listens to name query broadcasts and then queries the WINS server on behalf of the requesting client computer.

The actual configuration of a computer to use LMHOSTS for NetBIOS name resolution is not done by using the WINS console or a Group Policy Object, as you might expect. Instead, you must actually configure it computer by computer by setting the options available to you on the WINS tab of the Advanced TCP/IP Settings dialog box.

# PLANNING, IMPLEMENTING, AND MAINTAINING ROUTING AND REMOTE ACCESS

Routing is the process of taking data from one network and sending it to another network.

A static routing environment is one in which all routing entries in a routing table are entered manually. In other words, if you want the router to know that the destination for all traffic is not local to the subnet that the router is connected to, you must manually enter the route into the router's table so it can be used.

You create a dynamic routing table with a routing protocol such as Routing Information Protocol (RIP) or Open Shortest Path First (OSPF). Understanding the routing table first is key to understanding the protocol because the protocol is responsible for building the table for you from information it is configured to learn. In other words, if you turn on RIP, the router builds a table from information it learns from other routers that are adjacent to it.

Routing tables are used to compute the next hop for a packet. Remember that a routing table must have two fields: the IP prefix and the next hop address, which also needs to be valid. The router in which the packet is leaving and going to must be able to reach this valid address. You must be connected; otherwise, the router will not work. Lastly, if you do not have a match (a packet comes in and does not have a routing table entry match), the packet is discarded, and you will most likely get an Internet Control Message Protocol (ICMP) notification that the destination host was unreachable.

Following are some pros and cons of the different routing types:

▶ Static routing is tedious. You must know exactly what you want to do because any mistake causes the router to either not work properly or make routing errors.

▶ You may want to implement static routing if you have only a few routes to maintain. Remember, each time a packet enters the router, the router needs to process it, so tables that are very long can cause the router to take longer to make a routing decision, which in turn could slow down your network. When you use dynamic routing protocols, it is possible to have a router learn as many as hundreds of routes, depending on network size.

▶ Static routes are more secure because only a few required routes are in the table, so no one can see too much information. In this case, if the router is compromised by an attacker, he or she cannot

glean too much information from your compromised router. The attacker may know only a default route back to the core network, for example; whereas if the attacker compromises a core router with 300 networks in the table, he or she can map your whole network from that one router.

▶ Dynamic routing is easy to configure and, once configured, is easy to maintain. If changes are made to the network, more than likely the routers will learn the changes, and they can quickly establish convergence on the network. Convergence occurs when all routers know all other routers on the network, and the topology is accurate.

▶ Dynamic routing is becoming more secure as more and more routing protocols provide ways to encrypt and authenticate updates between peers. However, configuring dynamic routes requires that the administrator have a greater level of knowledge and experience than when configuring static routes.

A Link State routing protocol ensures that each router on the network maintains a map of the network. For example, say one of your WAN links has a problem that results in two routers losing contact with each other. Both can (through the routing protocol) adjust for this loss of the link between them because they are programmed to do so. When your router link fails, it is programmed to sense the loss of carrier on the line and then, through the routing protocol, send updates to the other routers adjacent to them so that they all know that the link is down and the IP subnet that they maintained is no longer available for destination packets on the wire. When a network link changes state (up to down, or vice versa), a notification, called a link state advertisement (LSA), is flooded throughout the network. Routers all over the network address this change and make sure that their routing tables are adjusted accordingly. Another configurable option of Link State protocols is that they can use something other than hop count to determine their path through the network. Link State protocols can also determine that going over more routers may be quicker if the available bandwidth is higher instead of choosing the shortest path deemed solely on how many routers away the destination is.

Distance Vector protocols are easy to configure and maintain, but not as reliable or efficient as Link State protocols. Distance Vector protocols (such as RIP) allow for simple design and easy maintenance, but your bandwidth may suffer as a result. A Distance Vector protocol lets every router that is configured to use it inform every other adjacent router of its entire routing table. This means that each router on the network gets a full routing table from each neighboring router. These tables are used to create a metric based on hop count. Each router knows how far it is to another subnet in the network so that when incoming packets (when the router strips the header and reads the destination address) are read, the router will know the quickest way to get the packet there.

RIP is a Distance Vector routing protocol. Following are some details about RIP:

▶ RIP is limited to 15 router hops, with 16 hops being infinity. What does this mean? Picture a LAN with a PC that needs to communicate with a server on another LAN that is 15 routers away. The routers keep a list of which subnets are no more than 15 routers away, and if you try to expand the network past the 16$^{th}$ router, communications do not happen. Remember, you have a 15-hop minimum between networks, and the 16$^{th}$ is deemed infinity.

▶ RIP has problems with subnetted networks. In Chapter 2, we briefly covered what subnetted networks would resemble in your design. RIP was created and deployed before networks were subnetted to the degree that they are today, and because they have no direct support for RIP, your networks cannot support it. It really comes down to the information that each router sends to each other and what that packet contains. If the routing update does not contain a field in the packet to allow for subnetted networks, it does not carry over the information you may need it to. In other words, the RIP protocol is configured to look at the prefix of the IP address in the routing update and know whether it's either A, B, or C, and nothing more. If you subnet, your subnet will not be supported because RIP understands only that if a packet with an IP address of 10.0.0.1 comes in, it's automatically assigned a subnet of 255.0.0.0, even if you have it subnetted down to 255.255.255.0.

▶ RIP is bandwidth intensive, and although that isn't a problem on most networks, a smaller network with WAN links that are set small (such as Frame Relay links set with a 32KB committed information rate) could feel the effect of constant broadcasts every 30 seconds, especially if the routing table is large. If the routing table is too large, more than one update could be sent every 30 seconds, making it even more bandwidth intensive. For the 70-293 exam, remember that, by default, RIP broadcasts to its neighbors every 30 seconds lists of networks and subnets it can reach.

▶ RIP is not very secure. RIP contains no security features or configurable parameters to make it secure. Other protocols used today have configurable parameters to make them more secure; however, RIP does not contain any solution to make it secure by default.

RIP2, or RIP version 2, was created for RIP users to overcome problems with security. This version adds an option for authentication to the RIP packet as well as adding support for subnetted networks and allows for variable length subnetted networks to be passed through routing updates.

Open Shortest Path First (OSPF) is a Link State–based nonproprietary routing protocol. Following are some details about OSPF:

▶ OSPF is highly scalable. You will be hard pressed to build (or support) a network large enough to outdo OSPF. OSPF was designed to work in very large networks, and it works very well at that. It does not have a hop count restriction as RIP does. With OSPF's use of areas and a subdivided domain, the design possibilities are almost seemingly infinite.

▶ With RIP, you cannot use subnetted networks; with OSPF, you can.

▶ With OSPF, your bandwidth is spared. With RIP, an entire routing table is broadcast from every router on the network every 30 seconds. With OSPF (in stable environments that do not suffer from many changes), packets (called hello packets) are sent out intermittently to verify links between adjacent routers. This way, less bandwidth is used, and a major update check is performed only every 30 minutes.

OSPF divides the network (what it considers a routing domain) into areas. An area is a subdivision of the entire network and is given a label. Area 0 (zero) is considered the backbone of an OSPF network. If your network is small enough, you can set up the entire network to use Area 0, which is very important. For example, if the network becomes more subdivided (say you have three areas, including Area 0), you would need to know that if all traffic must travel between areas, the packets are first routed to the backbone, or

Area 0. When you plan a network this way, the design keeps subnets consolidated to areas, thus reducing the size of the link state database that is updated on every router in an OSPF network. This keeps your OSPF network running optimally.

Following is some other important information to remember about OSPF:

▶ OSPF sends out hello packets to each adjacent router connected to the network. OSPF uses hello packets to verify that the network is always ready to work as advertised. These hellos are sent out of every router interface every 10 seconds but are so small in size that they do not affect your available bandwidth.

▶ Link state advertisements provide other functionality, such as providing a solution for a scenario in which a router does not hear from its neighboring router for more than 40 seconds. The router then sends out LSAs marking the other router as down so that all the other routers can adjust their tables with the change.

▶ Hellos can be adjusted. A hello has a timer value that, when configured properly throughout the OSPF network, allows proper and accurate communications to take place. It is important to know that if a hello timer is misconfigured (not all timers are identical), problems can occur. Make sure that when you plan an OSPF network, you ensure that all the hello timers match. They must all be consistent across all routers on a network segment.

▶ Because LSAs age, it is important to get a refreshed routing table (or database) from a neighboring router just in case anything has changed. If nothing has changed on a particular router for 30 minutes, the router flushes its information and seeks an updated database from its adjacent routers. This means that the network reconverges every 30 minutes—a far cry from the forced reconvergence in a RIP network every 30 seconds!

Three forms of traffic traverse a network:

▶ *Unicast*—When a single node on the network sends data to its destination node under one single packet, it knows where the destination node is and gets the data to it. Remember *uni* as being a single transmission.

▶ *Broadcast*—Broadcasting (think of the word *broad*) occurs when the destination is not known or cannot be found, and that node (which needs to find the destination node) sends out packets to all nodes on the network segment to see whether it can find its destination node. This process is conducive to increased traffic, collisions on hubbed networks, and so on. Broadcasts are at times a necessary evil, but most of the time you should prevent them from happening often or control their number. Basically, broadcast traffic adds overhead to your network (bandwidth utilization) and its devices (processing packets they don't need to look at).

▶ *Multicast*—Multicast is the happy medium but still can cause problems. A multicast transmission is based on a group. In simple terms, think of 20 nodes on a network, 5 of which need to communicate at all times and 15 of which do not need to ever know what the other 5 are doing. Say these nodes are OSPF routers. OSPF routers send out updates to each other via a multicast, so you might ask, "What about devices that do not need to know this information?" If you use a multicast address, such as 224.0.0.5 (the all-OSPF routers multicast address) for OSPF-based networks, only those devices listen for transmissions from other nodes using this service. This reduces the problems caused by broadcast traffic and enables you

to cause one sender to get information to multiple (group) nodes without that message going to every node on the network. Consequently, multicasting is good, but as with any other technology, it can cause problems as well or require an advanced level of administration to make it work properly.

Considering multicast routing is very important because your network must be able to build packet distribution trees that allow sources to send packets to all receivers. These trees are meant to make certain that each packet on the network exists one time only and is found only on a specific network. If this limitation did not exist, you would have problems with IP multicast routing. Also, multicast routing, which is the propagation of multicast listening information, is provided by multicast routing protocols such as Distance Vector Multicast Routing Protocol (DVMRP) and Multicast Open Shortest Path First (MOSPF), which is an extension to OSPF that allows it to support IP multicasting. Such protocols ease manual configuration of VPN- and OSPF-based networks and are becoming the standard for these types of networks.

The Internet Group Management Protocol (IGMP) is an Internet protocol that allows nodes that are configured to use it to communicate as a group instead of individually. IGMP allows a node to report its multicast group membership (the group to which it is assigned) to adjacent routers. Multicasting allows a node to send data to many other nodes that have also identified themselves as being part of that group. This cuts down on broadcast traffic and bandwidth consumption. IGMP is detailed in RFC 2236.

When you want to access a network remotely, you must provide credentials. If you did not, security would not exist, and anyone could freely enter your network and exploit it. Based on this fact, you could say that Windows Server 2003 handles network access authorization based on account dial-in properties as well as remote access policies. Remote access polices are sets of rules (applied in an order) that define how incoming requests for authentication are handled—either accepted or rejected. Each policy is made up of profile settings and a remote access permissions setting.

Windows Server 2003 includes a new feature called Network Access Quarantine Control. This feature allows the delay of a remote access connection attempt to the Remote Access Server (RAS) until a script that verifies the configuration of the remote access computer runs. The connection attempt goes into quarantine until verified. The actual process is as follows: When a remote computer attempts to connect to the Remote Access Server, the computer is assigned an IP address to participate on the network. Then the user credentials are verified and authenticated, but the connection stays in quarantine until the remote computer is verified against the script. A script runs, and after it is completed, the server hosting quarantine releases the connection from quarantine after this information is verified. Network Access Quarantine Control is one of the newest features of Remote Access Security provided by default with Windows Server 2003.

Windows Server 2003 also provides Secure User Authentication. This means that security is obtained from the encrypted user credentials that are exchanged when you try to connect to a system. This can be done via the Point-to-Point Protocol (PPP) and its authentication-based protocols such as Extensible Authentication Protocol (EAP), Challenge Handshake Authentication Protocol (CHAP), and others. You can configure your Windows Server 2003 Remote Access Server to require specific secure authentication methods. The connection attempt is denied if the authentication credentials are not met.

EAP is a commonly used protocol on networks today; it is good at authenticating. EAP is responsible for creating an authentication method in which the authentication scheme to be used is negotiated by the remote access client and the authenticator, which could be either the Remote Access Server or even a RADIUS server. Windows Server 2003 Routing and Remote Access (RRAS) includes support for EAP-TLS by default; TLS stands for Transport Layer Security. It could be considered an EAP type, much like the wireless access protocol, called LEAP, provided by Cisco systems. There are many types of EAP, although they all perform similar functions, such as authentication; they just use different methods to do so.

Microsoft Challenge Handshake Authentication Protocol (MS-CHAP) is a nonreversible, encrypted password authentication protocol. MS-CHAP allows you to use Microsoft Point-to-Point Encryption (MPPE), which allows you to encrypt the data as well.

Version 2 of the MS-CHAP protocol provides stronger security for remote access connection attempts to your Remote Access Server. MS-CHAP version 2 solves a major issue with the cryptographically weak LAN Manager encoding used for backward compatibility and password changes because backward compatibility is no longer supported. This way, you don't have problems with crypto-based attacks on your networks that may break your security posture. It is for reasons such as this that you should opt to use version 2 over version 1.

Version 2 also solves other problems with version 1; for example, version 2 stops one-way authentication, which allows masquerading attacks on your Remote Access Server. Because two-way authentication is not available with version 1, such attacks are possible because the client that is trying to connect to a network remotely does not know whether it is dialing into the company's Remote Access Server or perhaps another server, one used for malicious intent. Again, you should use version 2 rather than version 1. MS-CHAP v2 provides two-way authentication, which is also called mutual authentication.

Challenge Handshake Authentication Protocol (CHAP) uses the industry standard Message Digest 5 (MD5) protocol. MD5 is a hashing scheme that encrypts your data in transit over the remote access network. CHAP does not allow you to change passwords during the authentication process, which may be a major issue, and one of the major reasons you would not want to include CHAP as part of your network.

The Shiva Password Authentication Protocol (SPAP) is an authentication protocol provided by a Shiva LAN Rover. If a Shiva client tries to connect to a Windows Server 2003 Remote Access Server, or a Windows client (such as XP) connects to a Shiva LAN Rover, SPAP is used. Because Shiva was prominent in the remote access market at one time, it is wise to include this support. Because PAP is used for cross-platform connectivity, it is not as secure as CHAP or even MS-CHAP. SPAP is even open to replay attacks (such attacks occur when data packets are captured in transit, examined, and then replayed to the server to gain access) because the same user password is always sent over the network in the same reversibly encrypted way each time. You should use SPAP only when you absolutely have to.

Routers keep routing tables. You can edit routing tables because if you use static routes, you have to enter them yourself, maintain them, and so on. You can use the RRAS console to manipulate this data, but nothing is faster or easier than using the route command. Within seconds, you can add a route in the routing table, adjust one, or take one out.

# PLANNING, IMPLEMENTING, AND MAINTAINING HIGHLY AVAILABLE SERVERS

When we discuss highly available solutions, we can look at the problem in two distinctly different ways: *hardware* and *software*. Windows Server 2003 provides two types of software-based high availability: *clustering* and *network load balancing (NLB)*.

*Clustering* is accomplished when you take a group of independent servers and put them together into one large collective entity that is accessed as if it were a single system. Incoming requests for service can be evenly distributed across multiple cluster members or may be handled by one specific cluster member.

The Microsoft Cluster Service (MSCS) in Windows Server 2003 provides highly available fault-tolerant systems through *failover*. When one of the cluster members (nodes) is unable to respond to client requests, the remaining cluster members respond by distributing the load among themselves, thus responding to all existing and new connections and requests for service. In this way, clients see little—if any—disruption in the service being provided by the cluster. Cluster nodes are kept aware of the status of other cluster nodes and their services through the use of heartbeats. A heartbeat keeps track of the status of each node and also sends updates in the configuration of the cluster. Clustering is most commonly used for database, messaging, and file/print servers. Windows Server 2003 supports up to eight nodes in a cluster.

Windows Server 2003 also provides *network load balancing (NLB)* in which all incoming connection requests are distributed to members of an NLB cluster using a mathematical algorithm. NLB clustering is best used in situations in which clients can connect to any server in the cluster, such as Web sites, Terminal Services servers, and VPN servers. You can configure how the client interacts with the NLB cluster as well, such as allowing the client to use multiple NLB cluster members during a single connection (acceptable for Web sites) or forcing the client to use the same cluster member for the entire connection period (a necessity for VPN and Terminal Services servers). Windows Server 2003 NLB clusters can contain as many as 32 nodes.

Although you can use both clustering and NLB in your final design, such as in the case of an e-commerce site that uses NLB for front-end Web servers and clustering for back-end SQL servers, you cannot use both technologies on the same server.

When a network load balancing cluster is created, port rules are used to determine what type of traffic is to be load-balanced across the cluster nodes. Within the port rule is the additional option to configure *port rule filtering*, which determines how the traffic will be load-balanced across each of the cluster nodes.

In an NLB cluster, every cluster node can answer for the cluster's IP address; thus, every cluster node receives all inbound traffic by default. When each node receives the inbound request, it either responds to the requesting client or drops the packet if the client has an existing session in progress with another node. If no port rule is configured to specifically define how traffic on the specific port is to be handled, the request is passed off to the cluster node having the lowest configured priority. This may result in decreased performance by the NLB cluster as a whole if the traffic is not meant to be or cannot be load-balanced.

Port rules allow you to change this behavior in a deliberate and controlled fashion. Think of port rules as the network load balancing equivalent of a firewall rule set. When you configure port rules to allow traffic on the specific ports you require to reach the NLB cluster and configure an additional rule to drop all packets not meeting any other port rules, you can greatly improve the performance of the NLB cluster by allowing it to drop all packets that are not allowed to be load-balanced. From an administrative and security standpoint, port rules allow for easier server monitoring due to the limited number of ports that must be monitored.

You can configure how NLB clusters load-balance traffic across cluster nodes; this process is referred to as *filtering*. By configuring filtering, you can specify whether only one node or multiple nodes within the NLB cluster are allowed to respond to multiple requests from the

same client during a single session (connection). The three filtering modes are as follows:

▶ *Single Host*—When this filtering mode is configured, all traffic that meets the port rule criteria is sent to a specific cluster node. The Single Host filter might be used in a Web site that has only one SSL server; thus, the port rule for TCP port 443 would specify that all traffic on this port must be directed to that one node.

▶ *Disable Port Range*—This filtering mode instructs the cluster nodes to ignore and drop all traffic on the configured ports without any further action. This type of filtering can be used to prevent ports and port ranges from being load-balanced.

▶ *Multiple Host*—The default filtering method, multiple host, specifies that all active nodes in the cluster are allowed to handle traffic. When Multiple Host filtering is enabled, the host affinity must be configured. Affinity determines how clients interact with the cluster nodes and varies depending on the requirements of the applications that the cluster is providing. The following three types of affinities can be configured:

- *None*—This affinity type sends an inbound client request to all nodes within the cluster. This type of affinity results in increased speed but is suitable only for providing static content to clients, such as static Web sites and FTP downloads. Typically, no cookies are generated by the applications running on the clusters that are configured for this type of affinity.

- *Class C*—This affinity type causes all inbound client requests from a particular Class C address space to a specific cluster node. This type of affinity allows a user's state to be maintained but can be overloaded or fooled if all client requests are passed through a single firewall or proxy server.

- *Single*—This affinity type maintains all client requests on the same node for the duration of the session (connection). This type of affinity provides the best support for maintaining user state data and is often used when applications are running on the cluster that generates cookies.

The mathematical algorithm used by network load balancing sends inbound traffic to every host in the NLB cluster. The inbound client requests can be distributed to the NLB cluster nodes through one of two methods: unicast or multicast. Although both methods send the inbound client requests to all hosts by sending them to the media access control (MAC) address of the cluster, they go about it in different ways.

When you use the *unicast* method, all cluster nodes share an identical unicast MAC address. To do so, NLB overwrites the original MAC address of the cluster network adapter with the unicast MAC address that is assigned to all the cluster nodes. When you use the *multicast* method, each cluster node retains its original MAC address of the cluster network adapter. The cluster network adapter is then assigned an additional multicast MAC address, which is shared by all the nodes in the cluster. Inbound client requests can then be sent to all cluster nodes by using the multicast MAC address.

The unicast method is usually preferred for NLB clusters unless each cluster node has only one network adapter installed in it. Recall that in any clustering arrangement, all nodes must be able to communicate not only with the clients, but also among themselves. Recall that NLB modifies the MAC address of the cluster network adapter when unicast is used; thus, the cluster nodes cannot communicate among themselves. If only one network adapter is installed in each cluster node, you need to use the multicast method.

NLB uses a group of between 2 and 32 servers to distribute inbound requests among them in a fashion that permits the maximum amount of loading with a minimal amount of downtime. Each NLB cluster node contains an exact copy of the static and dynamic content that every other NLB cluster node has; in this way, it doesn't matter which NLB cluster node receives the inbound request, except in the case of host affinity where cookies are involved. The NLB cluster nodes use heartbeats to keep aware of the status of all nodes.

Clustering, on the other hand, uses a group of between 2 and 8 servers that all share a common storage device. Recall that a cluster resource is an application, service, or hardware device that is defined and managed by the cluster service. The cluster service (MSCS) monitors these cluster resources to ensure that they are operating properly. When a problem occurs with a cluster resource, MSCS attempts to correct the problem on the same cluster node. If the problem cannot be corrected—such as a service that cannot be successfully restarted—the cluster service fails the resource, takes the cluster group offline, moves it to another cluster node, and restarts the cluster group. MSCS clusters also use heartbeats to determine the operational status of other nodes in the cluster.

Two clustering modes exist:

▶ *Active/Passive*—One node in the cluster is online providing services. The other nodes in the cluster are online but do not provide any services or applications to clients. If the active node fails, the cluster groups that were running on that node are failed over to the passive node. The passive node then changes its state to active and begins to service client requests. The passive nodes cannot be used for any other purpose during normal operations because they must remain available for a failover situation. All nodes should be configured identically to ensure that when failover occurs no performance loss is experienced.

▶ *Active/Active*—One instance of the clustered service or application runs on each node in the cluster. If a failure of a node occurs, that instance is transferred to one of the running nodes. Although this clustering mode allows you to make use of all cluster nodes to service client requests, it can cause significant performance degradation if the cluster was already operating at a very high load at the time of the failure.

Each resource group within the cluster has a prioritized listing of the nodes that are supposed to act as its host.

You can configure failover policies for each resource group to define exactly how each group behaves when a failover occurs. You must configure the following three settings:

▶ *Preferred nodes*—An internal prioritized list of available nodes for resource group failovers and failbacks. Ideally, all nodes in the cluster are in this list, in the order of priority you designate.

▶ *Failover timing*—The resource can be configured for immediate failover if the resource fails, or the cluster service may be configured to try to restart the resource a specified number of times before failover actually occurs. The failover threshold value should be equal to or less than the number of nodes in the cluster.

▶ *Failback timing*—Failback can be configured to occur as soon as the preferred node is available or during a specified period of time, such as when peak load is at its lowest so as to minimize service disruptions.

# MONITORING AND MAINTAINING SERVER AVAILABILITY

Periodic monitoring of your Windows Server 2003 network is important to the process of optimization. Monitoring helps to overcome the feeling-based assessment of your users. For example, by comparing current network performance against a previously established baseline, you have more information than the anecdotal "The network is slow today!" on which to base your actions. By gathering current information and comparing it against established norms for your systems (a baseline), you can detect bottlenecks, identify those system components that are slowing down server performance, and fix them before they become a problem to your users.

The importance of establishing a baseline before beginning to monitor performance can't be overstated. Although there are some guidelines as to what absolute performance numbers indicate, it is as you compare current performance against past performance (the baseline) that you will really be able to evaluate how well current demand is being met and whether you require more resources on your server. In addition, it is imperative that a baseline be established before problems begin to occur. If users are already beginning to complain, "The network is slow," it is too late to establish a baseline because the statistics gathered will include whatever performance factors are contributing to the dissatisfaction.

A baseline is a set of typical readings that define "normal" for your servers, client computers, or network under various operating conditions, such as no load, moderate load, and heavy load. Of course, what is normal is obviously open to interpretation, but you could say that normal is a server providing users with what they want in a time frame that they think is reasonable. By creating baselines early on, you have something that you can later look back at and compare current server operating conditions to. If your system is already to the point where you are seeing system degradation, it is really too late to establish a baseline.

To establish a baseline, you pick a time (or duration of time) that represents typical user interaction with the server. Then you create a log of important counters for the duration you have determined. Some of the more commonly used (and recommended) counters are summarized in Table 10.

## TABLE 10

### COUNTERS TO MONITOR FOR BASELINING AND BOTTLENECK TROUBLESHOOTING

| Server Component | Recommended Counters |
| --- | --- |
| Memory | Memory\Page Faults/sec |
| | Memory\Page Reads/sec |
| | Memory\Page Writes/sec |
| | Memory\Pages Input/sec |
| | Memory\Pages Output/sec |
| | Memory\Available Bytes |
| | Memory\Pool Nonpaged Bytes |
| | Process\Page Faults/sec |
| | Process\Working Set |
| | Process\Private Bytes |
| | Process\Page File Bytes |
| Processor | Processor\% Processor Time |
| | System\Processor Queue Length |
| | Process\% Privileged Time |
| | Process\% Processor Time |
| | Process\% User Time |
| | Process\Priority Base |
| | Thread\% Privileged Time |
| | Thread\% Processor Time |
| | Thread\% User Time |
| | Thread\Context Switches/sec |
| | Thread\Priority Base |
| | Thread\Priority Current |
| | Thread\Thread State |

| Server Component | Recommended Counters |
| --- | --- |
| Disk | PhysicalDisk\% Disk Time |
| | PhysicalDisk\Avg. Disk Queue Length |
| | PhysicalDisk\Current Disk Queue Length |
| | PhysicalDisk\Avg. Disk Sec/Read |
| | PhysicalDisk\Avg. Disk Sec/Write |
| | PhysicalDisk\Disk Read Bytes/sec |
| | PhysicalDisk\Disk Write Bytes/sec |
| | PhysicalDisk\Avg. Disk Bytes/Write |
| | PhysicalDisk\Disk Reads/sec |
| | PhysicalDisk\Disk Writes/sec |
| | LogicalDisk\% Disk Time |
| | LogicalDisk\Avg. Disk Queue Length |
| | LogicalDisk\Current Disk Queue Length |
| | LogicalDisk\Avg. Disk Sec/Read |
| | LogicalDisk\Avg. Disk Sec/Write |
| | LogicalDisk\Disk Read Bytes/sec |
| | LogicalDisk\Disk Write Bytes/sec |
| | LogicalDisk\Avg. Disk Bytes/Write |
| | LogicalDisk\Disk Reads/sec |
| | LogicalDisk\Disk Writes/sec |
| Network | Network Interface\Bytes Total/sec |
| | Network Interface\Bytes Sent/sec |
| | Network Interface\Bytes Received/sec |
| | TCPv4\Segments Received/sec |
| | TCPv4\Segments Sent/sec |
| | TCPv4\Frames Sent/sec |
| | TCPv4\Frames Received/sec |
| | Server\Bytes Total/sec |
| | Server\Bytes Received/sec |
| | Server\Bytes Transmitted/sec |

At a minimum, you must perform periodic monitoring on the following areas of your Windows Server 2003 computers: the hard disk(s), processor(s), memory, and network adapter(s). Regardless of which type of services the server is providing, these four areas interact to make your server efficient (thereby appearing fast) or inefficient. The actual speed or efficiency of each of the components varies in importance depending on the application. In some applications, memory is more important than processor speed or availability; in other applications, disk speed and availability are more important than fast network access.

Recognizing the need to be able to monitor the performance (and thus the health) of servers and client computers, Microsoft built the Performance Monitor into Windows Server 2003. Whether you are looking for real-time graphical views or a log you can peruse at your convenience, the Performance Monitor can provide the type of data you need to evaluate performance and recommend system modification if necessary.

On a daily basis, you may not want to monitor the full group of counters that were listed previously in Table 10. The counters in Table 11 present a smaller, and thus easier to manage, group of counters that you might consider monitoring on a daily basis to get a quick snapshot of your system and network performance.

### TABLE 11

#### COUNTERS TO MONITOR ON A DAILY BASIS

| Server Component | Recommended Counters |
| --- | --- |
| Memory | Memory\ Available Bytes |
| | Memory\ Cache Bytes |
| | Memory\ Pages/sec |
| | Memory\ Page reads/sec |
| | Memory\ Pool Paged Bytes |
| | Memory\ Pool Nonpaged Bytes |
| Processor | Processor\ % Processor Time (all instances) |
| | System\ Processor Queue Length (all instances) |
| | Processor\ Interrupts/sec |
| Disk | Physical Disk\ Disk Reads/sec |
| | Physical Disk\ Disk Writes/sec |
| | Logical Disk\% Free Space |
| | Logical Disk\% Disk Time |
| | Physical Disk\ Current Disk Queue Length (all instances) |
| | Physical Disk\ Split IO/sec |
| Network | Network Interface\ Bytes total/sec |

The following are some of the most common causes of bottlenecks that you might encounter while troubleshooting your network:

▶ The current level of provided resources is inadequate, thus requiring additional or upgraded resources to be added to the network.

▶ The available resources are not utilized evenly, thus requiring some form of load balancing to be implemented.

▶ An available resource is malfunctioning or stopped and needs to be repaired or restarted.

▶ An available resource is incorrectly configured, thus requiring a configuration correction.

After you have identified a problem, you should take care to avoid creating new problems while correcting the old one. You should make one change at a time to avoid masking the impact of changes. After each change, you should perform additional monitoring to determine the result and the effect of the change and reevaluate the status and condition of the previously identified problem(s). In addition, you can compare the performance of applications that are run over the network to their performance when run locally to determine how the network is affecting performance.

You should keep in mind the following general points when working with Windows Backup:

▶ You can back up to either a file or tape drive.

▶ You can back up files from either the local machine or remote computers, provided that you have access to the files you want to back up on the remote computer. The limitation of backing up a computer remotely is that system state information cannot be saved.

▶ To perform a backup, you must have Read access to the files or the user right of Backup and

Restore Files, which is granted by default to Administrators and Backup Operators.

▶ Special permissions are granted to the Administrators and Backup Operators groups to access all files for the purposes of doing backups. Even if members of these groups cannot access the data as users, they can back it up.

When you use the volume shadow copy, a copy of the original volume is created instantly at the time you initiate the backup. Data is then subsequently backed up to the backup media from this shadow copy instead of the original files. This new technology provides a means to back up open files that were in use at the time of the backup being initiated. When you use volume shadow copy, files that would normally be skipped during the backup are instead backed up in their current state (at the time of the shadow copy creation) and thus appear closed on the backup media. Any applications that are running during the backup process can continue to run during the backup process. After the backup has been completed, the shadow copy is deleted. The volume shadow copy feature requires the NTFS file system to be in use and can be disabled if you want. Another new use of the volume shadow copy feature is to create "snapshots" of shared network folders that can be used to roll back to a previous version of a file.

Automated System Recovery (ASR) is an advanced restoration option of the backup utility that you can use to restore your system if other disaster recovery methods fail or are not available for use. Using ASR, you can restore the operating system to a previous state, which allows you to start Windows Server 2003 in the event that other methods do not work. You should always consider ASR your last resort for recovery, after Safe Mode, the Recovery Console, and Last Known Good Configuration (LKGC). You should make a point to keep your ASR media up to date as you make configuration changes to your computer to minimize

the amount of recovery required should you ever need to use ASR.

ASR is a two-part process that uses a startup floppy disk to boot the Windows Server 2003 computer and a backup file (that must be accessible during ASR restoration) containing the system state, system services, and all disks associated with the operating system components. The startup disk contains information about the backup, the disk configurations, and the way the restoration is to be accomplished.

You should perform an ASR recovery only after all other available methods to start the server normally have failed. However, before starting the procedure, you need to locate the following items and have them readily available to you:

▶ The correct (up-to-date) ASR startup floppy disk.

▶ The correct (up-to-date) ASR backup media.

▶ The original Windows Server 2003 installation CD-ROM.

▶ Special drivers required for any mass storage controllers located in your server that are not available on the Windows Server 2003 CD-ROM; they also need to be available on floppy disk.

The usefulness of volume shadow copies is not just limited to its use within Windows Backup to create backups of open files; this feature also provides you with a way to archive copies of data over time, allowing users to locate and restore a specific file if they want. After the necessary configuration has been completed and the required software installed, users can view the volume shadow copies of shared network folders, including any previous versions in existence. Users can then copy any or all of the older files, allowing them to effectively restore a backup copy of the files from an earlier time.

As you might imagine, volume shadow copies can provide a number of benefits to your network users—the least of which is the ability to restore an older version should the current version of a file become corrupt or be deleted beyond recovery. You also can compare different versions of files to see what changes have occurred over time.

Files contained in a volume shadow copy are read-only while archived, preventing them from being modified and thus nullifying the benefits of the volume shadow copy. After a file has been extracted from a volume shadow copy archive, it can be modified or moved to any location desired for editing. Shadow copies are disabled by default but can be enabled and configured from the Shared Folders node of the Computer Management console.

Windows Server 2003 allows for only 64 volume shadow copies of a specific shared folder. When this limit is reached, the oldest copy is deleted to make room for a newer copy. Before your network clients can take advantage of this technology, they must have the Volume Shadow Client software installed. The client software is available on your Windows Server 2003 computer in the `%systemroot%\system32\clients\twclient\` folder.

After you've configured volume shadow copies, Windows Server 2003 computers and client computers with the Volume Shadow Client software installed can view the shadow copies available for a shared network folder.

Windows Server 2003 supports the following five backup methods:

▶ *Normal (full) backup*—This method copies all selected files and marks each file as having been backed up (the archive attribute is cleared). Only the most recent copy of the backup file is required to perform restoration.

▶ *Incremental backup*—This method copies only those files created or changed since the last normal or incremental backup; the archive attribute is then cleared. Using normal and incremental backups, you need the last normal backup and all incremental backups to be able to perform restoration.

▶ *Copy backup*—This method copies all selected files but does not mark each file as having been backed up (the archive attribute is not cleared). Copy backups have no effect on any other type of backup operation.

▶ *Daily backup*—This method copies all selected files that have been modified the day the daily backup is performed; the archive attribute is not cleared in this case. Using normal and daily backups, you need the last normal backup and all daily backups to be able to perform restoration.

▶ *Differential backup*—This method copies files created or changed since the last normal (full) or incremental backup; the archive attribute is not cleared in this case. Using normal and differential backups, you need the last normal backup and the last differential backup to be able to perform restoration.

The System State data contains information that is critical to the proper startup and operation of your Windows Server 2003 computer. The following items are included in the System State data:

▶ Registry

▶ COM+ class registration database

▶ Critical boot and system files

▶ System files that are protected by Windows File Protection

▶ Certificate Services database if the server is a Certificate Authority

▶ Active Directory directory service if the server is a domain controller

- SYSVOL directory if the server is a domain controller

- Cluster service information if the server is a member of a cluster

- IIS metadirectory if IIS is installed on the server

# Planning and Maintaining Network Security

Remote Assistance, first introduced in Windows XP, provides a built-in mechanism allowing an "Expert" to lend assistance to a "Novice" whether or not by request. The Expert can be located on the same internal network or even somewhere else on the Internet. Remote Assistance allows the Expert to create a connection to the Novice's computer, view the desktop, communicate with the Novice, and even take remote control of the Novice's computer if the Novice allows. Remote Assistance can be performed only on computers running Windows XP or Windows Server 2003—a good reason to consider that desktop upgrade to Windows XP. Before a computer is eligible to receive Remote Assistance, however, it must be enabled either locally or by Group Policy.

Users can request Remote Assistance in three basic ways: Windows Messenger, email (sends a URL), or file (creates a Remote Assistance request file). Note that Windows Messenger is not the same as Microsoft Messenger, although both use similar technologies. You can most easily send Remote Assistance requests by using the Help and Support Center, which you can access by clicking Start, Help and Support.

Remote Assistance, like all the Terminal Services and Remote Desktop Protocol–based applications, requires that TCP port 3389 be available to make a connection.

Remote Desktop for Administration, previously referred to as Remote Administration mode in Windows 2000, provides a built-in method to remotely administer and control servers. Provided you have the correct credentials, you can even remotely restart or shut down a server. Of course, you probably ought to warn any users who might be connected to it before doing so!

You can use Remote Desktop for Administration in one of two ways. The first and simplest (although less feature-rich) method is to use the Remote Desktop Connection utility, which you can find by clicking Start, Programs, Accessories, Communications, Remote Desktop Connection.

The second method for creating Remote Desktop for Administration connections is to use the new Remote Desktops Microsoft Management Console (MMC). This method offers two features that Windows administrators have been clamoring for since the introduction of Terminal Services:

- *Multiple connection profiles can be created*—You can configure multiple connections in the Remote Desktops MMC and then switch through them quickly and easily, all within the confines of a single window. The multiple windows required when using the Remote Desktop Connection utility or the Terminal Services client are not required.

- *Connections are made directly to the console session*—In the past, Terminal Services connections could not be made to the console session, preventing many administrators from using Terminal Services for remote administration or causing the use of third-party applications such as PC Anywhere or VNC. Windows Server 2003, using the Remote Desktops console, now creates connections to the console session, allowing administrators to view messages and pop-ups that are not redirected to any other session. There is no other way in Windows Server 2003 to connect to the existing console session and see these messages.

Remote Desktop for Administration, like Terminal Services Administration mode before it, is fairly restrictive in who can use it and how it can be used:

▶ Only administrators can create Remote Desktop for Administration connections by default; this is a good thing. You want the number of users with this power to be as small as possible to minimize the risk of an attacker gaining complete control over your network. Access control is handled through membership in the Remote Desktop Users group.

▶ Only two Remote Desktop sessions can exist on a computer, *and both* active and disconnected (but still running) sessions count toward this number. This restriction exists so that the number of concurrent changes being made to a computer is minimized to prevent configuration errors and conflicts. However, this does present a potential for a Denial of Service (DoS) attack against a computer—or at least the Remote Desktop portion.

In Windows Server 2003, administrators can now use Group Policy to design and implement security policies to secure 802.11 Wireless LANs. The use of both Wired Equivalent Privacy (WEP) and 802.1x authentication is supported. The Group Policy options that are configured in a GPO and applied to a computer then take precedence over any user-configured settings, thus ensuring that your configuration is applied. You can create policies for three types of Wireless LANs:

▶ *Access point (infrastructure)*—The most common type of Wireless LAN, the infrastructure mode WLAN, consists of wireless clients communicating directly with wireless Access Points (APs). No direct client-to-client communications exist. This is considered to be the most secure type of WLAN.

▶ *Computer-to-computer (ad hoc)*—Ad hoc WLANs consist of wireless clients communicating directly with each other without the use of an AP in the middle. This type of communication does not provide a direct path to the wired network.

▶ *Any available network access point preferred*—This option configures the policy to attempt a connection to an Access Point first if one is available. If an AP is not available, the client attempts to create an ad hoc connection if possible. This method is least preferred and usually most problematic over time.

The following are the standard features of the Windows Server 2003 IPSec implementation:

▶ IPSec in Windows Server 2003 is policy based. It cannot be configured without an IPSec policy being in place, allowing an administrator to more easily apply settings to groups of objects such as computers or users.

▶ IPSec on Windows Server 2003 can use Kerberos v5, a digital certificate, or a shared secret (string) for user authentication.

▶ IPSec mutually authenticates computers prior to any data being exchanged.

▶ IPSec establishes a security association (SA) between the two host computers involved in the data transfer. An SA is the collection of a policy and keys, which define the rules for security settings.

▶ IPSec encrypts data using Data Encryption Standard (DES) or Triple DES (3DES).

▶ IPSec uses the MD5 or SHA1 algorithm for data hashing.

▶ IPSec is invisible to users. IPSec operates at the network level of the Open System Interface (OSI) model; therefore, users and applications do not directly interact with the protocol. After an IPSec tunnel has been created, users can connect to applications and services as if they were on the local network and not on the other side of a public network.

The IPSec Authentication Header (AH) provides three services as part of the IPSec protocol. First (as its name might suggest), AH authenticates the entire packet. Second, it ensures data integrity. Third, it prevents any replaying of the packet by a third party who might be trying to penetrate the IPSec tunnel. One service AH doesn't provide is payload encryption. AH protects your data from modification, but an attacker who is snooping the network would still be able to read the data. To prevent the modification of the data, AH uses two hashing algorithms to "sign" the packet for integrity:

▶ The Message Digest 5 (MD5) algorithm applies the hashing function to the data in four passes.

▶ The Secure Hash Algorithm (SHA1) is closely modeled after MD5. SHA uses 79 32-bit constants during the computation of the hash value, which results in a 160-bit key. Because SHA has a longer key length, it is considered more secure than MD5.

Encapsulating Security Protocol (ESP) provides confidentiality in addition to authentication, integrity, and anti-replay. This portion of the IPSec protocol encrypts the data contents of the packet. The format of the ESP varies, depending on the type and mode of encryption being utilized. ESP can be used alone, in combination with AH, or using Microsoft's implementation, nested within the L2TP.

Policies allow you to quickly and easily configure IPSec based on the settings required within your organization. Windows Server 2003 comes with the following three preconfigured IPSec policies that may or may not meet your needs:

▶ *Client (Respond Only)*—This policy requires IPSec provided security only when another computer requests it. This policy allows the computer to attempt unsecured communications first and switch to IPSec-secured communications if requested. This policy contains the default response rule, which creates dynamic IPSec filters for inbound and outbound traffic based on the requested protocol and port traffic for the communication that is being secured. This policy, which can be used on workstations and servers alike, provides the minimum amount of IPSec security.

▶ *Server (Request Security)*—This policy requests security from the other computer and allows unsecured communication with non–IPSec-aware computers. The computer accepts inbound unsecured traffic but always attempts to secure further communications by requesting IPSec security from the sending computer. If the other computer is not IPSec-enabled, the entire communication is allowed to be unsecured. This policy, which can be used on workstations and servers alike, provides a medium level of IPSec security.

▶ *Secure Server (Require Security)*—This policy is implemented on computers that require highly secure communications, such as servers transmitting sensitive data. The filters in this policy require all outbound communication to be secured, allowing only the initial inbound communication request to be unsecured. This policy has a rule to require security for all IP traffic, a rule to permit ICMP traffic, and the default response rule to respond to requests for security from other computers. This policy, typically used only on servers, provides the highest level of IPSec security on a network. This policy can also be used on workstation computers if you want. Non–IPSec-enabled computers cannot establish any communications with computers using this policy.

Filter actions define the type of security and methods by which security is established. The default methods are Permit, Block, and Negotiate Security. The Permit option passes the traffic without the requirement for security. This action is appropriate if you never want to secure traffic to which a rule applies. The Block action silently blocks all traffic from computers specified in the IP filter list. The Negotiate Security action specifies that the computer is to use a list of security methods to negotiate the appropriate security for the communication.

Often when policies are applied on multiple levels, results can conflict. Using the RSoP snap-in can help you to easily determine where the problem lies and the precedence (processing order) of the policies involved. RSoP can be used in one of two modes:

▶ *Planning Mode*—This mode allows you to simulate the effect of policy settings that you want to apply to a computer and user.

▶ *Logging Mode*—This mode allows you to determine the existing policy settings for a computer and user who is currently logged on.

# PLANNING, IMPLEMENTING, AND MAINTAINING SECURITY INFRASTRUCTURE

Windows Server 2003, when combined with a Windows XP Professional client computer in a Windows Server 2003 Active Directory–based network,

features several enhancements and improvements to Certificate Services.

▶ *Version 2 certificate templates*—Version 2 templates extend the range of properties that you can configure from those provided in Version 1 templates. You now can create new certificate templates (an option sorely lacking from Windows 2000), copy existing certificate templates, and supercede certificate templates that are already in use. You need a Window Advanced Server 2003 functioning as the Enterprise Root CA.

▶ *Integrated and enhanced key recovery*—Windows 2000 Server relied on a Data Recovery Agent (DRA) to decrypt files following the loss or damage of an encryption key. Additionally, the Exchange 2000 Server Key Management Service (KMS) ran on top of Windows 2000 Certificate Services and did not fully integrate. Windows Server 2003 allows the archival and recovery of private keys and allows the administrator to access data encrypted with a lost or damaged private key. Now Key Recovery Agents (KRAs) are used to recover lost or damaged private keys across Windows Server 2003 and Exchange Server 2003.

▶ *Delta Certificate Revocation Lists*—Windows Server 2003 supports RFC 2459–compliant Delta Certificate Revocation Lists (CRLs) that contain only the certificates whose status has changed since the last full (base) CRL was compiled. This results in a much smaller CRL, which can be more frequently published with no adverse effects on the network or client computers. Additionally, this provides more accurate CRLs due to reduced latency periods. In Windows 2000, CRLs were typically published once per week (the default setting). Delta CRLs allow you to publish one or more times daily as required.

▶ *CA qualified subordination*—Another part of RFC 2459, qualified subordination allows a parent CA to granularly configure what a subordinate CA is allowed to do. Examples include preventing the subordinate CA from signing a certificate for another subordinate CA.

▶ *Common Criteria role separation*—By separating common CA-related tasks between several different levels of administration, you can meet Common Criteria requirements and enhance task delegation. Because roles are separated, no one individual should possess the ability to compromise the services or operation of the CA.

▶ *Enhanced auditing*—Windows Server 2003 provides for more detailed auditing of Certificate Services by adding two new types of events: access check and system events. System events come from seven critical areas: CA service, backup and restoration, certificate requests, certificate revocations, CA security, key archival and key recovery, and CA configuration.

A Windows Server 2003 Enterprise CA has five key characteristics:

▶ The CA server may run on any Windows Server 2003 server in the domain. You should plan for activity, network load, and physical placement of the server for best implementation.

▶ Because the CA name is integrated into the certificates it assigns, the name of the server should be determined before implementing CA services.

▶ The Enterprise CA Authority is integrated into the Active Directory.

▶ When you've installed an Enterprise CA, a policy module is created. An administrator can edit the policy.

▶ Because the CA is crucial for the successful implementation of the PKI, it must have a fault-tolerance scheme and a schedule of regular secure backups.

A typical Standalone CA has these key characteristics:

▶ It doesn't require Active Directory interaction.

▶ It can be used with extranets.

▶ It doesn't verify the requests for certificates. (All requests are pending until an administrator approves them.)

▶ Users requesting a certificate from a Standalone CA must supply all user account information. This information is not required within an Enterprise CA because the user is recognized by the logon account in the Active Directory.

▶ No certificate templates are used.

▶ Windows Sever 2003 logon credential certificates are not stored on smart cards. Other certificates can be, however.

▶ An administrator must distribute the Standalone CA certificate to the Trusted Root Certificate Store.

If Active Directory exists on the network and a Standalone CA can access it, additional options are available:

▶ If a domain administrator with write access to Active Directory installs the Standalone CA, the standalone is added to the Trusted Root Certification Authorities Certificate Store. In this situation, you must make certain that the default action of pending requests isn't changed to allow the Standalone CA to automatically approve all requests for certificates. Do not change the default action of pending certificate requests on a Standalone CA.

▶ If a domain administrator group member of the parent domain (or an administrator with write access to Active Directory) installs the Standalone CA, the Standalone CA will publish the certificate and the Certificate Revocation list to Active Directory.

Windows Server 2003 PKI allows for and encourages a dispersed hierarchy of CAs. Building a tree of CAs allows for scalability with other organizations, internal and external resources, and compatibility with third-party CA implementations.

Ideally (for ease of administration), an enterprise would have one CA; this is not usually a reality, however. Each CA hierarchy begins with the Root CA, and multiple CAs branch from this Root CA in a parent-child relationship. The child CAs are certified by the parent CA all the way back to the Root CA. The parent CAs bind a CA public key to the child CA's identity.

In this parent-child relationship, child CAs are trusted by the parent. That parent is, in turn, trusted by its parent CA, all the way back to the originating Root CA. Also in this model, when an organization trusts a CA by adding its certificate in the Trusted Root Certification Authorities Certificate Store, the organization therefore trusts every Subordinate CA in the hierarchy. Should a Subordinate CA have its certificate revoked by the issuing CA, the revoked CA is no longer trustworthy.

CAs are responsible not only for issuing and signing digital certificates, but they are also responsible for maintaining an accurate and up-to-date listing of those certificates that are no longer valid and thus should not be trusted. This listing of invalid certificates is known as a Certificate Revocation List (CRL) and is itself digitally signed by the issuing CA to verify its authenticity.

When a certificate is issued, it has a set validity period attached to it, typically one year by default. Under normal circumstances, the certificate can be used for this period of time and will cease to be valid automatically should it not be renewed before the expiration date has been reached. Thus, it is only necessary to place certificates that have been revoked early for some reason on the CRL; certificates that have expired (that is, have passed their expiration date) are automatically considered invalid and do not need to be placed on a CRL.

In a parent-child relationship between CAs, the parent CA issues a certificate as part of the relationship to designate the child CA. Just like the certificate to a client, the certificate to a Subordinate CA includes a validity period.

When the validity period expires for a CA, its own certificate must be renewed before it can grant any certification requests from client computers. When organizing your PKI, take into account the time a certification in a parent-child relationship should last.

As a safety and security measure, Windows Server 2003 PKI is set up so that a CA cannot issue certificates to requestors that will last beyond its own certificate's expiration date. This measure is handy because it ensures, for example, that a CA scheduled to expire this October cannot issue a certificate that may expire later than October.

Even the Root CA's own certificate will eventually expire. Therefore, certificates that it issues to subordinates will be staggered from its own expiration date. In other words, when the Root CA expires, all Subordinate CAs will have expired as well. No Subordinate CAs are valid beyond the date of the originating CA.

Depending on the configuration of your network, you can choose from four different certificate enrollment options:

▶ *Certificate autoenrollment and renewal*—A Windows Server 2003 Active Directory domain with Windows XP Professional clients provides the most robust Certificate Services model. This is certainly the case when discussing certificate autoenrollment and renewal. Using these features, you can automatically issue certificates that enable PKI-based applications, such as smart card logon, EFS, SSL, and S/MIME to users and computers within your Active Directory environment. Through a combination of certificate template properties and Group Policy settings, you can opt to enroll computers when they start up and users when they log in to their domain on the network.

▶ *Certificate Request Wizard/Certificate Renewal Wizard*—Users of Windows 2000, Windows XP, and Windows Server 2003 computers can manually request certificates through the Certificates MMC snap-in. This snap-in can be added to any custom MMC. Alternatively, you can launch the Certificates management console by entering `certmgr.msc` at the command prompt.

▶ *Web Enrollment Web pages*—You can connect to a CA by entering `http://CAname/certsrv` in your browser. By default, the Web Enrollment pages, which consist of ASP and ActiveX controls and thus could be considered dangerous, are installed on a CA. You can, however, install these pages on any other Windows Server 2003 computer running IIS that you want. If you're up to it, you can also customize these Web Enrollment pages to suit your specific needs. The Web Enrollment pages provide an easy way to connect clients to your CA without using the Certificates management console. Although Standalone CAs also use the Web Enrollment pages, they cannot provide certificates for smart card logon and for autoenrollment—only Enterprise CAs. Also, when Standalone CAs are used with Web Enrollment pages, the requester must specifically specify all required information because Active Directory is not available to provide the information for the certificate template. Windows 2000, Windows XP, and Windows Server 2003 computers support the use of the Web Enrollment pages.

▶ *Smart Card enrollment station*—This is an advanced form of the Web Enrollment pages that allows trusted administrators to request and enroll smart card logon certificates for smart card users on the network. Only Windows XP and Windows Server 2003 computers support this form of enrollment.

You can choose from two basic options when you want to enroll smart card certificates:

▶ *Use an enrollment agent*—The use of an enrollment agent allows a trusted administrator to process all smart card certificate requests and ensures that smart cards and their certificates are created and installed properly. Although this can be a good thing from a user's point of view, it can quickly become an overwhelming task if too few enrollment agents are designated. The other disadvantage to using enrollment agents becomes apparent if one of the enrollment agents is later deemed to be untrustworthy. What do you do with all the smart cards that agent previously enrolled?

▶ *Allow self-enrollment by smart card users*—Although using enrollment agents is usually the best (and by far the most secure) method to enroll smart cards, in some cases you may need or want to have users perform this task themselves. In cases in which you cannot physically (and safely) distribute fully ready smart cards, you may want to consider issuing blank smart cards and allowing the user to self-enroll. Should you think that self-enrollment is completely insecure, recall that you can configure your CA to hold all new requests pending a manual administrative approval, thus allowing you a chance to examine and validate the request before allowing the smart card to be enrolled with its certificate.

When you use smart cards for increased security of your network, you can configure several Group Policy options to further enhance the security of your smart card implementation:

▶ *Interactive logon: Require smart card*—This option, located in the Computer Configuration\Windows Settings\Security Settings\Local Policies\Security Options node of the Group Policy Editor can be used to prevent users from logging in to the domain by using a standard Windows username and password. Although this setting provides enhanced security, it can leave users without network access if their smart cards become unavailable for any reason. You should apply this policy at the OU level, making each smart card user a member of a domain local group and placing that group within the OU. Mistakenly applying this setting to non-smart card users will have disastrous effects.

▶ *Interactive logon: Smart card removal behavior*—This option, also located in the Security Option node, can be used to define what Windows should do when a smart card is removed from its reader with the user logged in. Possible options include No Action, Lock Workstation, and Force Logoff. This option again presents both benefits and dangers. A user who mistakenly removes her smart card with open documents may well lose any changes made since the document was last saved. On the other hand, for computers located in kiosks or other insecure areas, this setting can greatly increase the security of the computer and your network. This Group Policy setting requires training on your part to ensure that your smart card users understand the consequences of their actions. Again, this setting should be configured on a OU containing only those users who have been issued smart cards.

▶ *Do not allow smart card device redirection*—This option, located in the Computer Configuration\Administrative Templates\Windows Components\Terminal Services\ Client/Server data redirection node of the Group Policy Editor, can be used to prevent users from logging in to a Terminal Server with a smart card. This can increase security and decrease loading on your Terminal Servers.

▶ *Account Lockout Policy*—The Account Lockout Policy node, located at Computer Configuration\Windows Settings\Security Settings\Account Policies\Account Lockout Policy in the Group Policy Editor, contains three useful Group Policy settings that you can use to enhance both smart card and standard Windows login. The Account Lockout Threshold setting can be configured to specify how many failed logon attempts should be allowed before that user account is locked out. The Account Lockout Duration setting specifies how long the account is to be locked out (barring an administrator's unlocking the account early). The Reset Account Lockout Counter After option specifies how much time must pass before failed logon attempts are no longer counted against the Account Lockout Threshold setting. These policies are typically applied at a high level in your organization, such as the root of a domain to cause them to apply to all users within the domain.

Realizing that it needed to become more proactive in helping Windows network administrators understand and correct the issues associated with the various security flaws that occur in the Windows operating systems, Microsoft has provided you with several tools that you can use to identify, categorize, and correct security-related issues on your network. The choice of what tool you use really depends on how you want to go about keeping your network updated. The following options are available for you to use in identifying and installing required security updates on your network's computers:

▶ *Microsoft Baseline Security Analyzer (MBSA)*—MBSA is an enhanced GUI version of the popular command-line HFNetChk application that can be used on Windows 2000, Windows XP, and Window Server 2003 computers to look for missing security updates, missing service packs, and weak security configurations in the supported Windows operating systems, Office, IIS, Structured Query Language (SQL) Server, and several other popular Microsoft applications. Even though MBSA cannot be run on a Windows NT 4.0 computer, it can be used remotely to scan a Windows NT 4.0 computer. MBSA does a good job of identifying and categorizing missing updates and security problems that it finds, but it does not provide any direct means to update required patches. The real strength of MBSA is that it can be used to scan many computers, even remote ones, at a time, providing a quick and easy-to-interpret graphical output.

▶ *Windows Update*—Windows Update, which has been around since Windows 98 arrived, provides an easy-to-use (although not always accurate) Web-based tool for determining the need to install newly available updates on a local computer. Automatic Update works in conjunction with Windows Update in instances in which SUS has not been installed; it provides automatic downloading and installation of required updates.

▶ *Software Update Services (SUS)*—Introduced for Windows 2000 and improved for Windows Server 2003, SUS allows you to provide one or more Windows Update servers that run inside your protected internal network. SUS allows an administer to exercise granular control over which updates are installed and which aren't by allowing only "approved" updates to be installed on network computers configured to use an SUS

server for updating. After installing SUS, you perform all management and configuration from within your Web browser for ease of administration.

▶ *Automatic Updates*—Automatic Updates is a new component of Windows XP SP1 and Windows 2000 SP3 that can download and install required updates from either the Windows Update Web servers or your internal SUS servers, depending on how it has been configured; the default configuration is to use the Windows Update Web servers. Automatic Updates is included in the default installation of Windows Server 2003. To configure Automatic Updates to use an internal SUS server, you must first install and configure at least one SUS server and then configure the appropriate Group Policy settings to require clients to use the designated SUS servers.

▶ *Systems Management Server*—SMS 2.0 was in use by a large number of organizations well before the release of Windows 2000 and its IntelliMirror and Active Directory technologies—the heart of software installation via Active Directory. SMS has been updated recently with the SMS 2.0 Software Update Services Feature Pack, which allows it to integrate into a SUS implementation without changing the configuration of the network clients. For many years, administrators have used SMS to manually push updates to clients; the feature pack allows this function to become more automatic. SMS is due for a new version in late 2003. This new version, which will be Active Directory integrated, promises many new features for software management and maintenance.

SUS is actually one part of a two-part system. The other part, the Automatic Updates client, runs on the servers and client workstations that you want to download updates. Although the Automatic Updates client was included in Windows XP (pre–Service Pack 1), it was not the correct version to participate in SUS. You need to install Windows 2000 Service Pack 3 (or higher) or Windows XP Service Pack 1 (or higher) on client workstations to get the updated version that can interact with SUS. Alternatively, you can install the updated version of the Automatic Updates client.

MBSA scans your computers not only for Windows security updates, but also for updates associated with other Microsoft products. MBSA 1.1.1 (the current version as of this writing) scans for security updates in the following products:

▶ Windows NT 4.0

▶ Windows 2000

▶ Windows XP

▶ Windows Server 2003

▶ Internet Explorer 5.01 and higher

▶ Windows Media Player 6.4 and higher

▶ IIS 4.0 and higher

▶ SQL Server 7.0 and 2000 (including Microsoft Data Engine)

▶ Exchange 5.5 and 2000 (including Exchange Admin Tools

Windows Server 2003 allows you to perform auditing of the following areas:

▶ *Audit Account Logon Events*—This option configures auditing to occur for user logons and logoffs. A successful audit generates an audit entry when a user successfully logs in, and a failed audit generates an entry when a user unsuccessfully attempts to log in.

▶ *Audit Account Management*—This option configures auditing to occur for each event of account management on a computer. Typical account management events include creating a user, creating a group, renaming a user, disabling a user account, and setting or changing a password. A success audit generates an audit entry when any account management event is successful, and a failure audit generates an entry when any account management event fails.

▶ *Audit Directory Service Access*—This option configures auditing to occur when a user accesses an Active Directory object that has its own system access control list (SACL). This setting is only for Active Directory objects, such as GPOs, not for file system and Registry objects. A success audit generates an audit entry when a user successfully accesses an Active Directory object that has an SACL specified, and a failure audit generates an entry when an unsuccessful access attempt occurs.

▶ *Audit Logon Events*—This option configures auditing to occur upon each instance of a user logging on to or off a computer. The audit events are generated on domain controllers for domain account activity and on local computers for local account activity. When both the Audit Logon Events and the Audit Account Logon Events options are configured, logons and logoffs that use a domain account generate logon or logoff audit events on the local computer as well as the domain controller. A success audit generates an audit entry when a logon attempt succeeds, and a failure audit generates an audit entry when a logon attempt fails.

▶ *Audit Object Access*—This option configures auditing to occur upon each user access of an object, such as a file, folder, printer, or Registry key that has its own SACL configured. To configure auditing for object access, you also need to configure auditing specifically on each object on which you want to perform auditing. A success audit generates an audit entry when a user successfully accesses an object, and a failure audit generates an audit entry when a user unsuccessfully attempts to access an object.

▶ *Audit Policy Change*—This option configures auditing to occur upon every occurrence of changing user rights assignment policies, audit policies, or trust policies. A success audit generates an audit entry when a change to one of these policies is successful, and a failure audit generates an audit entry when a change to one of these policies fails.

▶ *Audit Privilege Use*—This option configures auditing to occur upon every occurrence of a user exercising a user right. A success audit generates an audit entry when the exercise of a user right succeeds, and a failure audit generates an audit entry when the exercise of a user right fails.

▶ *Audit Process Tracking*—This option configures auditing to occur for events such as program activation, process exit, handle duplication, and indirect object access. A success audit generates an audit entry when the process being tracked succeeds, and a failure audit generates an audit entry when the process being tracked fails.

▶ *Audit System Events*—This option configures auditing to occur when certain system events occur such as computer restarts and shutdowns. A success audit generates an audit entry when a system event is executed successfully, and a failure audit generates an audit entry when a system event is attempted unsuccessfully.

This practice exam consists of 65 questions that are meant to help you assess what you have learned from this training guide. It also includes questions that are representative of what you should expect on the actual exam. The questions here are mostly multiple choice. Some question forms that you might see on the actual exam, such as those that appear with simulations, are difficult or impossible to implement in book form because of the limitations of pencil-and-paper testing. Still, this practice exam should help you find out how well you understood the material presented in this training guide and give you some experience with Microsoft-style questions. When you take this exam, you should treat it as you would the real exam: Time yourself (about 90-120 minutes), answer each question carefully, and mark the questions you want to go back and double-check. The answers and their explanations appear at the end of the practice exam.

After you have taken this exam, you should follow up with Que Certification's exclusive PrepLogic test engine on the CD-ROM that accompanies this book. For more information, see Appendix B, "What's on the CD-ROM," and Appendix C, "Using PrepLogic, Preview Edition Software."

# Practice Exam

# EXAM QUESTIONS

1. You are the network administrator for Gus Gus Gas Stations, Inc. You need to implement a more secure network environment across all servers, both domain controllers and member servers. What security templates could you use to provide a higher level of security for these servers and still leave room to increase security again if desired? (Choose two correct answers.)

   A. securews.inf

   B. hisecws.inf

   C. hisecdc.inf

   D. securedc.inf

   E. compatws.inf

2. Marshall is the network administrator for QBC Corp. He runs a network of 20 Windows Server 2003 systems on a network backbone, as well as 200 Windows XP Professional clients. Marshall is asked about using an IP address for a local LAN, whether an IP address is needed, as well as whether a MAC address is needed. Marshall claims that he can assign an IP address but not a MAC address. Why not?

   A. He needs only an IP address, not a MAC address.

   B. MAC addresses are not assigned; they come by default burned into the network device.

   C. MAC addresses work on top of physical IP addresses.

   D. Neither IP addresses nor MAC addresses are needed if Marshall has the DNS name.

3. You are a network consultant and have been hired by Carmen's Clown College, Inc. You have been given the task of designing a unique DNS namespace for Carmen's new Windows Server 2003 network. Carmen's already owns the clowncollege.com domain, and the company's ISP is hosting its Web site. Which of the following options represents the best unique DNS namespace?

   A. clowncollege.net

   B. corp.clowncollege.com

   C. clowncollege.corp.com

   D. clowncollege.com.corp

4. You are the network administrator for QBC Corp. The company has a network of 25 Windows Server 2003 systems on a network backbone, as well as 300 Windows XP Professional clients. You need to test the connectivity of a remote site that is currently four router hops away. You are experiencing a lot of latency. What would be the appropriate plan of action to take to solve this issue?

   A. Go from router to router and look at the routing table metrics. If any say one or more, you need to deal with a routing issue.

   B. Use a standard ping, see how long it takes to get to the target host, and then calculate the time difference between hops.

   C. Use netsh in the routing> prompt and send a ping to the host; then calculate the time it takes to get there.

   D. Use pathping to trace the route to the destination and then look at the calculations of latency times in milliseconds on each hop through the network. Find the problem link.

5. Which of the following gives the best description of clustering?

   A. Clustering distributes all incoming client connection requests to its nodes via a mathematical algorithm.

   B. Clustering distributes all incoming client connection requests to its nodes via a round-robin system.

   C. Clustering allows multiple nodes to appear as a single system to clients.

   D. Clustering allows multiple CPUs to be used in a server.

6. You are the network administrator for Tom's Travel, an international travel agency. You have been directed to create a backup plan that will ensure that all data on your file server is backed up every night, regardless of when the last modification was made to the data. Which of these backup types would meet your requirements?

   A. Incremental

   B. Daily

   C. Normal

   D. Differential

7. You are the network administrator for Roger's Rockets, a manufacturer of toy rocket kits. You want to require that all wireless clients have the correct WEP key to authenticate to your wireless LAN. What setting do you need to select in your WLAN security policy?

   A. Data Encryption (WEP enabled)

   B. Network authentication (Shared mode)

   C. The key is provided to me automatically

   D. Transmit per IEEE 802.1x

8. You are the network administrator for Flagston Enterprises. The company's Windows Server 2003 network consists of 8 domain controllers, 4 member servers, and 592 Windows XP Professional workstations. You have created a plan to implement a CA. You report to your supervisor that the first CA will be a Root CA. Your plans then call for an Intermediary CA. Your supervisors want to know why an additional CA is required. Of the following, which is a valid reason for adding an Intermediary CA?

   A. All Enterprise CAs require Intermediary CAs to communicate with other CAs.

   B. Enterprise CAs require Active Directory, and the Intermediary CAs do not. Intermediary CAs are used to function with CAs outside this domain.

   C. The Root CA would be secured and taken offline, whereas the Intermediary CA would remain online to issue certificates to certificate requestors.

   D. The Intermediary CA would handle all communication between the Subordinate CAs and the Root CA.

9. You are the administrator of a large Windows Server 2003 Active Directory network. Your network consists of 1,500 Windows Server 2003 servers spread out over 150 Organizational Units, with approximately 10 servers each. You have just finished creating a customized security template that specifies the Account Policy and Auditing settings that are required for specific departments by your organization's corporate policy. What is the best way for you to apply this template to only the Sales, Marketing, Production, and Engineering OUs?

A. Import the security template at the domain level into a Group Policy Object.

B. Import the security template into each required Organizational Unit using a Group Policy Object.

C. Script the `secedit.exe` command to apply the security template to the required computers.

D. Manually apply the security template to each of the computers.

10. Pete is the network engineer for RDT, Inc. He runs a network of 25 Windows Server 2003 systems on a network backbone, as well as 300 Windows XP Professional clients. Pete is not sure whether he should design and implement a new switch that connects his additional servers to his server farm and the core network and then connect a new router to route the traffic from VLAN to VLAN. Unaware of any design options, he considers the following options. What should Pete use to connect his new systems to the core network?

A. Pete should implement a new Layer 3 switch.

B. Pete should implement a new Layer 2 switch only.

C. Pete should implement a new Layer 1 switch.

D. Pete should implement a new router only.

11. Helper Hal is a leading manufacturer of household goods. The CIO of Helper Hal has hired you to design a new DNS namespace for an upcoming Windows Server 2003 deployment. Helper Hal already owns the `helperhal.com` domain name. Helper Hal's corporate offices are in England, and satellite offices are located in the United States, Canada, India, Germany, and Japan. The corporate office contains five departments: Sales, Production, Support, Facilities, and Finance. Each satellite office has only Sales and Support departments. Which of the following FQDNs for a client named `FILESVR042` in the Production department represents the best designed DNS namespace?

A. `filesvr042.production.helperhal.com`

B. `filesvr042.uk.helperhal.com`

C. `filesvr042.production.uk.helperhal.com`

D. `filesvr042.helperhal.com`

12. Pete is the systems administrator for RDT, Inc. He runs a network of 25 Windows Server 2003 systems on a network backbone, as well as 300 Windows XP Professional clients. Pete wants to be able to set up a Windows Server 2003 server as a router using the RRAS console and needs to be able to connect up to three different network segments, which are 10.1.1.0 /24, 10.1.2.0 /24, and 10.1.3.0 /24. To do so, Pete needs to build the server as a trihomed unit. He connects three links and sets up the Routing Information Protocol. For some reason, one of the users on the 10.1.1.0 /24 network segment cannot communicate with a system on the 10.1.2.0 /24 segment. What could be the potential problem?

A. The routing table does not accurately show the route to the destination subnet in question. Pete needs to use the `route add` command to verify.

B. The routing table does not accurately show the route to the destination subnet in question. Pete needs to use the `route change` command to verify.

C. The routing table does not accurately show the route to the destination subnet in question. Pete needs to use the `route check` command to verify.

D. The routing table does not accurately show the route to the destination subnet in question. Pete needs to use the `route print` command to verify.

13. Which of the following gives the best description of network load balancing?

A. Network load balancing distributes all incoming client connection requests to its nodes via a mathematical algorithm.

B. Network load balancing distributes all incoming client connection requests to its nodes via a round-robin system.

C. Network load balancing allows multiple nodes to appear as a single system to clients.

D. Network load balancing allows multiple CPUs to be used in a server.

14. You are the network administrator for Tom's Travel, an international travel agency. You have been directed to create a backup plan that will ensure your company's critical data is backed up nightly. Your plan must minimize the time that is required each night to perform the backups. Your plan also should require the minimum amount of time and number of tapes possible during the restoration process. What combination of backup types should you use? (Choose two correct answers.)

A. Copy

B. Incremental

C. Normal

D. Daily

E. Differential

15. You are the network administrator for Jeff's Jeep Tours, an Australian tour company. While assisting one of your remote office users with a configuration issue on the user's computer, you have tried unsuccessfully to take control of the user's computer. Why are you not able to take control? (Select two correct answers.)

A. Your computer is not configured to allow it to initiate remote control sessions.

B. The remote computer is not configured to allow it to be controlled remotely.

C. A firewall is in place blocking the request.

D. The Novice is not allowing you to take control of his computer.

16. You are the network administrator for Fast Sloth Enterprises. After increasing the security of your network client computers, you need to implement an auditing system to keep track of times computers are restarted and shut down. Which of the following options should you configure to track these events?

A. Audit Process Tracking

B. Audit System Events

C. Audit Object Access

D. Audit Privilege Use

17. You are the network administrator of the Gidgets Widgets, LLC corporate network. You have instructed Andrea, your assistant administrator, to configure file access auditing for all files in the `CorpDocs` folder on your file server. Where will Andrea find the auditing options in the Group Policy Editor?

A. Account Policies

B. Local Policies

C. Restricted Groups

D. File System

18. Sally is the senior network administrator for Runners Corp. She runs a network of 20 Windows Server 2003 systems, as well as 250 Windows XP Professional clients. Sally needs to connect a server to the network. She has been given an IP address of 172.16.1.100 with a subnet mask of 255.255.255.0. She enters the IP address information given and tries to ping a server on a remote subnet. The IP address she is trying to ping is 172.16.2.100. What could the problem be?

    A. Sally needs to change her IP address to 172.16.2.101.

    B. Sally needs to add the default gateway address to the server.

    C. Sally needs to ping localhost to see whether she has IP connectivity.

    D. Sally has done nothing wrong; the problem is most likely with the host at 172.16.2.100.

19. You are planning a new DNS namespace for Lou's Loghomes, Inc. Security and redundancy are important factors in your design. Which of the following zone types should you choose to ensure the highest level of security and most redundancy possible?

    A. Standard primary

    B. Standard secondary

    C. Stub

    D. Active Directory–integrated

20. You are the network administrator for QBC Corp. The company has a network of 25 Windows Server 2003 systems on a network backbone, as well as 300 Windows XP Professional clients. You want to use a tool that can capture packets sent to and from a server. You decide to use Network Monitor, so you try to capture traffic from a remote server. Why are you failing to do so? (Choose only one answer.)

    A. You need to use System Monitor; it tells you what packets are traversing the LAN.

    B. Network Monitor is available only on Windows 2000; Network Analyzer is available on Windows Server 2003.

    C. Network Monitor is for system processes only; it does not pick up network packets.

    D. The version of Network Monitor included with Windows Server 2003 records only packets sent to and from this server and the LAN.

21. When discussing the process of convergence, what are you referring to?

    A. A network communication sent among individual cluster nodes at intervals of no more than 500 milliseconds that is used to determine the status of all cluster nodes.

    B. The process of a cluster group moving back to the preferred node after the preferred node has resumed cluster membership.

    C. The process by which NLB clustering hosts determine a new, stable state among themselves and elect a new default host after the failure of one or more cluster nodes.

    D. The process of a cluster group moving from the currently active node to another still-functioning node in the cluster group.

22. You are the network administrator for Tom's Travel, an international travel agency. You are currently performing backups using your approved corporate backup plan. The plan calls for a Normal backup to be made every Saturday night and Differential backups to be made on Monday through Friday nights. On Thursday

morning your file server crashes and must be rebuilt with a clean installation of Windows Server 2003. In what order should you use the backup tapes you have?

A. Friday, Monday, Thursday, Saturday

B. Tuesday, Monday, Friday

C. Saturday, Wednesday

D. Monday, Tuesday, Wednesday, Saturday

E. Saturday, Wednesday, Tuesday, Monday

23. You are the network administrator for Roger's Rockets, a manufacturer of toy rocket kits. You are configuring a new WLAN security policy for the wireless clients that are located in your Accounting OU. You want to provide the maximum level of security for your WLAN by requiring that all computers authenticate to the WLAN upon creating their wireless connection. You want the computer to authenticate using its computer account. You are using a RADIUS server to handle authentication, and the authentication database is Active Directory. What setting do you need to configure in the WLAN security policy?

A. Authenticate as guest when user or computer information is unavailable

B. Transmit per IEEE 802.1x

C. Data Encryption (WEP enabled)

D. Authenticate as computer when computer information is available

24. Andrea is the network administrator for the Think Pink Bike Company. She has recently finished implementing an auditing solution for her Windows Server 2003 network. Andrea wants to track unauthorized access attempts to the company network. After two weeks, she has not found any authorized access attempts, even though she

tried password-guessing several users' accounts just this morning. What is the most likely reason for the problem that Andrea is experiencing?

A. Andrea has not configured success audits for the Audit Account Logon events option.

B. Andrea has not configured failure audits for the Audit Account Management option.

C. Andrea has not configured failure audits for the Audit Logon events.

D. Andrea has not configured success audits for the Audit Policy Change option.

25. You are the network administrator for Good Faith Enterprises, LLC. You want to increase the security of your client workstations, which are all Windows 2000 Professional computers, without causing any adverse effect on network communications between computers. You have already completed this same configuration action on all your domain controllers and member servers. Which security template should you use to accomplish your goal?

A. `securews.inf`

B. `securedc.inf`

C. `compatws.inf`

D. `hisecws.inf`

26. You are the network administrator for QBC Corp. The company has a network of 25 Windows Server 2003 systems on a network backbone, as well as 300 Windows XP Professional clients. You are asked to connect a server to the network. You are given an IP address of 192.168.5.10/16 and a default gateway of 192.168.5.1. You set up the server and connect it to the network via a network cable. After testing all connectivity, you still cannot access resources on the network. The network you are attaching

to is 192.168.5.0/24. What do you think the problem may be?

A. You were given the incorrect IP address.

B. You were given the incorrect default gateway.

C. You were given the incorrect subnet mask.

D. You must have a routing issue; there is nothing wrong with this configuration.

27. A DNS resolver performs a recursive query against its local DNS server asking it to provide the IP address for the host `www.quepublishing.com`. Assuming that the local DNS server is not authoritative for the `quepublishing.com` domain, does not have the answer in its local cache, and is configured for forwarding, what will happen next?

A. The local name server will return an error to the DNS resolver stating that it could not resolve the name as requested.

B. A root name server will make an iterative query to determine the IP address of the `quepublishing.com` domain.

C. A root name server will make an iterative query to determine the IP address of the host `www.quepublishing.com`.

D. The local DNS server will make an iterative query to a root name server to determine the IP address of the host `www.quepublishing.com`.

28. Sally is the senior network administrator for Runners Corp. Sally runs a network of 20 Windows Server 2003 systems, as well as 250 Windows XP Professional clients. Sally would like to implement a new remote access feature called Network Access Quarantine Control on the Windows Server 2003 system. What does this new feature do?

A. The remote access sender's connection attempt goes into quarantine until verified.

B. The quarantine holds viruses trying to access your RAS server.

C. Network quarantine is a central repository that allows you to store antivirus updates deployed to your server.

D. This new feature enables you to set up a repository where you can store executables that are grabbed from users attempting to connect to your RAS server.

29. In regards to a network load balancing cluster, what desirable function do port rules provide?

A. They can be used to allow traffic only on specific ports to be load-balanced, dropping all other traffic.

B. They assign a unique numerical identifier to each cluster node.

C. They specify the IP address where the network load balancing cluster can be accessed.

D. They specify the IP subnet on which the administrative network adapter is to be located.

30. You are the network administrator for Jorge's Gyms, a health club company. You have been directed to create a backup plan that will back up all data on the Financial department's file servers. The data must be backed up even if it is currently in use by a user. You need to minimize the impact of the backup on user operations. How should you configure the backup plan?

A. Configure a backup job that backs up data in Remote Storage.

B. Configure a backup job that compresses data to save space.

C. Configure a backup job that verifies data after the backup is complete.

D. Configure a backup job that uses the volume shadow copy.

31. You are the network administrator for Jeff's Jeep Tours, an Australian tour company. A user in one of your remote locations has sent you an email request for remote assistance, but it expired before you were able to assist the user with her problem. You have called the user on the telephone and informed her of the problem with the expired request. You need to have this request answered. What is the easiest way to handle this situation?

   A. Have the user create a new request and send it to you.

   B. Have the user extend the lifetime of the initial request.

   C. Have the user delete the expired request, causing it to be re-created anew.

   D. Have the user resend the expired request to you again.

32. You are the network administrator for the Sunbrew Dairy Farms, Inc., corporate network. You have just completed the installation and configuration of SUS for your network. Your client computers are all running Windows 2000 Professional Service Pack 2, and your servers are all Windows Server 2003 computers. After a week passes, you notice that none of your clients have received any updates that are available from your SUS server. What is the most likely reason for this problem?

A. Your SUS server has lost network connectivity to the Internet and has not downloaded any updates from the Windows Update Web servers.

B. You have not correctly configured the Group Policy options for Automatic Updates.

C. The GPO in which you configured the Automatic Updates changes has not been replicated to the rest of the network.

D. Your client computers are not using the correct version of the Automatic Updates client software.

33. You are an assistant network administrator for the Nimbus Flying Broom corporation. You are responsible for 75 Windows XP Professional workstations and 5 Windows Server 2003 member server computers. You have been directed to perform a security analysis on each computer, comparing its settings to those contained in the `hisecws.inf` template. How you can accomplish your assigned task with the least amount of administrative effort and fewest number of trips to remote computers?

A. The only way to perform this analysis is to physically visit each computer and use the Security Configuration and Analysis snap-in.

B. You can create a script that runs Security Configuration and Analysis on each computer, collecting the results in a central location for later viewing.

C. You can create a script that runs the `secedit /analyze` command on each computer, collecting the results in a central location for later viewing.

D. You can analyze remote computers from the Security Configuration and Analysis snap-in by targeting it at the desired computer.

34. Sally is the senior network administrator for Runners Corp. She runs a network of 200 Windows Server 2003 systems, as well as 2,500 Windows XP Professional clients. Sally needs to connect her LAN to the Internet. She is running a large network that has a private addressing scheme of 10.1.0.0/16. To connect the Internet, Sally must set up what technology on the Internet firewall to get on to the public range of 12.1.1.0?

    A. IPSec

    B. NAT

    C. RIP

    D. BGP

35. What new feature of Windows Server 2003's DNS service allows you to configure multiple DNS forwarders depending on the destination domain?

    A. DNS forwarder

    B. DNS resolver

    C. Conditional forwarding

    D. Recursion

36. Pete is the systems administrator for RDT, Inc. He runs a network of 25 Windows Server 2003 systems on a network backbone, as well as 300 Windows XP Professional clients. Pete has a problem with a remote site (10.10.2.0) from his campus network. None of the users from a remote site company can access his Exchange server (10.10.1.10) in the core network he is responsible for. Pete needs to verify that this is a problem with the Exchange server, or something else. What is the best troubleshooting step Pete should take?

    A. Pete should have the remote users `ping` his default gateway. If he receives a response, it must be the users' problem.

    B. Pete should have the remote users `ping` his default gateway. If there is no response, it must be the Exchange server's problem.

    C. Pete should do a `tracert` to the Exchange server and see what path it takes and then `ping` the server to see if it replies.

    D. Pete should `ping` 10.10.1.10, `ping` 10.10.2.1 (default gateway), and then have a remote user `ping` 10.10.1.1 (default gateway).

37. You are preparing to implement a network load balancing solution for your company's Web site. You will be load balancing six Windows Server 2003 computers running IIS. Employees and customers using the FTP protocol use the IIS servers only to upload and download files. What type of affinity should you configure to ensure that clients receive the best overall possible service during their connection period?

    A. None

    B. Class C

    C. Multiple

    D. Single

38. You are the network administrator for Jorge's Gyms, a health club company. You have enabled volume shadow copy on your Financial department file server using the default configuration. With these settings, how many days' worth of historical data will be available to your users?

    A. 14

    B. 21

    C. 28

    D. 32

    E. 45

39. You are the network administrator for Herb's Happenings, a public relations firm. You are preparing to create a new IPSec policy that will be used to secure all internal network traffic. What available user authentication methods does IPSec in Windows Server 2003 offer? (Choose all that apply.)

A. NTLM v2

B. Kerberos v5

C. EFS

D. Digital certificate

E. Shared secret

F. WEP

40. You are the network administrator for the Wing Walkers, Inc., corporate network. You are configuring SUS for your network's client computers, which are all running Windows XP Professional Service Pack 1. You want all client computers to automatically download from your SUS server and install any required updates each night at 11:30 p.m. After the updates have been installed, you want the client computers to restart so that the updates can fully install and the computers will be ready for work the next morning. What must you do to ensure that updates will be installed each night and the computers will be restarted after the updates are installed? (Choose all that apply.)

A. You must configure the Automatic Updates client options on each of your Windows XP Professional Service Pack 1 client computers to download and install updates nightly.

B. You must set the Configure Automatic Updates option in Group Policy to Enabled and set option 4. You then need to configure a schedule for nightly updates at 11:30 p.m.

C. You must set the No Auto-Restart for Scheduled Automatic Updates Installations option in Group Policy to Disabled.

D. You must set the Specify Intranet Microsoft Update Server Location option in Group Policy to Enabled and enter the URL of your SUS server.

41. You are the network administrator for Fast Sloth Enterprises. You need to increase the security of your Windows XP Professional client computers and Windows Server 2003 servers. Which security template should you apply to your workstations to ensure they have the most secure configuration?

A. `securews.inf`

B. `hisecdc.inf`

C. `hisecws.inf`

D. `rootsec.inf`

42. Pete is the systems administrator for RDT, Inc. He runs a network of 25 Windows Server 2003 systems on a network backbone, as well as 300 Windows XP Professional clients. Pete has to connect all his internal clients to the Internet, but he has only one public IP address. He also needs to accelerate the speed of Internet access while at the same time minimizing impact on the Internet bandwidth. What device should he use on his network?

A. Layer 4 Router

B. SNA Server

C. Load Balancer

D. Proxy Server

43. You are concerned about the security of your organization's private internal network. As such, you have configured the firewall to allow traffic only on UDP and TCP ports 53 from one IP address: 192.168.100.133. Your firewall creates dynamic response rules that will allow valid return traffic back to the DNS server if it is a response back to traffic originating from the DNS server. Your internal network contains four internal DNS servers, and your network users must be able to perform external name resolution regardless of which DNS server their query is sent to. What should you to do ensure that only the DNS server with IP address 192.168.100.133 makes external DNS queries?

   A. Configure the other three DNS servers to forward name resolution requests for all domains other than the internal namespace to the DNS server with IP address 192.168.100.133. This server will then perform name resolution by using Internet DNS servers.

   B. Disable the other three DNS servers to prevent them from providing name resolution services.

   C. Configure all four internal DNS servers to be forwarders to an external DNS server.

   D. Configure all client computers to use the DNS server with IP address 192.168.100.133 as the primary DNS server.

44. You are the network administrator for QBC Corp. The company has a network of 25 Windows Server 2003 systems on a network backbone, as well as 300 Windows XP Professional clients. You have a problem with a remote server that does not seem to show up in one of your MMCs. You need to access this server, so you try to ping it but get no response. What is your next step? (Choose the best answer.)

   A. Try running a `tracert` to the remote server.

   B. Try using the `netsh` command with a `routing>` prompt and `ping` to the remote server.

   C. Try using the `arp -a` command to the remote server.

   D. Try using the `ipconfig /check` command on the remote server.

45. You are preparing to implement a network load balancing solution for your company's Web site. You will be load balancing six Windows Server 2003 computers running IIS. Why would you want to ensure that each server has two network adapters installed for this type of solution?

   A. To allow for double the load-balanced traffic

   B. To separate the load-balanced traffic from the administrative traffic

   C. To provide extra redundancy in case an adapter fails

   D. To allow a multicast MAC address to be used

46. You are the network administrator for Jorge's Gyms, a health club company. You have enabled volume shadow copy on your Financial department's file server using the default configuration. When you try to look at the previous versions of the shared folder locally at the file server using Windows Explorer, you do not have the Previous Versions tab on the share Properties dialog box. What is the reason for this problem?

   A. You did not install the Previous Versions Client on the server.

   B. The volume shadow copy has run out of free space on the disk.

C. The volume shadow copy service has stopped.

D. You can view shadow copies only over the network using My Network Places.

47. You are the network administrator for Jeff's Jeep Tours, an Australian tour company. You need to connect to the console session of one of your Windows Server 2003 computers to perform some configuration actions. What tool does Windows Server 2003 provide that allows you to do this?

A. The Remote Desktops console

B. The Web Interface for Remote Administration

C. The Remote Desktop Connection Web utility

D. The Remote Desktop Connection utility

48. Austin is the network administrator for Captain Bob's Ocean Fantasies, a retailer specializing in hard-to-find ocean-related collectible items. As part of his smart card solution, Austin has decided to limit the number of incorrect logon attempts that users can make within a specified amount of time. Where, within the Group Policy Editor, would Austin be able to locate the settings that he needs to configure?

A. Computer Configuration\Windows Settings\Security Settings\Account Policies\Account Lockout Policy

B. Computer Configuration\Windows Settings\Security Settings\Local Policies\Security Options

C. Computer Configuration\Administrative Templates\Windows Components\Terminal Services\Client/Server data redirection

D. Computer Configuration\Windows Settings\Security Settings\Public Key Policies

49. Hannah is the network administrator for Think Pink Bicycles, Inc. She is attempting to configure the Engineering Organizational Unit in her Windows Server 2003 network with the `securews.inf` template. There are 30 member file and print servers in this OU, along with approximately 500 Windows XP Professional workstations. Which of the following methods of applying the `securews.inf` template would be the most administratively efficient?

A. Using the Security Configuration and Analysis snap-in

B. Using the `secedit.exe` command

C. Using Group Policy

D. Using the Domain Controller Security Policy console

50. Marshall is the network administrator for QBC Corp. He runs a network of 20 Windows Server 2003 systems on a network backbone, as well as 200 Windows XP Professional clients. Marshall is asked to protect his network from Internet-based attacks. He needs to put in a device that will help him to secure his network from attack. What device would you recommend that Marshall install?

A. NIC

B. IPSec Client

C. Network Monitor

D. Firewall

51. Andrea is an administrator for Carmine's Circus Clowns, Inc. She was just recently hired after the last administrator, oddly enough, ran off to join the circus. Carmine's network includes two domain controllers and three member servers

providing file, print, and backup/restoration services. Carmine, the president of the company, has instructed Andrea to implement a more secure configuration on all five Windows Server 2003 servers. Andrea has decided to use the secure templates but is not sure what the current configuration is on each server because the last administrator did not keep any records. What is the best way for Andrea to go about configuring these servers with the secure templates?

A. Andrea should apply the default security template from one of her member servers to all five servers and then apply the `securews.inf` and `securedc.inf` templates to them.

B. Andrea should apply the default security template found on each computer to that specific computer. After doing this, she should then apply the `securews.inf` template to her domain controllers and the `securedc.inf` template to her member servers.

C. Andrea should reinstall Windows Server 2003 on all five servers and re-create the domain. After doing this, she should apply the `securews.inf` and `securedc.inf` templates to her servers.

D. Andrea should apply the default security template found on each computer to that specific computer. After doing this, she should then apply the `securedc.inf` template to her domain controllers and the `securews.inf` template to her member servers.

52. Sally is the senior network administrator for Runners Corp. She runs a network of 20 Windows Server 2003 systems, as well as 250 Windows XP Professional clients. Sally needs to deploy a multicasting solution that allows all multicast traffic to pass through her network and to the MBone, which is the multicast backbone on the Internet. How can Sally set up her Windows Server 2003 system to make sure that it can participate in the forwarding of multicast traffic?

A. Set up ICMP routing

B. Set up IGMP routing

C. Set up OSPF routing

D. Set up RIP routing

53. You are the network administrator for QBC Corp. The company has a network of 25 Windows Server 2003 systems on a network backbone, as well as 300 Windows XP Professional clients. You have a problem with a router a few hops away because it does not seem to be passing traffic past it. What tool can you use to troubleshoot with?

A. Use `Trace Route`.

B. Use `Traceroute`.

C. Use `Tracert`.

D. Use `Trace`.

54. You are the network administrator for Jorge's Gyms, a health club company. You have enabled volume shadow copy on your Financial department's file server using the default configuration. When you try to look at the previous versions of the shared folder from one of your Windows XP Professional workstations using My Network Places, you do not see the Previous Versions tab on the share Properties dialog box. What is the reason for this problem?

A. You did not install the Previous Versions Client on the client.

B. The volume shadow copy has run out of free space on the disk.

C. The volume shadow copy service has stopped.

D. You can view shadow copies only over the network using My Network Places.

55. You are the network administrator for Herb's Happenings, a public relations firm. You are preparing to create a new IPSec policy that will be used to secure all internal network traffic. What available data encryption methods does IPSec in Windows Server 2003 offer? (Choose all that apply.)

A. DES

B. SHA1

C. MD5

D. AES

E. 3DES

56. Austin is the network administrator for Captain Bob's Ocean Fantasies, a retailer specializing in hard-to-find ocean-related collectible items. Captain Bob's network currently has about 500 remote traveling users who connect to the network via Terminal Services using their smart cards for authentication. A new change in company policy requires that remote users will no longer be able to make Terminal Services connections to the network, but instead can create and use VPN tunnels to one of the available RRAS servers. In addition to announcing this policy change, what else can Austin do to ensure that his remote smart card users do not make Terminal Services connections?

A. Interactive logon: Require smart card

B. Interactive logon: Smart card removal behavior

C. Do not allow smart card device redirection

D. Account Lockout Policy

57. You have just completed an analysis of a computer using the Security Configuration and Analysis snap-in. When you examine the results, you notice several items that have an X icon next to them. What does this icon indicate?

A. The item is not defined in the analysis database and was not examined on the computer.

B. The item is defined in the analysis database and on the computer and matches the currently configured setting.

C. The item is defined in the analysis database but not on the computer.

D. The item is defined in the analysis database and on the computer, but does not match the current configured setting.

58. You are the network administrator for QBC Corp. The company has a network of 25 Windows Server 2003 systems on a network backbone, as well as 300 Windows XP Professional clients. You need to set up a new Windows Server 2003 system on your network. You are given an IP address, a subnet mask, and a default gateway. Your IP address is 10.0.1.10 /8, and the default gateway is 10.0.1.1. You are trying to connect to and ping the default gateway but are not able to. You analyze the router and find that it has the IP configured as 10.0.1.1 /24 on the Ethernet port. What do you think the problem is?

A. Bad IP address assignment

B. Bad default gateway assignment

C. Bad Ethernet port assignment

D. Bad subnet mask assignment

59. You are in the process of creating a customized security solution for your network's computers. You want to edit the `securedc.inf` template in a text editor. Where can you find the preconfigured security templates?

    A. `%systemroot%\system32\security`

    B. `%systemroot%\security\templates`

    C. `WINNT\security\templates`

    D. `%systemroot%\system32\templates`

60. Andrea is the network administrator of the Beachside Entertainment Group, Incorporated network. Beachside owns and operates several miniature golf centers in resort destinations. Andrea is preparing to implement a smart card solution for use by all Beachside Entertainment employees because their computers are often lacking in other forms of security, such as physical security. Beachside has locations in 5 eastern states with a total of 17 offices, including the corporate offices in Chincoteague, Virginia. Andrea has decided to use self-enrollment for her smart card users. Which of the following items must Andrea take into consideration for her self-enrollment plan to work effectively and securely? (Choose two correct answers.)

    A. Andrea must ensure that all required users get a blank smart card.

    B. Andrea should configure her CAs not to automatically issue smart card user certificates when requested.

    C. Andrea must ensure that all required users get a ready-to-use smart card.

    D. Andrea must ensure that only trusted users are tasked with the job of performing the smart card certificate enrollments.

    E. Andrea must ensure that she has selected enough enrollment agents to perform the smart card enrollments for users without becoming overburdened.

61. You are the network administrator for Herb's Happenings, a public relations firm. You are preparing to create a new IPSec policy that will be used to secure all international network traffic. You need to configure this new IPSec policy such that the computers at each end of the connection will communicate with each other and agree on the security parameters that are to be used. What filter action do you need to configure to ensure this behavior occurs?

    A. Permit

    B. Block

    C. Negotiate

    D. Open

62. You are the network administrator for Herb's Happenings, a public relations firm. You have decided to use one of the preconfigured IPSec policies that come in Windows Server 2003 to secure network traffic on your international network. Which of the following policies are included with Windows Server 2003? (Choose all that apply.)

    A. Client (Respond Only)

    B. Client (Request Security)

    C. Client (Require Security)

    D. Server (Respond Only)

    E. Server (Request Security)

    F. Server (Require Security)

    G. Secure Server (Respond Only)

    H. Secure Server (Request Security)

    I. Secure Server (Require Security)

63. You are the network administrator for Herb's Happenings, a public relations firm. You are preparing to create a new IPSec policy that will be used to secure all internal network traffic. What available data hashing methods does IPSec in Windows Server 2003 offer? (Choose all that apply.)

    A. DES

    B. SHA1

    C. MD5

    D. AES

    E. 3DES

64. You are the network administrator for Nebuchadnezzar Furnaces. The company's Windows Server 2003 domain consists of domain controllers, 2 member servers, and 765 Windows XP Professional workstations. Daniel, your supervisor, reports to you that he suspects that Sam is still accessing the network through the Internet, although he was fired from the company 12 days ago. He asks you to resolve the matter so that Sam cannot access the network remotely. What two actions can you perform that would ensure that Sam can no longer use his digital certificate to access the network?

    A. Delete Sam's previously assigned certificate.

    B. Revoke Sam's previously assigned certificate.

    C. Force Sam's certificate to expire early.

    D. Publish the CRL.

65. You are the network administrator for Phil's Fillup Stations, Inc. Your CIO has tasked you with increasing the security of all member servers on your network. After examining the security settings configured in the Secure and Highly Secure templates, you have decided that neither one of them completely meets your requirements.

You must configure the required settings as efficiently and safely as possible. Which of the following represent the two best available options that you could choose to configure your servers as required? (Choose two correct answers.)

    A. Create a new (empty) security template and configure the settings you need in it.

    B. Modify the `securews.inf` security template, changing and adding options as needed.

    C. Configure the member server settings from the Local Security Policy console on each member server.

    D. Configure the security settings you need directly into a Group Policy Object linked to the OU containing the member servers.

## ANSWERS AND EXPLANATIONS

1. **A, D.** By using the Secure templates (`securews.inf` for member servers and workstations and `securedc.inf` for domain controllers), you can increase the baseline security of your servers and still allow for increasing security later (if you want) through the use of the Highly Secure templates. For more information, see Chapter 1.

2. **B.** MAC addresses are not assigned; they come by default burned into the network device. A physical address is a 48-bit alphanumeric number that denotes the host's physical address. Also called a Media Access Control (MAC) address, the physical address is unique to the device it is assigned to. For instance, your PC has a MAC address of 00-08-74-97-0B-26; this is unique to that one device's NIC card. For more information, see Chapter 2.

3. **A.** The `clowncollege.net` namespace represents a unique DNS namespace. `clowncollege.net` would thus become the root of the Active Directory forest and domain structure. Unique DNS namespaces should, typically, be similar to the original namespace, in this case `clowncollege.com`. For more information, see Chapter 3.

4. **D.** Use `pathping` to trace the route to the destination and then look at the calculations of latency times in milliseconds on each hop through the network. Then find the problem link. For more information, see Chapter 4.

5. **C.** Clustering is accomplished when you take a group of independent servers and group them together into one collective entity that is accessed as if it were a single system. For more information, see Chapter 5.

6. **C.** A Normal backup ensures that all selected data is backed up and sets the archive bit, indicating the data has been backed up. Normal backups are typically used in combination with Incremental or Differential backups. For more information, see Chapter 6.

7. **B.** To use WEP to perform WLAN authentication, you need to select the Network Authentication (Shared mode) option. The Data Encryption (WEP enabled) option specifies that WEP is to be used to encrypt data placed on the WLAN; thus, answer A is incorrect. The option titled *The key is provided to me automatically* specifies that the key is dynamically assigned from a key server, such as a RADIUS server; thus, answer C is incorrect. The *Transmit per IEEE 802.1x* option is used to configure how the EAPOL-start message is sent and has nothing to do with WEP; thus, answer D is incorrect. For more information, see Chapter 7.

8. **C.** Creating an Intermediary CA allows the Root CA to be taken offline and secured. The Intermediary server would then issue certificates to other CAs. For more information, see Chapter 8.

9. **B.** The best way to apply the settings to only those computers that require them is to import the template into a Group Policy Object associated with each OU that requires the settings. Importing the security template into the domain-level GPO would apply the settings to all computers in the domain, most likely with unwanted side effects. For more information, see Chapter 1.

10. **A.** Pete should implement a new Layer 3 switch. In today's networks, the line has blurred between what a switch is and what a router is. For this exam (at this level), you should already know what a router is and what a switch is, but if you do not, you need to know that a switch operates on the first layer of the DoD model. A switch keeps a memory database of which device is plugged into which port on the switch. The memory in the switch can show via a table which MAC address (from the NIC) is plugged into which port, so when a device needs to communicate with another device, it doesn't need to broadcast across the whole network to find it; the switch makes the port-to-port connection and keeps traffic down to a minimum, as well as speeds up the transmission. Most devices on a segment can communicate via MAC addresses kept in their ARP cache. The Address Resolution Protocol maps IP addresses to MAC addresses, and the ARP cache is kept in just about every network device with TCP/IP installed. A router works at the Internet layer of the DoD model and basically forwards packets from one segment to another via a routing table kept in the router's memory. Because routers keep ARP caches, and switches can have routers installed in them, you

basically blur the lines, combine the two devices, and have a layer 3 switch. For more information, see Chapter 2.

11. **C.** The FQDN `filesvr042.production.uk.helperhal.com` represents the best designed DNS namespace. This FQDN allows you to quickly and accurately determine the location of the host within the network. Also, this DNS namespace is designed intelligently by using countries as the second-level domains and departments as the third-level domains. Alternatively, the `helperhal.com` domain could be delegated to create a `corp.helperhal.com` domain, with the countries becoming third-level domains and the departments becoming fourth-level domains. For more information, see Chapter 3.

12. **D.** The routing table does not accurately show the route to the destination subnet in question; Pete should use the `route print` command to verify. All other answers are incorrect. For more information, see Chapter 4.

13. **A.** Network load balancing distributes all incoming connection requests using a mathematical algorithm to members of the NLB cluster. For more information, see Chapter 5.

14. **C, E.** You should perform a Normal backup once a week during nonworking hours to set the initial state for the critical data that is being backed up. Each night, a Differential backup should be run to back up all the data that has been modified since that last Normal backup. Although Differential backups take slightly longer to perform each night than Daily backups, they provide the benefit of a two-tape restoration using the last Normal backup and the last Differential backup. For more information, see Chapter 6.

15. **B, D.** Of the given options, the most likely problems are that the Novice is not allowing you to take control, or the remote computer is not configured to allow you to take remote control. Your local computer is not an issue in the case of not being able to take remote control of an existing Remote Assistance session; thus, answer A is incorrect. Because you already have an existing Remote Assistance connection, the firewall is not the source of your problem; thus, answer C is incorrect. For more information, see Chapter 7.

16. **B.** The Audit System Events option configures auditing for certain system events, such as computer restarts and shutdowns. For more information, see Chapter 8.

17. **B.** The Local Policies node of the Group Policy Editor contains three subnodes: Audit Policy, User Rights Assignment, and Security Options. The Audit Policy subnode is the place where Andrea can find the auditing items she needs to configure. For more information, see Chapter 1.

18. **B.** Sally needs to add the default gateway address to the server. The IP address of the closest router on your network segment that can either route you off that segment or to another segment on the network is your default gateway. This makes a routing decision for you to a remote site, which is what Sally needed to make happen. If Sally enters the gateway address, the packets sent to 172.16.2.0 will be sent to the router, which will then forward the request to that host. Without a gateway address, the packet destined for the remote LAN will not be sent anywhere. For more information, see Chapter 2.

19. **D.** Active Directory–integrated DNS zones store the zone data within the Active Directory database itself, thus allowing for greatly increased security, manageability, and redundancy. When Active Directory–integrated zones are used, all DNS servers operate in a multimaster arrangement, allowing any DNS server to make changes to the zone data. If you have multiple DNS servers that are allowed to manage the zone data, dynamic updates are also more redundant because the failure of a single DNS server will not prevent dynamic updates from occurring. For more information, see Chapter 3.

20. **D.** Network Monitor is the tool you use to capture packets sent to and from this server. The version of Network Monitor included with Windows Server 2003 records only packets sent to and from this server and the LAN. For more information, see Chapter 4.

21. **C.** Convergence is the process by which NLB clustering hosts determine a new, stable state among themselves and elect a new default host after the failure of one or more cluster nodes. For more information, see Chapter 5.

22. **C.** To perform the restoration, you first need to use your last Normal backup (the Saturday tape) and then your last Differential backup (the Wednesday tape). For more information, see Chapter 6.

23. **D.** Selecting the Authenticate as computer when computer information is available option forces the computer to authenticate itself to the network as soon as the wireless network connection is made. If the computer cannot authenticate, no authentication is performed. The *Authenticate as guest when user or computer information is unavailable* option allows the computer to authenticate using the Guest account if it cannot authenticate using its computer account; thus, answer A is incorrect. The *Transmit per IEEE 802.1x* option is used to configure how the EAPOL-start message is sent and has nothing to do with WEP; thus, answer B is incorrect. The Data Encryption (WEP enabled) option specifies that WEP is to be used to encrypt data placed on the WLAN; thus, answer C is incorrect. For more information, see Chapter 7.

24. **C.** To track failed logon attempts, Andrea needs to configure failure auditing to occur for the Audit Logon Events option. For more information, see Chapter 8.

25. **A.** By applying the Secure template, `securews.inf`, you can increase the security of the client workstations without adversely affecting network communications. For more information, see Chapter 1.

26. **C.** The subnet mask is the other 32-bit set of numbers you place with an IP address to denote where the network starts and ends and the host-based addressing starts and ends. In other words, if you have a 10.1.1.0 /24 network, this really means you have a subnet mask of 255.255.255.0 assigned to the 10.1.1.0 IP address network. The network is 10.1.1 (24 bits mask it with 255.255.255.0), and the last octet, which is simply a zero, is assignable to hosts. For more information, see Chapter 2.

27. **D.** If the local DNS server is not authoritative for the requested domain and does not have the answer in its local cache, it will perform an iterative query to a root name server if it is configured as a forwarder. The root name server will likely not know the IP address of the host but will be able to provide the local DNS server with the IP address of another DNS server that is authoritative for the `quepublishing.com` domain. This DNS server then can provide the requested name resolution service for the local DNS server. For more information, see Chapter 3.

28. **A.** The connection attempt goes into quarantine until verified. Here's the actual process: When a remote computer attempts to connect to the Remote Access Server, the computer is assigned an IP address with which to participate on the network. Then the user credentials are verified and authenticated, but the connection will stay in quarantine until the remote computer is verified against the script. A script runs, and when it is completed, the server hosting quarantine will release the connection from quarantine after this information is verified. This is just one of the newest features of Remote Access Security provided by default with Windows Server 2003. For more information, see Chapter 4.

29. **A.** Port rules can be used to allow traffic only on specific ports to be load-balanced. If you configure explicit allow rules for specific ports and an explicit deny rule dropping all other traffic, only the desired traffic will be load-balanced. For more information, see Chapter 5.

30. **D.** By using the volume shadow copy feature of Windows Backup, you can back up all files—even the ones that are open and in use at the time of the backup. Open files are backed up in a closed state as of the time of the backup. This allows you to back up open files without closing them for the backup as previously required. For more information, see Chapter 6.

31. **D.** The easiest way to allow an expired request to be answered is to resend it again. This way, some of the information that was originally entered can be saved from the expired request. Creating a new request is not the easiest way to solve this problem; thus, answer A is incorrect. When a request has expired, it can only be deleted or resent; thus, answer B is incorrect. Deleting the request does not cause it be automatically re-created; thus, answer C is incorrect. For more information, see Chapter 7.

32. **D.** To participate in SUS, the Windows 2000 computers need to be updated to at least Service Pack 3, and any Windows XP computers need to be updated to Service Pack 1. You can, alternatively, install an updated version of the Automatic Updates client to achieve the same effect. For more information, see Chapter 8.

33. **C.** The easiest way to accomplish this task is to create a script that runs the `secedit/analyze` command on the computers and collects the results in a central network location. For more information, see Chapter 1.

34. **B.** Network Address Translation (NAT) turns one IP address into another, and the device that performs this NAT will keep a table of which IP addresses given from the NAT pool map to the one that was distributed. For more information, see Chapter 2.

35. **C.** A new feature in Windows Server 2003, conditional forwarding, allows you to configure a DNS forwarder with multiple forwarding IP addresses. As an example, you could have all name resolution requests for the `bigcorp.com` domain sent to one IP address and all other name requests sent to a second, completely different, IP address. This way, you can provide for both internal and external name resolution from within the internal network. For more information, see Chapter 3.

36. **D.** Pete should `ping 10.10.1.10`, `ping 10.10.2.1` (default gateway), and then have a remote user `ping 10.10.1.1` (default gateway). For more information, see Chapter 4.

37. **A.** Setting the affinity setting to None results in an inbound client request being sent to all nodes within the cluster. This type of affinity results in increased speed but is suitable only for providing static content to clients, such as static Web sites and FTP downloads. Typically, no cookies are

generated by the applications running on the cluster that is configured for this type of affinity. For more information, see Chapter 5.

38. **D.** When enabled with its default settings, volume shadow copy will create a shadow copy twice daily. Volume shadow copy is limited to a maximum of 64 copies; thus, the maximum number of days to retrieve the historical data is 32 days. For more information, see Chapter 6.

39. **B, D, E.** The Windows Server 2003 IPSec implementation can use Kerberos v5, digital certificates, or shared secrets to perform user authentication. NTLM v2 is used for network authentication with Windows 2000 and Windows Server 2003; thus, answer A is incorrect. The Encrypting File System (EFS) is used to encrypt files and folders to add extra security to them; thus, answer C is incorrect. WEP is used as both an encryption and authentication method on wireless LANs; thus, answer F is incorrect. For more information, see Chapter 7.

40. **B, C, D.** For SUS to operate, the SUS server must be provided to the Automatic Updates client computers via the Specify Intranet Microsoft Update Server Location option. In addition, you need to configure the schedule by using the Configure Automatic Updates option and configure for restarting by using the No Auto-Restart for Scheduled Automatic Updates Installations option. For more information, see Chapter 8.

41. **C.** Of the given choices, the `hisecws.inf` template will provide the most secure configuration to your Windows XP Professional clients. For more information, see Chapter 1.

42. **D.** A proxy server is a server-based application that serves as a go-between for the internal LAN clients and the public Internet. If you do not want all your internal hosts accessing the Internet and perhaps exposing all the internal IP addressing information to the world, you could put in a proxy server to act as the middleman when searching the Internet. A proxy server also caches the pages so that Internet response seems faster to internal clients. For more information, see Chapter 2.

43. **A.** If you configure the other three internal DNS servers to forward name resolution queries to the DNS server with IP address 192.168.100.133, only that one specific DNS server will make external DNS queries. For more information, see Chapter 3.

44. **A.** You should try a `Tracert` to the remote server. For more information, see Chapter 4.

45. **B.** The reason, and advantage, to having two network adapters installed in any cluster host is that this setup allows you to separate the load-balanced traffic from the administrative traffic by placing the adapters in different IP subnets. This increases security of the administrative traffic by not exposing it to the load-balanced front end and also improves the performance of the host by allowing more load-balanced traffic to be passed over its front-end load balancing network adapter.

46. **D.** Shadow copies can be viewed only when connecting to the shared folder over the network using My Network Places or locally on the server using My Network Places. On a Windows Server 2003 computer, you do not need to install the Previous Versions Client software to view shadow copies. For more information, see Chapter 6.

47. **A.** The Remote Desktops console can be used to connect to the console session if it is configured correctly. When you are creating the new connection, ensure that you select the Connect to Console option. The Web Interface for Remote Administration, the Remote Desktop Web utility, and the Remote Desktop Connection utility do

not provide access to the console session on a remote server; thus, answers B, C, and D are incorrect. For more information, see Chapter 7.

48. **A.** The Account Lockout Policy node contains three items that can be used to limit the number of incorrect logon attempts over a specified amount of time. The Account Lockout Threshold setting can be configured to specify how many failed logon attempts should be allowed before that user account is locked out. The Account Lockout Duration setting specifies how long the account is to be locked out (barring an administrator unlocking the account early). The Reset Account Lockout Counter After option specifies how much time must pass before failed logon attempts are no longer counted against the Account Lockout Threshold setting. These policies are typically applied at a high level in the organization, such as the root of a domain to cause them to apply to all users within the domain. For more information, see Chapter 8.

49. **C.** Although, in a sense, all the answers will produce some or all the results that Hannah needs, only by using Group Policy can Hannah quickly, accurately, and efficiently apply the `securews.inf` template to all the computers (member servers and workstations alike) located in the Engineering OU. To apply these settings to the computers located in the Engineering OU, Hannah will need to import the `securews.inf` template into an existing or new Group Policy Object. For more information, see Chapter 1.

50. **D.** A firewall is a device that protects the internal network from the external Internet, WAN, business partner, or anything else you may want to protect against. There are many different kinds, but you will be responsible for only the most basic information listed here for the exam. Make sure that you understand what a firewall is

because exam questions may have the term added into the scenario, but you need to know little other than that. For more information, see Chapter 2.

51. **D.** If Andrea does not know what the current security configuration is, she should apply the default security template to the computer. Each computer has its own default security template that is created at the time of Windows Server 2003 installation for workstations and member servers and at the time of promotion for domain controllers. Andrea should not apply the default security template from one computer to any other computer. After the security configuration is reset back to a known state by using the default template, the secure templates can be successfully applied to create the desired level of security. Recall that security templates are incremental and only build on the security configuration already configured; they do not reset the computer's security configuration back to the default settings before making any changes. For more information, see Chapter 1.

52. **B.** Sally should set up IGMP routing so that her server can forward multicast traffic up- and downstream to other multicast routers on the network. Windows Server 2003 does not support a multicast routing protocol, only a forwarding service. For more information, see Chapter 4.

53. **C.** If you want to troubleshoot remote problems on a multihop network, you need to use `tracert`. This tool can find latency and network holes that span more than a couple of router hops. For more information, see Chapter 4.

54. **A.** For your clients to be able to view and work with shadow copies, you need to install the Previous Versions Client software. For more information, see Chapter 6.

55. **A, E.** The Windows Server 2003 IPSec implementation uses DES and 3DES for data encryption. The Windows Server 2003 IPSec implementation uses SHA1 and MD5 for data hashing; thus, answers B and C are incorrect. Advanced Encryption Standard (AES) is not used in IPSec; thus, answer D is incorrect. For more information, see Chapter 7.

56. **C.** The quickest way to configure Captain Bob's network to prevent smart cards from being used to log in to Terminal Services servers is to configure the Do Not Allow Smart Card Device Redirection option, located in the Computer Configuration\Administrative Templates\Windows Components\ Terminal Services\Client/Server data redirection node of the Group Policy Editor. For more information, see Chapter 8.

57. **D.** An X icon next to an item in the Security Configuration and Analysis results indicates that the item is present in both the database and the computer, but does not match the current configured setting. For more information, see Chapter 1.

58. **D.** The subnet mask is the other 32-bit set of numbers you place with an IP address to denote where the network starts and ends and the host-based addressing starts and ends. In other words, if you have a 10.1.1.0/24 network, this really means you have a subnet mask of 255.255.255.0 assigned to the 10.1.1.0 IP address network. The network is 10.1.1 (24 bits mask it with 255.255.255.0), and the last octet, which is simply a zero, is assignable to hosts. For more information, see Chapter 2.

59. **B.** You can locate the preconfigured security templates in the `%systemroot%\security\templates` folder. For a clean installation of Windows Server 2003 on volume C of a computer, this would be `c:\windows\security\templates`. For more information, see Chapter 1.

60. **A, B.** For Andrea to make her smart card self-enrollment solution work efficiently and securely, she needs to ensure that all required users get a blank smart card. To increase the security of the solution, Andrea should configure her CAs so that they do not issue smart card user certificates automatically, but to instead place them into the Pending Requests folder awaiting manual administrative approval. Andrea should also take time to properly educate her users in the procedures to be followed to request a smart card certificate and to enroll the approved certificate. Also, all users will require training on the proper use, storage, and handling of their smart cards to prevent loss or damage. For more information, see Chapter 8.

61. **C.** If the Negotiate Security Action is selected, both computers must make an agreement on the security parameters to be used, meaning that they both must support at least one common set of security parameters from those in the list. The list entries are processed in order of preference from top to bottom. The first security method shared by both computers is used. The Permit option passes the traffic without the requirement for security; thus, Answer A is incorrect. This action is appropriate if you never want to secure traffic to which a rule applies. The Block Action silently blocks all traffic from computers specified in the IP filter list; thus, answer B is incorrect. There is no Open filter action; thus, answer D is incorrect. For more information, see Chapter 7.

62. **A, E, I.** The three preconfigured IPSec policies in Windows Server 2003 are Client (Respond Only), Server (Request Security), and Secure Server (Require Security); thus, answers B, C, D, F, G, and H are incorrect. For more information, see Chapter 7.

63. **B, C.** The Windows Server 2003 IPSec implementation uses SHA1 and MD5 for data hashing. The Windows Server 2003 IPSec implementation uses DES and 3DES for data encryption; thus, answers A and E are incorrect. Advanced Encryption Standard (AES) is not used in IPSec; thus, answer D is incorrect. For more information, see Chapter 7.

64. **B, D.** You should revoke Sam's certificate to prevent him from accessing any network resources. After the certificate has been revoked, you should publish the CRL to all CRL Distribution Points to ensure that all locations have the most up-to-date CRL. For more information, see Chapter 8.

65. **A, B.** Although all four of these options can be used to achieve the desired results, the creation of a new security template and the modification of an existing security template represent the best options available. You can opt to configure the settings using the Local Security Policy console, but this approach requires that you make the same changes on all member servers. You could also make the changes directly in Group Policy, but this approach does not give you the opportunity to test your configuration in a lab environment, thus locating problems before they have a chance to occur on the production network. For more information, see Chapter 1.

# Glossary

## NUMBERS AND SYMBOLS

**802.1x**   An IEEE standard that provides for port-based access control and thus authentication for both wired and wireless networks. 802.1x uses the physical characteristics of a switched LAN to authenticate devices (and users) that are attached to each switch port and to disallow access from that port in the event that the user or device cannot be successfully authenticated.

**3DES (Triple Data Encryption Standard)**   A more secure variant of the DES standard that encrypts data by using three different 56-bit keys in succession. 3DES thus extends the DES key to 168 bits, providing approximately $6.2 \times 10^{57}$ different keys.

**%systemroot%**   A universal reference to the directory in which the Windows system files are installed. Typically, %systemroot% is C:\Winnt or C:\Windows. By default, clean installations of Windows Server 2003 use the Windows directory. If multiple copies of Windows are installed in a multiboot system, each copy has its own %systemroot% directory.

## A

**Active Directory**   The directory services included with Windows Server 2003. Based on the DNS hierarchy, Active Directory provides a domain-based directory service for organizing all the objects and services in a Windows Server 2003 network.

**Active Directory–integrated zone**   A DNS zone file that is stored within the Active Directory data and replicated among other domain controllers running DNS as configured instead of being stored in a normal DNS text file.

**Active Directory Users and Computers**   A Microsoft Management Console provided in Windows 2000 and Windows Server 2003 Active Directory domains that can be used to administer Active Directory objects.

**Affinity**   The method used by network load balancing to associate client requests with hosts in the NLB cluster.

**AH (Authentication Header)**   A protocol in the IPSec suite that is used to authenticate IP traffic. The AH is inserted into the original IP packet immediately after the IP header.

**Application Data Partition**   A new directory partition type in Windows Server 2003 that can be used to store application-specific information in a separate partition that replicates only with the domain controllers that require this information. A common use of such partitions in Windows Server 2003 is for replication of Active Directory–integrated DNS zones.

**Auditing**   The process of logging information about network activities such as user logins, system shutdowns, and file access.

**Authentication**   The process of verifying a user's identity on a network.

**Automated System Restore (ASR)** The replacement for the Windows 2000 Emergency Repair Disk in which a boot floppy and a backup file can be used to restore a system to working order.

**Automatic Updates** The client side of the SUS solution. Automatic Updates can be configured to work with the Microsoft Windows Update Web servers or with internal SUS servers.

# B

**B-node (Broadcast Node)** A NetBIOS name resolution method that relies exclusively on broadcast messages and is the oldest NetBIOS name resolution mode. A host needing to resolve a name request sends a message to every host within earshot, requesting the address associated with a hostname.

**Back up** To make a reliable copy of critical data so that it can be recovered (restored) at a later date in the event of an emergency or casualty.

**Baseline** A set of collected data that is representative of the normal or beginning performance statistics. You can compare the current performance statistics against a baseline to troubleshoot problems.

**Bottleneck** A situation resulting from the inability of a computer system to meet or keep up with the demands placed on it.

# C

**Certificate** A credential that is used to authenticate the origin, identity, and purpose of the public half of a public/private key pair. A certificate ensures that the data sent and received is kept secure.

**Certificate Authority (CA)** A service that issues digital certificates to users and computers. Additionally, CAs maintain a current list of revoked certificates that are no longer considered valid.

**Certificate Revocation List (CRL)** A list maintained by Certificate Authorities that identifies all certificates that are no longer valid but have not yet reached their configured expiration date. Clients validating a certificate can check the CRL to determine whether a presented certificate is still valid.

**Change management** The planning and implementation processes by which changes are proposed within an organization.

**CHAP (Challenge Handshake Authentication Protocol)** An encrypted authentication scheme in which an unencrypted password is not sent over the network. CHAP is defined in RFC 1994 and is supported by RRAS to allow legacy and non-Windows clients to dial in and authenticate to a Windows Server 2003 Remote Access Server.

**Child domain** A Windows Active Directory domain that exists directly beneath a parent domain in a tree hierarchy.

**Class A network** The largest of the classes of IP networks. There are 126 Class A networks, each capable of addressing up to 16,777,214 hosts. Class A networks have a first octet between 1 to 126 with a default subnet mask of 255.0.0.0.

**Class B network** The second-largest class of IP networks. There are 16,384 Class B networks, each capable of addressing up to 65,534 hosts. Class B networks have a first octet between 128 and 191 with a default subnet mask 255.255.0.0.

**Class C network** The smallest class of IP networks. There are 2,097,152 Class C networks, each capable of addressing up to 254 hosts. Class C networks have a first octet between 192 and 223 with a default subnet mask of 255.255.255.0.

**Classless interdomain routing (CIDR)** A more efficient IP address management system than the original class-based system of Class A, B, and C networks. CIDR is typically used by routers and gateways located on the Internet backbone for routing packets across the Internet. CIDR allows any number of contiguous bits in the IP address to be used at the network ID, resulting in more IP addresses becoming available.

**Cluster** A group of two or more independent servers that operate together and are viewed and accessed as a single resource. Also referred to as *clustering*.

**Cluster resource** A network application, service, or hardware device (such as a network adapter or storage system) that is defined and managed by the cluster service.

**Cluster resource group** A defined set of resources contained within a cluster. Cluster resource groups are used as failover units within a cluster. When a cluster resource group fails and cannot be automatically restarted by the cluster service, the entire cluster resource group is placed in an offline status and failed over to another node.

**Cluster virtual server** A cluster resource group that has a network name and IP address assigned to it. Cluster virtual servers are accessible by their NetBIOS name, DNS name, or IP address.

**Compatible security template** A security template that provides a means of allowing members of the Users group to run applications that do not conform to the Windows Logo Program by modifying the default file and Registry permissions that are granted to the Users group.

**Conditional forwarding** A new feature in Windows Server 2003 DNS that allows administrators to direct DNS requests to other DNS servers based on domain. Also known as *intelligent forwarding*.

**Convergence** The process by which NLB clustering hosts determine a new, stable state among themselves and elect a new default host after the failure of one or more cluster nodes. During convergence, the total load on the NLB cluster is redistributed among all cluster nodes that share traffic handling on specific ports, as determined by their port rules.

**Copy backup** A type of backup operation that copies all selected files but does not mark each file as having been backed up (the archive attribute is not cleared). Copy backups have no effect on any other type of backup operation.

**Counter** Part of an object in the System Monitor that can have usage and performance statistics measured.

**Counter log** A log that can be created by using the Performance console for later viewing and comparison against current performance statistics.

**CRL Distribution Point (CDP)** A location to which Certificate Revocation Lists are published.

# D

**Daily backup** A type of backup operation that copies all selected files that have been modified the day the daily backup is performed; the archive attribute is not cleared in this case. Using normal and daily backups, you need the last normal backup and all daily backups to be able to perform restoration.

**dcpromo** The command-line command that is issued to start the process of promoting a member server to a domain controller.

**Default DC Security template** A security template that is automatically created when a member server is promoted to DC. It represents the file, Registry, and system service default security settings for that DC and can be used later to reset those areas to their default configurations.

**Default gateway** The configured router on a TCP/IP-enabled system that allows all packets destined for a remote network to be forwarded out of the local network. If a packet is bound for a remote network but no route is specified, the packet is sent to the default gateway address. Also known as the *default router*.

**Default Security template** A security template that is created during the installation of Windows on a computer. This template varies from one computer to the next, depending on whether the installation was performed as a clean installation or an upgrade. This template represents the default security settings that a computer started out with and thus can be used to reset portions of security as required.

**Delegation of Control** The process by which you can allow nonadministrative users to have some responsibility for some portion of Active Directory, such as delegating the ability to change users' passwords or add computers to the domain.

**DES (Data Encryption Standard)** A symmetric encryption scheme that requires the sender and the receiver to know the secret key. DES uses a 56-bit key that provides approximately $7.2 \times 10^{16}$ different key combinations.

**Differential backup** A type of backup operation that copies files created or changed since the last normal (full) or incremental backup and clears the archive attribute. Using normal and differential backups, you need the last normal backup and the last differential backup to be able to perform restoration.

**Discretionary Access Control List (DACL)** An internal list that is attached to files and folders on NTFS-formatted volumes that is configured to specify the level of permissions that are to be allowed for different users and groups.

**Distance-vector routing** A type of routing that calculates the best path in an OSPF environment.

**DNS forwarder** A DNS server that has been configured to forward to another DNS server name resolution queries it cannot answer.

**DNS resolver** Any computer that has been configured with one or more DNS server IP addresses and that performs queries against these DNS servers.

**DNS Security (DNSSEC)** A public key infrastructure–based system in which authentication and data integrity can be provided to DNS resolvers as discussed in RFC 2535. Digital signatures are used and encrypted with private keys. These digital signatures can then be authenticated by DNSSEC-aware resolvers by using the corresponding public key. The required digital signature and public keys are added to the DNS zone in the form of resource records.

**DNS slave server** A DNS forwarder server that does not try to resolve a resolution request if it doesn't receive a valid response to its forwarded DNS request.

**Domain** A container in the DNS name hierarchy or the network Organizational Unit for Windows Server 2003 networks.

**Domain controller (DC)** A server that holds a writable copy of the Active Directory data and manages information contained within the Active Directory database. Domain controllers also function as NS servers when Active Directory–integrated zones are used. The Kerberos Key Distribution Center (KDC) is located on every domain controller as well.

**Domain name system (DNS)** A service that dynamically provides name and address resolution services in a TCP/IP environment.

**DumpEL** A command-line based utility that can be used to quickly collect and search through event logs. This tool is found in the Windows Server 2003 Resource Kit.

**Dynamic Host Configuration Protocol (DHCP)**   A standards-based method of automatically assigning and configuring IP addresses for DHCP clients.

# E

**EAP (Extensible Authentication Protocol)**   An extension to the Point-to-Point Protocol (PPP) as specified in RFC 2284 that provides a means for the primary authentication method to be negotiated during the initiation of the PPP session.

**Encryption**   A mechanism for securing data in which data is translated into a secret code, which can be read only with the correct key to translate the secret code back to the original data.

**Enterprise Certificate Authority**   The first Certification Authority (CA) in a branch of CAs. It is responsible for assigning certificates to intermediary CAs and other subordinate CAs.

**ESP (Encapsulating Security Protocol)**   A protocol that is used in the IPSec suite to handle data encryption. ESP is usually used with AH to provide the maximum level of security and integrity for data transmitted in IPSec transmissions. ESP uses DES encryption by default, but it can be configured to use 3DES.

**EventCombMT**   A GUI-based utility that can be used to quickly collect and search through event logs. This tool is found in the Windows Server 2003 Resource Kit.

**Exterior Gateway Protocol (EGP)**   The original exterior protocol, which is used to exchange routing information between networks that do not share a common administration.

# F

**Failback**   The process of moving a cluster group (either manually or automatically) back to the preferred node after the preferred node has resumed cluster membership. For failback to occur, it must be configured for the cluster group, including the failback threshold and selection of the preferred node.

**Failover**   The process of a cluster group moving from the currently active node to a designated, functioning node in the cluster group. Failover typically occurs when the active node becomes unresponsive (for any reason) and cannot be recovered within the configured failure threshold period.

**Firewall**   A device that protects the internal network from the external Internet, WAN, business partner, or anything else you may want to protect against.

**Forest**   The logical structure that contains all domains in the Active Directory model.

**Forest and domain functional levels**   Levels of functionality for Active Directory forests and Active Directory domains that determine what unique features they can possess, such as the capability to remain forests and domains that are configured for Windows Server 2003 mode.

**Forest root**   The first domain created within an Active Directory forest.

**Fully qualified domain name (FQDN)**   The complete DNS name of a host, including the hostname and all domains that connect the host to the root domain. The FQDN is typically expressed without a trailing period, with the root domain assumed.

# G

**GPO (Group Policy Object)** A collection of security and configuration settings that are applied to a container in an Active Directory domain.

**Group Policy Editor** A subset of the Active Directory Users and Computers console that allows the editing of Group Policy Objects.

# H

**H-node (Hybrid Node)** A hybrid NetBIOS name resolution mode that favors the use of WINS for NetBIOS name resolution.

**Heartbeat** A network communication sent among individual cluster nodes at intervals of no more than 500 milliseconds (ms); used to determine the status of all cluster nodes.

**Highly Secure security template** A security template that imposes further restrictions on computers it is applied to. Whereas the Secure templates require at least NTLM authentication, the Highly Secure templates require NTLMv2 authentication.

# I

**IGMP Proxy mode** The mode used to configure a router that has two or more interfaces with different settings on different interfaces. One interface acts as a proxy multicast host that sends IGMP membership reports on one of its interfaces.

**IGMP Routing mode** The mode in which you can set Windows Server 2003 to listen for IGMP Membership Report packets as well as to track group membership.

**Incremental backup** A type of backup operation that copies only those files created or changed since the last normal or incremental backup; the archive attribute is then cleared. Using normal and incremental backups, you need the last normal backup and all incremental backups to be able to perform restoration.

**Interior Gateway Protocol (IGP)** A protocol that is used to pass routing information for routing networks that are under a common network administration.

**Internet Control Message Protocol (ICMP)** A protocol in the TCP/IP suite of protocols that is used for testing connectivity.

**Internet Group Management Protocol (IGMP)** One of the core protocols in the TCP/IP suite, a routing protocol that is used as part of multicasting.

**Internet Key Exchange (IKE)** An encryption scheme that allows disparate VPN servers to share encryption key information and make the IPSec protocol practical in today's environment.

**Internet Protocol (IP)** The portion of the TCP/IP protocol suite that is used to provide packet routing.

**IP address** The 32-bit binary address that is used to identify a TCP/IP host's network and host ID. IPv6 IP addresses are 128 bits in length.

**IP Security (IPSec)** A Layer 3 TCP/IP protocol that provides end-to-end security for data in transit.

**ipconfig** A command-line–based tool that allows you to view and modify the TCP/IP properties of installed network adapters. Some if its uses include releasing and renewing DHCP leases as well as clearing the local DNS resolver cache.

**ISAKMP/Oakley (Internet Security Association and Key Management Protocol/Oakley)** A protocol that is used to share a public key between sender and receiver of a secure connection. ISAKMP/Oakley allows the receiving system to retrieve a public key and then authenticate the sender using digital certificates.

**Iterative query**   A DNS query sent from a DNS server to one or more DNS servers in search of the DNS server that is authoritative for the name being sought.

# K

**Kerberos v5**   An identity-based security protocol based on Internet security standards used by Windows Server 2003 to authenticate users.

# L

**LAN Manager HOSTS (LMHOSTS)**   A file modeled after the TCP/IP HOSTS file and used to provide a static NetBIOS name to IP address resolution in a Windows environment. The HOSTS file was originally used for name resolution in a TCP/IP network environment. As the HOSTS file was replaced by DNS, the LMHOSTS file was replaced by WINS.

**Layer 2 Tunneling Protocol (L2TP)**   A VPN protocol that is created by combining the Point-to-Point Tunneling Protocol (PPTP) and Layer 2 Forwarding (L2F) tunneling protocols. L2TP is used as the transport protocol in the Windows Server 2003 VPN service in conjunction with IPSec.

**Leaf**   The end object in a hierarchical tree structure.

**Link State**   An operation used by dynamic routing protocols to test the condition of a connection (link) between routers. OSPF is a Link State protocol.

**link-state routing**   Dynamic routing that tests the condition of a connection (link) between routers. OSPF is a Link State protocol.

**LSA (link state advertisement)**   A notification that is flooded throughout the network when a network link changes state (up to down, or vice versa).

# M

**M-node (Modified Node)**   A hybrid NetBIOS name resolution mode that first attempts to resolve NetBIOS names using the B-node mechanism. If that fails, an attempt is made to use P-node name resolution. M-node was the first hybrid mode put into operation, but it has the disadvantage of favoring B-node operation, which is associated with high levels of broadcast traffic.

**Microsoft Baseline Security Analyzer (MBSA)**   A utility that can be used to scan computers on a network looking for missing security updates and weak security configurations from either the command line or from within the GUI.

**Microsoft Management Console (MMC)**   A Microsoft Windows framework used for hosting administrative tools.

**Microsoft Point-to-Point Encryption (MPPE)**   A data encryption method used for PPP-based connections or PPTP VPN connections. MPPE supports strong (128-bit key) and standard (40-bit key) encryption.

**MS-CHAP (Microsoft Challenge Authentication Protocol)**   A Microsoft-specific variation of the CHAP authentication protocol. MS-CHAP is more secure than CHAP and comes in two variations: MS-CHAPv1 and MS-CHAPv2. MS-CHAPv1 supports one-way authentication and is used by Windows NT 4.0. MS-CHAPv2 is used with Windows 2000 or later and supports mutual authentication.

**Multicasting**   A method of sending a series of packets to a group of computers instead of to a single computer or all computers on a network. IGMP support is required to use multicasting.

**Multilink**   A capability included in Windows Server 2003 that allows the aggregating of multiple modem connections.

# N

**nbtstat**   A command-line utility that allows you to verify the current connections over the NBT protocol. It also allows you to check and load the NetBIOS name cache.

**netsh**   A command-line tool used on Windows 2000 and 2003 systems for configuring and troubleshooting networking-based issues.

**NetBIOS Name**   The computer name for NetBIOS networking. This name can be 16 characters long: 15 provide the hostname, and the 16th represents the service registering the name.

**NetBIOS Name Cache**   A list of system NetBIOS names that a host has resolved or that have been preloaded from the LMHOSTS file.

**NetBIOS node type**   The node type that determines the order of name resolution for NetBIOS names. There are four types: B-node, P-node, M-node, and H-node.

**NetBIOS over TCP/IP (NBT or NetBT)**   The name given to the process of running NetBIOS network services over TCP/IP.

**Network Address Translation (NAT)**   A process by which private IP addresses are mapped to public IP addresses and vice versa. The device that performs this NAT keeps a table of which IP addresses given from the NAT pool map to the one that was distributed.

**Network Basic Input/Output System (NetBIOS)** An Application layer networking protocol that works at the Application, Presentation, and Session layers of the OSI model. Legacy Microsoft networking used NetBIOS as the default Application layer protocol.

**Network interface card (NIC)**   A device installed into a PC or other host device to allow it to have a MAC address and be assigned an IP address. This device connects you to the network. Also referred to as a *network adapter*.

**Network load balancing**   A way to provide highly available solutions in which all incoming connection requests are distributed using a mathematical algorithm to members of an NLB cluster. NLB clustering is best used when clients can connect to any server in the cluster, such as Web sites, Terminal Services servers, and VPN servers.

**Node**   In regards to clustering, an individual server within a cluster. In regards to networking, a device that communicates on a network and is identified by a unique address. In hierarchies, a node is a container that contains other containers and data.

**Normal backup**   A type of backup operation that copies all selected files and marks each file as having been backed up (the archive attribute is cleared). Only the most recent copy of the backup file is required to perform restoration.

**ntbackup.exe**   The command-line version of the Windows Backup Utility.

# O

**Open Shortest Path First (OSPF)**   A routing protocol that allows routers to share their routing information, making them dynamic routers.

**Organizational Unit (OU)**   A container that provides for the logical grouping of objects within Active Directory for ease of administration and configuration.

# P

**P-node (Point-to-Point Node)**   A NetBIOS name resolution method that relies on WINS servers for NetBIOS name resolution. Client computers register themselves with a WINS server when they come on the network.

**PAP (Password Authentication Protocol)** A clear-text authentication scheme that provides no security for information passed over the connection. PAP is defined in RFC 1334.

**Parent domain** The domain that has one or more child domains under it that share the same DNS namespace.

**pathping** A command-line tool that provides the equivalent of the tracert command by allowing you to identify which routers are in the path the packets are taking. pathping also acts as the equivalent of the ping command by sending ping requests to all the routers over a specified time period and then computing statistics based on the packets returned from each router. pathping displays the number of packets lost at each router or link, allowing you to determine which routers and links (subnets) might be causes of connectivity troubles.

**Performance console** A preconfigured Microsoft Management Console that contains the System Monitor as well as Performance Logs and Alerts.

**Physical Address (MAC Address)** A 48-bit alphanumeric number, such as 00-08-74-97-0B-26, that denotes the host's physical address. Also called a Media Access Control (MAC) address, the physical address is unique to the device to which it is assigned.

**ping** A command-line utility that is used to troubleshoot TCP/IP problems. ping sends a packet with data, asking the remote system to echo the packet to the sender.

**Point-to-Point Tunneling Protocol (PPTP)** A protocol that is used by Microsoft and others to create VPNs.

**Port rules** A configuration that is used to determine what types of traffic are to be load-balanced across the cluster nodes.

**Primary DNS server** The name server that contains the master copy of a zone file. Also called a *primary master*.

**Primary master** See *primary DNS server.*

**Primary zone** A DNS zone that contains the master copies of resource records for a domain.

**Principle of least privilege** An administrative principle which states that users are given only the minimum privileges required to perform the specific set of tasks they have been assigned.

**Private IP address** An IP address range reserved for private (non–Internet-connected) networks. There are private address ranges in the Class A, Class B, and Class C address blocks.

**Proxy server** A server-based application that serves as a go-between for the internal LAN clients and the public Internet. A proxy server also caches the pages so that Internet response seems faster to internal clients.

**Public IP address** An IP address for use on the Internet or a private network that must be assigned via an organization or ISP so that no duplicates exist.

**Pull replication** The act of replicating a copy of the WINS database from a WINS replication partner by pulling data from the partner's database to the local database.

**Push replication** The act of replicating a copy of the WINS database to a WINS replication partner by pushing data from the partner's database to the local database.

**Push/pull replication** The act of replicating a copy of the WINS database to a WINS replication partner by allowing the replication partners to push and/or pull.

# Q

**Quorum disk**   The disk drive that contains the definitive cluster-configuration data. Clustering with MSCS requires the use of a quorum disk and requires continuous access to the data contained within the quorum disk. The quorum disk contains vital data about the nodes participating in the cluster, the applications and services defined within the cluster resource group, and the status of each node and cluster resource. The quorum disk is typically located on a shared storage device.

# R

**RADIUS (Remote Access Dial-in User Service)**   An industry-standard security protocol that is used to authenticate client connections.

**Recursive query**   A DNS query that is used to request an authoritative answer or an answer indicating that there is no resolution for a DNS lookup.

**Registered IP address**   Any block of addresses registered with Internet Assigned Numbers Authority (IANA).

**Remote Assistance**   A Remote Desktop Protocol–based service in Windows XP and Windows Server 2003 that allows a Novice to ask for and receive help from an Expert over a TCP/IP network connection.

**Remote Desktop for Administration**   A Remote Desktop Protocol–based service that allows administrators to remotely connect to and administer Windows XP and Windows Server 2003 computers. Remote Desktop for Administration replaces Terminal Services Administration mode in Windows 2000.

**Remote Desktop Protocol**   A terminal communications protocol based on the industry standard T.120 multichannel conferencing protocol.

**Replication partner**   A server in a WINS architecture that sends or receives a copy of the WINS database from another WINS server.

**Resource record**   A data record in a DNS zone. Many types of resource records are available. For example, an address resource record is the data record that describes the address-to-name relationship for a host.

**Restoration**   The process of replacing or re-creating data on a computer using a set of backup media.

**Resultant Set of Policies (RSoP)**   An MMC snap-in that allows you to determine how various Group Policies are applied to an object.

**Reverse lookup**   In DNS, an IP address-to-name resolution.

**Revoked certificate**   A digital certificate that has been taken out of use before its configured end of lifetime. Certificates can be revoked for any number of reasons, including loss of keys or employee termination.

**Role-based security**   The process of configuring network security for hardware and users based on the role they play in the network.

**Root**   In a hierarchy, the container that holds all other containers.

**Root Certificate Authority (CA)**   A Certificate Authority that forms the top of the CA hierarchy.

**Router**   A system or device that forwards or drops packets between networks, based on the entries in its routing table.

**Routing and Remote Access Services (RRAS)**   A service that allows for remote connection to a server.

**Routing Information Protocol (RIP)**   A protocol that dynamic routers use to share their routing tables. Similar to the OSPF and BGP protocols, RIP is an older, less-efficient routing protocol.

**Routing protocol** A type of protocol that is used by dynamic routers to share their routing tables with other routers.

**Routing table** A table that describes routing decisions that a host can make. Minimum entries in the routing table include routes to each local network and a default route.

**Routing table (`route`) utility** A utility that allows you to view and modify the routing table on a Windows computer.

# S

`secedit.exe` The command-line equivalent of the Security Configuration and Analysis snap-in.

**Secondary DNS server** A server that provides name resolution for a zone but cannot be used to modify the zone. It contains a read-only copy of the zone file. Also known as a *secondary master*.

**Secure dynamic update** A secure method used by Active Directory–integrated zones that allows DHCP to automatically update DNS when leases are granted and expired by the DHCP server.

**Secure security template** A security template that increases the level of security configured on a computer it is applied to above the default configuration. Secure templates prevent the use of the LAN Manager (LM) authentication protocol. Windows 9*x* clients need to have Active Directory Client Extensions installed to enable NTLMv2 to allow them to communicate with Windows 2000 and later clients and servers using these templates. These templates also impose additional restrictions on anonymous users, such as preventing them from enumerating account and share information.

**Security Configuration and Analysis snap-in** An MMC snap-in that is used to configure, analyze, and implement security templates on a local computer. It can be used to create templates that are imported into GPOs for application to larger groups of computers.

**Security log** A log that is found in the Event Viewer and that contains auditing entries.

**Security template** A text file that contains settings that configure the security settings of the computer or computers to which it is applied. Several preconfigured security templates come with Windows Server 2003, and you can edit and create your own custom ones as required.

**Security Templates snap-in** An MMC snap-in that can be used to safely create and modify security templates without danger of accidentally applying them to the local computer or the network.

**Site** A well-connected TCP/IP subnet.

**Snap-in** A tool that you can add to the MMC.

**SPAP (Shiva Password Authentication Protocol)** An encrypted password authentication protocol that was introduced for Shiva remote access servers.

**Split horizon** A mechanism that is used with RIP to prevent routing loops.

**Split horizon with poison reverse** A mechanism that broadcasts routes with an infinite routing metric.

**Standalone CA** A certificate authority that can be used with or without Active Directory. Certificate requests are set to pending until an administrator approves the request.

**Standard primary zone** A DNS zone file that holds the master writable copy of a zone and can transfer it to all configured secondary zones.

**Standard secondary zone** A DNS zone file that holds a read-only copy of the zone file and is used to provide increased reliability and performance.

**Start of Authority (SOA) record**   In a DNS zone file, a record that is used to provide the zone parameters to all the DNS servers for the zone. The SOA record also provides the name of the primary server and the person in charge of the domain.

**Stub zone**   A new DNS zone type in Windows Server 2003 that contains only the required resource records that are needed to identify the authoritative DNS servers for another zone.

**Subnet**   A subdivision of a TCP/IP internetwork that communicates with other subnets through routers.

**Subnet mask**   In TCP/IP, a mask that is used to determine what subnet an IP address belongs to. A subnet mask enables a host or a router to determine which portion of an IP address is the network ID and which is the host ID. The host can then use this information to determine whether to send a packet to a host on the local network or to a router.

**Subordinate CA**   Typically the lowest level in a Certificate Authority hierarchy. Subordinate CAs issue certificates directly to users and network hosts.

**Suffix**   A domain extension that indicates the root domain. For example, .com is a domain suffix.

**SUS (Software Update Services)**   An add-on service for Windows 2000 and Windows Server 2003 networks that provides the functionality of a Windows Update Web server on the internal network. SUS allows you to select which available updates are authorized for distribution to network clients, thus ensuring that only the updates you have tested and approved are installed.

# T

**Terminal Services**   An RDP-based service offered by Windows NT, Windows 2000, and Windows Server 2003 servers allowing thin clients to connect to the server and utilize applications stored on the server.

**Top-level domain (TLD)**   A domain that exists directly underneath the root domain.

**tracert**   A command-line utility that traces the route that packets travel between the local host and the destination host and displays it to the screen.

**Transmission Control Protocol/Internet Protocol (TCP/IP)**   The suite of communications protocols used to connect hosts on the Internet.

**Transport Mode**   The use of IPSec not in a tunnel (with two configured endpoints). Commonly used on a private network between two hosts.

**Tree**   A logical group of Windows Server 2003 domains that share a common DNS namespace.

**Tunnel Mode**   The use of IPSec in a mode where two endpoints have been configured to create a tunnel, such as when a VPN tunnel is created.

# U

**Universal Naming Convention (UNC)**   A naming convention that is used to define a resource on a Windows Server 2003 server network. A share named DOCS on the server SERVER1 could be accessed using the UNC path \\SERVER1\DOCS.

**User logon name**   Commonly referred to as the pre-Windows 2000 logon name, such as will.

**User principal name (UPN)**   The full DNS domain name of an Active Directory user account, such as will@corp.mcseworld.com.

# V

**Validity period**   The length of time a digital certificate is valid.

**Virtual private network (VPN)**   A mechanism for providing secure, private communications, utilizing a public network (such as the Internet) as the transport method. VPNs use a combination of encryption and authentication technologies to ensure data integrity and security.

**Volume shadow copy**   A new feature in Windows Server 2003 that provides distinctly different functions. The first function allows the Windows Backup Utility (or ntbackup from the command line) to back up open files as if they were closed. The second feature provides a means to create and store up to 64 historical versions of files located within a network share.

# W

**Windows 2000 mixed mode**   The mode that allows Windows NT 4.0 domain controllers to exist and function within a Windows 2003 domain. This is the default setting when Active Directory is installed, although it can be changed to native mode.

**Windows 2000 native mode**   The mode in which all domain controllers in a domain have been upgraded to Windows 2003 and there are no longer any NT 4.0 domain controllers. An administrator explicitly puts Active Directory into native mode, at which time it cannot be returned to mixed mode without removing and reinstalling Active Directory.

**Windows 2003 functional level**   The highest functional level of either the domain or forest in Windows 2003. This functional level implements all the new features of Windows 2003 Active Directory.

**Windows Internet Naming Service (WINS)**   A service that runs on a Windows Server 2003 server to provide NetBIOS name resolution. When you use WINS, name resolution is performed using directed transmissions, resulting in a reduction in broadcast traffic and the capability to find systems on different subnets. WINS replaces the LMHOSTS file in a fashion similar to the way DNS replaced the HOSTS file.

**Wireless LAN (WLAN)**   A local area network that uses one of the 802.11 standards, such as 802.11b or 802.11a.

**Workgroup**   A grouping of computers and resources that use a decentralized authentication and management system.

# Z

**Zone**   A domain for which a DNS server is authoritative.

**Zone transfer**   The process of copying DNS resource records from a primary zone to a secondary zone.

# What's on the CD-ROM?

This appendix is a brief rundown of what you'll find on the CD-ROM that comes with this book. For a more detailed description of the PrepLogic Practice Exams, Preview Edition exam simulation software, see Appendix C, "Using PrepLogic, Preview Edition Software."

## PrepLogic Practice Exams, Preview Edition

PrepLogic is a leading provider of certification training tools. Trusted by certification students worldwide, PrepLogic is, we believe, the best practice exam software available. In addition to providing a means of evaluating your knowledge of the Training Guide material, PrepLogic Practice Exams, Preview Edition features several innovations that help you to improve your mastery of the subject matter.

For example, the practice tests allow you to check your score by exam area or domain to determine which topics you need to study more. Another feature allows you to obtain immediate feedback on your responses in the form of explanations for the correct and incorrect answers.

PrepLogic Practice Exams, Preview Edition exhibits most of the full functionality of the Premium Edition but offers only a fraction of the total questions. To get the complete set of practice questions and exam functionality, visit PrepLogic.com and order the Premium Edition for this and other challenging exam titles.

Again for a more detailed description of the PrepLogic Practice Exams, Preview Edition features, see Appendix C.

# Using PrepLogic, Preview Edition Software

This Training Guide includes a special version of PrepLogic Practice Exams—a revolutionary test engine designed to give you the best in certification exam preparation. PrepLogic offers sample and practice exams for many of today's most in-demand and challenging technical certifications. This special Preview Edition is included with this book as a tool to use in assessing your knowledge of the Training Guide material while also providing you with the experience of taking an electronic exam.

This appendix describes in detail what PrepLogic Practice Exams, Preview Edition is, how it works, and what it can do to help you prepare for the exam. Note that although the Preview Edition includes all the test simulation functions of the complete, retail version, it contains only a single practice test. The Premium Edition, available at PrepLogic.com, contains the complete set of challenging practice exams designed to optimize your learning experience.

## EXAM SIMULATION

One of the main functions of PrepLogic Practice Exams, Preview Edition is exam simulation. To prepare you to take the actual vendor certification exam, PrepLogic is designed to offer the most effective exam simulation available.

## QUESTION QUALITY

The questions provided in the PrepLogic Practice Exams, Preview Edition are written to the highest standards of technical accuracy. The questions tap the content of the Training Guide chapters and help you review and assess your knowledge before you take the actual exam.

## INTERFACE DESIGN

The PrepLogic Practice Exams, Preview Edition exam simulation interface provides you with the experience of taking an electronic exam. This experience enables you to effectively prepare for taking the actual exam by making the test experience a familiar one. Using this test simulation can help eliminate the sense of surprise or anxiety you might experience in the testing center because you will already be acquainted with computerized testing.

## EFFECTIVE LEARNING ENVIRONMENT

The PrepLogic Practice Exams, Preview Edition interface provides a learning environment that not only tests you through the computer, but also teaches the material you need to know to pass the certification exam. Each question comes with a detailed explanation of the correct answer and often provides reasons the other options are incorrect. This information helps to reinforce the knowledge you already have and also provides practical information you can use on the job.

## SOFTWARE REQUIREMENTS

PrepLogic Practice Exams requires a computer with the following:

▶ Microsoft Windows 98, Windows Me, Windows NT 4.0, Windows 2000, or Windows XP.

▶ A 166MHz or faster processor is recommended.

▶ A minimum of 32MB of RAM (As with any Windows application, the more memory, the better your performance.)

▶ 10MB of hard drive space.

## INSTALLING PREPLOGIC PRACTICE EXAMS, PREVIEW EDITION

Install PrepLogic Practice Exams, Preview Edition by running the setup program on the PrepLogic Practice Exams, Preview Edition CD. Follow these instructions to install the software on your computer.

1. Insert the CD into your CD-ROM drive. The Autorun feature of Windows should launch the software. If you have Autorun disabled, click Start and select Run. Go to the root directory of the CD and select setup.exe. Click Open, and then click OK.

2. The Installation Wizard copies the PrepLogic Practice Exams, Preview Edition files to your hard drive; adds PrepLogic Practice Exams, Preview Edition to your Desktop and Program menu; and installs test engine components to the appropriate system folders.

## Removing PrepLogic Practice Exams, Preview Edition from Your Computer

If you elect to remove the PrepLogic Practice Exams, Preview Edition product from your computer, an uninstall process has been included to ensure that it is removed from your system safely and completely. Follow these instructions to remove PrepLogic Practice Exams, Preview Edition from your computer:

1. Select Start, Settings, Control Panel.

2. Double-click the Add/Remove Programs icon.

3. You are presented with a list of software installed on your computer. Select the appropriate PrepLogic Practice Exams, Preview Edition title you want to remove. Click the Add/Remove button. The software is then removed from your computer.

## USING PREPLOGIC PRACTICE EXAMS, PREVIEW EDITION

PrepLogic is designed to be user friendly and intuitive. Because the software has a smooth learning curve, your time is maximized, and you can start practicing almost immediately. PrepLogic Practice Exams, Preview Edition has two major modes of study: Practice Test and Flash Review.

Using Practice Test mode, you can develop your test-taking abilities as well as your knowledge through the use of the Show Answer option. While you are taking the test, you can expose the answers along with a detailed explanation of why the given answers are right or wrong. This way, you can better understand the material presented.

Flash Review is designed to reinforce exam topics rather than quiz you. In this mode, you are shown a series of questions but no answer choices. Instead, you are given a button that reveals the correct answer to the question and a full explanation for that answer.

## Starting a Practice Test Mode Session

Practice Test mode enables you to control the exam experience in ways that actual certification exams do not allow:

▶ **Enable Show Answer Button**—Activates the Show Answer button allowing you to view the correct answer(s) and full explanation(s) for each question during the exam. When this button is not enabled, you must wait until after your exam has been graded to view the correct answer(s) and explanation.

▶ **Enable Item Review Button**—Activates the Item Review button, allowing you to view your answer choices and marked questions. This button also facilitates navigation between questions.

▶ **Randomize Choices**—Randomizes answer choices from one exam session to the next. This feature makes memorizing question choices more difficult, thus keeping questions fresh and challenging longer.

To begin studying in Practice Test mode, click the Practice Test radio button from the main exam customization screen. Selecting this button enables the options detailed in the preceding list.

To your left, you are presented with the option of selecting the preconfigured Practice Test or creating your own Custom Test. The preconfigured test has a fixed time limit and number of questions. Custom Tests allow you to configure the time limit and the number of questions in your exam.

The Preview Edition included with this book includes a single preconfigured Practice Test. Get the complete set of challenging PrepLogic Practice Exams at PrepLogic.com and make certain you're ready for the big exam.

Click the Begin Exam button to begin your exam.

## Starting a Flash Review Mode Session

Flash Review mode provides you with an easy way to reinforce topics covered in the practice questions. To begin studying in Flash Review mode, click the Flash Review radio button from the main exam customization screen. Select either the preconfigured Practice Test or create your own Custom Test.

Click the Best Exam button to begin your Flash Review of the exam questions.

## Standard PrepLogic Practice Exams, Preview Edition Options

Depending on the options you choose, some of the buttons on your screen are grayed out and inaccessible or missing completely. Buttons that are appropriate remain active. The following list describes the function of each of the buttons you see:

▶ **Exhibit**—This button is visible if an exhibit is provided to support the question. An exhibit is an image that provides supplemental information necessary to answer the question.

▶ **Item Review**—This button leaves the question window and opens the Item Review screen. From this screen, you can see all questions, your answers, and your marked items. You also see correct answers listed here when appropriate.

▶ **Show Answer**—This option displays the correct answer with an explanation of why it is correct. If you select this option, the current question is not scored.

▶ **Mark Item**—This check box enables you to tag a question you need to review further. You can view and navigate your Marked Items by clicking the Item Review button (if enabled). When grading your exam, you are notified if you have marked items remaining.

▶ **Previous Item**—This button enables you to view the previous question.

▶ **Next Item**—This button enables you to view the next question.

▶ **Grade Exam**—After you have completed your exam, you click this button to end your exam and view your detailed score report. If you have unanswered or marked items remaining you are asked whether you would like to continue taking your exam or view your exam report.

## Time Remaining

If the test is timed, the time remaining is displayed on the upper-right corner of the application screen. The clock counts down minutes and seconds remaining to complete the test. If you run out of time, you are asked whether you want to continue taking the test or if you want to end your exam.

## Your Examination Score Report

The Examination Score Report screen appears when the Practice Test mode ends—as the result of time expiration, completion of all questions, or your decision to terminate early.

This screen provides you with a graphical display of your test score with a breakdown of scores by topic domain. The graphical display at the top of the screen compares your overall score with the PrepLogic Exam Competency Score.

The PrepLogic Exam Competency Score reflects the level of subject competency required to pass this vendor's exam. Although this score does not directly translate to a passing score, consistently matching or exceeding this score does suggest you possess the knowledge to pass the actual vendor exam.

## Review Your Exam

From your Score Report screen, you can review the exam that you just completed by clicking on the View Items button. Navigate through the items, viewing the questions, your answers, the correct answers, and the explanations for those questions. You can return to your score report by clicking the View Items button.

## GET MORE EXAMS

Each PrepLogic Practice Exams, Preview Edition that accompanies your training guide contains a single PrepLogic Practice Exam. Certification students worldwide trust PrepLogic Practice Exams to help them pass their IT certification exams the first time. Purchase the

Premium Edition of PrepLogic Practice Exams and get the entire set of all new challenging Practice Tests for this exam. PrepLogic Practice Exams—Because You Want to Pass the First Time.

## Contacting PrepLogic

If you would like to contact PrepLogic for any reason including information about our extensive line of certification practice tests, we invite you to do so. Please contact us online at www.preplogic.com.

## CUSTOMER SERVICE

If you have a damaged product and need a replacement or refund, please call the following phone number:

800-858-7674

## Product Suggestions and Comments

We value your input! Please email your suggestions and comments to the following address:

feedback@preplogic.com

## License Agreement

YOU MUST AGREE TO THE TERMS AND CONDITIONS OUTLINED IN THE END USER LICENSE AGREEMENT ("EULA") PRESENTED TO YOU DURING THE INSTALLATION PROCESS. IF YOU DO NOT AGREE TO THESE TERMS, DO NOT INSTALL THE SOFTWARE.

# Index

## SYMBOLS

3DES (Triple DES), 459
4 parameter
    pathping command, 280
    tracert command, 276
6 parameter
    pathping command, 280
    tracert command, 276

## A

a parameter (ping command), 277
ABC, Inc. case study, 123-124
Acceptable Use Policy (AUP), 526
access
    Active Directory audits, 572
    objects, auditing, 573, 629
    remote
        Network Access Quarantine Control, 270
        networks, 610-611
        RRAS, 288-289
        security. *See* security, remote access
    unauthorized, 256
Access Method dialog box, 260
Access Points (APs), 621
Account Lockout policy, 561
accounts
    logon events, 629
    management audits, 572
    policies, 595
Account Policies node, 61
Accounting to Payroll Security Policy Properties
  dialog box, 477
Active Directory, 29
    access audits, 572
    auditing, 629
    certificate publication configuration, 537, 540

integrated zones, 146, 601
permissions, 157-158
server security, 29
Active Policy node (IP Security Monitor snap-in), 491
active/active clustering, 326, 615
active/passive clustering, 325, 614
ad hoc WLANs, 621
adapters
    load balancing, 315
    network, 314, 318
adaptive exams, 22
Add Counters dialog box, 366-368
Add Objects dialog box, 374
Add Standalone Snap-in dialog box, 466
Add/Edit Port Rule dialog box, 317
adding
    certificate templates, 541
    counter logs, 378
    nodes
        MSCS clusters, 339-340, 351-352
        NLB clusters, 320-322, 350
    OSPF to RRAS, 237-239
    RIP to RRAS, 229, 232
    silent RIP to RRAS, 233-234
    static routes, 288
addresses
    IP, 97, 597
        administrative, 313
        classes, 102-103
        clusters, 313, 316
        configuring, 106
        host identifiers, 99
        IPv4, 97
        IPv6, 98-99
        loopback addressing, 101
        MSCS clusters, 335
        network identifiers, 99
        private, 96, 101-102
        private classes, 598

# E

# I

# M

*How can we make this index more useful? Email us at indexes@quepublishing.com*

## Q

## R

role separation, 624
Standalone CA, 624-625
version 2 templates, 623
certificates, 519-520
autoenrollment, 545-547
enrollment, 543-544
requests/renewal, 548-554
template management, 541-542
change and configuration management framework, 575-576
configuring servers, 25
Active Directory, 29
OUs, 29
roles, 26-27
CRLs, 580-581
default settings, 592
DNS, 155, 604-605
Active Directory permissions, 157-158
DNSSEC, 159-160
dynamic updates, 156-157, 604
server properties, 159
zones, 148, 158-159
dynamic updates, 156, 604
ESP, 622
filter actions, 472, 623
Group Policy, 55, 621
ICMP packets, blocking, 281
Internet connections, 120
IPSec, 456-459
Authentication Header, 460-461, 622
configuring, 464
custom policies, creating. See customizing, IPSec policies
ESP, 461-463
implementation, 621-622
IP Security Monitor, 457, 491-496
ISAKMP/IKE, 463-464
Jeff's Jeep Tours case study, 499
L2TP, 464
management console, creating, 466, 469
monitoring, 491
new features, 457-458
policies, 465, 469, 622-623

replaying, 462
RSoP snap-in, 497
Secure Server (Require Security) policy, 470, 474
standard features, 458-459
stateful filtering, 458
transport mode, 457
troubleshooting, 491, 498-499
tunnels, 457, 474
VPN connections, 457
monitoring, 571-574
networks, 109
PKI. See PKI
policies, 596
RDA, 445, 448
remote access, 252-253
authentication, 253-256
dial-in properties, 257-258
Network Access Quarantine Control, 270, 611
policies, 258-261, 264
profiles, 264-269
Secure User Authentication, 611
unauthorized access, 256
remote administration. See Remote Assistance
RIP, 608
Rockwell Financial Services case study, 577-578
role-based, 28, 72-73, 591
Baseline Policy, 73
Domain Policy, 73
Enterprise Client Policy, 74
High Security Policy, 74
Legacy Client Policy, 74
Role-Specific Policy, 73
Security Configuration Manager tools. See Security Configuration Manager tools
security templates, 50-54
server roles, 74-75
settings, restoring, 404
templates, 591-594
TLS, 611
updates, 562-564
installing, 628
maintenance, 569

# W

# X-Y-Z

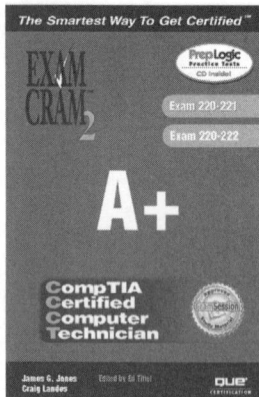